Outback Australia

Rob van Driesum   **Denis O'Byrne**
Pete Cruttenden   **Elizabeth Swan**
Mic Looby   **Martin Robinson**

D0993129

LONELY PLANET PUBLICATIONS
Melbourne • Oakland • London • Paris

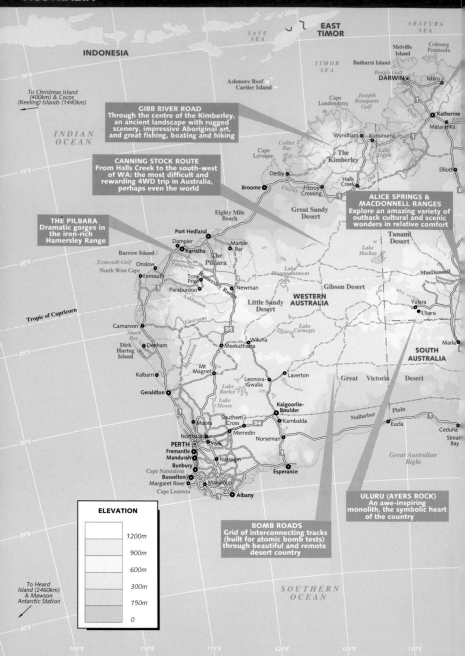

AUSTRALIA

GIBB RIVER ROAD
Through the centre of the Kimberley, an ancient landscape with rugged scenery, impressive Aboriginal art, and great fishing, boating and hiking

CANNING STOCK ROUTE
From Halls Creek to the south-west of WA: the most difficult and rewarding 4WD trip in Australia, perhaps even the world

THE PILBARA
Dramatic gorges in the iron-rich Hamersley Range

ALICE SPRINGS & MACDONNELL RANGES
Explore an amazing variety of outback cultural and scenic wonders in relative comfort

ULURU (AYERS ROCK)
An awe-inspiring monolith, the symbolic heart of the country

BOMB ROADS
Grid of interconnecting tracks (built for atomic bomb tests) through beautiful and remote desert country

INDONESIA

EAST TIMOR

SAVU SEA

ARAFURA SEA

TIMOR SEA

Ashmore Reef Cartier Island

To Christmas Island (400km) & Cocos (Keeling) Islands (1440km)

INDIAN OCEAN

Melville Island
Cobourg Peninsula
Bathurst Island
Beagle Gulf
DARWIN
Jabiru
Cape Londonderry
Joseph Bonaparte Gulf
Katherine
Mataranka

Cape Leveque
Collier Bay
The Kimberley
Wyndham
Kununurra
Lake Argyle
Elliott

Derby
Fitzroy Crossing
Halls Creek
Broome
Fitzroy

Eighty Mile Beach

Great Sandy Desert

Tanami Desert

Lake Mackay

MacDonnell

Port Hedland
Dampier
Karratha
Marble Bar
The Pilbara
Newman

Barrow Island
Exmouth Gulf
North West Cape
Onslow
Exmouth
Tom Price
Paraburdoo

Ashburton

Lake Disappointment

Little Sandy Desert

Gibson Desert

WESTERN AUSTRALIA

Yulara
Uluru

Carnarvon
Shark Bay
Dirk Hartog Island
Denham

Tropic of Capricorn

Gascoyne

Wiluna
Meekatharra

Lake Carnegie

SOUTH AUSTRALIA

Marla

Kalbarri

Murchison

Mt Magnet
Lake Barlee
Leonora-Gwalia
Laverton

Geraldton

Lake Moore

Kalgoorlie-Boulder
Kambalda

Great Victoria Desert

Moora
Southern Cross
Merredin
Coolgardie
Norseman

Nullarbor
Plain
Eucla
Ceduna
Streaky Bay

Northam
PERTH
Fremantle
Mandurah
York
Narrogin
Esperance

Bunbury
Busselton
Margaret River
Cape Leeuwin
Cape Naturaliste
Manjimup
Albany

Great Australian Bight

To Heard Island (2460km) & Mawson Antarctic Station

SOUTHERN OCEAN

ELEVATION

	1200m
	900m
	600m
	300m
	150m
	0

105°E   110°E   115°E   120°E   125°E   130°E

10°S   15°S   20°S   25°S   30°S   35°S   40°S

AUSTRALIA

KAKADU NATIONAL PARK
Superb wetlands, brilliant
aboriginal rock art and scenic
Arnhem Land Escarpment

CAPE YORK TRACK
Traverse Australia's last frontier,
from the rainforests near Cairns to the
unique Islander communities at the
northernmost tip of the continent

OODNADATTA TRACK
Relatively easy introduction
to outback travel along the
historic Ghan railway line,
from the Flinders Ranges
to the Red Centre

PAPUA NEW
GUINEA

SOLOMON
SEA

SOLOMON
ISLANDS

Torres Strait

Thursday
Island   Cape York

Wessel
Islands

Nhulunbuy
Cape Arnhem

Weipa

CORAL
SEA

Groote Eylandt
Alyangula

Coen
Cape York
Peninsula

Cape
Melville

Osprey
Reef

Gulf of
Carpentaria

Borroloola

Mornington
Island

Cooktown

WILLIS
GROUP

Lihou Reefs

Burketown

Normanton

Port Douglas
Mareeba Cairns

Innisfail
Tully
Hinchinbrook Island
Ingham

QUEENSLAND

Townsville
Ayr
Bowen
Airlie Beach
Proserpine

Marion Reef

Mt Isa Cloncurry

Charters
Towers

Hughenden

Mackay
Sarina

Winton

Moranbah
Clermont

Swains
Reef

Saumarez
Reef

Wreck Reef

Simpson
Desert

Birdsville

Longreach
Barcaldine

Emerald

Yeppoon
Rockhampton

Gladstone

GREAT BARRIER REEF
MARINE PARK
Cato Island

Tropic of Capricorn

Oodnadatta

Quilpie
Charleville

Roma

Biloela
Bundaberg
Hervey Bay
Maryborough
Gympie

Fraser
Island

Sandy Cape

Cunnamulla

St George

Chinchilla
Dalby
Toowoomba
Goondiwindi Warwick

Noosa Heads
Maroochydore

BRISBANE
Surfers Paradise
Tweed Heads
Byron Bay
Ballina

SOUTH
PACIFIC
OCEAN

To Norfolk
Island (610km)

Marree
Leigh
Creek

Milparinka

Bourke
Walgett

Moree
Inverell
Armidale

Lismore
Grafton
Coffs Harbour

Roxby
Downs

Broken
Hill

Wilcannia

Cobar

Narrabri
Gunnedah

Kempsey
Port Macquarie

Lord Howe Island

Woomera

NEW SOUTH
WALES

Nyngan

Tamworth

Taree
Forster

Port Augusta
Whyalla
Port Pirie
Peterborough
Ivanhoe

Parkes
Dubbo

Newcastle

Clare
Kapunda
Gawler

Mildura

Griffith
Hay
Narrandera

Bathurst
Cowra

Katoomba SYDNEY
Wollongong

ADELAIDE
Murray Bridge

Swan Hill

Wagga
Wagga

Goulburn
CANBERRA
ACT

Kingscote
Victor Harbor

VICTORIA

Bendigo

Albury

Batemans Bay

Kangaroo
Island

Encounter
Bay

Naracoorte

Horsham
Shepparton

Narooma

Eden

Millicent
Mt Gambier

Ararat
Ballarat
Geelong

MELBOURNE
Bairnsdale
Sale
Yarram

Cape
Howe
Mallacoota

Portland
Warrnambool

Cape
Otway

Wilsons
Promontory

Bass Strait

King Island

Flinders
Island

TASMAN
SEA

Smithton Burnie
Devonport Launceston

Queenstown

TASMANIA
HOBART

Lake Gordon

Bruny
Island

South East
Cape

To Macquarie
Island (1420Km)

0   250   500km
0   150   300mi

Outback Australia
3rd edition – May 2002
First published – November 1994

Published by
Lonely Planet Publications Pty Ltd ABN 36 005 607 983
90 Maribyrnong St, Footscray, Victoria 3011, Australia

Lonely Planet offices
Australia Locked Bag 1, Footscray, Victoria 3011
USA 150 Linden St, Oakland, CA 94607
UK 10a Spring Place, London NW5 3BH
France 1 rue du Dahomey, 75011 Paris

Photographs
Many of the images in this guide are available for licensing from
Lonely Planet Images.
Web site: www.lonelyplanetimages.com

Front cover photograph
Old petrol bowsers in the outback (Jason Edwards)

ISBN 1 86450 187 1

Printed through Colorcraft Ltd, Hong Kong
Printed in China

**Although the authors
and Lonely Planet try
to make the informa-
tion as accurate as
possible, we accept
no responsibility for
any loss, injury or
inconvenience sus-
tained by anyone
using this book.**

Contents – Text

THE SOUTH 267

THE NORTH-WEST 306

THE TROPICS 372

Contents – Maps

FACTS ABOUT THE OUTBACK

THE CENTRAL DESERTS

THE SOUTH

THE NORTH-WEST

THE TROPICS

The Authors

Rob van Driesum

Rob grew up in several Asian and African countries before moving to The Netherlands, where he studied modern history at the University of Amsterdam and worked as a history teacher, bartender and freelance journalist to finance his motorcycle travels. A motorcycle journey around the world was cut short in Australia, where he worked as a labourer, flower salesman, truck driver and motorcycle magazine editor – pursuing his passion for outback travel on the latest test bikes. He joined Lonely Planet to help set up its range of European titles and eventually became an associate publisher, but after more than a decade behind a desk he decided it was time to move on. He now does a bit of authoring and freelance teaching, and grabs every opportunity he can to head into the bush.

Peter Cruttenden

Normally a walker or mountain-biker, Pete found to his consternation that an extended 4WD trip can be a hell of a lot of fun, particularly in the remote and beautiful Central Deserts. After a four-year stint in LP's Melbourne office, Pete is now writing full-time and has contributed to *Read This First: Asia & India*, *Walking in Britain*, *East Coast Australia* and the first three editions of *Out to Eat Melbourne*.

Ronele & Eric Gard

Ronele and Eric Gard have travelled the Canning Stock Route once or twice a year for 22 years. What began as a 4WD club run fired an interest that became a passion resulting in their Western Desert Guides business and the writing of a guide book about the route. They believe in preserving the Canning Stock Route for future generations and in 1987 signposted the track for the WA Heritage Trails Network. As foundation members of Track Care WA, they have assisted in cleanups and the erection of a composting toilet at the ideal camp site, Durba Springs. They encourage all who travel the route to act as temporary caretakers.

Mic Looby

After what seemed like an eternity, Mic was born in Australia's Blue Mountains in 1969. Since then, he has been busy growing up, travelling, coming home, travelling again, and becoming a professional writer and freelance illustrator somewhere along the way. He has a degree in journalism, a graduate diploma in animation and interactive media, a 1968 Holden HK station wagon, and – until a recent water-filter disaster – a pet crayfish called Eric. Mic has illustrated several Lonely Planet phrasebooks and co-authored Lonely Planet's *Philippines* guidebook.

Denis O'Byrne

Now a resident of Darwin, Denis lived in Alice Springs for over 20 years and has travelled widely throughout the outback. He is a columnist for the national 4WD magazine *Overlander*, and has had many outback features published in this and various other publications.

Martin Robinson

Born in Britain, Martin is now a resident of New Zealand. He has had more than 30 employers but has spent most of his life escaping real work and the real world of mortgages and kids by travelling to odd places, writing, taking photographs and listening to Bob Dylan. His aim in life is to stay happily married and to continue finding people willing to pay him to roam around our small but complicated planet.

Elizabeth Swan

With bona fide gypsy ancestry, a travelling army dad and a taste for adventure, it's no surprise that Elizabeth has experienced life on almost every continent. After completing a degree in linguistics, she made the natural progression into a career as a 'Travel Agent to the Stars'. Consequently she has seen Status Quo's passport photos and knows Alice Cooper's minibar preferences. Tired of planning other people's trips, she opted instead to edit and write LP travel guides for other people's trips. She has made several visits to the Northern Territory over the years and it continues to rate as one of her top five favourite places.

FROM THE AUTHORS

Rob van Driesum Thanks to the many people who provided help and advice, in particular Kurt Weidner in Glenluce; Paul Fitzgerald in Wittenoom; Jamie Birnie in Millstream; Chris Perry and Terese Cooke in Warburton; and Katherine Ayres from the RFDS in Sydney. They'll know why.

Pete Cruttenden Thanks firstly to Harriet Gaffney for beer and beds in Alice Springs and to Jim Puckett for dinner and stories in Kalgoorlie. For stories just as good, thanks to Iain M Banks and Donald Westlake. In Leonora, it was a pleasure to meet Jasmin and watch her demolish any number of Skippy myths, and back in Alice Springs it was fun to catch up with Linda Jaivin. A big thanks to the old bloke outside Kintore who helped us out of a tight spot, and thanks, too, to Nola at Advance Rentals who was most gracious when her vehicle was returned scratched, scuffed and with 15,000km put on the clock (from a four-week rental). Thanks to Imogen Keen and Geoff Hinchliffe (and now Finbar) for lending me gear and, as always, my love and thanks to Rebecca Cole for her unswerving support, proof-reading and stoic endurance of my absences from the home fires. Greetings also to Gudrun Likar, who gamely endured dingoes in the campsite, no showers, a contrary tent and knee-deep mud during the days she was with us. The comforts of Vienna must have never seemed so far away! Finally, thanks to Stuart Partridge who displayed the cojones and foresight to chuck in a perfectly good job to come to the desert with me. Co-driver, cook, cyclist, hacker and conversationalist par excellence, Stu ensured a potentially gruelling slog became a rich and satisfying adventure.

Mic Looby Road trains of thanks to map guru Zed Senbergs, fellow Lonely Planet outback survivors Sarah Mathers and Pete Cruttenden, Quorn's very own Georgia, the Broken Hill expat medical team, and the Copley mechanic who welded my car's shock tower back together when it was 'slopping around like a dick in a shirt-sleeve'.

Denis O'Byrne Many people assisted by giving advice and information for this update and I'm grateful to them all. In particular, thanks go to Alan O'Keefe for his company on a two-week camping trip along the Oodnadatta, Birdsville and Strzelecki tracks.

Martin Robinson I would like to thank Toyota for manufacturing a good vehicle, Britz for renting it to me and Lonely Planet for paying the bills. Thanks also to Vince, Trudy, Kalum and Nathaniel for accommodation and to my wife for everything.

Elizabeth Swan Thank you to all the friendly Territorians up the Track and in the Top End, especially Dale Hudderson at Tourism Top End, Sean and Natalie at Salvatore's, Andy at Gondwana, Karen Holmes and Kylie Koeford at YHA Travel; and Monty the python and his mate, Steve, in Alice Springs. Special thanks to senior designer Corie Louise Waddell for kick-starting the outback dream; my sister Doll for the cackles over SFWs at Larry's during the write-up; and my dad, Garry, and my husband Mark Peters, who were wonderful companions for a third of the red-dust road trip.

This Book

LP's first guide to *Outback Australia* was co-ordinated by Rob van Driesum, with contributions from Jim Hart and Julian Barry. Denis O'Byrne co-ordinated the 2nd edition, with contributions from Ron & Viv Moon, Hugh Finlay, Jeff Williams and John Weldon.

Rob van Driesum co-ordinated this 3rd edition, as well as updating the introductory chapters (with the assistance of the other authors) and the sections on the Tanami Track, Gibb River Road, Broome, Dampier Peninsula, Pilbara and part of the Gunbarrel Highway. Ronele & Eric Gard updated the Canning Stock Route section of the North-West chapter.

Denis O'Byrne updated Alice Springs, MacDonnell Ranges, Finke Gorge, Plenty Highway, Sandover Highway, the Finke & Old Andado Tracks, Simpson Desert, Oodnadatta, Birdsville and Strzelecki Tracks.

Mic Looby updated the Flinders Ranges, Stuart Highway (south of Alice Springs), Silver City Highway, Kidman Way and Matilda Highway.

Pete Cruttenden expanded the section on Uluru, Kata Tjuta and King's Canyon, as well as the Bomb Roads, Eyre Highway and the rest of the Gunbarrel Highway.

Elizabeth Swan updated the Stuart Highway (north of Alice Springs), Darwin, Litchfield National Park, Kakadu National Park and Cobourg Peninsula.

Martin Robinson updated the sections on the Gulf Track, Cairns, Kennedy Highway, Cairns to Musgrave via Cooktown, Cape York and Thursday Island & Torres Strait.

From The Publisher

The 3rd edition of *Outback Australia* was produced in Lonely Planet's Melbourne office. Victoria Harrison was the coordinating editor and was assisted by Ann Seward, Michael Day, Simone Egger, Bruce Evans, Gina Tsarouhas, Anastasia Safioleas and Jane Thompson who, with Corinne Waddell, also commissioned the authors. Thanks to Jocelyn Harewood for help with the colour sections.

Barbara Benson coordinated the mapping and design of the book, with help from Sophie Reed, Clare Capell, Meredith Mail, and Kusnandar, who drew the climate charts. Final checks were done by Errol Hunt (senior editor), Corinne (senior designer), Tim Fitzgerald and Jane.

Thanks to Mark Germanchis, Chris Lee Ack, Lachlan Ross and Bibiana Jaramillo in Production Services for their invaluable assistance and patience, and to Matt King for the special section on Aboriginal art & culture. Thanks to Margie Jung and Andrew Weatherill for the front cover photo and design; and to Lonely Planet Images for their help with other photos throughout the book.

ACKNOWLEDGEMENTS

Many thanks to the travellers who used the last edition and wrote to us with helpful hints, useful advice and interesting anecdotes:

Julien Renney, Max Biesse, HM Boczech, Margaret Brown, Adrian Christen, Robert Colman, Wendy & John Daley, Hans-Werner Denzel, Nicholas Plunkett Dillon, Beate Fortenbacher, Patrick Gmuer, Robert Greenup, Adrian Haas, Dr J A Hayman, William Hemphill, Lyn Hinspeter, Vickie Hughson, Paul Jenkins, Jude Kelly, Sue Kemp, Paul Key, Monty & Leila Kleiman, Bodil Lindholm, Nicole Malkre, Tomas Maltby, Kerry McGinnis, Shirley Mills, Michael Moritz, Terrence Moss, Jill Mottram, Helen Mulholland, Luis Muller, Sarah O'Rourke, Seth Parks, Jerry Payne, Sharon Posket, Paul Prowting, Lyndsay & Kay Smith, Chris Strakosch, Jane Ward, Wanda Waugh, Michele Wecels and Jessica Wiegan

Foreword

ABOUT LONELY PLANET GUIDEBOOKS

The story begins with a classic travel adventure: Tony and Maureen Wheeler's 1972 journey across Europe and Asia to Australia. There was no useful information about the overland trail then, so Tony and Maureen published the first Lonely Planet guidebook to meet a growing need.

From a kitchen table, Lonely Planet has grown to become the largest independent travel publisher in the world, with offices in Melbourne (Australia), Oakland (USA), London (UK) and Paris (France).

Today Lonely Planet guidebooks cover the globe. There is an ever-growing list of books and information in a variety of media. Some things haven't changed. The main aim is still to make it possible for adventurous travellers to get out there – to explore and better understand the world.

At Lonely Planet we believe travellers can make a positive contribution to the countries they visit – if they respect their host communities and spend their money wisely. Since 1986 a percentage of the income from each book has been donated to aid projects and human rights campaigns, and, more recently, to wildlife conservation.

Although inclusion in a guidebook usually implies a recommendation we cannot list every good place. Exclusion does not necessarily imply criticism. In fact there are a number of reasons why we might exclude a place – sometimes it is simply inappropriate to encourage an influx of travellers.

UPDATES & READER FEEDBACK

Things change – prices go up, schedules change, good places go bad and bad places go bankrupt. Nothing stays the same. So, if you find things better or worse, recently opened or long-since closed, please tell us and help make the next edition even more accurate and useful.

Lonely Planet thoroughly updates each guidebook as often as possible – usually every two years, although for some destinations the gap can be longer. Between editions, up-to-date information is available in our free, quarterly *Planet Talk* newsletter and monthly email bulletin *Comet*. The *Upgrades* section of our web site (W www.lonelyplanet.com) is also regularly updated by Lonely Planet authors, and the site's *Scoop* section covers news and current affairs relevant to travellers. Lastly, the *Thorn Tree* bulletin board and *Postcards* section carry unverified, but fascinating, reports from travellers.

Tell us about it! We genuinely value your feedback. A well-travelled team at Lonely Planet reads and acknowledges every email and letter we receive and ensures that every morsel of information finds its way to the relevant authors, editors and cartographers.

Everyone who writes to us will find their name listed in the next edition of the appropriate guidebook, and will receive the latest issue of *Comet* or *Planet Talk*. The very best contributions will be rewarded with a free guidebook.

We may edit, reproduce and incorporate your comments in Lonely Planet products such as guidebooks, web sites and digital products, so let us know if you don't want your comments reproduced or your name acknowledged.

How to contact Lonely Planet:
Online: e talk2us@lonelyplanet.com.au, W www.lonelyplanet.com
Australia: Locked Bag 1, Footscray, Victoria 3011
UK: 10a Spring Place, London NW5 3BH
USA: 150 Linden St, Oakland, CA 94607

Introduction

Out 'back o' Bourke', way 'beyond the black stump', is Australia's outback. It may be hard to define but you'll certainly know it when you see it. It's the mythical Australia – the Australia of red dust, empty tracks, strange wildlife, endless vistas, tall tales and big thirsts. And, myth or not, it's ready and waiting for anyone with a spirit of adventure and some suitable transport.

Some of the routes that take you through the outback are modern sealed roads, like the east-west Eyre Highway and north-south Stuart Highway, but most of them are not. Some of them are not even maintained and it's only the passing of an occasional vehicle that keeps them open. Some of them are long and dreary, others provide a kaleidoscope of changes, but all of them traverse some of the most remote country on earth.

Improved equipment, from more reliable and readily available vehicles to better long-range radios, plus better track maintenance have made all the outback routes more accessible in recent years. Forty years ago a journey down the Birdsville Track required a sturdy 4WD, and a breakdown in summer could easily be a prelude to disaster. Today, with a little care, you can drive the Birdsville in the same car you use for suburban supermarket runs, although breaking down in the heat of summer is still not recommended. Forty years ago only Aborigines and a handful of hardy explorers with camels ever made it across the Simpson Desert. Today there's a steady trickle of 4WD parties crossing this awe-inspiring stretch of land. Even the Canning Stock Route, the three-week-long ultimate outback

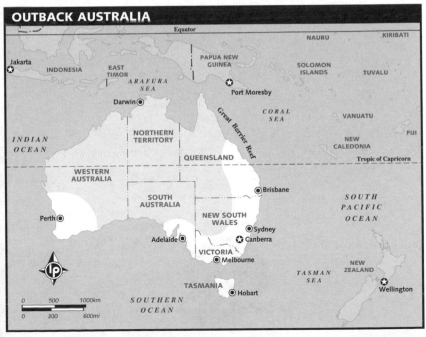

OUTBACK AUSTRALIA

trip, is feasible for any well-equipped group to tackle.

This book covers all of the outback; it explores the easily accessible places like Alice Springs and Kakadu but it also comes to grips with the 'real' outback, the rough and tough tracks where you'd better be equipped with plenty of fuel, plenty of water and plenty of spare tyres. There are full details on when to go (many of the tracks are strictly for the cooler months), what vehicle to use (hardy travellers have even conquered some of the tracks on bicycles or on foot), equipment requirements (tools, radios, spare parts), essential supplies (on the Canning Stock Route it's even necessary to arrange a fuel drop) and safety (foolhardy travellers sometimes still pay with their lives).

The year of publication of this 3rd edition coincides with the Year of the Outback, which means that the outback will offer more attractions and events than ever before. What are you waiting for?

Facts about the Outback

HISTORY

Australia was the last great landmass to be discovered by Europeans. Long before the British claimed it as their own, European explorers and traders had been dreaming of the riches to be found in the unknown – some said mythical – southern land (*terra australis*) that was supposed to form a counterbalance to the landmasses north of the equator. The continent they eventually found had already been inhabited for tens of thousands of years.

Aboriginal Settlement

Australian Aboriginal (which literally means 'indigenous') society has the longest continuous cultural history in the world, with origins dating back to the last ice age. Although mystery shrouds many aspects of Australian prehistory, it seems almost certain that the first humans came here across the sea from South-East Asia. Just when colonisation took place is the subject of hot debate; depending on who you talk to, Aborigines have been living here for at least 50,000 years, possibly as long as 70,000 years.

These early colonisers arrived during a period when the sea level was more than 50m lower than it is today. There was more land between Asia and Australia than there is now, but watercraft were still needed to cross some stretches of open sea. Although much of Australia is today arid, the first migrants found a much wetter continent, with large forests and numerous inland lakes teeming with fish. The fauna included giant marsupials, such as kangaroos that were 3m tall, and huge, flightless birds. The environment was relatively nonthreatening – only a few carnivorous predators existed.

Because of these favourable conditions, archaeologists suggest that within a few thousand years Aborigines had populated much of Australia, although the most central parts of the continent were not occupied until about 24,000 years ago.

The last ice age came to an end 15,000 to 10,000 years ago. The sea level rose dramatically with the rise in temperature. An area of Australia the size of Western Australia was flooded during a process that would have seen strips of land 100km wide inundated in just a few decades. Many of the inland lakes dried up, and vast deserts formed. Although the Aboriginal population was spread fairly evenly throughout the continent 20,000 years ago, the coastal areas became more densely occupied after the end of the last ice age and the stabilisation of the sea level 5000 years ago.

The Development of Culture Areas

The stabilisation of the sea level led to more stable patterns of settlement and the emergence of broad culture areas – Aboriginal groups that exhibited similarities in terms of language, social organisation, tools, art and the environment in which they lived. There is some disagreement among anthropologists about the definition of these areas, and their exact number. The Australian Institute for Aboriginal and Torres Strait Islander Studies (Aiatsis) recognises 11 regional subdivisions in Aboriginal Australia today, while individual anthropologists have identified up to 21.

Traditionally, most Aboriginal people lived either in the desert, in inland nondesert areas, on the coast, or in Tasmania. Throughout the desert, Aborigines exhibited a similar foraging pattern, spreading out over large tracts of land after rain, and retreating to permanent waterholes during dry periods. In the desert and inland nondesert areas, they foraged for insects, birds, reptiles and mammals. They also ate a variety of fruit, and collected various seeds that were ground and mixed with water before being either baked in the coals to make damper, or eaten as a paste.

Coastal Aborigines ate roots, fruit, small game, reptiles, fish and shellfish. In the

Archaeological Treasures

The early Aborigines left no stone buildings or statues to tickle our fancy, but archaeologists have unearthed many other treasures. The best known site by far is Lake Mungo, in the dry Willandra Lakes system in south-western New South Wales.

Mungo (the name is Scottish) is a living, evolving excavation. The archaeologists here are time and weather. This area was once a vast system of inland lakes, dry now for some 20,000 years. The embankment of sand and mud on the eastern fringe of the ancient lake system, named the 'Walls of China' by homesick Chinese workers, has been eroded by the wind in recent years, revealing human and animal skeletal remains, ancient campfires and evidence of trading.

The remains prove that ritual burial was practised here 15,000 years before the construction of the Egyptian pyramids. The fireplaces reveal that sophisticated, tertiary-chipped stone implements were fashioned by the dwellers at the edge of this now dry lake. The food they ate can be discovered in the fireplaces, and the long-extinct animals they preyed on are found in skeletal form on the dunes. This area is so important that Willandra Lakes is now a World Heritage area.

Another fascinating area of study has been Kow Swamp in northern Victoria. This site has a rich collection of human remains that date from the late Pleistocene epoch. One body, buried 12,000 years ago, had a headband of kangaroo incisor teeth. In the lunette of Lake Nitchie, in western New South Wales, a man was buried 6500 to 7000 years ago with a necklace of 178 pierced Tasmanian-devil teeth.

The west and north of Australia have many significant sites. Groove-edged axes dating back 23,000 years have been found in the Malangangerr rock-shelter in Arnhem Land. Other rich sources of artefacts are Miriwun rock-shelter on the Ord River in the Kimberley; the Mt Newman rock-shelter in the Pilbara; and the Devil's Lair near Cape Leeuwin in the far south-west of the continent. Fragments and stone tools dating back 38,000 years were found in the nearby Swan Valley.

Ice-age rock engravings (petroglyphs) have been found throughout the continent. Those in Koonalda Cave, on the Nullarbor in South Australia, are perhaps the oldest. Flint miners often visited the cave 24,000 to 14,000 years ago, and unexplained patterns were left on the wall – perhaps they are art, perhaps not. Other places where petroglyphs are easily seen are on the Burrup Peninsula near Dampier, Western Australia; Mutawintji National Park, between Tibooburra and Broken Hill in far western New South Wales; the Lightning Brothers site, Delamere, Northern Territory; and the Early Human Shelter near Laura in Queensland.

Josephine Flood's *Archaeology of the Dreamtime* (1983) provides a fascinating account of archaeological research into Australia's first inhabitants.

Warning: In Australia it is illegal to remove archaeological objects or to disturb human remains – look but don't touch.

Torres Strait Islands, between Cape York and New Guinea, people ate fish, shellfish, dugong (a relative of the manatee and walrus), fruit and yams. Many Aboriginal people and Torres Strait Islanders still eat traditional foods.

Aboriginal Society

The Aborigines were tribal people living in extended family groups. Many still live in clans, with clan members descending from a common ancestor. Tradition, rituals and laws link the people of each clan to the land they occupy. Each clan has various sites of spiritual significance on their land, places to which their spirits return when they die. Clan members come together to perform rituals to honour their ancestral spirits and the Dreamtime creators. These traditional religious beliefs are the basis of the Aborigines' ties to the land.

It is the responsibility of the clan, or particular members of it, to correctly maintain and protect the sites so that the ancestral beings are not offended and so will continue to protect and provide for the clan. Traditional punishments for those who neglect these responsibilities can still be severe, as their actions can easily affect the wellbeing of the whole clan – food and water shortages, natural disasters and mysterious illnesses can all be attributed to disgruntled or offended ancestral beings.

Many Aboriginal communities were seminomadic, others sedentary, one of the deciding factors being the availability of food. Where food and water were readily available, the people tended to remain in a limited area. When they did wander, it was to visit sacred places to carry out rituals, or to take advantage of seasonal foods available elsewhere. They did not, as is still often believed, roam aimlessly and desperately in search of food and water.

The traditional role of the men was that of hunter, tool-maker and custodian of male law; the women reared the children, and gathered and prepared food. There was also female law and ritual for which the women were responsible. Ultimately, the shared effort of men and women ensured the continuation of their social system. This is still the view of many Aborigines, particularly in northern and central Australia.

Wisdom and skills obtained over millennia enabled Aborigines to use their environment to maximum advantage. An intimate knowledge of animal behaviour and the correct time to harvest the many plants they utilised ensured that food shortages were rare. Like other hunter-gatherer peoples of the world, Aborigines were true ecologists.

Aborigines in northern Australia were in regular contact with the farming and fishing peoples of Indonesia, who came to collect trepang (sea cucumbers). Aboriginal people neither cultivated crops (though some practised insipient agriculture) nor domesticated livestock. Their only major modification of the landscape was through selective burning of undergrowth in forests and dead grass on the plains. This encouraged new growth, which in turn attracted game animals. It also prevented the build-up of combustible material in the forests, making hunting

easier and reducing the possibility of major bush fires. Dingoes assisted in the hunt and guarded the camp from intruders.

Similar technology – for example the boomerang and spear – was used throughout the continent, but techniques were adapted to the environment and the species being hunted. In the wetlands of northern Australia, fish traps hundreds of metres long made of bamboo and cord were built to catch fish at the end of the wet season. In the area now known as Victoria, permanent stone dams many kilometres long were used to trap migrating eels, while in the tablelands of Queensland finely woven nets were used to snare herds of wallabies and kangaroos.

Dwellings varied from simple windbreaks to more permanent structures. Stone was used in western Victoria, while in Tasmania conical thatched shelters that could house up to 30 people were constructed. Such dwellings were used mainly for sleeping.

Aboriginal people were also traders. Trade routes crisscrossed the country, dispersing goods and a variety of produced items. Many of the items traded, such as certain types of stone or shell, were rare and had great ritual significance. Boomerangs and ochre were other important trade items. Along these trading networks, large numbers of people would often meet for 'exchange ceremonies', where not only goods but also songs and dances were passed on. See the Religion section later in this chapter for more on Aboriginal ceremonies and sacred sites.

'Discovery' & Colonisation

Portuguese navigators had probably come within sight of the Australian coast in the first half of the 16th century, and the Chinese may well have visited long before that – a Chinese book, *Classic of Shan Mai*, written before 338 BC, notes kangaroos and dark-skinned people using boomerangs in a land to the south. In 1606 the Spaniard Luis Vaez de Torres sailed through the strait between Cape York and New Guinea that still bears his name, though there's no record of his actually sighting the southern continent.

In the early 1600s Dutch explorers began to map parts of the Australian coastline, and the southern continent became known to the world as New Holland – a name that stuck until the second half of the 19th century, when British settlers began using the label 'Australia'. Traders first and foremost, the Dutch found little of value in this 'barren' continent with its 'backward' inhabitants, and saw it as an obstacle to be avoided on their hazardous sea voyages to the rich East Indies.

Heading east from the Cape of Good Hope, Dutch captains intent on making time rode the Roaring Forties, the icy but powerful winds of the sub-Antarctic, for as long as they dared before changing course to the north. 'Dared' because longitude calculations were very much guesswork before the invention of the chronometer in the 18th century, and many of the more reckless captains smashed their ships into the Western Australian coast.

During the colonisation drive of the 18th century French and British explorers began to take a stronger interest in New Holland. Captain James Cook, with one of the first chronometers on board, 'discovered' the relatively fertile eastern coast that earlier explorers had overlooked, and the British government, to head off French claims, established a penal colony there in 1788 under the name of New South Wales.

Devastation of the Aborigines

When Sydney Cove was first settled by the British, it is believed there were about 750,000 Aboriginal people in Australia and that around 250 different languages were spoken, many as distinct from each other as English is from Chinese. Tasmania alone had eight languages, and tribes living on opposite sides of present-day Sydney Harbour spoke mutually unintelligible languages.

In such a society, based on family groups and with an egalitarian political structure, a coordinated response to the Europeans was not possible. Despite the presence of Aboriginal people, the newly arrived colonisers declared this new continent to be *terra nullius* – quite literally, a land belonging to no-one. Conveniently, they saw no recognisable system of government, no visible commerce or permanent settlements and no

evidence of landownership. (If the opposite had been the case, and if the Aborigines had offered coordinated resistance, the English might have been forced to legitimise their colonisation by entering into a treaty with the Aboriginal landowners, as happened in New Zealand with the Treaty of Waitangi.)

Many Aboriginal people were driven from their land by force, and many more succumbed to exotic diseases such as smallpox, measles, venereal disease, influenza, whooping cough, pneumonia and tuberculosis. Others voluntarily travelled to the fringes of European-settled areas in order to obtain new commodities such as steel and cloth, and to access hitherto unknown drugs such as tea, tobacco and alcohol.

The delicate balance between Aboriginal people and the environment was broken as the European invaders cut down forests and introduced numerous animals – by 1860 there were 20 million sheep in Australia. Sheep and cattle destroyed waterholes and ruined the habitats which had for tens of thousands of years sustained the Aborigines' food sources.

Competition for water and land often led to warfare between Aborigines and white settlers. Starving Aborigines speared sheep and cattle, and often settlers, and then suffered bloody reprisal raids. For the first 150 years of 'settlement' very few Europeans were prosecuted for killing Aborigines, although the practice was widespread.

In many parts of Australia, Aboriginal people defended their lands with desperate guerrilla tactics. Warriors such as Pemulwy, Yagan, Dundalli, Jandamarra and Nemarluk were feared by the colonists for a time, and some settlements had to be abandoned. Until the introduction of breech-loading repeater rifles in the 1870s, Aboriginal people sometimes had the benefit of superior numbers, weapons and tactics. The new rifles were accurate and reliable, and armed resistance was quickly crushed (although on isolated occasions into the 1920s, whites were still speared in central and northern Australia). Full-blood Aboriginal people in Tasmania were wiped out, and Aboriginal society elsewhere in Australia suffered terribly. By the

1880s only relatively small groups in the remotest outback were unscathed by the European invasion.

'Protection' & 'Assimilation' By the early 1900s legislation designed to segregate and 'protect' Aboriginal people was passed in all states. The legislation imposed restrictions on their rights to own property and seek employment. The Aboriginals Ordinance of 1918 even allowed the state to remove children from Aboriginal mothers if it was suspected that the father was non-Aboriginal. In these cases the parents were considered to have no rights over the children, who were placed in foster homes or childcare institutions. Many Aborigines are still suffering the effects of having been separated from their families and forced to grow up apart from their people. This practice continued up until the 1970s.

The processes of social change were accelerated by WWII, and after the war 'assimilation' became the stated aim of the government. To this end, the rights of Aborigines were subjugated even further – the government had control over everything, from where Aborigines could live to whom they could marry. Many people were forcibly moved to townships, the idea being that they would adapt to European culture, which would in turn aid their economic development. This policy was a dismal failure.

In the 1960s the assimilation policy came under a great deal of scrutiny, and white Australians became increasingly aware of the inequity of the treatment of Aborigines. In 1967 non-Aboriginal Australians voted to give Aborigines and Torres Strait Islanders the status of citizens and thus the right to vote, and gave the federal government power to legislate for them in all states. The states had to provide them with the same services available to other citizens, and the federal government set up the Department of Aboriginal Affairs to identify and legislate for the special needs of Aboriginal people.

In 1972 the assimilation policy was finally dumped and replaced with the government's policy of 'self-determination', which for the first time enabled Aborigines to participate in decision-making processes by granting them rights to their land. See Aboriginal Land Rights, later in this chapter, for more about government policies on Aboriginal people.

In 1997 a comprehensive, independent report by government and nongovernmental agencies on the removal of Aboriginal children from their families, titled *Bringing Them Home*, gave rise to the term 'Stolen Generations'. The trauma of separation from family and culture had wide-ranging consequences for those concerned and has been passed on to subsequent generations. However, the federal government criticised the report and in early 2000 released its own report claiming there was no Stolen Generation and that 'only 10%' of indigenous children were taken.

State and territory governments have now made formal apologies to Aboriginal and Torres Strait Islander people, but the federal government refuses to do so. Prime Minister John Howard has expressed his personal 'sincere regret' but firmly refuses to say sorry on behalf of the nation, believing that no-one should be held responsible for the actions of the past.

Meanwhile, many Aborigines still live in appalling conditions, and alcohol and drug abuse remains a huge problem. Aboriginal communities have taken up the challenge of eradicating these problems – many Aboriginal communities are now 'dry', and there are rehabilitation programs for alcoholics, petrol-sniffers and others with drug problems. Thanks for much of this work goes to Aboriginal women, many of whom have found themselves on the receiving end of domestic violence.

Health statistics highlight some of the most shocking disparities between Aboriginal and non-Aboriginal people. The average life expectancy of the latter is 78.3 years, while Aboriginal people can expect to live for 60 years. At the beginning of the 21st century, basic needs such as clean water, proper sewerage, access to decent health services, education and housing are still far from a reality for Aboriginal people.

In many ways contemporary Australia is a nation of contradictions – combining idealism and generosity with regressive attitudes towards Aborigines. The contempt of some non-Aboriginal Australians for Aborigines has its origins in the massacres that mar modern history. Unfortunately, these attitudes have often been uncritically absorbed by later migrants. In 2000, however, hundreds of thousands of non-Aboriginal people marched with Aborigines in support of reconciliation. There is a spirit of optimism and an obvious commitment from many in both communities to rectify the wrongs of the past.

White Exploration

Twenty-five years after the establishment of New South Wales, Gregory Blaxland, William Lawson and William C Wentworth crossed the mountains west of Sydney Cove and the white exploration of inland Australia began. Already the coast was fairly well known, with Matthew Flinders making his great circumnavigation of the continent in 1803 and Phillip Parker King's voyages between 1817 and 1822 filling in most of the blanks.

By the 1840s John Oxley, Hamilton Hume, William Hovell, Charles Sturt and

First Contact in the Western Desert

The Anangu people of the Western Desert were the last Aborigines to have first contact with non-Aboriginal people. The last Anangu to abandon their autonomous hunter-gatherer lifestyle were a small group of Pintupi, who in 1984 walked into Kintore, a community 350km north-west of Uluru (Ayers Rock).

First contact in other parts of the Western Desert is also relatively recent, even in the Uluru region that today receives 300,000 tourists annually. Although Ernest Giles passed through the Western Desert region in the 1870s, in the following 50 years non-Aboriginal visitation was so infrequent that many Anangu didn't see a white person until the 1930s or '40s or even later.

By the early 1950s most Anangu were living permanently or semipermanently on missions, or on pastoral properties where they often worked for no payment other than food and clothing. Up until the late 1960s they continued to spend considerable periods travelling around on foot or on camels, in many cases still hunting with kulata (spears) and miru (spear throwers).

Up until the 1960s, government patrol officers searched out groups of Anangu, many of whom had experienced little or no contact with non-Aborigines, and trucked them from remote parts of the Western Desert to various settlements. This was part of a government policy which stated that Aborigines should be encouraged to abandon their traditions and become assimilated into mainstream white society.

In other parts of the Western Desert, Anangu were forcibly removed to make way for the testing of military hardware. In 1946 a guided-missile range was established at Woomera, within what was then the Central Desert Aboriginal Reserve. Until at least 1966, groups of Anangu were brought in from areas where testing had taken place. In some cases these people had been traumatised by rockets but had not experienced face-to-face contact with whites.

As well as testing conventional weapons, in the 1950s the Australian government permitted the British to detonate atomic devices at Emu Junction, 500km south-west of Uluru; and at Maralinga a little further south. The authorities claimed that prior to detonation two patrol officers combed thousands of square kilometres, ensuring that no Anangu people were harmed by the tests. Anangu have another story: they say that as a result of these tests many people became sick and died.

Yami Lester is a Yankunytjatjara man who was a child at the time one of the British nuclear devices was detonated 180km from his home. As a result of radioactive fallout, Yami saw many of his relatives sicken and die; some years later, he went blind. Yami – The Autobiography of Yami Lester provides an excellent insight into many aspects of early Western Desert contact, and the struggle for land rights that took place some decades later.

Thomas Mitchell had blazed their trails of exploration across south-eastern Australia, opening up the country between Sydney and the newer settlements of Melbourne and Adelaide. Over in the west, explorers had set out from Perth to survey the land southwards close to present-day Albany and northwards to the Gascoyne River. In 1838 a group of men under Charles (later Sir) Grey landed on a rugged stretch of coast in the Kimberley at Hanover Bay and got nowhere, barely escaping with their lives in the forbidding terrain.

It is ironic that some explorers died of thirst and starvation in a land where Aborigines had survived for thousands of years. Rather than living with the land, they chose to conquer it the only way they knew: with weapons and supplies.

The 'Inland Sea' While trying to find a way into the centre of the continent, Edward Eyre explored the Flinders Ranges in South Australia in 1840. A vast salt lake that he called Lake Torrens blocked his way (in reality it was a number of lakes, now called Torrens, Eyre and Frome, to name a few). It was this so-called impassable barrier that forced Sturt, a few years later, to head east and then north.

Giving up on his quest for the centre of Australia, Eyre, in an epic feat, crossed from Port Lincoln in South Australia to Albany in the west. Although he was a little more successful than Grey and travelled a darn sight further, he too nearly died along the way. One of the only things he proved was that it was impossible to drive cattle from Adelaide to Perth via the coast.

In 1844, Charles Sturt, already a well-known and respected explorer, set out from Adelaide on his greatest expedition, to find what many thought would be an 'inland sea'. Following the Murray and Darling Rivers to a point near Menindee, his team struck north-west. Trapped by unbelievable heat and lack of water, the men spent months at Depot Glen, near present-day Milparinka, before pushing further inland, finally reaching a spot on Eyre Creek north of what is now Birdsville. Forced back by the unrelenting conditions, it was thanks to Sturt's skills that only one man died on this 18-month journey. Sturt's health never fully recovered, and although he was welcomed back to civilisation a hero and promoted to government positions, he soon had to retire because of deteriorating eyesight.

The Tropics The opening up of the Moreton Bay area in south-eastern Queensland to white settlement in 1842 soon led to pioneer pastoralists pushing further north and west. In 1845 the enigmatic Ludwig Leichhardt led his men from Brisbane to Port Essington (near present-day Darwin) in one of the great sagas of exploration, while Mitchell crossed the Darling River and pushed north into central Queensland. Mitchell went on to be knighted, but Leichhardt vanished without trace somewhere in central Australia soon after.

In 1848 Edmund Kennedy set off from Rockingham Bay, just south of Cairns, and headed north towards the tip of Cape York through the mountains and jungles of northern Queensland. Forced to split his men and leave them at camps along the way, Kennedy met his death when he and his Aboriginal friend Jackey-Jackey (Galmarra) were attacked by Aborigines near the headwaters of the Escape and Jardine Rivers, just a few kilometres south of where a boat was waiting for them. There were only two other survivors of the 14 people who had set out, and they owed their lives to Jackey-Jackey, who led the ship and the crew back to where they had been left.

In the mid- to late 1850s AC Gregory blazed a trail from the Victoria River, near the border of Western Australia and the Northern Territory, across the top of the continent and down the coast to Brisbane. A member of the team was Thomas Baines, an artist who had done extensive work in southern Africa, and his paintings of their adventures with crocodiles and hostile Aborigines in northern Australia still exist. AC Gregory's brother Francis discovered good pastoral land in Western Australia between Geraldton and the De Grey River, 1000km further north.

Burke & Wills In 1860 the stage was set for the greatest act in the white exploration of Australia. Some today would say that it was the greatest folly, but the Burke and Wills expedition was the largest, most lavish and best-equipped expedition ever to attempt to solve the riddle of inland Australia.

The lure of being the first to cross the continent was only part of the story. In 1859 the wonder of the telegraph line had reached India and was soon to head for Darwin. Depending on the route forged across the continent by an explorer, an overland telegraph line would finish either in Adelaide or Melbourne. Melbourne was the brashly rich capital of the colony of Victoria, where a gold rush fuelled the fires of progress. In South Australia, however, the government was offering £2000 to the first explorer who crossed the continent.

From Adelaide, John McDouall Stuart, who had been with Sturt on his central Australian expedition, was pushing his way further and further north in a series of small expeditions. The race was on!

With much fanfare Robert O'Hara Burke led the Victorian Exploring Expedition north out of Melbourne on 20 August 1860. Chosen by a committee of the Royal Society, Burke was neither an explorer nor a surveyor, had no scientific training, had never led an expedition of any kind, had never set foot out of Victoria since arriving there just a few years previously, and was considered to be, if anything, a very poor bushman. He also ignored the advice from earlier explorers to enlist the help of Aboriginal guides. So much for committees.

Leaving most of his group at Menindee (then at the outer limits of white civilisation), Burke and his new second-in-command, William John Wills, pushed north to Cooper Creek, where they set up a depot. From there Burke chose Wills, Charles Grey and John King to accompany him to the Gulf of Carpentaria, leaving the depot and the remainder of the expedition on 16 December 1860. At the height of summer, these men set out to walk 1100km through central Australia to the sea! It says something of their fortitude and sheer guts that, on 11 February 1861, they made it, reaching the mangroves that barred their view of the Gulf of Carpentaria. Camp No 119 was their northernmost camp and can be visited today.

Turning their backs on the sea, the rush south became a life-and-death stagger, with Grey dying at a place later called Lake Massacre, just west of the Cooper Creek depot. When Burke, Wills and King arrived at the depot they were astonished to find that the men there had retreated to Menindee that very morning! The famous Dig Tree, one of the most significant historic sites in inland Australia, still stands on the banks of Cooper Creek. The name relates to the message carved into the trunk of this coolabah by the departing men: 'DIG 3FT N.W. APR. 21 1861.' Unfortunately the buried supplies weren't enough to revive the explorers.

Trapped at Cooper Creek they wasted away, Burke and Wills dying on the banks of this desert oasis. King, who had been befriended by some Aborigines, was alive when the first of the rescue parties arrived in September 1861.

These rescue expeditions really opened up the interior for the Europeans, with groups from Queensland, South Australia and Victoria crisscrossing the continent in search of Burke and Wills. Howitt, McKinlay, Landsborough and Walker were not only better explorers than Burke, but experienced bushmen who proved that Europeans, cattle and sheep could survive in these regions.

Meanwhile, the determined Stuart finally crossed the continent, reaching Chambers Bay, east of present-day Darwin, in July 1862. So well planned and executed were his expeditions that the Overland Telegraph Line followed his route, as did the original railway line and road.

The Jardines Over in Queensland, the Jardine brothers battled their way north through the wilds of Cape York to the new settlement of Somerset in 1864. They took nine months to drive their mob of 300-odd cattle and 20 or so horses through plains scorched by the dry season in the southwestern Cape, across rivers flooded during the wet season in the central and northern

Cape, while fighting with hostile Aborigines all the way. Frank Jardine, the leader of the small group, stayed on at Somerset, where he died in 1919 after building an empire of cattle and pearls.

The 'Empty' West Explorer John Forrest crossed from Perth to Fowlers Bay in South Australia and from Geraldton to the Overland Telegraph Line, between 1869 and 1875. Meanwhile, William Gosse, leaving from the telegraph station at Alice Springs, had happened upon Ayers Rock while trying to find a route westwards.

Major Peter Warburton was also in Alice Springs around the same time, trying to find a route to the west. Pushed north by the harsh deserts and finally subsisting on a spoonful of flour and water for breakfast, a tough strip of dried camel meat for lunch and whatever they could collect from bushes for dinner, his team finally made it to the Oakover River. At one stage they were forced to eat the hide of the camels as well. As Warburton wrote in his book, *Journey Across the Western Interior of Australia*, camel hide needed 'about forty hours continuous boiling and is then very good'!

At the same time Ernest Giles was also trying to be the first to cross the western half of Australia. He was the first white man to see Kata Tjuta, naming it the Olgas after the queen of Spain. The lake that blocked his path he named Lake Amadeus, after the king. Forced back after the loss of his companion, Alf Gibson, Giles finally crossed the deserts further south. A few months later he crossed the continent again, this time from the Gascoyne River in the west to the Olgas and the telegraph line in the east. The year was 1876 and Giles died 20 years later, unknown, in the gold-rush town of Coolgardie. His two-volume book, *Australia Twice Traversed*, is regularly reprinted as a facsimile.

By then, the big picture of Australia was filled in. Some of the detail still needed completing, and during the 1890s the first of the 'scientific expeditions' sallied forth looking for minerals and studying flora, fauna, and the Aboriginal people who still lived according to their tribal ways in the vast interior.

The 1891 Elder Scientific Exploring Expedition, under David Lindsay, explored the area to the north-east of Coolgardie, and the 1894 Horn expedition explored south and west of Alice Springs. The Calvert Expedition, led by Lawrence Wells, met tragedy in the Great Sandy Desert of Western Australia in 1896, about the same time as a young gold prospector, David Carnegie, was blazing a trail north from Coolgardie to Halls Creek and back again. Carnegie died a few years later, not in the waterless wastes of Australia, but after being wounded by a poisoned arrow in Nigeria.

In 1906 Alfred Canning, using the knowledge of these explorers, mapped and then constructed his famous stock route from Wiluna to Halls Creek. Today this line of wells is one of the greatest 4WD adventures left on the planet.

The 20th Century Around the turn of the century, Baldwin Spencer, a biologist, and Francis Gillen, an anthropologist, teamed up to study the Aborigines of central Australia and Arnhem Land. The result was one of the most detailed records ever of a now-vanished way of life. Other expeditions to northern Australia and Arnhem Land were led by the British polar explorer GH Wilkins (in 1923) and Donald Mackay (in 1928). Donald Thomson led his first expedition to Arnhem Land in 1935 and his work in northern Australia still receives accolades from anthropologists and naturalists.

In 1930, the mapping of central Australia began in earnest, financed by Donald Mackay. Aerial surveys were carried out over the Simpson Desert, the only large stretch of the country not explored on foot. In 1939 CT Madigan led an expedition that crossed this forbidding landscape from Old Andado to Birdsville; today his unmarked route attracts experienced adventurers.

In 1948 the largest scientific expedition ever undertaken in Australia was led by Charles Mountford into Arnhem Land. Financed by the National Geographic Society and the Australian government, it collected over 13,000 fish, 13,500 plant specimens, 850 birds and over 450 skins, along with

The Lure of Gold

If the need for grazing land was the major reason behind European exploration and colonisation of the outback (see the boxed text 'The Cattle Kings' later in this chapter), the search for gold added to the impetus.

The first recorded find of gold in Australia was in 1823 in New South Wales, but it was not until early 1851, when Edward Hargraves vigorously promoted his meagre finds at Ophir, near Bathurst, that the first real rush started. A licensing system was introduced whereby each person paid 30 shillings, both to limit the number of diggers and to encourage the unsuccessful to return to their jobs.

The drift of the population northwards to the gold fields of New South Wales prompted the Victorian government, on 9 June 1851, to offer a £200 reward for the discovery of a payable gold field within 200 miles of Melbourne. Early the following month, the finds of James Esmond at Clunes were made public. In August diggers were flocking to Ballarat, later to be one of the greatest sources of gold. In September the rush was to the shallow fields around Mt Alexander (later Castlemaine). By December there were 20,000 diggers spread out around there and as far north as Bendigo.

The following years saw rushes to new discoveries in Victoria, especially in Eaglehawk Gully, the largely inaccessible creeks around Omeo in Gippsland, and the Buckland River on the rugged Ovens field. In 1854, Maldon, Avoca, Maryborough and Ararat were opened up.

The diggers came from all parts of the world and from a range of professions. They included people from England and Ireland, continental Europeans (especially Germans), some veterans of the Californian gold fields (the '49ers') and impoverished Chinese from Kwangtung province.

Melbourne was the new San Francisco, teeming with diggers infected with a golden wanderlust. Canvas Town, a sea of tents, was established between Princes Bridge and the bay beaches, to accommodate the migrants before they began the hazardous journey to the gold fields.

The introduction of a licence fee on the Victorian fields was met with resentment, especially the strict enforcement of fee collections with biweekly licence hunts. After a number of incidents that inflamed the mostly Irish miners of the Eureka lode near Ballarat, they erected the Eureka Stockade as a symbol of their own protection. Peter Lalor led the diggers' oath of allegiance to the flag of the Southern Cross. When the stockade was attacked by soldiers and police on 3 December 1854, about 30 miners and five soldiers were killed. None of the protesters were convicted and the diggers' stand hastened reform. The following year 'miner's right' was introduced – a document entitling the holder to search for and remove minerals from crown land in return for an annual registration fee of £1.

In 1858 diggers began to move north towards Rockhampton (also called Fitzroy, or Anoona). In the autumn of 1860 Victorians crossed the border and climbed high into the Snowy Mountains to

---

thousands of Aboriginal implements and weapons.

During the 1950s the Woomera Rocket Range and the atomic-bomb test sites of Emu Junction and Maralinga were developed. This vast region, which had been seen by few whites since Gosse, Giles and Canning, was opened up by the surveyor Len Beadell, widely regarded as the last Australian explorer. It was, as one of his books is called, the 'End of an Era'.

This is not to say that people haven't accomplished some amazing feats since then. In 2001, for instance, Jon Muir, a Victorian adventurer who had climbed Mt Everest and walked to the South Pole, spent 128 days walking 2500km from Port Augusta in the south to Burketown on the Gulf of Carpentaria, alone and unassisted – the first person to do so. In the process he crossed the Southern Simpson, Tirari, Western Strzelecki and Sturt Stony Deserts, as well as Lake Eyre. 'Nothing I've done before has been as hard as this,' he said.

GEOGRAPHY

Australia is the world's sixth-largest country. Lying between the Indian and Pacific

The Lure of Gold

the alpine rush at Kiandra. Winter snows forced the diggers to look elsewhere, which they did with success – Forbes and Young became rich fields.

Queensland's turn for such frenzy came in 1867, when the white quartz reefs of Gympie were discovered. Four years later, it was the rich fields of Charters Towers, then the steamy tropical forests of the Palmer River and the fields on Cape York, which lured only the desperate.

Discoveries in the Northern Territory followed, and a workable gold field at Pine Creek was announced in August 1872. Isolation, the high costs of mining, and the marauding Aborigines were problems. Coolies (indentured labourers) were brought in to work the fields, and when the work stopped they went over the alluvial deposits for a second time.

In 1886 the Croydon field was opened about 500km north-west of Charters Towers. Gold was discovered at Halls Creek in the remote Kimberley in 1885, and diggers on the Queensland fields soon made the anticlockwise trek to the new riches. The terrain in the Kimberley was inhospitable and the track from the wharves at Wyndham and Derby was the most ferocious that miners in Australia had yet negotiated. Still, they pushed across it and, unbelievably, many miners walked to it from the Queensland fields.

The Pilbara was the next to reveal its riches. The year 1888 saw diggers pouring over Pilbara Creek and fanning out through the dry gorges to Marble Bar, Nullagine and the Ashburton River. Despite the intense heat, the lure of gold held them fast and some diggers were rewarded with finds of huge nuggets.

Gold was found inland from Geraldton, near Nannine, in 1890. The Murchison field now bloomed and Cue, Day Dawn, Payne's Find, Lake Austin and Mount Magnet joined the huge list of gold towns in the outback.

More discoveries followed, especially around Southern Cross in Western Australia's Yilgarn district, first opened in 1888. Major strikes were made in 1892 at Coolgardie and nearby Kalgoorlie, the only large town left today in the Western Australian gold fields.

Coolgardie's period of prosperity lasted only until 1905 – many other gold towns went from nothing to populations of 10,000 then back to nothing in just 10 years. Western Australia profited from the gold boom for the rest of the 19th century (and still profits today). It was gold that put the state on the map and finally gave it the population to make it viable in its own right.

Depressions and unemployment often attracted fossickers back to the gullies and rivers, especially during the Great Depression in the 1930s. In other places, like the Golden Mile in Kalgoorlie-Boulder, mining never stopped.

Oceans, it measures about 4000km from east to west and 3200km from north to south, with a coastline 36,735km long. Its area is 7,682,300 sq km (about 5% of the world's land surface), similar in size to the 48 mainland states of the USA, and half as large again as Europe excluding the former USSR (Perth to Melbourne is the same distance as London to Moscow). Over 75% of the continent is generally referred to as 'the outback' (ie, very sparsely settled and remote from the coastal plains of the east, south-east and south-west, the regions where over 90% of Australians live).

Worn down by time, the often monotonous landscape of this island continent is the result of gradual changes wrought over many millions of years. Parts of the outback are among the world's oldest land surfaces. Its last great mountain-building events took place over 300 million years ago, and as a result its once-mighty highlands have long since been eroded down to their stumps.

Most of the outback of Australia is taken up by the Western Australian Shield, which lies west of a line drawn south from the east coast of Arnhem Land, around the western margin of the Simpson Desert and on to

Eyre Peninsula in South Australia. The shield is a vast plateau with an average elevation somewhere between 300m and 460m. It has been fractured into blocks, or cratons, some of which have subsided to form lowlands while others have been raised to form rugged uplands.

The latter include the Hamersley Ranges in the west, the ranges of the Kimberley region in the north-west, and the MacDonnell and Musgrave ranges of central Australia. At 1531m above sea level, Mt Zeil in the West MacDonnells is the country's highest point west of the Great Dividing Range. Scattered over large areas are striking flat-topped hills (mesas), such as Mt Conner in central Australia, whose tops represent the ancient land surface now largely removed by erosion.

The shield's lowlands include the Nullarbor Plain in the south – its name is derived from the Latin for 'no tree'. This flat, dry limestone area is largely devoid of scenic interest but has extensive cave systems, several of world class. Other arid lowlands are the Great Sandy and Gibson Deserts in the north-west and the Great Victoria Desert in the central shield area. Shaped by the prevailing winds, the directions of which they parallel, the long, linear dunes of these inhospitable areas, and the Simpson Desert further east, were formed about 10,000 years ago during a period of peak aridity.

East of the Western Australian Shield and butting onto the Great Dividing Range is a world of vast plains with few significant uplands – the spectacular Flinders Ranges in South Australia are a notable exception. Known as the Central Lowlands, this region overlies the world's largest reservoir of artesian water: the Great Artesian Basin. Its central west includes the Simpson and Tirari sand-ridge deserts and the gibber-plated desolation of Sturt Stony Desert, all in Australia's driest area. Even here artesian water makes low-density sheep and cattle grazing possible where the native vegetation is palatable.

The Western Australian Shield is generally lacking in surface drainage, except in the ranges of the north, central west and south-west. The Central Lowlands, on the

other hand, has the Cooper Creek and Diamantina River systems. These mainly dry, inland rivers rise in central and north-western Queensland respectively, and wend their way for around 1500km to Lake Eyre in north-eastern South Australia. Covering 9700 sq km, Lake Eyre is the largest of a number of huge, mainly dry salt lakes in this part of the state – at 15m below sea level, its bed is the continent's lowest point. These lakes are the remains of a shallow inland sea that once stretched south from the Gulf of Carpentaria.

More than one-third of Australia lies north of the Tropic of Capricorn and is thus technically within the tropics. However, only the extreme north – the Kimberley, Cape York and the northern part of the Northern Territory (the so-called Top End) – lies within the monsoon belt. The long dry season and infertile soils – not to mention remoteness from markets – have prevented the far north becoming a major agricultural producer, although suitable areas for farming do exist and are being developed. The most important is the Ord River irrigation scheme in the Kimberley, and there are other ones near Katherine and Darwin.

GEOLOGY

Along with Africa, South America, Antarctica and India, Australia once formed part of the supercontinent called Gondwana. It became a continent in its own right only about 100 million years ago, when it broke away from Antarctica. Since then it has been drifting north – its current rate of drift is about 55mm per year – and in another 100 million years it will collide with Indonesia. So in a very short time (geologically speaking) the continent will cease to exist as a separate entity.

Australia can be divided into two broad geological zones: the Tasman Fold Belt and the Australian Craton. These lie east and west, respectively, of a line drawn roughly between Kangaroo Island in South Australia and Princess Charlotte Bay, near Cooktown in far north Queensland.

Virtually the entire area generally referred to today as 'the outback' lies on a huge crustal block called the Australian Craton. The craton is geologically ancient, its basement metamorphic and igneous rocks ranging in age from 370 million to 3.7 billion years. Its oldest rock formations – in Western Australia's Pilbara region – contain crystals that formed 4.3 billion years ago, making them part of the earth's original crust. At North Pole, also in the Pilbara, are the fossil remains of stromatolites that lived 3.5 billion years ago. Still in existence after all this time, stromatolites are the world's oldest known form of life – see the Palaeontology section later in this chapter.

The Australian Craton is actually made up of several small crustal blocks of igneous material such as granite that became welded together about a billion years ago. Today these blocks are mostly buried by sedimentary material, although they emerge at places like Mt Isa, Broken Hill and in the Tanami Desert. All these areas contain rich mineral deposits that today sustain major mining developments. The eroded remnants of the original sandstone blanket form the rugged landscapes we now admire in the north-west Kimberley region and Kakadu, in the Top End. In the Pilbara, marine sediments laid down 2500 million years ago form huge deposits of iron oxide now being mined at Mt Tom Price, Mt Newman and elsewhere.

Other rocks in this ancient mantle include reminders of the vast ice sheets that covered Australia during ferocious ice ages 750 and 670 million years ago. Although much of this evidence is buried, exposures of glacial debris called tillite can be seen at Ellery Creek in the MacDonnell Ranges and Tillite Gorge, near Arkaroola in the Flinders Ranges. Deposits of tillite reach 5.5km in thickness in the northern Flinders. This was probably where the ice sheet met an inland sea, melting at the bottom and so dropping its load of rubble.

At that time Australia was still drifting around as a separate entity and was actually in the tropics. Gondwana was formed about 600 million years ago, when its various components bumped into each other and bonded. The collisions created shock waves that are thought to have caused the Petermann Event in central Australia. These forces buckled the crust into a chain of mighty mountains that stretched 2000km from the north-west to Broken Hill. Over millions of years, snow-fed torrents gouged deep into the mountains, washing huge quantities of debris into a shallow sea on their northern flank.

Today the original Petermann Ranges are mere hills, best seen on the road between Uluru-Kata Tjuta National Park and Laverton, in Western Australia. The outwash material originally deposited in the sea has likewise largely been stripped away by erosion, although several spectacular remnants still rise above the sand plain. Kata Tjuta is formed of large rocks, so this area must have been quite close to the original mountains. Eastwards, and further out in the ancient sea, Uluru is composed of coarse sand and gravel, while Mt Conner is capped by fine sand and silt.

During the Petermann Event the Tasman Fold Belt was a deep sea basin with volcanic islands. Then, about 500 million years ago, the first of a series of mountain-building episodes threw up an Andes-like mountain range along the Australian Craton's eastern side. Today the only remnants of it are the Transantarctica Mountains of Antarctica, and the Flinders Ranges. Over a period of 110 million years these events gradually pushed the coastline 1000km eastwards.

Meanwhile, the Australian Craton has been relatively stable, which helps explain why it is generally so flat. Over the past 500 million years the major interruptions to its stability have been periods of inundation by shallow seas, and the earth movements that formed the ancestral MacDonnell Ranges about 320 million years ago.

On the heels of this event, another period of global cooling brought glaciers and extensive ice sheets to Australia's southern half. Later bursts of warm, moist climate encouraged the growth of dense forests. Buried under thick layers of sediment, their remains turned into huge coal seams, producing large reservoirs of oil and gas. These are now being tapped around Moomba in north-eastern South Australia and in south-western Queensland.

Most of the Australian Craton was dry land between 250 and 140 million years ago, after which a major rise in sea level created an inland sea covering a third of the continent. Marine siltstones from this period contain precious opal, now mined at a number of places including Coober Pedy in South Australia and White Cliffs in New South Wales. Another inundation occurred 10 to 15 million years ago, creating the limestone deposits that today make up the Nullarbor Plain.

For further reading, *The Voyage of the Great Southern Ark* by Reg & Maggie Morrison tells the fascinating story of the four-billion-year journey of the Australian continent, and explains the evolution of its landscapes, plants and animals. The book is easy to understand and lavishly illustrated.

CLIMATE

Australian seasons are the antithesis of those in Europe and North America. Summer starts in December, autumn in March, winter in June and spring in September.

The climatic extremes aren't too severe in most parts of Australia. Even in Melbourne, the southernmost capital city on the mainland, it's rare for the mercury to hit freezing point, although it's different in the mountains around Canberra, the national capital.

As you head north the seasonal variations become less pronounced until, in the far north around Darwin and up in Cape York, you're in the monsoon belt where there are just two seasons: hot and wet, and hot and dry.

The centre of the continent has a typical desert climate – hot and dry during the day but often bitterly cold at night in the 'winter' months, when temperatures below freezing are not uncommon.

See the Planning section in the Facts for the Visitor chapter for information about the best times to visit the outback. See also the Bicycle section in the Getting Around chapter if you want to take advantage of the prevailing winds, which can make a big difference in fuel costs.

FLORA

Australia's tropical north is largely covered with forest, despite the fact that at least seven months of the year are hot and dry. The climate is much harsher in the arid inland, of course, but even the Simpson Desert is well vegetated – tourists expecting to marvel at endless expanses of naked sand and rock will be disappointed. The Mac-Donnell Ranges near Alice Springs, close to the Simpson's north-western corner, contain nearly 600 native plant species, including a number of rainforest relicts.

Plants have to be tough to cope with the harsh conditions, which might seem ideal for succulent plants such as the cactus. However, Australian deserts, unlike most of those overseas, have very few true water-holding plants and none are related to the cactus. This type of plant requires a reliable supply of water – even if it is scanty – and Australian deserts don't provide this.

Origins

Australia's distinctive vegetation began to take shape about 100 million years ago when Australia broke from the southern supercontinent of Gondwana, drifting away from Antarctica to warmer climes. Then, Australia was completely covered by cool-climate rainforest, but due to its geographic

ALICE SPRINGS

Elevation – 546m/1791ft

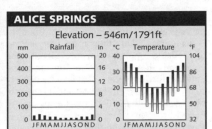

BROOME

Elevation – 17m/55ft

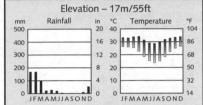

COEN

Elevation – 160m/524ft

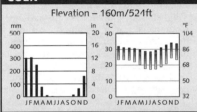

COOBER PEDY

Elevation – 215m/705ft

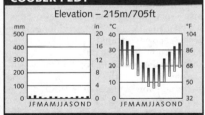

DARWIN

Elevation – 31m/101ft

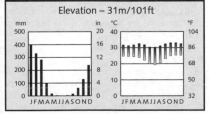

GILES

Elevation – 598m/1961ft

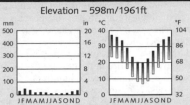

KALGOORLIE

Elevation – 360m/1181ft

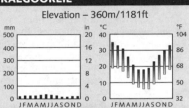

KUNUNURRA

Elevation – 47m/154ft

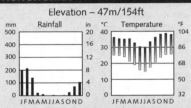

MT ISA

Elevation – 343m/1125ft

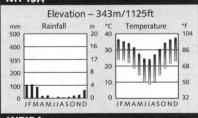

WEIPA

Elevation – 20m/65ft

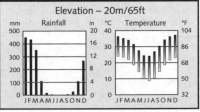

isolation and the gradual drying of the continent, rainforests retreated, plants such as eucalypts (gum trees) and acacias (or wattles) took over and grasslands expanded. Eucalypts and wattles were able to adapt to the warmer temperatures, increased natural occurrence of fire and later the use of fire by Aboriginal people for hunting and other purposes. Now many species benefit from fire, relying on it to crack open their tough seed casings.

The arrival of Europeans two centuries ago saw the introduction of new flora, fauna and land-management practices. Even in the outback, native vegetation has been displaced by pasture grasses or degraded by grazing pressure; Aboriginal burning practices have largely ceased; and soils have been severely damaged by hoofed imports such as cows, sheep and goats. As a result, there have been major, usually detrimental, changes to the native vegetation and its dynamics over vast areas.

Interesting books on Australian flora include *Field Guide to Native Plants of Australia* and *The Greening of Gondwana* by Mary E White. Good places to see outback plants are Brisbane's Mt Coot-tha Botanic Gardens, the Adelaide Botanic Garden, Port Augusta's Australian Arid Lands Botanic Garden and the Alice Springs Desert Park.

Eucalypts

Large eucalypts (gum trees) are among the most distinctive features of the Australian landscape, and the smell of burning eucalyptus leaves and twigs is guaranteed to make any expatriate Aussie homesick. The gum tree features in Australian folklore, art and literature, its flowers support the bee industry, its wood has many uses and its oil is used for pharmaceuticals and perfumed products.

There are around 560 species of the eucalyptus genus in Australia but only 60 or so are found in the arid zone, where, not surprisingly, most are rather stunted. However, some species can grow into huge trees that make a spectacular sight in their dry setting. Mallee, a multistemmed form of gum, is very common, and the roots of fallen mallees will burn seemingly forever in a campfire.

River red gums, usually called river gums or red gums, are generally confined to watercourses where their roots have access to a reliable supply of moisture. Given good conditions they can grow to 40m high and may live for 1000 years. This species is fairly easily identified by its habitat and its smooth, often beautifully mottled grey, tan and cream bark; its timber is dark red, hence the name. River gums are found throughout Australia. They have a habit of dropping large limbs, so while they may be good shade trees it's certainly not wise to camp under them.

The ghost gum is a great favourite thanks to its bright green leaves and glossy white bark. Although these often majestic, spreading trees are common in tropical northern Australia, it's around Alice Springs that they've achieved most of their fame through the work of artists such as Albert Namatjira. In central Australia ghost gums are found on alluvial flats and rocky hills, where they are in vivid contrast to their red surroundings.

Coolabahs are a common feature of watercourses, swamps and flood plains right through the outback's drier areas. They are typically gnarled, spreading trees with a rough, dark-brown bark and dull, leathery leaves. Coolabahs can grow to 20m high and often provide excellent shade. All eucalypts are hardwoods and this species is said to have the hardest timber of all. It's also very strong and termite-resistant, which made it extremely useful for building fences and stockyards in the days before steel became readily available.

One of the dominant Top End gums is the Darwin woollybutt, which occurs on sandstone and lowland country from Broome right across to the east coast. This tall, spreading tree has rough, fibrous, dark-coloured bark on its lower trunk, a smooth, white upper trunk and branches and large clusters of bright orange flowers that occur from May to August.

Acacias

The Australian species of the acacia genus are commonly known as wattle, and they are common indeed. There are 660 species in Australia, but only about 120 are found in

Wattle is Australia's national floral emblem and is found everywhere!

Spinifex

Spinifex – the dense, dome-shaped masses of long, needle-like grass that you find on sandy soils and rocky areas – is among the hardiest of desert plants. There are many species but most share an important characteristic: in dry times their leaves roll into tight cylinders to reduce the number of pores exposed to the sun and wind. This keeps water loss through evaporation to a minimum, but even so, most plants will succumb during a really bad drought. Spinifex grasslands are very difficult to walk through – the explorer Ernest Giles called it 'that abominable vegetable production'. They cover vast areas of central Australia and support some of the world's richest populations of reptiles.

Grass Trees

The unusual looking grass trees, also known as blackboys or yaccas, are ancient plants of the lily family that are widespread in south-eastern and south-western Australia, mainly in sandy soils. They look like a patch of grass atop a slow-growing trunk, with a distinctive, spear-like flower spike up to 3m tall, with tiny flowers massed along the upper half of a long stem. These flowers yield considerable nectar. They can live up to 600 years and are very slow growing. They're well adapted to fire (the name blackboy refers to the trunk that's normally burnt black

the arid zone. They tend to be fast-growing, short-lived and come in many forms, from tall, weeping trees to prickly shrubs. Despite their many differences, all wattles have furry yellow flowers shaped either like a spike or a ball. If you see a plant with a flower like this you'll know it's a wattle.

Most species flower during late winter and spring. Then the country is ablaze with wattle and the reason for the choice of green and gold as Australia's national colours is obvious. Wattle is Australia's floral emblem.

Mulga, probably the most widespread of the arid-zone wattles, occurs in all mainland states except Victoria. Although young mulga can look a little like small pines, the adults, which are 10m tall at their best, are more of an umbrella shape with a sparse crown of narrow grey leaves. Mulga sometimes forms dense thickets (the explorer John McDouall Stuart complained that the scrub near Alice Springs tore his clothes and pack saddles to bits) but usually it's found as open woodland. Mulga leaves are very resistant to water loss, and the tree's shape directs any rain down to the base of the trunk where roots are most dense. With these attributes, mulga is a great drought survivor, but being good fodder for stock puts it at risk from overgrazing.

by repeated fires), and prolific flowering is often seen in the spring following a bushfire.

Saltbush

Millions of sheep and cattle living in the arid zone owe their survival to dry, shrubby plants called saltbush, which get their name from their tolerance to saline conditions. There are 30 species of saltbush which is extremely widespread and can dominant vast areas of land. On the Oodnadatta and Birdsville Tracks you'll often see nothing else for considerable distances.

Desert Oak

Its height, broad shady crown, dark weeping foliage and the sighing music of the wind in its leaves make the desert oak an inspiring feature of its sand-plain habitat. These magnificent trees are confined to the western arid zone and are common around Uluru and Kings Canyon, near Alice Springs and along the Gunbarrel Highway. Young desert oaks resemble tall, hairy broomsticks – they don't look anything like the adult trees and many people think that they're a different species altogether.

Wildflowers

After good autumn or winter rains the normally arid inland explodes in a multi-coloured carpet of vibrant wildflowers that will literally take your breath away. The most common of these ephemerals, or short-lived plants, are the numerous species of daisy.

In a miracle of nature, the seeds of desert ephemerals can lie dormant in the sand for years until exactly the right combination of temperature and moisture comes along to trigger germination. When this happens, life in the desert moves into top gear as the ephemerals hurry to complete their brief life cycles and woody plants likewise burst into bloom. The sand hills, plains and rocky ridges come alive with nectar-eating birds and insects, which adds up to a bumper harvest for predators as well. Everywhere the various forms of wildlife are breeding and rearing their young while food supplies are abundant. For nature lovers this is definitely the best time to tour the inland.

Water Lilies

Although the Top End can't match the visual spectacle of the desert in full bloom, it nevertheless has many spectacular wildflowers. One such is the water lily, which forms floating mats of large, roundish leaves on freshwater lagoons and swamps right across the tropical north. Its root stock is prized as a food by Aboriginal people.

Boabs

The grotesque boab is only found from the south-western Kimberley to the Northern Territory's Victoria River, where it grows on flood plains and rocky areas. Its huge, grey, swollen trunk topped by a mass of contorted branches make it a fascinating sight, particularly during the dry season when it loses its leaves and becomes 'the tree that God planted upside-down'. Although boab trees rarely grow higher than 20m, the circumference of their moisture-storing trunks can be over 25m. The content of the large, gourd-shaped fruit is edible and has a pleasant, fizzy taste similar to cream-of-tartar, though it feels as if you're chewing on powdered milk. Boabs are closely related to the baobab of Africa.

Weeds

By the 1920s the introduced prickly pear had choked millions of hectares of central Queensland before an effective biological control was found in the form of the cactoblastic moth. Today, in tropical Australia, weeds such as mimosa bush and rubber vine are threatening huge areas, while salvinia has begun to choke waterways. In central Australia, the Finke River has been invaded by athel trees that threaten to swamp its entire ecosystem. Introduced weeds can destroy wildlife habitats as well as make pastoral and cropping land unusable. Right across Australia, their cost in environmental and economic terms is incalculable.

Preventing the Spread of Weeds Studies have shown that motor vehicles are a major culprit in the spread of weeds. In 1990 a check of 222 tourist vehicles entering Kakadu National Park revealed that

70% were carrying a total of 1511 seeds from 84 different species.

The implications of this are obvious when you consider the millions of vehicles that travel Australia's roads and tracks each year. The question is: How can you avoid being responsible for an outbreak?

First, you need to be able to identify the various weeds as well as their seeds and seed capsules. This is easy: get hold of a weeds pamphlet from a state department of primary production or shire office. Second, if possible avoid driving through weed infestations – pay particular attention to quarantine signs, which should be observed to the letter. Third, immediately after leaving an infested area give your vehicle a thorough check for seeds and pieces of plant that may propagate. It's a good idea to carry out such checks on a regular basis regardless of whether you think you've been near weeds. Whenever you go walking or camping in the bush, carefully check the dog, your clothing, tent and bedding for burrs and seeds.

Seeds can become lodged in various places in the vehicle such as its undercarriage, engine compartment, radiator, wiper blades, gutters and around lights and doors. Don't forget the interior. For safety's sake, vehicles should only be washed on a proper wash-down area complete with sump and hard stand, not in places where weeds can grow.

If you find any seeds of noxious plants, seal them in a plastic bag and hand them in to the appropriate authorities for disposal; simply throwing them on the campfire is inadvisable, as fire promotes the germination of some species. It's always a good idea to inform the authorities of isolated outbreaks in remote areas as they may not be aware of them. If you're uncertain about identification, take along a cutting, which ideally will include fruit, seeds or flowers.

FAUNA

What can you say about the wildlife of an area with such a tremendous range of habitats and climates as the Australian outback? Obviously some areas are more rewarding than others when it comes to observing the local fauna. For example, the Top End rivers are like giant aviaries, particularly in early morning, and national parks inside the Dog Fence (see Dingoes later in this section) seem inundated with kangaroos. Even the barren gibber plains of northern South Australia have much to offer those prepared to put some time and effort into their wildlife-watching.

In most areas away from water the casual observer will wonder if anything lives there at all, apart from bushflies and ants. This is because the birds tend to be small and secretive, and native outback mammals are mostly nocturnal as a means of avoiding heat stress and water loss. It's unusual to see reptiles in winter south of the Tropic of Capricorn, as cold weather sends them into hibernation.

Almost all Australian native mammals apart from seals, bats, rodents and dingoes belonged to the order of marsupials. Marsupials are also found in Central and South America (opossums), but have had evolution to themselves in Australia, where they were isolated from the rest of the world for 55 million years or so. Marsupials are an order of mammals who lack a placenta: The young are born in an immature state, barely more than an embryo, climb through their mother's fur to her pouch *(marsupium)* and attach themselves to a teat to continue their development.

Australia is also home to the order of monotremes (egg-laying mammals), which consists of only the platypus and echidna. The semi aquatic platypus lives in eastern Australia and Tasmania, but within that area it can be found from near-freezing southern mountain streams to the Atherton Tablelands in far north Queensland. It has a duck-like bill and lays eggs in grass-lined nests.

MARTIN HARRIS

When the first reports of the platypus were sent back to England, the eminent scientists of the day thought they were a hoax.

The echidna, or spiny anteater, is a small, four-legged creature, covered on the back with long, sharp spines but on the underside by fur. It feeds on ants and termites, and is found in a great range of habitats, from hot, dry deserts to altitudes of 1800m in the Australian Alps, and also in New Guinea. The female carries her eggs in a pouch (that faces backwards because echidnas burrow), and on hatching, the young remain there and suckle, only being evicted when their spines become too sharp for mum.

Since European settlement of Australia, many mammal species once widely distributed through the outback's drier parts are now either extinct or endangered. Some, such as the greater stick-nest rat, are now found only on offshore islands. The reasons for this unhappy record seem to be competition from and predation by introduced animals, and the cessation of Aboriginal fire-stick farming throughout the spinifex grassland areas.

Kangaroos & Wallabies

Australia's national symbol and its smaller relative, the wallaby, generally spend the daylight hours in hidden places sheltering from the sun. For this reason they are seldom seen by most outback travellers except as road kills or as large shapes that suddenly appear in the headlights at night. Kangaroos tend to inhabit open woodlands and plains, while wallabies are more at home in dense scrub and forests – though some kangaroos and wallabies prefer rocky habitats.

There are six species of kangaroo, of which the red kangaroo is the largest, with adult males weighing an average of 66kg. Kangaroo numbers have exploded in many outback pastoral areas, owing to the extermination of dingoes and the increase in watering points and grasslands for sheep and cattle. To the horror of many animal-lovers, about three million are shot each year as a means of population control.

Kangaroo meat is a traditional food eaten by Aboriginal people and is beginning to be accepted and enjoyed by other Australians. Until the 1990s it was only sold as pet food in some states.

Although kangaroos are not generally aggressive, males of larger species, such as reds, can be dangerous when cornered. In the wild, boomers, as they are called, will grasp other males with their forearms, rear up on their muscular tails and pound their opponents with their hind feet, sometimes slashing them with their claws. Such behaviour can also be directed against dogs and, very rarely, people. If there's a dam or waterhole nearby, a boomer being pursued by dogs may hop into deep water and hold its tormentors under water until they drown.

In general, kangaroos are considered a serious hazard to motorists driving at night on outback roads – be careful.

Bandicoots

The small, rat-like bandicoot has been one of the principal victims of the introduced fox and pussy cat. A number of species have been either totally wiped out or are in danger of heading that way.

Bandicoots are mainly nocturnal, but can occasionally be seen scampering through the bush. They are largely insect eaters but also eat some plant material. Their large claws are put to good use scratching for insects, including centipedes and scorpions.

One of the most common varieties is the short-nosed bandicoot, which is found in eastern and western Australia. Others, such as the eastern-barred bandicoot, are these days found in very limited areas. The rare bilby, or rabbit-eared bandicoot, survives mainly in northern Western Australia and the Northern Territory. Efforts are being made to ensure its survival.

KATE NOLAN

Rabbit-eared bandicoot

Dingoes

Whether they tagged along with early Aborigines migrating from South-East Asia or were introduced fairly recently by Indonesian fishermen, the dingo, or wild dog, has been here long enough to be considered a native animal.

Dingoes differ from domestic dogs in various subtle ways – for example, dingoes breed only once a year while domestic dogs breed twice – but they can interbreed and this is the main threat to their survival as a pure strain. They're considered a threat to the sheep industry and in some areas have a price on their heads.

Dingoes are most numerous north and west of the Dog Fence, the world's longest man-made barrier. Between 1.4m and 2.4m high, the fence runs for about 5400km from near the Gold Coast in Queensland to near Ceduna in South Australia. Largely patrolled by government inspectors, the fence's sole purpose is to protect the sheep flocks of south-eastern Australia. A pair of dingoes acting together can kill dozens of sheep in a night, so any that make their way through the fence are vigorously pursued with bullets, traps and poison baits. Although dingoes do prey on calves, their depredations aren't considered a serious threat to the beef-cattle industry, which becomes dominant on the other side of the fence.

Crocodiles

There are two species: the large saltwater (estuarine) crocodile and the smaller freshwater variety. 'Salties', which can grow to 7m, will attack and kill humans. They're found in northern coastal areas from Broome around to Mackay, though there

KATE NOLAN
Saltwater crocodile

KATE NOLAN
Freshwater crocodile

have been sightings further south. Contrary to their name, salties aren't confined to salt water; they can be found in freshwater habitats more than 200km inland. Bush wisdom states that if you can catch barramundi, the prized fish that also lives in salt and freshwater environments, salties can get there too – though some people dispute this.

'Freshies' are smaller than salties – any over 3m should be regarded as a saltie crocodile. They are also more finely built and have much narrower snouts and smaller teeth to suit their fish diet. While generally harmless to humans, they have been known to bite in defence of their nests; keep children and pet dogs away from them.

Both species of crocodiles were once hunted almost to extinction, but since they were proclaimed a protected species they have become abundant. By some miracle, very few people are killed by salties and attacks still make headlines.

There are simple rules to avoid being attacked and the most important one is to stay out of the water whenever you're in saltie territory. This can be rather difficult after a hot, muggy day's travel along a dusty track, but you'll just have to put up with it. Observe the guidelines contained in national park brochures and you'll be quite safe.

Snakes

Only about 10% of Australia's 140 snake species are genuinely dangerous to humans, but at the same time many of the world's most venomous snakes are Australian. The most toxic land snake in the world is the 'fierce snake' or inland taipan of south-western Queensland and north-eastern South Australia – one dose of its venom is enough to kill a quarter of a million mice. It's a relative of the more famous and almost as deadly taipan. The tiger snake is highly

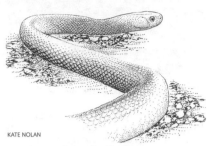

KATE NOLAN

Very deadly taipan

venomous too, and death adders, copperheads, brown snakes and red-bellied black snakes should also be avoided at all costs.

Many people spend months travelling in the outback without seeing a snake other than the occasional dead one on the road. Snakes tend to keep a low profile, but to minimise your chances of being bitten, always wear boots, socks and long, heavyweight trousers when walking through undergrowth. Walking in dry grass without shoes or long trousers in warm weather is inadvisable. Tramp heavily and they'll usually slither away before you come near. Don't put your hands into holes and crevices, and be careful when collecting firewood.

Always leave snakes alone – most people are bitten while doing something silly like trying to kill them, or stepping over them when they're asleep. In the unlikely event that you see a snake, the best approach is to either walk around it at a safe distance or to stand quietly until it's made its escape. In most cases it'll be as frightened as you,

although if it feels cornered it may well strike in self-defence.

There are 30 species of sea snakes in Australian coastal waters. Although their venom can be 10 times as toxic as that of a cobra, they're shy creatures and usually won't attack if left alone.

First Aid Contrary to popular belief, snake bites do not cause instantaneous death. A snake bite is often shallow and injects little venom – the fangs may not penetrate the skin properly for many reasons (thick clothing, or the victim pulling away at the last moment), and a snake rarely injects a full dose of the stuff anyway. Don't panic. Antivenenes are usually available but may not be close at hand.

Tourniquets and sucking out poison are now completely discredited. Instead, keep the patient calm and still. This is very important, as excitement and movement accelerate the spread of venom. Wrap the bitten limb tightly, as you would for a sprained ankle. Start at the bite, work your way down to the fingers or toes, and then back up to the armpit or groin. Finally, attach a splint to immobilise the limb. This has the effect of localising the venom and slowing its spread. Then seek medical help, if possible with the dead snake for identification. Don't attempt to catch it if there is even a remote chance of being bitten again.

Ideally, the patient should not be moved, but if you're in the middle of nowhere you may have no choice. Never leave the patient alone. If the bite is serious they may experience breathing problems that require artificial respiration, and you should be well-prepared for this.

Lizards

The outback hosts an amazing variety of lizards, from giant perentie goannas (Australian iguanas, or monitor lizards) to tiny skinks and geckoes. The ones you're most likely to see are the various large goannas and dragons, which like to sun themselves in exposed situations such as bitumen roads. Unable to generate their own heat, most lizards need to lie in the sun on cool

KATE NOLAN

Brown snake

days until their blood reaches the desired temperature for hunting etc.

Goannas are sleek, heavily built lizards with longish, narrow heads. The perentie – the world's second-largest lizard – is found in the kinder habitats of central Australia and is easy to identify by the regular pattern of large yellow spots on its back. Perenties can grow to 3m long but you're most unlikely to see one over 2m, which is still a big lizard. The large grey goannas found along the banks of northern rivers are water monitors.

Two of the more common dragons are the bearded dragon of arid Australia and the Top End's famous frilled lizard. Some people like to tease the latter to make its neck frill stand out (an attempt to make itself look large and fierce) but such behaviour is pretty thoughtless. You'll notice how the bearded dragon flattens its body when sunbaking so as to warm up in the shortest possible time.

Another unusual lizard is the thorny devil, or mountain devil. Found on the sandy plains of the western arid zone, this fat, brightly coloured little creature has an almost indescribably ferocious appearance, thanks to its armour-plated coat of horns and spikes. However, it's quite harmless to humans, as it lives on a diet consisting entirely of tiny black ants.

Finches
Australia has 18 species of native finch, of which most are found in the tropics – only two (the zebra finch and painted firetail) have adapted to arid conditions. Zebra finches are most commonly seen near permanent water sources as, being seed-eaters, they need to drink most days when it's cool and every day when it's hot. If you run out of water in hot weather and there are zebra finches around, you can be fairly sure there's a supply within a short distance.

The Gouldian finch's gorgeous colours make it one of Australia's most stunning birds. It was once common across the far north from the Kimberley to Cape York but is now scarce, largely because of its vulnerability to an introduced parasite that affects its respiratory tract. Trapping may also have contributed to its decline.

Honeyeaters
Arguably the most common and widespread variety of bird in scrubland and timbered areas, Australia's 67 species of honeyeaters come in many shapes, sizes and colours, from large, drab, bald-headed friarbirds to the small, brilliantly coloured scarlet honeyeaters. They are generally active, noisy birds with longish curved bills that are designed for extracting insects and nectar from flowers. Their morning wake-up calls are a feature along inland watercourses, where they are often dominant.

Parrots & Cockatoos
There is an incredible assortment of these birds in the outback. With the exception of the galah, cockatoos tend to be large, loud and not very colourful. The raucous screeching of cockatoos grates on the nerves, and makes you wonder why they're so popular as pets.

Parrots, on the other hand, are inoffensive and often very beautiful: the mulga parrot of the southern arid zone and the north's hooded parrot are typical examples. The latter, which nests in termite mounds, is now rare, so it's a treat to see one. Budgerigars are extremely widespread and often occur in vast flocks as they follow the favourable seasons across the arid inland.

Yellow-tailed black cockatoo

MARTIN HARRIS

Osprey

Birds of Prey

Being on top of the feathered food chain, the various eagles, goshawks, kites, harriers, falcons and kestrels are usually the most commonly seen of all outback birds. Largest of all is the wedge-tailed eagle, which you'll often notice feeding on road kills. The name refers to its distinctively pointed, diamond-shaped tail. With a wingspan approaching 3m, they soar high on the thermals while scanning the ground for prey such as rabbits and young kangaroos. Their eyesight is so keen that they're thought to be able to see a rabbit quite clearly from a distance of 1.5km. On remote coasts, watch for ospreys and white-bellied sea eagles.

Emus

The world's second-largest bird, the flightless emu is found in large numbers in less-inhabited areas inside the Dog Fence. These birds tend to be mobile and will often create problems for cereal growers when drought forces huge numbers in from their outlying haunts. They are extremely curious and you can sometimes attract them right up to the vehicle by waving a handkerchief or flashing a mirror. Attempts are being made to farm them for their meat, hides and feathers. The emu features with the kangaroo on Australia's coat of arms.

Cassowaries

A slightly smaller relative of the emu, the Australian cassowary is restricted to northern Queensland's wet tropical rainforests and some isolated areas in north-eastern Cape York (two other species live in Papua New Guinea and adjacent islands). Its glossy-black plumage (which looks like hair), tall helmet and brilliant red-and-blue neck are quite distinctive. Adults can stand up to 2m tall but usually they're a bit smaller. It's an endangered species and perhaps no more than 1500 remain in the wild. They're solitary creatures and will aggressively defend their territory.

Insects

It will come as no surprise to outback campers that Australia has by far the world's largest number and richest diversity of ant species. In fact, scientists come from all over the world to study them here.

These do not include white ants, which are more correctly called termites and aren't related. Termite mounds (each mound is the upper part of a nest) are often a spectacular feature of the tropical north. One species builds a large tombstone-shaped mound that points north-south, as a means of regulating the temperature within the mound. Another builds an immense pillar-like mound over 6m high.

Bushflies can be an unbelievable nuisance and at times your arm will feel like dropping off from giving the great Aussie salute. Why do they persist in crawling on you? The main answer is that they want to drink your sweat and tears to obtain protein, but they're also waiting for you to go to the toilet behind a bush. Flies lay their eggs in fresh animal droppings, which gives the maggots food to grow until they pupate. A single cow on good pasture can drop enough in one day for 2000 flies to develop. Bushflies become even more numerous after rain, and are at their worst during the warmest months.

Some shops sell the Genuine Aussie Fly Net (probably made in Korea), which is rather like a string onion bag but is very effective. Repellents such as Aerogard and Rid go some way to deterring the little bastards. Fortunately they disappear when it gets dark, which makes those outback nights around the campfire all the more enjoyable. They're also less numerous the further away you are from pastoral areas.

Mosquitoes can be a problem, especially in the warmer tropical and subtropical areas.

The risk of malaria is negligible but there's a small risk of Ross River Fever, a virus with symptoms similar to glandular fever. Avoid bites by covering bare skin and using an insect repellent. Insect screens on windows and mosquito nets on beds offer protection. Mosquito coils give mixed results.

Most Australian spiders bite but very few are actually dangerous. The redback spider, a relative of the American black widow, is widespread, poisonous (possibly deadly for children but rarely serious for an adult) and has a legendary liking for toilet seats. For first-aid treatment, apply an ice compress to lessen the pain and transport the victim to a medical facility for antivenene. Pain occurs rapidly but the venom acts slowly. Serious problems are unlikely in under three hours.

There are three species of scorpion in Australia, but they're not very venomous compared with overseas varieties – so far only one human is recorded to have died as a result of an Australian scorpion sting. Scorpions often shelter in shoes or clothing – always give your shoes a good shake-out before donning them in the morning, especially when camping.

Fish

Best known of all the outback's fish is the mighty barramundi of northern Australia. See Barramundi Fishing under Activities in the Facts for the Visitor chapter for more about this prized catch.

Surprisingly, the arid zone also has its share of fish, although most are very small. The major exception is the yellowbelly, or golden perch, which can grow to over 20kg. Yellowbellies are found in the Cooper Creek and Diamantina River systems, both of which drain into Lake Eyre.

The outback's most widespread fish is the spangled perch, which weighs about 0.5kg and is found in the coastal and inland streams of all the mainland states – it's one of the largest of the 10 species found in central Australia's Finke River. Among the least widespread are three species of fish known only from the hot pools of Dalhousie Springs, on the edge of the Simpson Desert.

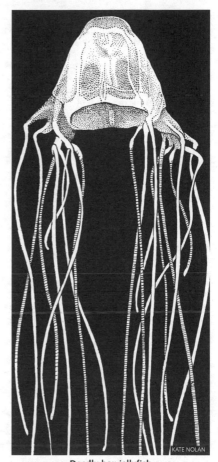

Deadly box jellyfish

Box Jellyfish

One sea creature you should be aware of is the box jellyfish, also known as the stinger or sea wasp. It inhabits coastal waters and estuaries north of the Tropic of Capricorn, and is particularly prevalent between October and mid-May. Its bell-shaped, translucent body is often difficult to spot, and its long, sticky tentacles discharge a highly potent venom that kills an average of one person a year and causes excruciating pain to many others.

If someone is stung, they are likely to run out of the sea, screaming, and collapse on the beach, with weals on their body as though they've been whipped. They may stop breathing, in which case artificial respiration is called for.

Douse the stings with household vinegar (available from first-aid boxes on many beaches, or from nearby houses); this will deactivate the tentacles, which can then be carefully removed with tweezers. Apply a compression bandage over the affected area to localise the venom as for a snake bite, and then seek medical help as soon as possible. Above all, stay out of the sea when the sea wasps are around – the local people are ignoring that lovely water in the muggy season for an excellent reason.

Introduced Animals

Soon after foxes and rabbits were introduced to Australia for sport in the mid-1800s it became apparent that a dreadful mistake had been made. Both spread far and wide with remarkable speed and it wasn't long before they became pests. Rabbits have had a devastating effect on native plants and animals, particularly in the arid zone, while foxes – along with domestic cats gone wild – have chewed great holes in the populations of Australia's smaller marsupials. Feral cats are now found throughout the mainland but rabbits and foxes have yet to establish themselves in the tropical north. There are hopes that the recently introduced calicivirus, which is specific to European grey rabbits, will provide a permanent control on the feral rabbit population. Researchers are working on a biological control for foxes and cats.

At least 18 introduced mammal species are now feral in Australia and many have become pests. Oddly enough, the dromedary (one-humped camel) seems to have had the smallest impact, even though it's the largest feral animal. Australia's estimated 100,000 wild camels are descendants of those released by their owners when the camel trains that supplied the outback for 50 years were replaced by motor vehicles in the 1920s and '30s. Now forming the world's only wild population of this species

(the other 13 million or so in North Africa and the Middle East are domesticated), Australian camels are being exported to the Middle East to improve the local gene pool.

Other introduced feral pests include the pig, goat, donkey, water buffalo, horse, starling, sparrow, blackbird and cane toad, all of which have multiplied rapidly in the wild through lack of natural enemies. The cane toad in particular has overrun vast areas of Queensland and, much to the horror of environmentalists, has recently made its way across the top to the lush wetlands of Kakadu National Park near Darwin. Biologists are observing with great interest what impact they'll have there.

Sparrows and starlings have yet to reach Western Australia – starling shooters are employed on the border near the south coast to prevent them entering the state and posing a threat to agriculture. The vast herds of water buffalo that devastated large areas of the Northern Territory's Top End have now been destroyed – these days the only buffalo you're likely to see are tame ones in a paddock.

PALAEONTOLOGY

Australia has abundant evidence of earlier life forms, but the search is not easy, as much of it is conducted in outback regions where conditions are harsh.

Palaeontologists distinguish four main eras – Precambrian (2300 to 570 million years ago), Palaeozoic (570 to 225 million years), Mesozoic (225 to 65 million years) and Cainozoic (65 million years to the present) – and many more periods which are subdivisions of the four eras.

The theory of continental drift says that the earth's landmass started as a supercontinent called Pangaea. About 200 million years ago, Pangaea broke into the northern and southern continents of Laurasia and Gondwana respectively; the latter consisted of what we now call Africa, South America, Australia, Antarctica and the Indian subcontinent. It eventually broke apart too, and Australia began its lonely journey northwards – see the Geology section earlier in this chapter.

In the Beginning...

The layered, mainly limestone deposits known as stromatolites, in the saline Hamelin Pool near Shark Bay in Western Australia, are still formed by the blue-green algae that are believed to have developed over three billion years ago. This makes them the oldest form of life on earth.

Australia also has some of the oldest rocks on earth and embedded in them are some of the oldest fossils. Australia's most primitive vertebrate fish, *Arandaspis* from the Ordovician period (500 to 435 million years ago), were found in the Stairway sandstone deposits of the Amadeus Basin in the Northern Territory.

Australia is also known for its cornucopia of Devonian fish (395 to 345 million years old). The Devonian Reef national parks of the Kimberley are a good source of fossils. Gogo Station, near Fitzroy Crossing, is the site of bony-plated placoderms such as the vertebrate *Rolfosteus canningenis*, which fed on fish and invertebrates in the ancient reef environment of the Devonian period.

In 240-million-year-old (Permian) coal deposits near Blackwater, central Queensland, curious fish with an upturned snout (*Ebenaqua ritchiei*) were uncovered in a large open-cut mine.

Amphibian life forms thrived during the Triassic period (230 to 195 million years ago). The Blina Shale of the Erskine Range, between Fitzroy Crossing and Derby, has revealed two interesting examples: *Deltasaurus kimberleyensis*, a fish predator similar to a crocodile in appearance; and *Erythrobatrachus noonkanbahensis*, another fish-eater with an elongated skull.

The first dicynodont (literally, two canine teeth) fossil was found in an area known as The Crater, near Carnarvon Gorge, Queensland. It was the first mammal-like reptile (theraspid) known to Australia, and became known as the 'Creature from the Crater'.

Dinosaurs & Friends

The Jurassic period (195 to 140 million years ago) was the heyday of the dinosaurs. There are possibly three groups: saurischians, ornithischians and a mixture of both. In 1924 a fair amount of bone material belonging to a four-footed, long-necked, long-tailed reptile (or sauropod) known as *Rhoetosaurus brownei* was found near Roma in Queensland, the first Jurassic example in Australia.

Other creatures of the Jurassic period were the pliosaurs and plesiosaurs – marine reptiles. Remains of a freshwater pliosaur were found near Mount Morgan in Queensland and the remains of two plesiosaurs were recovered from the Evergreen formation, 70km north of Wandoan in south-eastern Queensland.

One interesting tale of the naming of bones relates to the opalised skeleton of Eric, a pliosaur from the Cretaceous period (140 to 60 million years ago) who tours the country feted like a celebrity. Eric was unearthed near Coober Pedy, South Australia and, after a national campaign, purchased for all Australians. Why 'Eric'? Well, the person who lovingly pieced together the jigsaw of bones was a John Cleese fanatic: the fish bones found in the plesiosaur's stomach contents were named Wanda, and the devourer of the fish, Eric.

The skeleton of a bulky dinosaur, *Muttaburrasaurus langdoni*, was found in a cattle-mustering area on the banks of the Thomson River near Muttaburra, 100km north of Longreach, Queensland. The bones surfaced in early Cretaceous marine deposits and before they were gathered up, cattle had trodden into the dust what local souvenir hunters had failed to gather.

After a public appeal the jigsaw began to take shape and the bone-detectives realised that they had chanced upon an ornithischian (bird-hipped) dinosaur of the Ornithopoda (Bird-foot) suborder. What's more, it was closely related to the group of iguanodontids of the northern hemisphere. See for yourself when passing through Brisbane, as 'Mutta' is displayed in the Queensland Museum and an artist's steel and plaster rendition also lives outside the general store-cum-petrol station in Muttaburra.

Kronosaurus queenslandicus was quite a spectacular Cretaceous reptile. Its first fragments were found near Hughenden,

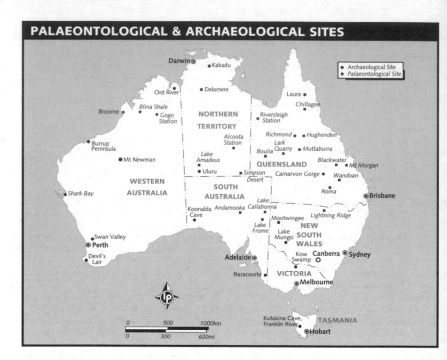

PALAEONTOLOGICAL & ARCHAEOLOGICAL SITES

Queensland. It is thought to be the largest known marine reptile, and the name is derived from the Greek god Kronos, who ate his children so they could not take over his throne. 'Krono' is a bulky pliosaur with its head accounting for a quarter of its length.

Bones of Cretaceous ichthyosaurs have been found in a number of places; the broad-finned *Platypterygius australis* was found near Richmond, Queensland, and other sites throughout the Great Artesian Basin.

Only two specimens of Cretaceous sauropods have been found and one named: *Austrosaurus*. Their bone fragments were found in central Queensland. Two of the impressive carnivorous theropods, similar to the overseas *Allosaurus*, lived in the Cretaceous period: *Rapator ornitholestoides*, found near Lightning Ridge; and *Kakuru kujani*, found near Andamooka.

There is also evidence of where these huge creatures passed. Preserved footprints of a 3m-high specimen are found at Gantheaume Point near Broome. More spectacular is the dinosaur stampede discovered at Lark Quarry south of Winton, Queensland. The prints were made when about 130 small dinosaurs were scared at a waterhole by a 5m-long carnosaur dinosaur.

In the air, Australia boasted some mean-looking pterosaurs, or winged reptiles. In 1979, near Boulia in western Queensland, fossils were excavated from early Cretaceous marine limestones; more recently, jaws were discovered near Boulia and Richmond. The pterosaurs had a wingspan of 2m and were small sea-going fish-eaters.

During the Eocene period (38 to 26 million years ago), the giant lungfish *Neoceradotus gregoryi*, known from central Australia and south-eastern Queensland, would have been crunching on water plants and freshwater snails. In the middle Miocene (16 to 14 million years ago), *rhabdosteids*, a type of river dolphin, inhabited the inland waterways – the bones of about six of them have been found in sediments in the Lake Frome district of South Australia.

There were huge flightless birds as well, such as 'giant emus' – the Mihirungs of Aboriginal mythology, which fossil evidence now seems to substantiate. *Dromornis stirtoni* was probably the world's largest bird. At 3m in height and over 300kg in weight it was much larger than Madagascar's extinct elephant bird; fossils from the Miocene were found at Alcoota Station near Alice Springs.

Alcoota has been a rich source of fossil material of the late Miocene (14 to seven million years ago). It has provided information on the oldest known meat-eating thylacinids: a marsupial lion called *Wakaleo alcootaensis*, and a cow-sized diprotodontid, *Plaisiodon centralis*.

Mammals

In Europe, mammals have been known for 200 million years (from the Triassic onwards), but in Australia they are relative newcomers. Australia's oldest fossil mammal is a relatively recent discovery: a monotreme, *Steropodon galmani*, found in Cretaceous opal near Lightning Ridge and believed to be 110 million years old. Until then, the oldest known monotreme was *Obdurodon insignis*, similar to a modern-day platypus, discovered in 15-million-year-old deposits from the Simpson Desert.

Marsupials that have long since become extinct include the Diprotodonta and related families – for example, *Ngapakaldia*, whose 14-million-year-old remains were retrieved from Riversleigh in north-western Queensland; or *Neohelos*, a browsing herbivore found in the Lake Eyre Basin, Bullock Creek in the Northern Territory and Riversleigh.

The biggest of the marsupials was *Diprotodon optatum*, about 3m long and 2m high at the shoulder. This bulky creature ranged all over the continent and is thought to have disappeared between 25,000 and 15,000 years ago. Evidence of the largest of the wombats, *Phascolonus gigas*, from the Pleistocene, has been found at Cooper Creek, Lake Callabonna and Lake Eyre.

Riversleigh World Heritage Fossil Site is a treasure trove of fossils, some of which

Stromatolites

The dolphins at Monkey Mia didn't contribute to the listing of Shark Bay as a World Heritage area; one of the main reasons was the existence of stromatolites (rocky formations) at Hamelin Pool. These structures are several thousands of years old but are built by the oldest living things on this planet, the blue-green algae (one-celled plants) that evolved over 3.5 *billion* years ago.

Hamelin Pool is suited to the growth of stromatolites because of the clarity and hypersalinity of the water; the latter prevents other organisms from attacking the algae. In essence, each stromatolite is covered in a form of cyanobacterial microbe shaped like algae, which waves around during daily photosynthesis. At night the microbes fold over, trapping calcium and carbonate ions dissolved in the water. The sticky chemicals they exude add to the concretion of another layer on the surface of the stromatolite.

These are the most accessible stromatolites in the world, spectacularly set amid the turquoise waters of Hamelin Pool. Please don't disturb them.

are on display in Mt Isa. The remains of *Wabularoo naughtoni* joins a number of other species of kangaroo found here. It is a type of rat-kangaroo that became extinct when browsing kangaroos evolved 10 to five million years ago.

Also found in recent times at Gag Site, Riversleigh, is an entirely new order of mammals, loosely named *Thingodonta* for a while but now known as *Yalkaparidon coheni*. The fossil remains of a 7m-long snake were named *Montypythonoides*.

The Queensland Museum (W www.qmuseum.qld.gov.au) in Brisbane houses the country's best collection of outback-related fossil and dinosaur material. Read more about this fascinating subject in the following books: *Prehistoric Australia* by Brian Mackness; *The Antipodean Ark*, edited by Suzanne Hand & Michael Archer; and *Prehistoric Animals of Australia*, edited by Susan Quirk & Michael Archer.

NATIONAL PARKS & RESERVES

Australia has more than 500 national parks – protected wilderness areas of environmental or natural importance. Each state defines and runs its own national parks, but the principle is the same throughout Australia.

Public access is encouraged but safety and conservation regulations must be observed. The codes of behaviour may vary slightly from state to state and park to park, but essentially all plants and animals are protected, and you're asked to do nothing to damage or alter the natural environment. Among other things, this means driving only on established tracks, camping only in designated areas, disposing of rubbish properly and taking care with fire.

Some outback parks and reserves, such as South Australia's Gammon Ranges National Park, are so isolated, rugged and harsh that they aren't recommended unless you're an experienced bushwalker or 4WD motorist. Others, however, are among Australia's major attractions. Some of the most beautiful have been included on the World Heritage Register – a Unesco list of natural or cultural places of world significance that would present an irreplaceable loss to the planet if they were altered.

In Australia, the register includes: the Great Barrier Reef; Daintree rainforest and Riversleigh fossil site (at Lawn Hill National Park) in far north Queensland; Kakadu and Uluru-Kata Tjuta National Parks in the Northern Territory; the Willandra Lakes region of far western New South Wales; Naracoorte Caves in South Australia; and Shark Bay on the Western Australian coast. The Australian Conservation Foundation is one of a number of bodies lobbying to have further places listed, including the Lake Eyre Basin and Cape York Peninsula.

Most of these parks are accessible by vehicles, although many are restricted to 4WD. While camping is generally allowed, facilities at the more remote, less-visited parks are either minimal or nonexistent; details on camping are found in the descriptions of tracks and destinations later in this book. For details on outback parks, contact the appropriate state management authority – see Useful Organisations in the Facts for the Visitor chapter.

South Australia has several enormous conservation areas. They include Witjira National Park (7770 sq km), which protects a unique concentration of artesian mound springs on the edge of the Simpson Desert. In the state's north-east, the Innamincka Regional Reserve (14,000 sq km) has plenty of variety – you'll see gibber plains of the Sturt Stony Desert, sand hills of the Strzelecki Desert, and semipermanent wetlands and large permanent waterholes along the Cooper Creek system. Other South Australian parks include the beds of huge, mainly dry salt lakes (eg, Lake Eyre National Park and Lake Torrens National Park) and vast tracts of sand ridge desert country (eg, Unnamed Conservation Park in the west, and the Simpson Desert Regional Reserve).

Parks in Western Australia's Hamersley Ranges, South Australia's Flinders Ranges and the Northern Territory's MacDonnell Ranges near Alice Springs offer some of the Australian arid zone's most dramatic landscapes, which support a surprising variety of plant species. Also near Alice Springs, Finke Gorge National Park contains lush remnants of a vanished rainforest along one of the world's oldest river systems. Mutawintji National Park near Broken Hill is a good place to learn about Aboriginal traditions in an arid environment.

As can be expected, the main features of the parks and reserves in tropical northern Australia typically reflect the monsoonal climate of the region. Right up the east coast from Cairns to the tip of Cape York, a series of parks offers rainforests, wetlands or the wonders of the Great Barrier Reef. These include Lakefield (Queensland's second-largest national park), the Daintree rainforest and Lizard Island (one of the state's most beautiful).

Kakadu National Park, near Darwin, is most famous for its Aboriginal heritage and the teeming birdlife that congregates around its wetlands come the late dry season. Gregory National Park in the Northern Territory's north-west has a network of remote 4WD tracks; further west, the Kimberley region's Purnululu (Bungle Bungle) National Park is best-known for its sandstone 'beehive' formations and deep, narrow gorges.

Finally, for a place with no trees, hills or rivers at all, try the Nullarbor National Park and adjoining regional reserve on the Nullarbor Plain in south-western South Australia. *Nullarbor* is bad Latin for 'no tree', and that's no exaggeration here. The plain seems endlessly flat and bare, and there's a mind-blowing sense of space and isolation.

ABORIGINAL LAND RIGHTS
Britain founded the colony of New South Wales on the legal principle of *terra nullius* (land belonging to no-one), which meant that Australia was legally considered unoccupied. The settlers could take land from Aborigines without signing treaties or providing compensation. The European concept of land ownership was completely foreign to Aboriginal people. In their view, people belonged to the land, were formed by it and were a part of it like everything else.

After WWII, Australian Aborigines became more organised and better educated, and a political movement for land rights developed. In 1962 a bark petition was presented to the federal government by the Yolngu people of Yirrkala, in north-eastern Arnhem Land, demanding that the government recognise Aboriginal peoples' occupation and ownership of Australia since time immemorial. The petition was ignored, and the Yolngu people took the matter to court and lost. In the famous Yirrkala Land Case (1971), Australian courts accepted the government's claim that Aborigines had no meaningful economic, legal or political relationship to land. The case upheld the principle of *terra nullius*, and the common-law position that Australia was unoccupied in 1788.

Because the Yirrkala Land Case was based on an inaccurate (if not outright racist) assessment of Aboriginal society, the federal government came under increasing pressure to legislate for Aboriginal land rights. In 1976 it eventually passed the Aboriginal Land Rights Act (NT), often referred to as the Land Rights Act.

State Land Rights Acts
The Land Rights Act (NT) of 1976, which operates in the Northern Territory, remains Australia's most powerful and comprehensive land rights legislation. Promises were made to legislate for national land rights, but these were abandoned after opposition from mining companies and state governments. The act established three Aboriginal Land Councils that are empowered to claim land on behalf of traditional Aboriginal owners.

However, under the act the only land claimable is unalienated Northern Territory land outside town boundaries – land that no-one else owns or leases, usually semi-desert or desert. Thus, when the traditional Anangunangu owners of Uluru (Ayers Rock) claimed traditional ownership of Uluru and Kata Tjuta (the Olgas), their claim was disallowed because the land was within a national park and thus alienated. It was only by amending two acts of parliament that Uluru-Kata Tjuta National Park was handed back to the Anangu owners on the condition that it was immediately leased back to the federal government as a national park.

At present almost half of the Northern Territory has either been claimed, or is being claimed, by its traditional owners. The claim process is extremely tedious and can take many years to complete, largely because almost all claims have been opposed by the Territory government. Claimants must prove that under Aboriginal law they are responsible for the sacred sites on the land being claimed. A great many elderly claimants die before the matter is resolved.

Once a claim is successful, Aboriginal people have the right to negotiate with mining companies and ultimately to accept or reject exploration and mining proposals. This right is strongly opposed by the mining lobby, despite the fact that traditional Aboriginal owners in the Northern Territory generally reject only about a third of these proposals outright.

The Pitjantjatjara Land Rights Act 1981 is Australia's second-most comprehensive land rights law. This gives Anangu Pitjantjatjara and Yankunytjatjara people freehold title to 10% of South Australia. The land, known as the Anangu Pitjantjatjara Lands, is in the far north of the state.

Just south of the Anangu Pitjantjatjara Lands lie the Maralinga Lands, which comprise 8% of South Australia. The area, much of which was contaminated by British nuclear tests in the 1950s, was returned to its Anangu traditional owners by virtue of the Maralinga Tjarutja Land Rights Act 1984.

Under these two South Australian acts, the Anangu can control access to land and liquor consumption. However, if traditional owners cannot reach agreement with mining companies seeking to explore or mine on their land, they cannot veto mining activity; an arbitrator decides if mining will go ahead, and if so, will bind the mining company with terms and conditions to ensure reasonable monetary payments to Anangu.

In South Australia, other Aboriginal reserves exist by virtue of the Aboriginal Land Trust Act 1966. However, this act gives Aboriginal people little control over their land.

Outside the Northern Territory and South Australia, Aboriginal land rights are extremely limited. In Queensland, less than 2% of the state is Aboriginal land, and the only land that can be claimed under its Aboriginal Land Act 1991 is land that has been gazetted by the government as land available for claim. Under existing Queensland legislation, 95% of the state's Aborigines can't claim their traditional country.

Since the passing of Queensland's Nature Conservation Act 1992, Aborigines in the state also have very limited claim to national parks. If Aborigines successfully claim a Queensland park, they must permanently lease it back to the government without a guarantee of a review of the lease arrangement or a majority on the board of management. This is quite different from the arrangements at Uluru-Kata Tjuta National Park, where the traditional owners have a majority on the board, with a 99-year lease-back that is renegotiated every five years.

In Western Australia, Aboriginal reserves comprise about 13% of the state. Of this land, about one-third is granted to Aborigines under 99-year leases; the other two-thirds are controlled by the government's Aboriginal Affairs Planning Authority. Control of mining and payments to communities are a matter of ministerial discretion.

In New South Wales, the Aboriginal Land Rights Act 1983 transferred freehold title of existing Aboriginal reserves to Aborigines and gave them the right to claim a minuscule amount of other land. Aborigines also have limited rights to the state's national parks, but these rights fall short of genuine control and don't permit them to live inside parks.

Land rights are extremely limited in Victoria and Tasmania, though in 2001 the Victorian government issued more-flexible guidelines for mounting native title claims.

Mabo & the Native Title Act

In May 1982 five Torres Strait Islanders led by Eddie Mabo began an action for a declaration of native title over one of the Murray Islands, off the tip of Cape York. They argued that the legal principle of *terra nullius* had wrongfully usurped their title to land, as for thousands of years Murray Islanders had enjoyed a relationship with the land that included a notion of ownership. In June 1992 the High Court of Australia rejected *terra nullius* and the myth that Australia had been unoccupied. In doing this, it recognised that the principle of native title existed before the arrival of the British.

The high court's judgment became known as the Mabo decision, one of the most controversial decisions ever handed down by an Australian court. It was ambiguous, as it didn't outline the extent to which native title existed in mainland Australia. However, it was hailed by Aborigines and the prime minister at the time, Paul Keating, as an opportunity to create a basis for reconciliation between Aboriginal and non-Aboriginal Australians.

To define the principle of native title, the federal parliament passed the Native Title Act in December 1993. Despite protests to the contrary from the mining industry, the act gives Aboriginal people very few new rights. It limits the application of native title to land

Hill Stockmen's Strike of 1966

Aboriginal stockmen played an essential role in the early days of the pastoral industry in the Northern Territory. Because they were paid such paltry wages (which often never even materialised), a pastoralist could afford to employ many of them, and run his station at a much lower cost. White stockmen received regular and relatively high wages, were given decent food and accommodation, and were able to return to the station homestead every week. In contrast, Aboriginal stockmen received poor food and accommodation, little or no money, and would often spend months in the bush with the cattle.

In the 1960s Vincent Lingiari was a stockman on the huge Wave Hill station, owned by the British Vesteys company. His concern about the way Aboriginal workers were treated led to an appeal to the North Australian Workers' Union (NAWU), which had already applied to the federal court for equal wages for Aboriginal workers. The federal court approved the granting of equal wages in March 1966, but it was not to take effect until December 1968.

The decision led Lingiari to ask the Wave Hill management directly for equal wages. This was refused, and, on 23 August 1966, the Aboriginal stockmen walked off the station and camped in nearby Wattie Creek. They were soon joined by others, and before long only stations that gave their Aboriginal workers not only good conditions but also respect, were provided with workers by Lingiari and the other Gurindji elders.

The Wattie Creek camp gained a lot of local support from both white and Aboriginal people, and it soon developed into a sizeable community with housing and a degree of organisation. Having gained the right to be paid equally, Lingiari and the Gurindji people felt, perhaps for the first time, that they had some say in the way they were able to live. This victory led to the hope that perhaps they could achieve something even more important – title to their own land. To this end Lingiari travelled widely in the eastern states campaigning for land rights, and finally made some progress with the Whitlam government in Canberra. On 16 August 1975, Prime Minister Gough Whitlam attended a ceremony at Wattie Creek that saw the handing over of 3200 sq km of land, now known as Daguragu.

Lingiari was awarded the Order of Australia Medal for service to the Aboriginal people, and died at Daguragu in 1988.

Symbolic gesture by Gough Whitlam to Vincent Lingiari

that no-one else owns or leases, and to land with which Aborigines have continued to have a physical association. The act states that existing ownership or leases extinguish native title, although native title may be revived after mining leases have expired. If land is successfully claimed by Aborigines under the act, they will have no right of veto over developments, including mining.

The Wik Decision

Several months before the Native Title Act became law, the Wik and Thayorre peoples had made a claim in the federal court for native title to land on Cape York Peninsula. The area claimed included two pastoral leases, neither of which had ever been permanently occupied for that purpose. The Wik and Thayorre peoples, however, had been in continuous occupation of them. They argued that native title coexisted with the pastoral leases.

In January 1996 the federal court decided that the claim could not succeed, as the granting of pastoral leases under Queensland law extinguished any native title rights. The Wik people appealed that decision in the high court, which subsequently overturned it.

The high court determined that, under the law that created pastoral leases in Queensland, native title to the leases in question had not been extinguished. Further, it said that native title rights could continue at the same time that land was under lease, and that pastoralists did not have exclusive right of possession to their leases. Importantly, it also ruled that where the two were in conflict, the rights of pastoralists would prevail.

Despite the fact that lease tenure was not threatened, the Wik decision brought an outcry from pastoral lessees across Australia. They demanded that the federal government protect them by legislating to limit native title rights, as was intended in the original act. Aboriginal leaders were equally adamant that native title must be preserved.

In late 1997 John Howard's government responded with its so-called Ten Point Plan, a raft of proposed legislative amendments to the Native Title Act which further entrenched the pastoralists' position. The Native Title Amendment Act 1998 is an improvement on the government's intended bill, but it removes the 'right to negotiate' the way that pastoral leases and reserved lands are used.

ECONOMY

Australia is a relatively affluent, industrialised nation but most of its wealth still comes from agriculture and mining. It has a small domestic market and a comparatively weak manufacturing sector. Nevertheless, a substantial proportion of the population is employed in manufacturing, and for much of Australia's history it has been argued that these industries need tariff protection from imports to ensure their survival.

Today, however, tariff protection is on the way out and efforts are being made to increase Australia's international competitiveness. This has become more important as prices of traditional primary exports have become more volatile.

In the outback, where so much of the economy is dependent on wool, meat and mining, this volatility has resulted in a roller-coaster ride of boom and bust. Alongside the huge cattle and wool enterprises (Australia is the world's largest exporter of wool) and the billion-dollar mining conglomerates, there are thousands of struggling cow cockies, hard-partying opal diggers and reclusive gold-panning hermits. More often than not, these interesting characters fight a hard battle for survival in a harsh environment, but very few of them would dream of surrendering their freedom.

A typical cattle or sheep station in the outback covers tens, if not hundreds, of thousands of hectares, and the larger ones are the size of small countries – Anna Creek station in South Australia is the size of Belgium! Large stations may have one or more semi-independent outstations. The headquarters of a station is the homestead, which is where the owner (or manager) and staff live. The livestock is often left to fend for itself, though the owner will ensure that there are sufficient watering points where additional fodder and salt may be left. Once or twice a year the livestock is mustered to check on their general welfare and take stock of births and deaths, but they may be mustered more often for sale or to move them to other paddocks. Sheep are shorn twice a year – firstly the main shearing and then later on the stragglers; cattle are mustered once a year for ear-marking.

One of Australia's greatest economic hopes is tourism, especially in the economically depressed outback, with the numbers of visitors rising each year and projections for even greater numbers in the future. Almost five million foreigners visited the country in 2000, generating more than $12 billion in foreign exchange.

More than half of Australia's exports go to the Asian region. Japan is Australia's biggest trading partner, but the economies of China, Korea and Vietnam are becoming increasingly important. Regionally, Australia has initiated the establishment of the Asia-Pacific Economic Cooperation (APEC) group, a body aimed at furthering the economic interests of the Pacific nations.

The government has sought to restrain real wages and is trying to stimulate new manufacturing and service industries. This policy has seen the creation of new jobs while many people employed in traditional sectors have joined the dole queues, and unemployment is currently around 7%. However, prospects for the future are cautiously optimistic – the economy is growing at an annual rate of around 4% (very high by developed-world standards) and inflation is relatively low, at around 2%.

Although most non-Aboriginal Australians enjoy a relatively high standard of living, the same cannot be said for most of their Aboriginal counterparts. Many Aborigines still live in deplorable conditions, with infant mortality and outbreaks of preventable diseases running at an unacceptably high rate – higher even than in many Third World countries. Progress has definitely been made with the recent native title legislation (see Aboriginal Land Rights earlier), but there is still a very long way to go before Aborigines can enjoy the lifestyles of their choice.

POPULATION & PEOPLE

Australia's population is about 19 million. The most populous states are New South Wales and Victoria, which also have the two largest cities – Sydney (four million) and Melbourne (3.3 million). The population is concentrated along the east coast from Adelaide to Cairns and in the much smaller coastal region of south-west Western Australia. The centre of the country is very sparsely populated.

Until WWII, Australians were predominantly of British and Irish descent, and there was a sprinkling of Chinese settlers, but that has changed dramatically. Since the war, heavy migration from Europe has created major Greek and Italian populations, but also German, Dutch, Maltese, Yugoslav, Lebanese, Turkish and other groups.

More recently, Australia has had large influxes of Asians, particularly Vietnamese after the Vietnam War. In proportion to its population, Australia probably took more Vietnamese refugees than any other Western nation. Australia accepts about 85,000 migrants annually and, despite some opposition, most Australians pride themselves on the nation's multiculturalism.

At the time of the 1996 census (2001 census figures were not available at the time of writing), around 386,000 people identified themselves as Aboriginal or of indigenous origin, most of whom live in northern and central Australia This figure is growing at an annual rate of about 2% – a large increase on previous census figures and perhaps a reflection of the fact that people are now far more willing to declare their indigenous origins. Most of the 28,000 Torres Strait Islanders, primarily a Melanesian people, live in northern Queensland and on the islands of Torres Strait between Cape York and Papua New Guinea.

ARTS
Literature

For white Australian writers, a somewhat undelineated outback has always been an important source of inspiration, with its 'frontier' image. For Aborigines, however, the outback was not remote or dangerous: it was their life, and the focus of a rich oral tradition; creeds and practicalities were passed on from generation to generation by word of mouth in songs, stories and accompanying rituals. See the Religion section for more on Aboriginal song and narrative.

Modern Aboriginal Literature Most of the big issues in Aboriginal Australia are covered in Aboriginal writing. A good introduction is James Miller's *Koori: A Will to Win*. It's a history of European settlement in Australia from a Koori perspective, combining personal insights with historical analysis. Philip McLaren, a Sydney-based writer, has used the crime-fiction genre to cover many of the aspects of contemporary Aboriginal life.

Ruby Langford's *Don't Take Your Love to Town* is about the struggle of an Aboriginal woman trying to raise a large family by herself, and the drift of rural Aborigines to the cities. It deals with the impact of urban life on young Aborigines, police harassment and the continuing importance of Aboriginal spirituality for city-dwelling Aborigines.

Rita and Jackie Huggins' *Auntie Rita*, much more than a story of an individual life, tells how Aborigines were rounded up and moved on to missions and government reserves. It gives a rich account of Aboriginal lives in postwar Queensland. Other life narratives worth looking at include Ida West's *Pride Against Prejudice* and Ellie Gaffney's *Somebody Now*.

The University of Queensland Press (UQP) has been a leader in publishing indigenous writing. Aboriginal writers who've been published by UQP include Bill Rosser and Herb Wharton. Two especially significant books published under the UQP label are *Paperbark* and *The Honey-Ant Men's Love Song*. Edited by Jack Davis, Adam Shoemaker, Mudrooroo & Stephen Muecke, *Paperbark* is an anthology of Aboriginal writing going back to the 19th century. It includes a petition from the Kaurna people of South Australia to Governor Gawler, a traditional story dealing with the Myall Creek massacre, and contemporary writing.

Bob Dixon and Martin Duwell have edited a superb collection of Aboriginal song-poems in *The Honey-Ant Men's Love Song*. As well as being great literature, these song-poems provide the reader with insights into often unsuspected dimensions of Aboriginal traditional life.

Black Hours is the true story of Wayne King, an Aboriginal man growing up gay in Ipswich – at one time the headquarters of Pauline Hanson's One Nation Party, which was opposed to Aboriginal rights. King escapes and makes an exciting life for himself as he travels overseas, but when he comes home he finds he has unfinished business – many others besides himself have been scarred by Australian racism. Sam Watson's *The Kadaitcha Sung* is one of those books best described as 'gripping'. Combining science fiction, crime fiction, fantasy, social analysis and historical references, it has enjoyed something approaching cult status among Australian readers.

Kakadu Elder Bill Neidjie's *Story about Feeling* has been described as narrative philosophy and provides an Aboriginal perspective on stars, trees, rocks, animals and people. It's a message about connectedness for all people, including city folk. In *Gularabalu*,

Paddy Roe, a Broome Elder, tells stories that illustrate the power of the Aboriginal 'clever man' – sometimes in relation to settlers and their law, sometimes in relation to lawbreakers in the Aboriginal community. Both books use Kriol – a poetic language that draws on traditional Aboriginal languages and English. It may seem a little difficult to understand at first but it's worth persevering.

In terms of 'classics', the poetry of Oodgeroo Noonuccal (Kath Walker), written in the early 1960s, still makes great reading. You may not be able to find copies of *We Are Going* and *The Dawn Is at Hand*, but Kevin Gilbert's *Inside Black Australia* has remained in print. It's long been one of Australia's most popular anthologies of Aboriginal poetry.

One of the success stories of Aboriginal publishing is Magabala Books. It's based in Broome and achieved early success with *Wandering Girl* by Glenyse Ward. It has continued to publish strong works such as Magdalene Williams' *Ngay Janijirr Ngank – This is my Word*. It's a senior woman's testimony with its own charm that makes use of bilingualism and weaves the narrator's Christian spirituality with traditional Aboriginal spirituality and history.

Jinangga, the autobiography of Monty Walgar, is in most respects quite a different story. Walgar tells of his love affair with alcohol – but he's no victim: Monty has since reformed and given up his fighting and drinking. What's unexpected is that the author always comes across as a decent and ethical person in spite of his wild excesses.

Sally Morgan's *My Place* is one of the most popular books ever written by an Aborigine. It's the story of Morgan's mother and grandmother, who try to pass Sally and her brother and sisters off as 'Indian' – anything but Aboriginal – in an attempt to evade the government policy of removing 'part-Aboriginal' children from their families and institutionalising them. As such it anticipated the inquiry and report on the Stolen Generations by over a decade. Morgan sets out to uncover and reclaim her repressed identity as an Aborigine.

[Continued on page 49]

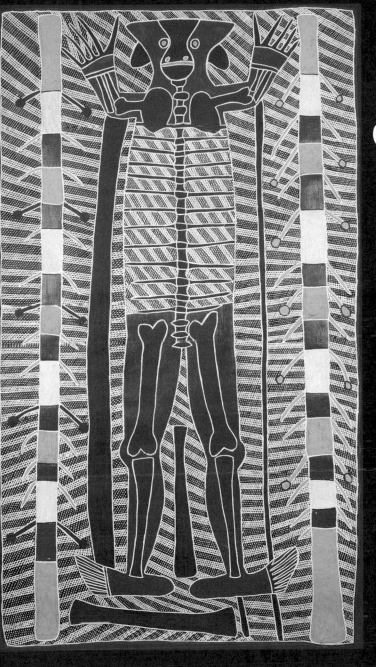

Aboriginal Art

Visual Art

Visual imagery is a fundamental part of indigenous life, a connection between past and present, between the supernatural and the earthly, between people and the land. The early forms of indigenous artistic expression were rock carvings (petroglyphs), body painting and ground designs, and the earliest engraved designs known to exist date back at least 30,000 years.

indigenous art was either largely ignored by non-indigenous people or simply seen as an anthropological curiosity. Then, in 1971 an event took place that changed non-indigenous perceptions of indigenous art. At **Papunya**, north-west of Alice Springs, a group of senior men from the community, led by Kaapa Mbitjana Tjampitjinpa (Anmatyerre/ Arrernte; 1925–89), along with Long Jack Phillipus Tjakamarra (Pintupi/Luritja/Warlpiri) and Billy Stockman Tjapaltjarri (Anmatyerre) were encouraged to paint a mural on one of the school's external walls. Other members of the community became enthused by the project and joined in creating the mural named *Honey Ant Dreaming*. Government regulations later saw the mural destroyed, but its effect on the community was still profound. Images of spiritual significance had taken on a permanent and very public form. From this quiet beginning in a remote Aboriginal community one of the most important art movements of the late 20th century grew and spread.

There's a huge range of material being produced across Australia; including paintings, batik and wood carvings from the central Australian Aboriginal communities; bark paintings from Arnhem Land; ironwood carvings and silk-screen printing from the Tiwi Islands north of Darwin; and didgeridoos (*yidaki*) – wind instruments made of branches hollowed out by termites.

While the art of the more traditional communities differs in style from urban works, a common theme that appears to run through all the works is the strong and ancient connection indigenous people have with the

Warning

Readers should be aware that the names of deceased members of the Aboriginal community are cited in this section. Naming or showing images of recently deceased people can cause offence in some communities; however, after a suitable period of mourning has passed family and community representatives allow the name and the artwork of the deceased to be reproduced.

land, mixed with a deep sense of loss occasioned by the horror of the last 200-plus years. Ultimately, however, the viewer is left with a sense of indigenous cultural strength and renewal.

Rock Art In Australia's tropical Top End, **Arnhem Land** is an area of rich artistic heritage. Recent finds suggest that rock paintings were being produced as early as 60,000 years ago, and some of the rock-art galleries in the huge sandstone Arnhem Land plateau are at least 18,000 years old.

The paintings contained in the Arnhem Land rock-art sites range from hand prints to paintings of animals, people, mythological beings and European ships, constituting one of the world's most important and fascinating rock-art collections. They provide a record of changing environments and lifestyles over the millennia.

In some places they are concentrated in large galleries, with paintings from more recent eras sometimes superimposed over older paintings. Some sites are kept secret – not only to protect them from damage, but also because they are private or sacred to the Aboriginal owners. Some are believed to be inhabited by malevolent beings, who must not be approached by those ignorant of the indigenous customs of the region. However, two of the finest sites have been opened up to visitors, with access roads, walkways and explanatory signs. These are **Ubirr** and **Nourlangie** in Kakadu National Park.

Rock paintings show how the main styles succeeded each other over time. The earliest hand or grass-prints were followed by a 'naturalistic' style, with large outlines of people or animals filled in with colour. Some of the animals depicted, such as the thylacine (Tasmanian tiger), have long been extinct on mainland Australia.

Then came the 'dynamic' style, in which motion was often depicted (a dotted line, for example, to show a spear's path through the air). In this era the first mythological beings appeared, with human bodies and animal heads.

Title page: Devil Devil Corroboree *by Djambu Barra Barra (1999); 191x110cm; acrylic on linen; Ngukurr, Northern Territory – Barra Barra combines X-ray and crosshatching techniques with the distinctive bright palette made famous by the Ngukurr artists. Photo courtesy of Alcaston Gallery, Melbourne*
Left facing page: George Wallaby working on a painting that represents his country, Barragoo (Lake Gregory). Photo by Richard I'Anson
Right: X-ray art examines the internal structure of its subject – this fish is in the Kakadu National Park. Photo by Tom Boyden

The next style featured simple human silhouettes. It was followed by the curious 'yam figures', in which people and animals were drawn in the shape of yams (or yams in the shape of people and animals!). Other painting styles, including the 'X-ray' style, which displays the internal organs and bone structures of animals, also appeared around this time.

From around 400 years ago, indigenous artists depicted newcomers to the region – intially Macassan traders, then Europeans.

The art of the **Kimberley** is perhaps best known for its images of the Wandjina, a group of ancestral beings who came from the sky and sea and were associated with fertility. These beings controlled the elements and were responsible for the formation of the country's natural features.

Wandjina images are found painted on rock as well as on more recent contemporary media, with some of the rock images being more than 7m long. They generally appear in human form, with large black eyes, a nose but no mouth, a halo around the head (representative of both hair and clouds) and a black oval shape on the chest.

In **Northern Queensland** rock art again predominates. The superb Quinkan galleries at Laura on the Cape York Peninsula, north-west of Cairns, are among the best known in the country. Among the many creatures depicted on the walls are the Quinkan spirits, which are shown in two forms – the long and stick-like Timara, and the crocodile-like Imjim with their knobbed, club-like tails.

Painting In central Australia, painting has flourished to such a degree that it is now an important source of income for communities. It has also been an important educational tool for children, through which they can learn different aspects of religious and ceremonial knowledge.

Western Desert painting, also known as dot painting, partly evolved from 'ground paintings', which formed the centrepiece of dances and songs. 'Paints' were made from pulped plant material, and the designs were made on the ground using dots. Dots also outline objects in rock paintings, and highlight geographical features or vegetation.

Dot paintings depict Dreaming *stories*. (The Dreaming is a complex concept that forms the basis of Aboriginal spirituality, incorporating the creation of the world and the spiritual energies operating around us. A *story* is a tale from the Dreaming that taps into the concepts of legend, myth, tradition and the law.) While the paintings may look random and abstract to the outsider, they can be read in many ways, including as aerial landscape maps. Many dot paintings feature the tracks of birds, animals and humans, often identifying the ancestral

Albert Namatjira

Probably Australia's best-known Aboriginal artist, Albert Namatjira (1902–59) was a Western Arrernte who lived at the Hermannsburg Lutheran Mission, west of Alice Springs. He was introduced to the technique of European-style watercolour painting by a non-Aboriginal artist, Rex Batterbee, in the 1930s.

Namatjira successfully captured the essence of the Centre with paintings that were heavily influenced by European art. At the time non-Aboriginal people saw his pictures purely for what they appeared to be – renderings of picturesque landscapes. The reality was that he only chose subjects associated with the deeds of his totemic ancestor.

Namatjira supported many of his people with the income from his work, as he was obliged to do under Western Arrernte law. Because of his fame, he was allowed to buy alcohol at a time when this was otherwise illegal for Aboriginal people. In 1957 he was the first Aboriginal person to be granted Australian citizenship, but in 1958 he was jailed for six months for supplying alcohol to Aborigines. He died the following year, aged 57.

Although Namatjira died disenchanted with white society, he did much to change the extremely negative views of Aboriginal people which prevailed at the time. At the same time he paved the way for the Hermannsburg painting movement, which emerged a decade after his death.

beings. Subjects may be depicted by the imprint they leave in the sand – a person is depicted by a simple arc (the print of the buttocks left by someone sitting), a *coolamon* (wooden carrying dish) by an oval shape, a digging stick by a single line, and a camp fire by a circle. Men or women are identified by the objects associated with them – digging sticks and coolamons for women, spears and boomerangs for men. Concentric circles usually depict Dreaming sites, or places where ancestors paused in their journeys.

While these symbols are widely used, their meaning within each painting is known only to the artist and the people closely associated with him or her – either by clan or by the Dreaming – and different clans apply different interpretations to each painting. In this way sacred stories can be publicly portrayed, as the deeper meaning is not revealed to uninitiated viewers.

Top facing page: The Wandjina are ancestral spirits with the power to summon the great storms of the Wet season – here their images are photographed at Gibb River in the east Kimberley. Photo by Mitch Reardon
Top inset: Albert Namatjira (1952). Photo by Wendy Hart

Bark painting is an integral part of the cultural heritage of Arnhem Land indigenous people. It's difficult to establish when bark was first used, partly because it is perishable, so very old pieces don't exist. The paintings were never intended to be permanent records.

The bark used is from the stringy-bark tree *(Eucalyptus tetradonta)*. The pigments used in bark paintings are mainly red and yellow (ochres), white (kaolin) and black (charcoal). These natural pigments give the paintings their superb soft and earthy finish.

One of the main features of Arnhem Land bark paintings is the use of *rarrk* (crosshatching) designs. These designs identify the particular clans, and are based on body paintings handed down through generations. The paintings can also be broadly categorised by their regional styles. In the region's west the tendency is towards naturalistic images and plain backgrounds, while to the east the use of geometric, abstract designs is more common.

The art reflects Dreaming themes that vary by region. In eastern Arnhem Land the prominent ancestor beings are the Djang'kawu Sisters, who travelled the land with elaborate *dilly* bags (carry bags) and digging sticks (for making waterholes), and the Wagilag Sisters, who are associated with snakes and waterholes. In western Arnhem Land Yingarna, the

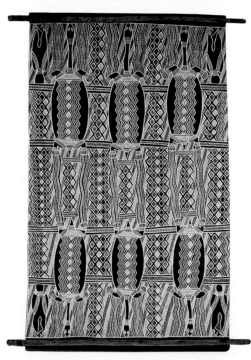

Rainbow Serpent, is the significant being (according to some clans), as is one of her offspring, Ngalyod. Other groups paint Nawura as the principal ancestral being – he travelled through the rocky landscape creating sacred sites and giving people the attributes of culture.

The Mimi spirits also feature in western Arnhem Land art. These mischievous spirits are attributed with having taught the indigenous people of the region many things, including hunting, food gathering and painting skills.

Contemporary Painting Since the late 1980s the artists of **Ngukurr**, a settlement near Roper Bar in south-eastern Arnhem Land, have been producing works using acrylic paints on canvas. People from a number of language groups live at Ngukurr. This is reflected stylistically in the art created, as can be seen in paintings by Ginger Riley Munduwalawala (Mara), Amy Johnson, Willie Gububi/Gudapi (Mara; 1916–96) and Gertie Huddleston (Nameratjara). Ancestral beings feature prominently; other subject matter includes bush tucker and reference to missionaries. The works of these artists are contemporary in their use of vibrant palettes, and differ markedly from the bark painting and associated art in other regions of Arnhem Land.

Contemporary art in the eastern **Kimberley** sometimes features elements of the works of the indigenous people of central Australia, a legacy of the forced relocation of people during the 1970s. The community of Warmun, at Turkey Creek on the Great Northern Hwy, has been particularly active in ensuring that Aboriginal culture, through painting and dance, remains strong. Renowned artists from this region include Rover Thomas (Wangkajungka/Kukatja; 1926–98), Queenie

Left facing page: Minhala at Gangan *by Nawurapu Wunungmurra; earth pigments on bark. Photo courtesy of Buku Larrngay Arts (Yirrkala)*
Right: Driving to Iltjiltjari *by Bessy Liddle (2000); acrylic on linen – some Aboriginal artists choose to express traditional stories in a figurative style that can appear similar to naive European art. Courtesy Desart and Jukurrpa Artists Photo by Steve Strike*

McKenzie (Kija [Gija]/Gurindji; 1930–99) and Paddy Tjamintji (Kija [Gija]; 1912–86), among others.

On the edge of the Great Sandy Desert, **Balgo** was established as a Catholic mission in 1939. It was not until the mid-1980s that Balgo artists embraced painting for people outside the community. Balgo's art is characterised by the vivid use of colour, as best seen in works by Kukatja artists such as Peter Sunfly 'Sandfly' Tjampitjin (1916–96), Susie Bootja Bootja Napangarti, Donkeyman Lee Tjupurrula (1921–93), Eubena Nampitjin, Wimmitji Tjapangarti (1925–2000) and Lucy Yukenbarri.

In the late 1980s, members of the **Utopia** community north-east of Alice Springs started to paint on canvases with acrylics. While some men in the community paint, Utopia is best known for the work produced by its women artists, in particular Emily Kame Kngwarreye (Anmatyerre; 1910–96), Ada Bird Petyarre (Anmatyerre), Kathleen Petyarre (Anmatyerre/Eastern Alyawarre) and Gloria Tamerre Petyarre (Anmatyerre).

Of this group, Emily Kame Kngwarreye holds a special place. Her life as an artist only commenced when she was in her late 70s. Kngwarreye's paintings are closely connected to her people's relationship with the land. The beautiful use of textured colour in her paintings is reminiscent of expressionist paintings of the non-indigenous art world.

The work of indigenous metropolitan and rural artists is at times deeply confronting. Content often focuses on the terrible injustices of the past 200-plus years while raising issues of dispossession; access to language, cultural practices and land; contemporary indigenous culture; and the artist in the modern postcolonial world.

Notable artists include Queenslanders Fiona Foley (Badtjala), Judy Watson (Waanyi) and Gordon Bennett. From New South Wales there is HJ Wedge (Wiradjuri), Michael Riley (Wiradjuri), Rea (Gamilaroi/Wailwan), Richard Bell (Gamilaroi) and Lin Onus (Wiradjuri; 1948–96). South Australian artists include Trevor Nickolls, Yvonne Koolmatrie (Ngarrindjeri) and Ian Abdulla (Ngarrindjeri). Julie Dowling (Badimaya) and Sally Morgan (Palyuku) work in Western Australia. Others are based in places outside their traditional regions, such as Destiny Deacon (Kuku/Erub/Mer) in Victoria and Brenda L Croft (Gurindji) in Western Australia, or travel frequently for work, like Palawa artist Julie Gough from Tasmania.

Artefacts & Crafts
Objects traditionally made for practical or ceremonial uses, such as weapons and musical instruments, often featured intricate symbolic decoration. In recent years, many communities have also developed nontraditional craft forms, and the growing tourist trade has seen demand and production increase steadily.

The most widespread craft objects seen for sale these days are **didgeridoos**. Originally they were (and still are in many communities) used as ceremonial musical instruments by indigenous people in Arnhem Land (where they are known as yidaki). The traditional instrument was made from particular eucalypt branches that had been hollowed out by termites. The tubes were often fitted with a wax

mouthpiece made from sugarbag (native honeybee wax) and decorated with traditional designs.

Boomerangs are curved wooden throwing sticks used for hunting and also as ceremonial *clapsticks* (percussion instruments). Contrary to popular belief, not all boomerangs are designed to return when thrown – the idea is to hit the animal being hunted! Returning boomerangs were mostly used in south-eastern and western Australia. Although they all follow the same fundamental design, boomerangs come in a huge range of shapes, sizes and decorative styles, and are made from a number of different wood types.

Traditionally, most **wooden sculptures** were made to be used for particular ceremonies. Arnhem Land artists still produce softwood carvings of birds, fish, animals and ancestral beings, which are engraved and painted with intricate symbolic designs. Tiwi artists create impressive carvings from ironwood, which is said to be impossible for termites to bore through.

Also very popular are **scorched carvings**, wooden carvings that have designs scorched into them with hot fencing wire. These range from small figures, such as possums, up to quite large snakes and lizards. Many are connected with Dreaming stories.

There are many types of traditional weapons, including spears, woomeras (spear-throwers), nulla-nullas and bundis (types of clubs), and shields. **Ceremonial shields** were made from timber or bark in different shapes and sizes, and were often richly decorated with carved and painted surfaces showing the owner's ancestry or Dreaming. Though mainly used for ceremonial purposes, they were also put to practical use when fighting between clans occurred.

Fibre craft and weaving are major art forms among women, although in some regions men also made woven objects as hunting tools. String or twine was traditionally made from bark, grass, leaves, roots and other materials, hand-spun and dyed with natural pigments, then woven to make dilly bags, baskets, garments, fishing nets and other items. Strands or fibres from the leaves of the pandanus palm (and other palms or grasses) were also woven to make dilly bags and mats. While all these objects have utilitarian purposes, many also have ritual uses.

Left facing page: Didgeridoo by Djambu Barra Barra; private collection – Didgeridoos come from the Top End of the Northern Territory, where the Yolngu know them as yidaki. Photo by Bethune Carmichael, courtesy Alcaston Gallery, Melbourne
Top: Paddy Bedford, a member of the Juwulinypany community in the east Kimberley, painting a boomerang. Photo by Jason Davidson

Music

To make cermonial music, Aboriginal people traditionally beat the ground with hunting sticks, clap boomerangs together, and use their hands and feet to keep the beat.

Traditional Aboriginal Instruments
Many coastal and inland tribes have different musical instruments because of the different natural resources in their tribal areas. Today Aboriginal tribes still use percussion with different shaped **clapsticks** or message sticks, which are hit together to make different pitches.

The **didgeridoo** comes from the top end of the Northern Territory and its Yolngu name is yidaki. The 'didg' is created from a tree or tree trunk that has been eaten out by white ants or termites, leaving the tree hollow inside. It is cut down to a metre or more in length and then carved and shaped so it fits into the palm of your hand. When the didg is blown it creates a rhythmic droning sound; expert players can make bird and animal sounds as well.

The Yirkala Mirning tribe uses **gong stones** – musical stones from the caves and cliff faces of the Great Australian Bight area. The gong stones come in all shapes and sizes. Different pitches of sound are made by hitting the gong stones with smaller stones.

Traditional Torres Strait Instruments
The many islands in the Torres Strait all have their own unique *stories*, with their own songs and dances. But what they all have in common is the beautiful harmonies of the men and women singing in English or traditional languages.

The Torres Strait **island drum** has a deep sound and is held in one hand while the palm of the other hand is used to create a rhythmic pounding sound with a hypnotic echoing.

The **kulup** is a hand-shaker made up of black seeds tied together with special twine from the islands to make a sound of shells being shaken.

Contemporary Music Modern indigenous musicians have managed to create unique styles by incorporating traditional instruments into modern rock and pop formats. All the political concerns of indigenous Australians can be heard in their song lyrics.

If you're having a hard time finding a CD of an Aboriginal or Torres Strait Islander artists, you can check out CAAMA, Australia's only indigenous record company. You can e-mail them (**e** c.shop@caama .com) or check out their website (**W** www.caama.com.au).

Dance

There was an arresting moment in the opening ceremony of the Sydney Olympics which encapsulates indigenous dance today. The performance represented a nation-wide gathering of tribes, smoothly performing their respective traditional dances in harmony to the strains of the didgeridoo from the north, clapsticks from the south, kulups from the Torres Strait, and a songman from Arnhem Land.

An essential part of ceremonies, indigenous dance incorporates music, song and art.

A dance performance will tell a story of the Dreaming, an ancestor spirit or the passing down of a law. As most spirit ancestors were animals or birds, dancers imitate the movements and sounds of these creatures.

Top facing page:
Clapsticks are usually made of hardwood. Illustration by Martin Harris
Middle facing page:
Didgeridoos have a wax mouth-piece to give a good lip grip. Illustration by Martin Harris
Lower facing page:
Island drums can be very simple or elaborately decorated with island designs. Illustration by Martin Harris
Top right: Kulups are a special kind of island rattle. Illustration by Martin Harris
Bottom right: Aborigines from the Tjapukai Aboriginal Cultural Park recreate fire-making for visitors to the Creation Theatre. Photo by Dave Levitt

Cycles of Dance Every member of the clan participates in dance, which is a communal event. Children learn dance and song at an early age and are expected to perform during certain ceremonies. Some dances are gender-specific – men and women will perform separately as they tell a story that is significant to each group.

Sacred dances and songs are performed in seclusion during rituals These dances include the initiation ceremonies of young boys and girls, and fertility rituals for women and the earth (to increase food available for gathering by some tribes). An initiation ceremony is also a time of great communal celebration, of singing, dancing and music. Dancing is also a part of death rituals.

Regional Styles Dancing styles vary across regions and tribes. Most dances are accompanied by traditional music. The didgeridoo (yidaki) provides music to the fast–moving 'shake-a-leg' dance of Cape York Peninsula and the rhythmical stomp of Arnhem Land.

In the Torres Strait the energising militaristic style is categorised into three forms: social dances, ceremonial dances and war dances. There is a strong Polynesian influence in Islander dance, music and song.

Unfortunately, in New South Wales, Victoria and Tasmania many of the dances, along with languages and songs, were lost during colonisation.

Contemporary Dance Aboriginal and Torres Strait Islander contemporary dance combines traditional and Western dance and draws on traditional and contemporary themes.

This unique and mesmerising blend of dance is expertly performed by the Sydney-based Bangarra Dance Theatre, Australia's premier indigenous dance company. Credited with international and Olympic performances, Bangarra has collaborated with the Australian Ballet in *Rites*, a highly acclaimed work blending two vastly different cultural expressions in movement.

The award-winning Tjapukai Aboriginal Cultural Park at Smithfield, north of Cairns, showcases the highly entertaining and informative traditional dance and culture of the Tjapukai people of northern Queensland.

Bottom far left: Bangarra Dance Theatre, Corroboree, photo by Greg Barrett
Bottom left: Bangarra Dance Theatre, Fan The Flame, photo by Gerald Jenkins

[Continued from page 48]

Jack Davis and Kim Scott are probably Australia's finest Aboriginal writers. Any reading of one of Davis' plays (such as *No Sugar* or *In Our Town*) is amply rewarded, and if you ever have the chance to see his work performed, don't miss it. Scott shared the prestigious Miles Franklin award for *Benang* in 2000. This and his earlier novel, *True Country*, are books that are fundamental to Australia's self-understanding. They're complex but you'll find them dense with feeling and intelligence if you persevere.

The Aborigine in White Literature

Aboriginal people have often been used as characters in white outback literature and unfortunately early examples were usually demeaning. A common subject was sexual relationships between white men and Aboriginal women.

Rosa Praed, in her short piece *My Australian Girlhood* (1902), drew heavily on her outback experience and her affectionate childhood relationship with Aborigines. Jeannie Gunn's *Little Black Princess* was published in 1904, but it was *We of the Never Never* (1908) which brought her renown. Her story of the life and trials on Elsey Station includes an unflattering, patronising depiction of the Aborigines on and around the station. Ownership of the station was returned to the Mangarayi people in 2000.

Catherine Martin, in 1923, wrote *The Incredible Journey*. It follows the trail of two black women, Iliapo and Polde, in search of a little boy who had been kidnapped by a white man. The book describes in careful detail the harsh desert environment they traverse.

Katharine Susannah Prichard contributed a great deal to outback literature in the 1920s. A journey to Turee Station in the cattle country of the Ashburton and Fortescue rivers, in 1926, inspired her lyrical tribute to the Aborigine, *Coonardoo* (1929), which delved into the then almost taboo love between an Aboriginal woman and a white station boss. Later, Mary Durack's *Keep Him My Country* (1955) explored the theme of a white station-manager's love for an Aboriginal girl, Dalgerie.

The Chant of Jimmy Blacksmith (1972) by Thomas Keneally depicts the rage of a young Aboriginal man in white society early last century. It was made into a major feature film.

More-recent works exploring Aboriginal themes include Rodney Hall's *The Second Bridegroom* (1991), Thomas Keneally's *Flying Hero Class* (1991) and David Malouf's *Remembering Babylon* (1993). Carolyn Wadley Dowley's *Through Silent Country* (2000) tells the story of a group of Aboriginal people from Laverton who escaped a concentration camp in the 1920s.

Outback Explorers

When John Oxley published an account of his discoveries in 1820 he stimulated the myth of the 'inland sea', and others set about to find it. Charles Sturt gave the first written description of places in the interior such as the Simpson Desert.

Other accounts worth mentioning are the journals recalling Edward John Eyre's epic journey in 1841 across the Great Australian Bight; the account by Aboriginal Jackey-Jackey (Galmarra) of the death of Edmund Kennedy during an expedition to Cape York in 1848; and the writings of Ernest Giles from the period 1874 to 1876. Giles' matter-of-fact, unembellished descriptions of remote parts of Australia's arid heart, like the Gibson Desert, are among the most literary and perceptive of explorers' writings.

Much more recent is Robyn Davidson's description in *Tracks* (1980) of her solo journey, accompanied only by camels and a dog, into the outback. Her account of the characters she encountered along the way revealed that Australia's 'dead heart' was still populated by mythical 'bushies'.

You can find most of these accounts, either in full or condensed form, in major public libraries.

Bush Ballads & Yarns

The bush, in particular the outback, was a great source of inspiration for many popular ballads and

The Cattle Kings

More than any other enterprise, it was pastoral activity in general, and the cattle industry in particular, that led to European settlement of inland Australia. Given the vast distances, marginal country and harsh climate, it was an arduous and often risky business to establish stations and rear cattle. Yet there was no shortage of those prepared to give it a go, and some made major contributions.

Sir Sidney Kidman

Sid Kidman was the undisputed cattle king of Australia. He was born in Adelaide in 1857 and when he ran away from home at the age of 13, headed north for the 'corner country' of north-western New South Wales, where he found work on outback stations. Over the years he became an expert bushman and stockman.

In the latter part of the 19th century, the vast expanses of the outback were settled. The infrastructure was virtually nil and getting cattle to markets in good condition was a major problem. Kidman came up with a bold yet simple solution: 'chains' of stations along strategic routes that would allow the gradual movement of stock to the coastal markets – in effect, he split the entire outback into a number of paddocks.

Starting with £400 that he inherited at the age of 21, Kidman traded in cattle, horses and later Broken Hill mines until he built up a portfolio of land-holdings that gave him the envisaged 'chains'. Eventually he owned or controlled about 170,000 sq km of land (an area 2½ times the size of Tasmania) in chains, one which ran from the Gulf of Carpentaria south through western Queensland and New South Wales to Broken Hill and into South Australia, and another from the Kimberley into the Northern Territory, down through the centre and into South Australia. Such was his stature as a pastoralist that at one time the north-western area of New South Wales was known as 'Kidman's Corner'. His life was portrayed, somewhat romantically, in Ion Idriess's book *The Cattle King*. Kidman was knighted in 1921, and died in 1935.

The Duracks

Another name that is firmly linked with the cattle industry and the opening up of inland Australia is the Durack family. Brothers Patrick (Patsy) and Michael Durack took up land on Cooper Creek in

stories. These were particularly in vogue at the turn of the 20th century, but they have an enduring quality.

Adam Lindsay Gordon was the forerunner of this type of literature, having published *Bush Ballads and Galloping Rhymes* in 1870. The two most famous exponents of the ballad style were AB 'Banjo' Paterson and Henry Lawson. Paterson grew up in the bush in the second half of the 19th century and became one of Australia's most important bush poets. His pseudonym 'The Banjo' was the name of a horse on his family's station. His horse ballads were regarded as some of his best, but he was familiar with all aspects of station life and wrote with great optimism. *Clancy of the Overflow* and *The Man From Snowy River* are both well

known, but Paterson is probably most remembered as the author of Australia's alternative national anthem, *Waltzing Matilda*, in which he celebrates an unnamed wanderer of the bush.

Henry Lawson was a contemporary of Paterson's, but was much more of a social commentator and political thinker and less of a humorist. Although he wrote a good many poems about the bush – pieces such as *Andy's Gone with Cattle* and *The Roaring Days* are among his best – his greatest legacy is his short stories of life in the bush, which seem remarkably simple yet manage to capture the atmosphere perfectly. Good examples are *A Day on a Selection* (a selection was a tract of crown land for which annual fees were paid) and *The Drover's Wife*; the

The Cattle Kings

western Queensland in the 1860s, and were soon joined by members of their extended family.

With the discovery of good pastoral land in the Kimberley, the Duracks took up land around the Ord River in 1882. A huge cattle muster was organised and in June 1863 four parties of drovers with a total of 7500 head of cattle set off from the Cooper Creek area. On the map the trip was a neat 2500km, but in 'drover's miles', meandering from water to water and grass to grass, it was much further.

It took 28 months to make the journey, and men and cattle suffered greatly along the way – at one point they were held up for months at a waterhole waiting for the drought to break. Many cattle were lost to pleuropneumonia and tick fever.

Nevertheless, the party reached the Ord in September 1885 and still had enough cattle to establish three stations: Rosewood, Argyle and Lissadel.

Patsy Durack's granddaughter, Mary, became a popular author, and many of her novels were set in the Kimberley. Her most well-known work is *Kings in Grass Castles*, in which she describes the great trek.

Nat Buchanan

Although Nathaniel Buchanan was not a great land-holder in the mould of the Duracks or Sidney Kidman, he was a great cattleman and drover, responsible for the settlement of huge areas of the outback. Known as Old Bluey because of his shock of red hair, Buchanan led many drives through Queensland and the Northern Territory and was responsible for what was probably the largest cattle drive ever to be undertaken in Australia: the movement of 20,000 head from Aramac in Queensland to Glenco Station near Adelaide River in the Northern Territory.

In 1896, at the age of 70, Buchanan set off from Sturt Creek, in northern Western Australia, trying to find a direct route across the Tanami Desert to Tennant Creek that was suitable for cattle, rather than having to take them much further north. Although the cattle route didn't eventuate, this was probably the first European crossing of the Tanami Desert.

Buchanan was accompanied on some of his drives by his son, Gordon, who wrote about his experiences in the book *Packhorse & Waterhole*.

latter epitomises one of Lawson's 'battlers' who dreams of better things as an escape from the ennui of her isolated circumstances.

There were many other balladeers. George Essex Evans penned a tribute to Queensland's women pioneers, *The Women of the West*; Will Ogilvie wrote of the great cattle drives; and Barcroft Boake's *Where the Dead Men Lie* celebrates the people who opened up never-never country where 'heat-waves dance forever'.

Standing alone among these writers is Barbara Baynton. She is uncompromising in her depiction of the outback as a cruel, brutal environment, and the romantic imagery of the bush is absent in the ferocious depiction of the lot of 'Squeaker's Mate' in *Bush Studies* (1902). Squeaker's mate, crippled while clearing her selection and powerless to do anything, has to endure the indignity of her husband flaunting his new mistress. More terrifying though is the murder of a mother by a marauding swagman in 'The Chosen Vessel', also in *Bush Studies*.

Outback Raconteurs Many journalists and travel writers proudly proclaimed the outback to be the 'true' Australia. One of the least known is CEW Bean, Australia's official war historian of WWI. Two of his books, *On the Wool Track* (1910) and *The Dreadnought of the Darling* (1911), evocatively describe the outback of far western New South Wales.

Ion Idriess was an immensely popular writer in his time. His string of stories were eagerly awaited and their heroes were unashamedly outback: *Cattle King: Story of Sir Sidney Kidman*; *Flynn of the Inland;* and *Lasseter's Last Ride*. In *Nemarluk: King of the Wilds* (1941) he chronicles the exploits of an Aboriginal resistance fighter in the Top End.

One of the best-known travel writers was Ernestine Hill, whose *The Territory* (1951), it was said by the prolific Western Australian writer JK Ewers, 'ought to be in the swag of every Australian'. Her first publication, *The Great Australian Loneliness* (1937), described five years of travel through the outback.

Another writer in the vein of Idriess was Bill Harney. He married an Aborigine and was exposed to many aspects of Aboriginal culture. Much of his knowledge of the Top End was learned from the 'school of hard knocks', including a session in the Boorooloola lock-up for cattle-duffing. He later became the first park ranger at Uluru, a position he held for many years. His books, written in the 1940s and '50s, include: *Tales from the Aboriginals*; *To Ayers Rock and Beyond*; *Songs of the Songmen: Aboriginal Myth Retold;* and *Life among the Aborigines*.

George Farwell's *Ghost Towns of Australia* is a great source of outback yarns and history, and his travel books include *The Outside Track*, *Cape York to Kimberley* and *Traveller's Tracks*. Bill Wannan's *Hay, Hell and Booligal*, *A Dictionary of Australian Folklore* and *Bullockies, Beauts & Bandicoots* all have good titbits on the outback.

HM Barker's *Droving Days* (1966) looks into the exploits of the droving pioneers, the Aboriginal stockmen who accompanied them, and colourful characters such as horsebreakers and drifters.

More recently, Patsy Adam-Smith depicted the outback in her popular titles *The Shearers* (1982), *The Rails go Westward* (1969), *Across Australia by Indian Pacific* (1971) and her study of famous and ordinary lives in *Outback Heroes* (1981).

In *Sean and David's Long Drive* (1996), published in the Lonely Planet 'Journeys' series, Sean Condon describes his road journey through the outback. To a certain extent it debunks the myth of the 'great beyond' that lies a few hours' drive from the eastern seaboard. The journey is fuelled by alcohol, boredom, sex and distance. Has anything really changed?

Outback Novelists The author's name, if not the content, would have encouraged many overseas visitors to read DH Lawrence's *Kangaroo* (1923) which, in places, presents his frightening images of the bush. Later, Nevil Shute's *A Town Like Alice* (1950) would have been the first outback-based novel that many people read. Other Shute titles with outback themes are *In the Wet* (1953) and *Beyond the Black Stump* (1956).

Perhaps the best local depicter of the outback was the aforementioned Katharine Susannah Prichard. She produced a string of novels with outback themes into which she wove her political thoughts. *Black Opal* (1921) was the study of the fictional opal-mining community of Fallen Star Ridge; *Working Bullocks* (1926) examined the political nature of work in the karri forests of Western Australia; and *Moon of Desire* (1941) follows its characters from Broome to Singapore in search of a fabulous pearl. Her controversial trilogy about the Western Australian gold fields was published separately as *The Roaring Nineties* (1946), *Golden Miles* (1948) and *Winged Seeds* (1950).

Xavier Herbert's *Capricornia* (1938) stands as one of the great epics of outback Australia, with its sweeping descriptions of the north. His second epic, *Poor Fellow My Country* (1975), is an overlong documentary of the fortunes of a northern station owner.

One of the great non-fiction pieces is Mary Durack's family chronicle, *Kings in Grass Castles* (1959), which depicts the white settlement of the Kimberley ranges. The sequel is *Sons in the Saddle* (1983).

Australia's Nobel prize-winner Patrick White used the outback as the backdrop for a number of his monumental works. The most prominent character in *Voss* (1957) is an explorer, perhaps loosely based on Ludwig Leichhardt; *The Tree of Man* (1955) has all the outback happenings of flood, fire and drought; and the journey of *The Aunt's Story* (1948) begins on an Australian sheep station.

Kenneth Cook's nightmarish novel set in outback New South Wales, *Wake in Fright* (1961), was filmed in 1971 and has recently been reissued.

Painting

See the special 'Aboriginal Arts' colour section for information about Aboriginal visual art and craft.

In the 1880s a group of young artists developed the first distinctively Australian style of watercolour and oil painting. Working from a permanent bush camp in Melbourne's (then) outer suburb of Box Hill, the painters of the Heidelberg School captured the unique qualities of Australian life and the bush. In Sydney, a contemporary movement worked at Sirius Cove on Sydney Harbour. Both schools were influenced by the French plein-air painters, whose practice of working outdoors to capture the effects of natural light was very appropriate for capturing the fierce light and pastel hues of the Australian landscape. The main artists were Tom Roberts, Arthur Streeton, Frederick McCubbin, Louis Abrahams, Charles Conder, Julian Ashton and, later, Walter Withers. Their works can be found in most of the major galleries in Australia and are well worth seeking out.

In the 1940s, under the patronage of John and Sunday Reed at their home in suburban Melbourne, a new generation of artists redefined the direction of Australian art. This group included some of Australia's most famous contemporary artists, such as Sir Sidney Nolan and Arthur Boyd. More recently the work of painters such as Fred Williams, John Olsen, Robert Juniper, Russell Drysdale, Lloyd Rees and Brett Whitely has also made an impression on the international art world. Whiteley, probably Australia's best-known modern artist, died in 1992.

Broken Hill has been the popular focus of outback art for a number of years. Local painter Pro Hart has achieved international renown for his idiosyncratic style and his son, landscape artist Kym Hart, is following the family tradition.

Cinema

Many people have been introduced to the outback through films such as *Crocodile Dundee* and the *Mad Max* series, which depict the outback in all its glory.

The first Australian colour film to show a glimpse of the outback was *Jedda* (1955), a bleak yet compelling story of an Aboriginal girl, partly filmed at Katherine Gorge. Highly acclaimed films such as *The Chant of Jimmy Blacksmith* (1978) and Bruce Beresford's *The Fringe Dwellers* (1986) deal with Aboriginal people struggling to find their place in white society. Nicolas Roeg's cult classic *Walkabout* (1971) touches on the spectre of the outback and how it affects one's survival and culture.

Some outback films have the 'pioneering' feel of a John Ford western. Stories of conflict and struggle, of innocence and the loss of innocence abound. Look out for *We of the Never Never* (1982), filmed near Mataranka, which tells the true story of Jeannie Gunn and her experiences on a 19th-century outback property; and *Mr Electric*, about the effect of the first light bulbs on a very remote farm. *The Picture Show Man* (1977) tells the tale of a travelling projectionist who is constantly driven further up the road by the advance of technology.

For outback horror, see *Razorback*, the story of a giant killer hog; for a psychological thrill, see *Wake in Fright* and a man mysteriously unable to leave the eerie, sweltering town in which he finds himself marooned. *The Adventures of Priscilla, Queen of the Desert* (1994) is the often hilarious, sometimes sad story of three flamboyant drag queens crossing the macho outback in a pink bus, bound for a gig in Alice Springs. *Paperback Hero* (1998) is an amiable romantic comedy about an outback truckie who writes a best-seller of the Mills & Boon variety while trying to hide his identity.

Radiance (1988), directed by Aboriginal director Rachel Perkins, is the moving story of three sisters who reunite for their mother's funeral somewhere in far north Queensland.

Another recent Australian film, *Rabbit-Proof Fence* (2002), tells the true story of three young Aboriginal girls who were removed from their family in 1931, and their subsequent escape.

Music

Australia's participation in the flurry of popular music since the 1950s has been a frustrating mix of good, indifferent, lousy, parochial and excellent. However, little of the popular music created here has been noticeably different from overseas music, though there have certainly been exceptions.

The last decade or so has seen huge success for Aboriginal performers. The first name that springs to mind is Yothu Yindi, whose song about the dishonoured white man's agreement, *Treaty*, perhaps did more than anything else to popularise Aboriginal land-rights claims. The band's lead singer, Mandawuy Yunupingu, was proclaimed Australian of the Year in 1993.

Other Aboriginal talent includes Blekbala Mujik, Coloured Stone, Kev Carmody, Archie Roach, Ruby Hunter, Jimmy Little, Bart Willoughby, Scrap Metal, the Sunrise Band, Christine Anu (from Torres Strait), and the bands that started it all but no longer exist, No Fixed Address and Warumpi Band. Lately, Arrernte band NoKTuRNL from Alice Springs has introduced Australia to its brand of political rap-metal. Folk-rock performer and regular on the live music circuit Frank Yamma, a Pitjantjatjara man, usually performs in his native language.

Australian country music owes much to Irish heritage and American country influences, often with a liberal sprinkling of dry outback humour. Big names over the years have included Slim Dusty, Ted Gean, John Williamson, Gondwanaland, Smokey Dawson and Lee Kernaghan. Names to look out for now are Gina Jeffreys, James Blundell and Adam Brand. Kasey Chambers (who grew up in the outback) has received much acclaim for her original contemporary style of country.

Similarly, Australian folk music is derived from English, Irish and Scottish roots. Eric Bogle is one of Australia's great folk musicians. Fiddles, banjos and tin whistles feature prominently in bush bands, and then there's the 'lagerphone', a percussion instrument made from beer-bottle caps nailed to a stick that is shaken or thumped on the floor. Another popular instrument is the single-string, tea-chest bass. If you have a chance to go to a bush dance or folk festival, don't pass it up.

See the 'Aboriginal Arts' colour section in this book for information about traditional Aboriginal dance and music, and contemporary dance.

OUTBACK LIFE

Life in remote communities has been much improved by modern developments such as the Royal Flying Doctor Service, the School of the Air and the expanding national telephone network, but all outback places are still affected to a greater or lesser degree by the tyranny of distance. Not many city people can imagine living 200km or more from the nearest doctor and supermarket, or their children sitting down in front of a high-frequency (HF) radio transceiver to go to school.

School of the Air

Until recent times, outback children living away from towns either attended boarding school or were educated through written correspondence lessons. In 1944, Adelaide Meithke recognised that HF radio transceivers could be used to improve the children's education, as well as their social life, by giving them direct contact both with trained teachers and their fellow students. Her idea for a classroom of the airwaves, using the Royal Flying Doctor Service (RFDS) radio facilities, became a reality when Australia's first School of the Air opened in Alice Springs in 1951.

Today there are 14 Schools of the Air scattered about the outback and most use the RFDS network as their classroom. The major education method is still correspondence lessons – materials and equipment are sent to students, who return set written and audio work by mail – which are supplemented by radio classes lasting 20 to

Blue Heelers

As you travel around the outback you'll probably see a 4WD traytop or utility with a medium-sized, blue-speckled dog with a red or black face and white-striped forehead sitting alertly in the back. This is the Australian cattle-dog, or blue heeler, the world's only pure breed of cattle-dog.

The blue-heeler breed was established in 1890 to suit large-scale cattle raising in Australian conditions. It had originated some 50 years earlier, when a NSW squatter named Hall crossed smooth-coated Scottish collies with dingoes and produced a type that proved very suitable for working cattle. The dogs were silent and tireless, with the instinct to creep up behind an obstinate beast and nip it on the heel.

However, these early 'Hall's heelers' were deficient when it came to working the head of a mob, and to standing guard over their master's horses and gear. So dog breeders crossed them with Dalmatians to give them the instinct for guarding, and kelpies (an Australian breed of sheep-dog) so that they'd work a mob from the head as well as the back and sides.

The standard for blue heelers was drawn up in 1897 and has been only slightly varied since then.

Flying Doctor

Established by the Reverend John Flynn with a single aircraft in 1928, the original Flying Doctor has grown into a national organisation, the Royal Flying Doctor Service, which provides a comprehensive medical service to all outback residents. Where people once feared sickness and injury, even the most isolated communities are now assured of receiving expert medical assistance within two or three hours instead of weeks.

Before the rapid spread of telephone lines and the Internet, the RFDS' HF network played an important social function. Anyone could send and receive telegrams or take part in special broadcasts known as galah sessions. Like party lines, these open periods of radio time allowed distant neighbours to keep in touch with each other and events around them.

Shopping

Many small communities are far from even the most basic facilities such as post offices, libraries and shops, and often neighbours can be 50km or more apart. They may only receive mail and newspapers either weekly or fortnightly when the mail plane or mail truck does its rounds. Perishable groceries and minor freight can be sent out with the mail, but for really isolated people a shopping expedition can mean a round trip of 1000km or more to the nearest decent shops.

It's Not All Bad

Most of the outback's difficulties can be attributed to isolation, but as the famous Australian poet Banjo Paterson wrote in *Clancy of the Overflow*, bush people do 'have pleasures that the townsfolk never know'. One of these is the ready access to wide-open spaces untainted by air pollution, traffic and crowds. Another is the sense of self-reliance and independence that's still strong in the outback.

Being forced to make their own entertainment encourages people living hundreds of kilometres apart to get together (usually by telephone) for functions such as horse-race meetings, camp drafts (rodeos)

30 minutes. Students speak to their teachers daily and each has a 10-minute personal session with their teacher once a week. Although face-to-face contact is limited, students and teachers do meet at least once a year on special get-togethers, and teachers visit each of their students on patrols by 4WD vehicles and light aircraft.

With 14 teachers and eight support staff, the Alice Springs School of the Air teaches about 140 children in nine grades, from pre-school to Year 7, over a broadcast area of 1.3 million sq km. The student living furthest away is 1000km from Alice Springs. In 1992 the school broke new ground once again when it beamed 'live' lessons by satellite to its students.

The Flying Doctor

Before the late 1920s the outback's far-flung residents had little or no access to medical facilities. The nearest doctor was often weeks away over rough tracks, so if you fell seriously ill or met with a bad accident your chances of recovery were slim. Difficult pregnancies and illnesses such as rheumatic fever and acute appendicitis were almost a death sentence. If you were lucky you fell ill near a telegraph line, where your mates could treat you (or operate) under instructions received in Morse code. This pointed to another harsh truth of life in the outback: reliable and speedy communications over long distances were available to very few.

In 1912 the Reverend John Flynn of the Presbyterian Church helped establish the outback's first hospital, at Oodnadatta. Flynn was appalled by the tragedies that resulted from the lack of medical facilities and was quick to realise that the answer lay in radios and aircraft. However, these technologies – particularly radio – were still in their infancy and needed further development.

Flynn knew nothing of either radios or aviation but his sense of mission inspired others who did, such as radio engineer Alf Traeger. In 1928, after years of trial and error, Traeger developed a small, pedal-powered radio transceiver that was simple to use, inexpensive and could send and receive messages over 500km. The outback's great silence was broken at last.

Aircraft suitable for medical evacuations had become available in 1920 but it was the lack of a radio communication network that delayed their general use for this purpose. Traeger's invention was the key to the establishment of Australia's first Flying Doctor base in Cloncurry, Queensland, in 1928. Cloncurry was then the base for the Queensland and Northern Territory Aerial Services (Qantas), which provided the pilot and an aircraft under lease.

The new service proved an outstanding success and areas beyond the reach of Cloncurry soon began to clamour for their own Flying Doctor. However, the Presbyterian Church had insufficient resources to allow a rapid expansion. In 1933 it handed the aerial medical service over to 'an organisation of national character' and so the Royal Flying Doctor Service (RFDS) was born. Flynn's vision of a 'mantle of safety' over the outback had become a reality.

Today there are 19 RFDS base stations providing a sophisticated network of radio communications and medical services to 80% of the continent, an area as large as Western Europe and more than two-thirds the size of the USA. Emergency evacuations of sick or injured people are still an important function, but other services include routine clinics at communities that are unable to attract full-time medical staff. The RFDS also supervises numerous small hospitals that normally operate without a doctor; such hospitals are staffed by registered nurses who communicate by telephone or radio with their RFDS doctor.

The administration of RFDS bases is divided between four largely independent sections, each of which is a nonprofit organisation funded by government grants and private donations.

To get an idea of the RFDS' scope of operations, let's take a look at its Central Section, which covers virtually the entire outback of South Australia and the Northern Territory's bottom half. With its headquarters in Adelaide and base stations at Port Augusta, Alice Springs and Yulara, it operates 10 sophisticated twin-engine aircraft and employs around 100 staff, including 24 pilots, seven aircraft engineers, six doctors, 22 flight nurses and seven radio operators.

The service established by the Reverend John Flynn nearly 75 years ago is still a powerful force in the outback, enabling its residents to live secure in the knowledge that medical help is just a telephone or radio call away.

and gymkhanas. This strong sense of community spirit, even when the 'community' may be spread over a vast area, means that even neighbours who don't get on will usually assist each other in a crisis.

SOCIAL CONDUCT
Cross-Cultural Etiquette
Many of the outback's original inhabitants lead lives that are still powerfully influenced by ancient traditions. These will be almost incomprehensible to the average tourist, who may be almost entirely ignorant of Aboriginal social customs. Aborigines will make allowances for the ignorance of other people, but it does no harm to observe a few simple rules. One of the most important is to act naturally.

You won't go far wrong if you treat outback Aborigines as potential friends. Humour is a mainstay of the interactions between indigenous Australians, so keep it light where appropriate.

Paying a Visit You've arrived at a small Aboriginal community on a back road in the middle of nowhere. The front area outside each dwelling is the occupants' private space, a sort of outdoor living room. Park at a reasonable distance (say, 30m) so as not to intrude on this space, then get out of the vehicle and wait for someone to come over. That person will most likely speak at least reasonable English and will be able to point you in the right direction. If this approach yields no results, try walking over to the nearest house or shelter and calling out to attract attention.

Sometimes you'll find the residents sitting around in a circle, which usually indicates some sort of business in progress. Instead of barging in, stand a little way off – you may be beckoned over, or someone may come up. Don't hang around if it's obvious that your presence isn't wanted.

Most larger communities have a store staffed by white people, and this is the place to go first for information. The store may not be easy to find, in which case ask someone rather than head off on an unauthorised sightseeing tour. One sure way to wear out

a welcome is to drive around raising dust and taking photographs without permission.

Many tourists feel extremely uncomfortable when visiting their first Aboriginal community, and this can find expression in rudeness. For example, there's a tendency for tourists to race down the road with their faces expressionless and eyes fixed straight ahead. Aborigines won't think you're immoral if you smile and wave; the fact is they'll generally appreciate it and you'll get a positive response.

People Skills Having got to first base, you need to watch your body language. For example, wrinkling your nose at someone else's odour is unlikely to win any friends. Desert dwellers naturally place washing well down on the list of priorities; people who eat a lot of kangaroo meat can also develop a distinctive and fairly strong body odour. To put a different perspective on this, well-soaped people can smell unpleasantly like a wet sheep to desert people. However, being invariably polite, they'll give no indication that they find your personal aroma to be anything other than what you imagine it to be.

Western society regards a firm handshake and eye contact as important in creating a favourable first impression – just ask any salesperson. However, both are signs of aggression in Aboriginal society. Their usual greeting is a soft clasp of the hands with little or no arm movement, and there may be no eye contact at all until a friendly relationship is established. The best approach is to take eye contact as it comes. If the other person isn't looking directly at you, it's polite not to look at them.

It's also unwise to rush or be pushy, as the usual Aboriginal way is to engage in sociable small talk before getting down to the matter at hand, even if this takes time. While they won't expect you to waffle on at length about the drought or scarcity of kangaroos, a pleasantry or two gets the conversation flowing and establishes your unselfish interest in that person. This works well in white outback society too.

Aboriginal people tend to tolerate more silence in conversation than the average

Western person. If no-one says anything for a few minutes, don't feel compelled to fill the silence with idle chatter. Be content to wait and to listen.

It's also important to remember that English is very much the second language on most remote communities and may not be spoken at all well. This doesn't mean you should lapse into broken pidgin to make yourself understood. Not only is this demeaning to the people you're talking to, but they might think you're some sort of idiot. The correct approach is to speak distinctly and reasonably slowly, using straightforward English and a normal tone of voice. Be careful not to make the mistake of addressing your audience as you would a slow learner with a hearing problem. See the Language section later in this chapter for more advice on communicating with Aboriginal people.

Purchasing A visit to an Aboriginal community presents an ideal opportunity to purchase traditional paintings or other works of art directly from the artist. However, bargaining such as takes place in an Indian bazaar is foreign to this society, and in any case the prices asked are usually very reasonable.

If you're tempted to drive the price down, remember that there's no sport in this as the seller's inherent politeness may force him or her to accept your unreasonably low offer rather than offend you. On the other hand, Aboriginal artists are waking up fast to the value of their work and the devious ways of many tourists.

Alcohol Many Australians believe that most Aborigines drink to excess, but in actual fact a smaller percentage of Aborigines drink than do non-Aborigines. However, there's no denying that alcohol has had a devastating effect on many communities and often still does.

Aborigines who consume alcohol are more likely than their non-Aboriginal counterparts to drink in public. One reason for this is that Aboriginal councils have banned the possession and consumption of alcohol in many Aboriginal communities. As a result, many outback Aborigines have irregular access to alcohol, and only drink when they go to town where they'll indulge. Unfortunately, this is the only time many non-Aboriginal people (and tourists) see Aborigines.

Throughout Australia, Aboriginal people are actively involved in the fight against alcohol. They have persuaded some outback hotels and takeaway outlets not to sell alcohol to local Aboriginal people, and signs at such outlets explain that Aboriginal elders ask tourists to not buy alcohol for Aborigines. Also, some outlets may refuse to sell you alcohol if you're heading towards an Aboriginal community. Please respect such efforts to combat alcoholism.

In the eloquent words of Noel Pearson, a respected Cape York Aboriginal leader:

What we're facing now is an epidemic. An epidemic of grog and drug addiction. It's like a whirlwind in the communities. It sucks in everyone. Even kids from stable families...You can't get away from the fact that it's the grog and the drugs that are central to nearly all our problems, making us powerless to deal with other issues...

Pastoral Properties

It's a hot, sweaty day out on the wide brown land and you're bouncing along a dusty road in your 4WD. You've never felt more in need of a bath, particularly after changing that last tyre back in the bulldust.

Then you spy a lonely windmill in the scrub beside the track. There's a large steel tank beside it and the thought of a bath brings instant good cheer. Off come your clothes, you climb onto the edge and with a glad cry leap into the water. To your horror the concussion bursts the wall, but you manage to escape fearful mutilation by clinging to the edge as the tank's precious contents gush out through the jagged hole.

This sort of thing doesn't happen very often (thank goodness) but it's an example of how people from an urban environment can come undone in the unfamiliar world of the outback. Most visitors want to do the right thing; following are some simple rules on how to avoid upsetting the people who live there.

Water Most pastoralists are happy for travellers to make use of their water supplies, but they do ask that they be treated with respect. This means washing clothes, dishes and sweaty bodies in a bucket or basin, not in the water supply itself. Always remember that animals and people may have to drink it when you've finished.

Camping right beside watering points is also to be avoided. In the outback the stock is often half wild and will hang back if you're parked or have your tent pitched right where they normally drink. They'll eventually overcome their fear through necessity, which means you'll be covered in dust as the thirst-crazed mob mills around your camp at midnight. If you must camp in the vicinity, keep at least 200m away and stay well off the paths that animals have worn as they come in to drink.

Much the same applies if you drive up to a bore or dam and find the stock having a drink. Stay well back until they've finished, then you can move in for your share. The thing to remember at all times is that this isolated pool or trough might be the only water in a radius of 30km or more.

For more about water, see Health in the Facts for the Visitor chapter.

Gates The golden rule with any gate is to *leave it as you find it*. You must do this even if a sign by an open gate says to keep it closed – it may have been left open for any number of reasons, such as to let stock through to water. It's fairly common for animals to perish because tourists have closed gates that a pastoralist left open.

Unfortunately, some home-made wire gates can seem like the work of the devil and on occasion their tricky tensioning designs will turn nasty, entangling you in barbed wire as you struggle to close them. When you arrive at one of these things, take careful note of how it works while opening it; closure should then be a relatively simple matter. Never throw up your hands in defeat and drive off leaving it either insecurely fastened or, worse, lying on the ground. Having opened it, you must persevere until you've worked out how to close it.

If you're driving in a convoy it's accepted procedure that, on coming to a gate, one of the lead vehicles remains on the spot until all others are through. That way there won't be any mistakes with gates not being left as they were found.

Floods Sometimes the outback receives a large part of its annual rainfall in a matter of days. Unsealed roads and tracks can become extremely slippery and boggy. The correct thing to do in this event is either to get out before the rain soaks in or to stay put on high ground until the surface dries out. To do otherwise may see your vehicle gouging great ruts in the road surface, which of course won't endear you to the locals who must live with the mess you've made. Quite apart from that, you'll probably get well and truly stuck in some dreadful place far from anywhere. This is another reason to carry plenty of extra stores on an outback trip. If a road is officially closed because of heavy rain, you can be fined for travelling on it – the norm is $1000 per wheel!

Fire The outback usually experiences drought, during which time many grasses dry off to form standing hay. This, along with the foliage of trees and bushes, carries the stock through to the next rains. Under extreme weather conditions a careless camper can start a bushfire that might destroy the vegetation over many hundreds of square kilometres of grazing land. To avoid being responsible for such a disaster, always take care with your campfire by siting it at least 5m from flammable material, keeping it small and making certain it's out before you leave camp. The best way to guarantee the latter is to completely cover the ashes with soil.

For more about fire, see Dangers & Annoyances as well as Camping and Food in the Facts for the Visitor chapter.

Dogs The tourist's best friend is a contentious issue in the outback at the best of times. There's no doubt that the best way to avoid dog-related hassles is to keep your pet on a leash at all times when in sheep and cattle country. If nothing else, this will save it from an untimely and unpleasant end.

First, dogs like to chase things. After a day cooped up in the back of a vehicle you'd probably want to chase something yourself, but the difference is that Rover might put a flock of sheep through the fence while he's trying to round it up. The distress caused by being chased and worried by domestic dogs is a major contributing factor in stock deaths each year. For this reason, pastoralists who find a strange dog on their properties tend to shoot first and ask questions later.

Second, dogs are great scavengers, and no matter how well fed or bred they are they'll gobble up any old piece of meat or carcass they find lying around. Fox and dingo poisoning is widely practised throughout the outback, with bite-sized chunks of meat being a common bait. Rover won't be able to resist that one last meal.

Rubbish The best way to dispose of all noncombustible rubbish is to store it in a heavy-duty plastic bag and carry it with you to deposit at an authorised dumping place. Many tourists believe they're doing the right thing by burying their garbage, but few dig a deep enough hole. Any scraps buried under less than a metre of soil will be dug up by goannas and dingoes. Crows will then scatter it everywhere and the end result is an unsightly mess. If you must bury your rubbish, any cans or other food containers should always be burned first to get rid of the tantalising smells.

See also Camping in the Facts for the Visitor chapter.

Common Courtesy These days most outback pastoralists are on the telephone and it's a common courtesy to contact them before you invade their property. Straight-through travel on established roads is not a problem, but if you're thinking of going camping or fishing in some remote spot, the land-holder will expect you to ask permission. You'll usually rise in the estimation of the more isolated people if you drop off some very recent newspapers, or ask if

there's anything they'd like brought out from town. Always remember to take-your-own-everything, as station folk seldom organise their shopping around the needs of ill-prepared visitors.

RELIGION

A shrinking majority of people in Australia (around 58%) are at least nominally Christian. Most Protestant churches have merged to become the Uniting Church, although the Church of England has remained separate. The Catholic Church is popular (almost half of Australian Christians are Catholics), with the original Irish adherents joined by large numbers of Mediterranean immigrants.

Non-Christian minorities abound, the main ones being Buddhist and Muslim (each representing just over 1% of the population) and Jewish (0.45%). Almost 20% of the population describe themselves as having no religion.

Aboriginal Spirituality

Traditional Aboriginal religious beliefs centre on the continuing existence of spirit beings that lived on earth during the creation time (Dreaming), which occurred before the arrival of humans. These beings created all the features of the natural world and are the ancestors of all living things. They took different forms but behaved as people do, and as they travelled about they left signs to show where they had passed.

Despite being supernatural, the ancestors were subject to ageing and eventually they returned to the sleep from which they'd awoken at the dawn of time. Here their spirits remain as eternal forces that breathe life into the newborn and influence natural events. Each ancestor's spiritual energy flows along the path it travelled during the Dreamtime and is strongest at the points where it left physical evidence of its activities, such as a tree, hill or claypan. These features are called 'sacred sites'.

Sacred Sites Every person, animal and plant is believed to have two souls – one mortal and one immortal. The latter is part of a particular ancestral spirit and returns to the sacred sites of that ancestor after death, while the mortal soul simply fades into oblivion. Each person is spiritually bound to the sacred sites that mark the land associated with his or her spirit ancestor. It is the individual's obligation to help care for these sites by performing the necessary rituals and singing the songs that tell of the ancestor's deeds. By doing this, the order created by that ancestor is maintained.

Aboriginal people traditionally believe that to destroy or damage a sacred site threatens not only the living but also the spirit inhabitants of the land. It is a distressing and dangerous act, and one that no responsible person would condone.

These days the importance of sacred sites is more widely recognised among the non-Aboriginal community, and most state governments have legislated to give these sites a measure of protection. However, their presence can still lead to headline-grabbing controversy when they stand in the way of developments such as roads, mines and dams.

Some sacred sites are believed to be dangerous and entry is prohibited under traditional Aboriginal law. These restrictions often have a pragmatic origin. One site in northern Australia was believed to cause sores to break out all over the body of anyone visiting the area. Subsequently, the area was found to have a dangerously high level of radiation from naturally occurring radon gas. In another instance, fishing from a certain reef was traditionally prohibited. This restriction was scoffed at by local Europeans until it was discovered that fish from this area had a high incidence of ciguatera, which renders fish poisonous.

Throughout much of Australia, when pastoralists were breaking the Aborigines' link to the land, many Aborigines sought refuge on missions and became Christians. However, becoming Christian has not, for most Aborigines, meant renouncing their traditional religion. Many senior Aboriginal law men are also devout Christians, and in many cases ministers.

Culture & Ceremonies Early European settlers and explorers usually dismissed all Aborigines as 'savages' and 'barbarians'. It was quite some time before the Aboriginal people's deep spiritual bond with the land, and their relationship to it, even began to be understood by other Australians.

In traditional practice, religion, history, law and art are integrated in complex ceremonies that depict the activities of the Aborigines' spirit ancestors, and prescribe codes of behaviour and responsibilities for looking after the land.

The links between the people and their spirit ancestors are totems, each person having their own totem, or Dreaming. These totems take many forms, such as trees, caterpillars, snakes, fish and magpies. Songs explain that the landscape contains these powerful creator ancestors, who can exert either a benign or a malevolent influence. They tell of the best places and the best times to hunt, and where to find water in drought years. They can also specify kinship relations and identify correct marriage partners.

Traditional ceremonies are still performed in many parts of Australia.

Song & Narrative Aboriginal oral traditions are loosely and misleadingly described as 'myths and legends'. Their single uniting factor is the Dreaming, when the totemic ancestors formed the landscape, fashioned the laws and created the people who would inherit the land. Translated and printed in English, these renderings of the Dreaming often lose much of their intended impact. Gone are the sounds of clap sticks and the rhythm of dance that accompany each poetic line; alone, the words fail to fuse past and present, and the spirits and forces to which the lines refer lose much of their animation.

At the turn of the century, Catherine Langloh Parker was collecting traditional Aboriginal legends and using her outback experience to interpret them sincerely but synthetically. In 1902 she compiled the book *Australian Legendary Tales: Folklore of the Noongah-burrahs*.

TGH Strehlow was one of the first methodical translators, and his most important works include *Aranda Traditions* (1947) and *Songs of Central Australia* (1971). Equally important are the combined efforts of Catherine and Ronald Berndt. There are 188 songs in the collection *Djanggawul* (1952), 129 sacred and 47 secular songs in the collection *Kunapipi* (1951), and *The Land of the Rainbow Snake* (1979) focuses on children's stories from western Arnhem Land.

More recently many stories from the Dreaming have appeared in translation, illustrated and published by Aboriginal artists. Some representative collections are *Joe Nangan's Dreaming: Aboriginal Legends of the North-West* (1976) by Joe Nangan & Hugh Edwards; *Milbi: Aboriginal Tales from Queensland's Endeavour River* (1980) by Tulo Gordon & JB Haviland; *Visions of Mowanjum: Aboriginal Writings from the Kimberley* (1980) by the Kormilda Community College, Darwin; and *Gularabulu* (1983) by Paddy Roe & Stephen Muecke.

As you drive through the outback, realise that many of the features you see in the landscape have an oral history. They live, have a past and a present. You are, in effect, driving through the pages of the world's most ancient illuminated manuscript!

LANGUAGE

English is the main language of Australia but languages other than English are in common use – as you'd expect in a country with such a diverse ethnic mix. The 1996 census found that 240 languages other than English were being spoken at home, and almost 50 of these were indigenous languages. This amounts to a language other than English being used in 15% of Australian households.

The most commonly used non-English languages are, in descending order, Italian, Greek, Cantonese, Arabic and Vietnamese. Languages rapidly growing in use are Mandarin, Vietnamese and Cantonese, while those most in decline include Dutch, German, Italian and Greek.

Some words have completely different meanings in Australian English than they have in other English-speaking countries; some commonly used words have been shortened almost beyond recognition. Others derive from Aboriginal languages, or from the slang used by early convict settlers. The Glossary in the back of this book will help.

There's a slight regional variation in the Australian accent but it's minute compared with variations in, say, the USA. The main difference between city speech and that in the country or outback is speed.

Some of the most famed Aussie words are hardly heard at all – 'mates' and 'pals' are more common than 'cobbers'. Rhyming slang is used occasionally ('hit the frog and toad' for 'hit the road', 'Oxford scholars' for 'dollars'), so if you hear an odd expression that doesn't seem to make sense, see if it rhymes with something else that does.

Aboriginal Languages

Before Europeans arrived there were about 250 Aboriginal languages comprising about 700 dialects. It is believed that all the languages evolved from a single language family as the Aborigines gradually moved out over the entire continent and split into new groups. There are a number of words that occur right across the continent, such as *jina* (foot) and *mala* (hand), and similarities also exist in the often complex grammatical structures. Today at least 100 Aboriginal languages are still spoken to various extents, and many have a number of dialects. Some languages are actually growing as populations expand and dominant languages replace others.

Most Aboriginal languages have about 10,000 words – about the same number of words used by the average English speaker. Many words reflect the close relationship that Aboriginal people have with their environment. For example, the Western Desert Pintupi dialect has 18 words for 'hole': an ant burrow, a rabbit burrow, a goanna burrow, a small animal burrow etc. Traditionally, all Aboriginal adults could identify and name hundreds of plants and animals. This is still the case in many parts of outback and northern Australia, and one reason why Aboriginal people are central to much contemporary biological research.

Many Aboriginal words don't correspond directly to English words – they often cover a different classification of the natural world and express concepts particular to Aboriginal culture. However, dozens of Aboriginal words have been incorporated into Australian English: barramundi, boomerang, budgerigar, brolga, coolabah, corroboree, dingo, galah, jarrah, kangaroo, kookaburra, mallee, mulga, perentie, quandong, wallaby and yakka, to name a few. Similarly, Aboriginal languages have absorbed many English words, which are invariably adapted to suit Aboriginal grammar and sound systems. For example, many central Australian Aboriginal people use the words 'taraka' (truck), 'tiipii' (TV), 'riipula' (rifle) and 'ruuta' (road).

Aboriginal Kriol is a language that has developed since European arrival in Australia. It's spoken across northern Australia and has become the 'native' language of many young Aborigines. It contains many English words but, once again, grammatical usage is along Aboriginal lines. For example, the English sentence 'He was amazed' becomes 'I bin luk kwesjinmak' in Kriol.

Lonely Planet's *Australian phrasebook* gives a detailed account of Aboriginal languages, and there's also good coverage in Lonely Planet's *Aboriginal Australia & the Torres Strait Islands*.

Aboriginal English In many parts of outback Australia, including the Western Desert region and Arnhem Land, many Aborigines do not speak English regularly or fluently. Access to formal secondary education is often limited and many people emerge from school without basic English literacy or oracy. English is seldom used in their communities, and when in towns or shops they can get by without it.

Others may be fluent in an English dialect known as Aboriginal English. There's a wide array of Aboriginal English ranging from forms close to standard English to varieties very close to Kriol. It mostly uses English vocabulary but takes some sounds, features of grammar and many cultural meanings from the Aboriginal languages of its speakers.

Because of the differences between Aboriginal and English sound systems, many Aborigines have difficulty pronouncing some English words. For example, many Aboriginal languages do not include the sounds 's', 'z', 'v', 'sh' or 'th' and do not distinguish between 'b' and 'p', or 'd' and 't'. This is one of the reasons why the names of some languages have several spellings, such as Walbiri/Warlpiri, which is spoken in central Australia. Conversely, it's difficult for some English-speaking people to roll their r's, or to distinguish between retroflexed (made with the tongue curled back on the roof of the mouth) and non-retroflexed sounds that are typical of most Aboriginal languages.

Most Aboriginal languages have no words for hello, please or thank you. Although more people are now using the English thank you, thanks is traditionally expressed in actions rather than words, such as by doing something for a person at a later date. However, people will appreciate you using these terms as usual, as they show your friendly intentions.

Many Queensland Aborigines refer to themselves as Murris, many New South Wales and Victorian Aborigines call themselves Kooris, Western Desert speakers are Anangu, Warlpiri speakers Yappa, and north-eastern Arnhem Landers Yolngu. Nunga is used to refer to the people of coastal South Australia, and Nyoongah is used in the country's south-west. Aborigines appreciate non-Aboriginal people using these terms – provided that the correct term is used for the appropriate group.

See the Social Conduct section earlier in this chapter for specific advice on meeting Aboriginal people.

Facts for the Visitor

HIGHLIGHTS

In an area as broad and geographically diverse as Australia's outback the list of highlights is virtually endless, although one person's highlight can easily be another's disappointment. There are, however, a number of features in each state that shouldn't be missed.

In northern Queensland there's Cape York Peninsula, with wild savanna country and tracts of rainforest that run right down to the beach, and the Great Barrier Reef just offshore. In central Queensland, the Stockman's Hall of Fame in Longreach is a moving testimony to the people who opened up the outback.

The Northern Territory has the obvious attraction of Uluru (formerly Ayers Rock), probably Australia's most readily identifiable symbol after the Sydney Opera House. There's also the World Heritage–listed Kakadu National Park with its wealth of flora and fauna and superb wetlands. The Territory is also where Australia's Aboriginal cultural heritage is at its most accessible – the rock-art sites of Kakadu, and Aboriginal-owned and run tours of Arnhem Land and Uluru are just a few of the possibilities.

Then there's Western Australia with its vast distances and wide-open spaces. The remote Kimberley region in the far north is as ruggedly picturesque as any you'll find – the Purnululu (Bungle Bungle) National Park here is unforgettable. The 1700km Canning Stock Route across the Gibson and Great Sandy deserts is the nation's longest 4WD track – a true adventure.

South Australia's major outback drawcard is the Flinders Ranges, which offer superb bushwalking and stunning scenery. Further afield you can get a real taste of the outback along the Strzelecki, Oodnadatta and Birdsville tracks. There's also the unique opal-mining town of Coober Pedy, where many people work and live underground.

New South Wales has the outback mining town of Broken Hill, once the world's largest silver-lead-zinc mine and now a convenient base for outback excursions. Nearby is a treasure trove of early Aboriginal history at Mungo National Park.

PLANNING

The success of any trip to a vast, remote and sparsely populated area like the outback will depend largely on the research and planning you do before you go. Among other things, you need to find out about the best time to go, the availability of drinking water, services and facilities, the likely condition of roads and tracks, and whether or not your vehicle will be suitable. You'll probably regret it if you leave your planning until you get there.

This book focuses on the outback and assumes its readers are already familiar with Australia and the basics of travelling within it. Overseas readers planning a visit may wish to consult one or more of Lonely Planet's guidebooks, such as *Australia.*

When to Go

Roughly speaking, January is the middle of summer in the lower three-quarters of Australia and July is the middle of winter (see Climate in the Facts about the Outback chapter). Up in the monsoon belt, where temperatures remain relatively constant all year, 'summer' is the wet season and 'winter' is the dry season. The best time to visit the Centre and northern Australia is May to September; mid-winter (June–August) is ideal, but many people know that and the popular spots fill up fast.

The Centre isn't recommended in summer unless you love extreme heat, carry plenty of water and stick to the busy routes – every year inexperienced travellers die or become extremely ill because of heat and dehydration. Daytime shade temperatures usually hover around 40°C at the height of summer and can reach 50°C in the hotter parts. On hot days, physical activities such as cycling and walking are pretty much out of the question unless you do them early.

The northern wet season occurs between November and May – the rains can be late or early and their unpredictability is a popular topic of discussion. Once the wet sets in, tracks can become bottomless mud, dry creeks become raging torrents and low-lying areas are flooded. Vast areas can be cut off from the rest of the world for weeks at a time.

However, the wet season can be a good time to visit the far north: the vegetation is at its best, the waterfalls and rivers are at their most spectacular, and you'll never forget those fierce electrical storms. If you can handle hot and humid conditions and don't plan on driving (or can stay on sealed roads), you'll find quiet tourist facilities and bargain package deals. The biggest drawback is that you can't cool off in the sea because of the dreaded 'stingers', or box jellyfish (see the Fauna section in the Facts about the Outback chapter).

For current weather conditions and forecasts, check W www.bom.gov.au.

Another major consideration is school holidays. Australian families take to the road (and air) en masse at these times and many places are booked out, prices rise and things generally get a bit crazy. Holidays vary somewhat from state to state – see the Public Holidays section later in this chapter.

What Kind of Trip

As public road transport in the outback is limited to main through routes such as the Stuart and Eyre highways, the only real option if you want a good look around is to have your own vehicle. This being the case, you will probably want to do a fair amount of camping, particularly in the more remote areas where there is little or no commercial accommodation. Bush camping is cheap and it's a wonderful way to experience the real outback.

If you have a 4WD but don't want to drive the tougher tracks by yourself, consider a tag-along tour led by an expert guide. If time is an issue, consider one of the more adventurous coach options, or do a combination of localised tours/car rental, with bus/plane travel between major centres.

The Getting Around chapter gives details on transport options including buying your own vehicle, car rental and organised tours.

Maps

Maps are essential on any outback trip. The maps in this book will give you a good overview of the various tracks. The individual track descriptions list some of the most appropriate maps on a case-by-case basis, and you'd be well advised to try and get hold of them.

There's no shortage of touring maps available. Lonely Planet publishes the *Australia Road Atlas*, and the various oil companies – Shell, BP, Mobil etc – publish road maps that are available from service stations. They're quite good for major roads but begin to let you down off the beaten track.

The state motoring organisations (see Useful Organisations later in this chapter) produce maps that are often free (if you're a member) or cheaper than the oil company maps, and their maps and track-note sheets of outback regions in their own states can be very good. Don't forget the state tourist offices listed later in this chapter either: They sometimes have lovingly produced outback maps that are virtual works of art, though they won't be free.

Westprint maps are excellent and provide copious detail on points of interest, tracks and historical and tourist information. The Westprint catalogue of 25 outback maps covers many of the tracks mentioned in this book. They're available from specialist map shops, local information centres and various other outback outlets, such as service stations, or through Westprint Heritage Maps (☎ 03-5391 1466, fax 5391 1473, W www.westprint.com .au) at 6 Park St, Nhill, Vic 3418.

Hema's regional touring maps are attractive, informative and give a wide coverage of the outback. They're usually available at local outlets, or contact Hema Maps (☎ 07-3290 0322, fax 3290 0478, W www .hemamaps.com.au) at PO Box 2660, Logan City DC, Qld 4114

If you want the best, get the topographic sheets put out by the National Mapping Division of Geoscience Australia (formerly known as the Australian Surveying & Land Information Group or AUSLIG). They may be many years out of date, with indicated tracks long since abandoned and new ones formed, but their detail is staggering. The more popular sheets are often available over the counter at shops that sell bushwalking gear and outdoor equipment. Geoscience Australia also has special interest maps showing various types of land use such as population densities or Aboriginal land. For more information, or a catalogue, contact Geoscience Australia (☎ 02-6201 4201, fax 6201 4366, Ⓦ www.auslig.gov.au) at PO Box 2, Belconnen, ACT 2616 or its interstate sales outlets.

Every state capital has a number of shops that specialise in maps and guidebooks.

What to Bring

What you should bring will depend on what sort of trip you're doing. At one extreme is independent travel into the middle of nowhere, where you'll need to BYO everything. At the other end is an organised bus trip – all you may need to bring here is appropriate clothing (see Organised Tours in the Getting Around chapter). The check lists at the back of this book will give you some ideas.

RESPONSIBLE TOURISM

For information on responsible behaviour for travellers, see Social Conduct in the Facts about the Outback chapter, and Bush Camping later in this chapter.

TOURIST OFFICES

There are various sources of information and you can easily drown yourself in brochures and booklets, maps and leaflets.

Local Tourist Offices

Most states and the Northern Territory have a main office in the capital cities, as well as regional offices in main tourist centres and also in other states.

As well as supplying brochures, price lists, maps and other information, the state offices will often book transport, tours and accommodation. Unfortunately, the opening hours of the city offices are very much of the 9-to-5 weekdays and Saturday-morning-only variety. Addresses of the main state tourist offices relevant to the outback are:

New South Wales
The Rocks Visitor Centre
(☎ 13 20 77, Ⓦ www.visitnsw.com.au)
106 George St,
The Rocks. NSW 2000
Northern Territory
Northern Territory Tourist Commission
(☎ 08-8999 3900, Ⓦ www.nttc.com.au)
43 Mitchell St, Darwin, NT 0800
Queensland
Queensland Tourism (☎ 13 88 33,
Ⓦ www.queenslandtravel.com.au)
30 Makerston St, Brisbane, Qld 4000
South Australia
South Australia Information & Travel Centre
(☎ 1300 655 276, Ⓦ www.southaustralia.com)
18 King William St, Adelaide, SA 5000
Western Australia
Western Australian Visitor Centre,
(☎ 1300 361 351, Ⓦ www.westernaustralia.net)
Forrest Place, Perth, WA 6000

A step down from the state tourist offices are the local or regional tourist offices. All major outback towns and many minor ones maintain a tourist office or visitor information centre of some kind – see the individual track descriptions in this book. These often have a great deal of information not readily available from the state offices. Otherwise try hotels, police stations, park ranger offices and roadhouses.

Tourist offices will be happy to provide bookings and put you on to tour operators, but they usually know little about independent outback travel unless it earns them a commission. The automobile associations (see Useful Organisations later in this chapter) are a better bet; their head and regional offices are usually well stocked with maps and brochures of the outback in their own state.

TRAVEL PERMITS

If you intend to travel through the outback on your own, see the Getting Around chapter for information about the permits you may need to enter Aboriginal land or camp in national parks.

MONEY
Changing Money

Changing foreign currency or travellers cheques is no problem at most city banks and licensed money changers. However, banks in smaller outback towns aren't always geared up for complicated transactions and it can be a long way between banks. Before heading bush, foreigners should make sure they have sufficient Australian funds, preferably a mixture of travellers cheques (some outback shops and businesses will accept travellers cheques denominated in Australian dollars), credit cards and cash. Open a Commonwealth Bank passbook (see Passbook Account later in this section) and you'll have money at your disposal almost anywhere.

Credit Cards

Credit cards are widely accepted in the outback but by no means everywhere – this particularly applies to remote small businesses that may insist on travellers cheques or cash. Visa and MasterCard are the most commonly recognised, American Express and Diners Club less so.

Cash advances from credit cards are available over the bank counter and from many automated teller machines (ATMs), depending on the card. If you're planning to rent cars, a credit card is looked upon more favourably than nasty old cash; most agencies simply won't rent you a vehicle if you don't have a card.

Cash Cards, ATMs & Eftpos

Most people these days have a bank account that includes a cash card that can be used to access cash day or night from ATMs. Many of the larger outback towns have at least a couple of ATMs from different banks; major roadhouses may also have an ATM of some description.

All post offices and post-office agencies represent the Commonwealth Bank, and almost all of them, even in remote areas, have the electronic facilities to handle Commonwealth Bank cash cards at the counter. If you have a choice, this is the one to go for.

Even in the outback many businesses are linked into the Eftpos (Electronic Funds Transfer at Point Of Sale) system. At places with this facility you can use your cash card to pay for services or purchases direct, and sometimes withdraw a limited amount of cash as well. Cash cards and credit cards can also be used to make local, STD and international phone calls on special pay telephones found in many towns.

Passbook Account

Probably the most reliable way of obtaining cash in the outback is with a Commonwealth Bank passbook. This is one of those old-fashioned booklets that you may have had when you were a kid, where your transactions are typed in. All post offices and post-office agencies such as newsagencies and general stores – even the very remote ones that don't have the electronic facilities to handle cash cards – will handle a passbook, which makes this option particularly useful.

A passbook account can be opened on the spot at any Commonwealth Bank branch.

Costs

The biggest cost in any outback trip is transport, simply because it's such a vast country. If there's a group of you, buying a second-hand car is probably the most economical way to go. Fuel is cheap by world standards but you'll need lots of it.

Freight charges increase the cost of everything in the outback, up to 20% to 30% over city prices even in a major centre like Alice Springs. Fuel is also more expensive, not just because of freight but because most roadhouses and the like have to produce their own electricity using diesel generators.

Another problem is the difficulty of attracting reliable labour; relatively few people who aren't intent on escaping something (whether it be the law, their spouse or personal problems) are interested in leaving the comforts of town life to work in the bush. Tourists who complain about the high prices charged by remote roadhouses seldom have any appreciation of what it costs to provide the service.

Tipping & Bargaining

Tipping isn't entrenched in Australia and is uncommon in the outback. It's only customary to tip in more expensive restaurants and then only if you want to. If the service has been especially good, 10% of the bill is considered generous. Taxi drivers don't expect tips (of course, they won't hurl it back at you if you decide to leave the change).

Bargaining is not common, and most times you'll have to pay the indicated price. On the other hand, it's common practice (though not in the big chain stores) to ask for a discount on expensive items when paying cash – not that you're guaranteed to get one. You can try bargaining in markets and second-hand shops.

POST & COMMUNICATIONS
Post

Australia's postal services are reasonably efficient. It costs $0.45 to send a standard letter or postcard anywhere within Australia. Airmail letters up to 50g cost $1 to the Asia-Pacific region and $1.50 to the rest of the world; postcards cost $1 and aerograms $0.78 to any country.

Post offices are open from 9am to 5pm Monday to Friday, but you can often get stamps on Saturday mornings from post-office agencies that operate from local newsagencies or general stores, or from the Australia Post shops found in large cities.

Receiving Mail All post offices will hold mail for visitors, which can be collected on presentation of some form of identification (passport, driving licence). You can also have mail sent to you at American Express (AmEx) offices in big cities if you have an AmEx card or travellers cheques. Although Australia Post's delivery speed compares favourably with that in many other countries, add one or two weeks for mail to or from isolated outback towns – and always specify air mail.

Mail Runs One of the great outback traditions is the weekly mail run. For many isolated people, their visit from the postie may be their only regular contact with other people for weeks or even months on end. Even with the rapid advances in communication technology, the postie is still an important link in the spread of information, news and gossip in the outback.

During the northern wet season, when roads are often cut for weeks and long-distance travel by vehicle is not possible, the weekly mail plane becomes the only traffic in and out of many communities.

Other mail runs are done by truck, usually along hundreds of kilometres of often dusty and bumpy roads. The arrival of the mail truck is a keenly awaited event, for not only does it bring the mail, but also much needed station supplies – everything from groceries to vehicle spare parts to a new refrigerator come with the mail.

Joining a mail run is a great way to experience the outback – see the Getting Around chapter for details.

Telephone

Thanks to advances in satellite communication technology, even the outback is well serviced by telephones.

The Australian telecommunications industry is deregulated and there are a number of providers offering various services. Private phones are serviced by the two main players, Telstra and Optus, but it's in the mobile (cell) phone and pay phone markets, where companies such as Vodafone, Global One and AAPT are also operating, that you'll find the most competition.

Pay Phones & Phonecards There's a wide range of local and international phonecards. Lonely Planet's eKno global communication service provides low-cost international calls – for local calls you're usually better off with a local phonecard. eKno also offers free messaging services, email, travel information and an online travel vault, where you can securely store details of all your important documents. You can join online at W www.ekno.lonelyplanet.com, where you'll find the local access numbers for the 24-hour customer-service centre. Once you have joined, always check the eKno Web site for the latest access numbers for each country and updates on new features. The current dial-in numbers for Australia are: Sydney ☎ 02-8208 3000; Melbourne ☎ 03-9909 0888; and elsewhere (toll free) ☎ 1800 114 478.

There are plenty of other phonecards on the market that you can buy at newsagents and post offices for a fixed dollar value (usually $10, $20, $30 etc). These can be used with any private or pay phone by dialling a toll-free access number and then the PIN on the card. Then there are Telstra phonecards (again sold in various dollar amounts), which you can insert into most (Telstra) pay phones. The important thing is to know exactly how your calls are being charged, as the charges vary from company to company. An explanatory booklet should be available from the card outlet.

Some pay phones in the major outback centres conveniently accept credit cards, although you need to keep an eye on how much the call is costing as it can quickly mount up.

Local Calls Local calls from pay phones cost $0.40, while most local calls from private phones cost $0.25. In both cases you can talk for an unlimited time. In the outback, however, the term 'local' might be irrelevant and calls often cost more because they are actually over such a long distance. Calls to mobile phones attract (far) higher rates and are timed. Blue phones or gold phones that you sometimes find in hotel lobbies and outback shops usually cost a minimum of $0.50 for a local call.

STD Calls & Area Codes Long-distance or STD (Subscriber Trunk Dialling) calls can be made from virtually any public phone. STD calls are cheaper in off-peak hours (usually between 7pm and 7am), and different service providers have different charges.

Australia has four STD area codes. All regular numbers (ie, numbers other than mobiles, toll-free or information services) have an area code followed by an eight-digit number. Long-distance calls (ie, to more than about 50km away) within these areas are charged at long-distance rates, even though they have the same area code. Broadly, the 02 area code covers NSW and the ACT; 03 Victoria and Tasmania; 07 Queensland; and 08 SA, WA and the NT. Keep in mind that area code boundaries do not necessarily coincide exactly with state borders – for example, NSW uses each of the four codes.

International Calls From most STD phones you can also make ISD (International Subscriber Dialling) calls. Dial 0011 to get out of Australia, then the country code (44 for Britain, 1 for the USA or Canada, 64 for New Zealand etc), the city code (171 or 181 for London, 212 for New York etc), and finally the subscriber number. Have a phonecard, credit card or plenty of coins to hand.

International calls from Australia are among the cheapest you'll find anywhere, and there are often specials that bring the rates down even further. For instance, with Telstra (from a private phone) you can call the UK between 7pm and 7am and speak for 30 minutes for $6. Off-peak times, if available, vary depending on the destination – call ☎ 1800 113 011 for more details or check the Telstra web site (**W** www.telstra.com).

Toll-Free Calls Many businesses and some government departments operate a toll-free service (prefix 1800), which means it's a free call no matter where you are ringing from around the country. These numbers may not be accessible from certain areas (certainly not from outside Australia) or from mobile phones, in which case you'll have to dial the normal number.

Many companies, such as airlines, have numbers beginning with 13 or 1300, and these are charged at the rate of a local call. Often these numbers can be used Australia-wide, or they may be applicable to a specific state or STD district only. Unfortunately, as with 1800 numbers, there's no way of telling without actually ringing the number. Calls to these services still attract higher charges if you are calling from a mobile phone.

To make a reverse charge call within Australia from any private or pay phone, dial ☎ 1800 801 800. For international reverse-charge calls dial ☎ 12 550.

Information Calls Other odd numbers you may come across are those starting with 190. These numbers, usually recorded information services and the like, are provided by private companies, and your call is charged at anything from $0.35 to $5 or more per minute (more from mobile and pay phones).

Mobile (or Cell) Phones Numbers with the prefix 04xx or 04xxx are mobile or car phones. Calls to and from mobile numbers are charged at special STD rates and can be expensive.

Cellular (mobile) phone services cover 90% of Australia's population but only 7% of its landmass, which makes them next to useless in the outback. However, you can use mobile phones in many of the larger centres such as Alice Springs, Mt Isa and Port Hedland. The coverage provided by Telstra's service is more extensive than the Optus one, and often extends to (major) outback towns.

Radio Communications

Radio communications play an important role in the outback. Most travellers manage perfectly well without a radio, but in the more remote areas it is an important safety feature. When travelling in convoy, the ability to communicate with each other on the move can make the trip more enjoyable too.

EPIRB If you don't carry a radio, it's worth carrying an EPIRB (Emergency Position Indicating Radio Beacon) for peace of mind. This emits a distress signal that's picked up by commercial aircraft flying overhead and can be used to pinpoint your position. Originally designed for yachts, they've become a common emergency device in the outback. Many rental vehicles set up for outback travel include one in their standard kit (or at least they should).

An EPIRB costs $250 to $300 and can also be hired (try marine suppliers). Keep it

serviced and make sure the battery hasn't reached its expiry date. Needless to say, EPIRBs are for life-threatening emergencies only (eg, two flat tyres may be inconvenient but it's not a matter of life and death). Setting off an EPIRB unnecessarily can end up being very expensive for you.

CB Radio CB radio comes in two forms, working in two frequency bands. The cheaper of the two is AM in the 27MHz frequency range, while the dearer is UHF in the 477MHz band. Both bands have 40 channels to choose from; channel 9 is reserved for emergency contact on the 27MHz band, and channel 5 on the UHF sets.

The cheapest sets on the market are the pure AM sets (from under $100), but these are limited in what they can do. The better 27MHz set is an AM/SSB (single sideband) unit (from $200), and while both units can talk to one another and are good for inter-vehicle communication, the SSB facility gives a longer range. This function may be unreliable and completely unpredictable, but is of some use as a safety feature.

The UHF sets can be expensive ($300 to $800), and while they give good and clear intervehicle communication, they are only a line-of-sight device. In the more settled areas of Australia their range has been improved by the use of repeater towers, but you need to know the required channels in the respective areas.

For anybody travelling with another vehicle, a CB radio is a great boon. You can yarn to one another, warn the second vehicle of the need to close a gate, of a large dip in the road, or whatever. CBs don't need to be licensed, and there are no restrictions on normal day-to-day operations.

Call signs, which identify the caller or recipient, use the phonetic alphabet used by radio operators, eg, call sign 7VAB would be spoken as 'Seven Victor Alpha Bravo'.

HF Outpost Radio For those travelling the remote areas of Australia, a HF (high-frequency) radio is the way to go. 'Outpost' refers to any building or vehicle that does not have direct contact with the normal telephone service. People without radio qualifications can get units that are set up for the Royal Flying Doctor Service (RFDS) or several other professional safety organisations. For emergency situations the RFDS HF set is your best option.

These radios are expensive: a reliable second-hand unit can cost at least $1000, while a new unit is $3000 to $5000. They can also be hired from radio outlets in the capital cities and major outback centres for about $80 a week – the RFDS no longer rents them out. McKay's Communications (☎ 02-6884 5237) at 25 Douglas Mawson Rd, Dubbo, NSW 2830, will deliver to your door. Whether you buy one or hire one, you'll need a Mobile Outpost Station Licence issued by the Australian Communications Authority (☎ 02-6219 5555, fax 6219 5353, Ⓦ www.aca.gov.au) at PO Box 78, Belconnen, ACT 2616. It has offices in each state capital as well as some major regional centres.

Tonecall facilities (basically a distress signal) should be available on any HF set worth its salt, though it won't provide a fix on your position like an EPIRB will. Selcall (a more complex version of Tonecall, which allows the base to call *you*) is available on the better sets and this does make it easier to call the required station.

HF sets are mainly meant for long-distance communication up to 3000km. You can talk from one mobile unit to another or to an RFDS base. The RFDS system provides emergency medical aid right throughout the outback and is on call, for an emergency, 24 hours a day, 365 days a year. Each RFDS base operates a number of channels and these are detailed in the individual track descriptions later in this book.

If you're planning to travel along a particular track, it's a good idea to contact the relevant RFDS base beforehand to ask whether there's anything you need to know (channel changes, road closures etc). They're usually very up to date with road information.

Several smaller organisations also provide HF networks. For instance, the VKS-737 network run by the Australian National 4WD Radio Network Inc (☎ 08-8287 6222,

Ⓔ info@vks737.on.net, Ⓦ http://4wdclubs .sofcom.com/au/an4wdrn) at PO Box 270, Elizabeth, SA 5112, covers much of the outback, but you have to be a member. It uses the following frequencies: 5455 (Ch 1); 8022 (Ch 2); 11612 (Ch 3); 14977 (Ch 4); and 3995 (Ch 5).

Calling a Station Before using the radio, spend a while listening to traffic so you become familiar with what's normal for each channel. Though you need to use call signs and the like, the base operators aren't going to get upset if you make mistakes. Select the RFDS station closest to you, choose the 'primary' or 'on call' channel, tune the antenna to that channel and listen before making your call. If the channel is busy, wait until it's clear or select another.

When it is free, make a call. If calling an RFDS base, such as Broken Hill, include its call sign by saying something like 'VJC Broken Hill this is Seven Victor Alpha Bravo calling. How do you read? Over.' Once you have established contact, ask for whatever you require.

If you don't succeed first time, try again. If you have no luck on one channel, try another. The time of day and other cyclic factors (eg, seasons and sunspot cycles) affect radio communication. Remember the rule of thumb: The higher the sun, the higher the channel number (or frequency). Longer distances also mean higher frequencies so you may have to try a few.

Satellite Phones (Satphones) These are the ultimate in modern communication and allow you to make a phone call from anywhere in the world. They're slowly making inroads but are expensive to purchase ($3000 to $6000, or upwards of $150 a week rental) and operate (more than $45 a month access fee plus $1.60 to $4 a minute call cost depending on the carrier and other factors). Despite advances in technology they're still fairly large and heavy – the size of a small briefcase, with smaller units several times the bulk of a mobile phone. Some 4WD clubs have satphones that their members can use, usually for a fee plus the cost of calls.

The Future HF radio will be a part of the communication scene for a long time to come and will get better as new options and service providers come on stream – some even put phone calls through your HF set. Contact the Australian Communications Authority for an update on service providers in your area of interest.

For the time being, the purchase or rental and especially operating costs of satphones put them out of reach for the casual user. This may improve as time goes on, though costs haven't come down much since these phones first made an appearance in the mid-1990s. By comparison, HF radios remain cheap to run and reliable.

Email & Internet Access

Email is a great way to keep in touch. Internet cafes are thin on the ground in the outback but their number is growing in the major towns, and public libraries will almost always have a few computers hooked up to the Internet. Hostels often have Internet access as well, as do some hotels and caravan parks. The cost ranges from $2 an hour in public libraries (the 'cheaper' ones) to $10 an hour in remote locations.

The most convenient way to send and receive email while travelling is to open an account with one of the free Web-based email services. Hotmail is plagued by junk mail these days but there are plenty of alternatives such as eKno (**W** www.ekno. lonelyplanet.com) or Yahoo (**W** www.yahoo .com). These services will allow you to access your mail from any Internet-connected machine running a standard Web browser, either using the Web-based account or by accessing your home account using your POP or IMAP address.

Hooking Up If you're bringing your palmtop or notebook computer along on the trip and want to get connected, there are plenty of ISPs (Internet Service Providers) to use, though some limit their dial-up areas to major cities or particular regions. Whatever enticements a particular ISP offers, make sure it has local dial-up numbers for the places you intend to use it. The last thing

you want is to be making timed STD calls every time you connect to the Internet. Telstra (Big Pond) uses a nationwide dial-up number at local call rates that seems to work very well from anywhere in the outback. Major ISPs include:

America Online (AOL; ☎ 1800 265 265, **W** www.aol.com.au) Also has log-in numbers in all capitals and many provincial cities.
CompuServe (☎ 1300 555 520, **W** www .compuserve.com.au) Check the web site or phone to get the local log-in numbers.
OzEmail (☎ 13 28 84,**W** www.ozemail.com.au)
Primus (☎ 1300 858 585, **W** www.iprimus .com.au)
Telstra Big Pond (☎ 13 12 82, **W** www.bigpond .com)

One problem is finding somewhere to connect. Mid-range and top-end hotels will have sockets but you'll be hit with expensive call charges. In cheaper places you'll probably find that phones are hardwired into the wall. If you just want to send and receive messages and have a local dial-up number, most camping grounds and hotel offices won't mind you unplugging their phone for a couple of minutes if you ask them nicely – though if they're running a private branch exchange you may need to use the separate fax line instead.

Foreigners should be aware that Australia uses RJ-45 telephone plugs and Telstra EXI-160 four-pin plugs. Neither are universal – electronics shops such as Tandy and Dick Smith should be able to help if your plug doesn't suit. See Electricity later in this chapter to check if your laptop will plug into the local power supply; a universal AC adaptor will enable you to plug it in anywhere without frying the innards. You'll also need a plug adaptor – often it's easiest to buy these before you leave home. Keep in mind too that your PC-card modem may not work in Australia. The safest option is to buy a reputable 'global' modem before you leave home, or buy a local PC-card modem once you get to Australia.

Some modems will die for good if you connect them to a digital phone line. As you don't always know whether the line is digital (unusual but they do exist), a protection device such as Modem Shield is a wise investment.

INTERNET RESOURCES
The World Wide Web is a rich resource for travellers. You can research your trip, hunt down bargain air fares, book hotels, check on weather conditions or chat with locals and other travellers about the best places to visit (or avoid).

At Lonely Planet (W www.lonelyplanet .com) you'll find succinct summaries on travelling around Australia, postcards from other travellers and the Thorn Tree bulletin board, where you can ask questions before you go or dispense advice when you get back. You can also find travel news and updates to many of our most popular guidebooks, and the subWWWay section links you to the most useful travel resources elsewhere on the Web.

A simple search using the key word 'outback' or 'outback travel' will throw up enough sites to keep you researching for a year. We try to list as many specific sites as possible throughout this book, but you can start with these general ones:

Aboriginal Australia Covers Aboriginal art, culture and tourism options. It's partly commercial – you can buy art and products online:
W www.aboriginalaustralia.com
Aussie Backpacker Standard backpackers site covering accommodation, tours, sights and employment:
W www.aussiebackpack.com.au
A-Z of Australia Off-beat site with information on everything from Aborigines to Zinc cream:
W www.australiaonline.com.au
Guide to Australia Maintained by the Charles Sturt University in NSW, a mine of information, with links to Australian government departments, weather information, books, maps etc:
W www.csu.edu.au/education/australia.html
The Aussie Index Fairly comprehensive list of Australian companies, educational institutions and government departments that maintain Web sites:
W www.aussie.com.au
The Australian The online version of Australia's only national daily newspaper:
W www.theaustralian.news.com.au

BOOKS
In almost every specialist bookshop in the country you'll find a section devoted to Australiana. The outback features prominently, especially among the coffee-table books: Penny van Oosterzee & Reg Morrison's *The Centre – The Natural History of Australia's Desert Regions* is one of the more affordable and informative; the two-volume *Australia's Wilderness Heritage*, published by Angus & Robertson, is quite affordable in its paperback version and is filled with stunning photographs. At the Wilderness Society shops in each capital city and the Government Printing Offices in Sydney and Melbourne you'll find a good range of wildlife posters, calendars and books.

Lonely Planet
Lonely Planet is based in Melbourne and has its home country well covered. Apart from the country guide, *Australia*, it has separate state guides to every state, city guides to Melbourne and Sydney, and *Islands of Australia's Great Barrier Reef*. There are also Out to Eat restaurant guides to Melbourne and Sydney, and a *Healthy Travel: Australia, New Zealand & the Pacific* guide.

Walking in Australia describes 72 walks of varying lengths and difficulty in various parts of the country, several of them in outback areas. The *Australian phrasebook* discusses Australian English but also has a large amount of detail on Aboriginal languages.

Watching Wildlife Australia is a comprehensive guide to Australia's fauna, parks and habitats. *Cycling Australia* describes 32 rides that take from a few hours to 31 days, to suit both the novice and experienced cycle tourist.

Sean & David's Long Drive is an offbeat road book by Melbourne author Sean Condon. The 'Pisces' diving guides include *Coral Sea & Great Barrier Reef*.

For an in-depth look at the indigenous population, *Aboriginal Australia & the Torres Strait Islands* is hard to beat. With contributions from more than 50 indigenous Australians, it provides an overview of the main issues affecting them today as well as a wealth of practical information.

Aboriginal People

Apart from the Lonely Planet title just discussed, *The Australian Aborigines* by Kenneth Maddock is a good cultural summary. The award-winning *Triumph of the Nomads* by Geoffrey Blainey chronicles the life of Australia's original inhabitants, and convincingly demolishes the myth that the Aborigines were 'primitive' people trapped on a hostile continent – the book is an excellent read.

For a sympathetic historical account of what happened to the original Australians since Europeans landed, read *Aboriginal Australians* by Richard Broome. *A Change of Ownership*, by Mildred Kirk, covers similar ground to Broome's book, but does so more concisely, focusing on the land-rights movement and its historical background.

The Other Side of the Frontier by Henry Reynolds uses historical records to give a vivid account of an Aboriginal view of the arrival and takeover of Australia by Europeans. His *With the White People* identifies the essential Aboriginal contributions to the survival of early white settlers. *My People*, by Oodgeroo Noonuccal (Kath Walker), is recommended reading for people interested in the experiences of Aboriginal people.

The Little Black, Red and Yellow Book is an invaluable pocket guide to the society, culture and politics of indigenous Australia. It's published by the Australian Institute for Aboriginal and Torres Strait Islander Studies (Aiatsis) and you can pick it up for free at the offices of many indigenous organisations. See Literature in the Facts about the Outback chapter for more literature by Aboriginal people.

History

For a good introduction to Australian history, read *A Short History of Australia*, a most accessible and informative general history by the late Manning Clark, the celebrated (and controversial) Aussie historian, or *The Fatal Shore*, Robert Hughes' best-selling account of the convict era.

Geoffrey Blainey's *The Tyranny of Distance* is an engrossing study of the problems of transport in this harsh continent and how they shaped the pattern of white settlement. For instance, transporting produce 160km by bullock cart from an inland farm to a port cost more than shipping it from there around the globe to Europe – a handicap that only wool and later gold were profitable enough to overcome.

Finding Australia by Russel Ward traces the story from the first Aboriginal arrivals up to 1821. The book is strong on Aborigines, women and the full story of foreign exploration, not just Captain Cook's role. There's lots of fascinating detail, including descriptions of the appalling crooks who ran the early colony.

The Exploration of Australia by Michael Cannon is coffee-table book in size, presentation and price, but it's also a fascinating reference book about the gradual European discovery of the continent.

Cooper's Creek by Alan Moorehead is a classic account of the ill-fated Burke and Wills expedition that dramatises the horrors and hardships faced by the early explorers.

The Fatal Impact, also by Moorehead, begins with the voyages of Captain James Cook, regarded as one of the greatest and most humane explorers, and tells the tragic story of the European impact on Australia, Tahiti and Antarctica in the years that followed. It details how good intentions and the economic imperatives of the time led to disaster, corruption and annihilation

John Pilger's *A Secret Country* is a vividly written book that deals with Australia's historical roots and its shabby treatment of Aboriginal people. It also posits an interesting theory on the dismissal of the Whitlam government in 1975.

Fiction

There's no shortage of excellent Australian fiction with an outback theme. See Arts in the Facts about the Outback chapter.

Travel Accounts

Tony Horwitz's *One for the Road* is an entertaining account of a high-speed hitchhiking trip around Australia (Oz through a windscreen). In contrast, *The Ribbon and the Ragged Square* by Linda Christmas, a

Publications

Most books are published in different editions by different publishers in different countries. As a result, a book might be a hardcover rarity in one country while it's readily available in paperback in another. Fortunately, bookshops and libraries search by title or author, so your local bookshop or library is best placed to advise you on the availability of the these recommendations.

UK journalist from the *Guardian*, is an intelligent, sober account of a nine-month investigatory trip around Australia. There's lots of background, history, first-hand reporting and interviews.

The late Bruce Chatwin's *The Songlines* tells of his experiences among central Australian Aborigines. It probably reveals more about the author than Aboriginal people, its best feature perhaps being some excellent, pithy anecdotes about modern Australia.

Bill Bryson's *Down Under* is another bestseller from the American travel writer. It's veteran Bryson humour and has some interesting insights.

The journals of the early European explorers can be fairly hard going but make fascinating reading. The hardships that many of them endured is nothing short of incredible. Men such as Sturt, Eyre, Leichhardt, Davidson, King (on the Burke and Wills expedition), Stuart and Jardine kept detailed journals. These accounts are usually available in public libraries and sometimes in bookshops.

Travel Guides
The track descriptions in this book mention literature relevant to the particular tracks. *Burnum Burnum's Aboriginal Australia* is subtitled 'a traveller's guide'. If you want to explore Australia from the Aboriginal point of view, this large and lavish hardback is the book for you.

Safe Outback Travel by Jack Absalom is a very practical little book with basic advice on subjects such as vehicle preparation and troubleshooting, general rules of outback travel, and the most important survival skills necessary.

There are a number of other books about vehicle preparation and driving in the outback, as well as survival skills and general bushcraft. In the latter category, *Stay Alive* by Maurice Dunlevy gives practical advice on survival techniques and first aid. *The Outdoor Companion* by Q & J Chester, Paddy Pallin's *Bushwalking & Camping* and Lex Lannoy's *The Australian Bushcraft Handbook* (endorsed by the Scout Association) are all good but mainly aimed at bushwalkers and cross-country skiers. The Western Australian police force produces an excellent book titled *Aids to Survival*, which covers map reading, first aid and survival techniques.

Jeff & Mare Carter's *The Complete Guide to Central Australia* has some beautiful photographs and provides lots of knowledgeable background on flora and fauna. Australian Geographic has several excellent publications dealing with life and travel in the outback, including *The Red Centre*, *Cape York*, *The Kimberley* and *The Canning Stock Route*.

NEWSPAPERS & MAGAZINES
Once upon a time virtually every Australian town of any significance had its own newspaper. Many outback centres still do, and these are a must if you want to know what's happening locally.

Respected big-city newspapers such as the *Sydney Morning Herald* and the Melbourne *Age* become harder to get the further you move into the outback. However, any reasonable newsagent will have that day's (or at least yesterday's) edition of The *Australian* (the country's only national daily) and the major big-city newspaper for that particular state. Rural newspapers are widely available and often have information relevant to the outback, such as employment and vehicle sales.

Weekly newspapers and magazines include an Australian edition of *Time* and a combined edition of the Australian news magazine the *Bulletin* with *Newsweek*. The *Economist* and the *Guardian Weekly* are sometimes available and good for international news. Most of the outback newsagencies also stock a wide variety of special-interest magazines including adventure and 4WD publications.

RADIO & TV

The national, advertising-free TV and radio network is the Australian Broadcasting Corporation (ABC). In most state capitals there are a couple of ABC radio stations and a host of commercial stations, both AM and FM, featuring the whole gamut of radio possibilities. There's also a wide variety of community radio stations that rely on volunteers and listener subscriptions.

In Sydney and Melbourne there are the ABC, three commercial TV stations and SBS, a government-sponsored multicultural TV station that beams to the state capitals and a growing number of regional centres. Around the country the number of TV stations varies from place to place; there are regional TV stations but in some remote areas the ABC may be all you can receive.

Imparja is an Aboriginal-owned-and-run commercial TV station that operates out of Alice Springs and covers one-third of the country (mainly the Northern Territory, South Australia and western New South Wales). It broadcasts a variety of programs, ranging from soaps to productions made by and for Aboriginal people.

Satellite pay TV is growing in popularity, especially in the outback. Many pubs and clubs have TVs or a big screen for showing sports on Pay TV.

PHOTOGRAPHY & VIDEO

In the outback, print film is usually available at general stores, supermarkets, pharmacies and petrol stations; but it can be expensive, the range is often limited and it may have been sitting on the shelf for a while – check the use-by date or stock up beforehand. Slide film probably won't be available in small outback towns at all. The largest outback towns have at least one camera shop and maybe even a camera repairer.

When taking photographs in the outback, allow for the exceptional intensity of the light. Best results are obtained early in the morning and late in the afternoon. As the sun gets higher, colours appear washed out, which you can compensate for to some extent with a polarising filter. You must also allow for the intensity of reflected light.

Do your best to keep film cool, particularly after exposure – don't store it in the car's glove compartment. Other film and camera hazards are dust and, in the tropical regions of the far north, humidity.

Lonely Planet's *Travel Photography: A Guide to Taking Better Pictures*, by respected travel photographer Richard I'Anson, offers a comprehensive guide to technical and creative travel photography.

Politeness goes a long way when taking photographs – ask before taking pictures of people. Many Aboriginal people don't like having their photographs taken, even from a distance, and are distressed by images of people who are no longer alive.

TIME

Australia is divided into three time zones: Western Standard Time (Western Australia) is plus eight hours from GMT/UTC; Central Standard Time (Northern Territory, South Australia and the Broken Hill area in New South Wales) is plus 9½ hours; and Eastern Standard Time (Tasmania, Victoria, New South Wales and Queensland) is plus 10. When it's noon in Western Australia it's 1.30pm in the Northern Territory and South Australia, and 2pm in the rest of the country. From October to March, things get slightly screwed up as daylight-saving time (when clocks are put forward an hour) does not operate in Western Australia, the Northern Territory or Queensland, and in Tasmania it starts a month earlier and finishes a month later than in South Australia, Victoria and New South Wales.

ELECTRICITY

The electricity supply is pretty reliable in most outback towns, even the smaller ones. However the smallest towns – and most roadhouses and homesteads – rely on their own generators that are often shut down at night to conserve fuel. Either way, if you pitch your tent or put your van near one of these the noise and diesel fumes can be unbearable, so check before you settle in.

WEIGHTS & MEASURES

Australia may be metric but many outback people still think in miles and imperial gallons and pints, and will often indicate distance by the time it takes to get there. Australia-wide, fuel consumption is still often referred to in miles per gallon (29mpg is roughly 10km per litre), and almost everybody still quotes tyre pressures in pounds per square inch (28psi is roughly 193kPa).

For those who need help with metric, there's a conversion table at the back of this book.

LAUNDRY

Most major outback centres have at least one dry-cleaning business and seven-day laundrette, and you'll usually find coin-operated washing machines and driers at caravan parks. Otherwise there will generally be at least a wash trough and cold water tap, although remote parks and reserves may have no facilities whatsoever. If you're camping away from it all, carry a bucket to wash your clothes in.

An alternative washing machine when travelling is a heavy-duty, sealable 20L plastic container, filled with water, soiled clothing and detergent, and carried in the car. The agitation as you drive along gets your clothes remarkably clean, particularly on corrugated roads.

HEALTH

Australia is a remarkably healthy country considering that such a large portion of it lies in the tropics. Tropical diseases such as malaria and yellow fever are unknown, diseases of insanitation such as cholera and typhoid are unheard of, and, thanks to Australia's isolation and quarantine standards, even some animal diseases such as rabies and foot-and-mouth disease are absent. However, there are some venomous creatures that you need to beware of – see the Fauna section in the Facts about the Outback chapter.

A few routine vaccinations are recommended worldwide whether you're travelling or not, and for the outback you might want to check whether your tetanus booster is still up to date.

Australia poses a significant risk for asthmatics, with air-borne allergens such as dust and pollen being the main culprits – in fact, Australia has one of the world's highest incidences of asthma. The main danger periods are winter in the south and April/May and October in the north. Inhalers (or puffers) are available without prescription at chemists.

If you have an immediate health problem, contact the casualty section at the nearest public hospital or outback medical clinic. For those equipped with a HF radio able to reach the nearest Flying Doctor base, expert medical advice is available 24 hours a day via the radio's emergency call button.

Lonely Planet's *Healthy Travel: Australia, New Zealand & the Pacific* is a handy, pocket-size guide packed with useful information including pre-trip planning, emergency first aid, immunisation and disease information and also advice on what to do if you get sick on the road.

Travel Insurance

Ambulance services can end up being frightfully expensive in the outback, so it would be wise to take out travel insurance. Make sure the policy specifically includes ambulance, helicopter rescue and a flight home for you and anyone you're travelling with. Also check the fine print: some policies exclude 'dangerous activities' such as scuba diving, motorcycling and even trekking. If such activities are on your agenda, you don't want that policy.

Medical Kit

Outback doctors and hospitals are few and far between, so you'd be wise to carry a first-aid handbook and a basic medical kit. Ideally, at least one person in your party will be a competent first-aider.

St John Ambulance Australia (☎ 13 13 94, W www.stjohn.org.au) has a selection of first-aid kits for car drivers, motorcyclists and bushwalkers, ranging in price from $39

Medical Kit Check List

Following is a list of items you should consider including in your medical kit – consult your pharmacist for brands available in your country.

- ☐ **Aspirin or paracetamol (acetaminophen in the USA)** – for pain or fever
- ☐ **Antihistamine** – for allergies, eg, hay fever; to ease the itch from insect bites or stings; and to prevent motion sickness. Some antihistamines can cause sedation and may interact with alcohol, so care should be taken when using them while driving.
- ☐ **Cold and flu tablets, throat lozenges and nasal decongestant**
- ☐ **Multivitamins** – consider for long trips, when dietary vitamin intake may be inadequate
- ☐ **Antibiotics** – consider including these if you're travelling well off the beaten track; see your doctor, as they must be prescribed, and carry the prescription with you
- ☐ **Loperamide or diphenoxylate** – 'blockers' for diarrhoea
- ☐ **Prochlorperazine or metaclopramide** – for nausea and vomiting
- ☐ **Rehydration mixture** – to prevent dehydration, which may occur, for example, during bouts of diarrhoea; particularly important when travelling with children
- ☐ **Insect repellent, sunscreen, lip balm, ear drops and eye drops**
- ☐ **Calamine lotion, sting relief spray or aloe vera** – to ease irritation from sunburn and insect bites or stings
- ☐ **Antifungal cream or powder** – for fungal skin infections and thrush
- ☐ **Antiseptic (such as povidone-iodine)** – for cuts and grazes
- ☐ **Bandages, Band-Aids (plasters) and other wound dressings**
- ☐ **Elastic or crepe bandages** – for sprains or snake bite
- ☐ **Water purification tablets or iodine**
- ☐ **Scissors, tweezers, ribber pointed eye probe and a thermometer** – note that mercury thermometers are prohibited by airlines
- ☐ **Pencil and note paper**

Optional
- ☐ **Indigestion tablets**
- ☐ **Vinegar** – for jellyfish stings (in the tropics)
- ☐ **Temporary tooth-filling mix** – to replace fillings and loose caps
- ☐ **Toothache drops**
- ☐ **Burn cream**
- ☐ **Airsplint** – for broken limbs or immobilising limbs after snake bite

---

to $158. They include a first-aid handbook and are well worth considering as a base kit to which you can add some of the above items. They're available from St John offices and motoring organisations.

Don't forget any medication you're already taking, and include prescriptions with the generic name rather than the brand one as it may not be available locally.

Health Precautions
Those ultraviolet rays from the fierce outback sun can have you burnt to a crisp even on an overcast day, so if in doubt wear protective cream, a wide-brimmed hat and loose-fitting cotton clothing that gives maximum skin coverage. Loose clothes allow the air to circulate around your skin and you'll find cotton to be much more comfortable and cooler than synthetics. Smother exposed areas of skin with a sunscreen (protection factor 30 or higher). Australia has the world's highest incidence of skin cancer (a fact directly connected to exposure to the sun) so be very careful.

Remember also that excessive ultraviolet light (direct or reflected) will damage the surface structure and lens of the eye. Good-quality sunglasses with lenses treated to filter out harmful ultraviolet radiation – are pretty well essential. Poor-quality glasses have limited filtering, and actually allow more ultraviolet light to be absorbed than if no sunglasses were worn at all. The Australian Cancer Society produces sunglasses that meet all the standard safety requirements and are for sale at most chemists and many newsagencies.

If you wear glasses or contact lenses, take a spare pair and your prescription. A Medic Alert tag is worth having if your medical condition is not always easily recognisable (heart trouble, diabetes, asthma, allergic reactions to antibiotics etc).

The contraceptive pill is available on prescription only, so a visit to a doctor is necessary. Doctors are listed in the *Yellow Pages* phone book or you can visit the outpatients section of a public hospital. Condoms are available from chemists, many convenience stores and often from vending machines in the toilets of pubs.

Basic Rules

Heat With the exception of southern areas, you can expect the weather to be hot throughout the outback from October to April inclusive, and travellers from cool climates may feel uncomfortable even in winter – 'hot' is a relative term depending on what you're used to. The sensible thing to do on a 'hot' day is to avoid the sun between mid-morning and mid-afternoon. Infants and elderly people are most at risk from heat exhaustion and heat stroke.

Water People who first arrive in a hot climate may not feel thirsty when they should; the body and 'thirst mechanism' often need a few days to adjust. The rule of thumb is that an active adult should drink at least 4L of water per day in hot weather, more when walking or cycling. Use the colour of your urine as a guide: if it's clear you're probably drinking enough but if it's dark you need to drink more (vitamin B supplements turn urine bright yellow, which is not the same and unfortunately masks this useful indicator). Remember that body moisture will evaporate in the dry desert air with no indication that you're sweating.

Tap water is generally safe to drink in the settled parts of Australia, including most outback towns, but in remote areas it may be unfit for human consumption – check with the locals before gulping it down. Bore water (ie, water pumped out of the ground) is often OK even if it tastes unpleasant, but children's stomachs in particular may have trouble coping with the high mineral content. (Note how soap often won't lather in outback showers.) There's nothing you can do short of actually distilling it – or carrying your own supply of drinking water. Outback residents normally save rainwater for drinking and use bore water for other purposes.

Be careful of drinking from streams and waterholes as they may be polluted by humans or animals. The surest way to disinfect water is to boil it – vigorous boiling for ten minutes should be satisfactory (it takes that long to kill giardia). On the other hand, there may be a risk of an upset stomach attached to drinking surface water but in an emergency this is preferable to dying of thirst.

Consider purchasing a water filter for a long trip. There are two main kinds of filter. Total filters take out all parasites, bacteria and viruses and make water safe to drink. They're often expensive, but they can be more cost effective than buying bottled water. Simple filters (which can even be a nylon mesh bag) take out dirt and larger foreign bodies from the water so that chemical solutions work much more effectively – if water is dirty, chemical solutions may not work at all. It's very important when buying a filter to read the specifications, so that you know exactly what it removes from the water and what it doesn't.

Simple filtering will not remove all dangerous organisms, so if you cannot boil water it should be treated chemically. Chlorine tablets will kill many pathogens, but not some parasites like giardia and amoebic cysts. Iodine is more effective in purifying water and is available in tablet form. Follow the directions carefully and remember that too much iodine can be harmful. Cordial or flavoured powder will disguise the taste of treated water and is a good idea if you're travelling with children.

Salt Sweating will also lead to a loss of salt. Excessive salt loss manifests itself in headaches, dizziness and muscle cramps. Salt tablets are not a preventative, but will quickly restore the balance if you show symptoms of salt loss. Add salt to your food to prevent this happening – a teaspoon a day should normally be enough in hot climates. If you're on a low-salt diet, check with your physician before you leave.

Food If you don't vary your diet, travel hard and fast and therefore miss meals, or simply lose your appetite, you can soon start to lose weight and place your health at risk, just as you would at home.

If you rely on fast foods dished out by roadhouses and takeaways, you'll get plenty of fats and carbohydrates but little else. Remember that overcooked food loses much of its nutritional value. If your diet isn't well balanced, it's a good idea to take vitamin and iron pills. Fresh fruit and vegetables are a good source of vitamins, provided they're available of course.

Health Problems

Prickly Heat Prickly heat is an itchy rash caused by excessive perspiration trapped under the skin. It usually strikes people who have just arrived in a hot climate and whose pores have not yet opened sufficiently to cope with greater sweating. Keeping cool, bathing often, using a mild talcum powder or even resorting to air-conditioning may help until you acclimatise.

Heat Exhaustion Dehydration or salt deficiency can cause heat exhaustion. Take time to acclimatise to high temperatures and make sure you do drink lots of (non-alcoholic) liquids – good old water is best. Think of your salt level too.

Anhidrotic heat exhaustion, caused by an inability to sweat, is quite rare. Unlike the other forms of heat exhaustion it is likely to strike people who have been in a hot climate for some time, rather than newcomers.

Heatstroke This serious, and sometimes fatal, condition occurs when the body's heat-regulating mechanism breaks down and the body temperature rises to dangerous levels. Long, continuous periods of exposure to high temperatures can leave you vulnerable to heatstroke. You should avoid excessive alcohol or strenuous activity when you first arrive in a hot climate.

The symptoms are feeling unwell, not sweating very much or at all and a high body temperature (39°C to 41°C or 102°F to 106°F). When sweating has ceased, the skin becomes flushed and red. Severe, throbbing headaches and lack of coordination will also occur, and the sufferer may become confused or aggressive. Eventually the victim will become delirious or convulse. Hospitalisation is essential, but meanwhile get patients out of the sun, remove their clothing, cover them with a wet sheet or towel and fan them continually. Give fluids if they are conscious.

Fungal Infections Hot-weather fungal infections are most likely to occur on the scalp, between the toes or fingers (athlete's foot), in the groin (jock itch or crotch rot) and on the body (ringworm). You get ringworm (a fungal infection, not a worm) from infected animals or from other people, for instance by walking on damp shower floors.

To prevent fungal infections, wear loose, comfortable clothes, avoid artificial fibres, wash frequently and dry carefully. Always wear plastic sandals or thongs in showers you can't completely trust. If you do get an infection, wash the infected area daily with a disinfectant or medicated soap and water, and rinse and dry well. Apply an antifungal powder like Tolnaftate. Try to expose the infected area to air or sunlight as much as possible, wash all towels and underwear in hot water, change them often and let them dry in the sun.

Motion Sickness Eating lightly before and during a trip will reduce the chances of motion sickness. If you are prone to motion sickness, try to find a place that minimises disturbance – near the wing in aircraft, near the centre in cars and buses. Fresh air and looking at a steady reference point like the horizon usually help, whereas reading and cigarette smoke don't. Pharmaceutical medications, which can cause drowsiness, have to be taken before the trip commences; when you're feeling sick it's too late. Ginger (available in capsule form) and peppermint (including mint-flavoured sweets) are natural preventatives.

Diarrhoea Major causes of diarrhoea (sometimes referred to as 'gastro' or 'the trots') are drinking mineralised bore water, eating contaminated food and handling contaminated objects (eg, money, door handles). Some 'gastro' disorders, such as shigella and giardiasis, are endemic in parts of the outback including Alice Springs and many Aboriginal communities. Hepatitis A (another locally endemic virus) can also be transferred from person to person on money, door handles and food as well as in water.

Small children are most at risk from diarrhoea and Hepatitis A – with the former they can quickly become dehydrated if fluids are not kept up. The best prevention is to be strict about personal hygiene: Always wash your hands (or use moistened tissues) after going to the toilet and before preparing meals or eating. Wash all fruit and vegetables as well, and try to keep the flies off your food – you never know where they've been!

Ross River Fever This debilitating virus is spread by mosquitoes, mainly across northern Australia but also in the south. While not life-threatening, its effects are comparable to chronic fatigue syndrome and can (rarely) last several years. It's best to avoid being bitten by mosquitoes: Wear loose-fitting, light-coloured long pants and long-sleeved shirts and apply repellent to exposed skin and clothing edges.

Worms These parasites are common in outback animals. The steak that you buy at the butcher's or get served in the roadhouse will be perfectly safe, but kangaroo or wild goat that hasn't been checked by the proper authorities can be risky, especially if undercooked. Worms may also be present on unwashed vegetables, and you can pick them up through your skin by walking in bare feet, particularly in the north.

Infestations may not show up for some time, and though they are generally not serious, if left untreated they can cause severe health problems. A stool test is necessary to pinpoint the problem, and medication is often available over the counter.

Sexually Transmitted Diseases The outback is generally a bastion of sexual conservatism, but there's a lot of alcohol about and a lot of short-term residents who don't mind partying on. Take care. Abstinence is the only 100% preventative, but using condoms is also effective (though not against pubic lice, also known as crabs).

Gonorrhoea and syphilis are the most common of these diseases; sores, blisters or rashes around the genitals, discharges or pain when urinating are common symptoms. Symptoms may be less marked or not observed at all in women. Syphilis symptoms eventually disappear completely but the disease continues and can cause severe problems in later years. The treatment of gonorrhoea and syphilis is by antibiotics.

Unfortunately there is no cure for herpes and there is also currently no cure for HIV/AIDS. Remember that it is impossible to detect the HIV-positive status of any person without a blood test.

There are numerous other sexually transmitted diseases, for most of which effective treatment is available. If you suspect anything is wrong, go to the nearest public hospital or medical clinic.

Cuts & Scratches Skin punctures can easily become infected in hot climates and may be difficult to heal. Treat cuts with an antiseptic solution such as povidone-iodine. Where possible, avoid bandages and Band-aids, which can keep wounds wet. Coral cuts are notoriously slow to heal, as the coral injects a weak venom into the wound.

Snakebite For first-aid information, see Snakes in the Fauna section of the Facts about the Outback chapter.

Women's Health

Poor diet and even contraceptive pills can lead to vaginal infections when travelling in hot climates. Maintaining good personal hygiene, and wearing skirts or loose-fitting trousers and cotton underwear will help to prevent infections.

Yeast infections (thrush), characterised by a rash, itch and discharge, can be treated with a vinegar or even lemon-juice douche or with yogurt. Nystatin, miconazole or clotrimazole pessaries or vaginal cream are the usual treatment.

Some women experience irregular periods when travelling because of the upset in routine. Don't forget to take time zones into account if you're on the pill. If you run into intestinal problems, the pill may not be absorbed. Ask your physician about these matters before you go.

WOMEN TRAVELLERS

Travelling in outback Australia is generally safe for women, but avoid walking alone late at night in any of the major cities and towns – particularly near pubs and clubs. Unfortunately, scores of Aussie blokes still slip into sexual-harassment mode in the company of women, especially if they've had a few beers. It's reasonably true to say that the further you move from the big cities, the more macho and less enlightened your average Aussie male is going to be about women's issues. On the other hand, the un-enlightened outback male will show great respect for creative swearing, a technique used to great effect by tough outback women.

Hitching is not recommended for solo women, and even pairs must exercise care at all times (see Hitching in the Getting Around chapter).

DISABLED TRAVELLERS

Generally speaking, disabled travellers are poorly catered for in the outback, although most towns, modern roadhouses and major parks have facilities designed for wheelchair access. However, these days there is a more enlightened appreciation of the needs of disabled travellers and the situation is improving all the time.

You're Never Too Old

Many first-time visitors to the outback are surprised by the high proportion of middle-aged and elderly couples exploring the most unlikely places by 4WD. The average age in many camp sites, no matter how remote, would have to be well over 50.

Val and Bill Griffiths, 67 and 73 years respectively, are good examples of this hardy breed. A farming couple from Mansfield in central Victoria, they began to travel the outback more than 20 years ago when their kids left home, and since then they've spent an average of two months every year doing so.

They get around in the 12-year-old Toyota HJ tray truck that Bill uses 'all the time' on the farm. The only modifications are a turbo ('because we thought it would help us get over the sand hills'), an HF radio (though 'it's not the friendly banter it used to be; sat-phones are taking over'), an extra 160-litre fuel tank and a water tank.

On their travels they used to camp in a tent, but the last 12 years they've opted for a fold-out camping unit with kitchen and other conveniences that bolts on top of the tray. It has extendable legs so they can drive the car out from underneath it, if required. They're now having a new one built to order because they want an inner-spring mattress.

Two thick planks that slide under the tray are called into service when they get stuck – 'we often use them.' They also carry a hand winch which they haven't used at all so far.

They've done some remarkable trips over the years, including the Canning (three times), all the Bomb Roads, Cape York, the Gulf Road (several times), the Kimberley, the Gunbarrel ('a real denture-rougher'), and on it goes.

Their favourite areas? Val loves the Kimberley and can't get enough of it. Bill agrees, 'though I do love the desert; Ruddall River is rather nice.'

Sometimes they travel alone, sometimes with others, and as Bill says, 'We're never lonely. The world is where you happen to be.'

There are a few organisations that can supply advice to disabled travellers, but most of them only operate within a single state. The exception is Nican (☎ 1800 806 769, fax 02-6285 3714, W www.nican .com.au) at 4/2 Phipps Close, Deakin, ACT 2600, which can help with advice on most matters and can put you in touch with state organisations, specialist travel agents, wheelchair and equipment hire, and access guides.

USEFUL ORGANISATIONS
Automobile Associations

Australia's national Australian Automobile Association exists mainly as an umbrella for the various state associations and to maintain international links. The day-to-day operations are handled by the state organisations, which provide breakdown service, literature, excellent maps and detailed guides to accommodation. The material they produce is usually of a very high standard, and relatively cheap or often free to members. The state organisations have reciprocal arrangements with each other and similar organisations overseas and provide the same services to each other's members. You'll need to bring proof of membership with you and, if from overseas, a letter of introduction.

The most useful state offices are:

New South Wales
National Roads and Motorists Association (NRMA, ☎ 02-9292 9222, fax 9292 8472, W www.nrma.com.au) 388 George St, Sydney, NSW 2000

Northern Territory
Automobile Association of the Northern Territory (AANT; ☎ 08-8981 3837, fax 8941 2965) 79–81 Smith St, Darwin, NT 0800

Queensland
Royal Automobile Club of Queensland (RACQ; ☎ 07-3361 2444, fax 3257 1863, W www.racq.com.au) 300 St Pauls Terrace, Fortitude Valley, Qld 4006

South Australia
Royal Automobile Association of South Australia (RAA; ☎ 08-8202 4500, fax 8202 4520, W www.raa.net) 41 Hindmarsh Square, Adelaide, SA 5000

Western Australia
Royal Automobile Club of Western Australia (RACWA; ☎ 08-9421 4444, fax 9221 2708, W www.racwa.com.au) Adelaide Terrace, Perth, WA 6000

4WD Organisations

Each state has an umbrella organisation for its various 4WD clubs. They can provide information on many 4WD tracks, including conditions and permit requirements, and will usually be happy to answer specific queries on outback touring. And of course, they can put you in touch with any 4WD clubs you want to contact.

These umbrella groups are run by volunteers and the telephone contacts given below are private numbers, so they're liable to change; also, please remember to ring at a decent time:

National
Australian National Four Wheel Drive Council (W www.anfwdc.asn.au) GPO Box 79, Canberra, ACT 2601

New South Wales
Recreational 4WD Clubs Association of NSW & ACT (☎ 1800 646 630, W www.rfwdca.asn.au) PO Box 1371, Parramatta, NSW 2124

Northern Territory
NT Association of 4WD Clubs (☎ 08-8927 1464) PO Box 37476, Winnellie, NT 0820

Queensland
Queensland Association of 4WD Clubs (☎ 07-3277 6071, W www.qafwdc.com.au) PO Box 174, Brisbane Markets, Qld 4106

South Australia
South Australian Association of 4WD Clubs (☎ 08-8359 0627, W www.saafwdc.asn.au) PO Box 178, Enfield Plaza, SA 5085

Tasmania
Tasmanian Recreational Vehicles Association (☎ 03-6244 5290, W www.users .bigpond.com/secretary.trva/) PO Box 662, Glenorchy, Tas 7010

Victoria
Victoria Association of Four Wheel Drive Clubs (☎ 03-9857 5209, W www.vafwdc.org.au) PO Box 596, North Balwyn, Vic 3104

Western Australia
Western Australian Association of 4WD
Clubs (☎ 08-9243 6839,
W www.pps.net.au/wa4wd)
PO Box 6029, East Perth, WA 6892

National Parks Organisations

Environment Australia (☎ 02-6274 2111, W www.ea.gov.au, GPO Box 787, Canberra 2601) at the John Gorton Bldg, King Edward Terrace, is the Commonwealth body responsible for Kakadu and Uluru-Kata Tjuta National Parks, some offshore areas such as the Cocos (Keeling), Christmas and Norfolk Islands, and also international conservation issues such as whaling.

The individual national park organisations in each state are not nationally run. They can be hidden away in their capital-city locations, but if you search them out they have excellent literature and maps on the parks. In the bush, national park offices are much more visible and are usually the best places for local information. The state offices for outback parks are:

New South Wales
National Parks & Wildlife Service
(☎ 02-9585 6444, W www.npws.nsw.gov.au)
43 Bridge St, Hurstville, NSW 2220

Northern Territory
Parks and Wildlife Commission of the
Northern Territory (☎ 08-8999 5511,
W www.nt.gov.au/paw, PO Box 496,
Palmerston, NT 0830)
Cnr Knuckey & Mitchell Sts, Darwin
CATIA office (☎ 08-8951 8211)
Gregory Tce, Alice Springs, NT 0870

Queensland
Queensland Parks and Wildlife Service
(QPWS) (☎ 07-3227 8186,
W www.env.qld.gov.au/environment/park/)
160 Ann St, Brisbane, Qld 4000

South Australia
Parks and Wildlife SA (☎ 08-8204 1910,
W www.sa.gov.au/environment/parks/, GPO
Box 1047, Adelaide, SA 5001)
77 Grenfell St, Adelaide, SA 5000

Western Australia
Department of Conservation and Land
Management (☎ 08-9334 0333,
1800 199 287, W www.calm.wa.gov.au)
50 Hayman Rd, Como, WA 6152

Australian Conservation Foundation

The largest nongovernmental organisation involved in conservation is the Australian Conservation Foundation (ACF; ☎ 03-9416 1166, fax 94160767, W www.acfonline.org. au) at 340 Gore St, Fitzroy, Vic 3065. It covers a wide range of issues, including the greenhouse effect and depletion of the ozone layer, the negative effects of logging, the preservation of rainforests, and the problems of land degradation. It frequently works in conjunction with the Wilderness Society and other conservation groups.

Wilderness Society

The Wilderness Society (☎ 03-6234 9799, fax 6224 1497, W www.wilderness.org.au) at 130 Davey St, Hobart, Tas 7000, was formed by conservationists who were determined to prevent the damming of the Franklin River in south-western Tasmania. This was one of Australia's first major conservation confrontations. In 1983, the High Court decided against the proposed dam.

The Wilderness Society is involved in issues such as forest management and preventing logging of old-growth forests throughout Australia. All its income is derived from memberships, donations and merchandising – there are Wilderness Society shops in most states.

Conservation Volunteers Australia

This nonpolitical, nonprofit group organises practical conservation projects for volunteers (including travellers) to take part in, such as tree planting, track construction and flora and fauna surveys. It's an excellent way to get involved with the conservation movement and, at the same time, visit some interesting areas. Past volunteers have found themselves working in outback places such as Finke Gorge, the MacDonnell Ranges, Kakadu and Broken Hill.

Projects are called Conservation Experience and typically last two, four or six weeks. Food, accommodation and transport are supplied in return for a contribution of $23 a night to help cover costs.

There are offices in every state and territory. For details, contact the head office (☎ 03-5333 1483 or ☎ 1800 032 501, **W** www.conservationvolunteers.com.au) at PO Box 423, Ballarat, Vic 3353.

WWOOF

There are about 1200 WWOOF (Willing Workers on Organic Farms) associates in Australia, although only a few qualify as 'outback'. The idea is that you do a few hours' work each day on a farm or cottage business in return for bed and board, often in the family home.

As the name says, the farms are supposed to be organic but that isn't always so – some places aren't even farms: you might help out at a pottery or do the books at a seed wholesaler. Whether participants in the scheme have a farm or just a vegetable patch, most are concerned to some extent with alternative lifestyles.

To join WWOOF (☎ 03-5155 0218, fax 5155 0342, **W** www.wwoof.com.au), send $45/50 for singles/couples to WWOOF, Mt Murrindal Co-op, Buchan, Vic 3885. They send a membership number and booklet listing WWOOF places across Australia.

DANGERS & ANNOYANCES

Australia is free of carnivorous wild mammals that tear you to shreds at night, but it does have more than its share of other potentially dangerous creatures such as crocodiles, snakes and poisonous spiders, and more annoying flies than you ever thought possible. See the Fauna section in the Facts about the Outback chapter for more about these hazards.

Other dangers include the climate and the extreme isolation if something goes wrong in a remote area. Plan your outback trips carefully. Beware of abandoned shafts in old mining areas – the holes are often very deep and can be difficult to see.

On the Road

Collisions with cattle, sheep, kangaroos and emus are all too common (as the many carcasses by the side of the road will attest) but there's a simple solution: don't drive at night. Unfortunately, other drivers are even more dangerous, particularly those who drink – which happens a lot in the outback. See the Getting Around chapter for more on driving hazards.

Bushfires

Bushfires happen every year in Australia. Don't be the idiot who starts one. In hot, dry, windy weather, be extremely careful with any naked flame – no cigarette butts out of car windows, please. On a Total Fire Ban Day (listen to the radio or watch the billboards along the roads), it's forbidden even to use a camping stove in the open. The locals will not be amused if they catch you breaking this particular law; they'll happily dob you in and the penalties are severe.

If you're unfortunate enough to find yourself driving through a bushfire, stay inside your car and try to park off the road in an open space, away from trees, until the danger has passed. Lie on the floor under the dashboard, covering yourself with a wool blanket if possible. The fire front should pass quickly. A diesel-engine vehicle is safer in this regard than a petrol one.

Bushwalkers should take local advice before setting out. On a Total Fire Ban Day, don't go – delay your trip until the weather

CLINT CURÉ

Not all of Australia's dangerous creatures will knock on your door!

has changed. Chances are that it will be so unpleasantly hot and windy, you'll be better off anyway in an air-conditioned pub sipping a cool beer.

If you're walking in the bush and you see smoke, even at a distance, take it seriously. Bushfires move very quickly and change direction with the wind. Go to the nearest open space, downhill if possible. A forested ridge is the most dangerous place to be. Eucalypts burn easily because of their high content of volatile oil and may literally explode into flames. Heat radiation is a big killer, so cover yourself up, preferably in a less flammable material such as wool.

Fire is a part of nature, and many Australian plants have come to rely on it for reproduction. In outback areas in particular, the authorities often leave bushfires to burn themselves out if there's no danger to humans. For more about the role of fire in savanna country – the landscapes of open trees and grasses that dominate so much of the continent, especially the top third – see W http://savanna.ntu.edu.au.

EMERGENCY

In the case of a life-threatening situation, dial ☎ 000. This call is free from any phone and the operator will connect you with either the police, ambulance or fire brigade. To dial any of these services direct, check the inside front cover of the local telephone book.

For other telephone crisis and personal counselling services (such as for sexual assault, poisons information or alcohol and drug problems), check the front pages of the local phone book.

If you have CB or HF radio or an EPIRB, see Radio Communications in Post & Communications earlier in this chapter.

SURVIVAL

The key to safe travel anywhere is preparation, and the only way you can be prepared is to research your destination – see the earlier Planning section. If you're unsure, particularly if you're heading off the beaten track, seek expert advice from local police or park rangers, you may not like what they say but you'd be foolish to ignore it.

There are plenty of books on bushcraft and survival, and it's worth buying one in advance and reading it; you never know when one of those neat little tricks may save your life. See the earlier Books and Maps sections.

There are a number of general survival tips to remember regardless of whether you're driving or bushwalking – and despite the outback's fierce reputation, there's plenty of excellent walking on offer.

Water

See the earlier Health section about your water needs and sources. The main thing is to carry sufficient water to get you through to the next supply point and still have plenty in reserve for emergencies; don't forget additional supplies for washing purposes and for refilling the vehicle's radiator. If you're planning a trip, allow 4L to 5L drinking water per day per person. On most tracks, around 20L per person is a sensible amount to carry if you want to be well prepared – provided you top it up when you can and store it in more than one container. Food is less important: The space might better be allocated to an extra spare tyre. You can survive for days without food but only hours without water.

If your vehicle breaks down and you run out of water, use the water in your radiator only if it's free of chemical additives. When walking, it's wise to carry at least one full canteen per person even on a short walk – you never know when you might need it. Tough, army-style canteens are ideal; flimsy plastic bottles such as fruit-juice containers are not.

Register Your Intentions

In the remote outback you should always let a responsible person know details of your proposed activities so that the police will know where to look for you. Generally the best person is someone who cares – parents, siblings and other close acquaintances. In the past, people used to check in with the police at the start and end of outback tracks, but the outback is so heavily travelled these days and so many people forget to check in at the end that this is no longer the reliable insurance it used to be. Obviously you'd register your intentions with a ranger when doing a serious walk in a national park.

Leave a map showing where you're going, how you're getting there and how long you expect to take. Always check in as arranged, otherwise you may spark an unnecessary search and rescue operation – in which case you'll be expected to pay the costs.

Safety in Numbers

It's better to travel in company, firstly for sharing experiences and secondly for safety. The minimum recommended number when bushwalking is three people: If someone is hurt, one person can stay to assist while the other goes for help. The silliest thing to do is to go bushwalking by yourself and not tell anyone your plans.

Getting Lost or Breaking Down

The best way to avoid getting lost is to have current, large-scale maps of the area and to keep track of where you are at all times. A hand-held GPS (Global Positioning System) unit, costing from $150 to $400, is a great accessory – some would say essential. When walking in unfamiliar terrain, always take note of the landmarks around you – including those behind in case you want to return by the same route – and the direction of the sun. Use a compass, or in an emergency, point the hour hand of your watch at the sun, and roughly halfway between the hour hand and 12 will be north (though if you're north of the tropic of Capricorn in summer, it could be south).

It's a good idea to keep a detailed running log when driving on remote tracks. Simply note each point of interest – an intersection, turn-off, windmill, gate or any obvious feature – and its distance from your starting point. Running logs enable you to backtrack with confidence and can also be used to advise fellow travellers.

If you do get hopelessly lost or the vehicle breaks down beyond repair it's essential not to panic, as this will more than likely make things worse. You will have told someone where you're going so the best idea is to sit

quietly in the shade and conserve water supplies until the search party arrives. If you call for help on the radio, remember that the most protracted searches are often for people who confidently claim to be where they are not; only report an approximate position of which you can be absolutely sure.

To assist aerial searchers, you can lay out a large 'V' (the recognised ground-to-air visual signal for requiring help) in an open area using any material of contrasting colour to the ground. As a general rule, *never* leave your vehicle and wander off to seek help: The car is much larger than you and will more easily be seen by searchers. It also provides shelter and other means of survival, though this may not be terribly obvious if you're impatient.

BUSINESS HOURS

Most outback shops close at 5pm or 6pm weekdays, and either noon or 5pm on Saturday, and some may be closed for lunch. In most larger centres Sunday trading is catching on, particularly where tourism is an important industry. In many larger towns there are one or two late-shopping nights – usually Thursday and/or Friday – when the doors stay open until 9pm or 9.30pm. In major centres, supermarkets are generally open till at least 8pm and sometimes 24 hours, but not in more remote areas.

Banks are generally open from 9.30am to 4pm Monday to Thursday, and until 5pm on Friday. Along major roads, service stations may stay open till 10pm or even 24 hours, but don't count on it.

PUBLIC HOLIDAYS

The Christmas holiday period is part of the long summer school vacation, but as this is the outback's slow season for tourism you're unlikely to be bothered by booked-out accommodation and long queues. There are three other, shorter school-holiday periods during the year but they vary by a week or two from state to state, falling from early to mid-April, late June to mid-July, and late September to early October. Generally, by far the outback's busiest tourist season is the mid-year break.

Like school holidays, public holidays vary quite a bit from state to state. The following are the main national and state public holidays:

New Year's Day 1 January
Australia Day 26 January
Labour Day (Vic) second Monday in March
Labour Day (WA) first Monday in March
Easter Good Friday to Easter Monday inclusive
Anzac Day 25 April
Labour Day (Qld) first Monday in May
May Day (NT) first Monday in May
Adelaide Cup (SA) third Monday in May
Foundation Day (WA) first Monday in June
Queen's Birthday (except WA) second Monday in June
Bank Holiday (NSW) first Monday in August
Picnic Day (NT) first Monday in August
Queen's Birthday (WA) last Monday in September
Labour Day (NSW, ACT & SA) first Monday in October
Melbourne Cup (Vic) first Tuesday in November
Proclamation Day (SA) last Tuesday in December
Christmas Day 25 December
Boxing Day 26 December

SPECIAL EVENTS

The year 2002 is being promoted as the Year of the Outback by an organisation of enthusiasts based in Queensland, and it's likely to see more than its usual share of events and festivities. The Outback 2002 organisation (☎ 07-3837 0202, Ⓦ www.out back2002.com) can provide a monthly listing of events and information about the relevant organisers.

Some of the most enjoyable Australian festivals are, naturally, the ones that are most typically Australian – like the outback rodeos, race meetings and bachelor-and-spinster balls, which draw together bush folk from hundreds of kilometres around including more than a few eccentric characters.

The following is just a brief overview of some of the more famous 'cultural' events in the outback. Check the track descriptions later in this book for more events, and contact the relevant state tourist authorities for exact dates, which tend to vary a bit from year to year.

Easter (March/April)
Great Goat Race (NSW) This is an annual wild-goat race through the main street of Lightning Ridge in outback New South Wales.

May
Outback Muster (Qld) Held at the Stockman's Hall of Fame in Longreach, this unusual three-day festival features a variety of events related to droving.

June
Barunga Wugularr Sports & Cultural Festival (NT) About 40 Aboriginal communities descend on Barunga, 80km south-east of Katherine, for this wonderful festival with sporting contests, traditional dancing, bush tucker and art and craft.
Blackrock Stakes (WA) This is a 122km race from Whim Creek to Port Hedland, in which contestants (teams or solo) push wheelbarrows weighed down with iron ore.
Darwin Beer Can Regatta (NT) Held over the Queen's Birthday weekend (the second weekend in June), this rowdy 'boat' race on Mindil Beach involves sailing vessels made of beer (or soft-drink) cans, carrying names like 'Tipsy Moth' and 'Cantiki'. Other events include 'ladies thong throwing' and 'iron person' races.
Merrepen Arts Festival (NT) Daly River's one-day event exhibits art, crafts and dance of the regional Aboriginal communities.

July
Beanie Festival (NT) An Alice Springs festival with cult status, this event was formed to honour the woolly beanie; there are prizes, exhibitions and workshops.
Boulia Desert Sands (Qld) This is a serious camel race (total prize money over $100,000), part of five races in Queensland throughout July and August.
Cairns Show (Qld) The highlights here are pig racing, including a steeplechase; there are also vertical races up a high pole – the world record is 10 seconds to climb up 25m.
Darwin to Bali Yacht Race (NT) An annual high-seas highlight, this race attracts keen sailors from around Australia and the world.
NT Royal Shows There are agricultural shows in Alice Springs (first Friday), Tennant Creek (second Friday), Katherine (third Friday) and Darwin (fourth Friday).

August
Cunnamulla Festival (Qld) This annual event centres around lizard races, although usually

someone has to chase them around to get them to participate.

Darwin Rodeo (NT) Whips crack as international teams compete in numerous events.

Festival of Darwin (NT) This festival reflects the city's large Asian and Aboriginal populations with a diverse program of arts and activities.

Flying Fox Festival (NT) Katherine's premier arts and cultural event kicks off with a parade, followed by concerts, exhibitions and festivities.

Gunbalanya (Oenpelli) Open Day (NT) Held on the 2nd Saturday in August, this day gives people a chance to experience Aboriginal art and culture within Arnhem Land.

Mt Isa Rodeo (Qld) This is three days of rodeo events and street parties.

Shinju Matsuri or Festival of the Pearl (WA) Held in the old pearling port of Broome during the week of the full moon, this great festival celebrates the town's Asian heritage.

Yuendumu Festival (NT) Aboriginal people from the central and western desert region meet in Yuendumu, northwest of Alice Springs, over a long weekend in early August for a mix of traditional and modern sporting and cultural events.

September

Birdsville Cup (Qld) The tiny town of Birdsville hosts the country's premier outback horse-racing event on the first weekend in September.

Henley-on-Todd Regatta (NT) This is a series of races for leg-powered bottomless boats on Alice Springs' (usually) dry Todd River.

Winton Outback Festival (Qld) This festival includes a dunny (toilet) derby: The dunnies are on wheels which makes it easier, but someone has to be inside sitting down.

October

Stompem Ground Festival (WA) Held in Broome, this is a month-long festival of Aboriginal culture and arts from the Kimberley.

ACTIVITIES

There are many great walks in the various national parks, where you can do bird-watching and other nature-based activities. Water isn't a feature of the arid zone, although there are plenty of swimming holes in its river systems. You can go snorkelling and scuba diving at a number of places around the coast such as on the Great Barrier Reef and Western Australia's Ningaloo Reef. Canoeing is a possibility on many tropical rivers.

In northern Queensland you can hire a horse and ride it through rainforests and sand dunes, and swim with it in the sea. Camel riding is available in many places – if you've done it in India or Egypt or you just fancy yourself as the explorer/outdoors type, then here's your chance.

You can cycle anywhere in the outback, although much of it is pretty boring when seen from a bike. For the well-prepared enthusiast there are long, challenging routes, and plenty of great day trips for the not-so-athletic. You can generally hire bikes in major tourist centres, such as Broome and Alice Springs. Most states have helpful bicycle societies with maps and useful tips and advice on outback cycling.

Windsurfing, paragliding, rafting, hot-air ballooning and hang-gliding are among the many other outdoor activities. For more information, see the Activities sections in the track descriptions in this book or contact any of the state tourist bureaus.

Two activities that draw many people to the outback are fossicking (hunting for gemstones and gold) and barramundi fishing (in the north). In fact, they're so popular that we'll deal with them separately.

Fossicking

The best places to fossick for gemstones are in areas where mountain-building has taken place. The rocks of such areas are often formed under conditions that are ideal for the development of large crystals.

Most important of these are pegmatites, which are the major hosts for a whole range of gemstones such as aquamarine, tourmaline, garnet, quartz and topaz. Pegmatites originate as molten, mineral-rich material that is injected into cracks in the earth's crust. Being more resistant to erosion they often form wall-like structures across the landscape.

Also important are rocks, particularly limestone, that have been chemically changed through coming into contact with an invading body of super-heated material – a process known as contact metamorphism. Rocks altered in this way are major hosts for many types of gems, including sapphire, ruby, aquamarine, garnet, epidote, sphene and zircon.

About 30% of Australia's land area consists of basins that have been filled with sediments, but with the notable exception of precious opal, these are poor in gemstones. Only about 15% has potential for fossickers and this lies in three interrupted zones that stretch roughly from north to south across the continent. The western zone includes the Kalgoorlie goldfields, the Pilbara and the Kimberley. The central zone runs from Kangaroo Island to Darwin and includes the northern Flinders Ranges, the Harts Range in central Australia and the Top End goldfields, while an offshoot covers the Broken Hill area. The eastern zone runs up the eastern highlands from Tasmania to Cape York.

Research A successful fossicking trip is usually dependent on good research. Without local information, an area's potential is best discovered in your armchair with large-scale geological maps, mines-department reports and any other literature you can find. The most popular areas are likely to be written about in the various fossicking guides available from mines departments and bookshops.

State-produced geological maps – the larger their scale the better – are essential as they show the types of surface rock and thus give a hint of the gems and minerals you may find there. They also show roads, homesteads, watercourses and the locations of old mines, prospecting areas and any interesting mineral occurrences. Make sure you get hold of the explanatory booklet that accompanies each map as this will contain additional information.

Fossicking Tools Successful fossicking doesn't require a trailerful of equipment, but you must have some basic tools. A minimum would include: a small spalling hammer or sledgehammer; a pick and shovel; a nest of aluminium sieves; a prospecting dish; a large basin or cut-down drum to wash gravel in; and a small crowbar. Most of these will earn their keep in other ways. If you can fit in a pry bar, a selection of rock

chisels, a magnifying glass and a gardening trowel, so much the better. A book on mineral identification is essential, of course.

Prospecting dishes come in a range of sizes and can be either metal or plastic; the best ones have a groove around the edge that is designed to catch heavy particles such as gold as material is washed out of the pan. A shiny metal pan should be blackened first so that the gold stands out – the easiest way to do this is turn it upside down on a smoky fire. You need water to use a pan effectively, but few outback gold deposits have a supply right next to them. This is where the cut-down drum or large basin comes in handy.

Sieves are essential when fossicking for gems in dirt or gravel. The most convenient ones are the small round aluminium sieves that can be fitted together to form a combination – three sieves of 12mm, 6mm and 3mm mesh fitted together are ideal for most purposes. Fossickers who are really serious and want to move a lot of material usually prefer a large wooden-framed sieve mounted on a tripod. The sieved material needs to be washed so that any gems will be easily seen.

Where to Look River deposits are good places as running water and gravity have already done the hard work of concentrating nature's treasures in one spot. Any situation that causes a drop in flow rate, hence deposition of heavier materials, should be checked. Rock bars often yield exciting finds as gold and gems, being heavy, move along the bottom during a flood and may become trapped in potholes or crevices in the bar. If necessary use your crowbar to gain access to crevices that should be cleaned out using your trowel and a brush. All material obtained should be either panned or sieved depending on whether it's gold or gems you're after.

The use of a prospecting dish is straightforward but requires some practice with ball bearings or steel shot to perfect the art. First, the dish must be submerged in water as it is water that helps concentrate the heavy particles on the bottom. Second, grasp the rim of the dish with both hands (one on either side) and tilt it slightly, the groove being downwards. Third, agitate the contents by gently shaking the dish sideways and back and forth so that the backwash carries the lighter material over the edge – don't be too vigorous or you'll lose the gold. As you progress you can sweep the larger stones out with your hand.

Eventually all that remains will be heavy particles, which you concentrate further by slowly rotating the dish so that the gold forms a tail. To remove the gold, simply moisten the end of a finger and press it on the specks, which you then transfer to a jar of water – just dip your finger in the water and the gold will drop off.

Digging and sieving around the base of suitable rock outcrops, particularly pegmatites, is worth trying. There are some outstanding areas of gem-yielding pegmatite in the outback, including the Pilbara region near Marble Bar, the Harts Range near Alice Springs and the northern Flinders Ranges.

Mine dumps that date from last century – or at least no later than the 1930s – are good sources of all kinds of secondary minerals, including gemstones. High costs and inefficient methods used during the early days often meant that only high-grade ore was worth mining.

Anything of poorer grade, including fine specimens, was usually thrown out with the waste, as were secondary minerals. A good example is the Harts Range mica field, where magnificent gems were tossed away because they had no monetary value. On the opal fields, precious opal with orange fire was out of favour late last century so the gougers threw most of it away.

The best way to fossick on old dumps is to either sieve material from untouched areas or drag down the sides with a rake. You can also find gemstones by closely examining the surface without necessarily disturbing it. This is best done soon after rain when the dust has been washed away leaving the gems readily visible.

Abandoned mines are dangerous. *Never* enter workings where the roofs are held up by old timbers or where there are signs of rock falls, and always stand well back from old shafts as your weight may trigger a collapse.

Mining Law Mining law differs between the states and territories but all have one thing in common: a fossicker must be in possession of a miner's right or fossicking permit to search for gems and minerals on crown (public) land. Permission to fossick on freehold land and mineral leases must usually be obtained from the owner or leaseholder. A miner's right may allow access to pastoral leases, but this should be checked with the relevant authority. Sadly, the actions of the thoughtless minority has brought the hobby into disrepute in many areas, and fossickers are no longer always welcome.

Information Contact these departments for information on mining laws, geological maps, reports and fossicking guides:

New South Wales
Department of Mineral Resources
(☎ 02-9901 8888, W www.minerals.nsw
.gov.au, PO Box 536, St Leonards, NSW 1590)
29–57 Christie St, St Leonards, NSW 2065

Northern Territory
Department of Mines & Energy
in Darwin (☎ 08-8999 5511,
W www.dme.nt.gov.au, PO Box 2901, Darwin,
NT 0801) Paspaley Centre Point, Smith St
Mall, Darwin, NT 0800
in Alice Springs (☎ 08-8951 5658)
Mineral House, 50 Todd St Mall, Alice
Springs, NT 0870

Queensland
Department of Natural Resources & Mines
(☎ 07-3237 1435, W www.nrm.qld.gov.au,
GPO Box 194, Brisbane, Qld 4001) QMEC
Building, 61 Mary St, Brisbane, Qld 4000

South Australia
**Primary Industries & Resources SA, Office
of Mineral & Energy Resources**
(☎ 08-8463 4154, W www.pir.sa.gov.au,
GPO Box 1671, Adelaide, SA 5001)
7th Floor, 101 Grenfell St, Adelaide, SA 5000

Western Australia
Department of Minerals & Energy
(☎ 08-9222 3333, W www.dme.wa.gov.au)
Minerals House, 100 Plain St,
East Perth, WA 6004

Barramundi Fishing

For many visitors to northern Australia, one of the primary motivations for getting off the beaten track is to find a waterhole where they can catch Australia's premier native sport fish, the barramundi. Sometimes it seems that every other 4WD you come across has a 'tinny' (aluminium dinghy) on the roof.

The 'barra' is highly prized mainly because of its great fighting qualities: once it takes a lure or fly, it fights like hell to be free. As you try to reel one in, chances are it will make some powerful runs, usually leaping clear of the water and shaking its head in an attempt to throw the hook. Even smaller fish (3kg to 4kg) can put up a decent fight, but when they are about 6kg or more you have a battle on your hands that can last several minutes.

The barramundi is also a prized table fish, although the taste of the flesh depends to some extent on where the fish is caught. Those caught in saltwater or tidal rivers generally have the sweetest flavour; those in landlocked waterways can have a muddy flavour and soft flesh if the water is murky.

Naturally, everyone has their own theory as to where, when and how barramundi are most likely to be caught. The fish is found throughout coastal and riverine waters of the Kimberley, Top End, Gulf Country and Cape York. The best time to catch them is just after the Wet, ie, from around late March to the end of May. At this time the rivers are receding and the fish tend to gather in freshwater creeks where there is plenty of food. The best method is to cast a lure around snags (eg, fallen trees) or places where food might be concentrated, such as creek junctions or channels below waterfalls.

The Dry, from June to September, isn't the best season for barra, but many roads and tracks are impassable at other times are open, and so the chances of reaching a good spot are much enhanced. Trolling close to banks, snags or rock bars with lures is best at this time as the barra tend to stay deep and are relatively inactive as the water is cool.

The build-up to the Wet, from October to late December, is another good fishing time. The water temperature is on the rise and

there are occasional storms, so the fish are more active. Coastal inlets and tidal rivers offer the best fishing at this time. Trolling lures is the best method, although live bait also gets good results.

During the Wet, from January to March, fishing is generally done from boats as many tracks and roads are flooded, making access by vehicle difficult. Casting lures into floodwater run-off or channels is the best method, but even fishing from a river bank or into large channels that feed the rivers is often successful.

In tidal rivers the barra seem to strike most during the last hour or so of the ebb tide, particularly if this is late in the day. The same applies to saltwater areas, although the first couple of hours of the rising tide are also good.

Life Cycle of the Barramundi Early in the Wet, the female barras spawn around the river mouths. The high tides wash the eggs into the coastal swamps. At the end of the Wet, juvenile fish migrate up the rivers to the freshwater areas. By the end of the first year, a barra weighs around 0.5kg and measures around 30cm. Here they stay until they are three to four years old (3.5kg and 65cm).

Maturing males start to head downstream at the beginning of the Wet, and once in the open water, mature males undergo an amazing transformation as they turn into females and start spawning! By the time the fish are about seven years old they weigh upwards of 7kg (around 90cm), and fish of up to 20kg are not uncommon.

Bag & Size Limits It's in everyone's interest to follow the legal restrictions when fishing for barra. In the Northern Territory and Western Australia, the minimum size is 55cm, and the bag limit is five fish per person. Barramundi may not be retained on a tether line at any time. Certain areas of the Northern Territory are closed to fishing between 1 October and 31 January. In Queensland, the closed season lasts from 1 November to 31 January, the minimum size is 50cm and there's a bag limit of five fish. Western Australia has no closed season.

Good Fishing Practices Apart from following the legal restrictions, there are a number ways to enhance the quality of barra fishing for yourself and others who follow.

When releasing fish, try to remove the hook while the fish is still in the water; use a net to land the fish for 'dehooking' and weighing. Where it's necessary to handle the fish, grip it firmly by the lower jaw ensuring your fingers don't get under the gill cover.

To store fish in top condition, they should be killed and bled as soon as possible. Bleeding by cutting the gills or throat is the best method, and if the fish is then placed in ice water this reduces clotting and aids bleeding. Rapid cleaning also preserves the quality, and it's helpful if you can avoid cutting into the flesh surrounding the gut region or rupturing the intestines. Chill the cleaned fish as soon as possible, as this slows the rigor mortis process; when rigor mortis takes place rapidly, violent muscle contractions result in loss of natural juices and the flesh has a tendency to fall apart when filleted.

Clean and rinse fish in a container if possible; doing so in the river may attract crocodiles.

Information The following addresses can provide all the local rules and regulations relating to barramundi fishing:

Amateur Fishermen's Association of the Northern Territory (☎ 08-8945 6455, fax 8945 6055, W www.afant.com.au) PO Box 40694, Casuarina, NT 0011

Fisheries Department (☎ 08-9192 1121, W www.wa.gov.au/westfish/) Broome District Office, 401 Port Drive, Broome, WA 6725

Northern Fisheries Centre (☎ 07-4035 0100, fax 4035 1401, W www.dpi.qld.gov.au/fishweb/) PO Box 5396, Cairns, Qld 4870

Organised Fishing Trips Various commercial operators across northern Australia offer barra fishing trips, either day or safari style, and in fresh or salt water – there are over a dozen in Darwin alone. Some are mentioned in the track descriptions later in this book. Contact state and local tourist bureaus for details, and check the *Yellow Pages* for

those that aren't registered with the tourist offices (many aren't because they refuse to pay the sometimes hefty commissions).

WORK

In outback areas, the difficulty of attracting labour means that there's still a fair bit of casual work available and potential employers won't ask too many questions about your background.

The best prospects include bar work, waiting on tables or washing dishes, other domestic chores at roadhouses, and nanny work. Health professionals, chefs (or just plain cooks), and tradespersons are also in demand.

Still, short-term work is not as easy to find as it once was, even in the outback, and many travellers who have budgeted on finding work are forced to return home early.

To find out what's available and where, check the classified section of local papers. The various backpackers publications and hostels are other good information sources – some local employers even advertise on hostel notice boards. Also keep an eye out for notices posted in shop windows, and ask around at pubs and roadhouses.

ACCOMMODATION

A typical outback town of any importance will have a basic motel at around $45/55 for singles/doubles, an old hotel with rooms (shared bathrooms) at $25/35, and a caravan park with tent sites for $8 to $15 and on-site vans or cabins for $25 to $30 for two people. If the town is a major centre, it'll probably have several of each as well as backpacker accommodation. Even small towns have backpackers 'bunk-houses' these days, particularly if there's a fair degree of tourist traffic. If you're in a group, the rates for four or more people in a hotel or motel room are worth checking, and often there are larger 'family' rooms or units with two bedrooms.

It's worth remembering that accommodation prices vary depending on the time of year. 'High season' or peak holiday rates can be 75% or more above 'low season' rates, so it might be worthwhile timing your visit to coincide with quieter times. Unless stated otherwise, the prices given in this book are high season.

For accommodation listings, though not comprehensive, the state automobile clubs produce directories of hotels, motels, holiday flats, caravan parks and even some backpackers hostels in almost every city and town in the country. They're updated regularly so the prices are generally current and are available from the clubs for a nominal charge if you're a member. Alternatively, some state tourist offices put out guides to local accommodation, but again, they're usually not comprehensive. Local tourist offices often have the most comprehensive information.

Camping

The camping story is partly excellent and partly rather annoying. The excellent side is that you can camp almost anywhere out in the bush for free, or at national park camping grounds for a nominal fee, and stop at a roadhouse for a shower (they often cost only a couple of dollars). And if you prefer hot showers and laundry facilities while camping, there's a great number of caravan parks where – peak periods aside – you'll almost always find space.

One of the drawbacks is that commercial camping grounds are often intended more for caravans, and tent campers get little consideration in these places. Equally bad is the fact that camping grounds in most larger towns are well away from the centre. However, this is not too inconvenient as you will have your own transport in the outback anyway. Still, it's not all gloom: Caravan parks tend to be well kept and excellent value. Many also have on-site vans and cabins that you can rent for the night.

Bush Camping Camping in the bush, either where you choose or at designated spots in national parks and reserves, is for many people one of the highlights of their outback trip. Nights spent around a campfire under the stars are unforgettable (we're talking about million-star camping grounds here), especially in the outback.

You won't need a tent most of the time, though in the far north, where the mozzies can be ferocious even in winter, tents with plenty of insect-screened windows (fine mesh is best) are recommended. Elsewhere, a pleasant option is a stretcher (camp bed), as follows: Park your vehicle about 3m from a tree or bush; between the two, erect the stretcher and roll out your sleeping bag, string up a mosquito net and tuck it in under the bag. This way you'll sleep off the ground, safe from creeping insects, mosquitoes and early-morning flies, and you can still look at the blazing stars as you doze off.

There are some basic rules to camping in the wild (also see Social Conduct in the Facts about the Outback chapter):

- Most of the land in Australia belongs to someone, even if you haven't seen a house for 100km. They own it – it's their back yard – and you need permission before you can camp on it. In national parks and on Aboriginal land, you'll need permits. On public land, observe all the rules and regulations.
- Select your camping spot carefully. Start looking well before nightfall and choose a spot that makes you invisible from the road. You'll notice any number of vehicle tracks leading off the main road into the bush: Explore a few and see what you find.
- Keep to constructed vehicle tracks – never 'bush bash'. Avoid areas that are easily damaged, such as sand dunes.
- Some trees (for instance, river red gums and desert oaks) are notorious for dropping limbs. Don't camp under large branches.
- Ants live everywhere, and it's embarrassingly easy to set up camp on underground nests. Also beware of the wide variety of spiny seeds that can ruin your expensive tent groundsheet with pinprick holes – sweep the area first, and erect your tent on a layer of thick agricultural plastic sheeting.
- Carry out all the rubbish you take in, don't bury it there. Wild animals can dig it up and spread it everywhere.
- Observe fire restrictions and make sure your fire is safe – dig a trench and keep the area around the fire clean of flammable material.
- Don't chop down trees or pull branches off living trees to light your fire. Also leave dead timber that has become termite habitat (it won't burn well anyway). If the area is short of suitable dead timber, go back down the track a

little and collect some there. If that isn't possible, use a gas stove for cooking.

- Respect the wildlife. This also means observing crocodile warnings and keeping at least 50m away from suspect river banks.
- Don't camp right beside a water point as you'll scare off the stock and wildlife that normally drink there – stop at least 200m away.
- Don't camp close enough to a river or stream to pollute it. The minimum distance is 20m.
- Don't use soap or detergent in any stream, river, dam or any other water point.
- Use toilets where they are provided. If there isn't one, find a handy bush, dig a hole, do the job and then fill in the hole. If you're staying a few days, dig a trench (long, narrow and deep) and use that as a toilet pit for everyone, with each individual covering their waste with a little dirt. Burning used toilet paper is a good idea, but don't start a wildfire in the process. Bury all human waste well away from any watercourse.
- If you have small children, disposable nappies are anything but disposable and are becoming a major item of pollution in the bush. Carry used disposables away with you in a heavy-duty plastic bag on the roof rack (they won't smell much if rolled up tight).

If you're doing your own cooking, see Cooking in the Bush later in this chapter.

Youth Hostels
Australia has over 130 Youth Hostels Association (YHA) hostels, including associates. They are all over the country, including the major centres in the outback. YHA hostels provide basic accommodation, usually in small dormitories (bunk rooms), although in more and more are providing twin rooms. The nightly charges are usually between $12 and $20 for members, and most hostels also take non-YHA members for an extra $3 charge. There are no age limits – in fact, YHAs are actively campaigning to attract an older clientele.

A Hostelling International (HI) card (for visitors to Australia) costs $30 for 12 months. Australian residents can become full YHA members for $84 for two years. You can join at a state office or at any youth hostel.

To stay in a hostel you must have bed linen (sleeping bags are usually not allowed). If you don't have a sleeping sheet

they can be hired at many hostels (usually for $3), but if you're staying for more than a few nights, it's cheaper to have your own. YHA offices and some larger hostels sell the official YHA sheet bag.

Most hostels have 24-hour access, cooking facilities and a communal area where you can sit and talk or watch TV. There are usually laundry facilities and, in the larger hostels, useful notice boards and travel offices. Many have a maximum-stay period (usually five to seven days).

The annual *YHA Accommodation & Discounts Guide* booklet, available from all local YHA/HI offices and from some YHA offices overseas, lists all of the YHA hostels in Australia, with maps showing how to find them. It also lists the discounts (eg, bus transport, car hire, activities, accommodation) that their members are entitled to. The head office of the Australian YHA (☎ 02-9565 1699, fax 9565 1325, Ⓦ www.yha .com.au) is at 10 Mallett St, Camperdown, NSW 2050.

Not all of the hostels listed in the handbook are actually owned by the state YHAs. Some are 'associate hostels' that generally abide by hostel regulations but are owned by other organisations or individuals. You don't need to be a YHA member to stay at an associated hostel. Others are 'alternative accommodation' and do not totally fit the hostel blueprint. They might be motels that keep some hostel-style accommodation available for YHA members, caravan parks with an on-site van or two kept aside, or even places just like hostels but where the operators don't want to abide by all the hostel regulations.

Backpacker Hostels
The number of backpacker hostels in the outback has increased dramatically in recent years. Some are just run-down hotels where the owners have tried to fill empty rooms. Others are purpose-built and these are usually the best places in terms of facilities, although sometimes they're simply too big and lack any personalised service. The best places are often the smaller, more intimate hostels where the owner is also the manager.

A dorm bed at a backpacker hostel is typically $14 to $21 and twin/double rooms are $35 to $50 (usually without en suite), both with a small discount if you're a member of YHA or VIP and sometimes Nomads (see Hostel Organisations below). There are rarely single rooms, and if you're travelling solo but want a private room you'll almost always have to pay the double rate.

As with YHA hostels, the success of a hostel largely depends on the friendliness and willingness of the managers. Some places – in independent hostels only, since it never happens in YHAs – will only admit overseas guests. This happens mostly in cities when the hostel in question has had problems with locals using it as a dosshouse and bothering the guests. Hostels that discourage or ban Aussies say it's only a rowdy minority that makes trouble, but it's certainly annoying, patronising and discriminatory for genuine people trying to travel in their own country. If you're an Aussie and encounter this kind of reception, insist that you're genuinely travelling the country and aren't just looking for a cheap place to crash. Belonging to one of the backpacker hostel organisations (even waving around your guidebook!) might help.

Hostel Organisations There are a couple of backpacker hostel organisations that can be worth joining if you're not already a member of YHA.

VIP Backpacker Resorts (☎ 07-3395 6111, fax 3395 6222, W www.backpackers .com.au) at PO Box 600, Cannon Hill, Qld 4170, has 136 hostel franchisees in Australia and many more overseas. For $29 you'll receive 12 months' membership that entitles you to a $1 discount on accommodation and a 5% to 15% discount on other products such as air and bus transport, tours and activities. You can join at VIP hostels or the larger agencies dealing in backpacker travel. Contact the VIP office or join online.

Nomads World (☎ 1800 819 883, fax 08-8363 7968, W www.nomadsworld.com) at 43 The Parade West, Kent Town, SA 5067, is a growing organisation with around 46 franchisees in Australia and more in New Zealand and elsewhere. Membership ($25 for 12 months) likewise entitles you to a range of discounts. You can join at any participating hostel, backpacker travel agency, online or through the head office.

Pubs
For the budget traveller, hotels are the ones that serve beer – commonly known as pubs and invariably found in the town centre. They're often the social heart of town where you'll meet all the local eccentrics. If there's nothing that looks like a reception desk or counter, or if it doesn't appear to be staffed, just ask at the bar. A 'private hotel', as opposed to a 'licensed hotel', really is a hotel and doesn't serve alcohol. A 'guesthouse' is much the same as a 'private hotel'.

In historic places like the gold-mining towns, the pubs can be magnificent, heritage-listed buildings, with extravagant facades and entry halls. The rooms themselves may be old-fashioned though, with a long walk down the hall to the bathroom.

A bright word about hotels (guesthouses and private hotels, too) is that the breakfasts can be excellent – big and filling. If your hotel is still into serving a real breakfast (as opposed to simple cereal and bread) you'll probably feel it will last you until breakfast next morning. Generally, hotels will have rooms from around $25 or $35. When comparing prices, remember to check if breakfast is included.

Hotels & Motels
Real hotels, which you'll really only find in cities or places frequented by lots of tourists, are generally of the business or luxury variety where you get a comfortable, anonymous room in a multi-storey block. These usually have a pool, restaurant, room service and all the rest. We quote 'rack rates' throughout this book, but with discounts and special deals (weekends are usually cheaper than weekdays) you'll rarely pay such high rates.

For comfortable, mid-range accommodation all over the country, motels (or motor inns) are the best way to go. Roadhouses along outback roads generally fall into this category. Prices vary and there's rarely a cheaper rate for singles, so it's ideal for couples or groups of three. Most motels are modern, low-rise and have similar facilities (tea- and coffee-making, fridge, TV, air-con, en suite) but the price will usually indicate the standard. There are cheap motels that cost $40, but mostly you'll pay between $50 and $100 for a room.

Stations
The outback is a land of large sheep or cattle farms ('stations') and one of the best ways to come to grips with Australian life is to spend a few days on one. With unpredictable commodity prices and economic decline in some rural areas, tourism offers the hope of at least some income for farmers, at a time when many are being forced off the land. Some stations have switched almost entirely to tourism. Many offer accommodation where you can just sit back and watch how it's done, while others like to get you more actively involved in the day-to-day activities.

Accommodation can range from camp sites and dormitories to four-star bungalows, and prices are pretty reasonable. Many stations that take guests are listed in the track descriptions later in this book, and the state and local tourist offices can also advise you on what's available.

Other Possibilities
If you're staying somewhere for more than a few days, it might be worth sharing a holiday unit or serviced apartment with a few travelling companions. This sort of accommodation is generally only available in the major tourist centres like Alice Springs, Darwin and Broome.

For longer-term accommodation, the first place to look for houses to share or rooms to rent is the classified ad section of the local newspaper; notice boards in hostels, supermarkets and popular cafes are also good places to look.

FOOD
Australia's food has improved markedly since Italians, Greeks, Yugoslavs, Lebanese,

Vietnamese and many others arrived and brought their food with them. In the larger outback towns you can have Greek moussaka, Italian saltimbocca and pastas, German dumplings or maybe even Middle Eastern treats. The Chinese have been sweet and souring since the gold-rush days, while more recently Indian, Thai, Vietnamese and Malaysian restaurants have been making their way into the Australian interior.

The outback produces mighty steaks. They may be a bit tough (like the cattle) but they taste terrific and you'll seldom complain about the size. Fish like John Dory and the esteemed barramundi are often available far inland, as are yabbies – the delicious crayfish that often thrive in outback dams and waterholes.

Vegetarians will find their options limited, though most good roadhouses, cafes and pubs will have a vegetarian dish on the menu. Even an outback salad will usually be fresh – so long as it hasn't spent too long on the truck getting there.

Where to Eat
Eating options are obviously limited in the outback away from the major centres. Some towns will have at least a Chinese restaurant, and the larger towns may offer other styles too.

For a quick meal, roadhouses and local takeaway shops offer straightforward fish and chips, or hamburgers 'with the lot', and many different sandwiches that might be a more wholesome alternative. Roadhouse fare is often ordinary though some do a decent job. On the main trucking routes, check which roadhouse has the most trucks parked outside at mealtime: they might not serve the most imaginative food but they'll be good value.

Decent food can also be found in some pubs and the more upmarket hotels. In the busier outback centres, some places are almost restaurant-like, with serve-yourself salad tables where you can have as much salad, French bread and so on as you wish.

One catch with pub meals is that they usually operate fairly strict hours, more so in the outback than in the capital cities.

Preparing Your Own

Roadhouse and pub meals can get a bit boring (and expensive) after a while, so you may prefer to prepare your own food. Most outback supermarkets have a reasonable range of supplies, although the freshness and availability of fruit and vegetables may not be all you could wish for. This particularly applies to small, remote centres such as Birdsville and Oodnadatta.

For this reason, it's usually best to stock up on perishables such as tomatoes, cheese, meat and milk at every opportunity. You have to be super-cautious with fresh fish and poultry, but most other perishables can be kept for a few days in an Esky (portable ice box) if your vehicle doesn't have a fridge – ice is often available at service stations, general stores and pubs. Blocks of ice last longer than cubed ice.

Fruit-fly roadblocks can be a problem when travelling interstate. Some fruit-fly inspection stations are staffed but usually they consist of 'honesty pits' where you're expected to dump all fruit and vegetable matter. Stiff penalties apply for not obeying the rules.

Cooking in the Bush

It's nice to be able to cook your meal on the coals like a real bushie, but in reality this is not an option in many parts of the outback – particularly in conservation areas and popular bush camping grounds. In some areas open fires are prohibited during summer fire-danger periods. As well, fallen timber is a habitat for many wildlife species (eg, reptiles and insects). For these reasons it's best to plan on cooking most of your meals on a portable gas stove – you can fill your gas bottle at most roadhouses and service stations.

If you must cook on an open fire, follow a few basic rules. First, it's much better to have good-quality cast-iron or steel pots rather than aluminium, which heats unevenly and isn't recommended for campfire cooking. A steel grate is useful to put your pots on. Next you should use dry, solid hardwoods (dead timber, of course) and allow plenty of time for them to burn down to a bed of coals. Avoid cooking over flames unless you're in a hurry or simply boiling the billy.

Dig a trench in which to lay your fire. The width and length will depend on your own cooking needs and size of your fire grate, but it should be about 30cm deep.

Bush Cooking in Style by Gayle Hughes explains all you need to know about bush cooking, including planning and packing. For a good range of basic recipes, get hold of *Rabbit on a Shovel* by Herb ('Lummo') Lummis. Jack & Reg Absalom's *Outback Cooking in the Camp Oven* has exotic recipes like kangaroo, and explains how to use a camp oven.

See the Checklist at the back of this book for general cooking equipment and essential campfire cooking items.

DRINKS

In the nonalcoholic department, soft drinks, flavoured milk and mineral water are widely available, sometimes surprisingly far off the beaten track. Tea and coffee in the outback usually means teabags and instant, though many places are now sophisticated enough to offer espresso and cappuccino.

Beer

Beer plays an integral role in the social fabric of the outback. Probably the most widely available brand is Victoria Bitter (VB) but often the local or state beer will predominate.

The containers it comes in and the receptacles you drink it from are all referred to by different names. Beer by the glass basically comes in three sizes – 200mL, 285mL and 425mL – but knowing what to ask for when the bar staff queries you with an eloquent 'Yeah, mate?' is not quite so simple. A 200mL (7oz) beer is a 'glass' (Qld), a 'butcher' (SA) or a 'beer' (WA or NSW) – but this thimble-sized glass is rarely used in the outback, where thirsts are large. The more common option is the 285mL (10oz) 'pot' (Qld), 'schooner' (SA), 'handle' (NT), or 'middy' (NSW and WA). Then there's the 425mL (15oz) glass, which is a 'schooner' (NSW and NT) or a 'pint' (everywhere else) In New South Wales they may also ask if you want new or old, 'new' being normal beer and 'old' being dark ale. A low-alcohol beer is called a light, while regular-strength beer can be called a heavy, or super.

The common beer bottle is the 375mL 'stubby' with a twist-top cap (sometimes called 'echoes' in South Australia), often sold by the 24-bottle carton or 'slab'. In the Northern Territory, a Darwin stubby is a whopping 1.25L bottle, which is really only bought as a novelty souvenir these days.

Australians are generally considered to be heavy beer drinkers, especially in the outback, but per capita beer consumption even in the notoriously hard-drinking Northern Territory has been falling faster than in any other developed country.

Wine

Wine is widely available but the choice becomes rather limited away from the major centres. White wines are almost always drunk chilled, and in the outback many people chill their reds too – room temperature is just too hot!

You can usually get reasonable muscats and ports to enhance those evenings around the campfire. Sparkling cider is a great and very popular outback thirst-quencher, available as dry, draught (medium-sweet) or sweet, in 375mL or 750mL bottles.

THINGS TO BUY

There are lots of things definitely *not* to buy in the outback, such as plastic boomerangs, fake Aboriginal-design ashtrays and T-shirts, and all the other stuff that fills tacky souvenir shops. Most of them come from Taiwan or Korea anyway. Before buying a souvenir, check it was actually made here!

Often the best souvenirs are the ones that have special meaning: the fly-net hat bought at Urandangi when the flies were driving you insane, the tiny gold nugget found near Kalgoorlie, or the 'antique' glass insulator picked up along the old Overland Telegraph Line north of Alice Springs.

Aboriginal Art & Artefacts

One of the best, most evocative reminders of your trip is an Aboriginal artwork or artefact.

By buying authentic items you're supporting Aboriginal culture and helping to ensure that traditional and contemporary expertise and designs continue to be of economic and cultural benefit for Aboriginal individuals and communities. Unfortunately, much of the so-called Aboriginal art sold as souvenirs is ripped-off, consists of appropriated designs illegally taken from Aboriginal people or is just plain fake, usually made overseas by underpaid workers. In 2000, the 'Label of Authenticity' was launched by the National Indigenous Arts Advocacy Agency to help protect the intellectual property and copyrights of Aboriginal artists. Look for the swing tag on merchandise.

The best place to buy artefacts is either directly from the communities that have art-and-craft centres or from galleries and outlets that are owned and operated or supported by Aboriginal communities. This way you can be sure that the items are genuine and that the money you spend goes to the right people. There are also many reputable galleries that have long supported Aboriginal art – usually members of the Australian Commercial Galleries Association (ACGA; W www.agca.com.au).

Didgeridoos are a hot item, and you need to decide whether you want a decorative piece or an authentic and functional musical instrument. The didgeridoos sold are not always made by Aboriginal people, and there are many stories of backpackers in Darwin earning good money by making or decorating didgeridoos. From a community outlet such as Manyallaluk in the Northern Territory you could expect to pay $100 to $200 for a functional didgeridoo that has been painted natural pigments. On the other hand, from a nonsupportive souvenir shop in Darwin or Cairns you could pay anything from $200 to $400 or more for something that looks pretty but is really little more than a painted bit of wood.

If you're interested in buying a painting, possibly in part for its investment potential, it's best to purchase the work from a community art centre, Aboriginal-owned gallery or reputable non-Aboriginal-owned gallery. Regardless of its individual aesthetic worth, a painting purchased without a certificate of authenticity from either a reputable gallery or community art centre will probably be hard to resell at a later time – even if the painting is attributed to a well-known artist.

See Cross-Cultural Etiquette in the Facts about the Outback chapter if you want to purchase works of art while visiting Aboriginal communities.

Australiana

For the benefit of our foreign readers, the term 'Australiana' is a euphemism for all those things you buy as gifts for friends, aunts and uncles, nieces and nephews, and other sundry bods back home. They're supposedly representative of Australia and its culture but many are just tacky.

Some of the more worthwhile items are wool products such as hand-knitted jumpers, sheepskin products, and jewellery made from opal. The seeds of Australian native plants are also worth considering – try growing kangaroo paws back home. Australian wines are well known overseas but why not try honey (leatherwood honey is one of a number of powerful local varieties), macadamia nuts (native to Queensland), or Bundaberg rum with its unusual sweet flavour – a 'Bundy & Coke' is a popular drink in the outback, especially in Queensland.

Clothing & Surf Wear Australia's major contribution to the fashion world (with all due respect to modern Aussie fashion designers) is 'bush wear' and surf wear. The former describes the stockman look – waterproof Driza-Bone coats, Akubra hats, moleskin pants and Blundstone boots. RM Williams is a well-known bush-clothing brand.

Surf-wear labels such as Rip Curl, Quicksilver, Mambo and Billabong make good buys. You can pick up printed T-shirts, colourful boardshorts and the latest beach and street fashion from surf and sports shops all over the country, especially on the east coast. Rip Curl and Quicksilver were both born in Torquay, Victoria, in the 1960s and are now internationally renowned surf brands, marketing wetsuits, boards and surf wear.

Opals & Gemstones The opal is Australia's national gemstone, and opals and jewellery made with it are popular souvenirs. It's a beautiful stone, but buy wisely and shop around – quality and prices can vary widely from place to place. Coober Pedy (SA) and Lightning Ridge and White Cliffs (NSW) are opal-mining towns where you can buy the stones or perhaps fossick for your own.

In Cape York and the Torres Strait Islands look out for South Sea pearls, while in Broome (WA), cultured pearls are produced and sold in many local shops.

Semi-precious gemstones such as topaz, garnets, sapphires, rubies, zircon and others can sometimes be found lying around in piles of dirt at various locations. The gem fields around Anakie, Sapphire and Rubyvale in Queensland are a good place to shop for jewellery and gemstones, and there are sites around rural and outback Australia where you can pay a few dollars and fossick for your own stones.

Getting Around

DRIVING THE OUTBACK

Public transport is almost nonexistent in most parts of the outback and for this reason alone having your own transport is the way to go. Buying or hiring a car need not cost a fortune if there are three or four of you and, provided you don't have a major mechanical problem, the benefits are great.

Inexperienced drivers conquer some of the most difficult tracks in unsuitable vehicles, but they just happen to do so under perfect conditions, with more than their fair share of luck (or help from passers-by). Other keen souls never make it and some even perish. Everyone has a bit of luck now and then; just be aware that your life is at stake if your luck runs out. There's simply no substitute for careful planning.

Popular Tracks

There are many tracks to choose from, and this book describes most of them. To help narrow down your choice, here are a few of the more popular ones:

Birdsville Track Running 517km from Marree in South Australia to Birdsville, across the border in Queensland, this is one of the best-known routes in Australia and these days is quite feasible in a well-prepared conventional vehicle.

Strzelecki Track This track covers much the same territory, starting south of Marree at Lyndhurst and travelling 460km north-east to Innamincka (where the hapless Burke and Wills died), close to the Queensland border. From there you can loop down to Tibooburra in New South Wales. The route has been much improved by work on the Moomba gas fields.

Oodnadatta Track This runs parallel to the old *Ghan* railway line to Alice Springs. It's 429km from Marree to Oodnadatta and another 216km from there to the Stuart Hwy at Marla. There are many historical sites and it's worth taking your time to see them. So long as there's no rain, any well-prepared vehicle should be able to manage this route.

Simpson Desert Crossing the Simpson from the Stuart Hwy to Birdsville is becoming increasingly popular but this route is still a real test.

Four-wheel drive is definitely required and you should be in a party of at least three or four vehicles equipped with HF radios. There are several routes: the French Line and a couple of easier but longer alternatives. Silence and space are the main attractions.

Great Central Road This route runs west from Uluru via the Aboriginal communities of Docker River and Warburton to Laverton in Western Australia. From there you can drive down to Kalgoorlie and on to Perth. A well-prepared conventional vehicle can complete this remote route through the typical red desert landscape of central Australia, though there are a few creek crossings where ground clearance can be a problem. There are plans to seal this road.

Gunbarrel Highway For 300km near the Giles Weather Station, the Great Central road and the Gunbarrel Hwy run on the same route. Taking the Gunbarrel north past Warburton all the way to Wiluna in Western Australia is a much rougher trip requiring 4WD. It goes through the Gibson Desert (stunning wildflowers in season) following in the tracks of the great road-builder, Len Beadell.

Tanami Track Turning off the Stuart Hwy just north of Alice Springs, the Tanami Track goes north-west across the Tanami Desert to Halls Creek in Western Australia. It's a popular short-cut for people travelling between the Centre and the Kimberley. The road has been extensively improved in recent years and conventional vehicles are usually OK, although it's long, rough and remote and you should take it easy. Fuel can be a problem: Yuendumu often only has diesel and Rabbit Flat roadhouse is only open from Friday to Monday.

Canning Stock Route This old stock trail runs between Halls Creek and Wiluna in Western Australia and is one of the world's great 4WD adventures. It crosses a number of deserts and since the track has not been maintained for over 30 years, it's a route to be taken seriously. There's deep, soft sand for much of the way, with over a thousand dune ridges to cross. Like the Simpson Desert crossing, you should only travel in a well-equipped party, and careful navigation is required.

Plenty & Sandover Highways These remote routes run east from the Stuart Hwy north of Alice Springs to Boulia or Mt Isa in Queensland. Though often rough, they provide a significantly shorter alternative to the sealed Barkly Hwy heading east above Tennant Creek and are usually suitable for robust conventional vehicles.

Cape York The Peninsula Development Rd up to the tip of Cape York, the northernmost point of mainland Australia, is a popular route through a unique part of the country. There are many rivers to cross and the track can only be attempted in the dry season, when water levels are low. The original Cape York Track along the old telegraph line definitely requires 4WD. Well-prepared conventional vehicles can take several bypass roads that avoid the most difficult sections, but 4WD is strongly recommended.

Gibb River Road This is the 'short cut' between Derby and Kununurra, running through the heart of the spectacular Kimberley region in northern Western Australia. Although rough and corrugated in places, it can usually be negotiated by conventional vehicles in the dry season. Nothing gets through in the Wet.

Travel Permits

If you're travelling independently, you may need special permits to pass through or visit Aboriginal land or to camp in conservation areas.

Aboriginal Land A glance at any recent land-tenure map of Australia shows that vast portions of the north, centre and south are Aboriginal land. Generally, the land has either government-administered reserve status or may be held under freehold title vested in an Aboriginal land trust and managed by a council or corporation. In either case, the laws of trespass apply just as with any other form of private land, but the fines attached can be somewhat heftier.

In some cases, permits won't be necessary if you stay on recognised public roads that cross Aboriginal territory. However, as soon as you leave the main road by more than 50m, even if you're 'only' going into an Aboriginal settlement for fuel, you may need a permit. If you're on an organised tour, the operator should take care of any permits – check before you book.

To make an application, write to the appropriate land council or government department, enclosing a stamped, self-addressed envelope and giving all details of your proposed visit or transit. If you're on

line, applying via the Web or email (where these facilities exist) is easier and usually much quicker.

Allow plenty of time: The application process may take a couple of weeks or even one or two months as the administering body generally must obtain approval from the relevant community councils before issuing your permit – there is no centralised Aboriginal land authority. Keep in mind that your application may be knocked back for a number of reasons, including the risk of interference with sacred sites or disruption of ceremonial business. As well, some communities simply may not want to be bothered by visitors.

Specific permit requirements are explained in the track descriptions in this book but the general requirements are set out here:

Western Australia The Aboriginal Affairs Department (AAD) is responsible for all Aboriginal land trusts in the state, including transit on the Great Central Road. For permission to visit Aboriginal freehold land you must apply directly to the owners; contact the Permits Officer (☎ 08-9235 8000, fax 9235 8093, W www.aad.wa.gov.au) at PO Box 7770, Cloisters Square, WA 6850.

South Australia Outside the Woomera Prohibited Area, virtually the entire region bordered by the transcontinental railway, the Stuart Hwy and the Northern Territory and Western Australia borders is Aboriginal land. The northern portion of this region is taken up by the Anangu-Pitjantjatjara lands, while to the south are the Maralinga-Tjarutja lands. The two are separated on the map by a line drawn east-west through Mt Willoughby on the Stuart Hwy, about 230km south of the Northern Territory border.

Independent travel is not encouraged in the Anangu-Pitjantjatjara lands, though you can visit on a guided tour with Yulara-based Desert Tracks – see Organised Tours at the end of this chapter. If you have a valid reason for going there independently, contact the Anangu Pitjantjatjaraku (AP) office (☎ 08-8950 1511, fax 8950 1510) at Umuwa, near Ernabella, for permission.

Permits to visit the Maralinga-Tjarutja Lands, which include access to the Unnamed Conservation Park and tracks in the Emu Junction area, can be obtained from the Administration Officer, Maralinga-Tjarutja Inc (☎ 08-8625 2946, fax 8625 3076) in Ceduna.

Northern Territory A transit permit for straightforward travel along an established route can usually be processed within 48 hours. An entry permit to visit a community or conduct any activity other than through-travel, can take two weeks to a month.

The Central Land Council administers all Aboriginal land in the southern and central regions of the Territory. Contact the Permits Officer (☎ 08-8951 6320, fax 8953 4345, W www.clc.org.au) at 31–33 Stuart Hwy, Alice Springs, NT 0870. The office is about 1km north of the town centre.

Arnhem Land and other northern mainland areas are administered by the Northern Land Council in Darwin. Contact the Permits Officer (☎ 08-8920 5100, fax 8945 2633, e permits@nlc.org.au) at 9 Rowling St, Casuarina, NT 0811. Permits for Oenpelli are issued on the spot at the Jabiru Northern Land Council office.

Queensland There's no formal permit system for entry to Aboriginal land in Queensland. Instead, you obtain permission directly from the community, as you would with most other land-holders. The Cape York Land Council (☎ 07 4053 9222, fax 4051 0097, W www.cylc.org.au), at 32 Florence St, Cairns, Qld 4870, is a good contact point for communities on the cape.

National Parks You usually need a permit to camp in, or sometimes even to visit, a national park and permits may have to be obtained in advance. Details of required permits are provided in the individual track descriptions in this book. If you're spending a lot of time in a particular state's national parks, it pays to check if there's an annual pass system in operation, what it covers and how many parks it's valid for. It could save you a fair bit of money. See National Parks

Organisations under Useful Organisations in the Facts for the Visitor chapter.

In South Australia, you can get a Desert Parks Pass (required for the parks and regional reserves in the north of the state, eg, Simpson Desert, Lake Eyre National Park, Innamincka Regional Reserve) at the Department for Environment and Heritage (☎ 1800 816 078, 08-8648 5300) at 9 Mackay St, Port Augusta (PO Box 78, Port Augusta, SA 5710).

Buying a Car

If you're buying a second-hand vehicle, reliability is all-important. Mechanical breakdowns in the outback are potentially dangerous and at least very inconvenient – the nearest mechanic can be a hell of a long way down the road. Buying through a dealer gives the advantage of some sort of warranty but this won't be much good in the outback. Used-car warranty requirements vary from state to state – check with the local automobile organisation.

Depending on which state you're in, registration can cost $250 to $400 a year for a conventional car and $350 to $800 for a 4WD, so it's really worth checking how much registration is still left when you buy second-hand. This includes third-party personal injury insurance but you'd be wise to take out separate third-party property insurance as well – minor collisions with other vehicles can be amazingly expensive. Also be aware of compulsory safety checks, which vary from state to state.

Stamp duty has to be paid when you buy a car and, as this is based on the purchase price, it's not unknown for buyer and seller to agree privately to understate the price.

Note that it's much easier to sell a car in the same state it's registered in, otherwise you (or the buyer) must re-register it in the new state, and that's a hassle. Vehicles with interstate plates are particularly hard to get rid of in Western Australia.

Finally, make use of the automobile organisations – see the Facts for the Visitor chapter for details. They can advise on local regulations, give general guidelines about buying a car and, most importantly, for a fee (usually under $100) will check a used car and report on its condition before you buy it.

What Type of Car? Many of the routes mentioned in this book are suitable for conventional vehicles that are well prepared, preferably with strong tyres (see Tyres later in this section), aftermarket suspension and good ground clearance. Other routes are recommended for 4WD only. This doesn't mean that any 4WD will do. The smaller, more car-like 4WDs such as Mitsubishi L300s and Subarus are better for rough dirt roads than the average conventional vehicle, but their low ground clearance and high gearing make them unsuitable for rocky conditions and heavy sand. The same applies to the current crop of 'soft road', 'all-wheel-drive' (AWD) or 'crossover' vehicles such as the Toyota RAV4, Honda CRV and even the upmarket BMW X5. Suzuki Sierras will go anywhere, but on a long trip their lack of cargo space can be a telling deficiency.

The most secure choice for serious outback travel is a 4WD with a separate chassis (like a truck) for better structural integrity on bumps and corrugations. Solid front and rear axles (also like a truck) are a good idea as well, because they tend to allow more wheel travel over serious bumps and holes than independent suspension setups. Independent suspension is more comfortable on the bitumen (asphalt or tar), however, and makes the vehicle handle more like a 'normal' car.

Another important consideration when choosing a particular make and model is the availability of spares. In the 4WD category, Toyotas and Nissans are a dime a dozen and there's usually a local mechanic who knows how they work. Old Toyota Land Cruisers, in particular, are common outback workhorses and easier to repair than the newer models. Not so common in the backblocks are Land Rovers, Mitsubishi Pajeros, Holden Jackaroos and the like, although parts are generally available in major towns.

The further you get from civilisation in a 2WD vehicle, however, the better it is to be in a Holden or Ford. New cars can be a whole different ball game of course, but if you're in an older vehicle, something that's likely to have the odd hiccup from time to time, then life is much simpler if it's a car for which you can get spare parts anywhere from Bourke to Bulamakanka. When your rusty old Holden goes bang, there's probably another old Holden sitting in a ditch with a perfectly good widget waiting to be removed. Every scrap yard in Australia is full of good old Holdens and Ford Falcons.

Expect to pay $1500 to $3500 for an old Holden or Ford and $3000 to $10,000 for an old 4WD. Obviously the closer you get to the lower figures, the more you need to know about cars and how to fix them. For a 4WD, about $18,000 should get you something reasonably new (around five years old) and reliable enough to take you to remote areas.

Buy-Back Schemes For overseas visitors, but also for some locals, one way of getting around the hassles of buying and selling privately is to enter into a buy-back arrangement with a dealer. This is fairly easy to arrange if you can afford to buy new, though you'll lose a lot of money. Also, some dealers will find ways of knocking down the price when you return the vehicle, even if it was agreed to in writing – often by pointing out expensive repairs that allegedly will be required to gain the dreaded safety check.

Travellers Autobarn (☎ 02-9360 1500, W www.travellers-autobarn.com.au) specialises in buy-back arrangements. It has offices in Sydney, Brisbane and Cairns, and offers a range of cars and camper vans. The basic deal is 50% of the purchase price if you have the vehicle for eight weeks, 40% for up to six months, or 30% for up to 12 months.

Car and motorcycle buy-backs for adventurous travellers are the speciality of Car Connection Australia (☎ 03-5473 4469, fax 5473 4520, e car@carconnection.com.au, W www.carconnection.com.au) at RSD Lot 8, Vaughan Springs Rd, Glenluce, Victoria. Rather than requiring you to outlay the full amount and then sell it back, you post a bond that is actually less than the value of the vehicle (credit-card imprint is fine) and only pay a fixed 'user fee' for any period up to six months (longer periods are calculated at pro rata rates, shorter periods still cost the full six months). It's basically a glorified long-term rental arrangement, but up to 80% cheaper than a normal rental because you pay for maintenance and repairs (though there's a limited 5000km warranty on the vehicle, which can be extended to the whole trip for $350).

On this basis, a second-hand Ford station wagon will cost you $2145. A Toyota HJ60 Land Cruiser, suitable for serious outback exploration, is $4950; a more modern and slightly more comfortable HJ80 is $7150; and a Toyota 4WD Bushcamper, with pop-up roof and the full camping interior including kitchen and fridge, is $9350. There are also 2WD Mazda or Toyota Hiace – based camper vans at $6050. A Yamaha XT600 trail bike is $2145 (for six months), and a BMW R1150GS is $6050 (for three months). Vehicles are fitted with tools and basic spares, and for an additional $250 you get a full set of camping gear (no sleeping bags) and, for the 4WDs, recovery equipment (high-lift jack, hand winch etc). Information and bookings are also handled by its European agent, Travel Action GmbH (☎ 0276-478 24, fax 47938), at Einsiedeleiweg 16, 57399 Kirchhundem, Germany.

Renting a Car

If you have the cash, plenty of car-rental companies are ready and willing to put you behind the wheel. The track and city descriptions in this book provide further details. Competition is pretty fierce so rates tend to vary and lots of special deals pop up and disappear again.

The three major companies are Budget, Hertz and Avis, with offices in most of the outback's larger towns. Second-string companies that are also well represented are Thrifty, National and Delta Europcar. Then there's a vast number of local firms or firms with outlets in a limited number of locations. The big operators will generally have higher rates than the locals but not always. Don't jump to conclusions before you've taken additional costs and restrictions into account. Comparison shopping is essential.

One advantage with the big operators is that they have better support services and are more amenable to one-way rentals; pick up a car in Adelaide and leave it in Cairns, for example. There are, however, a variety of restrictions on this and sometimes there's a substantial drop-off fee. Ask plenty of questions before deciding on one company over another. One-way rentals into or out of the Northern Territory or Western Australia may be subject to a hefty repositioning fee, although at the time of writing Britz was offering good deals for taking a car or camper van from Broome back to Perth.

The major companies offer a choice of deals, either unlimited kilometres or 100km or so a day free and charged so many cents per kilometre over this. Daily rates (including insurance) in major centres are typically about $55 a day for a small car (Holden Barina, Ford Festiva, Hyundai Excel), about $65 to $75 a day for a medium car (Mitsubishi Magna, Toyota Camry, Nissan Pulsar) or $80 to $100 a day for a big car (Holden Commodore, Ford Falcon). In the really remote outback (Darwin, Alice Springs and Broome are only vaguely remote), the choice of cars is likely to be limited to the larger, more expensive ones.

You must be at least 21 years old to hire from most firms – if you're under 25 you may only be able to hire a small car or have to pay a surcharge. It gets cheaper if you rent for a week or more and there are often low-season and weekend discounts.

Many places rent camper vans – they're especially popular in the Top End. Check out Backpacker Campervans (☎ 1800 670 232, Ⓦ www.backpackercampervans.com).

Insurance We can't emphasise enough that you should know exactly what your liability is in the event of an accident. Rather than risk paying out thousands of dollars if you do have an accident, you can take out your own comprehensive insurance on the car, or (the usual option) pay an additional daily amount to the rental company for an 'insurance excess reduction' policy. This brings the excess (the amount of money for which you are liable before the insurance kicks in) you must pay in the event of an accident down from between $2000 and $5000 to a few hundred dollars. It really pushes the cost of the rental up but gives you peace of mind. Most companies' insurance won't cover the cost of damage to glass (including the windscreen) or tyres. Always read the small print.

Be aware that if you are travelling on dirt roads you will not be covered by insurance unless you rent a proper 4WD – in other words, if you have an accident you'll be liable for all the costs involved. Many will prohibit you travelling on dirt roads anyway, though a well-maintained dirt road leading into a major tourist site is usually not a problem. Ask before signing the agreement.

4WD Rentals Renting a 4WD need not cost a fortune if a few people get together and share the cost. Something small like a Suzuki Vitara or Toyota RAV4 costs $80 or $100 per day, but the rental company will probably impose limitations on where you can take it. For a Toyota Land Cruiser with fewer or no limitations you're looking at $140 and up, which should include some free kilometres (typically 100km to 200km per day, sometimes unlimited).

Check the insurance policy conditions, especially the excess, as it can be onerous. In the Northern Territory $5000 is typical, although this can often be reduced to around $1000 (or even to nil) on payment of an additional daily charge (around $45). Read the fine print to check what is and isn't covered when travelling off bitumen.

Hertz, Budget and Avis have 4WD rentals, with one-way rentals possible between the eastern states and the Northern Territory. Their vehicles are generally fairly new and you pay for the privilege. Territory Thrifty Car Rental rents 4WDs from Darwin (☎ 08-8924 0000, fax 8981 5247) and Alice Springs (☎ 08-8952 9999, fax 8952 9797).

Britz Campervan Rentals (☎ 1800 331 454, fax 03-9687 4844, W www.britz.com) has fully equipped 4WDs fitted out as camper vans, and you'll see loads of these getting around. They start at around $140 (two-berth) or $230 (four-berth) per day

with unlimited kilometres, plus insurance ($45 per day to delete the excess), but the price climbs from there. Britz has offices in all the mainland capitals except Canberra, as well as in Alice Springs, Broome and Cairns, so one-way rentals are also possible.

Apollo (☎ 07-3260 5466, fax 3260 5475, W www.apollocamper.com.au) in Brisbane, Koala (☎ 08-8352 7299, fax 8234 2733, W www.koalarentals.com.au) in Adelaide and Maui (affiliated with Britz; ☎ 1300 363 800, fax 03-9687 4844, W www.maui -rentals.com) in Melbourne are other rental companies offering 4WD camper vans. Ring around to find the deal that suits you best.

Four-wheel-drive hire vehicles tend to be pretty basic and not always well prepared – check the tyre pressures (including the spare), equal disengagement of free-wheel hubs, standard tools etc. You'll probably have to organise extra equipment if you want to do a Simpson Desert trip but then again, you shouldn't be doing such a hard, remote trip if you haven't any experience. If you're travelling with a tour operator (see Organised Tours at the end of this chapter), they may be able to organise a self-drive vehicle for you.

Road Rules

Road rules still vary from state to state, though attempts are being made to standardise them and the differences aren't as great as they used to be. Get hold of a copy from any police station and study them.

The speed limit in built-up areas is usually 60km/h and out on the open highway it's usually 100km/h or 110km/h, depending on where you are. In the Northern Territory there's generally no speed limit outside of built-up areas, although you might still be booked for driving at a 'speed inappropriate to the prevailing conditions' (for instance 160km/h at dawn, dusk or night). In 2001, a speed limit of 110km/h was introduced for the Lasseter Hwy between Stuart Hwy and Uluru. The police use radar speed traps and speed cameras to raise revenue in the most unlikely places (such as across the Nullarbor near the border of South Australia or Western Australia), so don't think you're immune because you're away from civilisation. Oncoming drivers who flash their lights may be giving you a friendly indication of a speed trap ahead.

Driving standards in the outback aren't exactly the highest in the world, though because of the light traffic it's usually not a major problem. Drink-driving is a far bigger worry.

On the Road

You can drive all the way round Australia on Hwy 1 or through the middle from Adelaide to Darwin on bitumen, but you don't have to get very far off the beaten track to find yourself on dirt roads.

Outback folks love to boast about the bad standard of their dirt roads, but they're actually excellent compared with unsealed roads in Africa or South America that tend to see far more traffic. The major roads are graded fairly regularly, although heavy road trains can cause the surface to break up rather quickly. You may not even need a 4WD vehicle – a well-prepared, conventional 2WD car with sufficient ground clearance is usually all you need on the more established unsealed routes (it might lose some bits and pieces along the way though). The individual track descriptions in this book give an indication of the type of vehicle required.

That said, a sudden downpour can change a reasonable dirt road into a quagmire and cause flash floods that fill up the creek crossings – not just in the tropical north, where you would expect this, but also in the normally arid central and southern regions. Before setting off on a journey over unsealed roads, check conditions with the following road-report services:

Northern Territory ☎ 1800 246 199
  W www.nt.gov.au
Queensland ☎ 1300 130 595, 07-3361 2406
  W www.racq.com.au
South Australia ☎ 1300 361 033
  W www.transport.sa.gov.au
Western Australia ☎ 1800 013 314
  W www.mrwa.wa.gov.au

Signposting on the main roads between cities is quite OK, and on the more important outback tracks you'll usually find signposts where they matter. Be careful though, as what matters to you may not matter to an outback road crew, and a missed turn-off can have serious consequences. This is all the more reason to keep a running log when travelling in the outback (see Survival in the Facts for the Visitor chapter) and to have good maps.

Cattle, sheep and kangaroos are common hazards on outback roads at night. A collision is likely to kill the animal and seriously damage your vehicle. Kangaroos tend to seek shade during the day but are active at night, especially at dawn and dusk when they often come to feed along the road verges – there's usually more feed there because the drains act as traps for even light showers falling on the bitumen. Roos move in groups, so if you see one hopping across the road in front of you, slow right down: Its friends are probably close behind. If one hops out right in front of you, hit the brakes and only swerve to avoid the animal if it's safe to do so. Each year, numerous people are killed or injured in accidents caused by swerving to miss an animal. For this reason, it is recommend that you avoid travelling altogether between 5pm and 8am on outback roads.

Cattle grids take the place of gates on most major outback routes and these should be approached with care. Often there are potholes beside the grids or the grids might be raised above the road level. Others may be on top of sharp humps that will wreck your suspension and cause your vehicle to 'take off' if you hit them at speed. Also, pastoralists spend a lot of time and money repairing caved-in grid wells caused by thoughtless drivers.

Another hazard that's not so obvious is driver fatigue. Driving long distances (particularly in hot weather) can be so tiring that you might fall asleep at the wheel. Not only that, people can become so mesmerised by the road stretching endlessly ahead that they forget to turn the next corner! The best approach on a long haul is to stop and rest every two hours – do some exercise, change drivers or have a coffee. On most dirt roads, 300km to 400km a day is not bad going and is usually a sensible cut-off; on serious 4WD tracks, 100km to 150km a day might be all you can hope for without running yourself (not to mention your vehicle) into the ground. Pace yourself.

Some outback roads are only wide enough for one vehicle, which begs the question of what to do when someone comes towards you. First of all, slow down. It's common to move the left half of the vehicle off the edge and expect the oncoming vehicle to do the same. Wrong, because this gives both parties the worst of both worlds. Outback residents usually wait and see what the other vehicle does: If it moves off the edge, they'll stay on the bitumen and risk a broken windscreen from flying gravel; if it stays on the bitumen, they'll move off the edge and wear out their suspension and tyres. However, everyone moves aside for an oncoming truck or road train – they have to stay on the road for obvious reasons.

Finally, if an oncoming vehicle throws up so much dust that you can't see the road ahead, slow down (and turn on the lights) or stop. *Don't* overtake another vehicle in dust clouds.

Accidents

Generally speaking, if you have an accident with livestock on an outback road, it'll be you who is considered at fault, not the owner of the animal you've collided with. You'll also be expected to pay for the repair or replacement of gates, fencing and other property that you may damage with your vehicle. This makes third-party property insurance a good idea even if you're driving a bucket of bolts.

The best approach after you've had an accident of any sort involving property damage (including to your vehicle) is to inform the police as soon as possible; your vehicle insurance policy will probably require you to do this, anyway.

Fuel

Service stations generally stock diesel, super (now commonly called leaded or LRP for lead-replacement fuel) and unleaded, though super/leaded is on the way out and the more

remote places may only stock diesel. Liquid petroleum gas (LPG) is often available at large service stations along the main sealed roads, but check current availability with the state's automobile association.

Prices vary from place to place and from price war to price war, but generally they're in the $0.85 to $0.95 per-litre range and more than $1 a litre is not uncommon away from the major centres; diesel sometimes costs a few cents more and LPG significantly less. In the remote outback, the price can soar and some service stations are not above exploiting their monopoly position (then again, their transport and other costs are high too).

Distances between fill-ups can be long, and in some really remote areas deliveries can be haphazard – it's not unknown to finally arrive at that 'nearest station x hundred km' only to find there's no fuel until next week's delivery! Ring ahead if you want to be sure.

The track descriptions in this book will give an indication of the required fuel ranges. There are a few tracks where your vehicle will need a long-range fuel tank, but on the others you'll usually be able to scrape by on your vehicle's standard tank (maybe with one or two 20L jerry cans as backup).

Trailers & Caravans

Trailers and caravans come in all shapes and sizes and what you choose will depend on your wallet and personal preferences. There are many places where you cannot take a caravan, but a well-constructed luggage trailer designed for off-road work will go virtually anywhere – with a few big provisos.

First, the trailer must be well made. Every year, dozens fall apart on the tracks up to Cape York, through the Kimberley or across the Gunbarrel. Axles bend, springs and spring hangers break, tow couplings snap, chassis fall apart and, if that's not enough, they can make you lose control more easily. Second, trailers will slow you down and get you stuck. Third, they are banned in some places, such as Finke Gorge and Gurig National Parks. At times they're simply not worth the trouble.

Car Preparation

A well-prepared vehicle is of paramount importance, though you can easily go overboard in setting it up. There are a host of accessories for 4WDs, some of them next to useless. But if you intend to keep your vehicle for a long time, or are planning some of the harder trips in this book, then the following advice becomes useful.

Good driving lights are pretty well essential for night driving in the outback, though we don't recommend driving after dark. An aftermarket suspension helps the vehicle cope with heavy loads, and a long-range fuel tank takes the worry out of carrying fuel inside the cabin or on the roof (neither of which are recommended). Roof racks are useful for carrying light, bulky items such as tents and sleeping gear; heavy items upset the handling and make the vehicle prone to rolling over.

A dual battery (with isolating switch) under the bonnet is a great help to keep the fridge running, for starting your vehicle when the main battery goes flat or for some emergency welding.

Radios are an important accessory in really remote areas, but if you don't carry one, then carry at least an EPIRB – see Radio Communications in the Facts for the Visitor chapter.

Items such as spare parts, tools and recovery gear are included in the Checklists at the back of this book and depend, to some extent, on your trip. It goes without saying that someone in your group should know how to use them. You don't have to be a qualified mechanic but some knowledge and experience are a great help, particularly on the more remote tracks.

Have your vehicle serviced properly before the trip. Thoroughly check the cooling system, engine, complete drive train, suspension and brakes. There are 4WD specialist service centres in each state capital and major regional centres, many specialising in trip preparation.

It's possible to write a whole book on setting up and preparing your vehicle for the outback, but specialist magazines such as *4X4 Australia* and *Overlander* are useful

sources of the most current information on where to go, what the conditions are like, what preparation you need and who to see for specialist advice.

Keep a pair of work gloves under the driver's seat for dirty jobs like filling up with diesel, changing a tyres and collecting firewood.

Tyres Buying tyres in the bush is always expensive. If your tyres are on their last legs, buy new ones before you set out (eight-ply or 10-ply rated if you can afford them) to minimise flex and the risk of punctures. Light truck (LT) tyres used on commercial 4WDs are generally reliable. The ultimate bush tyre is a 14-ply or 16-ply LT tyre, but you'll have a rough ride on the bitumen and it's still no guarantee you'll never get a puncture.

Stick to common brands, preferably with solid, narrow profiles; wide-profile 'desert' tyres are more fragile and tend to damage easily because of their wide contact patch. Some experts are blunter and say you shouldn't venture into the outback with wide tyres at all. They also say you should stick with tube tyres, as tubeless tyres are more difficult to repair reliably; though this advice is debatable as tubeless tyres do run cooler and lose air more slowly when they puncture. If you do go with tubes, bush mechanics love split wheel-rims because they make tyre removal so much easier.

What about spare tyres and tubes? As a rule of thumb, if you travel for a day without passing a supply point, you'll need to carry more than one complete spare. For hard trips like the Simpson or Canning, you'll also need a tyre and tube repair kit and to know how to use it.

When you've changed a wheel, check the wheel nuts after about 50km as they can sometimes work loose. Don't do them up too tight or you may snap the wheel bolts. For this reason, better tyre repair services keep their 'rattle-guns' on a 'soft' setting and give the nuts a final tightening-up by hand with a wheel brace.

Carry a reliable tyre pump: Tyre pressures play a very important part in four-wheel driving. Too hard and the drive will be uncomfortable and you'll get bogged more often; too soft and you'll destroy tyres. our load will determine what pressure you use, but for general touring on unsealed roads, pressures between 210kPa and 280kPa (30psi to 40psi) are a sensible average. For long stretches on the bitumen you might want to pump LT tyres up beyond 280kPa.

4WD Techniques

Driving a 4WD vehicle properly, and to its capability, is definitely a skill that needs to be practised. It's certainly not something that can be explained here in just a few paragraphs. There are more detailed books and instructional videos around, and a basic 4WD course at an accredited training establishment ($180 to $350) is money well spent. Ask around at 4WD clubs, motoring organisations (see Useful Organisations in the Facts for the Visitor chapter) or check 4WD magazines. Above all, take your time to learn and remember to tread lightly wherever you go.

Most pre-1984 vehicles don't have power steering or great brakes. Their suspension is very truck-like, giving a harsh ride, a touch or more of understeer and on rough roads, a fair amount of bump steer. Later-model 4WDs are generally more sophisticated, with many being distinctly car-like in comfort and handling.

The Basics You should understand the operation of free-wheeling hubs and the transfer-box gear selection. On bitumen or hard dirt surfaces, the vehicle should be in 2WD, high ratio, or if it's a constant 4WD vehicle such as a Range Rover, leave it in normal gear without the centre diff locked.

Once the road or track gets sandy, muddy or just slippery, you can engage 4WD high ratio or lock the centre diff of a constant 4WD vehicle. When the going slows to a crawl and the road is rough, sandy or muddy, it's best to engage 4WD low ratio, or low ratio with the centre diff locked in a constant 4WD machine. This engagement should give you the ultimate in traction and power.

Some people engage 4WD as soon as they see dirt, which leads to unnecessary wear and tear and increased fuel consumption. So long as you can easily manage in 2WD, keep it there. In 4WDs with manual free-wheeling hubs, *always* disengage the hubs and shift back to 2WD on the bitumen.

Remember that a 4WD isn't a guarantee that you won't get bogged, but it will help you get bogged less often. The down side is that when you do get bogged, it's normally deeper and further into the quagmire than with a normal car.

Corrugations These are one of the things you'll begin to hate with a passion on dirt roads. They can be so bad they will seem to vibrate the vehicle to pieces. Going too fast can be dangerous, as well as detrimental to you and your car, while going too slow might not be as dangerous but will certainly be tiring on you and wearing on your vehicle.

In some cases the corrugations are so bad you have no choice but to slow down to a crawl. In most cases, however, a speed of around 80km/h is the optimum, as the vehicle will tend to 'float' across the hollows, giving a smoother ride. Mind you, what sort of ride you get will all depend on how good your suspension is: Poor shock absorbers will make you feel every bump. So will over-inflated tyres.

Off the Beaten Track If you're unsure of the ground ahead, especially if there is mud or water, get out and check.

Keep thumbs outside or on the edge of the steering wheel. Irregularities in the track can suddenly make the steering wheel turn with incredible force, bruising or even breaking a thumb in the process.

Don't change gear in the middle of a tricky section and if in doubt, always choose the lower gear.

Cross small ridges square-on; ditches should be crossed at a slight angle.

Steep Hills Low second or third gear is generally best for going uphill, while low first is best for steep downhills. Use the foot brake sparingly and with caution and keep

Lock in Those Hubs!

Free-wheeling hubs enable the 4WD front differential to be disengaged when driving conditions don't require off-road capability. This results in less wear to the differential and front running gear, and slightly better fuel economy. Not all 4WDs are fitted with manual free-wheeling hubs. Some are constant 4WD while others have automatic hubs.

However, if your vehicle has manual hubs you *must* lock them in *and* engage 4WD to get drive from the front as well as the rear wheels. Put another way, if you don't (a) lock in the hubs and (b) engage 4WD, the vehicle will remain in 2WD mode.

Many tourists visiting the outback have found themselves in potentially dangerous situations because they failed to engage their vehicle's free-wheeling hubs. This is usually either because they forgot or the car rental company neglected to explain this to them.

As an example, two overseas visitors recently became bogged on a remote track in a national park near Darwin. They spent a miserable night being sucked dry by mosquitoes before activating their emergency radio beacon the next morning. A police rescue party arrived in due course and found…you guessed it, 4WD had been engaged but the hubs hadn't been locked in. The police simply engaged the hubs and drove out. At last report there was talk of invoicing the red-faced duo for the cost of their rescue.

Sadly, a lack of understanding of this simple procedure can have tragic consequences. An overseas visitor perished near Lake Eyre several years ago when the vehicle she was in became bogged and she attempted to walk to safety. Again, the vehicle was simply driven out by the rescue party. The lesson is obvious: If you're buying or renting a 4WD for your outback odyssey, make sure you understand its operation before you leave the city.

your feet well away from the clutch. Don't turn a vehicle sideways on a hill and if you stall going uphill, don't touch the clutch or accelerator. See Stall Start or Key Start later in this section for what to do.

Sand Speed and flotation are the keys to success and high ratio is best, if possible.

Tyre pressure is important in the sand. Generally 140kPa (20psi) is a good starting point but if you're heavily loaded, this may be too low and 175kPa (25psi) could be more appropriate. If you're lightly loaded, 105kPa (15psi) may be the way to go. This doesn't so much give you a wider 'footprint' as a longer one, and makes driving in sand much easier. Don't forget to increase the pressure again as soon as you leave the sand or you'll ruin your tyres – or worse, have an accident.

Stick to existing wheel tracks, avoid sudden changes in direction and tackle dunes head-on. When descending a dune, avoid braking at all costs, keep the nose pointing downhill and don't travel too fast. Don't go so slow that the wheels stop.

If you do get stuck in sand, rock the vehicle backwards and forwards, building up a small stretch of hard-packed sand that you can move off from. Don't spin the wheels or you'll only dig yourself in deeper.

Water Crossings Always check the crossing before you plunge in. Walk through it first if you're unsure. A 4WD should be able to tackle a crossing of around 60cm deep without any problems or preparation, but a soft, sandy bottom or a strong current flow can change all that.

Spray electrical components with a water repellent such as WD40, loosen the fanbelt unless the fan has an auto clutch, and in deep water, fit a canvas blind to the front of the vehicle.

Enter the water at a slow, steady pace (low second gear is generally best) and keep the engine running even if you stop.

Don't forget to dry your brakes out after the water crossing, and if you were stuck, check all your oils for contamination.

Mud Speed and power are essential and in deep mud, low second or third are probably best. Keep a steady pace and if possible, keep out of ruts.

Stall Start or Key Start When you stop on a steep hill, don't panic; think and stay calm. Engage both the handbrake and the footbrake. Switch the engine off if it hasn't already stalled, ease the clutch in, select low-range reverse gear and ease the clutch out. Check to see if the track is clear and the wheels are pointing straight ahead, take off both the brakes, but keep your foot close to the footbrake just in case. Keeping your feet away from the clutch or the accelerator, start the engine and slowly back the vehicle down the hill. Slight stroking of the brake is possible but take care.

AIR

Australia's aviation industry (not to mention its tourism industry) was turned on its head in September 2001 when the nation's second biggest airline, Ansett, was dumped by its owner Air New Zealand amid mounting debt. This had immediate implications for outback residents as Ansett was the only major airline servicing many of the more remote destinations, especially in the west.

At the time of writing, attempts to rescue Ansett and return it to its former glories had failed. For now Qantas is the sole remaining airline covering all of Australia and 90% of the internal market, with newcomer Virgin Blue covering many east-coast routes (and providing some welcome competition with the recent additions of flights to Perth and Darwin).

For reservations with the two remaining airlines, contact Qantas (☎ 13 13 13 W www.qantas.com.au), and Virgin Blue (☎ 13 67 89 W www.virginblue.com.au). The airlines' Web sites allow you to look up fares and routes.

Minor Airlines

Australia has numerous smaller operators flying regional routes not serviced by the bigger airlines. In many cases, such as remote outback destinations or islands, these are the only viable transport option. Most of these airlines have operated as subsidiaries of Qantas or Ansett.

Ansett's subsidiaries included Airnorth in the Northern Territory, Kendell and Hazelton in the eastern states, Aeropelican in NSW and Skywest in Western Australia. At the time of writing, most of these operators were continuing to service essential routes, thought it's likely they will be sold in time.

Numerous operators, including Sunstate and Eastern Australia, operate under the Qantas Link banner serving regional routes in eastern and southern Australia. Macair (☎ 13 13 13), another Qantas subsidiary, is a major operator in outback Queensland. There are numerous other, smaller operators operating in the industry. See the individual track descriptions in this book for further details.

Cheap Fares

A major feature of the deregulated air-travel industry is random discounting, even in the current near-monopoly situation as Qantas tries to undercut Virgin Blue. The airlines often offer substantial discounts on selected routes; there are usually conditions attached to the discounted fares, such as booking 14 or more days in advance (called Advance Purchase Excursion/Apex fare), or only flying on weekends or between certain dates. To get the discounted tickets, you really need to book early – as a particular flight fills up, only the full-fare tickets remain.

On most domestic routes, the full economy fare will not be the cheapest way to go; the situation is fluid and the discount options so varied. Most of the cheapest options are only available from the airlines' Web sites.

All nonresident international travellers can get up to 80% discount on internal Qantas flights (called the Visit Australia fare) simply by presenting their international ticket when booking. This discount applies only to the full economy fare and in many cases it will be cheaper to take advantage of other discounts offered. The big difference is that you don't face the same restrictions as you do with discount fares. Ring around and explore the options before you buy.

There are also some relatively cheap deals with local and regional airlines as well as with Qantas, especially if they are booked as part of a package that includes accommodation. Travel agents will often have the most current details.

Air Passes

With discounting being the norm these days, air passes aren't great value. Qantas' Boomerang Pass can only be purchased overseas and involves buying coupons for either short-haul flights at $250 one way, or multizone sectors for $315. You must purchase a minimum of two coupons before you arrive in Australia, and once here you can buy up to eight more.

Outback Air Tours

Scenic flights are available in small aircraft at the more popular outback destinations. Prices are very reasonable, sometimes including pick-up and drop-off from where you're staying, and the experience is unforgettable – nothing beats the sight of Uluru or the Bungle Bungles from the air. See the track descriptions in this book for more information or contact the state or local tourist offices.

If you have money to burn, there are tour operators who will take you to the best attractions of the outback in six-seater Piper Aztecs and larger aircraft, such as 10-seater Piper Chieftains. Itineraries range from four-day trips to the Flinders Ranges from around $1600 per person to two-week outback tours of six states for $7500. Your accommodation is included and you may even have some input into the itinerary. The state tourist offices can provide details. One operator who has been around for a while is Air Adventure Australia (☎ 03-5572 1371, 1800 033 160, fax 03-5572 5979) based at Hamilton Pierre Point, Victoria.

Other Tour Options At most outback airfields there will be someone to take you flying, enabling them to get their hours on the board while you cover the costs. Just ask around. Also see the Mail Runs section later in this chapter for details on mail planes.

Flying Yourself

If you're a pilot, flying yourself can be an interesting option and a fairly efficient way to cover large distances.

Many flying schools and clubs hire out planes for private use and are the best places to meet other pilots and find out about local flying conditions. They're listed in the Yellow Pages phone book or just go out to the local airport and ask around. Most capital cities have a separate suburban airport for general aviation, such as Bankstown airport in Sydney and Moorabbin in Melbourne.

Renting a plane tends to be cheaper from country airports than from city airports. Typical single-engine hire charges start at around $135 an hour for a Cessna 152, or $155 for a Cessna 172 or Piper Warrior. From there, they increase roughly in proportion to cruising speed. If you want a twin, a Seminole is about $280 an hour. Rates are usually 'wet VDO', ie, engine hours inclusive of fuel and oil. You get a credit for any fuel you buy along the way, but only at the operator's local price, not what you paid for it. If you want to take the aircraft away overnight, the operator will probably expect a minimum average usage.

Flying Conditions Anyone planning to fly in Australia will need more information than can be covered in this book. Flying schools or hire companies have instructors who are qualified to explain local conditions and regulations. They will also brief you on current airspace rules. Many of these rules are under review to bring them into line with international standards and this process is close to finalisation.

Australia has a fairly low level of air traffic, especially compared with North America and Europe, mainly concentrated around a few cities and a couple of tourist areas. Elsewhere, the sky is pretty empty but unfortunately navigation facilities are equally sparse. Radar coverage is limited to regions around the major cities, with much of the country outside the range of VOR transmitters, so you have to rely on dead reckoning and the ADF for cross-country flying, especially in the outback, unless you are equipped with a global positioning system (GPS) device.

Much of central Australia is classified as a 'Designated Remote Area' because of its inaccessibility or being beyond the range of VHF communications; flights here must carry a higher level of on-board equipment, such as HF radio or an ELB. Australia generally uses metric measurements but some imperial units are used in aviation for consistency with other countries. The result is a mixture, with altitudes in feet, winds and airspeeds in knots, long distances in nautical miles, short distances like runway lengths in metres and fuel in litres. Don't worry, it's not as confusing as it sounds.

Flight Planning Charts and other planning documents can be obtained from the Airservices Australia (ASA) Publications Centre (☎ 1300 306 630, 03-9342 2000, fax 9347 4407, Ⓦ www.airservices.gov.au/publications) in Melbourne or from aviation supply shops at the larger general airports.

Most large country towns have a local airport with sufficient facilities for regional commuter airlines. Many smaller towns offer a licensed aerodrome, even if it's only a gravel strip, a windsock and (with luck) a public phone. ASA's *En Route Supplement – Australia* (commonly known as *ERSA*) has details of all licensed aerodromes, including runway diagrams, navigational aids and fuel availability.

There are also a number of private and unlicensed aerodromes (some are mentioned in *ERSA*) and, further down the scale, numerous private strips and landing areas. Prior permission to land at these is usually required from the owner of the plane and also from the landowner if it is private property.

Avgas is widely available but prior notice may be required in some places. The price varies from around $1 a litre in the cities, increasing with distance to almost double in remote outback towns. Expect to pay a call-out fee (typically $20) to refuel outside normal hours. As well, small suppliers (such as roadhouses) may expect you to purchase full 200L drums regardless of how much you actually need.

Licences Licensing and all of the other regulations are controlled by the Civil Aviation Safety Authority (Casa), which has regional offices at airports in capital cities and larger regional centres. Contact the head office (☎ 13 17 57, fax 02-6217 1209, ⓔ publicrelations@casa.gov.au, Ⓦ www.casa.gov.au) at GPO Box 2005, Canberra, ACT 2601.

If you have a current foreign licence, Casa will issue a Certificate of Validation that allows you to fly for up to three months. It costs $55 and is available over the counter from any regional office. While no medical or flying tests are required for visual flying, you must undertake a flight review with a qualified instructor and be able to speak English.

For longer periods of tavel, a Special Pilot Licence ($50) is available for private operations. Again there is no theory exam or flight test for VFR operations, but you do need a current overseas medical certificate and to have had a flight check within the previous two years. You can apply at any Casa regional office and the licence is mailed to you from Canberra.

With either method, if you have an instrument rating you will generally need to pass a written exam and flight test before flying IFR in Australia.

In addition to Casa's legal requirements, any company hiring you an aircraft will require a check flight with an instructor to get you familiar with local conditions. Instructor rates are usually around $60 an hour on top of the normal hire cost.

Airport Transport

There are private or public bus services at airports in major towns, but at smaller airports you may have to rely on taxis or friendly locals. If you've booked a motel or other accommodation, they might pick you up. Quite often, a taxi shared between three or more people can be cheaper than the bus.

BUS

Bus travel is generally the cheapest way from A to B. The bus networks are far more comprehensive than the rail system, though they tend to stick to the main, sealed highways. The buses all look pretty similar and are similarly equipped with air-conditioning, toilets and videos. See the track descriptions in this book for specific bus services. In most places there is just one bus terminal, and in very small towns there might not be a proper terminal, just a drop-off/pick-up point. Big city terminals are usually well equipped with toilets, showers and other facilities.

It's true to say there is only one national bus network now, since McCafferty's took over Greyhound Pioneer in late 2000. Although now one company, McCafferty's is continuing to operate both brand names for the time being. They publish separate timetables but the fares and terminals are identical. McCafferty's and Greyhound bus passes remain separate but if you are the holder of a Greyhound pass you can also ride on a McCafferty's bus, provided it's on the route covered by your pass. Confused? So are we. For the latest details and reservations contact McCafferty's (☎ 13 14 99, W www.mccaffertys.com.au) and Greyhound (☎ 13 20 30, W www.greyhound.com.au).

Many smaller bus companies operate locally or specialise in one or two main intercity routes and often have the best deals. In South Australia, Premier Stateliner (☎ 08-8415 5555) operates around the state including trips to the Flinders Ranges. Westrail (☎ 13 10 53) in Western Australia operates bus services to places the trains no longer go.

See also Backpacker Buses under Organised Tours at the end of this chapter for options that focus on outback sights.

Bus Passes

Greyhound and McCafferty's passes can be used on either bus service provided it's within the limitations of the pass. There's a 10% discount for pensioners, children and members of YHA, VIP, Nomads and other approved organisations, as well as card-carrying students. For more information, contact Greyhound/McCaffertys direct or your nearest travel agent.

Aussie Kilometre/Roamer Pass This is the simplest pass and gives you a specified amount of travel, starting at 2000km ($281) and going up in increments of 1000km to a maximum of 20,000km ($1975). The pass is valid for 12 months; you can travel where and in what direction you like, and stop as many times as you like. For example, a 12,000km pass ($1259) will cover a loop from Sydney to Melbourne, Adelaide, central Australia, Darwin, Cairns and back to Sydney. On the west coast you'll need 3000km to get from Perth to Broome and 5000km from Perth to Darwin.

You should phone at least a day ahead to reserve a seat if you're using this pass and bear in mind that side trips or tours off the main route (eg, to Kakadu, Uluru or Shark Bay) may be calculated at double the actual kilometre distance.

Aussie Day Pass With this pass you are limited by days of travel rather than by distance – not much good for short hops but OK if you're planning long hauls. Passes for seven ($672), 10 ($863) and 15 ($1004) days of travel are valid for 30 days; a 21-day pass ($1325) is valid for 60 days.

Aussie Explorer Pass This type of pass is a popular option, giving you from two to 12 months to cover a set route; there are 17 in all and the validity period depends on distance. You don't have the go-anywhere flexibility of the Kilometre/Roamer Pass (no backtracking), but if you can find a route that suits generally works out cheaper.

The Aussie Highlights This allows you to loop around the eastern half of Australia from Sydney, taking in Melbourne, Adelaide, Coober Pedy, Alice Springs, Darwin, Cairns, Townsville, the Whitsundays, Brisbane and Surfers Paradise for $1254, including tours of Uluru-Kata Tjuta and Kakadu National Parks. Or there are one-way passes, such as the Reef & Rock, which goes from Sydney to Alice Springs (and Uluru) via Cairns and Darwin (and Kakadu) for $968; Top End Explorer, which takes in Cairns to Darwin (and Kakadu) for $404; and Western Explorer from Perth to Darwin ($589).

Travel Australia Pass The McCafferty's version of the Aussie Explorer Pass, this is seven set-route passes, valid for between three and 12 months. The Best of the East & Centre costs $1116 ($1288 including

Uluru and Kakadu tours). The Outback Wanderer goes from Cairns to Adelaide via the Centre for $511 ($599 including tours).

TRAIN

Train travel in Australia today is something you do because you really want to and not because it's cheap or convenient, and certainly not because it's fast. But trains are more comfortable than buses and on some of Australia's long-distance journeys the romance of the rails is alive and kicking. Apart from the *Ghan* and *Indian Pacific,* discussed separately in this chapter, there are some great outback train journeys in Queensland, such as the *Spirit of the Outback* from Brisbane to Longreach and the *Gulflander* from Normanton to Croydon. See the Matilda Hwy and Kennedy Hwy sections, respectively, for more information.

Discounted tickets work on a first-come, first-served quota basis so it helps to book in advance. Students get a 50% discount on economy fares and there are hefty discounts for pensioners too.

Rail services within each state are run by that state's rail body, either government or private. However, the *Ghan* from Melbourne or Sydney to Alice Springs via Adelaide, the *Indian Pacific* between Sydney and Perth, and the *Overland* between Melbourne and Adelaide are operated by Great Southern Railway (☎ 13 21 47, Ⓦ www.gsr.com.au).

Great Southern Railway handles train travel in Western Australia, the Northern Territory and South Australia. For services in New South Wales and Queensland, contact Countrylink (☎ 13 22 32, Ⓦ www.country link.nsw.gov.au). A useful one-stop site for Australian train information is Ⓦ www .train-ticket.net/austral/.

Foreign travellers are eligible for some useful train passes on the Countrylink network that also extend to the *Indian Pacific*, *Ghan* and several other services, though these passes have to be purchased before arrival in Australia. With the Austrail Pass, for instance, you can travel anywhere in economy class for $660 (14 days), $860 (21 days) and $1035 (30 days). The Austrail Flexi Pass differs in that it allows a set number of economy-class travelling days within a six-month period – $550 for eight days of travel, $790 for 15 days, $1110 for 22 days and $1440 for 29 days. The eight-day pass can't be used for travel between Adelaide and Perth, or on the *Ghan*.

As the current railway booking system is computerised, any station (other than on metropolitan lines) can make a booking for any journey throughout the country.

The *Ghan*

The *Ghan* saga started in 1877 when authorities decided to build a railway line from Adelaide to Darwin. The railhead reached Marree in 1883, Oodnadatta in 1889 and Alice Springs in 1929, which is where it has stayed ever since. Recently the go-ahead was given for the final 1500km between Alice Springs and Darwin, to be finished by 2004 (though locals say that they'll believe it when they see it).

By the early 1970s, the South Australian state railway system was taken over by the federal government and a new line to Alice Springs was planned. This opened in 1982, and the old line was torn up. While the old *Ghan* took 140 passengers and, under ideal conditions, made the trip in 50 hours, the new *Ghan* takes twice as many passengers and does it in less than half the time. It's still the *Ghan*, but not the trip it once was.

For more on the history of the old *Ghan* see the Oodnadatta Track section of the Central Deserts chapter.

Fares Between Adelaide and Alice Springs, the *Ghan* costs $197 in coach class (no sleeper or meals); a sleeper with shared facilities and no meals is $624; the Gold Kangaroo Service with the lot (including self-contained sleeper) is $780. There are enormous discounts (up to 50%) for students and pensioners. Return fares are generally double the one-way fare. There are also fares from Sydney and Melbourne, and check for the availability of special deals, eg, tours to Uluru and Kings Canyon, Coober Pedy and outback mail runs.

The train leaves Adelaide Monday and Thursday at 3pm, arriving in Alice Springs the next morning at 10am. It leaves Alice Springs Friday and Tuesday at 1pm, and arrives in Adelaide at 9am the next day.

You can transport a car (accompanied only) from Adelaide to Alice Springs for $356, or $262 coming down (there's a special $99 deal with two Gold Kangaroo tickets), so you can take the train one way and drive the car back the other.

Bookings can be made by phoning Great Southern Railway (☎ 13 21 47) between 9am and 5pm Monday to Friday and changeable hours on weekends; or Countrylink (☎ 13 22 32) from 7am to 9pm, daily.

The *Indian Pacific*

Along with the *Ghan*, the *Indian Pacific* line is one of Australia's greatest train journeys: a 66-hour trip between the Pacific Ocean on one side of the continent and the Indian Ocean on the other. Travelling this way, you really appreciate the immensity of the country (or are bored stiff).

From Sydney, it crosses New South Wales to Broken Hill, and continues on to Adelaide and across the Nullarbor. From Port Augusta to Kalgoorlie, the seemingly endless crossing of the almost uninhabited centre takes 23 hours on the longest straight stretch of tracks in the world (478km).

History The promise of a transcontinental railway helped to lure gold-rich Western Australia into the Commonwealth in 1901. Port Augusta in South Australia and Kalgoorlie in Western Australia were the only state railheads in 1907, when surveyors set out to map a line between the two. In 1911, the Commonwealth legislated to fund north-south *Ghan* and east-west *Indian Pacific* routes across the continent.

The first sod was turned in Port Augusta in 1912 and, for five years, two self-contained gangs, a total of 3000 workers, inched towards each other. They endured sandstorms, swarms of flies and intense heat as they laid 2.5 million sleepers and 140,000 tonnes of rail. Picks and shovels were used to remove soil and rocks and the workers were supplied by packhorse and camel. The job was completed with a minimum of

mechanical aids, one of the few machines being the Roberts track-layer.

As Australia was embroiled in WWI, there was no great opening celebration when the track gangs met in the sand hills near Ooldea. The first *Transcontinental Express* pulled out of Port Augusta at 9.32pm on 22 October 1917, heralding the start of 'the desert railway from Hell to Hallelujah'. It arrived in Kalgoorlie 42 hours 48 minutes later, after covering 1682km.

The participants in the struggle to get the railway started are reflected in the names of the stations along the straight stretch: Forrest, Deakin, Hughes, Cook, Fisher, O'Malley and Barton; Bates commemorates Daisy Bates, who devoted herself to the welfare of Aborigines and for a time lived alongside the line near Ooldea; Denman was the governor-general who turned the first sod in 1917.

A good read is Patsy Adam Smith's *The Desert Railway*, with its many photographs of the building of the line. The line's history is covered exhaustively in *Road through the Wilderness* by David Burke.

Fares To Perth, one-way fares from Adelaide are $283 (seat only), $879 (sleeper cabin) or $1099 (Gold Kangaroo with the lot), with whopping discounts (up to 50%) for students and pensioners. From Sydney, they're $459, $1199 or $1499, and there are also fares from Melbourne; again, discounts for students and pensioners are substantial. Return fares are generally double the one-way fare, and check the availability of special deals.

Melbourne passengers connect with the *Indian Pacific* at Adelaide, after arriving on the *Overlander*. Cars (accompanied only) can be transported from Adelaide to Perth for $522, or $314 the other way – a good option for those not wishing to drive the Nullarbor in both directions. As with the *Ghan*, there's a special $99 car deal with two Gold Kangaroo tickets.

The distance between Sydney and Perth is 3961km. Westbound, the *Indian Pacific* departs Sydney at 2.55pm Thursday and Monday. Heading east, the train departs Perth at 10.55am Monday and Friday. Book at least a month in advance.

Meals are included in the Gold Kangaroo fare only, as well as a lounge compartment with piano; other passengers can purchase meals from the restaurant car.

See the Fares in the *Ghan* section earlier for booking details.

MOTORCYCLE

Much of the information in the Car section also applies to motorcycles. One of the major differences is that most of the 4WD tracks don't require an off-road motorcycle. True, the going will be much easier on an enduro or motocross machine, especially in sand, but you won't be able to carry the gear you need. On a motorcycle it's much easier to pick your way through or around an obstacle and if you get stuck, you can always get off and push.

Many bikers travel the outback alone, but for obvious reasons that's not something we can recommend. The ideal setup for serious outback travel is a small group of bikes with one or two follow-up vehicles for fuel, water and luggage; make sure one of the vehicles can carry a broken-down bike.

Unfortunately Australia has no national motorcycling organisation like the AMA (American Motorcyclist Association) to help with touring advice. State automobile

---

The Amazing Ellis Bankin

In a remote corner of the 4200 sq km that make up Curtin Springs station, along the Lasseter Hwy out to Uluru, is a post-and-rail enclosure with a grave and a simple headstone that reads: 'In memory of EM Bankin, who perished Jan 1935.'

Unfortunately the year is wrong: It should read 1936. In 1935 the then 31-year-old Ellis Bankin was still alive and well, teaching History and Geography at a school in Glenroy, Melbourne. His classes must have been interesting because he set out to experience the wonders of the world first-hand in order to teach about them (that was his excuse, anyway).

In 1926, he had procured a job as chief steward on a tramp steamer bound for Boston, and spent the next three years travelling and working his way around the USA and Canada. He then went back home to teach, but soon took a year off to ride his bicycle around Britain.

Back in Australia again, he began travelling by motorcycle and wasted no time clocking up the miles. In 1934, the first trip on his 350cc Model 3/1 side-valve Triumph took him across the Nullarbor to Perth and back in 36 days. In May and June of 1935 he rode from Broken Hill via Milparinka into Queensland and down the Strzelecki Track from Innamincka to Marree. A few months later, in September, he rushed from Melbourne via Adelaide and Coober Pedy to Alice Springs and back via the Oodnadatta Track in a mere 10 days (the only time available to him between school terms), averaging a staggering 480km a day!

By now he was sponsored by the Triumph agent and by the Vacuum oil company, and his remarkable exploits were widely reported in the press.

On what was to be his final journey, in 1935–36, he went from Marree via Birdsville to Urandangi in far western Queensland, then across to Alice Springs and down to Kulgera before turning towards Uluru (mind you, this was long before there were tracks he could have followed). His plan was to head north from the Rock to Tennant Creek, across to Mt Isa, and then down the middle of Queensland to Sydney and back to Melbourne.

He was last seen leaving Ernabella Station, south-west of Kulgera just across the South Australian border, in heatwave conditions on 13 January 1936. He didn't have much choice: The long school holiday required for this trip happened to be during the hottest time of the year.

He hit a rabbit warren and had a bad fall. Later, on a claypan, he lost sight of the camel track he was supposed to follow. He then made for Mt Conner, visible in the distance. Unable to find water there, he left the mountain and travelled south-east (maybe to retrace his tracks) but this took him deeper into sand-ridge country where he was to die 48 hours later. It's not known what went wrong.

associations are your best source for general information. Unfortunately they usually know very little about motorcycles.

Which Motorcycle?

The ideal motorcycle has a large-capacity dual-purpose machine: One that will handle the long distances to and from your chosen track with ease and won't be too disturbed by the track itself. Good choices available in Australia include the Yamaha XTs, TTs or Ténérés (the 'Land Rovers' of motorcycles – rugged, reliable and proven); Honda XLs, XRs, Transalps or NX650 Dominators (one of the best machines for the outback but let down by a small tank); Suzuki DRs; Kawasaki KLRs or other dual-purpose models; and BMW GSes.

Dual-purpose models from other brands (eg, Moto Guzzi, Cagiva and Triumph) will also do the job but getting parts may be difficult. A sturdy, uncomplicated road bike from the 1980s or '90s with a large front wheel (18 or preferably 19 inch) will generally be OK too, if a bit more of a handful in tough conditions. The narrower the tyre profile the better; today's wide road-tyres aren't much good on dirt.

Chances are you will meet only a few motorcyclists, often Japanese, riding on

The Amazing Ellis Bankin

Although he kept a diary there were no entries for those final two days.

His body was found by a search party a month later and was buried right there. His bike, still in perfect working order, was shipped back to the importers in Melbourne.

In a report to the coroner, the Northern Territory Deputy Administrator concluded that a 'heat wave was on at the time, and with the exertion of pushing the cycle over heavy sand hills, his water supply of two or three gallons was totally inadequate. It was obvious that he either perished from thirst or from weakness due to thirst and exertion or both.'

In the years that followed, the tragedy was largely forgotten, but in 1982 the grave was rediscovered during a muster in a remote part of Curtin Springs. A nearby cattle bore was renamed Bankin's Bore in his honour. In 1986, on the 50th anniversary of his death, a group of 25 bike enthusiasts visited the site to install a commemorative plaque.

You can only visit the grave on a guided tour from Curtin Springs station (☎ 08-8956 2906). The station offers full-day ($172) and half-day ($82.50) tours (maximum six people) around the property and out to Mt Conner. The grave isn't normally part of the itinerary but is included if people are interested. When you get there, you'll probably agree with what Peter Severin, the owner of Curtin Springs, said to me when we stood at this tranquil spot among the red sand dunes and dense scrub: 'That's the way I want to be buried.'

Bankin's biography, *Ellis Matthewman Bankin – Outback Motorcyclist Who Perished* (1997, updated edition 2001) by Richard Duckworth, is hard to find (both editions were limited) but some of the local libraries might have it.

Rob van Driesum

small-capacity dual-purpose bikes, proof that size isn't always important. A 250cc may be a bit tedious over the long roads in the outback though – especially if you're carrying gear and aren't lightweight.

Important points to consider are fuel consumption and tank size. Few bikes have a fuel range of more than 300km in favourable conditions, which is just enough to get you around and straight through the continent on the sealed roads but not enough for many outback tracks.

An electric start will make life easier: A stalled bike is often reluctant to start and the engine usually floods when you drop it. Water-cooling is fine, but if you're faced with the choice, go for a simpler and less sensitive air-cooled engine. The bike ideally should have spoked wheels as they absorb shocks and corrugations better than cast wheels (which have been known to crack under Australian conditions).

Obtaining a Motorcycle

If you live overseas, bringing your own motorcycle into Australia will require a *carnet de passages* and when you try to sell it here, you'll get less than the market price because it doesn't have Australian approval markings. The cost of shipping from just about anywhere is expensive, but may be worth looking into if you're serious.

With time up your sleeve, you can easily buy a motorcycle. The start of the southern winter is a good time to strike – perfect timing for the outback season. Australian newspapers and the lively local bike press have extensive classified advertisement sections where $3000 will easily take you around the country if you know a bit about bikes. The main drawback is that you'll have to sell the bike again afterwards.

An easier option is a buy-back arrangement with one of the large motorcycle dealers in major cities. Elizabeth St, Melbourne, is a good hunting ground. Basic negotiating skills plus a wad of cash (say, $5000) should secure a decent second-hand road bike with a guarantee they'll buy it back in good condition minus 40% to 50% after your four-month, round-Australia trip.

They'll probably haggle about what constitutes 'good condition' when you return , so don't tell them about your Gunbarrel trip. Popular brands for this sort of thing are BMWs (cheap ones) and the large-capacity, shaft-driven Japanese bikes. Dual-purpose bikes are cheaper, but very few dealers are willing to buy them back. See Buying a Car earlier for a company that does buy-backs on Yamaha XT600s and BMW R1150GSes.

If you can afford to buy new, buy-backs become a lot easier to organise but you still lose about 50%, and for that sort of money, you're probably better off shipping it home.

Preparation & Spares

The owner's manual for your bike often specifies oils of different viscosities for different conditions. Check the daytime temperatures for where you want to go, but in the outback it's best to use the highest ('thickest') viscosity listed, especially for serious off-road work.

Road-going tyres will generally see you through but dual-purpose tyres are a much better proposition. Off-road 'knobbies' are great on chewed-up tracks with deep ruts like the Cape York telegraph track and are less susceptible to punctures than other types of tyre, but you'll probably wear them out before you get to the start of the off-road bits and they're hair-raising in wet weather on bitumen.

Tubeless tyres are manageable if they're fairly narrow and you carry at least six carbon-dioxide cartridges in the appropriate repair kit (buy cheap soda-water cartridges and tap the threads or have that done). A tubeless tyre will never seat properly with a hand pump and you'll be pumping forever. Replace the gas in the tyre with air at the earliest opportunity.

The different ways of carrying luggage could fill a separate chapter. Carry your heaviest stuff, such as tools, in a tank bag, which puts the weight between the wheels. Lighter, more bulky gear can be carried over the rear wheel, preferably not high over the rear end but in panniers or side bags that lower the centre of gravity. Luggage racks should be quite solid and, if necessary, braced to withstand the road corrugations. Aluminium racks tend to crack and aren't easy to weld. Take plenty of elastic straps ('ocky' or octopus straps) to tie down your gear, and bring a few spare.

Outback dust, especially the powdery bulldust, has a habit of getting everywhere you don't want it. Make sure the air intake is completely sealed: Apply silicone sealant to the outside of any connections and grease the contact areas of the air filter and cover. Some motorcyclists stop oiling their chains in the outback, and with modern O-ring chains this may be an option but opinions are divided: Yes, oil attracts dust, but a dry chain runs very hot and the critical O-ring seals may not survive the punishment. We're in favour of oiling.

If you're travelling in sandy or muddy regions, a small steel plate welded to the bottom of the side stand prevents it sinking, though a flattened can or small wooden plank kept to hand in the tank bag also works.

Ensure that the brake and clutch levers can twist around the handlebars in case of a fall – if you do the clamps up tight, they'll break off. A headlight protector (plastic cover or steel grid) is a good idea to protect the expensive lens against stones thrown up by oncoming traffic.

It's worth carrying some spares and tools even if you don't know how to use them, because someone else often does. If you do know, you'll probably have a fair idea of what to take. The basics include:

- a spare tyre tube (front wheel size, that will fit in the rear but usually not vice versa); you must know how to fix a tyre
- puncture repair kit with levers and a pump, or tubeless tyre repair kit with a pump and enough carbon dioxide cartridges to fix two or three flats (at least two cartridges per flat)
- a spare tyre valve and a valve cap that can unscrew same
- the bike's standard tool kit for what it's worth (aftermarket items are much better); some extra tools – ask at a friendly bike shop if you don't know
- spare throttle, clutch and, if relevant, brake cables
- tie wire, cloth tape ('gaffer' tape) and nylon 'zip-ties'

- a handful of bolts and nuts in emergency sizes (M6 and M8), along with a few self-tapping screws
- one or two fuses in your bike's ratings and a few metres of electrical wire
- a bar of soap for patching-up tank leaks (knead to a putty with water and squeeze into the leak)
- most important of all, a workshop manual for your bike – even if you can't make sense of it, the local motorcycle mechanic will be able to

Minimum clothing requirements are sturdy boots, gloves, trousers, jacket and a helmet (ideally with a peak to cut out the sun early and late in the day). Full leathers tend to be too hot. Knee and elbow protectors are seriously worth considering (some would say essential) on unsealed roads. Pick up a cheap sheepskin at a saddlery shop and throw it over the seat. It's very effective at easing sore-bum syndrome.

Always carry water – at least 2L on sealed roads where someone is bound to come along soon if you strike a problem, much more off the beaten track. Beware of dehydration in the dry, hot air: Force yourself to drink plenty of water even if you don't feel thirsty, and keep checking the colour of your urine.

Finally, learn something about first aid and carry a first-aid kit. Graze wounds are common in bike get-offs and your kit should contain some special gauze for this.

Riding Techniques

If you've never ridden on unsealed roads, the outback could be a bad place to start because of the serious consequences if something goes wrong. If you're in a group with a few experienced riders, however, it can be great fun.

The first mistake that beginners make is to 'freeze' and lock solid onto the handlebars as soon as they see dirt. Wrong. The bike will want to 'wander' a bit and find its own way – let it. Move your weight slightly back on the seat, keep the power on and guide the bike loosely. If things seem to get out of control, stand on the footpegs a bit, this will lower the centre of gravity and calm things down, and if you grip the tank with your knees at the same time, you'll be surprised how well you can 'steer' the bike. Look reasonably far ahead on the track, not immediately ahead of the front wheel or you'll get nervous.

If a sandy patch comes up, these techniques are mandatory. It's important to keep the power on; move back on the seat, maybe shift down a gear and open the throttle a bit further. You don't have to accelerate as such; the important thing is to keep enough power onto the rear wheel to maintain momentum. This will help move the centre of gravity to the rear and prevent the front wheel sliding sideways or digging into the sand, twisting sideways and spitting you over the bars – the latter result is guaranteed if you close the throttle and thereby transfer weight to the front. Don't try to 'jump ruts' unless they're shallow; choose a particular rut and try to ride it out. Great fun once you get the hang of it!

The same techniques apply to deep gravel, often encountered on 'graded' or freshly levelled roads. Car drivers love these, but to motorcyclists the loose surface can be bad news – a bit like riding on marbles. Keep power onto the rear wheel but be careful not to overdo it because the rear will break sideways more easily than in sand. It's better to shift back on the seat a bit. The less 'off-road' your tyre tread, the more of a problem you'll have with gravel.

You can fight against sand and gravel but mud is a much more formidable adversary. In theory the same riding principles apply, but, unless you're on an enduro machine with knobby tyres, mud requires a delicate balancing act with the throttle: If the front wheel doesn't slide out from under you the rear wheel will, especially in the slippery red or black soil often encountered in the outback. 'Soften' the power delivery by selecting a higher gear than you normally would for that speed. Take it slowly with your feet out if things are really wet, or look for harder surface off the side of the road. Also beware of mud build-up under the rear mudguard (and the front if it sits low on the wheel) as the rear wheel could well lock up and if you try to keep going, you'll burn the clutch. All you can do is stop and clear out the mud, which may be necessary every few hundred metres in black soil.

On corrugated roads, car drivers tend to sit on relatively high speeds so they skim over the top and make life more comfortable for themselves and their suspension. The drawback is that the tyres lose grip, which is fine so long as the road is flat and there aren't any corners. But a motorcycle has less inherent stability and you could well find yourself drifting sideways out of control if you don't slow down. See how it goes, but if the corrugation is really bad it might be necessary to slow right down and ride on the side of the road or off the road altogether.

Beware: Road sides and ditches often contain nails, bits of glass and other meanies that lie in wait for unsuspecting tyres.

BICYCLE

Whether you're hiring a bike to ride around town or wearing out your chain-wheels on a Melbourne-Darwin marathon, the outback has some great places for cycling. There are bike paths in most large towns and also thousands of kilometres of open road that carries little traffic. Especially appealing is that in many areas it's possible to ride all day without encountering a hill. On the downside, you can ride even further and not see any decent scenery.

Bicycle helmets are compulsory wear in all states and territories.

If you're coming from overseas just to cycle, it makes sense to bring your own bike. Check with your airline for costs and the degree of dismantling and packing required. Within Australia, you can load your bike onto a bus or train to skip the most boring bits. Note that bus companies require you to dismantle your bike and some don't guarantee that it will travel on the same bus as you. Trains are easier but supervise the loading. If possible tie your bike upright, otherwise you may find that the guard has stacked crates of Holden spares on your fragile alloy wheels.

You can buy a reasonable steel-framed touring bike in Australia for about $400 (plus panniers), but if you want quality fittings or a good mountain bike, costs rise sharply. It may be possible to rent touring bikes and equipment from a commercial touring outfit. A touring bike is better than a mountain bike if you're staying on the tar.

For those who don't want to buy a bike or organise their own tour, consider options such as Perth-based Remote Outback Cycle Tours (☎ 08-9279 6969, fax 9248 4866, Ⓦ www.cycletours.com.au). It has a wide range of adventurous and quite affordable tours all over the outback, with backup vehicles and catering.

Planning

There are two ways to tour the outback by bike. The first is to stay on the few sealed roads. Although these are usually highways, they carry little traffic and generally offer good riding. However, distances between sources of food and water can be great, so plan carefully – for example, heading south on the Stuart Hwy, it's 252km between Coober Pedy and the next roadhouse.

The other approach involves planning a trip on one of the unsealed routes. You'll probably need a mountain bike, not only because of the rough surface but also because the wider tyres will help in soft conditions. Some roads may be impossibly deep in sand or dust and the only sure way to find out is to talk to another cyclist – if you can find one. Allow plenty of time and be prepared to change your plans. Riding on dirt roads can be very slow and tiring, so don't underestimate the time it will take to reach the next water supply.

The track descriptions in this book tell you who to contact about road conditions. Police are a good source of information, but they will have to deal with the results if something goes wrong and may try to dissuade you. Don't dismiss their advice lightly. They usually know about the local conditions better than anyone else.

Always check with the locals if you're heading into remote areas and notify the police if you're about to do something particularly adventurous. That said, don't rely too much on local knowledge of road conditions: Most people have no idea of

Always ensure you have a more than adequate supply of water

what a heavily loaded bike needs. What they think is a great road for cars may actually be pedal-deep in sand or bulldust. Flooded roads that stop cars might not be a problem for bikes. Then again, they might be!

You can get by with standard road maps but one of the government series (such as Geoscience Australia's) showing topography and handy features such as farm buildings helps you plan routes and gives a better appreciation of the surrounding country. The 1:250,000 series is the most suitable, although you'll need a lot of maps if you're covering much territory. The next scale up, 1:1,000,000, is usually adequate

Spares

It's rare to find a town of reasonable size that doesn't have a bike shop stocking basic parts, although whether they will be compatible with the more exotic machines is another matter. It might be worth talking with a specialist bike shop in a major city before you set out. They may be able to courier parts to you in a repair emergency.

Compulsory spares include: puncture repair kit; tubes and tyres (hot roads wear tyres quickly and Michelin World Tours start to get pretty thin after about 2000km); brake and gear cables; spokes (about 10 and in the correct gauge); both bearings and lubricants plus all the tools required to strip down and clean bearings; and perhaps a spare chain (if you're going a long way) and crank. You obviously should know how to perform routine repairs.

On the Road

Until you get fit, be careful to eat enough to keep you going – remember that exercise is an appetite-suppressant. It's surprisingly easy to be so depleted of energy that you end up camping in the spinifex just 10km short of a shower and a steak.

No matter how fit you are, water is vital. Death by dehydration is a real possibility on a remote track. Summer in inland Australia can be impossibly hot, as can early autumn and late spring. Take it easy, wear a hat and plenty of sunscreen and drink *lots* of water. Six litres a day isn't an unreasonable amount if you're working hard and you may well need more – check the colour of your urine. Heat exhaustion can also kill and you need to be aware of how your body is coping. Obtain good medical advice (perhaps from a sports medicine clinic) and learn how to recognise the symptoms of dehydration and heat exhaustion.

The first time you're passed by a road train will be an interesting experience. If you stick to sealed roads often the most dangerous vehicles will be buses, which use a lot of road and are surprisingly quiet. When you haven't seen another vehicle for a few hours, it's easy to be on the wrong side of the road when the Alice Springs express blasts through.

In the eastern states, be aware of the blistering 'hot northerlies', the prevailing winds that make a northbound cyclist's life very uncomfortable in summer. In April, the southerly trades begin to prevail and you can have (theoretically at least) tailwinds all the way from Adelaide to Darwin. If you're travelling across the Nullarbor, don't cycle from east to west against the westerlies: They're pretty strong all year and can soon wear you out. In fact it's not uncommon for trans-Nullarbor trucks to use 30% more fuel heading west rather than east.

Information

See Lonely Planet's *Cycling Australia* for more general and sometimes quite specific advice. In each state there are touring organisations that can help with information and put you in touch with touring clubs and private tour operators. The most relevant ones for the outback are:

New South Wales
Bicycle New South Wales (☎ 02-9283 5200, fax 9283 5246, **W** www.bicyclensw.org.au) 209 Castlereagh St, Sydney, NSW 2000

Queensland
Bicycle Queensland (☎/fax 07-3844 1144, **W** www.biq.org.au) PO Box 8321, Woolloongabba, Brisbane, Qld 4102

South Australia
Bicycle SA (☎ 08-8410 1406, fax 8410 1455, **W** www.bikesa.asn.au) 1 Sturt St, Adelaide, SA 5000

Western Australia
Bicycle Transportation Alliance
(☎/fax 08-94207210, **W** sunsite.anu.edu .au/wa/bta) 2 Delhi St, West Perth, WA 6849.

HITCHING

Hitching is never entirely safe in any country and it's not a form of travel we can recommend. People who decide to hitch should understand that they're taking a small but potentially serious risk. They will be slightly safer if they travel in pairs and let someone know where they're going. University and hostel notice boards are good places to look for hitching partners.

Just as hitchers should be wary when accepting lifts, drivers who pick up hitchers or cost-sharing travellers should also be aware of the possible risks involved.

Quite a few travellers hitch rides in the outback. The locals are generally pretty easy-going and friendly and often pick up hitchers for company. The drawback is that they may deposit them at the track leading to their property, usually a long way from anywhere – find out before it's too late! On the other hand, most car drivers in the outback are engaged in long-distance travel themselves and aren't able to pick up hitchers. For these reasons, hitching is really only feasible along the main sealed roads, where rides take you from town to town or roadhouse to roadhouse.

Trucks often provide the best lifts but they'll only stop if they're going slowly and can get started easily again. Truckies will say they're going to the next town but if they don't like you, will usually drop you anywhere. As they often pick up hitchers for company, the quickest way to create a bad impression is to jump in and fall asleep.

BOAT

A boat might not seem an obvious way to tour the outback but there's a whole subculture of mostly young people who work their way around the outback on yachts and trawlers. For most it's quite an experience as they can visit parts of the Australian coastline that can't be reached any other way.

Once upon a time there was quite a busy coastal shipping service but now this only applies to freight, and even that is declining rapidly. In south eastern inland Australia, long-distance freight used to go by river (as evidenced by the admiralty office in Bourke, a town in outback New South Wales) but modern rail and road transport have taken over completely.

It is, however, quite possible to make your way round the coast by hitching rides or crewing on yachts. It obviously helps if you're an experienced sailor however some people are taken on as cooks (not very pleasant on a rolling yacht). Usually you have to chip in something for food and the skipper may demand a financial bond as security. Many boats move north to escape the winter, so April is a good time to look for a berth in the southern harbours.

For those who know their way around a commercial fishing boat, there's temporary work on the many small trawlers operating the remote north-eastern and northern coastline. The pay can be excellent or lousy depending on the catch. Ask around at harbours, marinas, or yacht or sailing clubs – anywhere that boats call. Trawler crews are often amenable to hiring female cooks,

and women who pursue this option report good and bad experiences.

MAIL RUNS

You'll get a first-hand idea of what a mail run means to the people of the outback by going along for the ride (see Post & Communications in the Facts for the Visitor chapter for an explanation of mail runs). In Coober Pedy, the mail truck leaves on Monday and Thursday, covering 600km of dirt roads as it does the 12-hour round trip to Oodnadatta and William Creek at a cost of $90 (no lunch provided). For further details contact Outback Mail Run (☎ 1800 069 911, ℮ mailrun@ozemail.com.au) or Underground Books (☎ 08-8672 5558) in Coober Pedy.

Another possibility is to hitch a ride on the mail planes that service the outback's scattered communities. There are a few that take paying passengers but they're not cheap. Airlines of SA (☎ 08-8642 3100, ℮ augusta@dove.net.au), in Port Augusta, does a run on Saturday to Boulia in western Queensland, via Innamincka and Birdsville; the cost (air fares only) is $330/660 one way/return. In Cairns, Cape York Air Services (☎ 07-4035 9399, ⓦ www.cape yorkair.com.au), the local mail contractor, does mail runs on weekdays. If there's enough space, you can go along on any of six different routes for $240 to $670, depending on the distance covered, and you can also do one-way trips. Based in Mt Isa, West Wing Aviation (☎ 07-4743 2144) will take tourists on its mail runs.

ORGANISED TOURS

Many operators offer outback tours in a variety of vehicles and even on foot. Some 4WD safaris go to places you simply can't get to on your own without large amounts of expensive equipment. See the individual track descriptions for details.

Victoria's AAT Kings (☎ 03-9274 7422, 1800 334 009, ⓦ www.aatkings.com) at 29–33 Palmerston Crescent, South Melbourne, is one of the better known general tour operators. Most of it's tours are of the large, air-con bus variety but it has a good range of 4WD tours also. Bookings are accepted only through travel agents.

Perth's Amesz Tours (☎ 08-9250 2577, fax 9250 2634, W www.amesz.com.au) at 1/4 Elmsfield Rd, Midvale does outback tours of the western half of Australia. Check with YHA Travel offices in capital cities as their tours are usually good value.

Backpacker Buses

Several companies offer transport for budget travellers, mostly backpackers but young-at-heart will do too. Most of these are pretty much organised tours but they do get from A to B (sometimes with hop-on, hop-off services), and can be an interesting (if less comfortable) alternative to the big bus companies.

Get a taste of the South Australia and Northern Territory outback with Groovy Grape (☎ 1800 661 177, W www.groovy grape.com.au), which organises a seven-day camping trip from Adelaide to Alice Springs via the northern Flinders Ranges, Marree, William Creek, Coober Pedy and Uluru for $690 all-inclusive. Wayward Bus (☎ 1800 882 823, W www.waywardbus.com.au) does much the same route in eight days for $770 all-inclusive. Heading Bush 4WD Adventures (☎ 1800 639 933, W www.head bush.mtx.net) also does a similar route but this is a 10-day, small-group 4WD trip ($985 all-inclusive) and you can expect to pitch in and rough it a bit.

Remote Possibilities (☎ 1800 623 854, 08-8953 6633, W www.australiaoutback tours.com) does Alice Springs–Darwin runs several times a week in season for $198 (including accommodation and meals), with an overnight stop at Daly Waters. You can get on and off where you like.

Nullarbor Traveller (☎ 1800 816 858, W www.the-traveller.com.au) is a small company running relaxed minibus trips across the Nullarbor. The Adelaide-Perth trip ($891, nine days) follows the Western Australian coast from Esperance to Albany and through the southern forests to Perth. The return ($693, seven days) goes straight through Kalgoorlie. Prices include budget accommodation, entry fees and most meals.

West Coast Explorer (☎ 1300 88 7779, W www.westcoastexplorer.com.au) offers a zigzag trip from Perth up the coast to Darwin (18 days including two rest days in Broome) for $2142 including meals, tent and entry fees.

Oz Experience (☎ 1300 300 028, W www .ozexperience.com) is the biggest hop-on, hop-off backpacker bus network in the country and we get mixed reports on the service. It's regarded as a bit of a party bus for younger travellers, but to be fair, lots of backpackers rave about Oz Experience and have a great time meeting other travellers. The network covers all parts of central and eastern Australia (in the Northern Territory the service is taken over by Northern Territory Adventure Tours), but not Western Australia. Travel is only in one direction and the passes are valid for six months with unlimited stops. A Sydney-Darwin pass, via Melbourne, Adelaide and Alice Springs, is $830; while the mother of all trips, Cairns to Darwin right around the coast and up the Centre, is $1495.

Tag-along 4WD Tours

If you already have a 4WD and want to experience the remote country safely, easily and in the company of others, it's well worth considering one of the many guiding services or 'tag-along' operators. They may be able to set you up with a 4WD hire vehicle, if necessary, and a few may even take a passenger or two.

Some provide a catering service and can produce wonderful meals in the bush, including wine with the evening meal. Most of these operations expect a little help preparing the food, washing dishes and carrying some of the tucker, usually on an informal roster basis.

Other operations only provide a guiding service. These are much cheaper but you provide your own food and the enthusiasm and expertise to cook it in the bush.

Tag-along services provide experienced guides who are experts at driving and recovery and will give you all the necessary hints to get you through. Full radio gear and recovery equipment are carried. Also, many of the operators have access to areas not available to the independent traveller, know the worthwhile attractions and camping spots, and take care of permits.

Once you've decided where you'd like to go, contact the operators servicing that area. Details are usually available from state and local tourist information centres or the 4WD clubs, and we also mention several in the track descriptions in this book.

Motorcycle Tours

Several operators offer outback motorcycle tours, either tag-along or (more often) on bikes supplied by them. Check individual track descriptions in this book.

Bike-tour operators tend to come and go, but one that has been in business for 20 years is Bike Tours Australia, which offers long-distance tours on Yamaha XT600 trail bikes. These range from sightseeing trips on bitumen (eg, the three-week Melbourne-Darwin 'Outbacker', $3650) to expeditions for experienced riders (a five-week Darwin-Perth 'Total' via the Kimberley and Canning Stock Route, or Perth–Cape York 'Classic', for $6500 including fuel and food). Most of Bike Tours' clients are Europeans but anyone is welcome. The company also does car and motorcycle buy-backs under the name Car Connection Australia – see Buying a Car earlier in this chapter for details.

Aboriginal Culture Tours

Aboriginal involvement in the tourism industry has increased greatly in recent years. Considering that outback Aborigines are faced with few employment opportunities and that Aboriginal culture is of major interest to most people who visit the outback, this trend is likely to continue.

Such tours often give an introduction to traditional Aboriginal law, religion and lifestyle, as well as the Aboriginals' encyclopaedic knowledge of useful plants and animals, all of which remain strong in many parts of the outback.

The following tours are just some of the ones we've found particularly worthwhile. See the individual track descriptions for other options, or contact the state and

(especially) local tourist offices. If you go on any of these tours, please respect requests that Aboriginal guides make about appropriate behaviour.

Northern South Australia Desert Tracks (☎ 0410 644 480, ⊠ www.desert-tracks .com.au) is Aboriginal-owned and offers two- and seven-day tours of the Anangu-Pitjantjatjara lands from April to October at a cost of $350 per day. Few other tours offer such a deep insight into traditional Aboriginal culture, with Aboriginal elders acting as guides and teachers. Contact Desert Tracks well in advance of your preferred date of departure. Two-day tours depart from Ayers Rock Resort, seven-day tours from Alice Springs.

Northern Territory – Southern & Central Uluru-Kata Tjuta National Park's two hour Liru Walk ($52), by Aboriginal-owned Anangu Tours (☎ 08-8956 2123, ⊠ www.anangutours.com.au), leaves from the park's cultural centre near Uluru. This tour focuses on traditional bush skills and the Tjukurpa stories associated with the battle between Liru and Kuniya.

Oak Valley Tours (☎ 08-8956 0959) is also Aboriginal-owned and operated. The company offers day tours of the area south of Alice Springs ($133) and also does extended 4WD tours for small groups to Uluru.

West of Alice Springs, the Wallace Rockhole Aboriginal community (☎ 08-8956 7415) conducts several educational tours including the popular 1½-hour rock art and bush medicine tour. There's also a day tour looking for (and eating) bush tucker. Sahara Outback Tours (☎ 1800 806 240, ⊠ www .saharatours.com) does the 1½-hour rock art and bush medicine tour as part of a five-day camping trip.

In Alice Springs, the Aboriginal-owned and operated Aboriginal Art & Culture Centre (☎ 09-8952 3408, ⊠ www.aboriginalart .com.au) has a couple of good tours. Its four-hour Discovery Tour includes a bush tucker walk and also demonstrations of traditional Aboriginal dance.

Northern Territory – Top End From Darwin there are a number of tours with significant Aboriginal content. Tiwi Tours (☎ 1800 183 630, fax 8924 1122; e aussie adventure@attglobal.net) has excellent one/two-day tours to the Tiwi Islands, a short flight off the coast from Darwin, for $279/548 per person. The tours are owned by the Tiwi people and are run by Aussie Adventure Holidays.

Aussie Adventure Holidays (☎ 1800 811 633, fax 8924 1122, e aussieadventure@attglobal.net) also runs Peppi Tours. These are two-day, 4WD camping tours to a small Aboriginal community in the Daly River region south-west of Darwin.

Davidson's Arnhemland Safaris (☎ 08-8927 5240, e dassafaris@onaustralia.com.au) runs extended tours to western Arnhem Land for $385 per person per day including flights from Darwin.

Western Australia In Fitzroy Crossing, on the southern edge of the Kimberley, the Darlngunaya Aboriginal Corporation (part of the Junjuwa community), in collaboration with Headwaters (☎ 03-9478 9414, e paddlesports@paddlesports.com.au), offers six- or seven-day white-water rafting trips on the Fitzroy River (Grades 5 to 6) for $1680/1960. The first trip covers the upper Fitzroy gorges passing rainforest, rock art and waterfalls, ending with a helicopter ride out of Moll Gorge. The second trip from Milli Windie station to Dimond Gorge is much more adrenalin-pumping, finishing with a helicopter ride. Trips operate during the Wet (January to March) and Bunuba guides are on hand to explain the passing landscapes. An unforgettable experience.

Queensland In Rockhampton, check out one of the daily guided tours of the Dreamtime Aboriginal Cultural Centre (☎ 07-4936 1655). In far northern Queensland, at Kuranda, the Rainforestation (☎ 07-4093 9033) organises Aboriginal-guided walks and presents traditional performances by the Pamagirri dancers. From Cairns, Jowalbinna Bush Camp (☎ 07-4051 4777, W www.adventures.com.au) runs 4WD tours to the Quinkan rock-art galleries near Laura on Cape York Peninsula. Also from Cairns, Ku Ku Yelangi woman Nalba (Hazel) Douglas (☎ 07-4098 2206, fax 4098 1008, W www.nativeguidesafaritours.com.au) will take you on an excellent 4WD cultural adventure tour to Cape Tribulation for $120.

The Ang-Gnarra Aboriginal Corporation (☎ 07-4060 3200) at Laura offers guided tours of the rock-art galleries in that area but only by prior arrangement. The Tjapukai Aboriginal Culture Park (☎ 07-4042 9900) at Smithfield, near Cairns, features a museum, a cultural theatre and traditional dance performances.

The Central Deserts

With its awesome sense of space and few people, central Australia is a golden opportunity for getting off the beaten track. The region has all of Australia's deserts, the most inhospitable of which is the Simpson Desert – one of the world's most outstanding examples of a sand-ridge desert. These aren't true deserts like the Sahara, but they're extremely dry and only very sparsely populated. Where it occurs, primary production is limited to low-intensity sheep and cattle grazing. The few significant towns are all largely dependent on either tourism (eg, Alice Springs) or mining (eg, Mt Isa). Because of their isolation, even the smallest towns generally have an excellent range of facilities and services.

The region has some of the nation's remotest touring routes. For major adventure there are several challenging 4WD

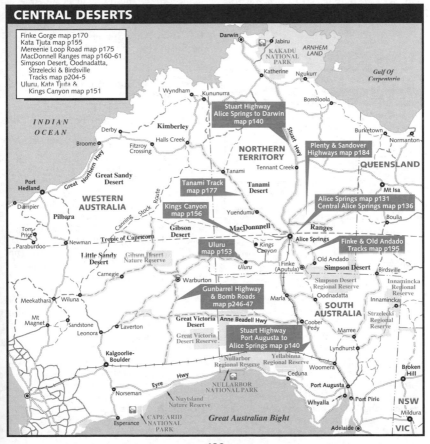

CENTRAL DESERTS

Finke Gorge map p170
Kata Tjuta map p155
Mereenie Loop Road map p175
MacDonnell Ranges map p160-61
Simpson Desert, Oodnadatta,
  Strzelecki & Birdsville
  Tracks map p204-5
Uluru, Kata Tjuta &
  Kings Canyon map p151

tracks, such as the French Line across the Simpson Desert and the Anne Beadell Hwy from Coober Pedy to Laverton. Routes such as these have no facilities whatsoever and are only recommended for experienced 4WD travellers. If you haven't got a 4WD, you can discover history in the footsteps of the cattle drovers along the remote Oodnadatta and Birdsville Tracks.

Explore some spectacular places in the central desert region without leaving the bitumen. The sealed Stuart Hwy crosses the continent from Port Augusta in the south to Darwin in the north. En route, sealed detours lead to Uluru (Ayers Rock), Watarrka National Park (and Kings Canyon) and the MacDonnell Ranges near Alice Springs.

Alice Springs

Highlights

- Discovering the biology of the arid zone at the Alice Springs Desert Park
- Checking out the stunning artwork on display in Alice's Aboriginal-owned arts-and-crafts shops
- Delving into history and enjoying a picnic at the old Telegraph Station

Alice Springs (also known as 'the Alice'; population 25,600), a pleasant, modern town with good shops and restaurants, is set among the rugged red hills and ridges of the MacDonnell Ranges. It's the major access point for the many tourist attractions of central Australia.

The growth of Alice Springs has been both recent and rapid. When the name was officially changed in 1933 (it was previously called Stuart), the population had only just reached 200! Even in the 1950s, Alice Springs was still a tiny town with a population in the hundreds. The road to Darwin was sealed during WWII, but it was only in 1987 that the rough dirt road south to Port Augusta was finally replaced by a sealed highway.

Information

Tourist Offices The well-stocked visitors information centre (☎ 08-8952 5800, fax 8953 0295, ⓔ visinfo@catia.asn.au, ⓦ www .centralaustraliantourism.com), operated by the Central Australian Tourism Industry Association (CATIA), is at the river end of Gregory Terrace in the town centre. It opens from 8.30am to 5.30pm weekdays and from 9am to 4pm weekends and public holidays.

National Parks The Parks and Wildlife Commission of the Northern Territory has brochures on most of the parks and reserves in the Centre. You'll find them at CATIA as well as at the Commission's main office (☎ 08-8951 8211, fax 8951 8268), at PO Box 1046, Alice Springs NT 0871, just off the Stuart Hwy about 7km south of the town centre.

Post & Communications The post office (☎ 08-8952 1020) is at 33 Hartley St, and there's a row of public phones outside. The telephone area code for Alice Springs is 08.

Internet Resources Most of the hostels include Internet access in their services – the Melanka Backpackers Resort and the Pioneer YHA have Internet outposts (see Places to Stay later).

The Alice Springs Library (☎ 08-8950 0555), on Gregory Terrace behind CATIA, opens from 10am to 6pm on Monday, Tuesday and Thursday, 10am to 5pm Wednesday and Friday, 9am to 1pm Saturday, and 1pm to 5pm Sunday. It charges $3 per 30 minutes for Internet access.

The Outback Travel Shop (☎ 08-8955 5288) at 2A Gregory Terrace charges $3.50 per 30 minutes. It opens from 8am to 8pm Monday to Friday, and 10am to 6pm Saturday and Sunday.

Training Solutions (☎ 08-8953 2157), in Shop 22 in the Coles complex (it's next to the interstate bus terminal) charges $2 for 15 minutes and $6 for an hour.

Books & Maps The best place to find books on the outback is the Arunta Art Gallery & Bookshop (☎ 08-8952 1544) at

ALICE SPRINGS

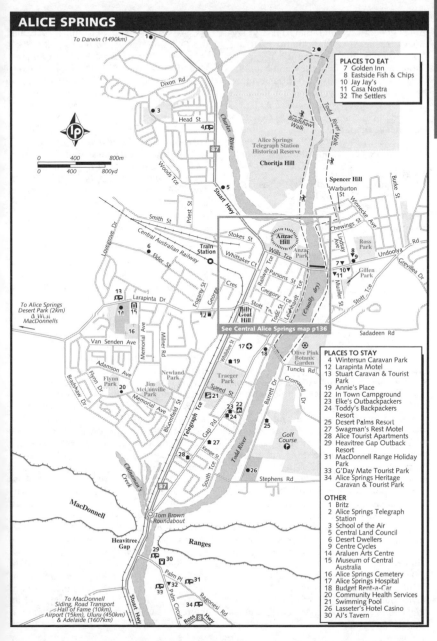

To Darwin (1490km)

Dixon Rd

Head St

Charles River

Bradshaw Walk

Alice Springs Telegraph Station Historical Reserve

Choritja Hill

Woods Tce

Stuart Hwy

Smith St

Central Australian Railway

Train Station

Stokes St

Whittaker Ct

Wills Tce

Anzac Hill

Anzac Park

Spencer Hill

Warburton St

Chewings St

Lindsay Ave

Ross Park

Undoolya Rd

Burke St

Winnecke Ave

Grevillea Dr

Gillen Park

Mueller St

Stott Tce

Sadadeen Rd

Priest St

Lovegrove Dr

Elder St

Fogarty St

George Cres

Railway Tce

Parsons St

Gregory Tce

Stott St

Leichhardt Tce

Todd St

(usually dry)

Billy Goat Hill

See Central Alice Springs map p136

Larapinta Dr

To Alice Springs Desert Park (2km) & West MacDonnells

Van Senden Ave

Memorial Ave

Milner Rd

Adamson Ave

Newland Park

Flynn Park

Jim McConville Park

Memorial Ave

Bloomfield St

Telegraph Tce

Gap Rd

Speed St

Traeger Park

Waldine St

Barrett Dr

Tuncks Rd

Cromwell Dr

Olive Pink Botanic Garden

Golf Course

Kempe St

South Tce

Todd River

Stephens Rd

Tom Brown Roundabout

Heavitree Gap

MacDonnell

Ranges

Chinaman Creek

Bradshaw Dr

Flynn Dr

Palm Pl

Palm Circuit

Ragonesi Rd

Ross Hwy

To MacDonnell Siding, Road Transport Hall of Fame (10km), Airport (15km), Uluru (450km) & Adelaide (1607km)

See Central Alice Springs map p136

0   400   800m
0   400   800yd

PLACES TO EAT
7 Golden Inn
8 Eastside Fish & Chips
10 Jay Jay's
11 Casa Nostra
32 The Settlers

PLACES TO STAY
4 Wintersun Caravan Park
12 Larapinta Motel
13 Stuart Caravan & Tourist Park
19 Annie's Place
22 In Town Campground
23 Elke's Outbackpackers
24 Toddy's Backpackers Resort
25 Desert Palms Resort
27 Swagman's Rest Motel
28 Alice Tourist Apartments
29 Heavitree Gap Outback Resort
31 MacDonnell Range Holiday Park
33 G'Day Mate Tourist Park
34 Alice Springs Heritage Caravan & Tourist Park

OTHER
1 Britz
2 Alice Springs Telegraph Station
3 School of the Air
5 Central Land Council
6 Desert Dwellers
9 Centre Cycles
14 Araluen Arts Centre
15 Museum of Central Australia
16 Alice Springs Cemetery
17 Alice Springs Hospital
18 Budget Rent-a-Car
20 Community Health Services
21 Swimming Pool
26 Lasseter's Hotel Casino
30 AJ's Tavern

72 Todd St, just south of Todd Mall. For more general reading material try Dymocks, in the Alice Plaza on the mall, and Alice Springs Book City, in the Yeperenye Shopping Centre off Hartley and Bath Sts.

The Department of Infrastructure, Planning and Environment (☎ 08-8951 5316) on Gregory Terrace near CATIA has all kinds of maps – it is a sales outlet for Geoscience products.

Other Services Useful addresses include:

Medical Facilities
    Alice Springs Community Health Centre
    (☎ 08-8951 6711) Flynn Dr
    Alice Springs Hospital
    (☎ 08-8951 7777) Gap Rd
    Royal Flying Doctor Service
    (☎ 08-8952 1033, PO Box 2210, NT 0871)
    8–10 Stuart Terrace

Aboriginal Land Permits
    Central Land Council
    (☎ 08-8951 6320, fax 8953 4345,
    PO Box 3321, NT 0871) 33 Stuart Hwy

Police
    Alice Springs Police Station
    (☎ 08-8951 8888) Parsons St

Things to See

Alice Springs has plenty of attractions, and it's worth putting aside some time to see the more interesting ones.

The restored 1870s **Alice Springs Telegraph Station** (☎ 08-8952 3993; adult/child $6.25/3.25; open 8am-5pm daily) is beside the Todd River (Lhere Mpamtwe) 2km north of the town centre. There's a small museum, and the lawns along the river are a great spot for a picnic or barbecue – the picnic areas are open until 9pm daily. The entry fee includes a guided tour.

Anzac Hill (Untyeyetweleye), at the northern end of Hartley St, offers fine views over Alice Springs to the surrounding hills and ridges.

There are several historic buildings in the central town area including the **Old Stuart Town Gaol** (☎ 08-8952 4516, Parsons St; adult/child $2.20/free; open 10am-12.30pm Mon-Fri), built in 1907; **The Residency**

(☎ 08-8951 5688, Cnr Parsons & Hartley Sts; open 10am-5pm daily), built in 1926; and the **Old Courthouse**, built in 1928, which now houses the **National Pioneer Women's Hall of Fame** (☎ 08-8952 9006, Cnr Parsons & Hartley Sts; adult/child $2.20/free; open 10am-5pm daily, closed mid-Dec to 31 Jan). **Adelaide House** (1926), the town's first hospital, is now a museum (☎ 08-8952 1856, Todd Mall; adult/child $4/free; open Mon-Fri 10am-4pm, Sat 10am-noon Mar-Nov).

Also in the town centre, **Panorama Guth** (☎ 08-8952 2013, 65 Hartley St; adult/child $5.50/3.30; open 9am-5pm Mon-Sat, noon-5pm Sun, closed Sun mid-Dec to 31 Jan) is a stunning 360-degree panoramic painting, 6m high and 60m in circumference, that depicts various central Australian landscapes by artist Henk Guth.

The **Royal Flying Doctor Service** (☎ 08-8952 1129, 8-10 Stuart Terrace; adult/child $5.50/2.20; open 9am-4pm Mon-Sat, 1pm-4pm Sun) is close to the town centre and there are tours daily.

Also open daily, the **School of the Air** (☎ 08-8951 6834, 80 Head St; adult/child $3.50/2.50; open 8.30am-4.30pm Mon-Sat, 1.30pm-4.30pm Sun) broadcasts school lessons to children in remote communities. It's about 3km north of the town centre.

About 2km west of the town centre, the **Alice Springs Cultural Precinct** (☎ 08-8951 1120, Cnr Larapinta Dr & Memorial Ave; adult/child/family $7/4/18; open 10am-5pm daily) has some of the town's most interesting cultural and historical attractions. These include the **Araluen Arts Centre**, which houses a collection of paintings by Albert Namatjira, and the **Museum of Central Australia**. The latter has some fascinating natural history exhibits, including the fossilised remains of the largest bird that ever lived.

MacDonnell Siding (☎ 08-8955 5047, Norris Bell Ave; adult/child entry $5.50/$3.30, entry & train ride $16.50/9.90; open 9am-5pm daily), off the Stuart Hwy 10km south of town, is a working museum that includes a train station (built to the design of the original Alice Springs station) and an impressive collection of railway memorabilia including the old *Ghan* train, which

KATE NOLAN

The old *Ghan* still runs.

trundles up and down on a 23km section of the original railway track.

Right next door, the **Road Transport Hall of Fame** (☎ 08-8952 7161, Norris Bell Ave; adult/child $6/3; open 9am-5pm daily) features early motor vehicles including Australia's first motorised road train.

The impressive **Alice Springs Desert Park** (☎ 08-8951 8788, Larapinta Dr; adult/child/family $18/9/40; open 7.30am-6pm daily) backs onto the red walls of Mt Gillen on the western outskirts of town. Here you can learn about Aboriginal traditions from local guides, and study Australia's unique flora and fauna. There are habitat walks, raptor displays, huge walk-in aviaries and a large nocturnal house. It's easy to spend four or five hours here. The nocturnal house displays 20 arid-zone mammal species. About half of these are either endangered or extinct in the wild on mainland Australia; several species that have vanished from the mainland since European settlement are now found only on small islands off the coast. The residents of the nocturnal house are most active in the morning. There's a *cafe* where you can buy lunch and coffee.

Organised Tours

There are literally dozens of tours available from Alice Springs. Listed here are some of the more interesting. See also the Organised Tours sections in the individual track descriptions and the Getting Around chapter.

Aboriginal Art & Culture Centre (☎ 08-8952 3408, e aborart@ozemail.com.au, w www.aboriginalart.com.au, 86 Todd St) This Aboriginal-owned-and-managed enterprise has some good tours that delve into Aboriginal culture. Its four-hour Discovery Tour, which includes a bush tucker walk, costs $82.50/44 per adult/child.

Central Rock-Rat

There was great excitement among central Australian naturalists late in 1996, when conservation volunteers working on the Larapinta Trail west of Alice Springs trapped an unusual yellow-brown rodent. About the size of a rat, the animal had a swollen hairy tail shaped like a carrot. It turned out to be a central rock-rat (*Zyzomys pedunculatus*), a species so rare that in the previous hundred years only five sightings of it had been recorded.

Apparently confined to the rocky ranges around Alice Springs, the central rock-rat was discovered by science in 1894. However, despite intensive searches, no confirmed sightings had been made since 1960, when a single animal was caught raiding a stockman's camp about 300km west of town. As a result, it was listed nationally as critically endangered, although many naturalists considered it probably extinct.

Subsequent to its rediscovery, rangers visited the area and managed to trap three adult rats. These formed the nucleus of a captive breeding program at the Alice Springs Desert Park, where the first litter of three arrived in April 1997. A secure breeding colony is now being established there to enable scientific study of the animal's behaviour and habitat requirements. Except in the spring breeding season, central rock-rats are on display in the park's nocturnal house.

Frontier Camel Farm (☎ 08-8953 0444, e info@cameltours.com.au, w www.cameltours.com.au, Ross Hwy) The farm offers yard and one-hour camel rides as well as the popular 'take a camel out to breakfast/dinner' tours ($65/98).

Trek Larapinta (☎ 08-8953 2933, e charlie@treklarapinta.com.au, w www.treklarapinta.com.au) Experienced guides offer fully catered one- to seven-day walks on the Larapinta Trail. These walks cost from $120 per day, and a minimum of two walkers is required.

The Camp Oven Kitchen (☎ 08-1800 659 574) This tour offers a four-course meal cooked on a campfire under the stars (adult/child $82/66). Bar facilities are available.

Sunrise balloon trips are popular; these cost from $160, which includes breakfast and a 30-minute flight. The local operators are: *Alice Springs Balloon Flights* (☎ 1800 677 893, 08-8953 4800, e spinifex@balloon flights.com.au); *Ballooning Downunder* (☎ 08-8952 8816, e sales@ballooning downunder.com.au, w www.ballooningdown under.com.au); and *Outback Ballooning* (☎ 1800 809 790, 08-8952 8723, e bal loons@topend.com.au).

Special Events

The Camel Cup, a series of camel races, takes place in July. In August there's the Alice Springs Rodeo.

The event that probably draws the biggest crowds of all takes place in September: the Henley-on-Todd Regatta. The boats are all bottomless, so the crews simply run up and down in the (usually) dry riverbed!

Held in September 2001, the Yeperenye Festival – a major celebration of Aboriginal culture from across Australia – was such an overwhelming success that there is talk of holding it on a biennial basis. Check with CATIA (☎ 08-8952 5800) for an update.

Places to Stay

Camping Most of the caravan parks close to town are centred on Palm Circuit just south of Heavitree Gap (Ntaripe). The ones listed here are within 5km of the town centre.

In Town Campground (☎ 1800 359 089, 08-8952 1545, e anniesplace@octa4 .net.au, Cnr South Terrace & Breaden St) Unpowered sites $16. Within walking distance of the town centre, this place has grassed sites, a communal kitchen and off-street parking.

Alice Springs Heritage Caravan & Tourist Park (☎ 08-8953 1418, e heritage cp@bigpond.com.au, w www.heritagecp .com.au, Ragonesi Rd) Unpowered/powered sites $16/22, on-site vans $46, cabins $80. This isn't the most attractive caravan park in town, but there's good shade and the amenities are clean and well maintained. It also allows pets.

G'Day Mate Tourist Park (☎ 08-8952 9589, Palm Circuit) Unpowered/powered sites $18/20, cabins $62. G'Day Mate is 4km south of the town centre. It's an attractive place with grassed sites and good shade.

Heavitree Gap Outback Resort (☎ 08-8950 4444, e headoffice@aurora-resorts .com.au, w www.aurora-resorts.com.au, Palm Circuit) Unpowered/powered sites $12/15, 4-bed bunkhouse $65, motel-style rooms $85-110. There's a *supermarket*, *tavern*, *restaurant* and fuel station in this complex, which is about 3km from town.

MacDonnell Range Holiday Park (☎ 08-8952 6111, e macrange@macrange.com.au, w www.macrange.com.au, Palm Place) Unpowered/powered sites $18.50/23, cabins $65-111, budget units $44. This place has a high standard and an excellent range of amenities. It's a little over 4km from town.

Wintersun Caravan Park (☎ 08-8952 4080, Stuart Hwy) Unpowered/powered sites $17/20.50, cabins $45-90. Wintersun has a good range of cabins, and its camp sites are grassed and shaded. It's 2km north of the town centre.

Hostels & Guesthouses There is a good range of hostels and guesthouses in Alice Springs.

Pioneer YHA (☎ 08-8952 8855, e alice pioneer@yhant.org.au, Cnr Parsons St & Leichhardt Terrace) YHA members/non-members dorm beds $18/21, doubles/twins $70/80. This place is very friendly and efficient, and is right in the middle of town. All rooms have shared facilities, and there's Internet access ($5 for 30 minutes).

Annie's Place (☎ 1800 359 089, 08-8952 1545, e info@mulgas.com.au, Cnr Traeger Ave & Willshire St) Beds in 6-bed dorm $16, doubles $55. All rooms in this converted motel have private facilities and TVs. It's a friendly place with an Internet cafe ($6 for an hour), cheap *meals* ($7), a *bar* and a swimming pool.

Melanka Backpackers Resort (☎ 1800 815 066, 08-8952 4744, e backpackers @ melanka.com.au, 94 Todd St) Beds in a 4–8-bed dorm $16, singles, doubles & twins $42. This place has a public *bar* and is said to be good for parties. An Internet cafe in the complex charges $7 an hour.

Toddy's Backpackers Resort (☎ *08-8952 1322,* e *toddys@saharatours.com.au, 41 Gap Rd)* Rooms with shared/private bathroom $40/52, dorm beds with shared/private bathroom $12/15. Toddys has a communal kitchen, and there are cheap 'all you can eat' evening **meals**. Other facilities include bicycle hire, Internet access, a **bar** and a courtesy bus.

Elke's Outbackpackers (☎ *1800 633 354,* 08-8952 8422, e *outback@outback holiday.com.au, 39 Gap Rd)* Dorm beds $18, doubles & twins $50, triples $56, motel units $75. Each two rooms share a TV, bathroom and cooking facilities; the motel units also have cooking facilities and sleep up to five persons. All rates include a continental breakfast.

Hotels, Motels & Holiday Units Alice Springs has numerous motels, but not so many hotels or holiday units.

Todd Tavern (☎ *08-8952 1255,* e *info@ toddtavern.com.au,* W *www.toddtavern.com .au, 1 Todd Mall)* Rooms with shared/ private bathroom $41/54. This traditional-style hotel, right by the river, can be noisy when there are bands playing, but otherwise it's quite a reasonable place to stay. There is some off-street parking.

Swagman's Rest Motel (☎ *08-8953 1333, 67 Gap Rd)* Singles/doubles $76/87. Each unit is fully self-contained, with a good kitchen and full-size bath.

Alice Tourist Apartments (☎ *08-8952 2788, Cnr Gap Rd & Gnoilya St)* Singles/doubles $72/110. The units are comfortable and each has cooking facilities; the larger ones have a full-size bath.

Desert Palms Resort (☎ *08-8952 5977,* e *despalms@saharatours.com.au,* W *www .saharatours.com.au, 74 Barrett Dr)* Singles & doubles $92, triples $102. With its palms and tropical-style villas this place is more like a Pacific island than the arid outback. Units are spacious and each has an electric frying pan and a microwave oven.

Desert Rose Inn (☎ *08-8952 1411, 15 Railway Terrace)* Rooms with private shower

$54, singles/doubles with private toilet & shower $88/97, singles/doubles with private facilities & kitchenette $115/125. The rooms here are comfortable and spacious, and it's just a short walk from the centre of town.

Larapinta Motel (☎ *08-8952 7255, 3 Larapinta Dr)* Singles/doubles $82/88. This place is near the train station. All rooms have a microwave oven and fridge, and there's a communal kitchen upstairs.

Places to Eat

As a major tourist destination, Alice Springs has a huge range of places to eat. If you're self-catering, there are a number of **supermarkets** in the CBD and out in the suburbs. Close to the post office are: a supermarket in the Coles Complex off Bath St and Railway Terrace; a Woolworths supermarket in the Yeperenye Shopping Centre off Hartley and Bath Sts; and a Bi-Lo supermarket in the Alice Plaza off Todd Mall. All three open seven days – Coles is open 24 hours.

Snacks & Fast Food The town centre has numerous places for a snack or light meal, particularly along Todd Mall. Several put tables and chairs outside – perfect for breakfast in the cool morning air. Takeaway addicts will be thrilled to know that the usual fast-food chains are well represented.

Red Dog Cafe (☎ *08-8953 1353, 64 Todd Mall)* Cooked breakfasts $8-12, light lunches $7-12. At the southern end of the mall, this place opens at 6am for breakfast, which you can eat either inside or at outside tables. There's a bakery on the premises.

Alice Plaza (☎ *08-8952 9666, Todd Mall)* At the mall's northern end, this shopping centre has four lunchtime eating places offering Asian, Australian and Italian fare. They share a central seating area – a popular meeting spot for visitors and locals alike.

Golly It's Good (☎ *08-8952 8388, Springs Plaza)* Light meals $5-10. Across the mall from the Alice Plaza, this place offers snacks and light lunches such as gourmet sandwiches, quiches and salads.

Yeperenye Shopping Centre (☎ *08-8952 5177, Hartley St)* The centre has a bakery and several cafes and takeaways.

CENTRAL ALICE SPRINGS

PLACES TO STAY
1 Desert Rose Inn
5 Todd Tavern; Pub Caf
26 Pioneer YHA Hostel
54 Melanka Backpackers Resort

PLACES TO EAT
8 Al Fresco's
9 Oscar's
11 Golly It's Good
14 Firkin & Hound
31 Red Dog Cafe
32 Bar Doppio
33 Red Dog
42 La Casalinga
44 Keller's Swiss & Indian Restaurant

45 Uncle's Tavern
49 Overlanders Steakhouse
53 Oriental Gourmet
55 Bluegrass

OTHER
2 Anglican Church
3 Catholic Church
4 Shell Service Station
6 Alice Springs Cinemas
7 Alice Plaza; Bi-Lo Supermarket
10 Westpac Bank
12 ANZ Bank
13 Old Courthouse
15 Old Stuart Town Gaol
16 Coles Supermarket
17 Training Solutions

18 Interstate Coach Terminal
19 Yeperenye Shopping Centre
20 Avis
21 Hartley St School
22 The Residency
23 Commonwealth Bank
24 Ansett Building/Puccini's
25 Qantas
27 National Australia Bank
28 Adelaide House
29 Flynn Church
30 Alice Springs Disposals
34 Department of Lands, Planning & Environment
35 Visitor Information Centre (CATIA)
36 Library
37 Aboriginal Art & Culture Centre

38 Bojangles
39 Papunya Tula Artists
40 Arunta Art Gallery & Bookshop
41 Outback Travel Shop
43 Warumpi Art
46 Panorama Guth
47 Thrifty
48 Hertz
50 Department of Business, Industry & Resource Development
51 Kmart
52 Pioneer Cemetery
56 Jukurrpa Artists
57 CAAMA Shop
58 Stuart Memorial
59 Royal Flying Doctor Service

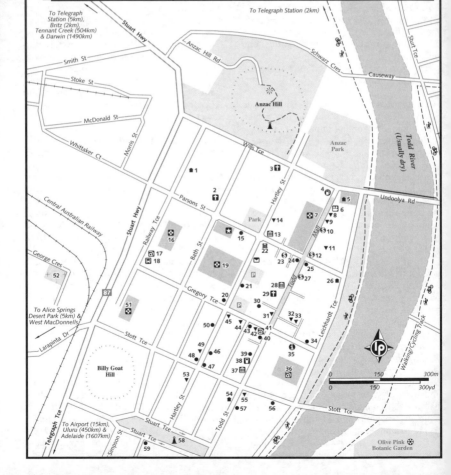

Eastside Fish & Chips (☎ 08-8952 3336, 10 Lindsay Ave) Single serve $5.50. Across the river, this is considered the best fish takeaway in town. There's a French *bakery* next door.

Pubs You might expect that Alice would be full of pubs, but in fact there are only a few venues where you can buy pub-style meals. The following are worth trying.

Todd Tavern (see Places to Stay earlier) is a popular place for pub food, with meals (mains $10 to $15) available daily in either the bar or the slightly more formal *Pub Cafe*. The food and serves are good, and there are usually specials.

Uncle's Tavern (☎ 08-8952 8977, Diplomat Hotel, Cnr Hartley St & Gregory Terrace) Mains $13-20. The food here is good, but Uncle's is better known as an after-work meeting place.

The Firkin & Hound (☎ 08-8953 3033, 21 Hartley St) Mains $13-25. This place prides itself on being a genuine English pub. Naturally the menu features traditional English fare such as bangers and mash, and beef-and-Guiness pie.

Restaurants Alice Springs has a number of restaurants worth trying, and overall there's a wide range of cuisines on offer.

Bluegrass (☎ 08-8955 5188, Cnr Stott Terrace & Todd St) Mains $19-23. This popular eatery has a very interesting menu (including vegetarian dishes) and a pleasant atmosphere. Car parking is off Stott Terrace.

Casa Nostra (☎ 08-8952 6749, Cnr Undoolya Rd & Sturt Terrace) Mains $11-18. Across the river from the town centre, this is a very popular pizza and pasta specialist. It has a BYO licence.

Al Fresco's (☎ 08-8953 4944, Todd Mall) Mains $15-22. Located in the cinema complex, this is a good pasta place, also popular for coffee and cake.

Oscar's (☎ 08-8953 0930, 86 Todd Mall) Mains $22-35. Specialising in Italian, Oscar's has an extensive menu and is noted for its large servings.

La Casalinga (☎ 08-8952 4508, 105 Gregory Terrace) Open 5pm-1am daily.

Mains $8-17. This place is an Alice institution for pizza and pasta.

Puccini's (☎ 08-8953 0935, Cnr Todd Mall & Parsons St) Mains $17-33. This is one of Alice's finest restaurants and has also won many awards. There's a cheaper *bistro* on the premises.

Bar Doppio (☎ 08-8952 6525, Fan Arcade) Mains $6-10. This is a very casual, alternative BYO place with an emphasis on Greek dishes. It's off the mall's southern end.

The Olive Tree (☎ 08-8952 5522, Fan Arcade) Light meals from $8. Next door to Bar Doppio, The Olive Tree is open for breakfast (from 8am) and does a mean ploughman's lunch.

Oriental Gourmet (☎ 08-8953 0888, 80 Hartley St) Mains $14-25. This place has extensive menus for both eat-in and takeaway meals. It's probably the most popular of the local Chinese eateries.

Golden Inn (☎ 08-8952 6910, 9 Undoolya Rd) Mains $13-30. Also enjoying a good reputation, this restaurant has a rather garish exterior, but once you're inside it the atmosphere is great.

Overlanders Steakhouse (☎ 08-8952 2159, 72 Hartley St) Mains $18-26. This is a local institution for steaks, and not just beef ones either – it also offers crocodile, kangaroo, barramundi, camel and emu.

Jay Jay's (☎ 08-8952 3721, Cnr Lindsay Ave & Undoolya Rd) Mains $15-20. This restaurant specialises in European, Chinese and Thai cuisine. Its children's menu is excellent.

Keller's Swiss & Indian Restaurant (☎ 08-8952 3188, Diplomat Hotel complex, Gregory Terrace) Mains $14-22. For something a little different, Keller's gives you the chance to try two vastly different cuisines, including vegetarian dishes, in the one place.

Old Ghan (☎ 08-8955 5047, Norris Bell Ave) Dinner $49. On Saturday night you can take a ride on the Old Ghan train and enjoy a three-course dinner cooked on its wood-burning stove.

Entertainment

The *Centralian Advocate* is the local paper, is published every Tuesday and Friday and has details of what's on in and around town – check out the gig guide in the paper's entertainment section.

Todd Tavern (see Places to Stay earlier) has the popular Jam Session on Monday night featuring local and walk-up talent.

Alice Springs Cinemas (☎ 08-8952 4999, Todd Mall) Near the Todd Tavern, the complex has three cinemas with multiple showings daily.

Bojangles (☎ 08-8952 2873, 80 Todd St) This **restaurant** and nightclub serves great food, and has live music and entertainment most nights. A reader described the clientele as being 'a nice mix between local rednecks and backpackers'.

AJ's Tavern (☎ 08-8950 4444, Palm Circuit) Known for Australian country-style music, this bar has live entertainment on most nights.

Lasseter's Hotel Casino (☎ 08-8950 7777, 93 Barrett Dr) For gambling there's Lasseter's, but dress up as rules are strict.

The Settlers (☎ 08-8953 4333, Palm Circuit) Show $16, mains $12-19. Well-known local character and raconteur Ted Egan puts on a performance of tall tales and outback songs four nights a week.

Araluen Arts Centre (☎ 08-8951 1122, Larapinta Dr). The centre holds a wide range of events including temporary art exhibits, theatre and music performances, and films.

Shopping

Aboriginal Arts Naturally, Alice Springs has a number of outlets for Aboriginal arts and crafts.

Central Australian Aboriginal Media Association (CAAMA) shop (☎ 08-8952 9207, 101 Todd St) This is a good place to buy Aboriginal CDs and cassettes (many produced by CAAMA), books, painted ceramics and various products with local Aboriginal designs.

Aboriginal Art & Culture Centre (☎ 08-8952 3408, 86 Todd St) This gallery and shop, established by Southern Arrernte people, offers a good range of paintings, woodcarvings, didgeridoos, T-shirts and the like. For $11 you get an hour's tuition in playing the didgeridoo.

The following places are owned and run by the art centres that produce the work on sale there.

Jukurrpa Artists (☎ 08-8953 1052, Stott Terrace) This women's art centre gives you a chance to watch artists at work as well as discuss your purchases with them.

Papunya Tula Artists (☎ 08-8952 4731, 78 Todd St) Representing artists from Papunya, this long-established shop deals mainly with fine arts. If you're looking for an investment this is a good place to start.

Warumpi Arts (☎ 08-8952 9066, 105 Gregory Terrace) You'll find the work of some prominent Papunya artists here, but there's also a range of art by lesser-known people.

Camping Equipment You'll find a wide range of camping gear, including swags, tents and cooking utensils at ***Desert Dwellers*** (☎ 08-8953 2240, 38 Elder St), Also try ***Alice Springs Disposals*** (☎ 08-8952 5701, Reg Harris Lane, off Todd Mall).

Getting Around

To/From the Airport The Alice Springs airport is 15km south of town, about $25 by taxi.

An airport shuttle bus (☎ 08-8953 0310) meets flights and takes passengers to all city accommodation places and also to the train station. It costs $10/17 one way/return.

Car Rental There are a number of car-rental companies with offices in Alice Springs. These include:

Advance Car Rentals (☎ 08-8953 3700)
  9 Railway Terrace
Avis (☎ 08-8953 5533) 52 Hartley St
Boomerang Rentals (☎ 08-8955 5171)
  3 Fogarty St
Britz (☎ 08-8952 8814) corner of Stuart Hwy
  and Power St, north of town
Budget (☎ 08-8952 8899) 10 Gap Rd
Delta Europcar (☎ 08-8955 5994) 10 Gap Rd
Hertz (☎ 08-8952 2644) 76 Hartley St
Thrifty (☎ 08-8952 9999) corner of Hartley St
  and Stott Terrace

Most have 4WD vehicles, with available models ranging from Suzuki Sierras to

Toyota Troopcarriers. Competition is fierce and different packages are available.

Alice Springs is classified as a remote area so car hire can be expensive, particularly if you want to drive down to Uluru or further afield. Generally, none of the companies allow their 2WDs to go off sealed roads – if you do, and have a crash, you're liable for all the damage. A sobering thought!

A 4WD is much more expensive, but it's the only option if you want to leave the bitumen and visit places like Palm Valley and Chambers Pillar. It costs around $150 per day for a small Toyota RAV4, including insurance and 100km per day. For a Land Cruiser or similar, the price jumps to around $200 per day. Discounts apply for longer rentals (more than four to seven days).

The 4WD outback specials offered by Hertz are worth investigating if you're planning to fly into Alice Springs and want to do a camping trip. Its Troopcarriers cost $228 per day including 300km per day for seven days or more, and hiring a full set of camping equipment for four people costs $50 per day.

Britz has fully equipped 4WD bush campers for three adults, starting at $168 per day for a trip of four to 20 days. Get the company's written permission before tackling many of the tracks described here.

Remember that conditions vary from company to company, and from rate plan to rate plan within the same company. Always read them carefully, particularly insurance matters.

Avis, Budget, Hertz and Thrifty have counters at the Alice Springs airport.

Bus Alice Springs has a public bus service (ASBUS; ☎ 08-8950 0500). Timetables and route maps are available from CATIA (☎ 08-8952 5800).

The Alice Wanderer (☎ 08-8952 2111) runs a town shuttle service ($25) that allows you to get on or off at many of the local attractions.

Bicycle Alice Springs has a number of bicycle tracks, including a 17km sealed path from Flynn's Grave to Simpsons Gap

(see the later MacDonnell Ranges section). Several places rent bikes, including most of the backpacker hostels – typical rates are $13/18 per half/full day. The main cycle shop is Centre Cycles at the corner of Undoolya Rd and Lindsay Ave – it also hires bikes.

Stuart Highway

While no longer a true outback track now that it's sealed and well served by roadhouses, the 2700km Stuart Hwy does go straight through the heart of the outback. It also gives access to many of the tracks described in this book and has a number of worthwhile sights of its own. If you are spending any amount of time travelling in Australia's harsh interior, it's almost guaranteed some of that time will be spent on 'the Track', as it's affectionately called.

History

The highway was named after John McDouall Stuart who, in 1862, was the first European to cross Australia from south to north. In the early days those heading into the interior were dependent on the availability of water, and so the route that initially developed was what is known today as the Oodnadatta Track, some distance to the east of the current highway, where water supplies were more reliable.

With the decline of vehicle traffic along the Oodnadatta Track due to the completion of the railway line to Alice Springs in 1929, the discovery of opals in Coober Pedy in

STUART HIGHWAY
Port Augusta to Alice Springs

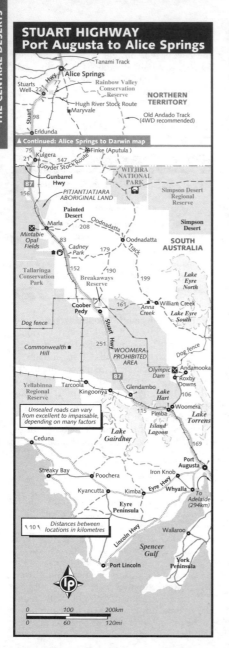

STUART HIGHWAY
Alice Springs to Darwin

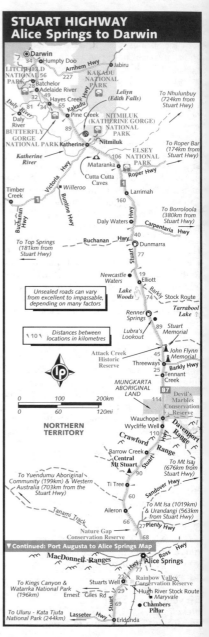

1915 and later the development of the Woomera Rocket Range in 1947, the main road developed further west along today's route. Surfacing work on the section from Port Augusta to the Northern Territory border was only completed in 1987.

From Alice Springs to Darwin the highway basically follows the route of the Overland Telegraph Line, which was built in 1872 largely along the route that Stuart had taken a decade before.

Information

There are no special requirements for travelling on the Stuart Hwy. The main thing you need to be aware of is that from Woomera (175km north of Port Augusta) to Glendambo (a distance of 115km) the highway skirts the southern edge of the Woomera Prohibited Area, and from Glendambo to Coober Pedy (251km) it cuts right through it. Travelling off the main road into this area without a permit from the Area Administrator in Woomera is prohibited.

For those with HF radios, the Royal Flying Doctor Service (RFDS; ☎ 08-8642 5555) at Port Augusta (call sign VNZ) monitors the following frequencies from 6am to 9pm daily: 2020kHz, 4010kHz, 6890kHz and 8165kHz. From Alice Springs RFDS (☎ 08-8952 5355, call sign VJD) there's 24-hour emergency coverage on 5410MHz, and the following frequencies are monitored from 7.30am to 5pm weekdays: 2020kHz, 5410kHz and 6950kHz. Darwin is no longer covered by the St John Ambulance Service. Contact Alice Springs for assistance.

THE ROUTE
Port Augusta

The Stuart Hwy starts the long haul north from the crossroads town of Port Augusta (population 14,600) at the head of Spencer Gulf. Port Augusta is an ideal place to stock up on supplies and equipment. It's also a good place to stock up on reasons to get out of big towns like Port Augusta.

For information on routes north of Port Augusta, check the Northern Road Conditions Report (☎ 1300 361 033, w www.transport.sa.gov.au/northern.htm).

Information Wadlata Outback Centre (☎ 08-8642 4511, 8641 0793 for tourist information, e wadlata@wadarid.mtx.net, w www.portaugusta.sa.gov.au) at 41 Flinders Terrace, is open 9am to 5.30pm weekdays, and 10am to 4pm weekends. There's masses of tourist information here, as well as an excellent interactive museum (adult/child/concession $8.95/5.50/7.95).

Port Augusta Public Library (☎ 08-8641 9151, Mackay St) offers free Internet access, but you should book ahead. It's open 9am to 6pm Monday and Friday, 9am to 8pm Tuesday to Thursday, 10am to 6pm Saturday and 2pm to 5pm Sunday.

PZ Computers Internet Cafe (☎ 08-8461 1086), at 7 Church St, has Internet access at $8.80 per hour. It's open 9am to 6pm weekdays and 10am to 2pm Saturday.

Other useful addresses include:

Port Augusta Post Office (☎ 13 13 18) 50 Commercial Rd
Port Augusta Police Station (☎ 08-8648 5020) Commercial Rd, near the town hall
Port Augusta Medical Centre (☎ 08-8641 1055) 17 Gibson St
Royal Flying Doctor Service (☎ 8642 2044, e tony.wade@flyingdoctor.net) 4 Vincent St

Port Augusta to Coober Pedy (536km)

The first stretch is 169km to the scruffy little settlement of **Pimba**, which sits on an almost treeless plateau and, despite its accessibility, is one of the most desolate places imaginable. The township of **Woomera** (population 1600) lies 6km north of the highway and in itself is hardly worth the detour, although you can pass through if you intend visiting the opal mining settlement of Andamooka. Woomera had its heyday in the 1950s and 1960s when it was the base for military and civil personnel involved in rocket-launching experiments. Although it will be the base for the world's first reusable launch vehicles for low-Earth satellites in 2003, it has something of a ghost-town feel about it, not unlike Canberra on a Sunday afternoon! The **Woomera Heritage Centre** (☎ 08-8673 7042) is in the middle of town, and houses a free museum. It's open 9am to 5pm daily.

From Pimba the highway swings west for the 115km run to **Glendambo**, along the way passing the usually dry salt lakes of Island Lagoon and Lake Hart and the massive Lake Gairdner. The road once again swings north for 251km, until it reaches the opal-mining town of Coober Pedy.

From Coober Pedy, unsealed roads lead east to **William Creek** (161km) and north to **Oodnadatta** (190km), both on the Oodnadatta Track – see the Oodnadatta Track section later in this chapter for more details. A short distance out of Coober Pedy, the road to Oodnadatta crosses the Dog Fence, and then traverses the flat, eerie and seemingly lifeless Moon Plain (featured in the movie *Mad Max III*).

Coober Pedy

Coober Pedy (population 2700) is as close as Australia gets to having a frontier town. The name is Aboriginal and said to mean 'white fellow's hole in the ground', which is apt, as a large proportion of the population live in dugouts to shelter from extreme temperatures.

The most dominant landmark is the **Big Winch**, which is a lookout over the town and has an extensive display of cut and uncut opals. The **Old Timers Mine** (*☎ 08-8672 5555,* **e** *oldtimersmine@ozemail.com.au,* **w** *www.oldtimersmine.com, Crowders Gully Rd; adult/child $5/free; open 9am-5pm daily)* and the **Umoona Opal Mine & Museum** *(Hutchison St; admission free; open 8am-7pm daily)* are also worth a look for their local history content.

A must-see is **Crocodile Harry's** *(17 Mile Rd; adult/child $2/free; open 8am-5pm daily)*, an interesting dugout home about 4km north-west of town, which has featured in a number of documentaries and movies, including *Mad Max III*. Not far either side of the Stuart Hwy at Coober Pedy is the world's largest sheep station (Commonwealth Hill at 10,567 sq km) and cattle station (Anna Creek at more than 30,000 sq km). See the Oodnadatta Track section for more about Anna Creek.

Information The tourist office (☎ 1800 637 076, fax 08-8672 5699) is open 9am-5pm weekdays; on the corner of Hutchison and Nicholas Sts, it's opposite the Ampol service station.

Gemstone Cafe & Bakery (☎ 08-8672 3177), on Hutchison St near the roundabout, has Internet access at $8.80 per hour with a $10 deposit, as well as good coffee. It's open 6am to 9.30pm daily.

Radeka's Downunder Underground Backpackers Inn & Underground Motel, on the corner of Oliver and Hutchison Sts, has slowish Internet booths at $12 per hour in the reception/bar area.

Other useful addresses include:

Coober Pedy Hospital (☎ 08-8672 5009)
    Hospital Rd
Coober Pedy Police Station (☎ 08-8672 5056)
    Wright St, near Ampol service station
Post Office (☎ 08-8672 5062) Hutchison St,
    opposite Westpac Bank and ATM

Fossicking In South Australia, fossicking (or 'noodling') doesn't require a permit, as long as your fossicking is a not-for-profit exercise that doesn't involve machinery, or disturb the land or water. You do need to obtain permission from landowners before you start sifting. Contact the South Australian Land Titles office (☎ 08-8226 3861) for details on private land owners.

You can also fossick in a registered mineral claim or lease (numerous in and around Coober Pedy) as long as you have approval from the claim or lease holder. Get in touch with claim or lease holders in South Australia through the Mineral Registration Branch (☎ 08-8463 3103). Quote the claim or lease number on the posts marking the boundaries of the claim or lease. In Coober Pedy, noodling for opals is generally discouraged, although a few tourist spots, such as the Old Timers Mine, have noodle pits open to the public.

Coober Pedy to Alice Springs (684km)

The Stuart Hwy continues from here through fairly unchanging country and passes the **Breakaways Reserve,** a stark but colourful area of arid hills and scarps (also known as the Painted Desert) about 33km by road north of Coober Pedy – you turn off the highway 22km from town. You can drive to a lookout in a conventional vehicle and see the white-and-yellow mesa known as the **Castle**, which featured in the films *Mad Max III* and *Priscilla, Queen of the Desert*. Entry permits ($2 per person) are available at the tourist office or Underground Books in Coober Pedy. The best time for photographs is late afternoon.

An interesting loop of 70km on mainly unsealed road from Coober Pedy takes in the Breakaways, the **Dog Fence** and the table-like **Moon Plain** on the Coober Pedy-Oodnadatta road. Underground Books has a leaflet and 'mud map' for $1; check road conditions before attempting this route.

About 152km from Coober Pedy, the Stuart Hwy passes the **Cadney Park Roadhouse**, from where a good dirt road strikes out east to Oodnadatta (179km).

The next settlement on the highway is the small town of **Marla** (population 250), 83km north of Cadney Park, and the head of the Oodnadatta Track (see the Oodnadatta Track section later in this chapter). The opal-mining fields of Mintabie, 35km to the west, are worth a quick visit, although permits need to be arranged from the Marla police station (☎ 08-8670 7020).

From Marla it's just a hop, skip and a jump (156km to be exact) to the Northern Territory border, and a further 2km to where one of the most famous outback tracks, the Gunbarrel Hwy, heads off into the great vastness of the western deserts (see the Gunbarrel Highway section later in this chapter).

Kulgera is next, and from here you can strike out east along a dirt road (which can be treacherous in the wet season) to **Finke**, from where there are a number of possibilities: east to Old Andado and then south to Mount Dare and Oodnadatta or north to Alice Springs; or head north to Alice Springs along the Finke Track, also known as the Old Ghan Track (see the Finke & Old Andado Tracks section later in this chapter).

From **Erldunda**, 75km north of Kulgera, you can head west along the bitumen road

to **Uluru (Ayers Rock)** (250km) and **Kata Tjuta (the Olgas)** (287km). From there the road is dirt for the journey to **Docker River** and the start of the Gunbarrel Hwy.

The old turn-off for Kings Canyon is 69km north of Erldunda, and from here the final stage into Alice Springs is 128km, passing through Stuarts Well along the way.

Alice Springs, set in the heart of the rugged and spectacular MacDonnell Ranges, is an oasis – a place to rest, restock, eat out and make repairs before heading bush again. A lively town with plenty to see, most people find that a few days here are well spent. With the biggest population in the outback, it's also the best place for mechanical repairs and spare parts. (see Alice Springs earlier)

Alice Springs to Tennant Creek (535km)

About 20km north of Alice Springs is the turn-off to the Tanami Track, and the sign here indicates that it's a long, lonely 703km to the Western Australian border. This road allows direct access to the Kimberley's Halls Creek via some of Australia's least populated land and is an increasingly popular option to the west. Most 2WD vehicles can pass with care (for details see the Tanami Track section later in this chapter).

The Plenty Hwy turn-off is a further 48km north, and this road heads east to the Queensland border, and then on to Mt Isa (742km). The Sandover Hwy, which branches off the Plenty Hwy 27km east of the Stuart Hwy, is an alternative to the Plenty, and it heads north-east into outback Queensland, with connections to Camooweal and Mt Isa (see the Plenty Highway and Sandover Highway sections later in this chapter).

Continuing north up the Stuart Hwy you pass through the roadhouse-settlements of **Aileron** (66km north of the Plenty Hwy turn-off), **Ti Tree** (a further 60km), **Barrow Creek** (a further 90km), **Wycliffe Well** (93km; the UFO capital of Australia...spooky!) and **Wauchope** (17km). It's about here that you bid farewell to the last sand dune of the Centre, and begin the gradual transition from the red soil of Australia's heart to the more densely vegetated and greener Top End. This section of the highway crosses the very eastern edge of the Tanami Desert, dominated by spinifex grass.

The **Devil's Marbles Conservation Reserve**, 9km north of Wauchope, consists of mammoth boulders scattered and stacked haphazardly over a large area and is a very photogenic spot. According to Aboriginal mythology, the 'marbles' are eggs laid by the Rainbow Serpent.

A further 19km along is the turn-off to the proposed 1120-sq-km **Davenport Range National Park**, encompassing the ancient Davenport and Murchison Ranges. The peaks are more than 1800 million years old and the area has that off-the-beaten-track appeal. There's a basic camping ground and the track is 4WD only – check for road conditions before you head off, especially in December to March.

Tennant Creek

Tennant Creek (population 3500), 114km north of Wauchope, is, apart from Katherine, the only sizeable town between Alice Springs and Darwin. Known as Jurnkurakurr by the local Aborigines, the town has an interesting history, including its role in the Overland Telegraph (there's an old telegraph station 12km from town) and the small gold rush here in the 1930s. Daily tours of a **gold-crushing plant and underground tunnel** *(admission $13/27 adult/family)* kick off at the visitor information centre on Battery Hill.

Useful addresses in Tennant Creek are:

Parks and Wildlife Commission (☎ 08-8962 4599) 2 Scott St
Post Office (☎ 08-8962 2196) 49 Paterson St
Tennant Creek Hospital (☎ 08-8962 4399) Schmidt St
Tennant Creek Police Station (☎ 08-8962 4444) Paterson St
Visitor Information Centre (☎ 08-8962 3388) Peko Rd, Battery Hill

Tennant Creek to Katherine (635km)

Twenty-five kilometres north of Tennant Creek, **Threeways** marks the junction of the

Stuart and Barkly Hwys, which is the only bitumen connection between the Northern Territory and Queensland. The brick **memorial** at this major junction commemorates the Reverend John Flynn, the founder of the Royal Flying Doctor Service.

About 45km north of Threeways there's the **Stuart Memorial** at Attack Creek, where the explorer turned back on the first of his attempts to cross Australia from south to north (see the Oodnadatta Track section later in this chapter). Just a few kilometres further north is a turn-off for the old Stuart Hwy, a hilly alternative route north good for breaking the monotony. Around 9km after you swing off the main highway is **Churchill's Head**, a rock that with a little imagination may remind you of Winston.

Back on the Stuart Hwy, you'll pass a flat-topped hill known as **Lubra's Lookout** as you approach the roadhouse at **Renner Springs**. A further 74km brings you to the turn-off to the **Barkly Stock Route**, a dirt road that joins up with the Carpentaria Hwy. Continuing through **Elliott** and passing by the ghost town of **Newcastle Waters** after 18km, you'll hit the area generally accepted as the dividing line between the desert landscape of the Red Centre and the Top End tropics. The highway here also divides the Tanami Desert on the west from the Barkly Tableland on the east.

Next in line along the Stuart Hwy and 77km past Newcastle Waters is **Dunmarra**, named after Dan O'Mara. Just beyond this roadhouse is the turn-off to the Buchanan Hwy, which heads west to **Top Springs**, **Victoria River Downs** and **Timber Creek** on the Victoria Hwy. Forty kilometres from Dunmarra, the sealed Carpentaria Hwy heads off east towards **Borroloola**, 380km away near the Gulf of Carpentaria and a popular place to hook a barra. **Daly Waters**, 8km north of the Carpentaria Hwy turn-off and 3km off the highway, is worth a detour. It's home to Australia's first international airfield and the eccentric *Daly Waters Pub* (1893), apparently the oldest pub in the Territory, with banknotes, bras and other assorted mementos dangling from the walls and rafters. Hot meals and cold beers are also available.

With its steep smooth flanks of red rock towering above the sand plain, Uluru is a remarkable sight. To visit it is like a pilgrimage. Uluru has tremendous spiritual significance to its owners, the Pitjantjatjara and Yankunytjatjara people, who call themselves Anangu. Powerful beings, the ancestors of the Anangu, created this rock and their biographies are etched into its features.

It rarely rains at Uluru, but when it does the desert springs to life (1). Each crevice and texture in the rock face is woven into Anangu stories, which you can learn on guided tours (2). Uluru is famous for its changing colours, which vary from bright orange to deep purple. At sunset the rock glows red (3, 5). The sacred red soils around Uluru are home to calandrines and other hardy wildflowers (4) .

INDRA KILFOYLE

GEOF BRANTON

RICHARD I'ANSON

CHRIS MELLOR

CHRIS MELLOR

Also known as the Olgas, this spectacular collection of 36 giant red domes is geologically linked to Uluru. It is of similar spiritual significance to the Anangu people who named it Kata Tjuta, meaning 'many heads'. Its weathered formations were mapped by events of the Creation time (Tjukurpa).

The rocks can appear strikingly different depending on the time of day (1, 5). Tiny but brilliant wildflowers (2). Shallow pools of water lie in the shadowed canyons of Walpa (Mt Olga Gorge) (3). Surrounding vegetation includes desert casuarina trees, mulga bush and black-barked desert oak (4). The distinctive rust red colour of the domes and the soil surrounding Kata Tjuta is caused by the oxidation of iron in the rock (6).

KRZYSZTOF DYDYNSKI

1

ROBYN COVENTRY

2

RICHARD I'ANSON

3

RICHARD I'ANSON

4

CHRIS MELLOR

5

PAUL SINCLAIR

Another 65km or so up the track, you can either whoosh past the tiny settlement of **Larrimah**, or stop at the popular *Fran's Devonshire Tea House (☎ 08-8975 9945; open 8am-9.30pm daily)*, in the old police station and museum.

About 80km north of Larrimah, the **Roper Hwy** splits from the Stuart Hwy and heads 174km east to **Roper Bar**, near the Roper River on the edge of Aboriginal land. It's an area that lures fishing enthusiasts, and all but about 40km of the road towards it is sealed. About 5km south of the Roper junction is the turn-off to the **Elsey Cemetery**. Here you'll find the grave of Aeneus Gunn, husband of Jeannie Gunn, whose novel *We of the Never Never* remains a classic novel about outback life at the turn of the 19th century.

The one-street town of **Mataranka** is on the Stuart Hwy, another 7km north of the Roper Hwy turn-off. One of the big draw-cards here is the **Mataranka Pool Nature Park**, 1.5km south of town, then 8km east of the highway along a bitumen road. The park's crystal-clear thermal pool ringed by pandanus is a good place for a tepid soak – though it can get crowded, especially when the big coaches pull in. Abutting the nature park is the 138-sq-km **Elsey National Park**, which takes in the Roper River and has walking paths meandering through monsoon forest. Also worth checking out a few kilometres north of town is **Bitter Springs**, a new addition to the Territory's thermal-pool trail.

From Mataranka the highway curves to the north-west and reaches Katherine after 106km. Just 27km before hitting Katherine is **Cutta Cutta Caves Nature Park** *(tours adult/child $10/5, 6 daily between 9am-3pm)*, home of the only Top End cave system open to the public and a great spot to explore while the bats are snoozing. The one-hour guided tour takes you 700m into tropical limestone caverns.

Katherine

Katherine has long been an important transit point and it continues to expand and prosper thanks to the town's important beef industry and the tourism generated by the Katherine Gorge and other nearby sites.

Interesting features of the town include the National Trust **railway station**, the small **Katherine Museum** *(☎ 08-8972 3945, Gorge Rd; adult/child $3.50/1)* in the old airport terminal building, and *Springvale homestead (☎ 08-8972 1355, Shadforth Rd; admission free)* 8km south-west of town (turn right off the Victoria Hwy after 3.8km). The historic homestead (1878) by the Katherine River is the oldest cattle station in the Northern Territory and today offers camping and motel accommodation. Five minutes' drive from town are the raved-about **Katherine Hot Springs**, surrounded by plenty of trees to shade your picnic blanket.

Katherine is also where the **Victoria Hwy**, part of Hwy 1 around Australia, joins from the west, connecting the Northern Territory with Western Australia.

Some useful addresses in Katherine include:

Katherine Hospital (☎ 08-8973 9211)
  Gorge Rd
Katherine Police Station (☎ 08-8972 0111)
  Stuart Hwy
Katherine Region Tourist Association
  (☎ 08-8972 2650) corner of Stuart Hwy and Lindsay St
Parks and Wildlife Commission (☎ 08-8973 8888) 32 Giles St
Post Office (☎ 08-8972 1439)
  corner of Katherine Terrace and Giles St

Nitmiluk (Katherine Gorge) National Park

The spectacular sandstone formation Nitmiluk (Katherine Gorge) in the eastern section of the Nitmiluk National Park is 29km north-east of the town of Katherine; its name means 'Cicada Dreaming' in Jawoyn, the language of its traditional owners. It is a remote, beautiful place and understandably one of the most visited sites in the Northern Territory. Within the park are opportunities to camp, canoe, swim (only freshwater crocs here) and walk any stretch of the 100km of tracks; there are also several *gorge cruises (☎ 1800 089 103 for reservations; 2-hour cruise adult/child $34/13.50; other tours available)*. The 12km-long gorge is in fact a series of 13 serpentine gorges, separated from each other by rapids of varying length.

Its sheer sandstone walls have been carved by the Katherine River, which rises in Arnhem Land. Further downstream it becomes the Daly River before flowing into the Timor Sea, 80km south-west of Darwin.

For information on walking tracks, canoe hire and wildlife, drop by the park's Visitor Centre (☎ 08-8972 1886), which is open 7am to 7pm daily.

Katherine to Darwin (355km)

From Katherine, travel 40km north and take the turn-off to **Leliyn (Edith Falls)**, 20km along a sealed road and part of Nitmiluk National Park. The waterfall is picturesque and the plunge pool is perfect for a swim. Make sure you walk to the lookout so you can look back at the falls from a distance.

Back on the Stuart Hwy, it's 49km to **Pine Creek**, an interesting gold-mining town with historic buildings, a mango winery and lots of accommodation. Pine Creek is set about 1km from the highway so it's quieter than other towns up the track; it's also the turn-off for the southern route into **Kakadu National Park** along the sealed Kakadu Hwy (see the Kakadu National Park section in The Tropics chapter).

Several kilometres beyond **Hayes Creek** (65km north of Pine Creek), a rough bitumen section of the Old Stuart Hwy leads you to a number of pleasant spots, but access to them is often cut in the wet season. To reach **Tjuwaliyn (Douglas Hot Springs) Nature Park**, turn south off the Old Stuart Hwy 5.5km after it branches from the Stuart Hwy and go 38km, the last 8km on a corrugated gravel road. The nature park here includes a section of the Douglas River, several hot springs flanked by pandanus and gums and a pretty camping area. If you like your springs hot (and less crowded), you'll be more content sitting in these waters than those at Mataranka. Check the temperature before hopping in as it can sometimes exceed 60°C.

Butterfly Gorge National Park is about 17km beyond Douglas Hot Springs along a rough 4WD track, which is often closed in the Wet. To reach the gorge from the carpark walk about 800m, including a steep climb over rocks (or a swim across the creek). As its name suggests, thousands of butterflies flutter around the rocks and paperbark trees of this quiet gorge.

Back on the Old Stuart Hwy, its around 27km to the turn-off to **Daly River**, a scenic spot about 81km west on a sealed road. The Daly is a favourite among barramundi hunters who flock here for the two annual major fishing competitions. Worth a peek are the **Jesuit mission ruins** (1886) on the grounds of the ***Mango Farm*** (☎ *1800 000 576, 08-8978 2464*), where you can also set up camp.

From Daly River you can continue north towards Darwin, or enter **Litchfield National Park** along the southern access track, which is strictly 4WD territory (see this park's section in The Tropics chapter).

Heading back towards the Stuart Hwy, the small **Robin Falls** are a mere trickle in the dry season, but gush down in the Wet. It's a short, rocky scramble to the plunge pool, set in a monsoon-forested gorge. The old highway rejoins the Stuart Hwy at the sleepy settlement of **Adelaide River**, with Australia's largest cemetery for those who made the 'supreme sacrifice' in the 1942–43 Japanese air raids on the Top End. Both sides of the highway between here and Darwin are dotted with WWII airstrips.

Twenty-eight kilometres north of Adelaide River is the turn-off to the regional centre of **Batchelor**, which is the main access point for Litchfield National Park. The highway then continues north through cleared farmland for the final 90km flat stretch into Darwin. The only feature of note along this section is where the **Arnhem Hwy**, the access road to Kakadu National Park and Arnhem Land, branches off the Stuart Hwy 34km south of Darwin.

For information on the capital of the Top End, see the Darwin section in The Tropics chapter.

DETOURS

While most of the detours off the Stuart Hwy are tracks in themselves, there's an interesting trip you can make from Woomera to Andamooka and the huge Olympic Dam mine at Roxby Downs. **Andamooka** (population 470) is a rough-and-ready opal-mining community, similar in many respects to Coober Pedy, but on a much smaller scale. However, due to its isolation, it is much less visited. It is 106km north of Woomera, and the road is sealed throughout.

The **Olympic Dam** uranium, gold, silver and copper mine was established in the early 1980s. It is the world's largest copper-uranium mine, and is currently one of only three uranium mines in the country. There are mine tours daily from the BP station at Roxby Downs township.

FACILITIES

Facilities are excellent all the way along the Stuart Hwy; the longest stretch without a fuel stop is 251km between Glendambo and Coober Pedy.

There are roadhouses with fuel (all types), food and accommodation, and mechanical repairs are available at most centres. While some roadhouses in the larger towns have 24-hour fuel, the smaller places are typically open from early morning to late evening. Apart from Alice Springs (see the start of this chapter) and Darwin (see the start of The Tropics chapter), facilities along the Stuart Hwy include:

Port Augusta

Many of Port Augusta's impressive old pubs have been turned into pokie machine shrines, making the caravan parks and dorm-style lodges best value.

Port Augusta Caravan Park (☎ 08-8643 6357, Brook St, Stirling North) Unpowered/powered sites $10/17 for 2 people, single/double on-site vans $24/28, standard cabins $37/47, railway carriage cabins $39/49. This is a good base for short trips into the Flinders Ranges, and pets are allowed. The park is 6km south-east of Port Augusta proper, off Quorn Rd.

Bluefox Lodge (☎ 08-8641 2960, e blue foxlodge@aussienet.net, Hwy 1, near cnr Trent Rd) Beds in 4-bed dorm $15. This is a fun and friendly former family home with great shared kitchen facilities, a free BBQ area, and imaginative tours and tourist info.

Pimba

Spud's Roadhouse Hotel Motel (☎ 08-8673 7473, fax 8673 7473, e spuds@internode .on.net, Stuart Hwy) Single/double & twin rooms $15/40. Accommodation here is strictly no-frills, but it has a pub with the lot. Fuel is generally dearer here than at nearby Woomera.

Woomera

Woomera Eldo Hotel (☎ 08-8673 7867, fax 8673 7700, Kotara Crescent) Air-con singles & doubles in 4-bed rooms with shared bathroom $66 (extra person $15), singles & doubles in 4-bed room with en suite $77 (extra person $15). This hotel is part of a large complex that has a bistro, bar and poker machines.

Woomera Travellers Village (☎ 08-8673 7800, fax 8673 7700, Old Pimba Rd) Unpowered/powered sites $5/7 per person, double on-site vans $35. This well-run place has plenty of tourist information.

Glendambo

Glendambo Tourist Centre Hotel Motel & Camping (☎ 08-8672 1035 for caravan park, ☎ 8672 1030 for motel, e gtc@ camtech.net.au, Stuart Hwy) Unpowered/powered sites $9.50/14.50 for 2 people, dorm beds $15.40, singles/doubles with en suite $94/94. This place has a range of comfortable accommodation available and very tourist-friendly roadhouse.

Coober Pedy

Accommodation is both above and below ground. Cuisine options include Greek and Chinese.

Oasis Caravan Park (☎ 08-8672 5169, Cnr Hutchison St & 17 Mile Rd) Unpowered/powered sites $13.20/17.60 for 2 people, standard double cabins with shared bathroom/en suite $52.80/64.90, deluxe double cabins $72.60-83.60. There's a pool here, and plenty of shade by Coober Pedy standards.

Stuart Range Caravan Park (☎ 08-8672 5179, fax 8672 5148, Hutchison St) Unpowered/powered sites $6/10 per person, double cabins & vans with shared bath/en suite $45/55. This place, near the Stuart

Hwy turn-off, offers a pool and an on-site pizza joint.

Radeka's Downunder Underground Backpackers Inn & Underground Motel (☎ *08-8672 5223,* e *radekadownunder@ ozemail.com.au, Cnr Oliver & Hutchison Sts)* Dorm beds $18, doubles & twins with shared bathroom $48, singles/doubles with en suite $77/88. Although some of its motel rooms are rather cramped, this is a palatial and popular backpacker establishment with great underground dorm accommodation, a bar, TV room and shared kitchen.

Opal Inn Chinese Restaurant (☎ *08-8672 5430, Paxton St near Hutchison St roundabout)* Mains $9.50-13.50. Open noon-2.30pm & 5pm-late daily. This is a deservedly busy place with a big range of fresh and tasty dishes to eat in or take away.

Cadney Park

Cadney Homestead Motel & Caravan Park (☎ *08-8670 7994, Stuart Hwy)* Unpowered/ powered sites $6/8.50 for 2 people, double cabins $35, singles/doubles with en suite $70/77. There's also a pool and bar.

Marla

Marla Travellers Rest (☎ *08-8670 7001, fax 8670 7021,* e *marla@internode.on.net, Stuart Hwy)* Unpowered/powered sites $5/7 for 2 people, dorm beds $20, single/twin cabins $30/40, air-con en suite singles $70-80, air-con en suite doubles $75-85. This is a roadhouse complex with the works, including a supermarket and 24-hour fuel.

Kulgera

Kulgera Roadhouse Motel & Caravan Park (☎ *08-8956 0973, fax 8956 0807,* e *loraine_mason@bigpond.com, Stuart Hwy)* Unpowered/powered sites $5/7 for 2 people, backpacker singles/doubles (with linen) $22/33, air-con en suite singles/doubles & twins $55/66. This place offers refurbished rooms and a huge camping ground.

Erldunda

Desert Oaks Motel (☎ *08-8956 0984, fax 8956 0942,* e *erldunda@bigpond.com, Cnr Stuart & Lasseter Hwys)* Air-con en suite

singles/doubles & twins $72/85. The grounds of this comfortable motel include a pool, BBQ area and tennis court.

Aileron

Aileron Hotel & Roadhouse (☎ *08-8956 9703, Stuart Hwy)* Camp sites $8.50, van sites $17, both powered until 10pm. Beds in 10-bed dorm $30. Self-contained singles/ doubles $78/88. Fuel is available 7am to 9.30pm daily. The pub serves meals 365 days a year (7am to 9.30pm) and the shop is very well stocked (check if the coffin – on sale for $600 – is still perched on the Coke machine!).

Ti Tree

Ti Tree Roadhouse (☎ *08-8956 9741, Stuart Hwy)* Double unpowered/powered sites $11/17, dorm beds $14, single/double motel rooms $65/72. Fuel is available 6am to 10pm daily. Rooms have TV and air-con but no phone. Kick back at Flo's Bar, 'the most central pub in Australia', which boasts a jukebox and a pool table.

Barrow Creek

Barrow Creek Hotel & Caravan Park (☎ *08-8956 9753, Stuart Hwy)* Powered sites $10, single/family cabins $20/40. Fuel available 7am to 11pm daily. At the time of writing there were brand-new motel units here. The colourful pub serves a mean 'Bullshit Burger' with the lot ($8).

Wycliffe Well

Wycliffe Well Holiday Park (☎ *1800 136 084, 08-8964 1966,* e *info@wycliffe.com .au, Stuart Hwy)* Single/double unpowered sites $12/16, powered sites $16/20, range of cabins, chalets & motel units $28-99. Fuel is available 7am to 8pm daily. This complex has an absolutely mind-boggling range of accommodation, including shaded sites and self-contained chalets. It has a pool, games room, animal park and UFO paraphernalia.

Wauchope

Wauchope Roadhouse (☎ *08-8964 1963, fax 8964 1567, Stuart Hwy)* Unpowered sites $5 per person, powered sites $14.50, double motel rooms $70. Fuel is available 6am to 1am daily. The rooms here are simple but clean; there's also a pool, tennis court, and a beer garden where guests can unwind.

Tennant Creek

Tennant Creek Caravan Park (☎ 08-8962 2325, Paterson St) Unpowered/powered sites $8/15, double 'bunkhouse' rooms $25, cabins $40-62. Owned by people with their priorities right, ie, clean bathrooms and well-tended grassy sites, this place also has a pool and a mini-mart.

Safari Lodge Motel & YHA Hostel (☎ 08-8962 2207, 12 Davidson St) Dorm beds $16, hostel rooms $38, single/double motel rooms $55/65. The hostel is across the road from the pool-less motel – both sections are well maintained and will do the job for a few days' stay in town.

Bluestone Motor Inn (☎ 08-8962 2617, 1 Paterson St) Single/double standard rooms $85/90, deluxe $91/97, executive lodges $105/115. Up just a notch from Safari, this place has plenty of comfortable rooms, complete with all the mod cons.

Places to eat include the *Top of Town Cafe (☎ 08-8962 1311)*, next to the Transit Centre, which is open from 8am to 8pm daily, but much later on weekends. It does big brekkies, good salad-crammed sandwiches and the best coffee between Alice and Katherine. Nearby on Paterson St are *Chompin' Charlie's (☎ 08-8962 2388)* and *Rocky's Pizza (☎ 08-8962 2049)* for stock-standard takeaway foods. One of the locals' favourites (and part of Tennant Creek Hotel) is *Margo Miles (☎ 08-8962 2006)*, where juicy steaks and home-made pastas can be yours for between $14 and $18.

Threeways

Threeways Roadhouse Motel & Caravan Park (☎ 08-8962 2744, fax 8962 2426, Stuart Hwy) Camp sites $7.70 per person, cabins $30-61. Open 24 hours for check-ins. Fuel is available 5.30am to midnight daily. The grassy camp sites, pool and pub provide three ways to spend your time here.

Renner Springs

Renner Springs Desert Motel (☎ 08-8964 4505, fax 8964 4525, Stuart Hwy) Unpowered/powered sites $5.50/13.75 per person. Single/double motel rooms $66/77, cabins $55/66. Fuel is available 6am to 11pm daily. This accommodation is nothing flash, but with a bed and air-con it'll do the trick for one night.

Elliott

Midland Caravan Park (☎ 08-8969 2037, Stuart Hwy) Camp sites $6 per person, cabins from $60. Fuel is available (Mobil) 6am to 8pm Monday to Saturday, 7am to 5pm Sunday. If you need to stay in Elliott, this is probably your best bet. Check out the open-air toilets!

Dunmarra

Dunmarra Wayside Inn (☎ 08-8975 9922, fax 8975 9981, Stuart Hwy) Unpowered/powered sites $11/16.50, single/double motel rooms $55/65. Fuel is available 6am to 11pm daily.

Daly Waters

Daly Waters Pub Hotel & Caravan Park (☎ 08-8975 9927, 3km off the Stuart Hwy) Unpowered sites $3.30 per person, powered sites $11, single/double motel rooms $33/44. Enjoy the pub's beef 'n' barra barbie – it's a lot of food for $15.40. A warning – it's wise to wear thongs (flip-flops) in the showers at the caravan park. Fuel is available 7am to 11pm daily.

Larrimah

Larrimah Wayside Inn & Caravan Park (☎ 08-8975 9931, Stuart Hwy) Unpowered sites $3.30 per person, powered sites $11, single motel rooms without/with en suite $25/35. Fuel is available nearby 7am to 9pm daily. The cheaper units are like cells – pay a bit more and you get an en suite. The old pub, shaded by trees, is a cool place for an afternoon drink.

Mataranka

Mataranka Homestead Motel (☎ 1800 089 103, 08-8975 4544, Near Mataranka pool)

Camp sites $8 per person, with power extra $4 per site, dorm beds $17, double self-contained cabins $93, double motel rooms $93. Booking in advance is recommended.

Territory Manor (☎ 08-8975 4516, Stuart Hwy) Powered sites $16, single/double motel rooms $74/86. The Manor is 300m east off the highway, heading in the direction of Katherine.

Katherine

Kookaburra Backpackers (☎ 1800 808 211, 08-8971 0257, Cnr Lindsay & Third Sts) Dorm beds $16, doubles & twins $45. This quiet place runs like a well-oiled machine, with squeaky-clean facilities, friendly staff and lots of help with trips and tourist info.

Beagle Motor Inn (☎ 08-8972 3998, Cnr Lindsay & Fourth Sts) Single/double budget rooms (no en suite) $50/60, motel rooms $60/70. With a quiet location and adequate rooms, it's all you need for a comfortable stay.

Knott's Crossing Resort (☎ 08-8972 2511, fax 8972 2628, ⓔ reservations@ knottscrossing.com.au, Ⓦ www.knottscross ing.com.au, Cnr Giles & Cameron Sts) Unpowered/powered sites $20/22 for 2 people, double self-contained cabins $75, single/ double motel rooms $110/120. A recommended, well-maintained accommodation complex, with the reputable Katie's Bistro with its $15 buffet and other fresh meals. The poolside bar is a bonus.

Places to eat include the *Cinema Cafe (☎ 08-8971 0594, 17 First St)*, in the cinema complex, which is one of the best spots for home-baked breads and cakes, breakfasts and excellent espresso; it's open Monday to Saturday from 8am until various hours. Quite good is *Olympia Cafe (☎ 08-8971 0422, 7 Victoria Hwy)*, where you can sit inside or out scoffing pizzas ($13.90) and large servings of pasta (from $12). *Cafe Enio's (☎ 08-8972 2255, 385 Katherine Terrace)* serves fabulous food and coffee but its hours are disappointing – opens early, closes early and on weekends. In town takeaway food outlets abound, and self-caterers can rejoice – there's a big Woolworths *supermarket* at the southern end of Katherine Terrace.

Pine Creek

Diggers Rest Motel (☎ 08-8976 1442, fax 8976 1458, 32 Main Terrace) Single/double units $65/75. Diggers Rest offers self-contained units with veranda, a pretty BBQ area and an attached laundrette.

Pine Creek Motel & Caravan Park (☎ 08-8976 1217, Moule St) Unpowered/powered sites $16/20 per double, single/double motel rooms $20/30. The 14 motel rooms have air-con, en suite and TV. Off-street parking is available.

Hayes Creek

Wayside Inn & Caravan Park (☎ 08-8978 2430, Stuart Hwy) Unpowered sites $4.50 per person, powered sites $15 for 2 people. Single/double/triple motel rooms $34/50/65. Fuel is available 5.30am to 11pm daily. Spartan rooms await you here, but it's a decent spot and the pub's fish and chips are great.

Adelaide River

Adelaide River Inn & Caravan Park (☎ 08-8976 7047, Stuart Hwy) Camp sites $6 per person, singles/doubles $55/75. Fuel is available 5am to around 10pm daily.

ALTERNATIVE TRANSPORT

As you'd expect on such a major highway, there are daily scheduled bus services all the way from Adelaide to Darwin (via Uluru/Ayers Rock) with McCafferty's/Greyhound (☎ 08-8087 2735, 1800 801 294, Ⓦ www.greyhound.com.au). These buses can drop passengers anywhere along this route, but will only pick up passengers at Glendambo, Coober Pedy, Cadney Park, Marla, Indulkana, Bulgunnia, Bon Bon, Coondambo and Wirraminna. Contact McCafferty's/Greyhound for timetables.

Premier Stateliner (☎ 08-8642 5055, Ⓦ www.premierstateliner.com.au), at 21 Mackay St, Port Augusta, has buses that make regular trips between Port Augusta and Roxby Downs (via Pimba/Woomera). It is also possible to take the *Ghan* train from Port Augusta to Alice Springs (see the separate entry on the *Ghan* in the Getting Around chapter).

Uluru, Kata Tjuta & Kings Canyon

Highlights

- Standing in awe at the imposing grandeur of the world's second-largest monolith
- Experiencing the mystery of Kata Tjuta on the Valley of the Winds walk
- Seeing the surprising variety of nature in the microclimates of Kings Canyon

Uluru, Kata Tjuta and Kings Canyon are the 'big three' drawcards of the Red Centre and attract hundreds of thousands of visitors every year. While Uluru (Ayers Rock) is the undisputed number-one attraction and the focus of a multitude of tours and events, nearby Kata Tjuta (the Olgas) has a majestic beauty all of its own and offers a more

intimate experience. Some 300km to the north-east, Kings Canyon (in Watarrka National Park) takes some getting to, but its sheer cliffs, spectacular views and hidden pools are well worth the effort.

ULURU-KATA TJUTA NATIONAL PARK

The main feature of this 1325 sq km desert park is the World Heritage–listed Uluru. At 3.6km long, and with steep, smooth flanks of red sandstone that tower 348m above the surrounding sand plain, it's an unforgettable sight. The 'many moods' of Uluru are well documented, but it's still remarkable to witness the progressive change in its colours between dawn and dusk. For this reason alone, it's worthwhile spending a couple of days exploring the park. You're much better off travelling independently to the park, as organised tours tend to be regrettably brief.

Ensure you also leave a day or so to visit the park's other principal attraction, Kata Tjuta (literally 'Many Heads'), 42km to the

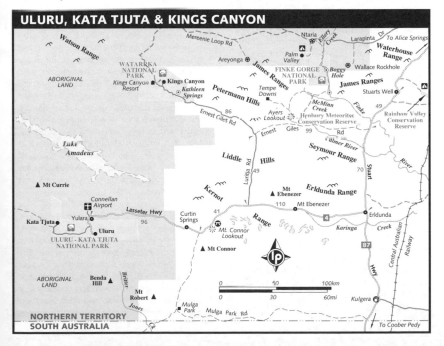

ULURU, KATA TJUTA & KINGS CANYON

west. As the name suggests, it's a collection of bulbous rock formations, principally made up of basalt and granite conglomerate. Individually, these are much smaller than the Rock, but are still spectacular – the tallest, Mt Olga, is about 200m higher than Uluru. You can easily while away a day wandering through its many gorges.

History

Archaeologists suggest that Aboriginal people have inhabited this part of Australia for at least 22,000 years, but according to traditional belief Anangu have been there since time began. According to the law laid down during the Tjukurpa (Creation Time), all landscape features were made by ancestral beings, and, as the descendants of these beings, the Anangu are responsible for the wellbeing of their ancestral lands.

A number of totemic ancestors are associated with Uluru, and their deeds are told in the marks and other natural features on and around the Rock. These ancestors include Kuniya (the woma python), Kurpany (an evil, dog-like creature), Liru (the poisonous snake), Lungkarta (the bluetongue lizard) and Mala (the rufous hare-wallaby). Their Tjukurpa stories are introduced at the park's excellent cultural centre and on Anangu-guided walks in the area.

The first white settlers came to the area in the 1870s. By the 1920s, increasing contact and conflict between the settlers and the Anangu prompted the Northern Territory, Western Australian and South Australian governments to set aside the area as part of Great Central Aboriginal Reserve. The modern national park was excised from the reserve in 1958, but it took until 1973 for Anangu to become involved in its management and a further 12 years – and the intervention of the federal government – before the freehold title was granted to the area's traditional owners. However, it was granted only on the condition that the park was leased back to Parks Australia for 99 years. The transfer of ownership took place on 26 October 1985.

Today the park is managed by a 10-person board, of which six members are Anangu

nominees. The traditional owners also receive an annual rent of $150,000 plus 25% of the park entrance fees.

Information

The Uluru-Kata Tjuta Cultural Centre (☎ 08-8956 3138) is found 1km before the rock on the road from Yulara. The organic curves of the two buildings represent the ancestral figures of Kuniya (woma python) and Liru (poisonous snake) and contain an arts and crafts gallery, arts centre (where artists from the Mutitjulu community come to paint), cafe, Anangu Tours booking desk and information desk. There are also excellent multilingual displays on the flora, fauna, history, geology, climate, walking trails, ancestral stories and art associated with Uluru and the Anangu. Good-quality information packs covering all of the above are available for $5.

This really is a well-designed, intriguing place, and you can easily spend an hour wandering around. The centre is open daily

A Question of Respect

For years, climbing Uluru has been the highlight of a trip to the Red Centre and has become almost a rite of passage for many visitors. For the Anangu, however, the path up the side of the Rock is part of the route taken by ancestral Mala men on their arrival at Uluru. As such, it's a place of considerable spiritual significance. The Anangu are also the custodians of these lands and take responsibility for the safety of visitors. All injuries and deaths that occur on the rock are a source of distress to them. For all of these reasons, the Anangu don't climb Uluru, and they ask that you don't either.

Ultimately, this is a question of respect – for the beliefs of the Anangu and for the people themselves. If you would respect Muslim or Christian beliefs by not striding through a mosque during prayer, or clambering over the altar in Notre Dame Cathedral, then content yourself with exploring this remarkable monolith from the ground. If such acts do not bother you, then go right ahead and climb that rock.

from 7am to 5.30pm (6pm in summer) and there's a free 1½-hour tour at 3.15pm on Monday, Tuesday and Wednesday.

The park itself is open daily from half an hour before sunrise to sunset. Five-day entry permits are $15 per person (children under 15 free) and are available from the Yulara visitor centre, or at the park's entry station on the road from Yulara to the Rock and the Kata Tjuta turn-off.

Bushwalking – Uluru

There are several walking trails around Uluru, plus guided walks delving into the plants, wildlife, geology and local Tjukurpa stories. Areas of special spiritual significance to Anangu are off-limits to visitors – these are marked with fences and signs.

Base Walk It can take up to four hours to make the 9.4km circumnavigation of Uluru's base, but this leaves plenty of time to check out the caves and rock paintings on the way.

Mala Walk This leisurely, 90-minute walk starts at the base of the climb and follows the Mala ancestral story through a series of significant sites, including caves, rock art

and a waterhole. You can do the walk on your own, or join a free guided walk from the carpark; they leave daily at 8am (10am May to September).

Liru Walk The two-hour, guided Liru Walk starts at the cultural centre and focuses on traditional uses of the area's plant and animal life, such as how to make bush glue, light a fire using dried kangaroo dung, make a *piti* (wooden dish) and carry the dish on your head. Operated by Anangu Tours, it leaves daily at 8.30am (earlier from October to March) and costs $47/24 for adults/children. Bookings are essential.

Mutitjulu Walk Mutitjulu, Uluru's most reliable waterhole and home to the ancestral water snake Wanampi, is reached during this self-guided, 45-minute, 1km walk, which also passes some excellent rock art.

Kuniya Walk This two-hour guided walk takes you from the cultural centre to the southern edge of Uluru, before joining up with the Mutitjulu Walk. On the way, Anangu guides discuss the Tjukurpa associated with the clash between Kuniya

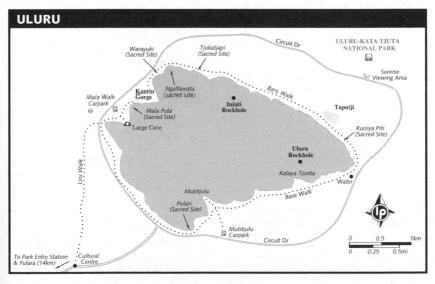

and Liru, two ancestral serpents; you also learn about the food and medicine plants found along the way. Anangu Tours has tours daily at 3.30pm (later from October to March) that cost $47/24 for adults/children.

The Climb If you insist on doing this, then be careful: it is a very demanding climb and there have been numerous deaths resulting from falls and heart attacks. Take plenty of water, cover up against the sun and be prepared to turn around if it's all getting too much. Also brace yourself for possible disappointment, as the climb is often closed due to rain, mist, extreme heat, strong winds or Anangu business. The climb itself is 1.6km and takes about two hours up and back, with a good rest at the top.

Uluru Viewing Areas
The sunset viewing area is just off the road to the left, 14km from Yulara on the way to Uluru. The sunrise viewing area is on the far side of Uluru almost exactly halfway around the base road.

Bushwalking – Kata Tjuta
Valley of the Winds Track The main walking trail at Kata Tjuta is aptly named Valley of the Winds and is a scenic 7.4km loop that takes about three hours to complete. The track wends its way through a number of gorges, giving excellent views of the domes. Although well constructed, the track is both rough and steep in places, so ensure you have sturdy footwear, plus drinking water and a hat.

Walpa (Olga Gorge) Walk This short, signposted track meanders gently into beautiful Walpa (Olga Gorge) from the carpark. The 2.6km return trip takes around an hour to complete and again offers good views.

Kata Tjuta Viewing Areas
There's a fine viewing area on your right, 36km along the road to Kata Tjuta. A five-minute stroll on a boardwalk takes you to a platform overlooking a sandy plain of spinifex and desert oak with Kata Tjuta looming impressively in the background.

There are signs informing about the complex dune environment. A few kilometres before Kata Tjuta is a left-hand turn to the sunset viewing area and picnic grounds.

Organised Tours
Anangu Tours (☎ 08-8956 2123, fax 8956 3136, ℮ lbanangu@bigpond.com, ⓦ www .anangutours.com.au) offers a range of tours led by local Aboriginal guides. These include the Liru Walk and Kuniya Walk (see Bushwalking – Uluru earlier); there are fancier versions that include breakfast at the cultural centre, and other combinations that take in a morning or afternoon at Kata Tjuta with AAT Tours. Prices for adults/children range from $47/24 to $160/110.

AAT Kings (☎ 08-8956 2171, ⓦ www .aatkings.com) offers a broad range of tours out of Yulara from $29/15 per adult/child, plus some useful connections with Alice Springs (see the Getting There & Around section later), while *Discovery Ecotours* (☎ 1800 803 174, ℮ bookings@ecotours .com.au) includes meals in its tours and charges from $83/65 to $306/227. There are several other outfits that offer sunrise, sunset, night sky, camel, motorbike, plane or helicopter tours to both Uluru and Kata Tjuta. For details and booking information, contact the Yulara Visitor Centre (☎ 08-8956 2240), drop into the Tour and Information Centre at the Yulara shopping centre or speak with resort hotel staff. There's also a slew of operators in Alice Springs that offer all sorts of tours; contact CATIA (☎ 08-8952 5800) for details.

Facilities
The Uluru-Kata Tjuta National Park is serviced by the resort town of Yulara, 18km north of Uluru, which offers several levels of accommodation, plus restaurants, shops, a bank, supermarket, post office and other facilities. It's the fourth most populous place in the Northern Territory, with up to 5500 people when it's busy.

Ayers Rock Resort (☎ 1300 139 889, 08-8957 7888, fax 02-9332 4555, ℮ reser vations@voyages.com.au, ⓦ www.ayers rockresort.com.au) This resort offers six

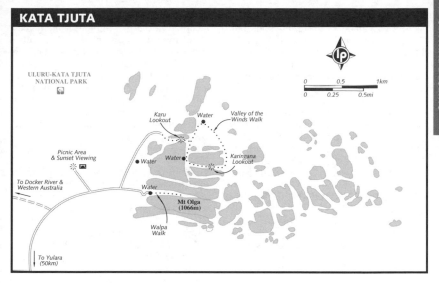

KATA TJUTA

ULURU-KATA TJUTA
NATIONAL PARK

Karu
Lookout

Water

Valley of the
Winds Walk

Picnic Area
& Sunset Viewing

Water

Water

Karingana
Lookout

To Docker River &
Western Australia

Water

Mt Olga
(1066m)

Walpa
Walk

To Yulara
(50km)

0   0.5   1km
0   0.25   0.5mi

---

levels of expensive accommodation, from camping to top-end luxury, in sprawling, attractive grounds. Each options is detailed below and can be booked through the resort's reservations line.

Ayers Rock Campground (fax 08-8956 2260) Unpowered/powered sites for two people $24.20/28.60, 6-bed cabins $132. This well-appointed camping ground is the least expensive accommodation available at the resort. The facilities are good and include a camp kitchen and a few nice patches of lawn, but it gets seriously over crowded in the high season.

Outback Pioneer Hotel & Lodge (fax 08-8957 7615) Beds in 4-bed/20-bed lodge dorm $32/38, 4-bed cabins $154, budget/standard hotel rooms $154/348. The lodge's dorms with kitchen, Internet and lounge facilities replace the budget rooms in the defunct Spinifex Lodge.

Emu Walk Apartments (fax 08-8957 7742) 4-person/8-person units $359/445. Designed for families, these self-contained units aren't bad value, with rollaway beds available for extra kids.

Lost Camel Hotel (☎ 08-8957 7888) Doubles $365. The old Spinifex Lodge is now a boutique hotel aimed squarely at the double-income, no kids market.

At the top of the tree are *Desert Gardens Hotel (fax 08-8657 7716)* and *Sails in the Desert Hotel (fax 08-8956 2018)*. Standard doubles at the Desert Gardens are $383/449, while Sails charges $464/543 and also has deluxe suites for $819. These are all beautifully appointed top-end rooms, filled mostly by overseas tourists.

In the town square you will find a good *supermarket*, a *takeaway* outlet, ANZ bank, several ATMs, post office, tour and hire-car booking service, newsagency and *Geckos Cafe* – one of 11 absurdly expensive eateries in the resort. The service station (☎ 08-8956 2229) near the camping ground has unleaded, super, diesel and LPG, plus a small selection of spare parts.

For more detailed information on all the facilities, tours and nightlife offered by the resort, contact the Yulara Visitor Centre (☎ 08-8957 7377).

Getting There & Around

Uluru-Kata Tjuta National Park is accessed via the Lasseter Hwy. Yulara is 247km from the Stuart Hwy turn-off at Erldunda; Uluru is a further 18km down the same road. To get to Kata Tjuta, take the turn to your right 8km past Yulara and follow it for 45km. All the roads are sealed.

If you're not travelling independently, there are a number of operators that provide connections to Yulara, Uluru and Kata Tjuta. ATT Kings (☎ 08-8956 2171) has a daily service from Alice Springs to Yulara for $99/50 per adult/child, but a much better bet is Uluru Express (☎ 08-8956 2152), which offers hourly services to Uluru for $30 and Kata Tjuta for $45 (both return fares) and you can stay as long as you wish.

WATARRKA NATIONAL PARK & KINGS CANYON

The 100m-high, sheer cliffs of Kings Canyon and the beautiful microclimates within its sheltering walls make a visit to Watarrka National Park an absolute must for the visitor to the Uluru–Alice Springs area.

More than 600 plant species have been recorded in the park, giving it the highest plant diversity of any place in Australia's arid zone. At the head of the 1km gorge is the lush vegetation and cool pools of the spring-fed Garden of Eden, while the narrow, rocky bed of Kings Creek along the canyon floor is covered with tall ghost gums. The gorge is carved from a towering sandstone plateau that's dotted with bizarre, weathered sandstone domes.

History

The Luritja Aboriginal people have lived in this area for at least 20,000 years and there are a number of registered sacred sites within the park. There are also three communities of Aboriginal people living within the park boundaries.

In 1872 Ernest Giles named the George Gill Range after his brother-in-law, who also helped fund his expedition. Kings Creek he named after his friend Fielder King. As the

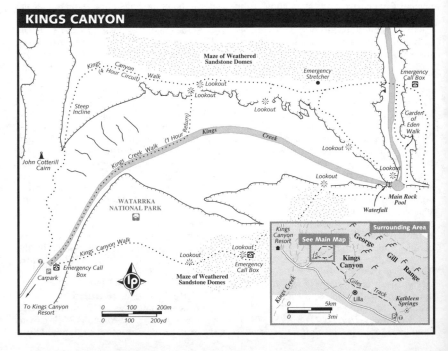

KINGS CANYON

first European to explore the area, Giles had first option on applying for a pastoral lease, and this he did in 1874. It covered almost 1000 sq miles and included the area of the modern park. The first tourism venture in the area was set up by Jack Cotterill in 1960 on Angus Downs station, but it wasn't until 1989 that the national park was established.

Information

There are some useful displays at the resort's reception centre, including maps for the walks. At the canyon, there are information boards, shelter, water and toilets at the carpark. Slide shows are held weekly at the resort and twice weekly at nearby Kings Creek station between May and October – check with resort staff for dates and times.

Bushwalking

The best way to appreciate Kings Canyon is to walk – either through the gorge or, if you're feeling energetic, up onto the plateau and around the canyon edge. There's another short walking trail to Kathleen Springs, about 17km to the east, plus the excellent two-day Giles Track that links Kings Canyon with Kathleen Springs. If you're attempting this one, contact the rangers (☎ 08-8956 7488) beforehand for a map and further information.

Kings Canyon Walk This is the best way to see everything the canyon has to offer, including the maze of eroded domes, sheer cliff faces, the tranquil pools of the Garden of Eden and stunning views to the west. The 6km track is well marked, but the initial climb is very steep and the entire track requires a decent level of fitness; you should allow about four hours to complete it. Take plenty of water, cover up in the sun and watch your step around the rim of the canyon – the cliffs are unfenced.

Kings Creek Walk This one-hour, 2.6km walk takes you along the rocky bed of Kings Creek. While you do get some good views of the canyon walls through the ghost gums, it's not a patch on those from the canyon rim. There is wheelchair access for the first 700m.

Kathleen Springs A beautiful, spring-fed rock pool at the base of the range is the reward for this one-hour, 2.5km, wheelchair-accessible walk. There's also a picnic ground with barbecues, shade, water and toilets.

Giles Track This is an easy overnight trail that follows the ridge from Kings Canyon to Kathleen Springs. It's 22km one way, but if you don't want to do the whole two days, you can do a day walk from Lilla about halfway along the trail. There's a designated *camp site* along the ridge above Lilla. You can register with the rangers (☎ 1300 650 730) if you wish.

Organised Tours

Lilla (☎ 08-8956 7442) is an Luritja-owned tour company that runs a couple of trips from the Kings Canyon Resort. A four-hour guided Kings Canyon Walk is available on demand. It costs $38.50/27.50 for adults/children and leaves at 7am.

The *Willy-Wagtail Tour* is a two-hour tour that takes in cave paintings and an introduction to Luritja traditions. Tours depart daily at 9am, 11am and 4pm and cost $39/28 for adults/children. Both tours can be booked at the resort reception centre.

Many operators in Alice Springs offer tours to Kings Canyon. Contact CATIA (☎ 08-8952 5800) for details.

Facilities

Kings Canyon Resort (☎ 1800 817 622, 08-8956 7442, fax 8956 7410, **e** *reserva tions@voyages.com.au,* **w** *www.voyages .com.au)* is a well-maintained place with plenty of facilities, including three levels of accommodation, two restaurants, a cafe, bar and a service station with a small shop.

A camp site for two people costs a hefty $26 ($29 with power), but there is a nice patch of lawn plus the use of a pool, barbecue and laundry. Next up, beds in clean, well-appointed four-or five-bed dorms are $42, and twin lodge rooms with shared facilities are $97. The hotel rooms are where you want to stay, though. Thoughtful design and siting makes it feel like you're in a cabin alone in the bush, and they don't stint on the luxuries either, and neither should they at $320/378 for standard/deluxe double rooms.

If you're on a budget, you're much better off avoiding the resort completely and staying at *Kings Creek station (☎ 08-8956 7474)*, 34km before the canyon turn-off on Ernest Giles Rd. Unpowered/powered camp sites among shady desert oaks cost $21/ 23.50 or two-bed tent-cabins go for $45 per person, including a cooked breakfast. There's also a small shop, camp kitchen and evening meals until 7pm.

Getting There & Around
Most people take their own vehicle or join a tour out of Alice Springs, but AAT Kings does offer daily bus services between Kings Canyon and Alice Springs (adult/child one way $103/52) or Yulara ($92/46). If you stay at the resort, there's a regular shuttle bus to the canyon itself for $9.50/4.50 return.

If you're driving from Alice Springs, you have to go via Erldunda if you want to stay on a sealed surface. Taking the dirt Ernest Giles Rd will save you about 150km, but a better option is to head west from Alice via Larapinta Dr and take the Mereenie Loop Rd, ideally exploring the West MacDonnell and Finke Gorge National Parks on the way – see the Finke Gorge section earlier in this chapter for details about this route and the required permit. Coming from Yulara, it's sealed road all the way via the Lasseter Hwy, Luritja Rd and Ernest Giles Rd.

Adelaide River
Adelaide River Inn & Caravan Park (☎ 08-8976 7047, Stuart Hwy) Camp sites $6 per person, singles/doubles $55/75. Fuel is available 5am to around 10pm daily.

ALTERNATIVE TRANSPORT
As you'd expect on such a major highway, there are daily scheduled bus services all the way from Adelaide to Darwin (via Uluru/Ayers Rock) with McCafferty's/ Greyhound (☎ 08-8087 2735, 1800 801 294, W www.greyhound.com.au). These buses can drop you anywhere along this route, but will only pick up passengers at

Glendambo, Coober Pedy, Cadney Park, Marla, Indulkana, Bulgunnia, Bon Bon, Coondambo and Wirraminna.

Premier Stateliner (☎ 08-8642 5055, W www.premierstateliner.com.au), at 21 Mackay St, Port Augusta, buses make regular trips between Port Augusta and Roxby Downs (via Pimba/Woomera). You can also take the *Ghan* train from Port Augusta to Alice Springs (see the separate entry on the *Ghan* in the Getting Around chapter).

MacDonnell Ranges

Highlights

- Experiencing the remoter parts of the ranges on an overnight trek along the Larapinta Trail
- Being enthralled by the superb evening and early morning views from Mt Sonder Lookout
- Marvelling at the rich colours of the landscape on a sunny winter's day
- Appreciating the hardships faced by the pioneers at the old Arltunga goldfield

Sweeping east-west for over 400km, the timeless MacDonnell Ranges form a rugged red barrier across the vast central Australian plain. The ranges consist mainly of a parallel series of long, steep-sided ridges that rise 100m to 600m above the valley floors. Scattered throughout are deep gorges carved by ancient rivers that meander south into the Simpson Desert. Here also are the four highest peaks west of the Great Dividing Range: Mt Zeil, the highest, is 1531m above sea level and 900m above the surrounding plain.

Although arid, the ranges are home to a huge variety of native plants, including many tall trees, such as the majestic ghost gum. In hidden, moist places are relics of the rainforest flora that covered this region millions of years ago. Wildlife enthusiasts will delight in the chance to observe 167 species of birds, and 85 reptile, 23 native mammal, 10 fish and five frog species; a number of the mammals are rare or endangered elsewhere in the arid zone.

Alice Springs is conveniently situated almost centrally in the ranges. Many of the most spectacular landscapes and important biological areas are now included in national parks and reserves, which are easily reached by conventional vehicle. Largest of these is the 2100-sq-km **West MacDonnell National Park**, which stretches 160km west from the outskirts of Alice Springs. To the east of town, a string of mainly small parks extends for nearly the same distance.

Most parks have basic picnic facilities, many excellent walks and superb scenic highlights but opportunities for vehicle-based camping are rather limited – most bush camping grounds bulge at the seams during the cooler months. Resorts at Ross River (to the east) and Glen Helen (to the west) offer services such as meals, motel accommodation, camping and fuel.

Information
Tourist Offices The best place for general information on all aspects of the MacDonnell Ranges is CATIA's visitors information centre in Alice Springs. See the Alice Springs section earlier in this chapter for details.

For in-depth information on national parks and reserves, contact the Parks and Wildlife Commission in Alice Springs (☎ 08-8951 8211, fax 8951 8268). Alternatively, contact the rangers direct at:

Alice Springs Telegraph Station (☎ 08-8952 1013) For Emily and Jessie Gaps Nature Park
Arltunga (☎ 08-8956 9770) For the Arltunga Historical Reserve and Ruby Gap Nature Park
Ormiston Gorge (☎ 08-8956 7799) For the western half of the West MacDonnell National Park
Simpsons Gap (☎ 08-8955 0310) For the eastern half of the West MacDonnell National Park
Trephina Gorge (☎ 08 8956 9765) For Corroboree Rock Conservation Reserve, N'Dhala Gorge Nature Park and Trephina Gorge Nature Park

Radio Frequencies As the main roads of the MacDonnell Ranges are fairly busy most of the year, an HF radio isn't generally considered necessary. The major exception would be a visit to remote Ruby Gap in the off-peak season (October to April), when a radio could prove useful.

The region is serviced by the Alice Springs RFDS base (call sign VJD; ☎ 08-8952 1033), which monitors 5410kHz and 6950kHz between 7.30am and 5pm weekdays. Use 2020kHz (best at night) and 5410kHz for after-hours emergency calls.

Books Sadly, there are no good books on the MacDonnell Ranges, although Jeff & Mare Carter's *The Complete Guide to Central Australia* does have a fair-sized section devoted to touring the area. This comprehensive, well-written book is a worthwhile purchase, particularly if you're travelling further afield in the Red Centre. Penny van Oosterzee & Reg Morrison's *The Centre – The Natural History of Australia's Desert Regions* contains some interesting material on the central ranges.

Maps For topographic information Geoscience Australia's *Hermannsburg* and *Alice Springs* 1:250,000 sheets are reasonably detailed. For bushwalkers, their 1:50,000 series of orthophoto (based on aerial photographs) maps, covers the ranges east of Serpentine Gorge.

The map-guide *MacDonnell Ranges*, by Westprint Heritage Maps, is a useful planning and touring reference. It also produces the map-guide *East MacDonnells*, which covers the ranges from Alice Springs east to Ruby Gap Nature Park. It highlights the 'Explorer Territory' 4WD route from the Ringwood Beef Road through to the Plenty Hwy via Ross River homestead and Arltunga.

For the MacDonnell Ranges west of town, get hold of the *West MacDonnell National Park* map-guide produced by the Department of Infrastructure, Planning and Environment. There's plenty of useful information and a good map at a scale of 1:250,000.

Geoscience Australia's maps are available from the Department of Infrastructure,

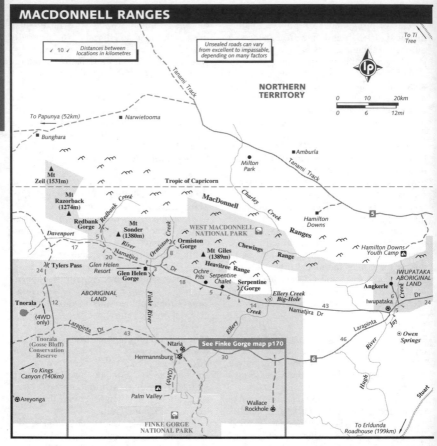

MACDONNELL RANGES

Planning and Environment in Alice Springs. Other maps are available from numerous outlets around Alice Springs, including CATIA, newsagencies and service stations.

Emergency In an emergency, you can obtain assistance at the park offices listed earlier in this section – provided there's someone there. The resort at Ross River usually has staff trained in first aid and, like the rangers stations, is in telephone contact with the outside world. In more remote areas, hail a tourist coach – they are invariably fitted with HF radios and first-aid kits.

WEST FROM ALICE SPRINGS

Spearing between high ridge-lines, the road from Alice Springs through the West MacDonnells is sealed as far as the Finke River crossing near Glen Helen, 135km from town. West of here the road is normally rough dirt, with numerous wash-outs after a heavy rain. Along the way are a number of spectacular red gorges and several deep waterholes, most of which are within the West MacDonnell National Park. During the dry season, all the main tourist attractions desribed here can easily be reached by conventional vehicle.

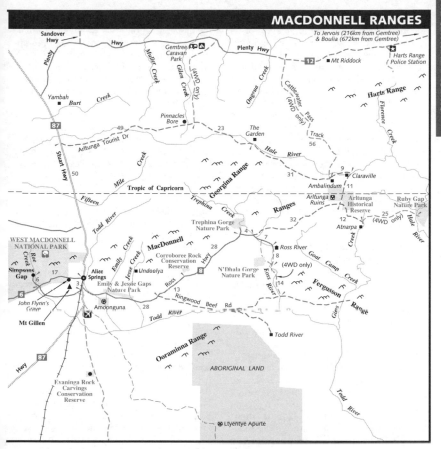

Simpsons Gap

Heading out on Larapinta Drive you pass the Alice Springs Desert Park (see the earlier Alice Springs section), then you're at the **grave** of Rev John Flynn, founder of the RFDS and the Australian Inland Mission. On a low rise with ghost gums and a magnificent view of nearby **Mt Gillen**, the great man's last resting place is just outside the eastern boundary of the West MacDonnell National Park.

At Simpsons Gap (☎ *08-8955 0310; open 5am-8pm daily*), 23km from town, Roe Creek has gouged a narrow gorge with towering red cliffs through Rungutjirba

Ridge. It's popular with picnickers and has some nice walks – there's also a sealed cycling path that winds through the bush from Flynn's grave (see Activities later in this section). In the early morning and late afternoon look for rock-wallabies among the jumble of huge boulders right in the gap.

Angkerle (Standley Chasm)

From the Simpsons Gap turn-off, you cross Aboriginal land for the next 30km to Angkerle (☎ *08-8956 7440; adult/child $5.50/ 4.50; open 7.30am-6pm daily*). Owned and managed by the nearby Iwupataka Aboriginal community, this deep narrow cleft has smooth, vertical walls and is famous for its midday light display – for a brief period at noon, reflected sunlight causes the rocks to glow red. A *kiosk* sells snacks, coffee, souvenirs and Aboriginal crafts.

The walk from the kiosk to the chasm follows the bed of a rocky gully and takes about 15 minutes. The gully's lower levels are crammed with moisture-loving plants such as river red gums, cycad palms and ferns – unexpected lushness in this arid world of craggy bluffs and spinifex. It's one of the outback's most interesting walks, but most visitors are in too much of a hurry to notice. For a real walking challenge with many rewards, you can return to Alice Springs along the Larapinta Trail (see Activities later).

Ellery Creek Big-Hole & Serpentine Gorge

Leaving the Angkerle turn-off, you pass through a scenic gap in the Heavitree Range before swinging right onto Namatjira Drive. Larapinta Drive continues straight on past Hermannsburg and eventually links up with the Natmatjira Drive again near Tnorala (Gosse Bluff) Conservation Reserve (see Alternative Routes later in this section).

Ten kilometres from the intersection is the **Hugh River**, with its large river red gums, then you enter a steep-sided valley that takes you all the way to Glen Helen, 79km further on. John McDouall Stuart travelled along the Hugh through the MacDonnell Ranges on his expeditions to and from the north between 1860 and 1862. Stuart named the ranges after the then governor of South Australia.

Ellery Creek Big-Hole, 91km from Alice Springs, is a popular swimming hole in summer. However, being shaded by high cliffs it's generally too cold for comfort – several swimmers have drowned here in recent years, so take care. There's a small camping ground (see Camping under Facilities later), and the 20-minute **Dolomite Walk**. An information shelter at the carpark explains the area's fascinating geological history, which is exposed in the creek banks downstream from the waterhole.

The next stop is Serpentine Gorge, where the main attraction lies a 1km walk from the carpark. A waterhole blocks the gorge entrance, but if you swim through (brrr!), walk up the rocky creek past large cycads to a second waterhole. The stunning scenery here can also be enjoyed from a lookout above the main entrance.

Section eight of the Larapinta Trail (see Activities – West of Alice Springs later in this section) starts at the carpark, goes via **Counts Point Lookout** to the Serpentine Chalet dams and **Inarlanga Pass**, with a detour to the Ochre Pits.

Ochre Pits

Six kilometres past Serpentine Gorge is the turn-off to **Serpentine Chalet**, where concrete slabs are all that remain of a 1950s tourist camp. In those days tourists had to be tough. The rough 4WD access track takes you past a number of bush camp sites suitable for winter use (see Facilities later). For details of walks in the area, pick up the brochures for sections eight and nine of the Larapinta Trail.

The nearby Ochre Pits have some interesting information relating to ochre and its importance to Aborigines. Except for a small deposit of yellow ochre, which is still used by local Aborigines, the material at this minor quarry site is of poor quality. Nevertheless, the swirls of red and yellow ochre in the walls of this little ravine make an attractive picture in the afternoon sun. From here a walking track takes you to the Larapinta Trail at Inarlanga Pass (see Activities – West of Alice Springs later).

Ormiston Gorge

From the Ochre Pits it's 26km to Ormiston Gorge (☎ 08-8956 7799), where soaring red cliffs, tall gums and a deep waterhole form some of the grandest scenery in the central ranges. Most visitors congregate at the gorge entrance. If you want to explore further afield there are several walks that start and finish at the information centre (see Activities – West of Alice Springs).

This gorge has been carved out by Ormiston Creek, and if you walk (and scramble) upstream from the waterhole for about 30 minutes you'll come to Ormiston Pound. Clothed in spinifex, this large, basin-like feature is bounded by high red cliffs and steep-sided ridges, with rugged Mt Giles rising above its eastern end.

Ormiston Gorge is a good spot for wildlife enthusiasts thanks to its variety of habitats – they include mulga woodland, spinifex slopes, rock faces, large gum trees and permanent water. Its small camping ground (see Facilities later) makes an ideal base for exploring the western half of the West Mac-Donnells. There's a picnic area with gas barbecues at the information centre.

Glen Helen Gorge & Resort
The Glen Helen Resort, 135km from Alice Springs, has the only major commercial facilities in the West MacDonnells. Nearby Glen Helen Gorge, where there's another large waterhole, has been carved out by the Finke River; a major flood in 1988 backed up so high that it flooded the resort. It's a 10-minute stroll from the resort down to the gorge entrance – if you want to go further you'll have to either swim through the waterhole or climb around it. The view from nearby **Mt Sonder Lookout** is one of the best in the central ranges – the turn-off is just west of the Finke crossing on Namatjira Drive. Bush camping is permitted in the Finke River upstream from the crossing (see Facilities later in this section).

Redbank Gorge
The bitumen ends at the Finke River crossing about 250m past the Glen Helen turn-off. For the next 20km to the Redbank Gorge turn-off you're on dirt with numerous sharp dips.

From Namatjira Drive it's 5km to the Redbank Gorge carpark, with the gorge a 20-minute walk away up a rocky creek bed. Redbank Gorge is extremely narrow, with polished, multihued walls that close over your head to block out the sky. You need an air mattress to get through as its deep pools are freezing even in summer, but it's worth doing. The colours and cathedral atmosphere inside are terrific.

Redbank Gorge is the starting point for section 12 of the Larapinta Trail, which ends at the summit of nearby Mt Sonder (see Activities – West of Alice Springs later). There are two camping areas at Redbank Gorge (see Facilities later).

EAST OF ALICE SPRINGS
The road from Alice Springs to Arltunga is extremely scenic for the most part, taking you through a jumble of high ridges and hills drained by gum-lined creeks. Along the way are several parks and reserves where you can explore rugged gorges, Aboriginal culture and abandoned mining areas.

Most points of interest in the East Mac-Donnells are reached off the sealed Ross Hwy, which links Alice Springs to the Ross River homestead, 83km from town. Further east, the historic Arltunga goldfield and Ruby Gap are accessed by unsealed routes which can be quite rough – as can the alternative route via Ambalindum station (see Altunga Tourist Drive under Alternative Routes later).

Access to John Hayes Rockhole (in Trephina Gorge Nature Park), N'Dhala Gorge and Ruby Gap is suitable for 4WDs only. The region's other main attractions are normally accessible to conventional vehicles.

Emily & Jessie Gaps
Leave Alice Springs, head south on the Stuart Hwy through Heavitree Gap, then turn east onto the Ross Hwy. Paralleling a high quartzite ridge to the north, the road heads out through the South Alice tourist and farm area before, finally, you're in the bush.

Emily Gap, 10km from the Stuart Hwy, is a beautiful spot with Aboriginal **rock paintings** and a deep waterhole in the narrow gorge. Local drunks have caused numerous problems here over the years, particularly on weekends, so check the situation before leaving your car to go sightseeing. Jessie Gap, 8km further on, is equally scenic, and a much quieter place to enjoy nature.

Corroboree Rock
Past Jessie Gap you cross eroded flats with the Heavitree Range looming large on your left, then enter a valley between red ridges.

Corroboree Rock, one of a number of unusual, tan-coloured dolomite hills scattered over the valley floor, is 41km from the Stuart Hwy. A small cave in this large dog-toothed outcrop was once used by Aborigines to store sacred objects.

Trephina Gorge

Sixty-three kilometres from the Stuart Hwy is the **Benstead Creek** crossing, with its lovely big gums. The many young river red gums that line the road near the Trephina Gorge turn-off, 6km on, germinated in the mid-1970s when the region received unusually high rainfall. This delightful picture is totally at odds with the common perception of central Australia.

Trephina Gorge Nature Park (☎ 08-8956 9765) offers some magnificent scenery, nice walks (see Activities – East of Alice Springs later), a deep swimming hole, abundant wildlife and low-key camping areas (see Camping under Facilities later). Its main attractions are Trephina Gorge, Trephina Bluff and **John Hayes Rockhole**. The rockhole, a permanent waterhole, is reached by a rough 4WD track that wanders 4km up the so-called **Valley of the Eagles**. Don't expect to see any of these large raptors.

With its restful atmosphere and grand views, Trephina Gorge is a great spot for a quiet picnic. There's a colony of black-footed rock-wallabies on the cliff above the waterhole – wander down first thing in the morning and you'll usually spot them leaping nimbly about on the rock face.

N'Dhala Gorge & Ross River Homestead

The sealed road ends at Ross River homestead, 83km from town. About 1km before the resort you pass the turn-off to **N'Dhala Gorge Nature Park**; the track winds down the picturesque **Ross River valley**, where a number of sandy river crossings make the going tough for conventional vehicles. As the sign says, towing is costly!

Rugged N'Dhala Gorge features thousands of ancient **rock carvings**, some of which can be viewed on a 1km walk from the carpark and camping ground (see

Camping under Facilities later). Continue on past the gorge to the Ringwood Beef Road, then head west to rejoin the Ross Hwy about 30km from Alice Springs.

Originally the headquarters for Loves Creek station, Ross River homestead boasts a pretty setting and offers a range of services and activities (see Facilities later).

Arltunga

Leaving the Ross Hwy, the first 12km of the Arltunga road passes through scenic **Bitter Springs Gorge**, where rumpled quartzite ridges tower above dolomite hills. This was the route taken by the early diggers as they walked from Alice Springs to Arltunga. The road can be quite rough at times and is impassable after heavy rain – watch out for road trains.

The **Arltunga Historical Reserve** (☎ 08-8956 9770) features significant evidence of the gold-mining activity that took place here between 1887 and 1913. Its major attraction is a partially restored ghost town containing the remains of a treatment plant and several stone buildings, including a police station and jail. Walking tracks take you past **old mines**, now complete with bat colonies – two underground mines are open to visitors, so make sure to bring a torch and some old clothes (see Activities later).

The richest area was **White Range**, a high quartzite ridge in the reserve's eastern section. In a remarkable display of short-sightedness, almost all the historic ruins and small mines that once dotted the ridge were destroyed during a short-lived open-cut mining operation in the early 1990s. Joseph Hele, who is credited with the discovery of gold at White Range in 1897, is buried in the nearby cemetery.

Arltunga is a fascinating place for anyone interested in history. To get some idea of what life was like for the early diggers, call in to the reserve's information centre and view its displays of old mining machinery and historic photographs. The centre is open from 8am to 5pm daily.

While prospecting isn't permitted within the historical reserve, there is a **fossicking reserve** in a gully just to the east where you may (with enormous luck) find some gold. A fossicking licence is required from the Department of Business, Industry and Resource Development (☎ 08-8951 5658) at 58 Hartley St, Alice Springs.

Ruby Gap

To reach Ruby Gap from Arltunga, head east towards Atnarpa homestead, then turn left at the gate 12km further on. The road deteriorates and is restricted to 4WD vehicles thanks to sandy creek crossings and sharp jump-ups. The **Hale River** is 25km beyond the gate; follow the wheel ruts upstream (left) along the sandy bed for about 5km to the turn-around point, which is through Ruby Gap and 3km short of rugged **Glen Annie Gorge**. These are the main scenic attractions in the **Ruby Gap Nature Park**. If you're first on the scene after a flood, always check that the riverbed is firm before driving onto it – beware of quicksand.

In 1886, Ruby Gap was the scene of a frantic ruby rush that crashed overnight when it was found that the rubies were actually only garnets. The scenery here is some of the wildest and most attractive in central Australia. And because it is remote and hard to get to, it doesn't have the crowds that often destroy the atmosphere at the more accessible places. Camping is allowed anywhere along the river bank (see Camping under Facilities later). Check road conditions with the rangers at Arltunga before continuing on.

ALTERNATIVE ROUTES
Tnorala (Gosse Bluff)

Having explored Redbank Gorge you can backtrack to Alice Springs the way you came, or return via Tnorala and Hermannsburg. To take the latter option, continue west then south along Namatjira Drive to meet up with Larapinta Drive, then turn left (east) to Hermannsburg and Alice Springs. The road between the Redbank Gorge turn-off and Hermannsburg is generally not recommended for conventional vehicles.

About 25km past the Redbank Gorge turn-off you come to Tylers Pass, where a **lookout** offers a 360-degree panorama that includes Tnorala to the south. Rising abruptly from a table-flat plain, this unusual feature resembles a ridge truncated at both ends, but it's actually the remnant of a huge impact crater that resulted when a comet plunged to Earth 130 million years ago. In local Aboriginal mythology it's a wooden dish belonging to some star ancestors that fell from the sky during the creation time. Tnorala is in a conservation reserve managed by the rangers at Ormiston Gorge (☎ 08-8956 7799); check with them about access into the crater – usually 4WD only.

For details of Hermannsburg and the Mereenie Loop Road, which links the western end of Larapinta Drive to Kings Canyon in Watarrka National Park, see the section on Finke Gorge later in this chapter.

Arltunga Tourist Drive

The Arltunga Tourist Drive is a 123km dirt road from Arltunga via **Ambalindum** station to the Stuart Hwy, which it meets 50km north of Alice Springs. It's an interesting alternative to a return along the Ross Hwy. You'll need fuel for at least 400km to drive from Ross River homestead to Alice Springs, with side trips to Arltunga and Ruby Gap. Check road conditions with the rangers at Arltunga before continuing.

En route, detour to the **Harts Range gem fields** (see the Plenty Hwy section later) via a 4WD track that turns off opposite Ambalindum. Fuel and camping facilities are available at the Gemtree Caravan Park on the Plenty Hwy.

ACTIVITIES – WEST OF ALICE SPRINGS
Walking

The Larapinta Trail By 2003 it's expected that a continuous series of walking tracks and marked routes, often through remote and rugged country, will link Alice Springs to the top of Mt Sonder. The following stages were open in 2001:

Section 1 Alice Springs Telegraph Station to Simpsons Gap (25km)
Section 2 Simpsons Gap to Jay Creek (24km)
Section 3 Jay Creek to Standley Chasm (15km)

Section 4 Standley Chasm to
  Birthday Waterhole (15km)
Section 5 Birthday Waterhole to
  Hugh Gorge (12km)
Section 8 Serpentine Gorge to
  Inarlanga Pass (15km)
Section 9 Inarlanga Pass to
  Ormiston Gorge (31km)
Section 10 Ormiston Gorge to
  Glen Helen (13km)
Section 11 Glen Helen to
  Redbank Gorge (33km)
Section 12 Redbank Gorge to
  Mt Sondersummit (9km)

Each section has its own distinctive high-lights: wildlife, rare plants, high lookouts, gorge scenery, deep waterholes or shady creeks. Experienced enthusiasts will enjoy them all, but most sections are too remote and rugged for inexperienced walkers without a guide.

Each section is covered by a detailed brochure, available from CATIA (☎ 08-8952 5800) in Alice Springs, and the rangers at Simpsons Gap (☎ 08-8955 0310) and Ormiston Gorge (☎ 08-8956 7799).

Anyone intending to do an overnight hike should make use of the Bushwalker Registration Scheme (☎ 1300 650 730). There's a security fee of $50/200 per person/group, but this is refunded provided you don't forget to report in at the completion of the walk – a search will be initiated if you fail to deregister. You can register by telephone, in which case you'll need to provide credit card details, or in person at CATIA, the Parks and Wildlife Commission office in Alice Springs (see that section earlier), or with the rangers at Simpsons Gap and Ormiston.

Simpsons Gap There are many walking opportunities here, with the short track up to the **Cassia Hill Lookout** recommended for starters. You can do day walks on the Larapinta Trail – peaceful **Bond Gap** (to the west) and **Wallaby Gap** (to the east) are both worthwhile – or take the Woodland Trail to **Rocky Gap**. The Woodland Trail continues on to Bond Gap via the Larapinta Trail, but it's hard walking through rough hills and won't appeal to many.

Ochre Pits A 4km walking track goes from the Ochre Pits to meet the Larapinta Trail at scenic Inarlanga Pass, at the foot of the Heavitree Range. The section 9 brochure for the Larapinta Trail has a lot of information on local Aboriginal bush foods and medicine, and you might find some along the way. Inarlanga Pass is interesting, as is the old Serpentine Chalet dam an hour's walk east along section 8 of the Larapinta Trail.

Ormiston Gorge One of the best short walks in the MacDonnell Ranges is the three-hour loop from the information centre at Ormiston Gorge into remote **Ormiston Pound** and back through Ormiston Gorge. Do it first thing in the morning in an anticlockwise direction so you can enjoy a sunlit view of the high cliffs in front.

Two other excellent but much longer cross-country excursions are mentioned in the *Walks of Ormiston Gorge and Pound* brochure ($1.10), available from CATIA in town and the Ormiston Gorge information centre. The return walk up Ormiston Creek to **Bowmans Gap** takes at least one day, while the **Mt Giles** route is a two-day affair. If you're an experienced bushwalker, do yourself a favour and spend a night on Mt Giles – the dawn view across Ormiston Pound to Mt Sonder is sensational.

Section 10 of the Larapinta Trail winds over rocky hills and along gum-lined creeks from Ormiston Gorge to Glen Helen, with fine views to Mt Sonder en route. Section 9 links Ormiston Gorge to Inarlanga Pass. It passes through remote, rugged country in the Alice Valley and is suitable only for experienced hikers.

Mt Sonder The full-day return walk along the ridge top from Redbank Gorge to the summit of Mt Sonder will appeal to the well-equipped enthusiast. The route is mostly unmarked and the trek itself is nothing to rave about – it's rather monotonous and seems never-ending. However, the view and sense of achievement once you get there are ample reward. The rangers at Ormiston Gorge (☎ 08-8956 7799) suggest that you register with them before doing this walk;

you'll find route details in the brochure on section 12 of the Larapinta Trail.

Cycling
Simpsons Gap The 17km sealed cycling path between Flynn's grave and Simpsons Gap wanders along timbered creek flats and over low rocky hills, with occasional kangaroos to keep you company. There are many bush picnic spots en route, and beaut views of Mt Gillen, Rungutjirba Ridge and the rugged Alice Valley. The path is suitable for novice cyclists, but don't go too fast – there are some sharp corners.

Flynn's Grave is 7km from the town centre, and do this first part along Larapinta Dr. For the best views (not to mention comfort), cycle out in the early morning and return in the afternoon. Carry plenty of drinking water in warm weather, as there is none along the way.

ACTIVITIES – EAST OF ALICE SPRINGS
Walking
Trephina Gorge There are several good walks within the nature park, ranging from 30 minutes to five hours. You can enjoy a stroll among the big gums along Trephina Creek, take the scenic rim walk around Trephina Gorge or, for a rewarding challenge, try the marked route over the main range from Trephina Gorge to John Hayes Rockhole. For details, see the *Walks of Trephina Gorge* brochure ($1.10), available from CATIA in town.

Arltunga Four interesting walks in the Arltunga Historical Reserve give access to various old mining areas. One track leads to the MacDonnell Range Reef Mine, where you can climb down steel ladders and explore about 50m of tunnels between two shafts. The adjoining walk to the nearby Golden Chance Mine is also worth doing for its varied content. You'll find details on these walks in the free reserve leaflet available at the visitor information centre.

Ruby Gap There are no marked walks here, but for the experienced enthusiast a climb around the craggy rim of Glen Annie Gorge features superb views of this beautiful spot. You can ascend on the southern side and return along the sandy floor, or vice versa. The grave of a ruby miner is hidden away at the gorge's northern end.

ORGANISED TOURS
Day tours of the MacDonnell Ranges are very popular and there are numerous operators and tours to choose from. Costs vary, but expect to pay from $80 for a day tour with lunch included; ask about standby rates during the off season. Extended camping safaris incorporating places such as Palm Valley and Kings Canyon are also available.

See the CATIA visitor information centre in Alice Springs for details of tours in the MacDonnell Ranges and further afield.

FACILITIES
West of Alice Springs
Glen Helen Resort (☎ *1800 896 110, 08-8956 7489,* e *glenhelen@melanka.com.au, Namatjira Dr)* Unpowered/powered sites $18/22, rooms with shared facilities without/with linen $19/29 per person, motel units $143. A high red cliff provides a dramatic backdrop to this resort, built on the site of an early homestead of Glen Helen station. It offers a range of services, including a good ***restaurant*** (three-course dinner $45), ***bar***, fuel sales (diesel, super, unleaded) and helicopter flights (from $35 per person for six minutes).

Camping There are several camping areas in the West MacDonnell National Park, with fees payable into honesty boxes. None are suitable for caravans, and you have to take your own firewood and drinking water.

Contact the rangers at Ormiston Gorge (☎ 08-8956 7799) for an update on the places listed here.

Ellery Creek Camp sites per adult/child/family $3.30/1.65/7.70. This is a small and often crowded camping area with wood-burning barbecues, tables, pit toilet and limited shade. It's just a short walk from the Ellery Creek Big-Hole.

Serpentine Chalet has 11 sites, all free, scattered through the mulga and mallee along the track past Serpentine Chalet. They have wood-burning fireplaces and a sense of isolation. These are ideal for winter camping but are too exposed in hot weather. The first five sites are accessible to conventional vehicles with care, the rest to 4WD only.

Ormiston Gorge Camp sites adult/child/family, $6.60/3.30/15.40. This small, relatively upmarket camping ground offers hot showers, toilets, picnic furniture and gas barbecues. Water restrictions may apply during droughts. The entrance to Ormiston Gorge is a short walk away.

Finke Two Mile has bush camping in the Finke River upstream from the crossing on Namatjira Dr. There are no facilities but the views and atmosphere are first class. Access is restricted to 4WD; you can camp anywhere in the riverbed within 3km of the crossing.

Two camping areas along the access road to Redbank Gorge offer entirely different experiences.

Redbank Woodland Adult/child/family $3.30/1.65/7.70. There are 13 attractive bush sites with wood and gas barbecues, picnic tables and pit toilets – most also have good shade. An early morning stroll downstream beside the nearby Davenport River is a nice way to start the day.

Redbank Ridgetop Adult/child/family $3.30/1.65/7.70. This much smaller area is on an exposed rocky ridge with nice views across to the main range. Facilities include wood-burning barbecues and a pit toilet.

East of Alice Springs

Ross River homestead (☎ 08-8956 9711, [e] *rrhca@ozemail.com.au*) Unpowered/powered sites $10/20, bunkhouse beds without/with linen $15/22, twins & doubles $85. Set among rumpled hills beside one of the region's most attractive rivers, the resort offers a variety of services including ***meals***, a ***bar***, fuel sales (diesel, super, unleaded) and a landing strip. The motel units (all with air con and private facilities) are built of local timber.

Activities include horse rides ($20 to $50), camel rides, sunset wagon rides, campfire cook-outs, boomerang throwing and the obligatory billy-tea-and-damper for morning tea. There's good potential for walks along the river.

Camping Camping is permitted at Trephina Gorge, N'Dhala Gorge and Ruby Gap Nature Parks. Sites cost $3.30/1.65/7.70 per adult/child/family (payable into honesty boxes), regardless of whether or not there are facilities. You have to take your own firewood to all places.

The Trephina Gorge Nature Park has attractive camping grounds at Trephina Gorge, the Bluff and John Hayes Rockhole. These offer a variety of camping experiences to outback travellers.

Trephina Gorge (ranger ☎ 08-8956 9765) The relatively large camping area here is in a timbered gully a short stroll from the main attraction. It has drinking water, pit toilets, wood-burning and gas barbecues, picnic furniture and some good shade. It is suitable for caravans.

Trephina Bluff (ranger ☎ 08-8956 9765) This area is about five minutes' walk from Trephina Gorge. It has similar facilities to the camping area there, but is not suitable for caravans. It also boasts a more spectacular setting under tall gums in front of a towering red ridge.

John Hayes Rockhole (ranger ☎ 08-8956 9765) There are just the two camp sites (neither with any shade) about 150m from the waterhole; facilities are limited to wood-burning barbecues, tables and a pit toilet. The most obvious thing about this restricted area is that fact that it's home to a large population of ants.

N'Dhala Gorge (ranger ☎ 08-8956 9765) There are three camp sites at the gorge entrance. Facilities are limited to wood-burning barbecues, tables and a pit toilet, and there is no shade.

Ruby Gap (ranger ☎ 08-8956 9770) A major attraction of this area is remote bush camping along the Hale River. Visitors should BYO everything as there are no facilities of any kind.

Finke Gorge

Highlights

- Exploring the fascinating history of the old Hermannsburg Mission
- Seeing the evidence of climate change over ages past at Palm Valley
- Experiencing the pleasures of bush camping on a trip down the Finke River
- Discovering Aboriginal culture on a tour at Wallace Rockhole

The historic Hermannsburg Mission is by the Finke River, 122km west of Alice Springs. From here 4WD tracks head south to Palm Valley and Boggy Hole in the 460-sq-km Finke Gorge National Park. Both routes take you through Finke Gorge, where central Australia's largest river has carved a long, meandering passage through the ranges. Much of the time you're actually driving in the sandy riverbed, so a 4WD vehicle and experience are essential. This particularly applies to the rugged Boggy Hole Track, which continues past Boggy Hole to join up with the Ernest Giles Rd to Watarrka National Park.

Famous for its rare palms, Finke Gorge National Park is one of central Australia's premier wilderness areas. It has plenty to offer those who enjoy bushwalks and remote camping, and the landscape is spectacular and colourful. The main gorge features high red cliffs, stately river red gums, cool waterholes, plenty of clean white sand and clumps of tall palms. Combine this tremendous natural beauty with the area's fascinating history and you have an excursion that's packed with interest.

Anyone intending to drive out from Alice Springs to the old mission, visit Palm Valley, and then continue on to Watarrka National Park via Boggy Hole and Illamurta Springs, should have a minimum fuel range of 650km – this allows for heavy going in the Finke River. Otherwise you must refuel at Hermannsburg, as the only other outlet between there and Watarrka is at Kings Creek, 35km before Watarrka.

History

For thousands of years the Finke River formed part of an Aboriginal trade route that crossed Australia, bringing goods such as sacred red ochre from the south and pearl shell from the north to the central Australian tribes. Far from being desert, the area around Hermannsburg had an abundance of game animals and food plants. It was a major drought refuge for the Western Arrernte people, who were able to find water by digging shallow wells in the dry riverbed. As the Finke River becomes saline during drought, the Western Arrernte call it 'Lhere Pirnte' (hence Larapinta), which means 'salty river'. Comprehensive knowledge of its freshwater soaks enabled them to survive in the harshest droughts.

In 1872, the explorer Ernest Giles travelled up the Finke on his first attempt to cross from the Overland Telegraph Line to the western coast. To his amazement he found tall palms growing in the river, which had been named 12 years earlier by John McDouall Stuart, and went into raptures over the beauty of its scenery. Giles later briefed the Lutheran Church of South Australia on his visit to the northern end of Finke Gorge. The Lutherans were keen to start missionary work among Aboriginal people in central Australia. After talking to Giles they applied for a lease over the area.

In 1876, fresh from the Hermannsburg Mission Institute in Germany, pastors AH Kempe and WF Schwarz left Adelaide bound for central Australia with a herd of cattle and several thousand sheep. Eighteen months later they arrived at the new mission site, having been trapped by drought at Dalhousie Springs for nearly a year. It was a nightmarish introduction to the harsh central Australian environment, but the pastors were committed to bringing Christianity and 'civilisation' to the Aborigines.

Despite incredible difficulties and hardships, including strong opposition from white settlers to their attempts to protect the Aborigines from genocide, the missionaries

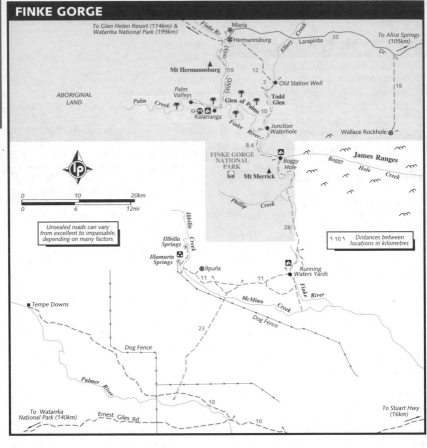

FINKE GORGE

To Glen Helen Resort (114km) &
Watarrka National Park (199km)

To Alice Springs (105km)

ABORIGINAL LAND

Mt Hermannsburg

Palm Valley

Palm Creek

Kalarranga

Glen of Palms

Todd Glen

Old Station Well

Junction Waterhole

FINKE GORGE NATIONAL PARK

Mt Merrick

Boggy Hole

Wallace Rockhole

James Ranges

Boggy Hole Creek

Phillip Creek

Unsealed roads can vary
from excellent to impassable,
depending on many factors

0   10   20km
0   6   12mi

Ilbilla Creek

Illbilla Springs

Illamurta Springs

Ilpurla

Running Waters Yards

10 Distances between
locations in kilometres

Tempe Downs

McMinn Creek

Finke River

Dog Fence

Dog Fence

Palmer River

To Watarrka
National Park (140km)

Ernest Giles Rd

To Stuart Hwy
(16km)

established the first township in central Australia. At one time Hermannsburg had a population of 700 Western Arrernte people, a cattle herd of 5000 and various cottage industries, including a tannery.

The mission continued to operate until 1982, when the Lutheran Church finally handed its lease back to the Western Arrernte people. Since then most of its residents have left Hermannsburg and established 35 small outstation communities on traditional clan territories. Although about 200 Aborigines still live at Hermannsburg, its main function is to provide support and resources for the outlying population in the area.

Information

Tourist Offices The best source of in-depth information on Finke Gorge National Park is the Parks and Wildlife Commission's Alice Springs office (☎ 08-8951 8211). Alternatively, ring the Palm Valley ranger (☎ 08-8956 7401).

Brochures on Finke Gorge, Hermannsburg, Wallace Rockhole and local tours are available from CATIA in Alice Springs (☎ 08-8952 5800).

For an update on conditions along the Boggy Hole Track, contact the rangers at Palm Valley.

Radio Frequencies As Palm Valley is a popular tourist attraction, you shouldn't require a HF radio (except possibly in summer, when visitor numbers drop dramatically). The Boggy Hole Track is much less used, and there can be a week between vehicles when the weather is hot. It's definitely a good idea to carry a HF radio if you're intending to make this trip in summer.

This region is serviced by the Alice Springs RFDS base (call sign VJD; ☎ 08-8952 1033), which monitors 5410kHz and 6950kHz between 7.30am and 5pm weekdays. Use 2020kHz (best at night) and 5410kHz for after-hours emergency calls.

Permits The Boggy Hole Track crosses Aboriginal land for the 16km from Hermannsburg to the national park boundary. Although there is no requirement for a permit to use the road, camping is not allowed in the area and visitors must stay on the main route. Likewise, you can visit the commercial facilities and historic mission at Hermannsburg without a permit, but residential areas are out of bounds.

Maps The Parks and Wildlife Commission's brochure *Finke River 4WD Route* covers the Boggy Hole Track from Hermannsburg to the Ernest Giles Rd, including the detour to Illamurta Springs. It's available on request from the rangers at Palm Valley and Watarrka National Park.

For topographic detail refer to Geoscience Australia's *Henbury* 1:250,000 map sheet, available from the Department of Infrastructure, Planning and Environment office in Alice Springs.

Emergency In the event of a medical emergency, you can obtain assistance at the Hermannsburg health clinic, which has skilled nursing staff. The rangers at Palm Valley and most coach drivers have training in first aid, and their vehicles are generally equipped with HF radios.

Special Preparations

The Boggy Hole Track is definitely not suitable for 4WD vehicles lacking low-range gearing or good ground clearance. Even experienced off-road drivers can get bogged on this one, so pack a high-lift jack and base-plate, long-handled shovel, tyre-pressure gauge and good-quality tyre pump. A winch (or at least a strong tow rope) might also come in handy. Anyone who attempts the track in summer should carry plenty of drinking water and travel in the company of at least one other vehicle.

In recent times the rangers at Palm Valley have rescued numerous visitors (some from potentially life-threatening situations) whose lack of preparation and experience have resulted in vehicles becoming badly bogged. Seek their advice before setting out.

THE ROUTE
Hermannsburg Mission

Shaded by tall river red gums and date palms, and with a view over the normally dry, shimmering bed of the Finke River, the old Hermannsburg Mission (☎ 08-8956 7402; adult/child/family $4.50/3/12; open 9am-4pm daily except 24 Dec-2 Jan) is a fascinating monument to the skill and dedication of early Lutheran missionaries. The group of 11 whitewashed stone buildings includes a church, a school and various houses and outbuildings. Dating from 1882, and restored in 1988, the buildings are probably as good an example of traditional German farmhouse architecture as you'll find anywhere outside of that country.

For an additional $3.50 you can take a guided tour of the **art gallery** which provides an insight into the life and times of Albert Namatjira, the Western Arrernte artist who opened the world's eyes to striking landscapes around Alice Springs. Examples of the work of 39 local watercolourists, including three generations of the Namatjira family, are also exhibited.

Hermannsburg to Palm Valley (18km)

The Palm Valley Track turns off Larapinta Drive on the Finke River's western bank about 1km west of Hermannsburg, and keeps to the riverbed for most of the next 11km. Deep corrugations and soft, sandy sections are normal conditions here, while a flood can close the track for days. However, the major hazards are large 4WD tourist coaches, which have right of way on the narrow track – when you see one heading towards you, either pull right over or reverse back until you can get off the track without bogging yourself. With 70,000 tourists visiting Palm Valley each year, the track can be fairly busy in peak periods.

Finke River Floods After about 1km, the track enters the red-walled confines of Finke Gorge and hits the first patch of soft sand – this is where visitors in conventional vehicles who've ignored the warning signs invariably come to grief. For the next 10km the track dives in and out of the river, passing occasional small waterholes and tall river red gums that make a cool contrast to the arid hills on either side.

There were many more big gums in the river prior to 1988, when one of the greatest floods in centuries swept many of them away. The debris piled against surviving trees gives you an idea of the river's force when it's in full flood. The scars high up on their trunks illustrate that Finke Gorge is no place to be when heavy rain sets in. The Finke runs on average about once a year, but relatively few floods reach the Stuart Hwy bridge south of Alice Springs. Even the largest floods simply vanish into the Simpson Desert which, if you count every twist and turn, is about 650km from the river's headwaters in the Mac-Donnell Ranges.

Cabbage Palm

Palm Valley

Leaving the Finke at its junction with Palm Creek, head west past the old rangers station (the abandoned houses were flooded in 1988), and 1km further on arrive at **Kalarranga**. En route, a small information bay introduces some of the walks in the area (see Activities later). Kalarranga, a semicircle of striking ochre-coloured sandstone formations, was sculpted by a now-extinct Palm Creek. Be there early morning or late afternoon for the best views.

Leaving Kalarranga you soon pass the camping ground, after which the track is extremely rough for the final 5km to Palm Valley. A worthwhile stop is **Cycad Gorge**, where a chocolate-coloured cliff towers over tall, slender palms. The gorge is named after the large number of shaggy cycads found growing on and below the cliff face.

Lending a tropical atmosphere to their barren setting, these palms and cycads are leftovers from much wetter times in central Australia. These plants only survive here because a reliable supply of moisture within the surrounding sandstone means they can escape the harsh realities of drought.

About 2km past Cycad Gorge is the Palm Valley carpark, with the first palms just a stone's throw away. The valley is actually a narrow gorge, which in places is almost choked with lush oases of **red cabbage palms** (*Livistona mariae*) up to 25m high. Found nowhere else in the world, this species grows within an area of 60 sq km and is nearly 1000km from its nearest relatives. There are only 1200 mature plants in the wild, so the rangers ask that you stay out of the palm groves – tiny seedlings are hard to see and are easily trampled underfoot.

The gorge is home to over 300 plant species, of which about 10% are either rare or have a restricted distribution. It's a botanist's paradise!

Hermannsburg to Boggy Hole (31km)

Heading out along Larapinta Drive from Alice Springs, you come to the Boggy Hole Track on your left just 50m or so before the main turn-off to Hermannsburg. For the first 12km the track is graded but rough, spearing across a red sandy plain past small outstation communities.

The graded section stops abruptly at an outstation at the foot of the range on the back of Ellery Creek; go past the houses (keep them on your left), ignore the track on the left and continue straight on into the gorge. The latter is officially called Todd Glen but is more usually known as Ellery Gorge. From this point the track is simply a pair of wheel ruts winding along the creek bed. Although the going is often rough, the colourful scenery and sense of discovery make it all worthwhile.

Ten kilometres after entering Todd Glen you arrive at **Junction Waterhole**, where Ellery Creek meets the Finke River. When full, the hole is a picture to gladden any eye. Unfortunately, however, the waterhole is empty as often as not.

Boggy Hole

At Junction Waterhole, enter Finke Gorge for the final 8.4km slog to Boggy Hole. A haven for migratory waterbirds such as swans and pelicans, Boggy Hole stretches for 2.5km after a flood but shrinks to only about 300m during droughts. It's one of only a handful of permanent waterholes in the Finke system, so has immense conservation value – believe it or not, 10 species of mainly small fish live here. The bank is rocky and the river red gums suffered badly in the 1988 flood, so good camp sites with shade are scarce near the water.

In the 1880s, Boggy Hole was the site of a police camp from which Mounted Constable William Willshire and his Aboriginal troopers rode the ranges, quelling resistance to European settlement. Their method was to shoot as many Aborigines as possible, prompting a Hermannsburg missionary to write in 1885: 'In ten years time there will not be many blacks left in this area and this is just what the white man wants'.

A year later the missionaries were protesting vigorously at the alarming decrease in the Aboriginal male population. It was thanks largely to their efforts that the police were moved to Illamurta Springs in

1893, and Willshire brought to trial for his alleged excesses. He wasn't convicted, but the trial meant the end of his career in the Northern Territory. The stone remains of the police camp (not to be confused with those of a more recent safari camp) are on the waterhole's eastern bank.

Boggy Hole to Ernest Giles Rd (72km)

The river's character changes continuously in the 28km from Boggy Hole to the old Running Waters cattle yards. One minute you're driving along a broad valley or through red sand hills, the next you're hemmed in with cliffs on either side. These narrow sections act as chokes when the river is in flood, the water banking up to submerge the flats on either side under metres of water. At one point, about 8km past Boggy Hole, scars 8m or higher up in the river red gums show where flood-borne debris, including huge trees, has bashed against their trunks. Looking around at the normally parched surroundings, it's difficult to imagine that such things can happen here.

Running Waters Twenty kilometres from Boggy Hole, a gate in a grove of desert oaks marks the boundary of **Henbury** station. Five kilometres further on, at the southern end of Finke Gorge, a couple of metal huts on the left mark the deserted Aboriginal outstation at Running Waters. The riverbed is littered by tree trunks dumped by floods. A solitary palm rises from the bulrushes lining the waterhole which is quite shallow in contrast to others in the river. The track continues downstream for a short distance to a set of old timber yards where you turn right (west) along the southern foot of the James Ranges.

Picturesque ghost gums are the major scenic highlights between the yards and the turn-off to Ernest Giles Rd – continue straight if you want to visit the Illamurta Springs Conservation Reserve (see Detours later). From the turn-off the track heads south-west across red sand hills covered with desert oaks; the going is soft in parts and so badly corrugated in others it'll make your teeth rattle. Around 21km further on you arrive at a claypan that heralds the start of the **Palmer River flood plain**. Although devastated by rabbits and cattle over the past century, its desolate claypans, scattered crimson dunes and skeletons of dead trees do have a certain awful beauty.

Another 2km and you swing left (east) onto the Tempe Downs Access Rd. From here it's about 10km to the Ernest Giles Rd, where you turn either east to the Stuart Hwy (53km) or west to Kings Canyon (140km) in Watarrka National Park.

DETOURS
Wallace Rockhole
The Arrernte community of Wallace Rockhole, off Larapinta Drive about 30km east of Hermannsburg, offers several *tours* including a good rock art and bush medicine tour (adult/child $9/5) lasting about 1½ hours, and a day out looking for bush tucker ($30/20). Book through the caravan park.

Wallace Rockhole Tourist Park & Camping Ground (☎ 08-8956 7993, e *info @wallacerockholetours.com.au,* W *www .wallacerockholetours.com.au)* Unpowered/ powered sites $18/22, cabins $85. This is a pleasant spot with lawned camp sites and good facilities; the cabins have private facilities. There's a *general store* and *arts & crafts outlet* close by.

Mereenie Loop Road
Larapinta Drive heads west from Alice Springs to the Areyonga turn-off, about 195km from town, where it becomes the Mereenie Loop Rd. From here it continues west for 60km, before swinging south to Kings Canyon in Watarrka National Park.

The Mereenie Loop Road provides an exciting opportunity for a circuit tour of the western central ranges. From Alice Springs you can drive out through the West MacDonnell National Park, continue on to Watarrka National Park via Tnorala (Gosse Bluff), then head back to town via Ernest Giles Rd and the Boggy Hole Track. The circuit, covers 800km or more (including detours), and will appeal to the more adventurous 4WD traveller with time to

spend. Most allow at least a week to do it properly.

The Mereenie Loop Road passes through a variety of semi-desert landscapes, including sand dunes and rocky ridges. It is, however, generally only suitable either for 4WDs or conventional vehicles with heavy-duty suspension and good ground clearance – wash outs are a hazard after heavy rain. The road is not recommended for caravans. Contact the Road Report Hotline (☎ 1800 246 199) for an update on road conditions.

To travel on this route you need a permit called the Mereenie Tour Pass ($2.20), which doubles as a visitor information guide. It's available at Hermannsburg (the Larapinta Service Station), the resorts at Kings Canyon and Glen Helen, and the CATIA office in Alice Springs.

You'll need sufficient fuel for at least 300km between Hermannsburg (the last fuel stop) and Watarrka National Park, including a detour to Tnorala. Note that camping is not permitted along the route.

Refer to the MacDonnell Ranges section earlier for details on Tnorala.

Illamurta Springs
At the foot of the James Ranges, 22km west of Running Waters yard, this remote conservation reserve is excellent for bird-watching, thanks to its permanent spring and variety of habitats. Hidden away in thick mallee near the spring are the evocative stone remains of what must have been one of the Territory's loneliest police outposts. It makes you wonder what crimes constables were guilty of to be posted here! The station opened in 1893 and closed in 1912.

The Ilpurla Aboriginal community near Illamurta Springs has pleasant *camp sites*, some with power. Contact Barry Abbott at Ilpurla on ☎ 08-8956 7902 for details.

ACTIVITIES
Bushwalking
There are good walking tracks in Finke Gorge National Park, although few visitors do more than a couple of short ones in the Palm Valley area. If you're camped at Boggy Hole, a walk to the top of **Mt Merrick** is

recommended for the view but there is no marked track. A stroll along the Finke offers colourful scenery and solitude, particularly in the **Glen of Palms** between Palm and Little Palm Creeks.

Unfortunately, there are no large-scale topographic maps of Finke Gorge National Park, shown in broad detail on Geoscience's *Henbury* 1:250,000 sheet. Before doing any long walks, ask the ranger for advice on routes, conditions and preparation.

Palm Valley Walking Tracks There are several walking tracks in the Palm Valley area, all suitable for families and each with its own particular attractions. The most popular is the **Arankaia Walk**, a 2km loop through Palm Valley and back around the gorge rim to the carpark. It offers terrific views down the gorge and gives a different perspective of local environments.

Another good one is the **Mparra Track**, a 5km loop from the Kalarranga carpark that takes in Kalarranga, the Finke River and **Palm Bend**. It leads you in the footsteps of a mythological hero from the Aboriginal creation time, whose adventures are explained by signs along the way.

ORGANISED TOURS

Day tours from Alice Springs to Hermannsburg and Palm Valley are run by: *AAT Kings* (☎ 08-8952 1700, W *www.aatkings .com; adult/child $103/52); NT Luxury Day Tours* (☎ 08-8952 7751, W *www .ntluxurydaytours.com.au; $180/130 includes Simpsons Gap & Standley Chasm); Palm Valley Day Tours* (☎ 8952 0022, 1800 000 629, e *tours@palmvalleytours .com.au, W www.palmvalleytours.com.au; $80); and The Alice Wanderer* (☎ 08-8952 2111, 1800 669 111, e *alicwand@ozemail .com.au, W www.ozemail.com.au/~alicwand; $125/100 including Wallace Rockhole).*

Sahara Outback Tours (☎ *1800 806 240,* W *www.saharatours.com.au) visits those places as part of a five-day camping tour (adult/child $625/564) of Uluru, Watarrka National Park and the West MacDonnell Ranges.

FACILITIES
Hermannsburg
Kata-Anga Tea Room (☎ *08-8956 7402; open 9am-4pm daily except 24 Dec-2 Jan)* Light lunches $6. This tea room in the old missionary house is the best place to start a

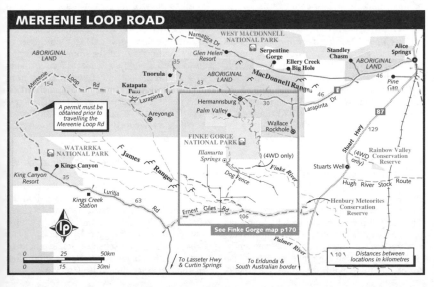

MEREENIE LOOP ROAD

visit to the historic precinct. It serves sandwiches of chunky home-made bread; relax with a bottomless cup of tea or coffee and a large slice of home-baked cake ($4.50) – the traditional apple strudel is highly recommended.

The tea room exhibits a collection of traditional and watercolour paintings, wooden carvings and pottery, all the work of local people. The quality is often very good, and the prices more appealing than those in most Alice Springs souvenir outlets.

Ntaria Supermarket (☎ *08-8956 7480*) Open 8.30am-5.30pm Mon-Sat, 10am-5.30pm Sun. This well-stocked shop is right at the entrance to town – it has an Eftpos facility but doesn't accept credit cards. The adjoining service station (☎ 08-8954 6007) sells diesel, super and unleaded fuel and can help with mechanical repairs. It opens from 8.30am to 4pm weekdays; it doesn't accept credit cards either.

Tjuwanpa Outstation Resource Centre (☎ *08-8956 7404*) is open 8am-5pm Monday to Thursday and 8am-3pm Friday. It's off Larapinta Drive opposite the Palm Valley turn-off, and sells fuel and does mechanical repairs. It accepts major credit cards.

Palm Valley

Palm Valley Camping Ground (☎ *08-8956 7401*) Camp sites adult/child/family $6.60/3.30/15.40. Beside Palm Creek, this relatively upmarket camping ground offers hot showers, flush toilets, picnic furniture and wood-burning barbecues. Water restrictions may apply during droughts, and firewood is not provided. It's an attractive spot with good shade just a short walk from Kalarranga.

Bush Camping

You'll find some magnificent camp sites with good shade and beautiful gorge scenery along the Finke River between Junction Waterhole and Running Waters. The most popular spot (though by no means the best) is Boggy Hole, which attracts many Alice Springs residents on weekends.

As waterholes in the Finke are vital to the survival of many wildlife species, the rangers ask that you do your washing in a bucket and camp well back from the water's edge. All rubbish should be carried out. Please don't make new vehicle tracks on the banks – it's unsightly and creates an erosion problem.

Tanami Track

The Tanami Track cuts right through the heart of the Tanami Desert and some of Australia's least populated country. It connects Alice Springs in the Centre with Halls Creek in the Kimberley in the country's far north-west.

In spite of the remoteness, or perhaps because of it, the Tanami Track is an increasingly popular route for those who want to get off the beaten track, and it can save hundreds of kilometres backtracking to visit both the Top End and the Kimberley from Alice Springs. It's also possible to leave the Tanami Track at the Tanami Mine and head north along Lajamanu Rd for Lajamanu and Kalkaringi on the Buntine Hwy, from where there are a number of possibilities: north-east to Katherine and the Stuart Hwy, west to Halls Creek or north along the Buchanan Hwy to Victoria River Downs and on to Timber Creek on the Victoria Hwy.

The Lajamanu Rd is best attempted with a 4WD, although the local Aborigines often manage with their trusty Ford Falcons (see Alternative Routes later in this section).

The Tanami Track is officially called the Tanami Rd in the Territory and McGuires Track in Western Australia but it's also universally known as the Tanami Track.

Apart from the sense of achievement of crossing the Tanami Desert, the highlights of the track are the Wolfe Creek Meteorite

Central Australia has an awesome sense of space. The region includes the most inhospitable Simpson Desert, one of the world's outstanding sand-ridge deserts. The other central deserts aren't like the Sahara, but are extremely dry with sparse vegetation.

Chambers Pillar, or to the local Aboriginal people the remains of Itirkawara, a gecko ancestor of great strength, is carved with the names of early explorers (1). Sturt's Desert Pea, the floral emblem of South Australia (2). The Finke River and Mt Sonder, from above – Glen Helen Gorge, Northern Territory (3). Old man emu (4). Off/on road vehicles cross the Simpson Desert on the QAA track which contains the steepest and often bumpiest dunes of the entire route (5). Magnificent and ancient palms in Finke Gorge National Park – Northern Territory (6).

PAUL SINCLAIR

1

CHRISTOPHER GROENHOUT

2

JOHN P BAER

3

M TCH REARDON

4

TONY WHEELER

5

TREVOR CREIGHTON

6

Some of the nation's remotest touring routes pass through the central desert region, each with its own unique attractions. Learning about the zone's plants and animals, and the local Aboriginal culture, is all part of its charm.

A magnificent ghost gum (1). Yellow-spotted Goanna takes a good look (2). One of the majestic road trains parked on the side of an unsealed road, while the driver checks the tyres – Northern Territory (3). The Breakaways punctuate the Outback's vast open space, Coober Pedy – South Australia (4). An international direction sign (5). A camp site on the pan at the base of a huge outcrop of sandstone that catches the setting sun, displaying a rich array of colours - Rainbow Valley, Northern Territory (6).

PAUL SINCLAIR

MITCH REARDON

HUGH FINLAY

1

2

3

RICHARD NEBESKY

HUGH FINLAY

RICHARD NEBESKY

4

5

6

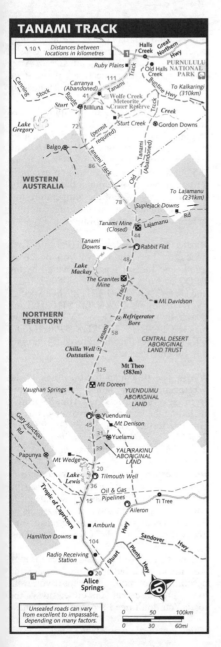

TANAMI TRACK

Distances between locations in kilometres

Unsealed roads can vary from excellent to impassable, depending on many factors.

Crater and the sheer vastness of the spinifex plains liberally sprinkled with millions of red termite mounds, many of which are over 3m high. The country is mainly gently undulating plains, with occasional low rock outcrops and areas of sand dunes.

The Tanami Desert is the traditional homeland of the Walpiri Aboriginal people, and for much of its length the Tanami Track passes through Aboriginal land.

History

The first European exploration of the Tanami Desert was undertaken by surveyor and explorer AC Gregory (later Sir) in 1855. His party headed south from the Victoria River to what is now Lajamanu, then headed west until they came to a dry watercourse near the present Western Australia–Northern Territory border, which Gregory named Sturt Creek, after the explorer. He followed the creek south-west to a lake south-west of Balgo, which he humbly named after himself, before returning to his Victoria River base.

The first white crossing of the desert was probably in 1896 when the pioneering drover Nat Buchanan crossed from Tennant Creek to Sturt Creek. Buchanan was responsible for some amazing cattle drives from Queensland, and he hoped to find a route suitable for stock so they didn't have to detour so far north. Although he crossed the desert without undue difficulty (largely thanks to his Aboriginal guides), no sources of permanent water were found and the hoped-for stock route never eventuated.

Allan Davidson was the first European to explore the Tanami Desert in any detail. In 1900 he set out looking for gold, and mapped, with amazing accuracy, likely-looking areas. Gold was discovered at a couple of sites in the Tanami and for a few brief years there was a flurry of activity as hopefuls came in search of fortune. The extremely harsh conditions and small finds deterred all but the most determined, and there were never more than a couple of hundred miners in the Tanami. The biggest discoveries were at Tanami and the Granites, and after many years of inactivity, the latter was reopened in 1986 and is still mined today; the Tanami Mine closed in 1994.

Pastoral activity in the area has always been a precarious proposition, although some areas are suitable for grazing. Suplejack ('soo-pull-jack') Downs and Tanami Downs, 60km north-west and south-west of Rabbit Flat respectively, are two that have survived. Suplejack is one of the few pieces of non-Aboriginal land in the Tanami Desert; Tanami Downs is owned by the Mangkururrta Aboriginal Land Trust.

During the 1920s geologist Michael Terry led a number of expeditions across the northern half of Australia in vehicles as well as on camels, searching for minerals. During his 1928 expedition, when he used a couple of Morris six-wheel trucks on what were the first motorised trips through this part of the continent, he travelled from Broome, via Halls Creek (Old Halls Creek today) down to the Tanami Mine and then south-east to Alice Springs. His book, *Hidden Wealth and Hiding People*, recounts his adventures and what life was like for the prospectors and the Indigenous inhabitants back then.

Some of the facts and figures he states regarding his vehicles still make interesting reading. Oil consumption was down to 250 miles to the gallon, while fuel consumption was down to less than five miles to the gallon. Mind you, that was across country, as all there was to follow was a camel pad. He also states, regarding tyres, 'the Australian Dunlops stood up very well', even though he recorded 57 punctures and tyre pressures of 80psi! It must have been a hard trip.

Information

Road Reports The 1000km track has been greatly improved in recent years, and if you're reasonably experienced on unsealed roads you can cover it in a well-prepared 2WD vehicle driven with care. But it's still quite rough in places and if you're lucky enough to make it through without damage, you'll know your vehicle is pretty well corrugation-proof! A sturdy 4WD is far less likely to come to grief.

The Northern Territory section is wide and usually well graded, but between the Western Australia–Northern Territory border and Halls Creek, some sandy patches and creek crossings require care; a high-clearance vehicle is advisable. After rain (rare in winter), sections of the track around Sturt Creek near Billiluna can become impassable for weeks on end.

In the cooler months there's quite a bit of traffic (up to 80 vehicles a day pass through Rabbit Flat) so a breakdown need not be cause for alarm if you're well prepared with water and food. There are many road trains too but don't expect them to stop except in a true emergency. In summer the heat can be extreme – days where the temperature hits 50°C are not uncommon – so think carefully before setting off at this time.

Radio Frequencies An HF radio isn't necessary but might give you peace of mind. The Tanami Track is covered by the RFDS in Alice Springs (☎ 08-8952 1033) and Derby (☎ 08-9191 1211); Alice Springs (VJD) monitors 2020kHz, 5410kHz and 6950kHz, while the Derby (VJB) frequencies are 2020kHz, 2792kHz, 5300kHz and 6925kHz. These are monitored 24 hours a day for emergencies.

Maps The best map for the track is the Westprint *Tanami Track* map, available from several outlets in Alice Springs, including the visitors information centre on Gregory Terrace. Hema Maps' *Great Desert Tracks – North East Sheet* includes the Tanami and is pretty good as well.

Registration It isn't compulsory to register with the police at either end of the Tanami Track (and they'd probably tell you not to worry so much), but travel in this area is no Sunday-school picnic and you should at least notify someone reliable of your travel plans.

Permits Much of the track passes through Aboriginal land, but it's a public road and permits are not required except if you want to venture more than 50m either side of the road. You don't need a permit to purchase fuel at Yuendumu or Rabbit Flat, both of which are a little way off the road.

Work out your fuel requirements because fuel availability can be a bit tricky (see the later Facilities section).

THE ROUTE
Alice Springs to Rabbit Flat (592km)

The Tanami Track starts at the Stuart Hwy, 20km north of Alice Springs. Here the somewhat daunting sign informs you that it's 703km to the Western Australian border, the first 127km of which are sealed.

The first point of interest is the masts of the Defence Department's **radio receiving station** off to the north of the road (entry prohibited). On the southern side of the road is the rugged northern face of the **West MacDonnell Ranges**.

Shortly after passing the receiver station the road crosses the **Hamilton Downs** station boundary fence, and passes the turn-off to the Apex youth camp at the foot of the ranges. The station was established early this century and named by the explorer John McDouall Stuart. The road then enters Amburla station (and crosses the Tropic of Capricorn) and, 104km from the Stuart Hwy, there's the turn-off to the Aboriginal community of **Papunya**, 96km to the west along a good dirt road (permit required). This leads to the Gary Junction Rd, also known as the Kintore Rd (see the Bomb Roads section later in this chapter).

A further 15km brings you to the crossing of the underground gas pipeline, which takes natural gas from near Palm Valley to Katherine and Darwin. It's another 36km to the first fuel and supply stop along the track, the modern Tilmouth Well Roadhouse on the banks of the (usually) dry Napperby Creek (see the later Facilities section).

On from Tilmouth the track passes through the **Stuart Bluff Range**, one of the few rocky outcrops before the turn-off for Mt Wedge homestead, 20km away. The boundary of the **Yalpirakinu Aboriginal land** is reached after 15km, and a further 24km goes to the turn-off to the **Yuelamu (Mt Allan)** community in the Ngalurbindi Hills.

It's then another 45km before you reach the turn-off to the Aboriginal community of **Yuendumu**, which lies 2km north of the track. Visitors are welcome to buy fuel or provisions from the store, but permits are required to visit elsewhere, and alcohol is prohibited (see the later Facilities section). Yuendumu has a thriving art community, and the work put out by the Warlukurlangi artists is highly regarded. It's not possible, however, to visit the artists without a permit. The town also has the highly sophisticated Tanami Network, a satellite TV conference network that can link Yuendumu with Darwin, Alice Springs and even overseas.

From Yuendumu the track crosses into **Mt Doreen** station and soon skirts the southern edge of the **Yarunganyi Hills**. On the northern side of the hills and close to the road is the site of the abandoned Mt Doreen station. Although originally built in the 1920s, it was later abandoned due to the unreliable water supply. These days the station is run from Vaughan Springs station, which lies about 80km west of the track at this point.

Chilla Well Outstation and the turn-off to **Mt Theo Outstation** are reached 125km north-west from Yuendumu, and from there it's 58km to **Refrigerator Bore**, off to the right (north) of the track. Up until the early 1970s there was a stock route that went from Refrigerator Bore, passing through Tanami Downs (then Mongrel Downs) and on to Balgo and Halls Creek. This route was pioneered in the early 1960s and a series of wells dug along its length to supply the cattle. Once trucks took over from droving, the route was no longer used.

By now you're in the vast expanses of the **Central Desert Aboriginal Land Trust**. The spinifex grass and anthills often stretch as far as the eye can see, and there's little to break the monotony – just the occasional acacia tree and the Telstra microwave towers at 45km to 50km intervals. You know you've bitten another chunk off your journey when you pass one.

Just before the gold mine of the Granites, you pass a low rocky outcrop on the left of the road where a couple of **old ruins** can be seen. These date back to the 1930s. Nearby are older relics, the most important of which is an ore stamper, or crushing battery.

What those early miners went through is vastly different from what today's workers experience, flying in and out from Alice Springs on their weekly shifts.

Granites Gold Mine is the next major point of interest, 82km along the track from Refrigerator Bore, although there is no public access or facilities except in an emergency. Although small-scale mining had occured in the area since the early 1900s, the mine site was first pegged in 1927 and operated until 1947. The returns were small with a yield of only about 28kg per year. In 1986 the mine reopened after exploratory drilling by North Flinders Mines proved gold reserves were still there. Production is currently running at around 5000kg of gold per year, from both the Granites site and the area known as Dead Bullock Soak, 45km to the west. The ore from Dead Bullock Soak is carted to the Granites site for treatment along a new bitumen road (the only one for hundreds of kilometres!) on huge four-trailer road trains, each carting well over 100 tonnes of ore. These monsters travel at great speed and require at least 1km to stop.

It's just 48km from the Granites to the most famous place in the Tanami, the Rabbit Flat Roadhouse, 1km or so to the north of the track. The roadhouse was established by Bruce Farrands and his French wife Jacqui in 1969 and has served travellers on the Tanami Track ever since. It's not an attractive place, just a couple of breeze-block buildings and a few fuel tanks, but it's the social centre of the Tanami, not least because it's the only place for hundreds of kilometres where people can buy a drink. On Friday and Saturday nights it can get pretty lively with all the workers back from the mines. Note that the roadhouse, along with the access track, is closed Tuesday, Wednesday and Thursday and there won't be fuel or anything else (see the later Facilities section) available.

Rabbit Flat to Halls Creek (448km)

From Rabbit Flat the track continues north-west for 44km to the **Tanami Mine**. The story here is much the same as that at the Granites

Gold Mine – early interest and small yields were followed by a period of inactivity from the 1930s to the 1980s. Modern techniques made the prospect viable once again. In 1987 Zapopan NL commenced operations and until March 1994 when was again shut down, around 10,000kg of gold were taken from the earth. There's no public access to the mine site.

Just 1km or so past the Tanami Mine, the **Lajamanu Rd** heads off north (see Alternative Routes later in this section). After the turn-off, the Tanami Track swings due west for the run to the Western Australian border and beyond. In the days of the area's minor gold rush, the track continued north-westerly, passing through Gordon Downs station and on to Halls Creek, but this route was abandoned once the rush was over. The route the current track takes between the Tanami Mine and Billiluna Aboriginal community was established in the 1960s by Father McGuire from what was then the Balgo Aboriginal Mission, and is sometimes still referred to as McGuire's Track.

It is 78km from the Tanami Mine to the Western Australia–Northern Territory border, and another 86km will see you at the junction of the road to **Balgo** Aboriginal community, nearly 40km to the south. Visiting Balgo requires a permit and there are no facilities except in an emergency. A fainter track heads north from this point across Aboriginal land to Sturt Creek homestead and finally to the **Buntine Hwy**, 70km east of Halls Creek. The 170km trip north to this highway requires a permit.

Near the Balgo turn-off the occasional sand ridge can be seen from the track, which now becomes a little sandier. The track begins to swing north the further west you travel, and 24km from the junction a very faint track heads south to Balgo. Although it is still marked on many maps, this track has been abandoned.

The track continues for another 48km through several floodplains to the crossing of **Sturt Creek**. Here is one of the few reasonable spots to camp along this route, with a couple of pleasant spots on the western bank, just north of the road crossing. The creek has a concrete causeway and the crossing should not present a problem if there's water about, which happens occasionally. The floodplains to the south will be far more daunting.

When Sturt Creek flows, its floodwaters end up in **Lake Gregory**, 70km to the south. When this occurs, the lake becomes one of the great habitats for birds in inland Australia. During one bird-surveying expedition more than 240,000 water birds of 57 species were counted, including cormorants, pink-eared ducks, plumed whistle-ducks, coots, darters, egrets and brolgas, to name just a few.

Just 2km past the crossing, a track comes in from the south. This leads a short distance to **Billiluna** Aboriginal community and the start (or the end) of the **Canning Stock Route** (see The North-West chapter). Billiluna has no facilities for travellers except in an emergency.

From here the road improves and swings almost due north, and the sand ridges slip away to the south-west. The abandoned Carranya Roadhouse comes up on the right, 41km north of the Sturt Creek crossing. It marks the turn-off to travel the 20-odd kilometres to Wolfe Creek Meteorite Crater and the small reserve that surrounds it. This station track leads 16km east, with some fierce corrugations, to the deserted Carranya homestead which you pass close to, before continuing on another 5km to the small parking area at the base of the crater wall.

Wolfe Creek Meteorite Crater This impact crater is the second-largest of its type in the world. Known to the Aboriginal people as the place where some of their Dreamtime ancestors originated, early explorers and the first aviators across this vast region knew of it long before its significance was recorded by geologists in 1947. It was first gazetted as a reserve in 1969.

The rim of the crater is about 850m across and up to 35m above the surrounding sand plain. While the outer walls of the crater are relatively steep, the inner walls are much more so and descend, in places, via sheer cliffs, over 50m to the crater floor. Once it would have been much deeper, but sand has filled the crater in.

When was it formed? Sometime within the last two million years, and possibly the last 500,000 years. Scientists tell us that this meteorite would have had to weigh thousands of tonnes and be travelling at around 900km per minute to create such a crater!

There are no facilities at the crater, not even a tree to cast shade, but the view from the crest of the rim is worth the short walk. Clamber down into the crater with care and explore the flat interior. The centre of the crater is a natural water trap and shrubs have grown up in profusion where the water is closer to the surface.

Halls Creek Back on the main road, there is still another 111km of dirt before the major T-intersection with Hwy 1 and the bitumen. The road passes through Ruby Plains station and the pretty McClintock Range (well, any hills are pretty after the Tanami), with several sudden creek crossings that shouldn't present a problem if you slow down. Once you get to the bitumen you are just 16km south-west of Halls Creek and all the facilities of this small but major town. There is a choice of fuel outlets, repair places, a supermarket, police station, hospital and more. For further information on Halls Creek, see the Canning Stock Route section in the North-West chapter.

ALTERNATIVE ROUTES
Lajamanu Road
The Lajamanu Rd heads north off the Tanami Track at the Tanami Mine, although it's not even marked on many maps. It's generally kept in good condition, but it does get sandy towards Lajamanu, and there are numerous creek-bed crossings and the occasional wash-out. A 2WD car will have trouble getting through.

The road offers an interesting alternative to the Tanami Track and takes you through country that has very little tourist traffic. It passes through the Central Desert Aboriginal Land and the Lajamanu Aboriginal Land. A permit is not required to traverse the road, or to get fuel and supplies at Lajamanu.

From the Tanami Mine it's 231km to the small Aboriginal community of **Lajamanu**, and the trip usually takes around six hours. The road goes through some very pretty countryside, especially in the area around Suplejack Downs station, and is generally a lot more interesting to travel than the Tanami Track itself.

The Lajamanu service station (☎ 08-8975 0644) sells unleaded and diesel 8.30am to noon, and 1pm to 5pm Monday to Friday, and 8.30am to noon Saturday. The adjacent *store* (☎ 08-8975 0896) is open 9am to noon, and 1pm to 5pm Monday to Friday, and 9am to noon Saturday. There's also a small *deli* open 5pm-7pm seven days a week.

North from Lajamanu, the road passes through spinifex plains until suddenly, about 10km before the Buntine Hwy, the countryside changes from the red of the Centre to grassed and lightly treed cattle country. The change is quite dramatic – like a line has been drawn delineating desert and grazing land.

The Lajamanu Rd joins the single-lane bitumen Buntine Hwy at an unmarked T-junction 8km east of **Kalkaringi**, which has a pleasant location on the banks of the Victoria River. At Kalkaringi there's a police station (☎ 08-8975 0790), medical clinic, caravan park, and a service station (☎ 08-8975 0788) with fuel (super, unleaded, diesel), takeaway food and provisions, including fresh bread daily. From there it's 105km and 1½ hours to the Buntine Hwy.

ORGANISED TOURS

The problem with the Tanami is that it's such a long track and tour operators can't get a good return on expenses. Several have tried in the past and given up.

Austour (☎ *1800 335 009,* e *Info@ austourtravel.com,* w *www.austourtravel .com, PO Box 1252, Frankston, Vic 3199)* includes the Tanami Desert as part of its wider tour six times a year in a 4WD Oka (maximum 12 people) from Alice Springs to Broome, the Bungle Bungles, Katherine and Litchfield National Park to Darwin. This takes 14 days and costs $2395 (tent all the way) or $2695 (cabin accommodation for all but three days); meals are included.

See also Organised Tours in the later Gunbarrel Highway section for a company

that does the challenging triangle consisting of the Tanami, Canning and Gunbarrel.

FACILITIES

Fuel supplies are well spaced out along the eastern end of the Tanami Track, but be warned that Rabbit Flat is only open from Friday to Monday, and that fuel availability at Yuendumu is unreliable due to petrol-sniffing problems (diesel may be all you can get). The longest stretch without fuel is nearly 500km from Rabbit Flat to Halls Creek, which includes a 50km round-trip detour to Wolfe Creek Meteorite Crater. Vehicles with long-range fuel tanks may be able to cover the 915km from Tilmouth Well to Halls Creek including the detour. It's recommended that you take it easy on the Tanami and don't go over 80km/h. If you follow this advice your fuel consumption will be pleasantly low.

Although there are a number of bores quite close to the track along the way, the water in some of these is undrinkable, so don't rely on them. Bring your own drinking water.

Tilmouth Well

Tilmouth Well Roadhouse (☎ *08-8956 8777)* Powered sites $5 per person, single/ double dongas $45/60. Open 7am-9pm daily. This modern roadhouse has fuel (super, unleaded, diesel), basic spare parts and accessories. There's also a bar and a licensed *restaurant* with takeaway tucker (great, freshly ground hamburgers), and an art gallery selling reasonable Aboriginal art. Out the back there's a very pleasant lawn, swimming pool and golf course. It's a veritable oasis for those who have just come down the Tanami from Halls Creek.

Yuendumu

Permits are not required to enter this Aboriginal community if you just want to get fuel and provisions.

Yuendumu Store (☎ *08-8956 4006)* Open 8.30am-5pm Mon-Fri, 9am-noon Sat & Sun. This store has unleaded and diesel and a fairly well-stocked supermarket.

Yuendumu Mining Company Store (☎ *08-8956 4040)* Open 9am-5pm Mon-Sat,

1pm-5pm Sun. This store has unleaded, diesel and Avgas, and is also fairly well stocked with supplies.

Rabbit Flat

Rabbit Flat Roadhouse (☎ 08-8956 8744) Open 7am-9pm Fri-Mon. This quirky roadhouse stocks fuel (super, unleaded, diesel) and oil. Although your attention will be drawn to it, note that the somewhat antiquated fuel bowsers for super and diesel (modern ones don't take kindly to the dust) can only register prices up to 99 cents per litre and the final price is doubled. The super/diesel currently costs $1.60/1.55 per litre (possibly and not surprisingly the most expensive in the country). The Farrands also sell basic provisions and beer ($56 for a warm carton, $65 for a cold one!), and there's a *bar*. *Camping* costs $3 per person; showers cost $3 as well. There are Eftpos facilities for cheque or savings accounts (no credit cards), and A$ travellers cheques are accepted.

Plenty Highway

Highlights

- Fossicking for gemstones at Mud Tank or the Harts Range
- Washing the dust down with a cold beer at Urandangi's bush pub
- Photographing the huge termite mound near Jervois homestead

Leaving the Stuart Hwy 70km north of Alice Springs, the Plenty Hwy skirts the northern fringe of the Simpson Desert before entering Queensland, where it becomes known as the Donohue Hwy. This 742km route, which terminates at the small town of Boulia, makes an adventurous alternative link between western Queensland and the Alice. Isolation is almost guaranteed, as even in winter you can drive the entire route and see fewer than a dozen vehicles. Signs of human habitation are rare and facilities are few and far between.

The first 103km are sealed, but after that the road can be extremely rough and corrugated; large bulldust holes are a common hazard on the Queensland side. The unsealed section is suitable for use only in dry weather and is normally not recommended for caravans.

Diesel, super and unleaded fuel are available at the Gemtree Caravan Park (140km from Alice Springs), Atitjere Aboriginal community (215km), Jervois homestead (356km), Tobermorey homestead (570km) and Boulia (812km).

History

The disappearance of the eccentric Prussian explorer Ludwig Leichhardt and his large, well-equipped party is one of Australia's great unsolved mysteries. Leichhardt vanished somewhere in the interior on his final expedition in 1848, and it's possible he crossed the area of the Plenty Hwy attempting to return to civilisation. The evidence that this actually happened was the discovery of marked trees in central Australia and far-western Queensland.

In 1886 the surveyor David Lindsay, of Simpson Desert fame, found trees in the Harts Range that had been carved with Leichhardt's distinctive mark. Many years later, more such trees were discovered along the Georgina River on Glenormiston station. Also of interest is the fact that the bones of several unknown Europeans had been found by a waterhole near Birdsville in the early 1870s, before the area was settled by white people.

Leichhardt had intended to cross northern Australia from east to west, but he may have been forced south by the waterless scrub west of the Roper River. Judging by the location of the carved trees, one theory goes, he reached the MacDonnell Ranges, headed east around the top of the Simpson Desert and then, on striking the Georgina, turned south once more. Reaching the junction of the Georgina and Diamantina Rivers he managed to upset the local Aborigines, who killed him and his remaining companions. No-one knows if the

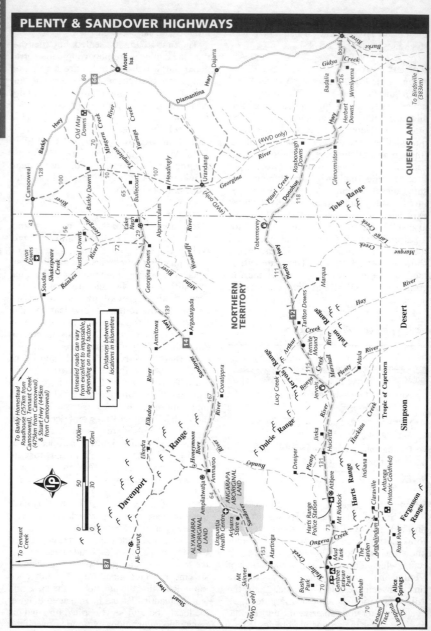

PLENTY & SANDOVER HIGHWAYS

bones found by that lonely waterhole belonged to Leichhardt and his men, but the theory is a fascinating and plausible one.

H Vere Barclay was one of the next Europeans on the scene. In 1878, while carrying out a trigonometric survey from Alice Springs to the Queensland border, he was north-east of the Harts Range when his water supply began to run out. He dug into a sandy riverbed – this being the usual method of finding water in dry outback rivers – and found ample supplies of the precious fluid. That is how the Plenty River got its name, and it's why the present beef road, which was first upgraded from a two-wheel track during the 1960s, is called the Plenty Hwy.

Information

Tourist Offices The Gemtree Caravan Park (☎ 08-8956 9855) can advise you on fossicking in the western Harts Range area. Boulia has the Min Min Encounter & Tourist Information Centre (☎ 07-4746 3386) – see Boulia later in this section.

Radio Frequencies Within the Territory call the Alice Springs RFDS base (call sign VJD; ☎ 08-8952 1033), which monitors 5410kHz and 6950kHz between 7.30am and 5pm weekdays. Use 2020kHz (best at night) and 5410kIIz for after-hours emergency calls. Once into Queensland try the RFDS in Mt Isa (call sign VJI; ☎ 07-4743 2800) on 5110kHz and 6965kHz between 8am and 5pm weekdays. Use 2020kHz (best at night) and 5110kHz for after-hours emergency calls.

Books & Maps Many of the fascinating reminiscences contained in *A Son of the Red Centre*, by Kurt Johannsen, involve the Plenty Hwy area. Johannsen, regarded as one of the pioneers of modern road-train transport, mined copper near Jervois and hauled huge loads from his mine to Mt Isa before there was a road.

If you're intending to look for gems in the Harts Range, you'll need *A Guide to Fossicking in the Northern Territory* by the Northern Territory Department of Mines and Energy (1986). It describes many of the range's fossicking areas and old mines,

including maps; although much of the information about access is out of date, it's still an essential reference. Copies of this guide are available from the Department of Business, Industry and Resource Development in Alice Springs.

At a scale of 1:1,000,000, the map-guide entitled *Plenty Hwy*, by Westprint Heritage Maps, makes a useful planning and touring reference. As a bonus, it includes the short cut from the Plenty Hwy to Mt Isa via Urandangi, and the direct route from Boulia to Birdsville. The guides are on sale at numerous outlets around Alice Springs and in good map shops everywhere.

Road Reports The Road Report Hotline (☎ 1800 246 199) will advise whether the highway is open to traffic. Contact Harts Range police station (☎ 08-8956 9772), Min Min Encounter (☎ 07- 4746 3386), Boulia police station (☎ 07-4746 3120) or Jervois homestead (☎ 08-8956 6307) for further information.

Emergency In the event of a medical emergency, you can obtain assistance from the health clinic at Atitjere Aboriginal community, where there's a registered nurse. The Boulia hospital is under the control of a matron, and an RFDS clinic is held there on a weekly basis. Cattle stations en route have RFDS medical kits and telephones.

Fossicking Permits You can find out more about fossicking in the Harts Range by calling in on the Department of Business, Industry and Resource Development (☎ 08-8951 5658) at 58 Hartley St. It can also issue you with a fossicking licence (free for 12 months).

THE ROUTE
Stuart Highway to Harts Range Police Station (143km)

From the Stuart Hwy to Harts Range police station, the road parallels the rugged northern flanks of first the Strangways Range and then the Harts Range. The scenery is attractive almost all the way, with several picturesque creeks in the 103km to Ongeva Creek. Most of these are worth stopping at if you feel like boiling the billy under a river red gum, although you'll generally need a 4WD vehicle to get off the road. There's also potential for quiet walks in the bush, and the chance of finding minerals such as zircon, quartz, garnet and staurolite. The road is single-lane bitumen as far as Ongeva Creek, where it changes to formed dirt.

Mud Tank At 70km you come to the Gemtree Caravan Park on the gum-lined banks of Gillen Creek (see Facilities later in this section). This is the only tourist facility of note on the Plenty Hwy. It offers guided **fossicking trips** to the zircon deposit costing $50 per set of equipment. They'll also take you to a garnet deposit for the same price.

At Mud Tank the top 80cm of soil conceals zircons of various colours (including yellow, light brown, pink, purple and blue), ranging in size from small chips to large crystals.

Provided they put their backs into it, even novices have a good chance of finding gem material with nothing more complicated than a shovel, a couple of small sieves (minimum mesh size 7mm) and some water for washing the stones. If you find anything worth faceting, Gemtree's gem-cutter can turn your find into a beautiful stone ready to be set in gold or silver.

The turn-off to the zircon field is on the right (south) at the big windmill about 7km east of Gemtree, and the fossicking area is 9km along the track. Deposits of gem-quality garnet also occur in the general area. The zircon field and one or two of the garnet deposits can be reached by conventional vehicles.

Mica Mines The Harts Range starts at **Ongeva Creek**, where a track on the right leads to the ominously named **Blackfellows Bones** mica mine. (Apparently, back in the 1870s, a group of Aborigines from the Sandover River were slaughtered nearby in reprisal for an attack on settlers.) From 1888 to 1960, mica was mined from pegmatites throughout the Harts Range, with literally dozens of small mines being developed. The field was never rich thanks

to its remoteness, the rugged terrain, lack of water and uncertain markets. However the miners, most of whom after the 1920s were Italians, persevered until cheaper imports eventually put them out of business. Now the old dumps are a magnet for fossickers, who come in search of the gems that were thrown out with the waste rock.

One of Australia's premier fossicking areas, the Harts Range yields a host of interesting gems and minerals, including mica, smoky and rose quartz, aquamarine, black and green tourmaline, sphene, garnet, sunstone, ruby, iolite and kyanite. However, the area is extremely rugged and the best spots for fossicking are hard to get to – high-clearance 4WD vehicles are required for most tracks. It's essential to carry plenty of water at all times.

Seven kilometres past Ongeva Creek, a signposted 4WD track leads to garnet deposits en route to Ambalindum station homestead, 60km to the south. A massive ochre-coloured ridge looms on your right, its steep bald flanks issuing an invitation to keen hill climbers. It's a tough scramble to the top of **Mt Riddock**, the highest point, but the view is well worth the effort. You can park your vehicle at Kong Bore, the turn-off to which is about 16km past Ongeva Creek. The tailings of abandoned mica mines in the near vicinity yield various minerals, such as black tourmaline, quartz, hornblende and epidote.

Harts Range Police Station High ridges and mountains keep you company for the final 40km to the Harts Range police station. The two police officers based here have the awesome task of preserving law and order over a sparsely populated area of 120,000 sq km – apart from constant travel, they do everything from investigating murders to issuing driving licences. They're kept busy controlling revellers during the annual Harts Range Races, which take place over the first weekend in August. This is good entertainment, with a barbecue and bush dance on the Saturday night. You need to get there early to find a bush camp site reasonably handy to the action.

From the racecourse, which is just south of the police station, a 4WD track gives access to a number of mica mines on and around the rocky slopes of **Mt Palmer**. At 600m above the northern plain, this is one of the highest points in the Harts Range and has many large cycads growing on its southern flank. It's well worth climbing – the atmosphere and sweeping panorama from the top are magnificent.

Mt Palmer first becomes visible past Mt Riddock homestead, 117km from the Stuart Hwy. Like a retreat for a goblin king from Tolkien's books, its jagged, misty-blue outline rising steeply above the plain makes an impressive sight. The two white patches you see high up on the western slopes as you get closer are the waste dumps of the **Billy Hughes** and **Oolgarinna** mica mines. Among the field's largest mines, they are best reached by walking along the old camel pads that wind up the mountainside from primitive mining camps at the bottom.

The **Disputed**, another of Mt Palmer's mines, is famous in mineralogical circles because of the many fine mineral specimens it has yielded over the years. In the 1930s, miners opened a cave-like cavity in the pegmatite and found it lined top and bottom with huge crystals of black tourmaline, mica, feldspar, quartz and beryl. Apparently the tourmaline crystals stuck up from the floor like fence posts! Known as the Jeweller's Cave, this sparkling wonderland was permanently sealed off by a mine collapse not long after its discovery.

A 4WD track takes you from the racecourse to the old Disputed camp, after which it's a half-hour walk along the camel pad to the dumps high above on the mountainside. En route you pass the **Spotted Dog Mine**, where two miners died in a rock fall in the late 1920s. Their simple grave is nearby, although hard to find.

Harts Range Police Station to the Queensland Border (357km)

The first 50km from the police station is extremely scenic, with attractive woodlands of whitewood and weeping ironwood fronting the crumpled ranges to the south.

Mulga and gidgee later become dominant. Past the ranges, only scattered low ridges, flat-topped hills and occasional gum-lined creeks break the line of the endless plain.

This section's highlight is right beside the road, 50km past the turn-off to Jervois homestead. Here a conical red **termite mound** nearly 5m high rears like a breaching whale above the stunted mallees and spinifex. It's the highest point around, and the white splashes on top tell you that it's a favourite perch for falcons. There are lots of similar, if smaller, termite mounds over the next 10km.

Pioneers & Poison Although explored in the 1870s, the area between the Harts Range and Queensland was one of the last parts of Australia to be settled by Europeans. The shortage of permanent surface water kept the pastoralists at bay until bore-drilling equipment became readily available in the late 1940s. Indiana, Jervois, Atula, Lucy Creek, Tarlton Downs and Marqua stations were all first taken up for cattle grazing between 1950 and 1960. Atula, on the Simpson Desert fringe, has since been handed back to its Aboriginal occupants.

Near Mt Riddock homestead you begin to notice clumps of **gidgee** beside the road. A tough acacia, this generally low, gnarled tree with dark-brown bark and dense grey foliage is the dominant species past Arthur Creek.

Although a valuable fodder plant in some areas, gidgee is extremely poisonous to cattle in others. At certain times its pods and young leaves carry a powerful toxin that causes any beast grazing on them to have a heart attack immediately after drinking – the unfortunate animal literally drops dead at the trough. In the early days, stations in this area often suffered devastating stock losses due to gidgee poisoning, but better fencing has brought the problem under control.

Queensland Border At the Queensland border, the road changes its name and becomes the Donohue Hwy. Crossing the border grid, you'll usually notice a dramatic change in road conditions – the Boulia Shire Council does its best, but it only takes a few road trains to break the surface and

THE CENTRAL DESERTS

form deep bulldust holes. After the first shattering experiences, learn to identify them and take due care.

Queensland Border to Boulia (244km)

Most of the final section to Boulia is a mix of gidgee scrub and open **Mitchell-grass** country, with variety provided by occasional stony undulations and coolabah creeks. Mitchell-grass habitats, which occur in a great arc from southern Queensland through the Territory's Barkly Tableland to the Kimberley, are the arid zone's most productive in terms of sheep and cattle grazing.

Georgina River At 118km from the border you cross the Georgina River. Other than vast expanses of empty space, this waterway is the highlight of the Queensland side. Its main channel features shady coolabahs, good camp sites and abundant **birdlife** – you'll see brolgas, emus and bustards, as well as large flocks of budgies, cockatiels, galahs and corellas. You can camp by the river on **Wirrilyerna** station, near Boulia (see Facilities later in this section).

Watch out for the Noogoora burr, that infests the river banks in some areas. It's an introduced noxious weed with prickly, cigar-shaped seeds that can easily hitch a ride on your clothing or swag. If you stop at the crossing, make sure you're not carrying any unwanted passengers before driving on.

Fed by summer monsoon rains, the Georgina River rises on the Barkly Tableland north-west of Camooweal and heads southward to join the Diamantina River near Birdsville. A large enough flood will eventually reach Lake Eyre, which is quite a journey by the standards of Australian rivers. The raised causeway means that major floods now only close the road for days, rather than weeks.

Boulia Thirty-three kilometres from Boulia you meet the bitumen, which means joyous relief from the bulldust and corrugations. By the time most travellers reach this point, they're ready to kill for a cold beer.

Situated on the **Burke River**, which the ill-fated Burke and Wills visited on their dash across Australia in 1861, Boulia is the administrative centre for the vast Boulia Shire. Covering about 60,000 sq km, the shire has a population of 250,000 sheep, 75,000 cattle and about 600 people, 300 of whom live in Boulia.

The towns has a good range of facilities, including a hospital, police station, post

Bustards

Mitchell grass areas along the Donohue Hwy are good places to see Australian bustards – also called bush turkeys. Tall (to 120cm), heavy-bodied, long-necked birds with a distinctive stately posture, they often gather there in pairs or small groups to feed on small animals and insects, particularly grasshoppers. Flocks of up to 200 birds are reported from the Kimberley, but I've never seen or heard of more than 10 or 20 in a group here.

The bustard's favourite habitat is tussock grassland, followed by low shrublands and lightly timbered woodlands with a grassy understorey. Stop if you see one near the road. It'll probably stand gazing haughtily at you for a bit, then walk slowly away with its head held high and beak pointing skywards. However, if it's been shot at or otherwise harassed it might take to the air straight away.

With a wingspan up to 230cm they're also impressive when in flight. Once widespread across the mainland, bustards are now scarce in the south because of shooting, habitat changes and introduced predators. However they are still widespread and reasonably common in the north and centre, although hunting pressure means few are to be seen near settlements. Despite the fact that the species is protected, as well as being endangered, many bush people regard it as 'good tucker' and often have one in the pot. Personally, I wouldn't jump over a roast chicken to get at one.

Denis O'Byrne

office, all-weather aerodrome, hotel, caravan park, and two garages. Banking facilities are limited to a Commonwealth Bank agency – the roadhouse, Min Min Store and hotel give cash out on Eftpos. See the Facilities section later for details of Boulia's commercial services.

The friendly Min Min Encounter & Tourist Information Centre (☎ 07-4746 3386, e bouliamin@bigpond.com, Herbert St) opens from 8.30am to 5pm weekdays and 9am to 2pm weekends. A *cafe* on the premises sells cappuccino, sandwiches and cake.

The Boulia Shire Library (☎ 07-4746 3408, Herbert St) charges $2 per hour to use its Internet facilities. It opens from 8.30am to 12.30pm and 1.30pm to 5pm weekdays.

There are a few tourist attractions in and around the town. These include the **Min Min Encounter** *(adult/child $11/7.70)*, a rather creepy 45-minute show featuring wax mannequins and anecdotes about the famous **Min Min Light**. It opens the same hours as the tourist office.

A ghostly luminous glow resembling a fluorescent football, the Min Min Light is said to float through the air like a lantern being carried in a mist. Many people in this area have seen the light but no-one has ever managed to get close enough to catch it. There is no scientific explanation for the phenomenon, and outsiders tend to scoff that a few ales must be imbibed before you'll see it. However, locals have no doubt that the Min Min Light exists.

There's also the **Stone House Museum** *(Cnr Pituri & Hamilton Sts; admission $2.20; open 8am-5pm Mon-Fri)*. Said to be one of the first houses built in western Queensland, this 1880s stone building holds an interesting collection of early household memorabilia, fossils and Aboriginal artefacts.

ALTERNATIVE ROUTE
Mt Isa via Urandangi (280km)
The road to Urandangi, which turns off the Plenty Hwy 493km from the Stuart Hwy, makes an excellent short cut to Mt Isa if the bulldust holes aren't too bad and conditions are dry. Gidgee scrub and open Mitchell grass plains keep you company for the 96km from the highway to the Georgina River crossing, after which tiny Urandangi is only about a minute or two away.

Once an important droving centre, this sleepy little outpost began its slow decline when road trains took over from the drovers in the 1950s and '60s. Large yellow belly live in the river, though getting them to bite is usually a challenge. There are plenty of shady bush camp sites near the crossing.

Leaving Urandangi, you endure similar road conditions for a further 110km, then turn onto the bitumen for the final 73km to Mt Isa.

Urandangi Hotel (☎ 07-4748 4988) Singles & doubles without air-con $44. This quaint old pub sells meals and fuel (diesel, super, unleaded), and also has free *camp sites* with showers and toilets.

FACILITIES
Gemtree
Gemtree Caravan Park (☎ 08-8956 9855, e gemtree@gemtree.com.au, w www.gemtree.com.au) Unpowered/powered sites $16/20, on-site caravans $44, cabins $55. This place offers good shade, a *shop* selling basic groceries and meat, a public telephone, and fuel sales (diesel, super and unleaded).

Games of paddymelon bowls, with tea and damper to follow, provide some light-hearted entertainment on Saturday night in the cooler months. Paddymelons, which look like small round watermelons, are often found beside outback roads.

There's also a nine-hole golf course ($5 including club hire).

Atitjere
Atitjere Community Store (☎ 08-8956 9773) Open 9am-noon & 3pm-5pm Mon-Fri, 9am-noon Sat. The store sells basic foodstuffs and cold drinks, as well as diesel, super and unleaded fuel. Ask here about the community's *bush camping ground* (camp sites $10). It has hot showers and pit toilets, and is close to a prime fossicking site.

Jervois
Jervois homestead (☎ 08-8956 6307) You can buy diesel, super and unleaded fuel at

Jervois homestead during daylight hours, seven days a week. Note that credit cards are not accepted.

Jervois also has a public telephone, and shower and toilet facilities are available (showers $2). You can stop overnight either at the turn-off, where there's a lay-by, or at a small **camping ground** (sites $5 per vehicle) at the first gate about 1km in on the homestead access road.

Next to the homestead is a huge **rocket-proof shelter** dating from the 1960s, when Blue Streak rockets were fired in this direction from Woomera. Instead of huddling inside as they were supposed to, the stationfolk preferred to stand on top of it to watch the fireworks. Similar shelters were provided for all the stations in this area. It seems to have been a huge waste of taxpayers' money, although a couple did come down near the highway.

Tobermorey

Tobermorey Homestead (☎ 07-4748 4996) Camp sites $20, air-con dongas $60. Just on the Territory side of the border, Tobermorey has a small **shop** (open 8am to 8pm daily) that sells drinks, snacks, minor grocery lines and diesel, super and unleaded fuel. Tyre repairs can also be attended to.

Wirrilyerna

Wirrilyerna Station Stay (☎ 07-4746 1253, e wirrilyerna@bigpond.com) Camp sites $6, bunk beds $25. Entry $25. This working cattle and sheep station, off the Donohue Hwy 45km from Boulia, has a bush camping area beside a beautiful, 22km-long, spring-fed waterhole in the Georgina River. There are wood-burning barbecues (firewood supplied) and pit toilets, but no showers. **Aboriginal guided tours** delve into the area's Indigenous culture with bush walks. The turn-off is 38km from Boulia (774km from Alice Springs).

Boulia

Min Min Store (☎ 07-4746 3158, 17 Herbert St) Boulia's largest store has a bakery, hardware section and well-stocked minimarket. Credit cards are accepted.

Boulia Caravan Park (Shell Roadhouse; ☎ 07-4746 3131, Winton Rd) Unpowered/powered sites $8.80/9.90, caravan sites $12.10. This place, which has grassed sites and good shade, is beside the Burke River just across the bridge on the road to Winton.

Australian Hotel-Motel (☎ 07-4746 3144, e bouliapub@hotmail.com, Herbert St) Single/twin/triple pub rooms $33/38/45, single/twin motel rooms $45/55. All pub rooms have air-con and share facilities, and the dining room serves breakfast, lunch and dinner.

Desert Sands Motel (☎ 07-4746 3000, Herbert St) Singles/doubles $70/80. All units have a TV and a fridge, and continental and cooked breakfasts are available.

Bush Camping

There are good camping spots in the mulga and gidgee scrub en route, although you'll generally need a 4WD vehicle to reach them. The sandy beds of Annamurra Creek (80km from the Stuart Hwy), the Plenty River (270km) and Arthur Creek (322km) have excellent camp sites among colourful river red gums. The best sites in Queensland are along the Georgina River, where coolabah trees offer good shade and firewood. Roadside stops with small shade shelters, wood-burning barbecues and water tanks are at the turn-offs to Jervois homestead and Urandangi.

ALTERNATIVE TRANSPORT
Air

Boulia is serviced each Saturday by Airlines of SA (☎ 08-8642 3100) on its mail run from Port Augusta in South Australia. The one-way fare costs $330. Macair (☎ 07-4729 9444) flies Mt Isa–Boulia on Monday and Thursday for $103 and Birdsville-Boulia on Tuesday and Friday for $202. Book through Qantas (☎ 13 13 13).

Bus

Down Under Tours (☎ 1800 079 119, 07-4035 5566, W www.desertventurer.com.au) includes Boulia and the Plenty Hwy on its thrice-weekly return runs from Cairns to Alice Springs. The one-way fare is $298 plus $50 for meals.

Sandover Highway

Highlights

- Experiencing remote travel on one of central Australia's loneliest roads
- Fishing for yellow belly in a Georgina River waterhole

Leaving the Plenty Hwy 96km from Alice Springs, the Sandover Hwy heads north-east across flat semi-desert for 552km and terminates at Lake Nash homestead, near the Queensland border. Named after the Sandover River, which it generally follows for about 250km, this wide ribbon of red dirt is an adventurous short cut between central Australia and north-western Queensland.

The Sandover Hwy offers a memorable if monotonous experience in remote touring. For almost the entire distance the only signs of human achievement are occasional communication towers, signposted turn-offs to a handful of isolated homesteads and Aboriginal communities, and the road stretching endlessly ahead. There's often light traffic as far as the Ammaroo turn-off, 217km from the Plenty Hwy, but beyond that it's a novelty to see another vehicle.

Prolonged heavy rain causes flooding that can keep the highway closed for days. In the late 1980s it was out to all traffic for several months after long sections were washed away in a terrific deluge. Although often rough, the road when dry is normally suitable for conventional vehicles with high ground clearance and heavy-duty suspension. However, it's definitely not recommended for caravans.

While tourist facilities are non-existent along the road, you can buy supplies and fuel at the Arlparra Store (249km from Alice Springs) and the Alpurrurulam Store (643km).

History

For most of its distance the Sandover Hwy crosses the traditional lands of the Alyawarra people, whose lives until recent times focused on the relatively rich environment of the Sandover River. White people arrived in the 1880s, when Lake Nash and Argadargada stations, near the Queensland border, were established for grazing. The country to the south-west wasn't permanently settled by Europeans until 40 years later; Ooratippra station wasn't taken up until the late 1940s.

As elsewhere in the outback, the loss of food resources and the fouling of precious water supplies by cattle caused bloody conflicts between pastoralists and Aborigines. The so-called Sandover Massacre of the 1920s resulted in the deaths of about 100 Alyawarra, either shot or poisoned as punishment for spearing cattle.

Atartinga station, about 75km from the Plenty Hwy, was taken up by RH (Bob) Purvis, father of the present owner, in 1920. Known as the Sandover Alligator because of his amazing appetite, RH was contracted in the late 1920s to sink wells along the newly gazetted Sandover Stock Route. This was intended to link far western Queensland stations with the Alice Springs rail-head. However, the water table's increasing depth caused the project to be abandoned near the halfway point. RH's last well, near present-day Ammaroo homestead, struck water at 80m. However this was far too deep for the simple windlasses that they used to raise water in those days.

The stock route was continued from Ammaroo through to Lake Nash after the 1940s, when heavy drilling equipment became readily available in central Australia. This meant that bores could be sunk at regular intervals regardless of depth. Nevertheless, the Sandover Hwy was, for the most part, little more than a bush track until the 1970s, when it was upgraded to a standard suitable for road trains.

Information

Radio Frequencies For most of the way you can call the Alice Springs RFDS base (call sign VJD; ☎ 08-8952 1033), which monitors 5410kHz and 6950kHz between 7.30am and 5pm weekdays. Use 2020kHz (best at night) and 5410kHz for after-hours emergency calls.

Nearer Lake Nash try the RFDS in Mt Isa (call sign VJI; ☎ 07-4743 2800) on 5110kHz and 6965kHz between 8am and 5pm weekdays. Use 2020kHz (best at night) and 5110kHz for after-hours emergency calls.

Maps There are no useful touring maps of the Sandover Hwy and its alternative routes at the Queensland end. The AANT's *Northern Territory* map is the most accurate of those available, but it's at a very small scale.

Road Reports The Road Report Hotline (☎ 1800 246 199) will tell you whether or not the highway is open to traffic. For more detail contact the Arlparra Store (☎ 08-8956 9910) and the Alpurrurulam council office (☎ 07-4748 4800).

Broken Down

I was about 50km past Ammaroo en route to Lake Nash when the engine cut out. I noticed a smell of burning, and a glance at the gauges showed the temperature in the red. With a sinking heart I opened the bonnet. My worst fears were realised: the radiator cap had come off and the radiator had boiled dry. I was carrying a spare cap, but my concern was that the engine might have overheated to the point where it was seriously damaged.

It took the engine over an hour to cool down sufficiently for me to refill the radiator. In the meantime I looked around at the stunted scrub, which offered little shade and no hope of water. The day was very hot, around 43°C, and utterly still, the only sound the incessant buzzing of flies. I hadn't seen another vehicle since the Arlparra Store, over 100km back, and no-one came along while I was stopped.

The Sandover Hwy is a very lonely road in summer, and although I had plenty of water, the silence and emptiness of the landscape caused my imagination to work overtime. You can appreciate my immense relief when I finally turned the ignition key and the engine, after coughing a bit, ran as sweetly as before.

Denis O'Byrne

Emergency In the event of a medical emergency, you can obtain assistance at the Urapuntja Health Centre (to the north of the road, 21km past the Arlparra Store), and at health clinics at the Ampilatwatja and Alpurrurulam Aboriginal communities. Homesteads en route have RFDS medical kits and telephones.

THE ROUTE
Plenty Highway to Ammaroo (217km)

Turning off the Plenty Hwy 26km from the Stuart Hwy, the Sandover crosses a vast plain virtually all the way to the Ammaroo turn-off. Indeed, the landscape is generally so flat that some low granite outcrops about 10km past the Atartinga turn-off become objects of great interest – the highest offers quite a nice view, so it's worth stopping to stretch. The road passes occasional attractive patches of shady white-barked gums, but the most common vegetation types are mulga woodland (on clay soils) and low mallee and spinifex (on sandy areas).

This is marginal cattle country – only about 25% of the area of the average station en route is useful grazing land, which explains why they're so huge. For example, Atartinga covers 2240 sq km but its 1200-head herd is concentrated on about 600 sq km. In semi-desert spinifex areas, a typical 10 sq km will support billions of termites but only one cow.

At 127km from the Plenty Hwy, cross the western boundary fence of the Aboriginal-owned **Utopia** station. The station is home to about 700 Alyawarra people, who live in 23 small outstations scattered over an area of 2500 sq km. These are governed by a council based at **Arlparra**, which you pass 27km further on. The fence 23km past Arlparra marks the boundary between Utopia and Ammaroo stations. Generally, the minor roads that turn off between the two fences lead to Aboriginal communities and are off-limits to the travelling public.

Ammaroo to Lake Nash (335km)

Past Ammaroo the country soon becomes undulating, with ˙ stony rises that give sweeping views over an ocean of grey-green scrub. This is the southern end of the **Davenport Range**, which sweeps north-west for 200km to the Devil's Marbles, south of Tennant Creek. At this point the **Sandover River** is 5km to the south. It's an extremely scenic watercourse, with attractive gums and a white sandy bed, but is only rarely visible from the highway.

About 60km further on you come to a red sandy plain covered by low mallee and spinifex, a scene that takes you almost all the way to Lake Nash. The main variation in plant communities occurs about 200km past Ammaroo, where you cross an outlier of the vast native grasslands of the Barkly Tableland to the north.

As elsewhere, this island of Mitchell grass grows on black clay, more commonly known as blacksoil. Blacksoil roads are typically hard as a rock when dry and incredibly sloppy when wet – it takes only a light shower to turn this short section of the Sandover Hwy into a skating rink. Mitchell grasslands form the arid zone's most productive cattle country – they cover only about 10% of the Northern Territory, yet carry up to 50% of its entire cattle herd.

More blacksoil and Mitchell grass appears 317km past Ammaroo, then the glittering iron roofs of the **Alpurrurulam** Aboriginal community come into view on the left. The end of the highway is just five minutes away, at **Lake Nash** homestead.

Largest of the Sandover's cattle stations, Lake Nash covers 13,000 sq km and carries, on average, 41,000 high-quality beef cattle. Everything about Lake Nash is big: it has the world's largest commercial herd of Santa Gertrudis, the property's bore runs are so long that the vehicles assigned to them travel a total of 96,000km per year, and the average paddock covers several hundred square kilometres. The workforce of around 30 people is also huge by local standards.

ALTERNATIVE ROUTES
The Sandover Hwy ends at Lake Nash homestead, and there's a choice of three routes beyond there: north to Camooweal, east to Mt Isa or south to Urandangi. All are classed as

minor dirt roads and their have blacksoil sections make them impassable after rain.

Caution must be exercised here, as sign-posting is poor throughout and available maps seldom show the roads' true positions. If in doubt, the best approach is to fill up with fuel at Alpurrurulam and ask for directions and an update on road conditions.

Lake Nash to Camooweal (183km)
The best route is via **Austral Downs** homestead, as it's a much better road than the alternative route further east via Barkly Downs. The former turns off the Sandover Hwy 13km before Lake Nash and heads mainly north over a vast grassy plain. Cross the **Ranken River** – where there's good shade for a meal break – and pass Austral Downs at the halfway mark. The road meets the Barkly Hwy 43km west of Camooweal.

Although very small, Camooweal township offers a wide range of services such as fuel sales, mechanical repairs, a general store, post office, police station and health clinic. There's a tourist information centre (☎ 07-4748 2022) in the main street (the Barkly Hwy).

Post Office Hotel (☎ 07-4748 2124, *Barkly Hwy*) Single/double pub rooms $30/45, single/double motel rooms $60/70. All rooms have air-con and the pub offers breakfast, lunch and dinner.

Lake Nash to Mt Isa (205km)
From Lake Nash, this route crosses the Georgina River and heads north-east to meet the Camooweal-Urandangi road at about 65km. Veer left towards Barkly Downs and Camooweal at this point. After about 10km you come to a series of three rough creek crossings, where you turn right onto the Old May Downs Rd. The turn-off is on a rise just past the third creek and, with no sign, is easy to miss. (Straight ahead leads to the Barkly Downs homestead.)

From here it's a straightforward run of about 70km, past windmills and the **Old May Downs** homestead ruins, to meet the Barkly Hwy about 60km out from Mt Isa. This final section is relatively scenic thanks to the stark red ridges that typify the Mt Isa area.

A major regional centre, Mt Isa is home to one of Australia's largest mining companies and has a population exceeding 20,000. Contact the Riversleigh Fossils Interpretive Centre & Mt Isa Tourist Information Office (☎ 07-4749 1555, ℮ riversleigh@mountisa .qld.gov.au, www.riversleigh.qld.gov.au, 19 Marian St) for details on local services, amenities and points of interest.

Lake Nash to Urandangi (172km)
The main route heads north-east from Lake Nash, meeting the road from Camooweal to Urandangi at the 65km mark. Turn right here and drive south for 69km to **Headingly** homestead, where you go around the southern end of the airstrip, keeping the buildings on your right, and head through the gate.

The road is wide and dusty through low gidgee scrub for the final 38km from Headingly to Urandangi. For details on this tiny outpost see the Plenty Highway section.

FACILITIES
Arlparra
Arlparra Store (☎ 08-8956 9910) Open 9am-12.30pm & 1.30pm-5pm Mon-Fri, 9am-noon Sat. This remote store mainly serves the Aboriginal communities of Utopia station. It sells diesel, super and unleaded fuel and has a well-stocked *minimarket* with all basic food requirements. You can also buy hardware items, tools and vehicle parts.

Alpurrurulam
Alpurrurulam Community Store (☎ 07-4748 4860) Open 8am-11am & 3pm-5pm Mon-Fri, 8am-11am Sat. The store has similar stock to the Arlparra Store. Nearby is a service station (open 8am to 4pm weekdays) selling all fuel types, and which can attend to minor repairs – ask at the council office next to the store. Although you're welcome to use these facilities, do not proceed further into the community without permission.

Bush Camping
Good camp sites near the highway are few and far between, particularly past Ammaroo.

There are roadside stops with small shade shelters, barbecues and water tanks at the Ammaroo turn-off and about 30km before Lake Nash. As night traffic is virtually nonexistent, you're unlikely to be disturbed.

Finke & Old Andado Tracks

Enthusiasts will find the area covered by the Finke and Old Andado Tracks to be full of interest. The country is varied, with much of it dominated by the red sand dunes of the western Simpson. In early spring, after good rains, the whole area can be ablaze with wildflowers.

A number of tracks offer various options: You can do the two main tracks as a loop from Alice Springs, and it's also worth dipping down into South Australia to visit the Dalhousie Hot Springs in Witjira National Park.

The Old Andado Track heads through the Simpson Desert to link the Alice with Old Andado homestead, on the desert's western side. The homestead is a fascinating spot; a visit with its owner, Molly Clark, is a step back into the pioneering days.

The Finke Track (the first part of which is the Old South Rd) follows the route of the old *Ghan* railway (now dismantled) between Alice Springs and the Aboriginal settlement of Finke (Aputula).

The Old Andado Track can usually be negotiated with care by 2WD vehicles with good ground clearance. However, if you want to head along the old *Ghan* line, or continue on to Dalhousie or Oodnadatta, then a well-prepared 4WD is required.

History

Archaeological evidence suggests that Aboriginal occupation of this area dates back at least 40,000 years. These days there are Aboriginal communities at Ltyentye Apurte (Santa Teresa) and Finke (Aputula).

European exploration into the area started in the 1860s with the indefatigable explorer John McDouall Stuart, who passed this way on his travels to and from the north. His route was later followed by the Overland Telegraph Line. See the Oodnadatta Track section later in this chapter for more on Stuart and the Telegraph Line.

The next major development was the railway line construction between Port Augusta and Alice Springs, which made it as far as Oodnadatta in 1889. For the next 40 years supplies were carted by camel from the railhead there to outlying districts and Alice Springs. It eventually reached Alice Springs in 1929, but closed in 1980 when a new line was constructed some distance to the west.

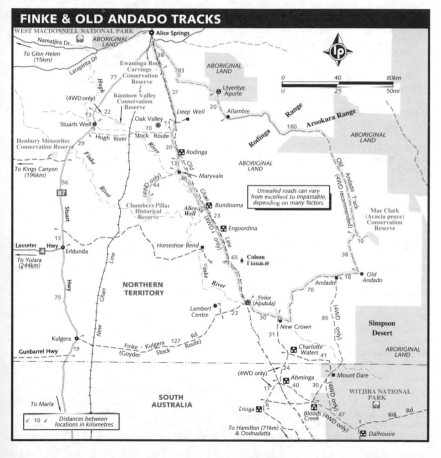

FINKE & OLD ANDADO TRACKS

Pastoral activity followed the opening up of the area that the Overland Telegraph Line brought. By early last century most of the suitable country was taken up with pastoral leases.

Information

Permits are not required to travel on any of the tracks listed below. However, if travelling on to Witjira National Park, permits must be obtained. The best place to buy one is at Mt Dare homestead; they are also available from the Pink Roadhouse in Oodnadatta if you are coming from the south.

This area is serviced by the Alice Springs RFDS base (call sign VJD; ☎ 08-8952 1033), which monitors 5410kHz and 6950kHz between 7.30am to 5pm weekdays. Use 2020kHz (best at night) and 5410kHz for after-hours emergency calls.

The best map of the area is once again the excellent Westprint series, this time the *Alice Springs–Oodnadatta* sheet. It is available from several outlets in Alice Springs, including CATIA (☎ 08-8952 5800).

THE ROUTE
Alice Springs to Finke (Aputula; 239km)

Heading south from Alice Springs along the Stuart Hwy it's 12km to the **Old South Rd**, where you turn off towards Ewaninga and Chambers Pillar. This unsealed route is generally fairly rough, with an abundance of bulldust holes and wash-outs.

After another 22km you pass the turn-off to **Ewaninga Rail Siding**. The railway from here to MacDonnell Siding is still intact and maintained by the Ghan Preservation Society. The old *Ghan* train makes regular trips along this section of line (see Things to See in the Alice Springs section earlier).

Just south of Ewaninga is the **Ewaninga Rock Carvings Conservation Reserve**, a small reserve that protects a number of Aboriginal rock peckings (or petroglyphs) carved into the smooth sandstone rocks. The peckings, which include concentric circles and animal tracks, are believed to date from between 5000 and 1000 years ago. There's a walking trail with interpretive signs,

barbecues and pit toilets. Bring your own firewood.

From Ewaninga the Old South Rd continues south for 37km to the **Deep Well** station turn-off, then it's a further 11km to the **Hugh River Stock Route**. This dirt road turns off just before the Maryvale station boundary fence and heads west for 70km to the Stuart Hwy. It's a good alternative access point to the Finke Track if you are coming from Kings Canyon or Uluru, or you can use it to make a good day-trip loop from Alice Springs, visiting Rainbow Valley and Ewaninga (see Alternative Routes later in this section).

The Finke Track proper turns off the Old South Rd about 20km south of the boundary fence. After 300m or so you pass the ruins of **Rodinga Siding**, one of a number of railway relics you encounter between here and Aputula. It is interesting to have a look around and get a feel for the loneliness the railway staff must have endured when posted to places such as this.

Maryvale homestead is 13km further south along the main road – keep straight on towards the homestead if you want to make the detour to **Chambers Pillar**. This trip is highly recommended (see Detours later in this section).

From Rodinga you follow the old railway line to **Bundooma Siding**, about 45km on, where whispering desert oaks surround a ruin and an elevated water tank. There are some extremely rough sections between the two sidings, so take things slowly. At Bundooma is the turn-off to **Alice Well**, the site of an early police station and now an Aboriginal outstation.

Another railway siding, **Engoordina**, is the next main feature, 23km south of Bundooma; from here it's a straightforward if slow 61km to the Finke River crossing. The track on this section at times deviates away from the old railway line. It can feel as if you are going in the complete wrong direction, but the two do eventually meet up again.

Once over the wide, sandy bed of the Finke River, it's just 4km to Aputula.

When driving along the old *Ghan* track, in many places you have the choice of actually driving on the old rail bed, or on the track alongside. While the old rail bed is obviously level and pretty straight, it is horribly corrugated; often you have to drive at a reckless speed to 'float' over the corrugations. You also have to concentrate like crazy and it just doesn't seem worth the effort.

The side track, on the other hand, varies from reasonable to sandy. In some places it has the most amazing corrugations, which must be at least 50cm deep and 1m long! Imagine a Matchbox car travelling over a sheet of corrugated iron and you'll get the picture! Obviously it's very slow going.

It's worth noting that the entire Alice Springs–Aputula route is closed over the Queen's Birthday weekend each year to allow the running of the **Finke Desert Race**. This major national event for off-road motor bikes and vehicles is the main cause of those huge corrugations.

Finke (Aputula) This small town started life as a railway siding and grew to have a European population of about 60. With the opening of the new *Ghan* line further west, administration of the town was taken over by the Aputula Aboriginal Corporation. These days the population of around 200 is almost entirely Indigenous. There's a store here (see Facilities later).

Aputula is linked to the Stuart Hwy, 150km to the west, by an often rough dirt road sometimes known as the Goyder Stock Route. It's a fairly dull stretch of road, although the Lambert Centre is an interesting curiosity (see Alternative Routes later).

Finke to Old Andado (118km)

From Finke, the road heads east along Goyder Creek, a tributary of the Finke River. After 30km you arrive at **New Crown** homestead (see Facilities later in this section). From here there are two choices: south to Charlotte Waters, Abminga and eventually Oodnadatta (with a possible detour to Dalhousie Springs; see Alternative Routes), or north and east to Andado and Old Andado.

Shortly after leaving New Crown, the road once again crosses the Finke River and then swings north for the 70km run to Andado

station. This stretch passes through some beautiful sand-dune country that is ablaze with wildflowers after good rains. For much of the way the track runs along the valleys between the sand dunes, but every now and then it swings up and over a dune to the next valley. While the road is generally in good condition, beware of speeding and keep well to the left when crossing the dune crests.

At **Andado** homestead, which has no tourist facilities, you are confronted with yet another choice: south along a sandy but very pretty and well-defined 4WD track to Mt Dare (85km; see Alternative Routes below), or east to Old Andado, the original homestead of Andado station. At over 10,000 sq km, Andado is the third-largest station in the Territory.

The 18km track to the **Old Andado** homestead (☎ 08-8956 0812, 8952 4034; admission $2) is often in a bad way – it's a private road that is rarely graded. It's quite sandy in places and requires a good deal of concentration if you want to maintain enough speed to get over the corrugations without the fillings in your teeth coming loose. Mercifully, it's only a short distance.

The homestead, the easternmost habitation on the western side of the Simpson Desert, is situated in a pretty valley between two huge lines of dunes. It's run as a tourist facility by the no-nonsense Molly Clark, one of the Centre's great battlers.

The Andado pastoral lease was first taken up by Robert McDill in 1909, who built the bush timber and corrugated-iron homestead in 1922. In 1955, Molly and husband, Mac, took up the management of the station from the 'new' homestead, 18km to the west. Pastoral activity on the edge of the desert is an even more marginal activity than elsewhere. When Mac and their eldest son died, and Molly was forced to clear the land entirely of stock for three years as part of the government brucellosis-eradication program, there seemed little future in it.

Despite these enormous setbacks, Molly Clark struggled on and eventually sold the property, while keeping the old homestead to run as a small-scale tourist operation. Today, visitors can camp or stay in dongas,

THE CENTRAL DESERTS

and eat meals cooked in the old homestead kitchen on a vintage combustion wood stove. Molly, now in her 80s but still going strong, does all the work around the place herself, and so needs advance warning of guests – don't expect much of a welcome if you just rock up unannounced (see Facilities later in this section).

Old Andado to Alice Springs (321km)

At Old Andado the track swings north for the 321km trip to the Alice. It takes around five hours to do in one hit, but it's worth stopping at the Mac Clark Conservation Reserve along the way. The majority of the route, pioneered by the Clarks and now generally known as the Old Andado Track, runs between two lines of dunes and is not difficult to negotiate.

Thirty-eight kilometres north of Old Andado a signposted track heads eastwards for 10km to the 30-sq-km **Mac Clark (Acacia peuce) Conservation Reserve**. The reserve, which is on a vast gravel plain, protects a large stand of tall waddy trees, a rare and unusual species found in only three places in the world: near Boulia and Birdsville in Queensland, and here on the western edge of the Simpson Desert. The trees survive in an environment where little else can – the average annual rainfall is just 150mm and summer daytime temperatures of 40°C are the norm rather than the exception.

Continuing past the reserve's turn-off, the track leaves the gravel plain and heads northward through sand-dune country, looping away to the west around the Arookara and Rodinga ranges, before arriving at **Allambie** homestead, 218km from Old Andado.

It's a further 20km to the Aboriginal community, **Ltyentye Apurte (Santa Teresa)**. A Catholic mission station was established here in the 1950s. A permit is not required to transit straight through, but visits to the community must be arranged in advance at the council office (☎ 08-8956 0999).

The community's *art centre (☎ 08-8956 0956)* produces some excellent work, such as acrylics on canvas, hand-painted silks and ceramics, and decorated wooden objects.

Tall Trees in the Desert

Waddy *(Acacia peuce)* grows very slowly to a height of up to 17m, and can live up to 500 years. Named after the Aboriginal fighting clubs that are said to have been made from its wood, the species has long, needle-like foliage that offers little shade. It's these leaves that are the key to the tree's survival: They suffer little moisture loss, as only a small surface of each leaf is exposed to the sun and wind. The adult trees have a spreading form similar to casuarinas, or she-oaks, while young trees are far more columnar.

The wood of *A. peuce* is extremely hard (it's next to impossible to drive a nail into) and very resistant to termites. Many trees were felled and used for fence and stockyard posts early this century. Fortunately, however, the species's rarity has been recognised and such activity is now discouraged. The reserve near Old Andado – named after the late Mac Clark, who had a great interest in protecting the trees – is one measure aimed at ensuring its survival.

Ring the centre if you'd like to arrange a visit to its workshop and gallery.

From Ltyentye Apurte it's about 82km to Alice Springs. The road is generally pretty rough and dusty from the community to the Alice Springs airport, 15km from town, where the bitumen is a welcome relief.

DETOURS
Chambers Pillar Historical Reserve

Chambers Pillar is a huge finger of sandstone that towers nearly 60m above the surrounding plain. The sandstone beds that form the pillar were formed over 350 million years ago, and subsequent erosion has left the pillar in its present form.

In the past it was an important landmark, first for European explorers and, later, for travellers heading north to Alice Springs from the railhead at Oodnadatta. In 1860, on his first attempt to cross the continent, Stuart was the first explorer to visit the pillar. He named it after James Chambers who, like Finke, was one of Stuart's Adelaide backers. Subsequent visitors included John Ross in 1870, who was on an expedition to determine the future route of the Overland Telegraph Line, and Ernest Giles, who, in 1872, passed the pillar while attempting to cross to the western coast of Australia.

Many of these early visitors carved their names into the rock, leaving a permanent reminder of their visit. This has given the pillar an interesting historical aspect. Unfortunately, however, many less-worthy graffiti artists have added to the gallery in recent times, at the same time defacing much of the historical significance. (Just in case you feel like immortalising yourself in stone, be warned that doing so will cost you a fine of up to $5000.)

Chambers Pillar also has great significance for Aboriginal people. It's said that the powerful gecko ancestor, Itirkawara, killed some of his ancestors and took a girl of the wrong skin group. They were banished to the desert where both turned to stone – Itirkawara became the pillar and the girl became **Castle Rock**, about 500m away.

The 4WD track to the pillar is signposted at Maryvale homestead, and is fairly straightforward throughout. You cross the Hugh River's wide sandy bed at 6km, then it's often slow going – mainly because of wash-outs – to the Idracowra boundary fence at about 33km. Here the track swings left (south) and climbs to the top of a high rocky ridge, from where you can see Chambers Pillar on the southern horizon. The track descends to the sand plain after 300m or so, and the final 10km are over red dunes.

Note that despite the existence of other station tracks in the area, the route described is the only public access to the pillar.

Chambers Pillar Camping Ground Camp sites $3.30/1.65/7.70 per adult/child/family. The camping area is in an attractive grove of desert oaks with a nice view of nearby Castle Rock. Facilities include an information board, wood-burning barbecues, picnic tables and long-drop dunnies. There is no water and firewood should be brought in from outside the reserve.

ALTERNATIVE ROUTES
Alice Springs to Old South Road via Rainbow Valley (217km)

The alternative to heading straight for the Finke Track and Chambers Pillar is to travel south along the Stuart Hwy, then head east along the Hugh River Stock Route to the Old South Rd. The main advantage of taking this route is that it allows you to visit the **Rainbow Valley Conservation Reserve** en route.

The turn-off to Rainbow Valley is 77km south of Alice Springs. From here it's 22km along a corrugated road (recommended 4WD only) to the park boundary, then another 2km to the carpark and camping area.

Just a short walk from here is a colourful cliff on the edge of a small claypan. Red, orange and yellow are dominant, and late in the day in winter there are some spectacular light effects. The darker colours are caused by iron-oxide staining, while in the lighter parts iron oxide has been leached out to a greater or lesser extent. You should get some stunning photos if you're lucky enough to visit when the claypans are full of water.

Rainbow Valley Camping Ground Camp sites $3.30/1.65/7.70 per adult/child/family. The camping area is rather small and cramped, but is close to the main attraction. Facilities include an information board, wood-burning barbecues, picnic tables and long-drop dunnies. There is no shade, and water and firewood must be brought in.

Back on the Stuart Hwy it's 13km to **Stuarts Well**, where there are camel rides, a garage and a *roadhouse* (meals, rooms, camp sites, tours and fuel sales).

From Stuarts Well it's a further 9km south along the highway to the **Hugh River Stock Route**, which heads east for 70km to the Old South Rd. This is generally in reasonable condition, although it's not as well maintained east of the Hugh River crossing about halfway along.

Oak Valley Camping Ground (☎ 08-8956 0959) Camp sites $9 per person. Owned and managed by local Aboriginal people, this camping ground is 10km west of the Old South Rd intersection and about 2km north of the stock route. It's a pleasant spot among desert oaks with shade shelters, showers, toilets and wood-burning barbecues (firewood supplied).

Finke (Aputula) to the Stuart Highway (150km)

The other option from Aputula is to head due west along the road to Kulgera, 150km away on the Stuart Hwy.

The only highlight worth mentioning along this route is the **Lambert Centre**. If you can imagine picking Australia up by the one point where it would balance (ie, the centre of gravity), this is it. Yippee! A team from the Queensland University spent two years doing computer calculations to come up with the exact spot. Exactly why they would want to do so is unclear. For those of you who like precision, the centre is at latitude 25°36'36.4"S and longitude 134°21'17.3"E.

The signposted turn-off is 23km west of Aputula. From the main road, you head 6.5km north along a well-defined track, passing Mulga Bore on the left. It's a further 8km west to the spot, which is marked by a replica of the flagpole atop Parliament House in Canberra!

It was named the Lambert Centre after Bruce Lambert, a surveyor and the first head of the National Mapping Council.

Charlotte Waters & Mt Dare Loop (240km)

While it's possible to travel direct between Aputula and Old Andado, it's much more interesting to head south from New Crown and loop around to Andado homestead by going through Charlotte Waters, Abminga, Bloods Creek and Mt Dare. This 4WD loop also gives access to the Dalhousie Mound Springs and the trans-Simpson Rig Rd (see the Simpson Desert section for details on Dalhousie and crossing the Simpson).

From New Crown, a normally good road heads due south to the remains of the 1870s **Charlotte Waters Telegraph Station**, 31km away and just shy of the South Australian border. The site was demolished many years ago to provide building materials for New Crown homestead.

At Charlotte Waters the choice is to head either east on the main road to Mt Dare

(41km), or continue south on the 4WD track to **Abminga Railway Siding** (24km).

The track forks at Abminga, the right taking you south to Oodnadatta via the ruin of **Eringa** homestead (23km), with its huge, picturesque billabong. The left fork heads direct to the site of **Bloods Creek** homestead, 40km to the south-east. Today, a windmill is all that marks the site of what was an important camping spot for workers on the Overland Telegraph Line. The strategic location meant that the site continued to be used after the line was finished; eventually a pub and store opened up.

It was from Bloods Creek homestead that the bushman Ted Colson and his Aboriginal companion set off on their camels to make the first successful crossing of the Simpson to Birdsville and back in 1936.

At the Bloods Creek windmill either continue south-east for the 47km run to **Dalhousie Mound Springs**, or head north-east to Mt Dare homestead, 30km away in **Witjira National Park**. Mt Dare offers a range of tourist facilities (see the Simpson Desert section later in this chapter).

From Mt Dare a road heads north and then west to Charlotte Waters (41km), or you can take the much more interesting route direct to Andado homestead. The latter crosses into the Northern Territory after 14km, and for the next 17km meanders about on the Finke River flood plain. This section is quite heavily treed and horrendously dusty; at the time of writing it was not being maintained.

Once off the flood plain the track heads on to Andado station, 54km away, passing at first through high sand dunes then through wide-open gravel plains to the homestead.

ORGANISED TOURS

A couple of outfits in Alice Springs run organised tours in this area.

Oak Valley Day Tours (☎ 08-8956 0959) This Aboriginal-owned and run organisation offers a tour at Oak Valley that takes in rock art, fossils and bush tucker (adult/child $19/10). They also have a day tour ($140/80) that takes in Ewaninga, Oak Valley and

Rainbow Valley, as well as 4WD charters of a day or longer.

The Outback Experience (☎ 08-8953 2666, ℮ 4wdtours@outbackexperience .com.au, Ⓦ www.outbackexperience.com.au) This long-established operator runs a day tour ($148) from Alice Springs to Chambers Pillar and Rainbow Valley.

FACILITIES
Maryvale
Maryvale Store (☎ 08-8956 0989) Open 9am-5pm daily including most public holidays. This small shop at Maryvale homestead sells refreshments, basic provisions and fuel (diesel, super, unleaded), as well as arts and crafts produced by the nearby Titjikala Aboriginal community. The shop has Eftpos and also accepts Mastercard, Bankcard and Visa.

Finke (Aputula)
Aputula Community Store (☎ 08-8956 0968) Open 9am-11.30am & 1.30pm-4.30pm Mon-Fri, 8.30am-11.30am Sat. The store sells grocery lines and refreshments.

Fuel (super, unleaded, diesel) is available during the same hours as the store, and basic mechanical repairs can be attended to.

New Crown Station
New Crown homestead (☎ 08-8956 0969) The road from Aputula to Andado passes right by the New Crown homestead. Even if you're not stopping, slow down enough so as not to shower the place in dust.

Fuel sales (diesel, unleaded) during daylight hours is the only service offered to travellers. Credit cards are not accepted.

Andado Station
Old Andado homestead (☎ 08-8956 0812) Camp sites $14. The camping area has showers and toilets, but little shade. There's reasonably priced twin accommodation in dongas, and you can get meals – rates are available on request and booking in advance is essential.

Note that there are no fuel sales or vehicle repairs, and credit cards are not accepted. There's an airstrip near the homestead.

Simpson Desert

Recognised as one of the world's most outstanding examples of a sand-ridge desert, the Simpson Desert sprawls across more than 150,000 sq km at the junction of the Northern Territory, Queensland and South Australian borders.

The desert's most obvious characteristic is its remarkable system of parallel dunes, which rise to 40m and stretch without a break for up to 200km. Their direction maintained by the prevailing winds, the dunes run south-south-east to north-north-west. They are made up of sand blown in from the flood plains and lakes that border the desert's eastern and southern margins.

There are 11 major dune systems and nine minor ones, each with its own characteristics – such as a specific dune height, length and width, crest shape, vegetation and the nature of the valleys between the dunes.

It receives an extremely unreliable average rainfall of only 130mm per year but the Simpson Desert is by no means ecologically boring. Sand ridges aside, it has a number of habitat types, including spinifex and gidgee woodlands, and coolabah floodouts. Collectively these are home to 800 plant species, and over 180 bird, 24 native mammal and probably 90 or more reptile species. In a good season the desert is an exciting place for wildlife enthusiasts.

One of Australia's last great wilderness areas, the desert was occupied by Aborigines until 1900 and was not crossed by a non-Aboriginal person until 1936. Only recently have tourists arrived, using the tracks that oil explorers carved through the desert during the 1960s. Several of these have since become popular 4WD routes, attracting increasing numbers of adventure travellers. Some are seeking a challenge, others spiritual refreshment in the endless horizons and awesome sense of solitude.

The recreation boom and a new awareness of the desert's fragility and unique values have led to the declaration of several conservation areas over most of South Australia's portion of the desert: Witjira National Park (7769 sq km) centres on Dalhousie Springs in the west, while the combined Simpson Desert Regional Reserve (29,640 sq km) and Simpson Desert Conservation Park (6930 sq km) stretch from Witjira to the Diamantina River on the desert's eastern flank. The Simpson Desert National Park (5550 sq km) occupies the south-western corner of Queensland. All these areas are crossed by one or more of the routes described below.

Before setting out on a Simpson Desert crossing, it's wise to reflect that in recent times several foolhardy travellers have paid the ultimate penalty for failing to prepare for its dangers. The hazards include great heat, lack of water and extreme isolation from human habitation and any facilities. Desert travel is not recommended from October to April, when shade temperatures in excess of 40°C are common.

History

In 1845 Charles Sturt was attempting to prove the existence of an inland sea when he became the first white person to visit the Simpson Desert. Crossing Sturts Stony Desert with a small party on horseback, he followed Eyre Creek (which he named) and struck westwards into the desert. On 14 August, at latitude 24.7°S, near the present border between Queensland and the Northern Territory, he was forced back by the waterless red ocean of sand ridges that stretched before him. Sturt wrote in his journal:

Grass had entirely disappeared and the horses wound about working their way through the pointed spinifex with which the ground was universally covered. Ascending one of the sand

ridges I saw a numberless succession of these terrific objects rising above each other to the east and west of me. Northwards they ran away from me for more than fifteen miles, with the most undeviating straightness, as if those masses had been thrown up with the plumb and rule.

Several expeditions nibbled at the desert's fringes in later years, but the first to penetrate it to any extent was led by David Lindsay in 1886. Accompanied by a white station owner and a desert Aborigine, he took camels from Dalhousie Springs via Approdinna Attora Knolls to about latitude 25.5°S on the Queensland and Northern Territory border. Here he turned around and returned to Dalhousie. He could easily have continued but didn't bother, as the area to the east was already well known to white people.

Assisted by Aboriginal informants, Lindsay found water at several of the native wells that were scattered through the desert's southern and eastern parts. The wells, sunk to depths of 7m, were located in depressions between the sand hills and gave access to freshwater soaks. They were the focus of life for the Aboriginal groups who then lived in the desert, providing them with security in drought. After good rains had filled the claypans, the Aborigines were able to leave the wells for extended periods and thus exploit the land's resources over a much wider area.

The first white person to cross the Simpson Desert's full width was pastoralist Ted Colson. In 1936, he took camels from Bloods Creek (near Mt Dare homestead) to Birdsville. Colson and his Aboriginal companion, Peter, travelled close to the Northern Territory border throughout their journey, visiting Approdinna Attora Knolls en route. Having reached Birdsville, the two men turned around and rode back across the desert to Bloods Creek. Colson received no support for this outstanding feat, which was accomplished without fanfare; it seems that he undertook the trek purely in the spirit of adventure.

The first scientific expedition into the Simpson was mounted in 1939 under the leadership of Dr CT Madigan. With eight men and 19 camels, he travelled northward from Old Andado homestead to the junction of the Hale and Todd rivers, then east to the Queensland border, where he turned south-east to Birdsville. Between the Hale River and Eyre Creek (a distance of 326km) the party crossed 626 sand ridges, many 30m high, and gathered much valuable data.

The desert's potential for oil exploration was recognised in the early 1960s, when Dr Reg Sprigg carried out gravity surveys in the region. As part of this work, Sprigg and his family completed the first motorised crossing of the Simpson Desert. They travelled from Mt Dare to Birdsville along the Northern Territory border, using fuel and supplies carried in by light aircraft. Two years later, by which time the French Line had been bulldozed, the Spriggs made a south-north crossing from Cowarie homestead to the Plenty River. These feats signalled the beginning of the current recreation boom.

Information

Tourist Offices For tourist information of a general nature, contact the Pink Roadhouse in Oodnadatta (☎ 08-8670 7822), Mt Dare homestead (☎ 08-8670 7835) and the Wirrarri Centre (☎ 07-4656 3300), in Birdsville. For details of the Wirrarri Centre see the Birdsville Track section later.

National Parks Conservation areas in the Simpson Desert within South Australia are managed by National Parks and Wildlife SA rangers based at Port Augusta. Ring the Desert Parks Hotline (☎ 1800 816 078) for the latest on all park matters.

Rangers are based at Dalhousie Springs during the cooler months, but they can be hard to reach by telephone. Try them on ☎ 08-8670 7773, or ☎ 8670 7901 if there's no answer.

For information on the Simpson Desert National Park contact the Queensland National Parks and Wildlife Service (☎ 07-4656 3272, fax 4656 3273) in Birdsville. The office is on Billabong Blvd.

Communications Due to the extreme remoteness and harsh conditions, it's commonsense to carry an HF radio fitted with

frequencies for the RFDS bases at Alice Springs and Port Augusta.

To speak to Port Augusta RFDS base (call sign VNZ), use 8165kHz between 7am and 5pm, or 4010kHz and 6890kHz between 7am and 9pm seven days. After-hours alarm frequencies are 2020kHz (best at night) and 4010kHz. Contact the base (☎ 08-8642 2044) for more details of its services.

The Alice Springs RFDS base (call sign VJD) can be reached on 5410kHz and 6950kHz between 7.30am and 5pm Monday to Friday, excluding public holidays. For after-hours emergency calls, use 2020kHz (best at night) and 5410kHz. For more information on services, contact the base (☎ 08-8952 1033).

The police at Oodnadatta (☎ 08-8670 7805) and Birdsville (☎ 07-4656 3220) hire satellite phones to travellers venturing out into the desert. Rental costs $21 per day and you simply hand it in when you get to the other end.

Road Reports The Desert Parks Hotline can advise on road conditions as can the Mt Dare homestead.

At the time of writing, Clifton Hills station had closed the eastern end of the Rig Rd until issues of public liability could be sorted out.

Books The only worthwhile reference on the desert as a whole is *The Simpson Desert* by Mark Shephard. It covers natural history, Aboriginal life, exploration and conservation issues, as well as giving sound advice on preparing for a crossing.

The *Natural History of Dalhousie Springs*, edited by W Zeidler & WF Ponder, is a fascinating explanation of the ecology and cultural history of these artesian springs on the edge of the Simpson.

Maps The map-guide entitled *Dalhousie and Simpson Desert*, published by Westprint Heritage Maps, covers the various tracks between Mt Dare and Birdsville. It's contained in the Desert Parks Pass package.

For a more detailed coverage, you'll need the *Dalhousie*, *Poolowanna* and *Pandie*

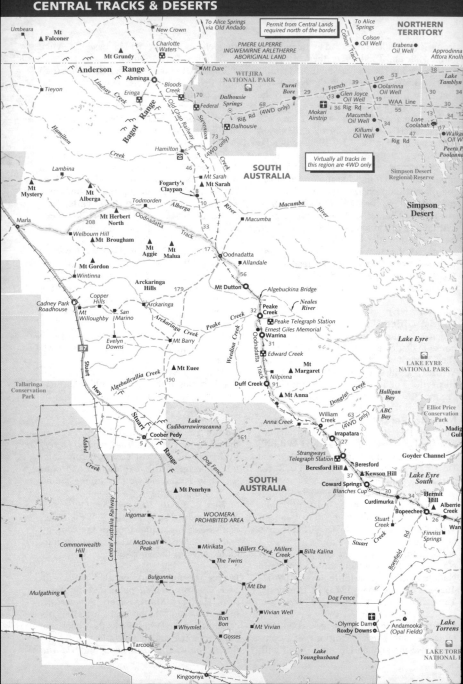

Eyre Creek
Goonamillera Crossing
To Bedourie (202km)
Diamantina River
Birdsville
Betoota
Developmental Rd
Cuddapan

Simpson Desert National Park
Flood Detour
Big Red Sandhill
28
Mt Hal
Haddon Corner
Planet Downs
Tanbar

Poeppel Well
18
Poeppel Corner
QAA Line (4WD only)
15
23
Birdsville
33
28
QUEENSLAND
Cadelga
Gilpeppee

K1 Line
Simpson Desert Conservation Park
Main Crossing Route
Pandie Pandie
Birdsville
Lake Yumma Yamma

awanna Well
102
86
Lake Uloowaranie
157
Lake
Cordillo Downs
Arrabury
Lake Pure
Durham Downs

Kuncherinna Oil Well
Inside Track (Closed when wet)
Alton Downs
Koonchera Waterhole
Page Family's Grave

Rig Rd (4WD only)
60
Goyder Lagoon
Koonchera Sandhill
94

Clifton Hills
18
19
60
Coongie Lakes
Innamincka Regional Reserve
Sturts Stony Desert
Lake Pure

8
7
11
16
27
Coongie
Kudriemitchie
106
Nappa Merrie
Karmona

Mt Gason
Mt Gason Bore
Sturts Stony Desert
Gidgealpa Oilfield
Innamincka Station
Dig Tree
28

Creek
46
Mirra Mitta Bore
Innamincka
17
Burke & Wills Bridge
Cooper Creek

Lake Howitt
Kalamurina
Cowarie
Crossing Track (4WD only)
62
47
48
Orientus

Warburton
55
36
Track closed at times check with NP & WS
Moomba
24
40
16
Bransby
Epsilon

Mungeranie Hotel
27
Lake Warrakatanna
50
69
Della Gas Field
Epsilon

Oorawillanie
13
Lake Hope
Strzelecki (4WD recommended)
10
Merty Merty
QUEENSLAND

Mulka Homestead & General Store
Tirari Desert
25
Cooper Creek
Strzelecki Regional Reserve
Old (4WD recommended)
45
Omicron
Naryilco
Mt Morris

Bethesda Mission
Ferry
12
Ferry Access only
Strzelecki Desert
Bollards Lagoon
Cameron Corner Store
Toona Gate
Warri Warri Gate

Etadunna
Cannuwaukaninna Bore
28
Lake Gregory
Strzelecki Crossing
87
15
STURT NATIONAL PARK

Muloorina
River Clayton
30
Dulkaninna
Strzelecki Creek
Lake Blanche
Cobbler
55
Strzelecki Desert
SOUTH AUSTRALIA

Lake Harry
10
Clayton
Blanchewater
Montecollina Bore
Tibooburra
Gum Vale

Frome River
12
31
Lake Harry
Marree
Mundowdna
40
21
Mt Hopeless
Lake Callabonna
Mt Poole
Depot Glen
Yandama
Milparinka

79
Murnpeowie
50
Dog Fence
Mt Hopeless
Hawker Gatehouse
NEW SOUTH WALES
Mt Shannon
Salt Lake

chelina
Farina
30
Mt Freeling Talc Mine
Unsealed roads can vary from excellent to impassable, depending on many factors.
Smithville House
Quinyambie
Lake Muck
Border Downs
Pimpara Lake

Mt Lyndhurst
76
Umberatana
North Mulga
Wooltana
Yankaninna
Arkaroola
Gammon Ranges
GAMMON RANGES NATIONAL PARK
Distances between locations in kilometres
10

Avondale Lyndhurst
Copley
Mt Serle
Flinders Ranges
Wertaloona
NANTAWARRINA ABORIGINAL LAND
Lake Frome
Lake Frome Regional Reserve
Pine Ridge
Yelka
Packsaddle Roadhouse
Nundora

Myrtle Springs
Leigh Creek South
To Port Augusta, Quorn & Lyndhurst
Broughams Gate
The Veldt
Silver City Hwy

0   25   50km
0   15   30mi

Pandie 1:250,000 topographic maps from Geoscience Australia. The QAA Line appears on the *Birdsville* sheet, while a small portion of the Rig Rd's western end lies on the *Gason* sheet.

Registration Despite the popular belief that travellers should register with the police at one end and sign off at the other, the police no longer wish to be involved in these matters. They suggest that you keep friends or relatives informed of your movements so that they can notify the authorities should you fail to report in on time. However, they're happy to provide advice, and travellers can leave messages with them for others to collect.

Permits If you're just visiting Dalhousie Springs overnight you'll need a day/night permit, which costs $18 per vehicle. However, wider travel in the Simpson Desert within South Australia requires a Desert Parks Pass ($80), which covers entry and camping fees – for details see the Travel Permits section in the Getting Around chapter.

The pass comes with a booklet that contains useful information on Witjira National Park, the Simpson Desert Regional Reserve and the Simpson Desert Conservation Park. They're available from the Pink Roadhouse in Oodnadatta, Mt Dare homestead, the ranger at Dalhousie Springs, Birdsville Fuel Services and Marree's Outback Roadhouse & General Store.

A camping permit ($3.85 per person per night) is required if you want to spend a night or two within the Simpson Desert National Park. This will mainly affect travellers intending to take the QAA Line from near Poeppel Corner east to the old rabbit fence. Permits can be obtained from the Queensland Parks and Wildlife Service ranger in Birdsville.

Emergency Birdsville has a well-equipped hospital staffed by registered nurses and doctors, but that's it. If you're heading into the desert it's wise to carry a good first-aid kit and HF radio fitted with RFDS frequencies, just in case!

Special Preparations

For the Simpson Desert driver, a lack of traffic, difficult driving conditions and remoteness from all facilities put a new emphasis on travel preparation.

For obvious reasons it's essential to carry ample drinking water – see the Survival section in the Facts for the Visitor chapter. You can fill up your containers at Mt Dare homestead and Birdsville as their water supplies are quite acceptable to all but the most sensitive stomachs. The water from Dalhousie Springs and Purni Bore is drinkable at a pinch.

Calculate fuel needs based on the distance of your chosen route, adding at least 30% for unexpected detours and the higher fuel consumption you can expect under 4WD conditions.

The French Line is particularly rough, thanks to the many inexperienced drivers who neglect to deflate their tyres to the recommended 20psi (140kPa) or less on soft surfaces. For this reason, trailers must be robust and all items should be packed to avoid breakages. Always place heavy items (such as full jerry cans) so they won't raise the vehicle's centre of gravity to dangerous levels – roof racks are not the place!

Owing to the many blind crests, the lead vehicle in each party should carry a flag (bright orange is ideal) on a long pole fixed to the bullbar. This will warn oncoming vehicles of your approach.

TRACK SUMMARY
The Rig Road

Built during the 1960s to a standard suitable for laden semi-trailers, the Rig Rd takes you right across the desert, from Mt Dare homestead to the Birdsville Track. It generally avoids the areas of higher dunes and has been sheeted with clay throughout. It is no longer maintained and is subject to guttering and drift sand, which make a 4WD essential. It is still by far the easiest route across the desert. The changing colours of its sand dunes (from tomato-red in the west to white in the south-east) and varied topography and vegetation also make it the most interesting.

The Rig Rd is lined by borrow pits where clay was extracted during its construction. These can hold water for a considerable period after heavy rain and at such times become a focus for desert wildlife.

The French Line & QAA Line
Bulldozed across the desert by the French Petroleum Company in 1963, the so-called French Line runs at right angles to the sand ridges. It was never intended to do more than provide temporary access for geological survey work. Kept open by 4WD traffic, its driving conditions are extremely difficult as it crosses literally hundreds of soft dunes – these are steepest on the eastern side, so travel in a west-to-east direction is recommended. The QAA Line was constructed in a like manner and also presents difficult conditions.

ROUTE OPTIONS
There are three major route options between Mt Dare homestead (the last resupply point on the desert's western side) and Birdsville. All tracks include clay surfaces which are closed when wet.

Via the French Line & QAA Line
This route involves a total distance of 507km, of which 275km includes soft dune crossings. The French Line is not recommended to inexperienced desert motorists.

Via the Rig Road, K1 Line & QAA Line
Covering a total distance of 696km, this route is mainly firm when dry, though 100km of it includes soft dune crossings.

Via the Rig Road & Birdsville Track
Except dune crossings, this route is mainly firm when dry and covers a total distance of 764km.

THE ROUTE
Mt Dare Homestead to Dalhousie Springs (70km)
Leaving Mt Dare, the rough, stony track to Dalhousie Springs crosses gibber uplands and sand ridges for the 44km to **Opossum Creek**, where coolabahs and gidgees make a pleasant spot to boil the billy. The creek was named after the brush-tailed possums that lived along its banks in earlier times. Sadly, this species has all but vanished from arid Australia over the past 60 years.

Eleven kilometres later and still in gibber country, you cross **Christmas Creek** with its depressing graveyard of dead trees. They died after nearby Crispe Bore, which flowed into the creek, was capped in 1987. This is one of many flowing artesian bores to have been capped in recent years following belated official awareness that the outback's major source of groundwater – the Great Artesian Basin – was being needlessly depleted. Collect firewood here if you're intending to camp at Dalhousie Springs.

Brush-tailed possum

Past Christmas Creek the track climbs up onto a barren gibber tableland 64km from Mt Dare. Here you look out over an eroded, salt-encrusted basin dotted with dense patches of tall reeds and dark scrub. These are the Dalhousie Springs, the only natural source of permanent surface water in an area as large as many European countries.

One kilometre further on is a T-junction, with the ruins of Dalhousie homestead 9km to the right and the Dalhousie Springs hot pool and camping area 4km to the left.

Dalhousie Springs Spread over an area of about 70 sq km, this group of 80 artesian springs is recognised as being of world significance because of its unique geological and biological values. The springs are so isolated from other permanent surface waters that they contain many species of aquatic fauna found nowhere else. This was one of the major reasons the surrounding 7769 sq km Witjira National Park was declared in 1985.

The main spring is a steaming oasis of deep water measuring about 150m by 50m and fringed by low paperbarks and reeds. A fantastic sight in its desolate setting, the pool attracts a large variety of wildlife, including goannas, water birds and dingoes. You can swim in the pool (great on a cold winter's morning) and there's a camping area nearby (see Facilities).

From here you can explore other springs in the area, including several – such as the one beside the old Dalhousie ruins – where the native vegetation has been choked out by date palms. The original palms probably grew from seed brought in by the Afghani camel drivers who once serviced this area.

The Rig Road – Dalhousie Springs to the French Line (97km)

Leaving the hot spring, you cross the aptly named Gluepot (a terror when wet) and pass extinct mound springs perforated with rabbit burrows. At 9km the track climbs onto a gibber tableland – these are the last gibbers you see until Big Red (near Birdsville), so make the most of them! At 20km you enter a large seasonal swamp,

where long, deep ruts tell a graphic story of what it's like to drive on when wet.

Ten kilometres later you pass some low mesas. The track now becomes sandier, with tall saltbush on either side. However, you don't enter the Simpson Desert proper for another 23km, when low sand ridges topped with cane grass appear beside the track. The dunes gradually become higher, and spinifex begins to appear on the flanks and in the swales, setting the scene for much of what follows. The distinctive large hoof prints of camels soon become apparent along the track – it's an unlucky traveller who doesn't see at least one of these animals during the crossing.

Purni Bore Cresting a sand ridge 68km from the hot springs, you arrive without warning at a large pool surrounded by luxuriant beds of reeds and bushy wattles. Clouds of steam and sulphurous smells billow from the near-boiling water that gushes from a pipe beside the track. Native hens scurry into the reeds as you approach. The tracks of camels, dingoes, donkeys, rabbits, hopping mice and many birds cover the nearby sand ridges. This is the little world of Purni Bore, an isolated wetland fed by a flowing artesian bore originally drilled in search of oil and gas. It's a beaut spot for **wildlife** enthusiasts – over 35 species of birds, including several water birds, have been sighted here. With time and patience you'll see most of them.

Unfortunately the dingoes around here haven't learned to fear people, so it's not a good idea to leave food or clothing lying around where they can get it. Near the pool is a camping area with a toilet and shower.

The Rig Road – French Line to the WBY Line (181km)

Twenty-nine kilometres past Purni Bore, the Rig Rd turns sharp right (south) at the beginning of the French Line, which spears straight ahead over a high sand ridge. After 13km of easy travel between the dunes you arrive at **Mokari airstrip**, used to service this area during the oil exploration days. The grave of Jaroslav Pecanek, an Oodnadatta identity who fell in love with the desert and asked to be buried here, lies under a low tree near the airstrip's southern end.

From Mokari you head eastwards once more across the sand ridges, with deep washouts running both along and across the road – just to make it interesting. Here the dunes are well vegetated with cane grass, spinifex and bushes, but shade is at a premium. Thirty-six kilometres from Mokari the Rig Rd turns southwards at the beginning of the **WAA Line**. This track continues due east across the dunes, meeting the **Colson Track** to Alice Springs about 2km from the intersection.

Heading south, the Rig Rd passes faint turn-offs to the Macumba and Killumi oil wells. It runs mainly in open swales before turning sharply east at 34km from the WAA Line. For the next 47km you cross low, orange dunes whose bare, scalloped crests resemble waves on a choppy sea. There is less vegetation than previously to hold the sand ridges together, and drift sand covers the dune crossings. These soft patches invariably drop sharply on their eastern side, so a careful approach is warranted. Drift sand worsens the further east you go on the Rig Rd.

Lone Gum & Eagles' Nests Eighty-one kilometres from the WAA Line, you turn north up a broad valley with scattered mulga trees, a number of which support the stick nests of wedge-tailed eagles. Some of these nests are an unbelievable size, the result of many generations of use. In winter and spring in a good season, this area used to be alive with eagles, breeding and rearing their young on the bountiful rabbit population. With the near demise of the rabbits due to calicivirus, the eagles' future is unclear.

Continuing on, you pass a lone coolabah tree growing on an area of gravel beside the road. Stunted by the harshness of its environment, the tree is an unexpected sight in its barren setting. Coolabahs are invariably confined to areas that are subject to flooding, so its presence here is a mystery. After 17km heading north, the road swings east again. At the bend, a huge eagle's nest almost covers the crown of a gnarled corkbark, making a fitting climax to this fascinating section.

From the nest, the road heads east across flatter country for 34km to the WBY Line, also called Knolls Track. This makes an ideal detour of about 40km each way to the Approdinna Attora Knolls. The final 5km on this section winds around small salt lakes, where suspension-busting gutters wait to trap the unwary motorist. At the T-junction with the WBY Line, you turn left (north) to the knolls or right (south) towards the K1 Line and the Birdsville Track.

The Rig Road – The WBY Line to the Birdsville Track (207km)

About 5km from the WBY Line you pass the **Poolawanna oil well**, which is conveniently located beside the road. It's one of six (including Purni Bore) to have been drilled in the southern Simpson Desert since the early 1960s.

For the next 40km the road wanders among low sand ridges and broad valleys, then a silent, almost coastal world of large, dazzling salt lakes and yellow dunes averaging 25m high. The bigger dunes offer extensive panoramas with Sahara-like foregrounds of bare, wind-sculpted sand – excellent vantage points for scenic photography. The dunes' paler colour indicates that the sand particles are relatively close to their source. As a grain of sand is blown further from its source the clay within it weathers, releasing iron oxide (rust) that covers the grain with a red skin.

Here the road skirts the shores of several lakes, a feature of which are eroded banks showing how sand has been deposited in layers over thousands of years. They show the classic signs of devastation by rabbits. Large areas of the Simpson have been almost denuded by these pests, but perhaps now that the rabbits have largely gone (hopefully permanently) the desert may recover.

About 90km from the WBY Line you leave the lakes and cross high dunes, where the road is covered by deep drift sand. This can be a problem, although tyre deflation will normally get you over without too much effort. Then, at 102km, you arrive at another T-junction: the K1 Line to Poeppel Corner (see Alternative Routes) and the

QAA Line are on your left (north); the Birdsville Track lies to the right.

Warburton Creek Turning south at the intersection, you almost immediately pass the turn-off to **Kuncherinna oil well**, then commence travelling down broad valleys between low dunes. At about 20km start looking for deposits of fossil bivalves and other shells, indicators of the shallow sea that once covered today's desert. Remember, the collection of fossils without a permit is illegal in South Australia.

Shortly after leaving these unusual deposits, the road enters a huge area of dead coolabahs and bare white sand. Probably killed by drought, these stark skeletons mark the northern edge of the Warburton Creek flood plain. Some trees have managed to survive, and provide the best shade since Dalhousie Springs. Drift sand now covers much of the road, making it necessary to deflate your tyres for easy progress.

At 60km from Kuncherinna oil well, the road turns abruptly north-east to parallel the main channel of Warburton Creek, which is about 8km to the east. Travelling now over blacksoil flats interspersed with coolabah channels, you reach the main creek crossing 37km further on. From here it is only 8km to the Birdsville Track, where you turn left to Birdsville or right to Marree – see the Birdsville Track section later in this chapter.

ALTERNATIVE ROUTES
The French & QAA Lines – Purni Bore to Birdsville (364km)
Leaving the Rig Rd 29km past Purni Bore, the French Line runs eastward for 175km to meet the K1 Line just past Poeppel Corner. Unlike the Rig Rd, the French Line has a natural surface, and cuts at right angles across literally hundreds of soft dunes that average 10m to 15m high. Although the crossings are straightforward when coming from the west (the usual direction of travel), the track's sandy sections have been deeply corrugated. This makes for slow, rough travelling.

The first 39km from the Rig Rd are difficult, thanks to very soft sand and high, steep ridges. Most travellers bypass this sec-

tion by taking the Rig Rd to the Colson Track, then heading 19km north to the French Line. Taking this option adds 35km to the total distance. Remember to deflate your tyres to a pressure of at least 20psi (140kPa) before entering this soft sand.

For anyone in a hurry, the French Line is a monotonous experience: As you crest each rise (and on average there are about four of these per kilometre), the view in front is of the track spearing endlessly away across an arid ocean of lesser ridges to reach the horizon at the next highest point. However, those with time to spare will find countless opportunities to soak up the desert atmosphere and discover such small attractions as wildflowers, bird life and innumerable animal tracks. Many of the valleys contain clumps of shady gidgee trees – good shelter for an overnight camp or a meal break.

Approdinna Attora Knolls About 89km past the Colson Track you cross the northern end of **Lake Tamblyn**, a typical salt lake fringed by gidgees and crowded by red dunes. Reg Sprigg once used the lake as a landing strip, flying tourists in to camp among the gidgees and to experience desert solitude.

Just past Lake Tamblyn, a turn-off on the right (the WBY Line) takes you about 8km to the Approdinna Attora Knolls. Named by Ted Colson, these two low, flat-topped hills of white gypseous rock are an important landmark in this world of sand ridges and saltpans. They also offer some of the best views in the Simpson Desert. An information sign explains that the knolls were once dunes formed of flour gypsum that later hardened to their present form.

To the south of the knolls lies **Wolporican Soak**, one of the rare permanent sources of fresh water that allowed the desert's original inhabitants to survive here. In 1886 David Lindsay found this soak, which was accessed by a well about 4m deep; on being cleaned out, it yielded 40L in an hour. Wolporican was a major habitation site for the Wang-kangurru people, who inhabited the desert's central and southern sections prior to 1900. Searching around the edge of claypans throughout the Simpson will often reveal evidence of Aboriginal occupation in the form of stone tools and grinding stones, all of which were carried in from far away. Note that the collection of such artefacts is illegal and hefty fines can result if you're caught with any in your possession.

Poeppel Corner For a change in scenery, the track cuts across the northern end of several long, narrow salt lakes in the 45km from the WBY Line to Poeppel Corner. After enduring the corrugations on the dunes, some people can't resist the temptation to go for a drive on the lakes' smooth surfaces. This is definitely not recommended: The bed may not be as hard as it looks, in which case your vehicle will become deeply bogged in saline mud.

A major objective simply because of its remoteness, the steel marker at Poeppel Corner shows the exact intersection point of the Northern Territory, Queensland and South Australian. Nearby is a replica of the original wooden marker installed in 1880 by surveyor Augustus Poeppel – he had just completed the daunting task of marking the border between South Australia and Queensland from Haddons Corner, about 300km to the east. Poeppel's corner post was a 2.1m-long piece of coolabah that he'd cut 90km away in the Mulligan River and dragged by camel to the intersection point.

Poeppel Corner to the Rabbit Fence (89km) Shortly after leaving Poeppel Corner you meet the K1 Line, which runs north-south to link the QAA Line with the Rig Rd. Turning north, the track now skirts a salt lake between the dunes, offering much easier going than the chopped-up sandy sections of the French Line. These conditions prevail for the 18km to the QAA Line, where once again you head eastwards over the dunes towards Birdsville.

Surveyed in 1979, the QAA Line crosses several salt lakes before entering the ancient flood plain of Eyre Creek. You notice an obvious improvement in the country – soft grasses begin to dominate between the sand ridges, which are higher and further apart

than those on the French Line. As a result, driving conditions are somewhat less severe, although the dune crossings are still rough.

The 66km section between the Northern Territory border, which you cross about 5km east of the K1 Line, and the rabbit fence lies within the 5500-sq-km Simpson Desert National Park.

Rabbit Fence Seventy-one kilometres from the K1 Line you pass through the remains of the great Queensland rabbit fence and enter cattle country. The fence, which once stretched for 800km, was built in the 1890s in an attempt to keep rabbits out of western Queensland; a census taken in 1890 showed 130 men working on its construction near Birdsville. It was maintained by boundary riders stationed roughly 80km apart until 1932, when they were paid off. Within 20 years much of the fence had either been buried by drifting sand, washed away in floods or corroded by salt. However, its remains are still plainly visible where it crosses the QAA Line. Here it forms the boundary between Adria Downs station and the Simpson Desert National Park.

Eyre Creek Continuing past the rabbit fence, you crest an orange-red sand ridge and find yourself looking out over a broad valley dotted with large coolabahs. This is part of Eyre Creek's present flood plain. Then, after more high dunes that separate blacksoil flats covered with trees and cane grass, you come to the creek's main channel, 15km from the fence. If the creek is flooded, you must head north on stony ground for 28km to **Goonamillera Crossing** at Dickery Waterhole, then back down along the creek to rejoin the main track. In good seasons the flood plain supports abundant birdlife, of which emus, bustards, brolgas, crested pigeons and galahs are the most obvious.

Big Red The country opens out past Eyre Creek, but then 23km later the Simpson Desert's last gasp rises in front of you as a towering wall of pale red sand: the Nappanerica Sand Dune. More commonly known as Big Red, this 40m-high monster is said to be the desert's highest. It's definitely the most difficult to drive over, although a detour 1km before the ridge goes over the same dune at a lower point. There's an information shelter on the Birdsville side, and from here it's 33km on a good road to town.

The WAA Line (85km)
There is no good reason to drive the WAA Line, which parallels the French Line, unless you want a somewhat more difficult run than that offered by the French Line. The track is little used and there are numerous steep ridges along the way, although it is generally less corrugated than the French Line.

The K1 Line (104km)
Forming a scenically attractive link between the Rig Rd and Poeppel Corner, this generally firm track runs up broad valleys between orange dunes averaging 13m high. For about 25km at its southern end, you hug the edge of a narrow salt lake; while small compared to others, it makes an impressive sight as you hurtle along at 60km/h. Extensive woodlands of gidgee, where you'll often see dingoes and camels, are another feature.

FACILITIES
Mt Dare homestead (☎ 08-8670 7835) Camp sites $12, singles/doubles $33/66. Situated in the middle of nowhere in Witjira National Park, Mt Dare homestead boasts a landing strip, public telephone, ice, a *bar*, minor mechanical and tyre repairs, and fuel sales (diesel, super, unleaded and Avgas). It's open every day, from early until late.

Accommodation in the homestead comes with shared facilities, which include a kitchen. Bookings are recommended. The camping area has shower and toilet facilities – showers cost $3 if you're not staying there.

Birdsville
See the Birdsville Track section later in this chapter for information on the facilities in Birdsville.

Airstrips
There are three airstrips – at Mt Dare, Dalhousie Springs and Mokari (on the Rig Rd). Use of the Mokari strip is permitted only in an emergency. For an update, contact the Desert Parks Hotline (☎ *1800 816 078)*.

Bush Camping
The only designated camping areas are at **Dalhousie Springs** (*seasonal ranger* ☎ *08-8670 7773, 8670 7901)* and **Purni Bore**, where facilities are limited to toilets and showers. You won't believe the bathroom block at Dalhousie – it must have cost a fortune to build way out here in the middle of nowhere. The camping ground is dusty and exposed, but only a short walk from the main hot pool. There's no shade, and firewood and drinking water must be carried in.

Past Purni Bore you'll find some good bush camp sites beside the various tracks described, though firewood and shade are often entirely lacking. The best ones are in the gidgee woodlands, and among the coolabahs on flood plain areas.

It's a good idea to carry a gas stove, and a tarpaulin or two that you can use as a shelter. A mosquito net over your bed will keep the flies out of your face first thing in the morning; you'll need a net as protection from mosquitoes around wetland areas such as Dalhousie Springs and Purni Bore.

KATE NOLAN

Emu family

Oodnadatta Track

One of Australia's most interesting outback routes, the 610km Oodnadatta Track links Marree to Marla via Oodnadatta in northern South Australia. Here, as you cross generally flat terrain of desert sand ridges and gibber plains, the sense of space is profound. There is little grand scenery, but in terms of heritage sites – both natural and cultural – it is well in front of other, more famous routes. Its many attractions include artesian mound springs, Lake Eyre National Park and numerous relics of the Overland Telegraph Line and the Great Northern Railway. If you're an enthusiast for such things, allow at least four days for the 413km drive between Marree and Oodnadatta. This section contains all the notable highlights.

Despite its name, the Oodnadatta Track is actually a fairly good road by outback standards. However, you can still expect plenty of corrugations, potholes and all the other hazards of an unsealed road, while flooded creeks can close the road for days following a big rain. Conditions are usually suitable for robust conventional vehicles with strong suspensions and good ground clearance, but a 4WD is best for some detours. Diesel, super and unleaded fuel are available at Marree, William Creek (203km), Oodnadatta (402km) and Marla (610km). LPG is sold only at Marla.

History

The track between Marree and Oodnadatta more or less follows the mound springs that form an arc from Lake Frome, through Marree and on to Dalhousie Springs. This is Australia's driest region and the springs are its major natural sources of fresh water. For Aborigines, explorers and settlers they were like stepping stones into the interior. Prior to white settlement the Aboriginal people used them as part of a major trade route that linked the Kimberley and Cape York to the southern coast via central Australia – the original Oodnadatta Track. For white settlers the springs became the focus of Australia's earliest attempts to develop the arid heart.

In 1858 South Australia's frontier was stalled about 80km east of the northern tip of Lake Torrens. What lay beyond was unknown to white people. Then, in the space of two years, the known country leapt 300km to reach the Davenport Range, about 60km north-west of Lake Eyre. This was almost entirely due to the explorations of Major Peter Edgerton Warburton (the South Australian Police Commissioner) and the Scottish surveyor John McDouall Stuart.

Warburton, who penetrated as far as Mt Margaret in the Davenports, was the first to report the existence of mound springs in the region. Stuart added substantially to these discoveries when he led two expeditions into the country west and north-west of Lake Eyre between April 1859 and January 1860. His efforts reduced the unknown by a further 150km – almost to the Macumba River, about 50km north of Oodnadatta.

Stuart was particularly impressed by the height of some of the mound springs and the amount of water flowing from them. He judged that the country would carry double if not treble the stocking rate of stations further south. However, what he didn't realise was that he'd seen the country after a succession of good rainfall years. Sadly for those who followed in his footsteps, the grim reality was an average annual rainfall of 130mm and an evaporation rate of 3600mm. Drought had reasserted itself by 1865. The grass withered, the sheep and cattle died in their thousands, and the newcomers went bankrupt.

Stuart also saw many well-used native pads, but seldom any of the people who'd made them – those he did see were usually

THE CENTRAL DESERTS

heading at top speed in the opposite direction. To them, the combination of a horse and rider must have seemed like some fearful monster straight from their worst nightmares. Once the explorers came upon an Aboriginal man hunting in the sand hills, and Stuart described the encounter thus:

What he imagined I was I do not know; but when he turned round and saw me, I never beheld a finer picture of astonishment and fear. He was a fine muscular fellow, about six feet in height, and stood as if riveted to the spot, with his mouth wide open and his eyes staring.

Stuart sent his Aboriginal guide forward to speak with the man, but didn't tell him to dismount. The terrified man stayed motionless until the awful apparition was within a few metres, whereupon he threw down his waddies and jumped up into a mulga bush. There, trembling violently on his precarious perch and with one foot only 1m from the ground, he awaited his fate. Imagine his relief when all the creature did was utter a few unintelligible sounds before walking away.

The reports of Stuart's explorations were received with great interest by the South Australian government. It was keen for Adelaide to be the ultimate destination for a proposed telegraphic link between Australia and Europe via India and Java. For this to happen, a practicable route had to be found across the unknown centre of the continent; Stuart had fuelled hopes that such a route might exist. Accordingly, the government offered a substantial reward for its discovery.

In March 1860 Stuart departed from Adelaide on what proved to be the first of three epic attempts to win the prize. He passed through the Alice Springs area, but hostile Aborigines and an acute shortage of rations forced his retreat near Tennant Creek. In January 1861 he set out again, only to be turned back by dense, waterless scrub further north, past Newcastle Waters. A final attempt brought success when, on 25 July 1862, he reached the Arafura Sea east of Darwin. Stuart returned in triumph, but the privations he'd suffered caused his premature death just four years later.

The Overland Telegraph Line (OTL)

Stuart's explorations gave impetus to South Australia's lobbying for a transcontinental telegraph line to be built entirely within its borders. It had gained control of the Northern Territory from New South Wales in 1863 and in April 1870, after overcoming heated opposition from Queensland, it signed a contract with the British-Australian Telegraph Company to build the line.

Under the terms of this agreement, the South Australian government had until 1 January 1872 to finance and construct 3000km of telegraph line between Port Augusta and Darwin. It had set itself an enormous task, as about 2000km of the proposed route would be through country known only from Stuart's journals.

With inspired optimism, the government raised a loan and set to work. For the sake of speed, the Overland Telegraph Line (OTL) was divided into three equal parts to be built concurrently. The southern section was to go north from Port Augusta to Marree, then follow the mound springs around the western side of Lake Eyre to meet the central section at the Macumba River, near Oodnadatta. This was by far the easiest section to construct. In fact, the only real difficulty proved to be a lack of suitable trees for use as poles. Most of the 10,000 poles required for this section were carted from the Flinders Ranges.

The first pole was erected at Port Augusta on 1 October 1870. By January 1872, the southern and central sections – a total distance of 1890km – were open for traffic, but there was still a gap of over 600km in the north. A pony express carried international messages between the operators at either end as 300 men laboured mightily to complete the line. The telegraph company made demands for compensation, but these ceased when their cable broke down in June. By the time it was repaired four months later, the two ends had been joined. The governor declared a public holiday to celebrate.

By now the route between Marree and Oodnadatta had become a well-established dray road along the seemingly endless line of white-capped telegraph poles. It was still very lonely country, however. Between the

Macumba and Lake Torrens – a distance of over 500km – there were only four or five rough homesteads, and new OTL repeater stations at The Peake Creek and Strangways Springs. Both telegraph stations were abandoned in the 1890s when relocated to the new railway line. Telegraph facilities moved from Strangways Springs to William Creek, and from The Peake to Oodnadatta.

Great Northern Railway After their success with the OTL, it seemed to South Australians that nothing could prevent the development of the north. This belief was strengthened when, in the early 1870s, a run of good seasons resulted in a wheat boom on the semi-arid plains north of Port Augusta. This coincided with a spectacular gold rush near Darwin.

With the bit between their teeth, the optimists now demanded a rail link across the continent. Would-be farmers were convinced that wheat could be grown all the way to the Centre; the plough, they said, would transform the outback into 'a wheat growers' golden glory'. This kind of emotive nonsense caught the public's imagination. Dissenting voices were drowned out by the ensuing clamour, which reached such a height that the government capitulated. So the Great Northern Railway was born.

By late 1883, when the railway reached Marree from Port Augusta, normal seasons had returned and the farmers were in full retreat to safer ground. It was now recognised that wheat fields would never stretch to the Territory border. Not only that, the colonies were in the grip of a general depression. In Adelaide alone there were thousands out of work.

Nevertheless, the South Australian government decided to press on with the railway as a means of relieving unemployment. Trainloads of jobless men were sent north to the railhead, which crept out from newly established Marree in July 1884. The immediate destination was Strangways Springs, although a transcontinental link was still the ultimate goal.

In those days, at least in South Australia, railways were built manually, with picks, shovels and wheelbarrows, assisted by dynamite and horse-drawn scoops. But these new navvies, many of whom were no longer young, were mostly soft-muscled clerks and shop assistants. With the flies swarming about their faces, they must have stared aghast at the shimmering stony wastes and quailed at what confronted them. Not surprisingly, they deserted in droves.

Yet many remained and became useful labourers. For some, however, the only reward was a violent death. Gruesome accidents, thirst and murders claimed many lives. In the worst accident, five navvies were killed when a ballast train collided with a mob of cattle. Typhoid epidemics raged, and soon the Oodnadatta Track was dotted with graves.

The Great Northern Railway was built on the cheap, with light rails and minimum ballast. Although hundreds were employed for the project, the work progressed at a snail's pace. In 1889 the line finally reached Oodnadatta, which was then just a place name on the OTL. It was hardly an epic in the annals of railroad construction.

Oodnadatta remained the railhead until January 1927, when the construction crews moved north towards Alice Springs. This time – to the relief of South Australian taxpayers – the federal government was paying. By now the service was known as 'the *Ghan*', after the Afghani camel drivers it had replaced. It had also become legendary for its inefficiency and the leisurely way it was operated. After all, what other major train service would stop so that its passengers could pick wildflowers?

In more recent times the *Ghan*'s faltering progress, laid-back style and old-world charm made it an anachronism in the modern age of transport. It also offered adventure, because passengers never knew how long their journey was going to take. The railway had been built through flood-prone areas, and heavy rains often resulted in wash-outs that closed it for weeks. The old *Ghan* may have provided an unforgettable experience for the tourists who travelled on it, but the service was a disaster for the treasury bureaucrats in Canberra.

The line closed for good in 1980, when the present rail service to Alice Springs was opened. It has since been dismantled – much of the track went to Queensland to be relaid in the sugar-cane fields – but many fascinating relics remain. These, along with remnants of the OTL, had been left to deteriorate until recently, when various restoration projects were launched to save the best examples for posterity.

Information

Tourist Offices The Oasis Cafe (☎ 08-8675 8352) in Marree, the William Creek Hotel (☎ 08-8670 7880) and the Pink Roadhouse (☎ 08-8670 7822) in Oodnadatta are useful sources of local knowledge on all touring matters.

Advice on tours, accommodation and the like is also available from the Wadlata Outback Centre (☎ 08-8641 0793, ☎ 1800 633 060, e wadlata@portaugusta.sa.gov.au; w www.flinders.outback.on.net) at 41 Flinders Terrace, Port Augusta. It's open from 9am to 5.30pm Monday to Friday, and 10am to 4pm Saturday and Sunday.

National Parks Conservation areas along the Oodnadatta Track are managed by National Parks and Wildlife SA rangers based at Port Augusta. Ring the Desert Parks Hotline (NPW SA; ☎ 1800 816 078) for the latest on all park matters.

Communications The track is well used in the winter months, when it may only be 30 minutes until another vehicle comes along. However, in summer it's an entirely different story: Vehicles can be hours apart, so an HF radio could come in handy, particularly if for those intending to visit out-of-the-way spots like Lake Eyre North.

The Port Augusta RFDS base (call sign VNZ; ☎ 08-862 2044) covers this part of the world. It monitors 8165kHz between 7am and 5pm and 4010kHz and 6890kHz between 7am and 9pm daily. Its 24-hour emergency service uses 4010kHz, 6890kHz and 8165kHz as daytime alarm frequencies, and 2020kHz (best at night) and 4010kHz between 9pm and 7am.

Thanks to the Oodnadatta Progress Association a UHF network now covers most main roads in the area between Marla, Oodnadatta, William Creek, Coober Pedy and Dalhousie Springs. For details contact the Oodnadatta police on ☎ 08-8670 7805.

Oodnadatta and Marree (☎ 08-8675 8346) police hire satellite phones to drivers venturing along the Oodnadatta Track. Rental costs $21 per day and the phones are simply handed in at the other end.

Road Reports For advice on the status of roads in this area contact the Outback Road Report Hotline on ☎ 1300 361 033.

Books If the dynamics of flooding in the Lake Eyre Basin are of interest, you can't go past the lavishly illustrated, large-format *Floods of Lake Eyre* by Victor Kotwicki. The photographs are superb – especially the series of full-colour satellite shots of Lake Eyre as it dries up after the 1984 flood.

Explorations in Australia – The Journals of John McDouall Stuart, by John McDouall Stuart, gives a fascinating day-by-day account of the great explorer's expeditions around Lake Eyre and on to the northern coast. It's a must for history enthusiasts.

Basil Fuller's *The Ghan – The Story of the Alice Springs Railway* makes interesting background reading.

Maps Westprint's *Oodnadatta Track* is a very useful basic reference for this trip. It covers the entire route from Lyndhurst (79km south of Marree) to Marla and includes brief details on its various highlights. It's available from various outlets in Alice Springs, Port Augusta, Leigh Creek, Marree, Oodnadatta and Marla. The map is part of the Desert Parks Pass package.

For more detailed map coverage of the Marree to Oodnadatta section, you'll need the *Marree, Curdimurka, Billakalina, Warrina* and *Oodnadatta* 1:250,000 topographic maps from Geoscience Australia. The *Marree* sheet only covers the first 6km. The *Wintinna* sheet covers the Oodnadatta-Marla section. The RAA's *Northern Areas* map is also quite useful.

Permits Entry to the conservation areas of outback South Australia requires a Desert Parks Pass ($80), which covers entry and camping fees – for details see Travel Permits in the Getting Around chapter.

The pass comes with a booklet that contains useful information on Lake Eyre National Park and Wabma Kadarbu Mound Springs Conservation Park. It's available from the Pink Roadhouse in Oodnadatta, the William Creek Store & Campground, and Marree's Outback Roadhouse & General Store in Marree.

If you're just visiting Lake Eyre overnight you'll need a day/night permit, which costs $18 per vehicle. Pick one up at the self-registration bay on the track in to Halligan Bay.

Emergency There are small, well-equipped hospitals at Marree, Oodnadatta and Marla.

Special Preparations
Water It's essential to carry an ample supply of drinking water – most springs and bores along the track yield water that tastes horrible and which has a laxative effect. It's pointless attempting to beg or buy rainwater from the locals, as they regard their scant supplies as being more precious than gold. Marree's water supply is undrinkable, as is William Creek's, but the Oodnadatta supply is palatable if served either chilled or in hot drinks. Marla's water is quite acceptable.

Flies & Mosquitoes Bushfly plagues are the track's downside in warm weather. A fly veil for your face and an insect-screened gazebo for meals are essential at such times; make sure to pack a net to cover any infants while they're having their daytime nap. Areas near wetlands (such as around springs and flowing bores) swarm with mosquitoes on warm nights.

THE ROUTE
Marree to William Creek (203km)
While there is some nice scenery on this section, the major attractions are old railway sidings, artesian mound springs and the world's sixth-largest lake: Lake Eyre. (See the later Birdsville Track section later for details on Marree.)

The Dog Fence Leaving Marree, the track spears westward over rolling gibber downs, passing through a rather ordinary-looking fence 42km from town. In fact, this is the famous Dog Fence, the world's longest man-made barrier – see the Fauna section in the Facts about the Outback chapter.

Alberrie Creek From about 5km from the Dog Fence you will notice what appears to be the silhouette of a giant Scottish terrier on the horizon. On closer inspection this puzzling object turns out to be a large, elevated water tank (the body) to which has been added a car (the head) and a tall thick pole (the tail).

The terrier – actually a dingo – is one of several weird and wonderful works of art in the **Mutonia Sculpture Park** *(Arabunna Centre;* ☎ *08-8675 8351; open 8am-5pm daily)*, at the Alberrie Creek Siding, 11km past the Dog Fence. Others include a windmill that has been turned into a huge wildflower, and two aeroplanes standing on their tails.

The Inland Sea Continuing on for a further 15km you pass a high hump-backed range on the right with a cairn on its highest point. This is **Hermit Hill**, climbed in 1858 by Benjamin Babbage, who thus became the first white person to cross the gap between Lake Torrens and Lake Eyre. Before then it was thought that these two great lakes were one and a massive barrier that would block any progress to the north.

Sixteen kilometres past Hermit Hill is a rough detour that leads to a **lookout** point, above the barren shore of Lake Eyre South. There's also another lookout 10km further on, where for a short distance the road runs right beside the lake with the old railway line in between.

Lake Eyre is actually two lakes – Lake Eyre North and Lake Eyre South – joined by the narrow Goyder Channel. Covering a total area of 9700 sq km, the entire lake bed is included within the 13,560-sq-km Lake

Eyre National Park. Although the lake has filled to near capacity only three times in the past 150 years (most recently in 1974), it does receive significant flooding once every eight years on average. This usually results from heavy rains over central and western Queensland.

Lake Eyre is so shallow that even a major flood like that of 1974 takes only two years or so to evaporate. In the meantime the lake becomes a vast breeding ground for swarms of pelicans, seagulls, terns and many other water birds; such a rare celebration of life in the desert is well worth a special trip in itself.

Most times, however, the lake is little more than a blinding expanse of white salt crust. In 1964 Britain's Donald Campbell set a world land-speed record of 648.6km/h on Lake Eyre North in his jet-powered car *Bluebird II*. However, it's not a good idea to drive on the lakebed yourself – your vehicle will soon break through the hard surface and sink deep into black saline slop.

Curdimurka Eight kilometres past Lake Eyre is Curdimurka Siding, whose name commemorates the fearsome kadimakara of Aboriginal belief – the kadimakara were thought to live under Lake Eyre and prey on anyone foolish enough to walk on it. The siding consists of a nine-roomed stone cottage, an elevated railway tank and a tower-like water softener. (The water tower removed harmful salts from bore water that otherwise caused heavy scaling in locomotive boilers.) Both the tank and tower lean alarmingly and seem imminent danger of falling over. Settlers based in this desolate place were responsible maintaining a 30km stretch of line that was noted for deep wash-outs after rain and drifting sand in drought.

In its day, Curdimurka was little different to most other sidings along the railway – what makes it remarkable now is the fact that it is still in one piece. This is entirely due to the unflagging enthusiasm of the Adelaide-based Ghan Railway Preservation Society (SA). This dedicated group has restored the entire complex, including 4km of railway and an adjacent section of the Overland Telegraph Line.

These days the siding really comes alive in October of even-numbered years, when up to 5000 people in evening dress attend the Curdimurka Outback Ball. A huge wooden floor is brought in for the occasion, and revellers dance the night away under the blazing stars. For details, contact the Ghan Railway Preservation Society, PO Box 311, Rundle Mall, SA 5000.

Mound Springs The road continues westwards for 29km from Curdimurka, at which point a side road heads south for 5km to flat-topped Hamilton Hill, in **Wabma Kadarbu Mound Springs Conservation Park**. At the

Living with Salt

It's difficult to imagine an environment more harsh than the sun-baked, wind-blown, salt-encrusted surface of Lake Eyre. In fact, it's generally so inhospitable to life that only a few vertebrate species have adapted to it. One of these is the Lake Eyre dragon (*Ctenophorus maculosus*).

Found only on the salt crusts of South Australia's inland lakes, this small (170mm-long) white lizard feeds mainly on the ants that live around the lake margins, as well as any other insects it can find there. It shelters from temperature extremes by wriggling under the salt crust; two to four eggs are laid in a steep burrow in moist sand at the shoreline. In the rare event of a flood, the dragon moves into adjoining sand dunes – if caught on a low island it can inflate its body and swim to higher ground, even in cold weather.

Unless you're very lucky you won't meet a Lake Eyre dragon in the wild – they're shy and well camouflaged for their life on the saltpan. However, you can see them at the Alice Springs Desert Park, which is the only place with specimens in captivity. (See the Alice Springs section at the start of this chapter for details.)

foot of this low but prominent feature is **Blanches Cup**, one of the many mound springs that line the track between Marree and William Creek.

Mound springs are natural outlets for the Great Artesian Basin – a vast sandstone aquifer shaped like a basin. Rainfall is soaked up where the basin's water-bearing rocks outcrop in the eastern ranges of Queensland and New South Wales. The water moves towards South Australia, taking an estimated 2.5 million years to reach the Oodnadatta Track.

Mound springs occur wherever the pressure in the aquifer is able to force water to the surface through cracks in the overlying impermeable rocks. The dramatic fall in pressure at the surface causes chemical changes in the water; magnesium, sodium and calcium carbonates are precipitated at the outlet and slowly build up to form hillocks usually several metres high. In this flat brown land, the white carbonate rock is visible for considerable distances.

Blanches Cup is considered a classic mound spring owing to the symmetry of its mound and the large circular pool on top. Like other springs, however, it has suffered greatly from introduced grazing animals and reduced flow rates, the latter resulting from the many bores that have been drilled into the aquifer. Nevertheless, the reed-fringed waterhole remains a beautiful paradox among the sun-baked salt flats. You can easily appreciate why the early explorers went into raptures when they first laid their eyes on it.

A few hundred metres to the north lies **the Bubbler**, so named because of the frequent eruptions of gas that disturb the otherwise tranquil pool over its outlet.

Coward Springs Back at the turn-off, continue for the remaining 11km to the old **Coward Springs Siding** (☎ *Apr-Oct 08-8675 8336; entry $1; open daylight hours)*. This was once an important little settlement with a hospital, hotel and store, as well as several railway houses. The South Australian government established a date plantation, but the bore water proved unsuitable and the palms failed to thrive.

Today, all that remains are the restored station master's and engineer's cottages – the latter houses interesting and informative displays, including the reminiscences of early residents and visitors. You can enjoy a bath in the nearby **hot pool**, which is fed by a flowing bore. The bore also feeds an extensive wetland that attracts many species of **waterbirds** – around 120 bird species have been recorded at Coward Springs. There's a bush camping area here (see Facilities) and you can do camel tours from April to September (see Organised Tours).

Extinct Springs Six kilometres from Coward Springs the road passes **Kewson Hill**, the largest active spring along the Oodnadatta Track. During his 1859 expedition, Stuart bogged his horse on top and had great difficulty getting it out again. An indication of what the flow from these springs must have been like way back in geological time is provided by Hamilton Hill and the much larger **Beresford Hill**, on your left 22km past Coward Springs. These huge mounds were formed by now-extinct springs.

About 2.5km past Beresford Hill you'll see a rare sight on the Oodnadatta Track: a large clump of shady trees around a **dam**. Built to supply water for steam locomotives, it is now used mainly by cattle and wildlife. There are usually plenty of native hens (black, bantam-like birds) running about, while screeching hordes of corellas frequently cover the trees.

Strangways Telegraph Station The capped bore 37km from Coward Springs marks the site of the old Strangways Siding. There is no longer any sign of this little settlement (it once had a pub and police station), but if you look to the west you may spot a ruin on the low ridge about 2km away. This was the Strangways Telegraph Station, one of 11 repeater stations constructed between Port Augusta and Darwin in 1871 to boost the morse signals that travelled along the Overland Telegraph Line. Unfortunately, vandals have been busy here: Only a large stone tank and some stone-walled sheep pens remain in good condition.

William Creek Two kilometres past Strangways Siding, cross salty Warriner Creek just downstream from a rusty railway bridge. Debris heaped against the piles shows what these streams are like in a flood. The track now leaves the gibber plains behind, and for the next 15km or so passes through large crimson sand ridges separated by claypans and gravel flats. Like other sandy areas in the region, it's a great spot for wildflowers. The dunes, which cut out 17km before William Creek, are outliers of the Simpson Desert dunefield 100km to the north-east.

Seven kilometres before William Creek is a large mulga tree from which is hung the bodies of numerous feral cats, all shot in this area.

William Creek (population 10) is South Australia's smallest town. It consists of a pub, a store and several residences set on a shimmering saltbush flat between two red dunes. As the rainfall is measured in drops, there isn't much in the way of lawns and gardens here. As well, the local bore water is fit only for sheep and cattle.

The attraction of bush pubs like the **William Creek Hotel** lies in the fact that what they lack in frills they more than make up for in character and atmosphere. It was built in 1887 as a support station for camel drivers working on the Overland Telegraph Line. While the weathered, single-storey, metal-clad structure may not look too prepossessing from the outside, once through the door you find a friendly haven away from the flies and sun's glare. The pub offers a range of services to travellers (see Facilities).

You can do scenic flights and camel rides here (see Organised Tours). Another highlight is the annual William Creek Cup, held on the weekend before Easter.

William Creek to Oodnadatta (199km)

On this section the track wanders generally northward over much the same terrain as before. Although there are no more mound springs beside the road past William Creek, abandoned railway sidings and other relics provide plenty of interest.

Anna Creek Having torn yourself away from William Creek, you soon pass the turn-off to Anna Creek homestead and Coober Pedy. Anna Creek station covers around 24,000 sq km and is the world's largest pastoral lease – most years it runs around 16,000 head of cattle (which, at an average value of $500 per head, is a huge investment in stock). The average carrying capacity of this country is less than one beast per sq km and most years you'll wonder how it supports even that many.

Anna Creek is leased by the Kidman Pastoral Company, which was established by the legendary cattle king, Sir Sidney Kidman. The company's holdings have been much reduced since its heyday, but it still operates a string of stations around the southern fringe of the Simpson Desert.

The Peake Telegraph Station There are a number of mainly small creeks in the 111km between William Creek and the **Ernest Giles Memorial**. Most are lined by coolabahs, river red gums or gidgees; several offer good shade and camping in welcome contrast to the gibbers on either side. The Ernest Giles Memorial is a simple cairn commemorating Giles' arrival here in 1876 after his epic crossing with camels from the western coast. The ruins and water-softening plant at **Edward Creek Siding** (91km from William Creek) are worth investigating, while the nearby creek is an excellent spot to boil the billy.

Heading east from the Giles Memorial, a rough 4WD track takes you 16km to The Peake ruins at Freeling Springs. The Peake homestead was South Australia's northernmost outpost of settlement in 1870, when construction of the Overland Telegraph Line began. A year later a telegraph station was built beside the homestead, and in 1873 a police station was added. This made The Peake a sizeable community for both its time and its place. It was abandoned 18 years later when operations were moved to Oodnadatta.

Some restoration work has been carried out at this fascinating site, which is situated on a rocky terrace overlooking a broad, shallow valley. There are nine stone ruins, of which the seven-room telegraph station is by far the largest and most sophisticated.

In the hills behind are several deep shafts dating from 1898, when mineral lodes assaying 70% copper and several ounces of gold per ton were discovered. A number of mines were developed and there was talk of employment for 3000 men. However, in the end it came to nothing, and activity ceased in 1904. By that time the smelter erected at great cost 300m south-west of the telegraph station had treated just 284 tonnes of ore, averaging 4% copper.

Algebuckina Thirty-two kilometres from the Giles Memorial is the **Neales River**, where the crossing over coolabah-lined channels is over 1km wide. This is by far the largest watercourse on the Oodnadatta Track. However, what really grabs your attention is the impressive, 578m-long **Algebuckina railway bridge** – the longest in South Australia. The **graves** of three railway workers lie beside the line at the bridge's northern end.

Excitement came to Algebuckina in October 1886 when gold was found on the Neales' northern bank close to the bridge. A small rush took place and five months later, by which time about 60 ounces had been won, 25 men were on the field. Sadly the rush proved a dud, as did the town site surveyed on the opposite bank at about the same time.

Also of interest here is a large salt waterhole on the downstream side of the road. This is a good spot for bird-watchers. The easy climb up to the cairn above the old **Algebuckina Siding**, about 1km south of the bridge, gives a good view over the Neales and surrounding country.

Leaving the river behind, the final 56km stage into Oodnadatta takes you through a mix of gibber plains, ochre-coloured hills and an area of yellow dunes inexplicably called the **Plantation Sandhills**. Some of this country is breathtakingly harsh, and you get a fine view of it from **Cadnaowie Lookout**, 17km from the Neales. With only 20km to go, you pass through **Duttons Gap**, where the sweating navvies toiled with picks and

shovels to maintain a suitable gradient. The thought of it gives you a powerful thirst that will last all the way to Oodnadatta.

Oodnadatta

Oodnadatta's heyday lasted from 1889 to 1927, when it was the terminus for the Great Northern Railway. From here, camel trains made round trips of up to 3000km to resupply communities as far away as Newcastle Waters, in the Northern Territory. However, the only obvious sign of this relatively prosperous era is an impressive sandstone **railway station**, which houses interesting displays of historic photographs. To gain entry, ask at either the general store, hotel or roadhouse for a key.

After the railway closed in 1980, most government functions were moved to Marla, on the new line, and the town was expected to die. However, it has managed to hang on and, despite its moribund appearance and small size, remains an oasis of unexpected comforts in a sea of gibbers. Today, half the town, including its hotel and general store, is owned by a council made up of Aborigines, who comprise the bulk of the population of about 200.

Oodnadatta has a hospital, post office agency, general store, garages, roadhouse, hotel, museum, police station and landing ground. There are Eftpos facilities at the Pink Roadhouse and general store. See Facilities for details of Oodnadatta's commercial services.

At the time of this update the Oodnadatta Progress Association was about to commence work on a telecentre that will have telephone, fax, photocopying, Internet access and Eftpos facilities. The telecentre will be opposite the hospital on the main street (Ikaturka Terrace), at the northern end of town.

The Oodnadatta Cup is held on Adelaide Cup Day in May.

Oodnadatta to Marla (208km)

Being of much more recent vintage, this final section is lacking in historic appeal. However, there's compensation in the fact that you've a good chance of seeing interesting wildlife such as emus, bustards, perenties, dingoes and red kangaroos. Most winters you will also see the bright crimson blooms of Sturt's desert pea, (pictured) which forms large mats on the ground, particularly in the east where the soils are sandier.

As before, there's not much variation in the topography. There are plenty of gibbers, patches of mulga and the odd low range, and these are interspersed with occasional tree-lined creeks. The final 50km past Welbourne Hill homestead takes you along the old Stuart Hwy, which was realigned to the west in the early 1980s.

Marla
The little township of Marla (the name is a corruption of the Pitjantjatjara word for red kangaroo) came into existence in 1980 as a regional centre to replace Oodnadatta. Being new and somewhat prefabricated, it has little outback character – it's basically a government town populated by public servants on short-term postings from the city. See Facilities later in this section.

DETOURS
Halligan Bay (63km one way)
Twenty-seven kilometres past Strangways Siding (7km before William Creek), a 4WD track leads off to the western shore of Lake Eyre North. This straightforward route terminates at Halligan Bay, where the desolation literally takes your breath away. Approaching the shore, you cross a wasteland of low breakaways entirely covered by small black stones. It's so ugly and lifeless that at first glance it seems as if some ghastly environmental disaster has befallen the place. On a satellite photograph, the area appears to have been scorched by a bushfire. But on the ground on a hot day, with the stillness and deathly silence working on your imagination, you can tell that in reality it's been seared by the furnaces of hell.

En route the track passes a **memorial** to an Austrian tourist who died of thirst here in December 1998. She had left her bogged vehicle at Halligan Bay and tried to walk back to William Creek for help. It's a grim reminder that lack of preparation in the outback can have fatal consequences.

Madigan Gulf (96km one way)
You can also visit Lake Eyre North by taking the 4WD track from Marree via **Muloorina** homestead to the shores of Madigan Gulf. This route turns off the Oodnadatta Track about 1.5km from Marree. From here it's easy travelling on a graded road across the gibbers to Muloorina (52km), where you turn off just before the homestead. The track now heads across the sand plain to Lake Eyre South (72km from Marree), then swings north along the shore to **Goyder Channel**. It ends at an information shelter by Madigan Gulf.

Muloorina Camping Ground (homestead ☎ 08-8675 8341) Bush camp sites $2 per vehicle. There's good shade and a waterhole, but no facilities at this camping area beside the River Frome – the fee is a donation to the RFDS. Bring your own drinking water and firewood.

Coober Pedy (161km one way)
The detour from William Creek to Coober Pedy, Australia's opal-mining capital, is worth taking if this is the only chance you'll have to visit the place. The turn-off to **Lake Cadibarrawirracanna** (Australia's longest place name) is about 70km from William Creek.

This road is remote and has no reliable fresh water, but is occasionally maintained and sees a bit of traffic now and then. Before setting out, get an update on road conditions from the William Creek Hotel. For more information on Coober Pedy, see the Stuart Highway section earlier in this chapter.

ALTERNATIVE ROUTES
At Oodnadatta you're faced with a number of options which will take you west to the Stuart Hwy, or north to Mt Dare and

ultimately either on to Alice Springs or Birdsville. The roads to Mt Dare, Cadney Park and Coober Pedy are normally suitable for conventional vehicles with good ground clearance. Check on road conditions at the Pink Roadhouse.

Oodnadatta to Coober Pedy (190km)

The main reason to take this road is as an alternative route to Coober Pedy. The country is flat, with gibbers almost all the way, and there are no facilities en route.

Oodnadatta to Cadney Park Roadhouse (179km)

The Arckaringa Hills or **Painted Desert**, about 80km from Oodnadatta, make this by far the most interesting route to the Stuart Hwy. Numerous colourful mesas provide some of the grandest scenery in outback South Australia and they also make fantastic subjects for photography during the early morning and late afternoon. Visitors are welcome in this area, but camping is not permitted.

Back of Beyond Tours (☎ 08-8672 5900, ⓔ *dapmburge@ozemail.com.au)* does a day tour from Coober Pedy to the Painted Desert ($120 including lunch).

Check with Cadney Park Roadhouse as to whether or not the *mail run* tour through the Painted Desert and on towards Oodnadatta is still being offered.

Copper Hills homestead (☎ 08-8670 7995) Camp sites $5 per person, cabins $8 per person. This homestead, 145km from Oodnadatta, offers pleasant bush camping with basic facilities, located next to a picturesque waterhole. There are basic aircon rooms in dongas.

Cadney Park Roadhouse (☎ 08-8670 7994) Bush camp sites free, powered sites $16 per site, single & double cabins without linen $30, single & double motel rooms $92. This roadhouse on the Stuart Hwy offers a range of services, including fuel sales (diesel, super and unleaded), a *restaurant*, takeaway meals, a *bar* and mechanical repairs. Cabin accommodation is basic and there is no air-con.

Oodnadatta to Mt Dare Homestead via Eringa (250km)

Take this slow but interesting route if you want to visit Dalhousie Springs, or head off to either Alice Springs or Birdsville via the Simpson Desert. As an option, you can take the 4WD short cut (73km) from Hamilton homestead to Dalhousie Springs, but this can be extremely rough in places. The turnoff is 1km north of the homestead and about 115km from Oodnadatta.

ORGANISED TOURS
Camel Safaris

Both these operators will take you to Lake Eyre, among other places.

Lake Eyre Camel Trekking (☎ 08-8675 8336 Apr-Sept, ☎ 03-5581 1903, ⓔ *coward camels@bigpond.com,* ⓦ *www.coward springs.com.au)* offers overnight ($150), four-day ($500) and seven-day ($900) camel treks from Coward Springs, or longer treks by arrangement.

Explore the Outback Camel Safaris (☎ 1800 064 244, 08-8672 3968, ⓔ *explore@ austcamel.com.au,* ⓦ *www.austcamel.com .au/explore.htm)* does camel treks from William Creek. A four-day ride costs $564, and longer ones are also available.

Scenic Flights

Wrightsair (☎ 08-8670 7962) flies over Lake Eyre from William Creek, charging $135/255 for a one-hour/two-hour flight.

Central Air Services (Oasis Cafe; ☎ 08-8675 8352, Railway Terrace South) in Marree offers flights over Lake Eyre from $130 for an hour. A longer flight includes Marree Man, the huge etching of an Aboriginal warrior carved into the desert a few years ago by persons unknown.

Aboriginal Culture Tours

The Aboriginal owned and operated *Arabunna Centre (☎ 08-8675 8351)* in Marree does a five-day camping tour of Arabunna country. Visit such places as Lake Eyre and various mound springs, and learn all about Aboriginal culture from a local Indigenous guide. The all-inclusive price of $1285 includes travel to and from Adelaide.

Bus Tours

Desert Diversity Tours (☎ 08-8672 5226, e info@desertdiversity.com, w www.desert diversity.com) does a day tour (adult/child $140/70) from Coober Pedy to William Creek and Lake Eyre North.

Back of Beyond Tours (☎ 08-8672 5900, e dapmburge@ozemail.com.au), also of Coober Pedy, offers a similar tour for a similar price.

Otherwise there's the *mail run* from Coober Pedy to Oodnadatta and return via William Creek (see Mail Runs in the Getting Around chapter).

Groovy Grape and *Wayward Bus* include the southern part of the track on their trips from Adelaide to Alice Springs (see Organised Tours in the Getting Around chapter).

FACILITIES
Marree

See the Birdsville Track section later in this chapter for information on Marree's facilities.

William Creek

William Creek Hotel (☎ 08-8670 7880, e williamcreek@ozemail.com.au, Oodnadatta Track) Camp sites per person/car $3.50/10, bunkhouse beds without/with linen $14/19, basic singles/doubles $25/50. The lonely William Creek Hotel dispenses ice, limited food lines, takeaway liquor, counter and dining room *meals* (from $15), very basic accommodation, minor mechanical repairs and fuel (diesel, super and unleaded). Its camping area has basic facilities and some shade. Normal trading hours for fuel are 7.30am to midnight daily (8pm Sunday).

William Creek Store & Campground (☎ 08-8670 7746, w www.williamcreek campground.com) Unpowered/powered sites $13/18, air-con rooms $40. This new camping area, across from the pub, has good facilities including a *takeaway food* outlet.

Oodnadatta

Pink Roadhouse (☎ 1800 802 074, 08-8670 7822, e Lynnie_Plate@bigpond.com, w www.biziworks.com.au/pink, Ikaturka Terrace) Unpowered/powered sites $14.50/ 19.50, bunkhouse beds $10, twin rooms

$45, self-contained cabins $80. At the Marree end of town, the distinctive Pink Roadhouse is the obvious tourism focus for this region – all routes leading to Oodnadatta are dotted with the distinctive information signs erected by proprietors Adam and Lynnie Plate. These long-time locals can give sound advice on all aspects of travel in the outback, so drop in for a coffee and a chat. You're welcome to browse through their private library of books, newspaper clippings and maps, all of which will add to your knowledge of the area.

Adam and Lynnie offer fuel (diesel, super and unleaded), takeaway and sit-down *meals*, a *minimarket*, minor mechanical repairs, a post office agency and a Commonwealth Bank agency. Accommodation facilities include a self-contained seven-bed shack, basic twin rooms and self-contained cabins with kitchen and TV. All units are air-conditioned.

Transcontinental Hotel (☎ 08-8670 7804, e oodnadattahotel@bigpond.com, Ikaturka Terrace) Single/double/triple hotel rooms $35/65/75; house $12 per bed. The hotel has air-conditioned but otherwise basic rooms, and there's a fully self-contained house across the street sleeping up to 12 people. The pub also offers hearty *meals*.

Oodnadatta General Store (☎ 08-8670 7802, Ikaturka Terrace) Next door to the pub, this reasonably priced minimarket offers hardware, takeaway meals as well as diesel, super and unleaded fuel. Check the fuel prices here and at the Pink Roadhouse, as there's usually a price war going on.

Marla

Now the major regional centre in northern South Australia, Marla boasts an excellent range of essential facilities. These include a supermarket, hotel-motel, caravan park, garage, police station, medical centre and airstrip.

Marla Travellers Rest (☎ 08-8670 7001, e marla@internode.on.net) Unpowered/ powered sites $10/17, single/double air-con cabins $30/40, single/double/triple/quad motel rooms $70/75/80/85 ($10 extra per person for TV and telephone). This place is a combination of hotel, motel, roadhouse, supermarket, garage and caravan park and has everything most travellers would require. The garage has a qualified mechanic, and fuel (diesel, super, unleaded and LPG) is available 24 hours. After 'normal' hours (6.30am-10.30pm daily), you can gain entry to the well-stocked *supermarket* by contacting the night watchman. The Commonwealth Bank agency in the supermarket has an Eftpos facility.

All guests have access to a swimming pool, and there are shady trees and lawns in the caravan park. The hotel section offers a choice of takeaway, a la carte or restaurant *meals*.

Bush Camping

Coward Springs Campground (☎ 08-8675 8336 Apr-Oct, ☎ 03-5581 1903 Nov-Mar, e cowardcamels@bigpond.com, w www .cowardsprings.com.au) Camp sites $6 per person. This sheltered camping area has toilets and showers, as well as shady trees and a hot pool. It's close to a wetland, so come prepared to do battle with mosquitoes at night. Pay the admission fee into the honesty box when the manager isn't there, which is most of the time between November and April.

Isolated bush camp sites with good shelter from both sun and wind aren't all that common. Popular spots such as Beresford Siding and the Neales River have generally been degraded by people-pressure. Avoid them if for no other reason than to protect your health. The best places to look for private sheltered sites are along creeks and in sand hill areas, but don't leave it too late in the day.

Firewood There's a general lack of dead timber between Marree and Oodnadatta, but the millions of sleepers along the railway are a great source of firewood. Most are old, easily splintered and make excellent coals for cooking. If you have the space, carry at least one with you, as the country away from creeklines is virtually devoid of dead timber. You'll also find that popular camping areas have long been stripped of firewood.

Birdsville Track

Highlights

- Discovering the history and scattered relics of the droving days
- Detouring to camp, fish and bird-watch along Warburton Creek
- Wondering at the dedication of the early missionaries at Bethesda Mission ruins

Seared by the relentless sun and scoured by countless raging dust storms, the 517km Birdsville Track between Birdsville and Marree earned notoriety as one of Australia's most hazardous stock routes. Linking a series of unreliable waterholes and artesian bores across the continent's driest region, it was a droving highway along which up to 50,000 head of cattle a year walked from Queensland to the railway at Marree.

The track's grim reputation was built on death; the lives of many people and entire mobs of cattle have been lost to its great heat and lack of water. Until relatively recent times it was little more than an ill-defined pad, with the bones of dead stock pointing the way to the next drink.

But progress has come to the Birdsville Track and it's now a much tamer version of earlier times. The drovers were replaced by road trains in the 1960s, and as a result the track has been upgraded to the point where it is now mostly a good dirt road. Catering mainly to tourist traffic, the air-conditioned Mungeranie Hotel, near the halfway mark, dispenses fuel and creature comforts such as cold drinks and soft beds. Purists might lament that the spirit of the track is dead, but those who live along it are unlikely to share that sentiment.

For the casual tourist there is little spectacular scenery in this desolate landscape of polished stones, sand ridges and occasional dried-up creeks. Many find the experience crushingly monotonous; for others, the loneliness, silence and vast empty spaces provide the opportunity for a unique adventure in outback touring. If you take the time – and an enthusiast could easily spend a week exploring the track – it's an opportunity to appreciate the courage of those who lived and worked here in the days when the drover was king. Those who aren't interested can drive its full length in one day and never know what they've missed.

History

The Diamantina River between Birdsville and Lake Eyre was explored by the surveyor John Lewis in 1874. However, the credit for pioneering the Birdsville Track was earned about six years later by EA Burt, the first Birdsville storekeeper. Burt's route gave the stations of south-western Queensland's channel country a link to Adelaide, their closest major market and supply point. In good seasons, mobs of up to 2000 cattle streamed south, taking an average of five weeks for the long walk to Marree.

The drovers' spartan needs were provided for by isolated stores at Mirra Mitta, Tidnacoordooninna, Cannuwaukaninna and Mulka; these, like the old homesteads at Lake Harry, Mt Gason, Apatoonganie and Oorawillanie, have long since been abandoned. Today, their scant remains and parched surroundings are starkly evocative of hard, lonely living and eventual failure in the face of overwhelming odds.

Apart from cattle, the track's main users until the 1930s were camel trains travelling to and from Marree. In the care of Afghani cameleers, strings of up to 75 animals carried virtually everything that Birdsville and the surrounding stations required in the way of stores, building materials and general cargo. The trek from Marree to Birdsville took about 24 days, with each beast carrying between 250kg and 450kg. However, by the late 1930s the camels had been replaced by road transport, and most were set free to wander in the desert.

In a land where water has sacred significance, only the foolhardy tempted fate by walking between the track's far-flung homesteads. Many such travellers were fatally ignorant of local conditions, and their epitaphs, if they were ever recorded, can be found among the terse entries in early police journals. On 22 December 1885 the Birdsville policeman wrote:

Traveller found a dead body. Three or four days old. Ten miles over the border in South Australia. Three men perished 10 miles from Clifton Hills station, ten or twelve days ago. No water.

More recently, the publicity surrounding the Page family's tragic demise served to enhance the track's fearsome reputation. In late December 1963 the Pages were en route from Marree to Queensland when their vehicle broke down at Dead Man's Sandhill, about 90km from Birdsville. Their water supplies were extremely limited, and in the great heat they waited with increasing desperation for help to arrive. However, in those days travellers were a rarity on the Birdsville Track in summer and the Pages had neglected to advise people of their movements. Tormented by thirst, they finally left their car in a despairing quest for water.

The abandoned vehicle was found several days later by a rabbit-shooter. A search party was quickly organised but it was too late for the Pages, whose bodies were located shortly afterwards. The parents and two of their three children had died in a dried-up waterhole, no doubt lured there by the coolabah trees and their false promise of salvation. The eldest son's body was found on a sand ridge about 1km away. Their lonely grave beside the waterhole is marked by a small metal cross bearing the stark inscription: 'The Pages Perished Dec 63'.

Information

Tourist Offices In Birdsville, the Wirrarri Centre (☎ 07-4656 3300, fax 4656 3302, www.diamantina.qld.gov.au) on Billabong Blvd houses a well-stocked tourist information office. From April to October inclusive it opens from 8.30am to 6pm Monday to Friday and 9.30am to 5.30pm weekends and public holidays – for the rest of the year it opens from 8.30am to 4.30pm weekdays only.

Other good sources of local knowledge are the Oasis Cafe (☎ 08-8675 8352) in Marree, and the Mungeranie Hotel (☎ 08-8675 8317).

Communications It's recommended that anyone travelling the track outside the busy season should carry an HF radio with frequencies for the RFDS bases at Port Augusta and Broken Hill; Port Augusta is the usual base for this region, but it doesn't hurt to have Broken Hill as a backup.

Port Augusta (call sign VNZ; ☎ 08-8642 2044) monitors 8165kHz between 7am and 5pm and 4010kHz and 6890kHz between 7am and 9pm daily. Its 24-hour emergency service uses 4010kHz, 6890kHz and 8165kHz as daytime alarm frequencies, and 2020kHz (best at night) and 4010kHz between 9pm and 7am.

The Broken Hill RFDS base (call sign VJC; ☎ 08-8080 1777) monitors 4055kHz and 6920kHz between 7am and 6pm weekdays. Alarm calls are received on 4055kHz and 6920kHz during business hours and on 2020kHz after hours.

The police at Marree (☎ 08-8675 8346) and Birdsville (☎ 07-4656 3220) hire satellite phones to travellers venturing up the Birdsville Track. Rental costs $21 per day and you simply hand it in when you get to the other end.

Road Reports For advice as to the status of roads in this area contact the Outback Road Report Hotline on ☎ 1300 361 033.

Books *Mail for the Back of Beyond*, by John Maddock, tells the fascinating story of the motor mailmen of the Birdsville Track. It gives you an appreciation of how easy motorists have it today. The Marree-Birdsville mail was carried by camels until 1936, when it was taken over by a motorised service, which lasted until 1975. Since then the mail has been carried by aeroplane. This book is out of print but copies can be found in libraries and second-hand bookshops.

Eric Bonython's *Where the Seasons Come and Go* is an absorbing read covering history, lifestyles and adventure in the Cooper Creek country up to the 1950s. The Bethesda Mission on Lake Killalpaninna is featured prominently.

Land of Mirage, by George Farwell, is a story of cattle-droving and station life along the track in the late 1940s, with plenty of history thrown in. It's definitely worth reading, although now out of print.

Maps The map-guide entitled *Birdsville and Strzelecki Tracks* published by Westprint Heritage Maps is a comprehensive if limited reference covering the major and minor tourist routes of South Australia's north-eastern corner. It's available from outlets in Birdsville, Marree, Innamincka and Leigh Creek, and forms part of the Desert Parks Pass package.

For detailed coverage, you'll need a copy of Geoscience Australia's *Marree, Kopperamanna, Gason* and *Pandie Pandie* 1:250,000 topographic maps – a small section of the track also falls on the *Cordillo* sheet.

Registration Despite the popular belief that travellers should register with police at one end and sign off at the other, the police no longer wish to do so. They suggest that you keep friends or relatives informed of your movements so that they can notify the authorities should you fail to report in on time. However, they're happy to provide advice, and travellers can leave messages with them for others to collect.

Emergency Marree and Birdsville both have well-equipped hospitals staffed by registered nurses.

Special Preparations

Water It's essential to carry ample drinking water at all times on the Birdsville Track. Although they can be used in emergencies, most of the track's artesian bores yield water that smells unpleasant and has a laxative effect when you're not used to it.

Marree's water supply is undrinkable, while Mungeranie's is best when chilled or drunk in tea and coffee. The Birdsville supply is quite acceptable and is regarded as the best bore water on the track. Always be careful collecting water from flowing artesian bores – it usually comes out of the ground at scalding temperatures.

Birdsville Races

Birdsville's big event each year is the two-day race meeting held in early September. Country races are often low-key occasions when the locals get together to bet on the horses and have a few beers, but Birdsville attracts thousands of people from all over the country. And they drink more than just a few beers.

The weekend is also notable for the hundreds of light aircraft that fly in. Normally one of the remotest runways in Australia, Birdsville aerodrome gets so busy that the Civil Aviation Safety Authority has to issue special flight rules to help control the traffic. So being a city-based private pilot, I decided that this was an experience we ought to try.

Things to Do

Getting drunk is the favourite activity, ahead of falling over and wearing tasteless T-shirts. Brawls used to be popular but these days the crowds are fairly good-natured.

Evening entertainment is provided by Fred Brophy's boxing troupe which set up in the centre of town, right across from the pub. This must be one of the last left in Australia, if not the world, and their days may be numbered as such acts are now outlawed in several states – not Queensland though. The bass drum booms out across the desert as the spruiker works the crowd ('Here's Mad Dingo. Who reckons he could fight Mad Dingo?'). There are always a few blokes drunk enough to try a few rounds against the professionals, and no shortage of others who will pay to see them try.

Oh yes, there are horse races too, on Friday and Saturday. The bookmakers work with speed and efficiency to take your money, though you may find they move a bit slower if your horse wins.

Places to Stay & Eat

Put your tent up right beside the plane, or just hang a plastic sheet over the wing. It can get cold at night and the ground is hard and stony so bring a good sleeping bag and mat.

The Diamantina Shire Council provides temporary toilets and showers, complete with hot running water straight from the bore. Your nose will remind you that the sewerage treatment pump runs 24 hours a day.

Don't count on eating at the pub, they're too busy selling beer. Hot dogs and steak sandwiches from the roadside stalls are as good as it gets, so bring your own.

Flies & Mosquitoes Bushfly plagues are the track's downside in warm weather. A fly veil for your face and an insect-screened gazebo for meals are essential at such times; make sure to pack a net to cover any toddlers while they're having their daytime nap. Except on cold nights, areas near wetlands usually swarm with mosquitoes.

THE ROUTE
Birdsville

With a population of around 120, Birdsville is set on a barren, stony rise overlooking the Diamantina River. So remote that it wasn't visited by a politician for its first 60 years, Birdsville is best known for its tremendous heat waves (temperatures of 50°C are common in summer), its annual race meeting and, of course, its association with the famous Birdsville Track.

Within 10 years of its founding in the late 1870s, Birdsville had a population of 90 whites and 180 Aborigines, as well as three pubs, a cordial factory and a border customs post. Prior to Federation in 1901, a duty was levied on all cattle leaving Queensland and on all goods that came up from Marree; smuggling, particularly of whisky, was rife.

Federation removed the town's status, and a terrible drought that followed saw the population drift away. Finally, in 1905, a tremendous wind storm levelled most of the town's less substantial buildings. After that

Birdsville Races

Getting There & Away

From Melbourne's Moorabbin Airport to Birdsville is about 1900km as the crow flies, and even further on the route we took in a single-engine Piper Arrow. We had planned a loop through central Queensland, but then rain arrived over most of eastern Australia so we headed for Arkaroola in the Flinders Ranges instead. Amended flight plans are a fact of life for small aircraft.

The manager at Arkaroola who refuelled the Arrow was surprised that we were going to the Birdsville Races. He said we seemed too intelligent.

Undeterred, we continued on the last leg, a two-hour flight that took us into a 'designated remote area'. The flat brown uniformity of the desert offers very few recognisable landmarks so we had to trust the instruments and were quite glad when a town finally appeared ahead of us.

This had to be Birdsville if only because no other town would have so many planes at the aerodrome.

Even if you're not a pilot or the friend of one, consider getting a few people together to charter a plane; check the *Yellow Pages* under 'Aircraft Charter' or 'Flying Clubs'. If you prefer a commercial carrier, Macair (book through Qantas ☎ 13 13 13) flies from Brisbane on Monday and Thursday, and Mt Isa on Tuesday and Friday, while Airlines of SA (☎ 08-8642 3100) flies up from Port Augusta on Saturday. You will need to book months ahead.

You can of course go by road, and several outback tour operators offer camping trips to the races. Buses will also take your camping gear if it's too heavy or bulky for the plane.

On Sunday morning the first engines start before dawn, waking everyone except the terminally inebriated, and from first light there is a steady stream of planes taking off. For some, an early start is essential if they are to get home in daylight, even though the passengers might prefer to be sleeping off their hangovers. By midday Birdsville is just about empty again except for the council workers who are already cleaning up.

Getting Around

The pub is right beside the aerodrome and you can walk to anywhere in the town in a few minutes. Shuttle buses will take you to the racecourse about 5km south of town for a $2 donation to the local hospital.

Jim Hart

---

disaster Birdsville almost expired, but it managed to hang on as a minor regional centre. Today, increasing tourism has restored much of its former prosperity.

For details on Birdsville's tourist office see Information earlier in this section. Open the same hours, the adjoining library has Internet access.

Attractions around town include: the **Diamantina River**; **Big Red** (the highest sand dune on the French Line-QAA crossing) 33km west; a stand of rare **waddy trees** (see the Finke & Old Andado Tracks section earlier) 14km north; and a coolabah tree carved by **Burke and Wills**, 2.5km south.

The town has several 1880s stone buildings, including its sole surviving pub and the ruins of the **Australian Inland Mission hospital** *(Cnr Adelaide & Frew Sts)*.

There's also the **Birdsville Working Museum** *(☎ 07-4656 3250, Waddi Dr; adult/child $6/4; open 8am-6pm daily)*. This interesting museum houses a large and varied collection of memorabilia – everything from Kodak box brownies to old fuel bowsers to horse-driven machinery. There are free guided tours daily at 9am, 11am, 3pm and 5pm.

Blue Poles Gallery *(☎ 07-4656 3221,* **e** *birdsvillestudio@bigpond.com,* **w** *www .birdsvillestudio.com.au, Cnr Graham & Frew Sts; open 8am-10pm Thur-Sat, 8am-5pm Sun-Wed, Mar-Dec only)* is opposite the big water tank; this gallery and coffee shop displays some stunning work by local artist Wolfgang John.

The famous Birdsville Races, which take place on the first weekend in September, see the population swell to 7000 or more as visitors from all over Australia fly in for the fun. See the boxed text earlier.

Birdsville to Clifton Hills (198km)

Known as the Outside Track, the section of the Birdsville Track past Pandie Pandie homestead to Clifton Hills is relatively new, having been constructed in the 1960s to allow trucks to detour around Goyder Lagoon. Generally the road surface is good, apart from bulldust patches on the Diamantina flood plain and rough sections through Sturts Stony Desert.

Leaving Birdsville, the track drops down onto the Diamantina River's coolabah-studded flood plain and almost immediately crosses its main channel. Rising in western Queensland, where it is fed by monsoon rains, the river heads south for 800km before flooding out in **Goyder Lagoon**. This extensive (1300 sq km) seasonal swamp is about 80km downstream from Birdsville. When full, it overflows into **Warburton Creek**, which meanders around the Simpson Desert's southern fringe to Lake Eyre.

Minor floods of the Diamantina are fairly common but cause little inconvenience. However, major events (above 8m) inundate large areas and can close the track for weeks at a time. The biggest flood in living memory occurred in 1974, when the river level reached 9.5m at Birdsville and completely swept away the Alton Downs homestead. While there have been at least 14 floods above 6m at Birdsville since 1970, there were none of that magnitude in the 15 years prior to 1970.

Past the Diamantina, the track spears southward for nearly 100km across broad blacksoil flats hemmed by long, yellow sand ridges. Clumps of coolabahs indicate that you're still on the flood plain, while lines of stunted coolabahs growing on some of the sand hills show how high the water can reach. However, there is usually no shade for anything much larger than a

rabbit. You may spot a flock of brolgas stalking purposefully among the lignum bushes, but more likely the only moving thing (apart from flies) will be a whirling column of grey dust dancing across the plain.

Page Family Grave At 85km from Birdsville you're opposite the grave of the Page family (see History earlier in this section), which is about 3km to the east of the road and on the opposite side of Dead Man's Sandhill. There is no track to the site, but you can walk over and climb the sand hill for a view over the area where they met their tragic end. The dune, which parallels the road at this point, earned its macabre name when five stockmen from Innamincka perished on their way to the Birdsville Races in the summer of 1912.

Sturts Stony Desert Approaching the 100km mark the track leaves the flood plain and enters the armour-plated desolation of Sturts Stony Desert. Squeezed between the sand ridges of the Simpson and Strzelecki Deserts, this enormous wasteland of polished stones was crossed by the explorer Charles Sturt on his search for the inland sea in 1845. He decided that it had 'no parallel on the earth's surface', and most people would agree with him. Sturt's description is as valid today as it was then:

The whole expanse appeared to be as level as the ocean, nor had it as far as we could see a single shrub or a blade of vegetation upon it. The stones indeed lay so thick on the ground, that it was impossible for any herb to have forced its way between them.

Sturt's north-easterly route into the Simpson Desert, where lack of water and a high sand ridges forced him to turn back, would have taken him across the Birdsville Track about 40km past the Koonchera Sandhill.

Koonchera Soon after entering Sturts Stony Desert, you cross the southern end of the mighty Koonchera Sandhill. Although no monster at this end, it grows to become one of the largest dunes on the Diamantina flood plain. A waterhole near its northern end was the scene of a massacre of Aborigines in the early years of settlement, when a state of open warfare existed in the region. Later, a mob of over 1000 cattle heading towards Marree perished near here during a ferocious dust storm.

Looking south-eastwards from the crossing point, you can see what appears to be a mighty range of fiery hills shimmering in the distance. The mirage magnifies and deceives, but that red, Sahara-like dune is still a spectacular sight close up. You drive close to it on the **Walkers Crossing Track** to Innamincka (see Detours later).

Clifton Hills Leaving Koonchera, you cross more sand hills and two or three coolabah creeks in the 33km to **Melon Creek**, where there are good sheltered camp sites among shady trees. Soon after, the track heads out onto a vast stony plain dotted with distant timers. This is the inhospitable setting for Clifton Hills homestead, 43km past Melon Creek. It was built here in the 1940s after an earlier site was buried by shifting sand – perhaps this why the station folk chose a moonscape of brown rocks on which to build their new home. Clifton Hills covers about 12,600 sq km and is the largest station on the Birdsville Track.

Clifton Hills to Cooper Creek (183km)

A few kilometres past the homestead the track crosses several low rises that offer views of much kinder country down on Warburton Creek's broad flood plain. Although it's difficult to imagine in drought times, a good rain or a flood transforms the flood plains of this region into the arid outback's finest cattle-fattening pastures. Between these rare events, cattle survive on the hardy but nutritious saltbush that dominates much of the local vegetation.

This section is the track's most interesting, thanks to its varied scenery and poignant evidence of human endeavour. Its major highlights are the Mt Gason and Mirra Mitta Bores, the Mulka ruins, Mungeranie Gap, Cooper Creek and a cold beer at the Mungeranie Hotel. However, this section of road is also the roughest, with bulldust holes and stony sections; heavy rain can render it impassable for days at a time. Past Mt Gason, the track follows almost exactly in the footprints of the early drovers.

Mt Gason Eleven kilometres past Clifton Hills is the turn-off to the 4WD **Rig Rd**, which crosses the southern edge of the Simpson Desert to Mt Dare homestead (see the earlier Simpson Desert section). Some shady trees in a nearby creek make a good spot to boil the billy before starting out on this remote trek.

For the next 15km the Birdsville Track winds over stony, undulating country on the edge of higher ground before arriving at a rare stand of the endangered **Mt Gason wattle** (*Acacia pickardii*). These low, tough-looking trees are known only from the Mt Gason area and another site near Old Andado homestead, in the Northern Territory. The stand has been fenced to determine whether or not cattle and rabbits have any effect on regeneration.

Twelve kilometres further on is the turn-off to **Mt Gason Bore**, on a stony rise 2km to the west. This is the first in a string of artesian bores spaced roughly 40km apart that took the mobs from Warburton Creek to Marree. Drilled in 1900, it reached a depth of 1350m and is the deepest bore between Clifton Hills and Marree. As at Mirra Mitta and Cannuwaukaninna, which you pass further south, scalding water smelling of sulphur gushes from a pipe into an open drain that takes it away to cool sufficiently for cattle to drink. In winter the steam billows up like bushfire smoke and is visible for considerable distances. The stone remains of the old Mt Gason homestead are on a rise a few hundred metres west of the bore. Permission from Clifton Hills (☎ 08-8675 8302) is required to visit the bore.

Mt Gason itself is about 5km south of the bore. Rising a mere 35m above the plain, this little mesa is one of the most prominent features along the track. However, it only looks mountainous when magnified by the mirage. It was named after Samuel Gason, the first police officer on the Birdsville Track.

Mirra Mitta Bore Leaving Mt Gason Bore, continue south across Sturts Stony Desert until, at 45km, you see a lush patch of tall reeds sprouting among the gibbers. This is watered by a drain fed by Mirra Mitta Bore, 1km further on. Although its setting is almost unbelievably hostile, the bore once boasted a drovers' store and eating house as well as a thriving vegetable garden. The store was little more than an iron shed, which meant that its occupants froze on winter nights and roasted in hell during the dust storms that lashed it in summer. Modern softies will find it amazing that people willingly spent years living in this unpromising spot.

Mungeranie Twenty-eight kilometres past Mirra Mitta is picturesque Mungeranie Gap, a scenic highlight of the Birdsville Track. In the early morning or late afternoon, it's worth going for a walk among these colourful low hills to capture their stark beauty on film. The country changes to patchy bare gibbers and low sand ridges in the next 8km to **Mungeranie Hotel,** where a cold beer or two does wonders for dust-caked throats.

The hotel is only a stone's throw from the **Derwent River,** where an oasis of shady trees is watered by a flowing bore. Like other wetland areas on the track, this is a beaut spot for bird-watchers. Half-dead coolabahs on the nearby sand hill are roosting places for screeching flocks of corellas. When they land, it seems as if the bleached limbs have miraculously burst into great masses of white flowers, although flowers were never so noisy. Water birds such as ducks, herons and native hens are also common here.

Mulka The gibber plain continues to soften past Mungeranie, with grass and shrubby patches becoming more common. At 27km is the old **Oorawillanie** homestead, now just a pile of rubble and scattered rubbish beside the road. Drought put the station out of business many years ago, and it now forms part of the Mulka lease.

Low sand ridges begin to dominate over the next 13km, then you're at the crumbling stone ruins of the Mulka homestead and general store off to your right. Once a substantial building for these parts, it was the home of Mr and Mrs George Aiston who'd previously lived at the Mungeranie police station. Aiston had been a mounted constable there from 1912 to 1924. On retirement he bought Mulka station and established the store, rather than be posted to Adelaide.

A remarkable man, Aiston co-authored the academic book *Savage Life in Central Australia* and became an honorary consulting anthropologist to the Australian Institute of Anatomy. Mrs Aiston stayed on and ran the store after his death in 1944, but finally abandoned it in the mid-1950s.

Natterannie Sandhills Eight kilometres past Mulka, you say goodbye to the gibbers of Sturts Stony Desert and enter a world of high yellow sand ridges that roll away on either side like jumbled waves on an ocean. Known as the Natterannie Sandhills, this area marks the convergence of the Strzelecki Desert to the east and the **Tirari Desert** to the west. Parts of the Tirari, which runs onto the eastern shore of Lake Eyre, are the closest thing Australia has to true desert.

Cooper Creek

After 17km of sand ridges the timbered Cooper Creek flood plain is a welcome sight, to say the least. Five kilometres wide at the crossing, its outstanding feature is an abundance of spreading coolabahs, which invite you to stop and boil the billy. Coolabahs are exceptionally hardy trees, but even they can be killed by drought, as you'll see at the crossing's northern end. On the positive side, this area of standing dead timber is a good source of firewood.

The Cooper rises in the central highlands of Queensland, and by the time its floodwaters flow into Lake Eyre they've travelled about 1500km. Floods seldom cut the Birdsville Track, but when they do the only way across is via a ferry 10km upstream from the road crossing. There are two things you must do on the ferry: Get out of the vehicle and wear a life-jacket. These rules are in response to an accident many years ago when a crosswind blowing against the side of a truck caused the ferry to capsize. The driver of the truck, sitting in his cabin, was drowned.

If a crossing on today's modest ferry is an adventure, you can imagine what its predecessor, the MV *Tom Brennan*, must have been like. This tiny steel craft was used to transport supplies across the Cooper after the 1949 flood, which was the first to reach the track in 30 years. After many years of occasional service, the boat is now permanently grounded on the southern bank as a memorial to the motor mail officers.

Cooper Creek to Marree (134km)

This section's major highlights are Cannuwaukaninna Bore, and a lookout and ruins at Lake Harry. Although sand hills and gibbers still dominate, the country is generally kinder south of Etadunna. The road surface is good throughout, if stony in parts.

The Missionaries Leaving the Cooper behind, the track spears across a rolling gibber plain until, at 12.5km from the *Tom Brennan* memorial, it passes a tall metal cross on the roadside at Etadunna homestead. This was placed in memory of the missionaries who came here in the 1860s to convert the local Aboriginal people to Christianity.

In 1866 a Moravian mission station was established at Lake Kopperamanna, 3km north-west of the Cooper Creek crossing. However, faced with a searing drought and an unfriendly reception from the Aborigines, the Moravians departed for good the following year. Just months after the Moravians arrived, Lutheran missionaries from Germany built their Bethesda Mission beside nearby **Lake Killalpaninna**. It too was abandoned, but the Lutherans later returned and established a permanent presence.

In its heyday in the 1880s, Bethesda had a population of several hundred Aborigines and a dozen whites. It was laid out like a small town, with over 20 mud-brick buildings including a church with a 12m-high tower. It survived largely on the income derived from its flocks of sheep, but rabbit plagues and drought eventually forced the missionaries to leave forever in 1917. Today only a sad little cemetery and a few timber uprights show that they were ever there. Nevertheless, when full the lake is a magnificent jewel among the sand ridges – you could easily spend several days here bird-watching, bushwalking and dining on yellow belly and bream.

Mail Run to Birdsville

The Natterannie Sandhills hold no terrors for today's motorist, but in the droving era their numerous boggy patches were a nightmare for anyone travelling in a motor vehicle. Even the famous Birdsville mail officer Tom Kruse – an expert in taking heavy vehicles through difficult country from the 1930s to '50s – found them tough going. It usually took Kruse eight hours or more to get through the worst section, which covered about 12km! Unfortunately, the tyre-deflation method couldn't be used when the truck became bogged, which it frequently did. This was because the effort involved in using a hand-pump to reinflate the big tyres put the driver at risk of heat exhaustion, or worse.

Kruse was forced to employ various strategies in his attempts to defeat the Natterannie Sandhills. Trucks fitted with dual rear wheels carried 6m lengths of 75mm bore casing which were laid on the sand such that the dual tyres could grip them and so find traction. Otherwise the slopes had to be laid with heavy iron sheets, although these were liable to fly up and damage the vehicle's underparts if tackled at speed. He even tried using conveyor belts to create a half-track vehicle, but with limited success.

The sand hills made for a fearful journey in hot weather, which is most of the time up here. The mailmen were forced to endure it every fortnight for many years until the road was finally upgraded.

Lake Killalpaninna is about 17km north-west of Etadunna and is accessible by a 4WD track that turns off opposite the cross. Directions and permission to enter must be obtained from the **Etadunna** (☎ 08-8675 8308; day/overnight pass $5/10 per vehicle plus $5 key deposit) homestead. Camping at the lake is permitted.

Cannuwaukaninna Past Etadunna the track crosses a vast saltbush plain for most of the 11km to Cannuwaukaninna Bore, where a small wetland attracts many birds. Once it had a drover's store, but that too has long since been demolished and carted away for use elsewhere. In this isolated country very little that's recyclable, such as sheets of corrugated iron, goes to waste.

Leaving Cannuwaukaninna, you pass **Dulkaninna** homestead at 28km; the power line stretching across the gibbers to the house carries electricity generated by a water-driven turbine at the flowing bore. Thirty kilometres further on, **Clayton** homestead is on the banks of a sandy river boasting the largest coolabahs between Marree and Cooper Creek.

Lake Harry Ten kilometres past Clayton is a grid in a rather ordinary-looking fence. This is, in fact, the world's longest artificial barrier: the famous **Dog Fence** – see the Fauna section in Facts about the Outback chapter. The claypan on your left at the grid is Lake Harry.

Soon after, the track passes close to a low mesa with twin wheel ruts climbing to its summit. Although only 40m above Lake Harry, the hill is arguably the most prominent feature seen along the track. From the cairn on top there's a view over a vast patchwork carpet of brown, yellow and dark green, with the road a narrow white ribbon stretching from horizon to horizon.

Eight kilometres further on, the remains of **Lake Harry** homestead are off on the left. Set amid a scatter of low, ochre-coloured hills, with the mirage giving an illusion of water in the nearby lake, this forlorn ruin dates from 1870, when it was an outstation of Mundowdna. Thirty years later it became a camel depot for the bore-sinking gangs then working along the Birdsville Track.

Around the same time, the South Australian government established a trial plantation of over 2000 date palms. The experiment looked promising at first, but failed due to poor water quality and a high labour requirement. Today not even a stump remains, but it's said Lake Harry palms still line the streets of Renmark and Mildura, both on the Murray River.

Twenty-two kilometres past Lake Harry you enter sheep country, as evidenced by the way the vegetation has been eaten out. Then the glittering iron roofs of Marree come into view across the plain and the end of the journey is just minutes away.

Marree

On a barren gibber plain 3km from Hergott Springs, Marree was a thriving railway town of 600 residents just two years after its establishment in 1883. The Great Northern Railway to Port Augusta had made Marree the focus for a vast area of the outback. In 1885 alone, between 40,000 and 50,000 head of cattle from Queensland and the Northern Territory were entrained for Adelaide. Meanwhile, camel trains carried supplies and general cargo to places as far away as the Gulf of Carpentaria. At one time Marree was home to 60 Afghani cameleers and their families, who lived in their own 'Ghantown', complete with mosque. In 1910, around 1500 camels were operating out of Marree.

However, progress sounded the death knell of Marree's role as a major regional centre when first the cameleers and then the droving teams were replaced by motor vehicles. Most people thought the end had come when, in 1980, the narrow-gauge railway to Alice Springs was replaced by the present service, which bypasses the town. Today, with a population of about 100, Marree clings to life as a minor regional centre and survives mainly on welfare cheques and tourism.

Despite its decline, Marree still has a good range of facilities such as a hotel, caravan parks, a landing strip, minimarkets, mechanical repairs, police and a hospital. See Facilities later for further details.

Several fine old residences, the abandoned **railway station** (complete with rusting locomotives) and an impressive hotel (1883) are graphic evidence of a more prosperous past.

Other points of interest include the small **Aboriginal heritage museum** *(☎ 08-8675 8351, Cnr Railway Terrace South & Sixth St; admission by donation; open 9am-4pm Mon-Fri)* in the Arabunna Centre and a large **sundial** in the form of a squatting camel (it's made of railway sleepers) near the railway station.

The Marree Picnic Races, held on the Queen's Birthday Weekend in June, attract a good crowd. Also popular is the Marree Australian Camel Cup, held on the first Saturday in July on odd-numbered years.

DETOURS
Kalamurina (55km one way)
The Kalamurina access road turns off the Birdsville Track 1.5km north of Mungeranie. It's generally rough, with plenty of bulldust patches, but is usually suitable for conventional vehicles in dry conditions. Many of the station tracks – including the White Bull Bore access – are 4WD only.

Kalamurina homestead (pronounced 'kallah-mer-nah'; ☎ 08-8675 8310, fax 8675 8321) Overnight/day passes $25/15 per vehicle. Camping is permitted along Warburton Creek between the homestead and White Bull Bore, about 55km downstream. There's a camping ground with toilets and showers near the homestead, or stay at sites with no facilities along the creek; both are the same price. The creek-bank environment offers interesting bushwalking and plenty of birdlife, particularly when the waterholes are full. They also contain many fat yellow belly and bream. At such times the contrast with the nearby sand hills and gibber flats is nothing short of fantastic.

Innamincka (229km one way)
The **Walkers Crossing Track** to Innamincka turns off the Birdsville Track 122km south of Birdsville. Winding across the Cooper Creek flood plain and through the big sand hills of the Strzelecki Desert, it offers a different experience in remote touring. En route you

pass infrastructure and wells of the Moomba oil and gas field. While the track is generally good in dry conditions, numerous sandy sections restrict its use to 4WD vehicles only.

The Walkers Crossing Track crosses Clifton Hills station (☎ 08-8675 8302), and the owner's permission is required to use it. The track was closed at the time of this update due to unresolved public liability issues.

The track also crosses the **Innamincka Regional Reserve**, so you'll need a Desert Parks Pass as well. These can be purchased in Birdsville, Marree and Innamincka – see the Travel Permits section in the Getting Around chapter.

For track information contact the Innamincka ranger (☎ 08-8675 9909). For details of Innamincka see the Strzelecki Track section later in this chapter.

ALTERNATIVE ROUTE
The Inside Track (157km one way)
Until the 1960s the Birdsville Track south to Clifton Hills wound among the channels of Goyder Lagoon. When wet, this black-soil swamp is a disaster for any sort of vehicle, so the present Outside Track was constructed to avoid it.

Known as the Inside Track, the original part of the old stock route covers about 157km, which makes it 25km shorter than the new road. It is the more scenic of the two, but is also slower, rougher and lonelier – in short, it's an attractive alternative for the more adventurous 4WD traveller. The Inside Track joins the Outside Track 60km west of the Koonchera Sandhill and 16km east of Clifton Hills homestead.

ORGANISED TOURS
Birdsville
Waddayawannado Tours (☎ 07-4656 3028, e waddayawannado@bigpond.com, 15 Gibber Court) does town tours ($10) as well as visits to Big Red ($20) and the waddy trees ($15).

Marree
For details of tours operating from Marree see the earlier Oodnadatta Track section.

FACILITIES

Birdsville

Being a regional centre, if one of only minor importance, Birdsville has a good range of facilities and services, including police, a hospital, hotel, general store, post office, airstrip and mechanical repairs.

Birdsville Hotel (*☎ 07-4656 3244,* **e** *birdsville@theoutback.com.au,* **w** *www .theoutback.com.au, 1 Adelaide St)* Singles/ doubles/triples/quads $70/90/105/120. Built in 1884, this stone pub has comfortable, air-conditioned motel-style units out the back, as well as a *restaurant* (mains $15 to $22, counter meals $8 to $18.). The licensee, who looks after the airstrip, is the local agent for Avgas – advance orders are appreciated.

Birdsville Auto Centre & General Store *(☎ 07-4656 3226, Cnr Frew & Adelaide Sts)* Open 8am-6pm Mon-Sat, 8am-5pm Sun. Birdsville Auto sells diesel, super and unleaded petrol, as well as grocery lines, frozen meat, fast food, ice, vehicle parts, tyres, camping equipment and maps. Vehicle repairs are available and they'll just about go anywhere to recover a stranded vehicle. Bankcard, Visa and MasterCard are accepted, and Eftpos is available.

Note that the availability of fresh fruit and vegetables depends on when the supply truck was last in – it comes in only once every two or three weeks.

Birdsville Fuel Service (*☎ 07-4656 3263, Adelaide St)* Open Apr-Oct 8am-6pm daily, Nov-Mar 7.30am-7pm daily. This place sells diesel, super and unleaded, and does mechanical and tyre repairs. It has Eftpos as well as the post office and Commonwealth Bank agency. Major credit cards are accepted.

Birdsville Caravan Park (*☎ 07-4656 3214,* **e** *birdsvillecvanpk@growzone.com .au, Florence St)* Unpowered/powered sites $12/18, cabins with shared facilities $60, cabins with own bathroom and kitchen $100. While lawns are unknown, the park does have shade shelters, modern bathroom and laundry facilities, electric barbecues, and powered sites with overhead lights and water. It overlooks a lagoon on the Diamantina River flood plain – a great spot for bird-watchers.

Mungeranie

Mungeranie Hotel (*☎ 08-8675 8317)* Camp sites $11, singles/doubles $38.50/62. This isolated place offers a wide range of services and amenities, including a landing strip, public telephone, ice, takeaway liquor, counter *meals* ($15 to $18), minor mechanical and tyre repairs, and fuel sales (diesel, super and unleaded). The normal trading hours for fuel are 8am to 8pm daily; Avgas should be ordered at least one month in advance. There's a camping area with some shade down by the Derwent River, and the pub has air-con twin rooms with shared facilities.

Marree

Marree offers a range of commercial facilities including a pub, two caravan parks and two stores.

Marree Hotel (*☎ 08-8675 8344,* **e** *marreehotel@bigpond.com, Railway Tce South)* Singles/doubles $39/55, 4-person room $110. This grand old pub offers counter and dining room *meals* (from $15) as well as old-style hotel accommodation.

Oasis Caravan Park (*☎ 08-8675 8352, Railway Terrace South)* Unpowered/powered sites $12/18, singles/doubles/triples $35/48/ 60. This park in the middle of town has grassed camp sites and some good shade. Its cabins have air-con and private facilities.

Marree Caravan & Campers Park (*☎ 08-8675 8371, Cnr Oodnadatta & Birdsville Tracks)* Unpowered/powered sites $12/16, bunkhouse beds $18, beds in twin room without/with private facilities $14/40, on-site caravans $30. This somewhat dustier alternative to the Oasis Caravan Park is at the start of the Birdsville Track about 1km south of town. It has grassed camp sites, a campers kitchen and air-con to all units. The park also sells diesel, super and unleaded fuel, and can attend to minor mechanical and tyre repairs.

There are two seven-day minimarkets, both with Eftpos: the **Oasis Cafe** (attached to the Oasis Caravan Park), which has a State Bank agency; and **Marree's Outback Store & Roadhouse** (*☎ 08-8675 8360, Railway Terrace North),* which has the post office and Commonwealth Bank agencies. Both sell takeaway meals and diesel, super and unleaded fuel; the roadhouse also has Internet access ($2.50 for 10 minutes).

Bush Camping

There are bush camp sites with basic facilities beside the road at the Clayton River (52km north of Marree) and the Cooper Creek (134km north of Marree). A donation to the RFDS, is paid into honesty boxes as a fee.

Otherwise, roadside camp sites offering good shelter aren't common. The best places are along coolabah creeks (such as between Koonchera and Melon Creek) and in sand hill areas, but don't leave it too late in the day. You can also camp at Lake Killalpannina, 17km north-west of Etadunna.

ALTERNATIVE TRANSPORT
Air

Birdsville is serviced each Saturday by Airlines of SA (☎ 08-8642 3100) on its mail run from Port Augusta to Boulia, in southwestern Queensland. The one-way fare costs $193/149 from Port Augusta/Innamincka.

Macair (Qantas ☎ 13 1313) flies to Birdsville from Brisbane on Monday and Thursday ($497 one way) and from Mt Isa on Tuesday and Friday ($273).

Strzelecki Track

Highlights

- Visiting the sites associated with Burke and Wills on Cooper Creek
- Canoeing and bird-watching on the gum-lined waterholes near Innamincka
- Absorbing the silent emptiness of the vast gibber plains

What does a Polish-born, sometime eccentric explorer who called himself a 'count' have to do with inland Australia? Not very much really, but his name is immortalised in the name of the track and the creek it follows through the arid expanse of north-eastern South Australia.

For most modern-day travellers the Strzelecki Track (pronounced 'stres-**lek**-ki'), which was originally a stock route, runs from Lyndhurst, a tiny hamlet on the northern edge of the Flinders Ranges 560km north of Adelaide, to Innamincka on historic Cooper Creek, a total distance of 483km. In times past the stock route continued north from Innamincka to Arrabury station, then on to meet the Birdsville Developmental Rd (between Birdsville and Windorah) 60km west of Beetoota.

The Strzelecki Track traverses extremely arid country, but like the Birdsville and Oodnadatta Tracks is well defined, graded and normally passable to conventional vehicles.

History

Long before the arrival of Europeans, Aboriginal people lived along the permanent waters of Cooper Creek. Little remains of their passing in this harsh desert country, but not far from Innamincka a spectacular array of rock engravings testify to the rich culture that was once here.

On 18 August 1845 the explorer Charles Sturt arrived at a creek which he named after Paul Edmund de Strzelecki. A self-taught geologist, Strzelecki had discovered and climbed Australia's highest mountain, Mt Kosciuszko, five years earlier. Obviously Sturt was impressed by his reputation!

Sturt was on the last legs of his central Australian trip, trying to find his elusive 'inland sea', when he stumbled across the life-saving waters of this ephemeral creek. He followed it north and discovered the more permanent waters of Cooper Creek, which, when in flood, feed Strzelecki Creek. The latter flows into Lake Blanche, but water rarely reaches far enough south to flood its normally dry, salt-encrusted bed.

The area around the junction of the Cooper and Strzelecki Creeks was to become etched into the Australian psyche by the death of explorers Burke and Wills in 1860 – see White Exploration in the Facts about the Outback chapter.

The route that was to become, for the most part, the Strzelecki Track, runs between the northern extremity of the Flinders

Ranges and Cooper Creek, and was pioneered by a bushman who happened also to be a cattle thief.

In the early days of settlement, some people regarded cattle-duffing (rustling) and the branding of cleanskins (unbranded cattle) as an easy way of stocking a station. But Harry Redford had bigger and better plans. With 1000 head of cattle stolen from Bowen Downs, north-east of Longreach in central Queensland, he set out on an ambitious drive over unknown country to sell the mob in South Australia.

Redford did dispose of the stolen cattle there, but a distinctive white bull in the mob was identified. Redford was arrested and brought back to face justice at the Roma court in Queensland in 1873. However, despite overwhelming evidence, public admiration at his exploit was such that the jury declared him not guilty! He went on to carve a name for himself as one of Australia's greatest drovers, with escapades in the Northern Territory and Far North Queensland.

Relying on waterholes and infrequent floods, the Strzelecki was always a much tougher route than the Birdsville Track, and in times of drought the track was not used for years. Travellers also had to cross the infamous Cobbler Desert, a sea of deeply furrowed and convoluted sand hills at the track's southern end.

Before the discovery of gas and oil in the Cooper Creek basin in the early 1960s, the track was largely unused. The development of gas and oil fields has transformed the area: Main roads have been upgraded, and a network of lesser routes crisscross the desert, some heading to wells and camps, others petering out in a sea of sand.

Information

Most of the adventure in travelling along the Strzelecki Track has been nullified since Moomba came into operation in the 1960s – although it's still a long way between drinks. For the most part the road has been rerouted away from the Strzelecki Creek flood plain. Unlike the rutted track of yesteryear it's a good dirt road on which it is usually quite easy to travel at 80km/h.

Contact the Outback Road Report Hotline on ☎ 1300 361 033 for current road conditions.

While there's no need to register with police, be aware that there are no supplies available between Lyndhurst and Innamincka. Moomba has no facilities for tourists, and only emergency assistance is given. There's a public telephone at the security gate at the entrance to Moomba.

As for most of the routes in this book, you need to be self-sufficient to travel the Strzelecki Track. Summer can be very hot, you will meet few other travellers, and a breakdown can be life-threatening.

There are no medical facilities or police stations in this remote region – the nearest are in Leigh Creek South. Innamincka is covered by the RFDS; in an emergency, call RFDS paramedics based at Moomba.

Lyndhurst Lyndhurst doesn't have an information centre, but the Lyndhurst Hotel (☎ 08-8675 7781) can certainly let you know about local attractions and road conditions.

The nearest medical facilities and police station are at Leigh Creek South, 38km south of Lyndhurst. The Leigh Creek hospital (☎ 08-8675 2100) and the Leigh Creek South police station (☎ 08-8675 2004) are in Black Oak Dr.

Innamincka The Innamincka Hotel (☎ 08-8675 9901) and the Innamincka Trading Post (☎ 08-8675 9900) can help travellers with information about the surrounding area.

The National Parks and Wildlife SA office (☎ 08-8675 9909), open from 8am to 6pm daily, in the old Australian Inland Mission hospital can give advice on all matters relating to the Innamincka Regional Reserve. It also houses interesting displays on early life in the district.

Books & Maps The best single map for the track is *Birdsville and Strzelecki Tracks* published by Westprint. It forms part of the Desert Parks Pass package.

A number of books cover the history of the surrounding area, including *Drought or Deluge: Man in the Cooper's Creek Region* by HM Tolcher. *Innamincka – The Town with Two Lives* (Innamincka Progress Association), by the same author, is a little beauty containing many historic photographs.

For a comprehensive insight into the natural order of things, try *Natural History of the North East Deserts*, edited by M Tyler, C Twidale, M Davies & C Wells.

Radio Frequencies If you have an HF radio with you, the important frequencies to have are the RFDS bases at Broken Hill, Port Augusta and Mt Isa, and the Telstra (OTC) base in Sydney.

For Broken Hill (call sign VJC), the primary frequency is 4055kHz with a secondary one of 6920kHz. Port Augusta (call sign VNZ) has a primary frequency of 4010kHz and secondary frequencies of 6890kHz and 8165kHz. Mt Isa (call sign VJI) has a primary frequency of 5110kHz and secondary frequencies of 4935kHz, 6965kHz and 7392kHz.

THE ROUTE
Lyndhurst

Lyndhurst, at the southern end of the Strzelecki Track, is 560km north of Adelaide and reached by a good bitumen road. It's considered by many to be the stepping-off point for the real outback. Here the bitumen ends; a dirt road heads north to Marree and the Birdsville and Oodnadatta Tracks, while the Strzelecki Track heads off to the east.

The town caters for travellers with fuel, food and accommodation (see Facilities later in this section).

Five kilometres north of the town, close to the Marree road, is an **ochre quarry** that was once worked by Aboriginal people. The ochre from this area was traded as far north as the Gulf of Carpentaria and south to the coast. Listed on the Register of the National Estate, this quarry, unlike many others, has never been mined by Europeans.

Turning off just opposite the general store, the Strzelecki Track passes the pub and crosses the old Great Northern Railway line before heading out onto the sea of gibbers that surrounds the township.

One of the characters of the north is **Talc Alf**, a local artist whose abode and gallery are just past the pub. He carves sculptures out of the soft talc stone mined at nearby Mt Freeling. Give him a chance and he'll let you know his views on politics, conservation, tourism, tourists and life in general.

Lyndhurst to Strzelecki Crossing (277km)

As you head north along the Strzelecki, the Flinders Ranges are a beckoning blue jumble of ridges and peaks on the southeastern horizon. The track passes through arid pastoral country made famous by Sir Thomas Elder who, in the 1860s, had taken up the expansive Murnpeowie station. Here he bred horses for the Indian Army and ran more than 100,000 sheep.

About 76km from Lyndhurst a track heads east off the Strzelecki Track towards the **Mt Freeling talc mine**. Less than 30km further north, the route passes through the Dog Fence. Sheep become scarce, and once through the fence you'll see only cattle.

Creek crossings are fairly common across these vast gibber plains. However, most are kept in good condition and the creeks only flow after rare, heavy rain. MacDonnell Creek is 50km north of the fence; the ruins of **Blanchewater** homestead are just north of the road and on the western bank.

In 1860, when the Burke and Wills tragedy was being played out, Blanchewater was the northernmost station in South Australia. It was this property that the explorers tried to reach after returning to Cooper Creek from the north. It was also where Harry Redford sold his ill-gotten cattle (see History earlier) rather than chance the saleyards in Adelaide.

Forty kilometres further on, a minor road heads south past the eastern flank of the Flinders Ranges to Arkaroola and the Gammon Ranges National Park. Another 7km later you wave goodbye to the gibbers and say hello to the sandy semi-desert that keeps you company almost all the way from here to Innamincka.

Montecollina Bore, the only bore drilled on the Strzelecki Track for the use of drovers, is just over 19km further north.

This is a popular spot to camp, but there are no facilities and you should bring your own firewood. The small wetland at the bore is a good spot for bird-watching.

Pushing ever north, the Strzelecki Track passes through the **Cobbler Desert**, its stark eroded forms being blamed on the rabbit plagues and heavy stocking rates of the late 19th century.

Strzelecki Creek is now just a few kilometres to the west, but the first time you see it will be some 50km further north at the **Strzelecki Crossing**.

About 3km south of the crossing a 4WD track heads west to **Yaningurie Waterhole**. This is a popular spot to *camp*, and with its water and trees is a better bet than trying to find a camp site by the road. Bring your wood in and *don't* cut trees down.

Shortly after, the road swings across the river and continues on the western side of the creek.

Strzelecki Crossing to Innamincka (206km)

The road continues north between dreary sand ridges to the Moomba turn-off, 95km past the crossing. At about 45km, a turn-off to the east heads towards **Merty Merty** station and the original Strzelecki Track. See Alternative Routes later.

From Moomba the main road heads east across the upper Strzelecki Creek flood plain, with its scrubby coolabahs and saltbush. It passes the **Della gas field** before meeting a major intersection 63km from Moomba. You turn left here for Innamincka, travelling between high red sand ridges until meeting the gibbers again 11km out.

Innamincka

On the banks of Cooper Creek is the tiny township of Innamincka. Here you can buy a cold beer, have a meal and shower, and fuel up. There's plenty to do in the surrounding area, so allow a bit of time to soak up the atmosphere and enjoy the scenery along the creek.

Close to the Queensland border, Innamincka owes its beginnings to the customs post which, prior to Federation in 1901,

taxed all the stock and goods travelling between the two colonies. A pub soon followed to help quench the thirst of the hard-working drovers. With their revelry came a need for a police station and lock-up, and by the turn of the century, Innamincka was a town of four or five buildings.

With the advent of free trade between the states as a result of Federation, the customs post went in 1901. But the years that followed saw Sidney Kidman, the 'Cattle King', build his empire. The Cooper fairly hummed with the clash of branding irons and the rattle of stirrup and spur. The pub and the police post were still required.

In 1928 the Australian Inland Mission (AIM) built a hostel there. Established in 1912, the AIM was a Presbyterian Church organisation that offered support to people living in the remote parts of Australia. Its first director was John Flynn, the founder of the RFDS. A few years later it and the Strzelecki Track played a part in John Flynn's establishment of the RFDS.

Until the beginning of WWII a mail truck ploughed its way up the track to Innamincka from Farina, now a ghost town south of Lyndhurst. Since the war the mail has come up every two weeks from Broken Hill via Tibooburra in New South Wales.

In 1951 the AIM closed the hostel, and within a year the police post and pub had gone as well. The town was dead. A couple of stations in the area claimed the remains – the pub became the stockmen's quarters for nearby Innamincka station, while the hostel was partly demolished and transported to Arrabury station, 160km north. About the only thing of substance left was the monster heap of empty beer bottles that stretched for over 200m and was over 1m high. It was obvious why there had been a police post.

With the 1960s came the search for oil and gas, and significant strikes of both occurred in the surrounding dune country.

Nowadays there are around 15 permanent residents of Innamincka, which is about as big as it's ever been. Mind you, there is a good chance you'll arrive when the place is seemingly overflowing with stockmen from the nearby stations, oil workers from Moomba, road workers from up and down the track, and more than a few travellers and holiday-makers.

A picnic race meeting is held each year, generally towards the end of August, and that really makes the place bounce. Then there may be over a thousand people in town! Needless to say, accommodation is stretched at these times and even camping close to town can be crowded.

Take the opportunity to visit **Coongie Lakes**, 106km to the north-west. When full this is often a spectacular wetland alive with birds. The lakes, which form one of the arid outback's greatest freshwater lake systems, rely on the occasional flooding of the Cooper to fill them. Coongie Lake itself is the southernmost in this complex, and the only one you can visit.

ALTERNATIVE ROUTES
Original Strzelecki Track (79km)
The turn-off to Merty Merty and the original Strzelecki Track is 45km north of the Strzelecki Creek crossing. From here a good road heads east over high, steep sand dunes to the Strzelecki flood plain, with its big coolabahs. At about 9km you pass the turn-off right to Merty Merty homestead, then arrive at the 'old' track on the left.

The road straight ahead leads to **Cameron Corner**, 105km away, where the borders of South Australia, Queensland and New South Wales meet. The *Cameron Corner Store* (☎ 08-8091 3872) sells liquor, ice, limited supplies, takeaway food and fuel (diesel, super and unleaded). It has basic bush camping with toilet and showers ($5 per vehicle).

The 'old' track – recommended 4WD – winds across the flood plain and is much more interesting than the modern version. Just how deep this country goes under water in a big flood is shown by the lines of coolabahs that grow on the flanks of some of the sand ridges. These 'flood levels' are up to 5m above the plain – it all seems rather improbable, but the evidence is there.

A few kilometres north from the aforementioned intersection you see the first signs of a producing oil field: Large, robotic arms wave to their computer master's beat,

pumping the liquid gold across the sand ridges to Moomba. Several of these pumps are just off to the east. Strictly speaking you shouldn't approach them, but most travellers are interested enough to do the short diversion. Please don't interfere with this equipment – the producers are concerned about vandalism, and access would definitely suffer if any damage was done.

Sixty-nine kilometres north of Merty Merty you meet the new road once more. Here you turn right to Innamincka (64km).

ACTIVITIES
Canoeing
Canoeing is excellent along the Cooper and at Coongie Lakes, where a host of water birds reagle with their variety and beauty.

One of the best canoe trips starts at Cullyamurra Waterhole, where vehicle access ends. From there you can take an easy paddle upstream as far as the Innamincka Choke and check out the Aboriginal engravings nearby, or head off downstream all the way to the causeway at Innamincka itself. It makes for a very pleasant day's outing.

The Innamincka Hotel hires two-person Canadian canoes for $20/30 per half/full day.

Fishing
Any decent-sized stretch of water here offers the chance of catching a feed of fish. Yellow belly is the prize catch of these waters, and it tastes delicious.

ORGANISED TOURS
Local tours can be arranged at the hotel or general store in Innamincka. Given enough warning, they can take you out to Coongie Lakes or along the Cooper to the Dig Tree and the other historic places scattered along the waterway.

Depending on numbers, *Cooper Discovery Tours* (☎ pub 08-8675 9901) runs a two-hour return cruise from the town common to King's Marker. Cruises leave at 9am and 4pm (adult/child $25/15).

A number of operators include the Strzelecki Track and/or the area around Innamincka in their itineraries. The pub can identify tours currently visiting the area.

Historic Sites of the Cooper

Aboriginal Sites

Aboriginal rock engravings can be found at the far end of Cullyamurra Waterhole, close to the bottleneck on the Cooper known as the Innamincka Choke. To find this spot, follow the vehicle track (that starts 8km from Innamincka on the road to Nappa Merrie) along Cullyamurra Waterhole to its end, then walk along the path to the rocky area that can be seen on both sides of the creek. If you are camped on the waterhole, there is no better way to get to the site than by canoe.

On sand hills all along the Cooper flood plain are old camp sites littered with stone chips and tools, and the evidence of past feasts. Note that the collection of such artefacts is illegal.

Explorers

Reminders of the earliest white explorers can also be seen in this region. Innamincka has a monument to Charles Sturt, who passed through this area in 1845, and Burke and Wills, who perished near here in 1860 (see History in the Facts about the Outback chapter for more about Burke and Wills).

The Burke and Wills expedition established a depot near a large coolabah now known as 'the Dig Tree' – this can easily be visited from Innamincka. Sitting here under the shady trees watching a

---

Regulars at Innamincka include *Dick Lang's Desert-Air Safaris* (☎ 08-8264 7200) of Adelaide and *Corner Country Adventure Tours* (☎ 08-8087 5142, e outback@rural net.net.au, W www.cornercountryadventure .com.au) of Broken Hill.

Ecotrek (☎ 08-8383 7198, e ecotrek@ ozemail.com.au, W www.ecotrek.com.au) does nine-day canoeing trips to the Innamincka area. These cost $1620, all inclusive.

FACILITIES
Lyndhurst

Lyndhurst Roadhouse (☎ 08-8675 7782) Open 7am-9pm daily. This place sells fuel (diesel, super, unleaded and LPG), take-away and sit-down *meals* ($9 to $14), Akubra hats, camping equipment, and limited grocery lines.

Lyndhurst Elsewhere Hotel (☎ 08-8675 7781, e lyndhursthotel@telstra.com) Railway carriages $45/50/60 per twin/double/ family, single/family hotel rooms $30/66. Meals $9-12. All rooms are air-con and have share facilities; tent and caravan sites were being developed at the time of this update. Eftpos is available.

Lyndhurst has no bank, post office or tyre and mechanical repairs; the nearest such facilities are at Leigh Creek South, 38km south.

Innamincka

Innamincka Hotel (☎ 08-8675 9901, e innamincka@theoutback.com.au, W www .theoutback.com.au) Singles/doubles/triples $45/66/88. The pub has air-con motel-style units, and offers breakfast, lunch and dinner daily (meals $8 to $19). Each week during the tourist season it puts on a couple of *barbecue nights* (both $15), and these are worth attending: Wednesday is 'Beef & Creek' night, when you feast on steak and fish, while Sunday is a roast night.

Innamincka Trading Post (☎ 08-8675 9900) Singles/doubles/triples $45/65/95. Open Apr-Oct 7am-7pm daily; Nov-Mar 8am-5.30pm. Next door to the hotel, the store sells daily requirements such as grocery lines, meat, fishing and camping gear, maps and books and also fuel (diesel, super and unleaded, camping gas and Avgas). There are three comfortable two-bedroom cabins, each with air-con and private facilities.

Innamincka has no banking or post office facilities, but Eftpos is available. Major credit cards (except Diners Club) are readily accepted at the hotel and trading store.

Just a stone's throw away are some excellent toilets and showers – a donation to help in the upkeep is greatly appreciated. Two solar-powered telephones are a link with the outside world.

Historic Sites of the Cooper

muddy river flow past, you cannot help but be struck by the irony of it all. The creek and its environs supported many hundreds of Aborigines and yet Burke and Wills starved to death.

The Dig Tree, which played such a pivotal role in the Burke and Wills saga, is arguably the most important reminder of early European exploration in Australia. A memorial to Wills can be found at the western end of Tilcha Waterhole; Burke's memorial is on the edge of Burke Waterhole – a pleasant spot to die.

About 7km west of Innamincka is a marker indicating the place where John King was found alive by Alfred Howitt's party. Howitt's depot camp on the Cooper is marked by a monument on the northern side of the river. This spot is best found by crossing the Cooper just below Cullyamurra Waterhole, then walking upstream to the monument. Be prepared for wet feet!

Other Sites
In Innamincka itself, the Australian Inland Mission nursing home stood in ruins for many years, but has now been restored. These days it houses the National Parks and Wildlife SA office, and has interesting displays of old photographs and historic memorabilia.

Camping is allowed by the creek on the town common. To camp elsewhere in the area (and there are plenty of good spots to camp), you will need a Desert Parks Pass ($80), available from either the ranger in the old Australian Inland Mission Hospital (☎ 08-8675 9909) or the store. For more details on the pass, see the Travel Permits section in the Getting Around chapter.

The camping rate within the Innamincka zone is a donation of $5 per vehicle, payable at the store or pub – the money allows upkeep of the facilities.

Bush Camping
There's camping at Montecollina Bore and Yaningurie Waterhole between Lyndhurst and the Strzelecki Crossing. See this section earlier for details.

Along the Cooper There are numerous camp sites spread along the river both up and downstream from Innamincka. One of the most popular sites is *Cullyamurra Waterhole*, about 13km east of Innamincka, a spectacular waterhole, stretching upriver for at least 6km to a natural rock bar called the Innamincka Choke. This waterhole is reputedly the deepest waterhole in central Australia – its depth has been measured at 28m. It has never been known to dry up.

Large gnarled gums line the creek and offer shade, but wood for fires is scarce. Much damage has been done in recent years to the magnificent trees along this section of river by unthinking people chopping down branches and even whole trees to feed their fires. If you must have a camp fire, bring in the firewood from elsewhere.

West of Innamincka, along the 15-Mile Track (this is another route to Moomba), is *Queerbidie Waterhole*, 2.5km away. A further 1.5km on, a turn-off towards the river leads to a number of camp sites spread along a short section of waterway.

Heading west from Innamincka, the 15 Mile Track passes a number of turn-offs that lead into camp sites along the Cooper. These include Queerbidie Waterhole (2.5km from Innamincka), *Ski Beach* (8km), *King's Marker* (10km), *Minkie Waterhole* (12km) and *Tilcha Waterhole* (16km).

All rubbish must be disposed of at the public refuse pit in Innamincka.

Coongie Lakes The track out to Coongie Lakes, 106km north-west of Innamincka, is usually restricted to 4WD. You need a Desert Parks Pass to travel this road and to camp.

Along the way are some pleasant camping spots: *Bulyeroo Waterhole* (37km from Innamincka), *Scrubby Camp Waterhole*

(45km) and *Kudriemitchie Waterhole* (85km). Wood fires, and even generators and dogs, are allowed as far as Kudriemitchie; further north these are all banned.

Don't forget that this area is part of a working cattle station and cattle may be seen along the way. Take care.

Just before the track ends at Coongie, a couple of turn-offs to the east lead to some camp sites along the lake shore. Only gas fires are allowed out here. Rubbish can be dumped only at the rubbish disposal pits at Kudriemitchie and Scrubby Camp.

Airstrips

Every homestead along the Strzelecki has an airstrip close by. These are meant for light aircraft and can be dotted with anthills, potholes and animals.

Innamincka has a well-used airstrip that sees many people flying in for a weekend or longer. The airstrip is on the highest ground around and is only a short distance from the pub. At times, when the Cooper is running a banker, this is the only way supplies and people can move in and out of the tiny outpost. Avgas is usually available – contact the Trading Post for more details. If you are flying in and will need fuel, it's best to check beforehand.

ALTERNATIVE TRANSPORT
Air

Innamincka is serviced each Saturday by Airlines of SA (☎ 08-8642 3100) on its mail run from Port Augusta to Boulia. The one-way fare costs $193.

Gunbarrel Highway

The Gunbarrel Hwy was the first link between central Australia and Western Australia. Built to service the Woomera Rocket Range and the Giles weather station, it was completed in 1958.

Today much of the 'real' Gunbarrel is out of bounds to normal travellers – in fact, the section from the Heather Hwy Junction west to Carnegie station is the only remaining stretch that's easily accessible. The original Gunbarrel actually began near Mt Cavenagh, 97km south of Erldunda on the Stuart Hwy, and swung down into South Australia before looping back to a point 28km east of Giles. Today, this section passes through Anangu Pitjantjatjara land and you need a very good reason to be granted a permit. The next original section from Giles (also known as Warakurna these days) to Jackie Junction is officially abandoned, but accessible under stringent conditions (see the boxed text 'The Abandoned Gunbarrel' later in this chapter).

This text describes today's accepted Gunbarrel Hwy route, which begins at Yulara (the resort servicing the endless stream of visitors to Uluru) and follows the Great Central Rd through Docker River (Kaltukatjara) and Warburton, up the Heather Hwy and along the original track to Carnegie station. Unlike the Great Central Rd, which is a well-maintained dirt highway, this last section is a rough, remote track that passes through beautiful parts of the Gibson Desert.

Also covered is the alternative route that continues along the Great Central Rd to Laverton, instead of heading up the Heather Hwy. While you're not taking in much of the original track this way, it's still a pleasant journey and you end up a good 300km closer to Kalgoorlie and Perth.

The Great Central Rd itself is gradually being improved to all-weather status and there are grand plans one day to seal it all the way to Winton in Queensland. This 2000km-long Laverton-Winton link is being promoted as the Outback Highway by enthusiastic government officials.

History

There was a flurry of activity in this region back in 1873 when three explorers vied for the honour of discovering what lay between the Overland Telegraph Line (which stretched across central Australia from north to south) and the Western Australian coast. Major Peter Warburton pushed north-west from Alice Springs, finally making the coast near De Grey north of present-day Port Hedland, but almost died in the attempt.

William Gosse left Alice eight days after Warburton had set out, but swung further south and he and his men eventually became the first whites to see Uluru, which Gosse named Ayers Rock. In his journeys south and west from Ayers Rock, Gosse also named the Mann and Tomkinson Ranges, before giving up his quest to cross the continent near Mt Squires in the Cavenagh Ranges of Western Australia.

Ernest Giles had already been in the region west of Alice in 1872. Later that year he tried to cross a vast salt lake he called Lake Amadeus. To the south he could see a cluster of rounded peaks, the highest of which he called Mt Olga. However, it was Gosse who actually got to Kata Tjuta (the Olgas) before him – by four weeks.

A year later, from Kata Tjuta, Giles and his men, who included William Tietkens as his second-in-command, pushed south-west into the desert, establishing a depot at Fort Mueller, west of the Tomkinson Ranges. Retreating to Circus Water in the Rawlinson Ranges, he tried to push west for the next three months. Time and again he was defeated.

During March 1874 Giles explored and named the Petermann Ranges and in April, from a depot he called Fort McKellar in the Petermanns, he gave his westward push one last effort. He took with him a young stockman by the name of Alf Gibson, and so one of the great stories of the white exploration of Australia began. About 140km west of Circus Water, Gibson's horse broke down. Giles gave him his own horse and, knowing that it was impossible to continue, sent Gibson back to bring help from their base camp. Gibson never made it. Giles, alone and on foot, with hardly a drop of water, did! Arriving at Circus Water, he drank his fill and came upon a dying wallaby. 'I pounced upon it and ate it,

living, raw, dying – fur, skin, bones, skull and all', he was to write later; his only regret was that he couldn't find its mother!

Two days later, Giles staggered into the depot at Fort McKellar to find that Gibson was missing. Tietkens joined him in a fruitless search that nearly claimed both their lives. Giles named the Gibson Desert in memory of the stockman. Retreating to civilisation, Giles arrived at Charlotte Waters in July 1874, and a couple of months later learnt that both Warburton and, further to the north, Alexander Forrest had crossed the western half of the continent.

Determined to write his name in the history books, eight months later Giles undertook a third expedition, this time from Fowlers Bay on the Bight to Finnis Springs south of Lake Eyre. Again he nearly died of thirst, but it proved to him that camels, of which he had two on that trip, were the best animals to use.

His fourth and most successful expedition left in May 1875. Striking north and west from Port Augusta, Giles used the waterholes he had discovered on the previous trip, passing the northern end of Lake Gairdner. Finally, after much hardship, he and his men crossed the Great Victoria Desert, discovering a life-saving spring that Giles called Queen Victoria Springs. In November the party was welcomed into Perth, and the celebrations followed. Giles, though, was still fired with the thought of exploring and finding rich pastoral land.

Leaving Perth in January 1876, he and his men pushed north along the Western Australian coast and then inland to the Ashburton River, about 480km from the coast. From a depot at this point in May, he turned his eyes and thoughts east – almost 800km away was where he and Gibson had parted.

Striking east, he finally reached the Alfred & Marie Range, the furthest point west he had sighted on his 1874 expedition. By late August the group was back on the Overland Telegraph Line at Peake, after passing along the old route through the Rawlinson, Petermann and Musgrave Ranges.

While Giles was the first explorer to cross the western deserts twice, he's probably

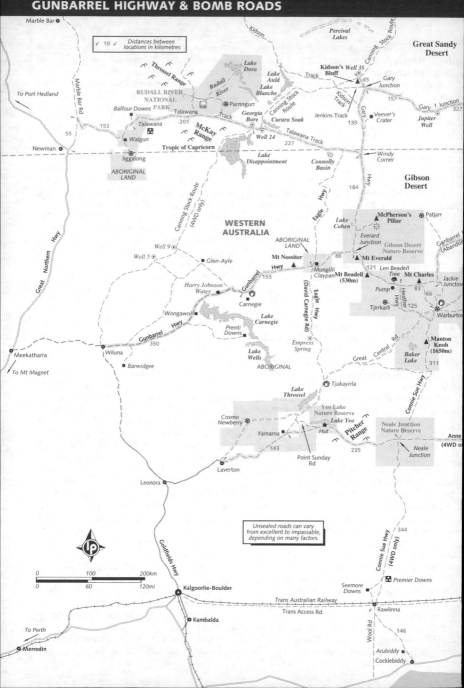

GUNBARREL HIGHWAY & BOMB ROADS

Marble Bar

To Port Hedland

Great Sandy Desert

Percival Lakes

Kidson

Throssel Range

Lake Dora

Lake Auld

Lake Blanche

Kidson's Bluff

Well 35

45

Gary Junction

Gary Junction 327

Marble Bar Rd

Rudall River

RUDALL RIVER NATIONAL PARK

Balfour Downs

Parnngurr

Georgia Bore

Curara Soak

Canning Stock Route

Jenkins Track

Kidson Track

139

Veever's Crater

Jupiter Well

Talawana

153

201

Talawana

Walgun

McKay Range

Well 24

Talawana Track

227

55

Newman

Jiggalong

Tropic of Capricorn

ABORIGINAL LAND

Lake Disappointment

Connolly Basin

Windy Corner

Gibson Desert

Canning Stock Route (4WD only)

WESTERN AUSTRALIA

Eagle Hwy

184

Hwy

Lake Cohen

McPherson's Pillar

Patjarr

Gunbarrel (Abandon

Well 9

Well 5

Glen-Ayle

ABORIGINAL LAND

Mt Nossiter

Hwy

Everard Junction

Gibson Desert Nature Reserve

Mt Everald

86

Harry Johnson Water

Gunbarrel

153

Mungilli Claypan

Mt Beadell (530m)

121

Len Beadell Tree

Mt Charles

Jackie Junction

Wongawol

Carnegie

Pump

83

66

Prenti Downs

Lake Carnegie

Eagle Hwy

(David Carnegie Rd)

Tjirkarli

Heather Hwy

125

Warburton

Gunbarrel Hwy

350

Wiluna

Empress Spring

Great

Central

Rd

Baker Lake

Manton Knob (1650m)

311

Meekatharra

To Mt Magnet

Barwidgee

Lake Wells

ABORIGINAL

Tjukayirla

Connie Sue Hwy

Lake Throssel

Cosmo Newberry

Yeo Lake Nature Reserve

Lake Yeo

Pitcher Range

Neale Junction Nature Reserve

Anne

(4WD o

Yamarna

Hut

235

143

Point Sunday Rd

Neale Junction

Laverton

Leonora

Unsealed roads can vary from excellent to impassable, depending on many factors.

Goldfields Hwy

Connie Sue Hwy

344

(4WD only)

0   100   200km
0   60   120mi

Kalgoorlie-Boulder

Kambalda

Seemore Downs

Premier Downs

Trans Australian Railway

Trans Access Rd

Rawlinna

Wool Rd

To Perth

Merredin

Arubiddy

Cocklebiddy

146

| ✓ 10 ✓ | Distances between locations in kilometres |

To Darwin

ABORIGINAL LAND

Lake Mackay

Stuart Hwy

Hwy

Sandover

ollock Hills

Burnt Out Ration Truck

Kiwirrkurra

Sandy Blight Junction

Gary Junction 255

Mt Liebig Rd

Papunya 110

Plenty Hwy

Lake MacDonald

Kintore

Tietkins Tree

Kintore Range

Ehrenberg Range

Mt Liebig

West Macdonnell National Park

Tropic of Capricorn

136

Sandy Blight Junction Rd

331

Lake Hopkins

Tjukurla

Meereenie Loop Rd

MacDonnell Ranges

Larapinta Dr

Alice Springs

Lake Christopher

Bungabiddy Rockhole

Giles Weather Station

Watarrka National Park

Kings Canyon

Finke Gorge National Park

NORTHERN TERRITORY

Rawlinson Range

Docker River

Uluru - Kata Tjuta National Park

Luritja Rd

Ernest Giles Rd

Warakurna

105

Lasseter's Cave

Great Central Rd

231

Yulara

Lasseter Hwy

Erldunda

at Central Rd

238

Petermann Ranges

Kata Tjuta

Uluru

4

(Roads closed to public access)

Mulga Park

Kulgera

Tomkinson Range

Gunbarrel Hwy

Victory Downs

(Roads closed to public access)

Mt Lindsay

ABORIGINAL LAND

Marla

SOUTH AUSTRALIA

Mt Davies Rd

Great Victoria Desert

353

Beadell

171 Hwy

159

Anne's Corner

Emu

Totem I & II

Tallaringa Conservation Park

Stuart

Serpentine Lakes

Vokes Hill Corner

Nuclear Test Viewing Area

233

Reenhouse Reserve

Sue Hwy

Tallaringa Well

Mabel Creek

46

Coober Pedy

Unnamed Conservation Park

Connie

ABORIGINAL LAND

WOOMERA PROHIBITED AREA

Dog Fence

Great Victoria Desert Natural Reserve

Maralinga

Commonwealth Hill

Central Australian Railway

Hwy

NULLARBOR PLAIN

Cook

Trans Australian Railway

Trans Access Rd

Malbooma

Tarcoola

161

Glendambo

Nullarbor Regional Reserve

Mt Finke

110

Goog's Track

To Port Augusta & Adelaide

Eyre Hwy

Eucla

Nullarbor National Park

ABORIGINAL LAND

1

Yumbarra Conservation Park

Yellabinna Regional Reserve

78

Goog's Lake

Pureba Conservation Park

Dog Fence

Penong

Lone Oak

Ceduna

Great Australian Bight

Australia's least-known successful explorer. He died penniless and unknown in 1897. His very readable book, *Australia Twice Traversed*, originally published in 1889, occasionally appears as a facsimile.

In 1891 David Lindsay, with Lawrence Wells as his lieutenant, led the Elder Scientific Exploring Expedition from northern South Australia. The group headed west to the Everard Ranges, Fort Mueller and Mt Squires, then south to Queen Victoria Springs and Esperance on the coast before striking north to Lake Wells. It was the first of the 'scientific' expeditions that were to fill in the gaps left by the earlier explorers.

Over the next 40 years, the country along the Overland Telegraph Line and around Alice Springs was taken up as pastoral country. By 1900 gold had been discovered in a couple of isolated regions north-west and east of Alice, and with the discovery of the untold riches at Kalgoorlie and Coolgardie in Western Australia, prospectors looked at the region along the Petermanns. One was Harold Lasseter, whose fabulous lost reef became the stuff of legend (see the boxed text 'Lasseter's Lost Reef' later in the chapter).

Apart from the occasional prospector, the next person on the scene was Len Beadell, who built the roads for the Woomera Rocket Range. The Gunbarrel Hwy, the first to run east-west across central Australia, took from 1955 to 1958 to complete and, for better or worse, ushered the modern world in to this ancient landscape.

Len Beadell – The Last Explorer

Len Beadell was born in 1923 in the Sydney suburb of West Pennant Hills. He was just 12 when he started his career as an unpaid assistant surveyor for the Sydney Water Board. He started working full-time with the board after finishing high school, but was conscripted in 1942. After serving in New Guinea, he rejoined the water board at the end of the war to help map remote Arnhem Land. A little later he was asked to do a job for the Defence Department: Lay out a rocket range!

This was the beginning of the town of Woomera and the Woomera Rocket Range, which later led to the A-bomb tests at Emu and Maralinga. It was also the beginning of the last phase of Australian exploration, during which Beadell and his men, whom he later christened 'the Gunbarrel Road Construction Party', carved out a series of roads through 2.5 million sq km of wilderness west of Alice Springs.

Beadell started to survey the Woomera range in 1947, but it was not until 1952 that he was called on to find a site for an A-bomb test; he decided on a flat claypan which he named Emu. The next year was taken up with building the road from Mabel Creek (then on the Stuart Hwy) to Emu, and then picking a new site that was to be called Maralinga. Surveying around Maralinga took up all of 1954 and much of the next year, and the remainder of 1955 was spent making the road between Emu and Maralinga. Later that year the first 160km of the Gunbarrel Hwy was completed, from Victory Downs to Mulga Park. This was Beadell's first major road, and also his most well known.

In 1956 the site for the Giles weather station was chosen and the Gunbarrel was continued out to this new site. Today the station is used to help amass information for weather forecasts and for aircraft flying 13,000m overhead, but its original purpose was to ensure that the days chosen for the big bangs at Emu or Maralinga were perfect and that the wind was blowing in the right direction.

Passing along the southern edge of the Rawlinsons, Beadell's route swung south to Warburton Mission. North of there he established a road junction for the last push, which ran west and then slightly north to Mt Everard before swinging south, passing the Mungilli Claypan and Mt Nossiter, and finally reaching the easternmost outpost of civilisation in Western Australia, Carnegie station.

Building an airstrip at Giles was next on the agenda, and the rest of the year was taken up with a new road south from Giles to Emu via Mt Davies, although that road wasn't finished until 1957. The last section of the Gunbarrel, west to Carnegie station, a little east of Wiluna in Western

Information

Tourist Offices Good sources of general information include the CATIA (☎ 08-8952 5800, e visinfo@catia.asn.au, w www.centralaustraliantourism.com) in Alice Springs and the Perth Visitor Centre (☎ 1300 361 351, e travel@westernaustralia.net, w www.westernaustralia.net) in Perth. There are also a couple of good web sites specifically about the Gunbarrel, including the Toyota Landcruiser Association (w www.tlca.org/virtual/gunbarrl/), and 4WD Online (w 4wd.sofcom.com/Places/Au/Gunbarrel/Highway.html).

Radio Frequencies There's no real need to carry an HF radio if you're sticking to the well-used Great Central Rd, but it might give you peace of mind on the Old Gunbarrel, and you should seriously consider carrying one if you're linking up with the Canning Stock Route or one of the Bomb Roads.

The RFDS base at Alice Springs (call sign VJD) has a primary frequency of 5410kHz and a secondary frequency of 6950kHz. Along the western section of the Gunbarrel Hwy, the base at Meekatharra is hard to beat (VKJ; 4010kHz and 6880kHz). If you're taking the alternative route to Laverton, try the Kalgoorlie base (VJQ; 5360kHz and 6825kHz).

Books & Maps Apart from Len Beadell's books on the area (see the boxed text), there are few others. *The Great Victoria Desert* by Mark Shephard covers the region to the south

Len Beadell – The Last Explorer

Australia, was pushed through during 1958. It was the first road link across central Australia and, as the name suggests, it was as straight as Beadell could make it – 'to keep the country looking tidy', as he said during his lecture tours. That same year he was awarded the British Empire Medal for his surveying work and his opening-up of this part of the country.

Other roads and sites followed. In 1960 the Sandy Blight Junction Rd was built, and the following year a road was pushed from Sandy Blight Junction east to the existing Northern Territory road system near Mt Liebig, 290km west of Alice Springs. In 1962 the road between Sandy Blight Junction and the Gary Junction via Jupiter Well was completed, as was the Anne Beadell in the south and the Connie Sue Hwy between Rawlinna and Warburton. In 1963 the Gary Hwy was pushed north and then west, via Well 35 on the Canning Stock Route, to Callawa, a little north-east of Marble Bar.

The last road graded by the Gunbarrel Road Construction Party was the Windy Corner–Talawana track, via Well 23 and Well 24 on the Canning. It was, as the title of Beadell's last book suggests, the end of an era.

Many of the roads bear the names of his wife and children. There's the Anne Beadell Hwy, after his wife, the Connie Sue Hwy, after their oldest daughter, the Gary Hwy after their son, and Jackie Junction after their youngest daughter.

A noted author, his seven books recount his times and adventures: *Blast the Bush*, *Bush Bashers*, *Beating about in the Bush*, *Too Long in the Bush*, *Still in the Bush*, *End of an Era* and *Outback Highways* have been reprinted many times. Illustrated with his own cartoon-like drawings and photos he took at the time, they capture the excitement and the adventure of those pioneering days.

On his retirement in 1988, Beadell was awarded the Order of Australia Medal, and the Mt Palomar Astronomical Observatory in California named an asteroid after him in recognition of the work he had done in opening up central Australia, enabling them to undertake their studies of meteorite impact craters. In 1989 he was presented with an Advance Australia Award, and was involved in three documentaries, including one on Woomera entitled *Beadell Country*.

Len Beadell remained active, often revisiting his beloved tracks as special guest on tag-along tours, until his death in May 1995. A year later, a memorial was unveiled on Mt Beadell, a low mesa just a stone's throw from the Gunbarrel Hwy.

of Warburton and is an excellent reference to the general area.

The whole route (including the alternative leg to Laverton) is covered by Hema's 1:1,250,000 *Great Desert Tracks* series. Features of this four-map series include useful GPS points, and the facilities and services available in towns, communities and roadhouses. You'll need the *South West* sheet and *North East* sheet. Alternatively, Westprint publishes a 1:1,300,000 map called *The Gunbarrel Highway* on tear-resistant and waterproof paper that includes loads of historical information and GPS points, but to do the whole route you'll also need the *Ayers Rock* map from the same series.

Registration It is not really necessary to register with the police in Alice Springs, Yulara or Wiluna before you set off – in fact, they probably won't want to know about it. They are, however, a good source of information on the latest conditions of the route, especially coming from the Wiluna end (from the other end you'll probably get better information at the Warburton Roadhouse). The Yulara Police Station (☎ 08-8956 2166) is on the Lasseter Hwy at Yulara; the Wiluna Police Station (☎ 08-9981 7024) is on Thompson St.

However, Carnegie station and the Warburton Roadhouse (see the later Facilities section) are happy to take your details and raise the alarm if you don't ring back from the other end by the agreed date. In fact, for those travelling alone or – not a smart thing to do – in the summer season, this is probably a good idea, but please don't forget to ring back.

Permits Permits are required to travel the enormous area of Aboriginal land in this region. For the Gunbarrel route described here, it's straightforward, although they can take about three weeks to be issued. There are, however, more specialist permits required for entry to closed communities and minor roads in the area and for very good reasons. To travel the full length of the Gunbarrel get a permit from the Central Land Council (☎ 08-8951 6320, fax 8953 4345, ⓔ permits@clc.org.au, ⓦ www.clc.org.au,

PO Box 3321, 33 Stuart Hwy, Alice Springs NT 0871) for the Northern Territory section, and another from the Western Australian Department of Indigenous Affairs (☎ 08-9235 8000, fax 9235 8088, ⓦ http:\\203.17.214.135/access.htm, PO Box 7770, Cloisters Square, Perth WA 6850) at 197 St Georges Terrace for the Western Australian section.

The Western Australia permit, however, is more easily obtained from the Ngaanyatjarra Council, which manages the area around Warburton and also issues permits for the Western Australian parts of the Gunbarrel itself; it has an office in Alice Springs (☎ 08-8950 1711, fax 8953 1892) at 6/58 Head St.

There is no charge for either permit and there is talk of scrapping them for the Great Central Rd. Indeed, it should only be a matter of time because few people seem to bother. For the real Gunbarrel west of Warburton, however, you still need a permit. The quickest method is to apply online or turn up in person at the relevant offices in Alice Springs or Perth (so long as the issuing officer is present, which may not always be the case). For more details on applications, see Travel Permits in the Getting Around chapter.

THE ROUTE

This route takes you from the upmarket resort at Yulara west to Warakurna and then southwest to the Warburton Aboriginal community. Soon after, you veer off the Great Central Rd and head for Carnegie station and Wiluna along the original track of the Gunbarrel Hwy. The total distance is 1408km.

Until you are west of Warburton, the track is fine for normal cars if there's been no rain (just take it easy in the creek crossings). Once on the Heather Hwy and the real Gunbarrel, the route deteriorates and a 4WD is required for ground clearance and sturdiness, not because you need drive to all four wheels (you normally don't anywhere along the route). Even then it can be slow going, and on some sections you may only average 20km/h or less – the corrugations are among the fiercest this author has encountered. If you're thinking of towing a trailer, be prepared to abandon it by the roadside as many earlier have done.

Note that the section of the real Gunbarrel west from Warakurna to Jackie Junction has been completely abandoned and can be impassable to all but determined convoys. The section from Jackie Junction to Mt Samuel and the Heather Hwy is now also being abandoned. All these sections require special permits that are hard to obtain. See the boxed text, 'The Abandoned Gunbarrel', later in this chapter for more information.

Travelling times between Yulara and places further west depend on how quickly you like to drive on sandy dirt and corrugated roads. Between Yulara and Warburton, allow seven to nine hours, though distances and driving times will decrease as the road is realigned and improved; between Warburton and Carnegie station, allow 14 to 16 hours (the people at Carnegie say it takes two overnight stops, it can be done within two days but that's pushing it); from Carnegie to Wiluna, allow five to six hours. Obviously these figures are for driving times only.

YULARA

Yulara is home to a modern and efficient tourist resort that has a monopoly on accommodation, food and other services for the hundreds of thousands of tourists who flock to see Uluru and Kata Tjuta each year. Situated on the edge of Uluru-Kata Tjuta National Park, the Ayers Rock Resort offers a broad range of somewhat overpriced accommodation, from the jam-packed camping ground to the alluring luxury of the Sails in the Desert Hotel. There's also a lesser array of definitely overpriced meal and bar options, as well as some breathtakingly hackneyed live entertainment. Other services include a shopping centre, library and free shuttle bus.

Really, the only reason to endure this seething press of humanity is to take in the extraordinary beauty of Uluru and Kata Tjuta, which can easily account for a few days of your time and is a great way to kick off your journey. See the Uluru, Kata Tjuta & Kings Canyon section earlier in this chapter for more information.

Yulara to Warburton (574km)

Head towards Uluru and enter the Uluru-Kata Tjuta National Park. If you're driving directly to Docker River, park officials will waive the entry fee on presentation of your permit. After 8km, take the right-hand turn to Kata Tjuta and Docker River.

Kata Tjuta soon dominates the skyline. If you don't have time to stop and explore, there's a fine viewing area across a plain thick with desert oak and spinifex about 28km from the turn-off. With the bulk of Mt Olga off to the right, turn left onto the dirt road at the junction 49km from Yulara.

Just over 83km of low desert country, punctuated by occasional stands of desert oak, takes you to **Irving Creek** where Lasseter died. Some 50m past the crossing, a track on the right leads 750m to a reliable, hand-operated water pump. Shaw Creek is crossed 26km further on, quickly followed by Chirnside Creek another 9km along. None of these crossings are difficult.

As you come up to the eastern bank of the Hull River, 191km from Yulara, a track on the left leads to the parking area for **Lasseter's Cave**, a poky nook that would have offered little comfort to the ill-fated explorer while he awaited rescue (see the boxed text 'Lasseter's Lost Reef'). Unfortunately, camping is no longer permitted along the river's attractive, shady banks; you'll have to push on to Kaltukatjara camping ground at Docker River, 40km away.

On the drive into Docker River note the orange-speckled slopes of the spectacular Petermann Ranges, and plains wreathed in desert oaks. Docker River is a partially closed community, with only the service station and store accessible to visitors (see the later Facilities section for details). The excellent camping ground is on the Gunbarrel a couple of kilometres past the turn-off into town.

The **Sandy Blight Junction Rd** leaves the main road 26km west of Docker River and heads north. Our route veers to the left, keeping to the main road. After a couple of creek crossings a signpost on the left, 13km past the junction, indicates you are at the **Schwerin Mural Crescent**, as Giles called this magnificent panorama of range country.

Lasseter's Lost Reef

Somewhere in the western deserts is a reef with gold as thick as 'plums in a pudding'…or so prospector Harold Lasseter insisted to his dying day. Lasseter's discovery and rediscovery of the fabulous reef, and his lonely, tragic death after he'd pegged his claim, are now the stuff of legend.

Lasseter claimed to have discovered a 23km-long gold reef in the late 1890s, but it was not until 1930 that the Central Australian Gold Exploration Company was formed, with Lasseter as a guide. The expedition was well equipped with an aeroplane, trucks and wireless, but things soon went awry. The aircraft crashed near Uluru and Lasseter, after an argument with another prospector, Paul Johns, eventually went out alone to look for the reef, heading west through the Petermann and Rawlinson Ranges to a point somewhere around Lake Christopher.

Lasseter states in his diary that he found and pegged the reef on 23 December. Retracing his steps, his camels bolted when he was about 50km east of the present-day Docker River Aboriginal community. Realising he couldn't make it back to the Olgas and safety, he stayed in a cave on the edge of Hull River for a few weeks, waiting in vain for a rescue party he was sure would be sent to look for him. Despairing, he finally set out on the impossible task, assisted by a local Aboriginal family, but he collapsed and died a few days later beside Irving Creek.

Lasseter's body and diary were later recovered and the legend of Lasseter's Reef was born. Many prospectors have since attempted to locate his fabled reef, but to no avail. Lasseter's adventure is chronicled in Ion Idriess' *Lasseter's Last Ride* (1931) and his name is perpetuated in the Lasseter Hwy, which runs west from the Stuart Hwy to Uluru.

At the T-junction 36km past the Schwerin Mural Crescent sign, you turn right onto the original Gunbarrel Hwy, now heading west towards Warakurna. Left takes you along the original Gunbarrel into South Australia, but you need a special permit.

Twenty-nine kilometres further on, you come to the Warakurna Roadhouse where you can camp, have a meal, refuel and top up with water. The turn-off to **Giles weather station** is less than 500m west of the roadhouse, and with advance permission (☎ 08-8956 7358, or inquire at the roadhouse) you can catch the launching of the weather balloon daily at 8.45am (kids love it). After the launch, if things are quiet, the staff are happy to show you around the high-tech control room and decidedly low-tech measuring field and explain what they do. The grader used by the Gunbarrel Road Construction Party is also on view, along with the remains of a rocket fired from Woomera. All in all, the weather station makes for an interesting one-hour stopover.

Continuing west along the Gunbarrel for another 16km brings you to where the original Gunbarrel veers off to the right. This is a definite 4WD route that's been completely abandoned, and you need a special permit to travel it (see the boxed text 'The Abandoned Gunbarrel' later for details). Continue south-west along the Great Central Rd and set your clocks back 1½ hours to Western Standard Time. Approaching the **Warburton** Aboriginal community the road swings hard right, past the centre of town to the Warburton Roadhouse on the right side of the road, 238km from Warakurna. There is accommodation and camping, plus the impressive **Tjulyuru Cultural & Civic Centre** *(☎ 08-8956 7966; open 8am-5pm Mon-Fri)* near the roadhouse that houses the shire offices, a shop selling high-quality regional Ngaanyatjarra art, and an art gallery that has the famous Warburton collection of 350 Aboriginal paintings – a must-see.

Warburton to Carnegie Station (486km)

The Heather Hwy turns off the Great Central Rd 41km south-west of Warburton and here you need to turn right, towards Tjirrkarli. At a T-junction 47km past this major turn-off, turn right again. The road immediately deteriorates and is very badly corrugated. All you can do is slow down to a crawl and ride the bumps one by one (going fast only leads to ruin). You'd better get used to it because there's more to come, though fortunately not all as bad as this. Thirty-seven kilometres later the rough Old Gunbarrel comes in from the right at a junction where you turn left to head for Carnegie and Wiluna.

A large gum tree, marked by Len Beadell in 1958 and sporting a plaque, is on the right, 11km west of the junction. A track off to the left leads 500m to a hand pump and water. It might not be brilliant, but if you were dying of thirst you'd love it. There's another pump just like it 25km further on.

Camp Beadell, 55km west of Beadell's tree, is a couple of hundred metres off to the left of the road. If you want a large, cleared area for a group camp, this could be it. There's a water bore here too, right next to a toilet pit! A hill on the left and a track towards it, 6km after the turn-off to Camp Beadell, brings you to **Mt Beadell**, with a monument to Len Beadell (see the boxed text earlier) and good views of the surrounding country.

Fifteen kilometres later you pass into the **Gibson Desert Nature Reserve**. If there has been some rain recently, the wildflowers can be stunning – stand along the roadside and you may be able to count 15 different species on a single square metre! Another 30km on, as you pass through the Browne Range, you'll see the red bluff of Mt Everard on the left. Just 7km further along the road is a major road junction, **Everard Junction**. At this point you're on a flat plain that is covered in spinifex all round, with scrub in the distance. The Browne Range rises to the east and the Young Range can be seen to the north-east. The Gunbarrel stretches away to the west.

The road north is the Gary Hwy, which leads to the Canning Stock Route. A Len Beadell plaque and a visitors book are on the left. See the section on the Bomb Roads later in this chapter for more details on this route.

You pass out of the Gibson Desert Nature Reserve 31km from the junction with the Gary Hwy. One kilometre later is the Geraldton Historical Society Bore on your

left, 150m off the road. The water isn't nice but it's drinkable.

The sign denoting the boundary of the **Mungilli Claypan Nature Reserve**, a unique Gibson Desert wetland, is passed 48km further on, while the claypan itself is crossed just a little over 4km later. When it contains water (which is often the case), a diversion track skirts the edge. Seven kilometres from the eastern boundary of the Mungilli Reserve (or 9km if you've taken the diversion), you cross the western boundary, and just before that you will have passed through a junction with the Eagle Hwy.

By now the road improves a bit as the Wiluna Shire grades it to a point around here. For the next 75km or so the Gunbarrel continues westward and becomes pretty good, although it can be washed out or rough in places. You might see the occasional camel on the road; they've been known to trot ahead of a car for up to 20km, stopping every time the car stops – no, they're not very intelligent! Sand hill country is met once again 85km from the western boundary sign of the Mungilli Reserve; the road can be sandy but it is no problem for a 4WD.

Just before you get to the turn-off to **Carnegie** station, you can see the station on your left, with the track junction a short distance later, 67km from first striking the sand ridge country and 486km from Warburton. At Carnegie you can buy fuel and limited supplies, and camp (see the later Facilities section). This is the end of the 'real' Gunbarrel, where Len and his men finished making their road across central Australia. For most, the trip continues westward for another 350km to Wiluna.

Carnegie to Wiluna (350km)
Heading west from Carnegie, the road is formed dirt and generally in better condition than the Gunbarrel. A Y-junction 30km from the station is where travellers heading for the Canning Stock Route at Well 9 must veer right, which takes them north for 45km via Glen-Ayle station to the stock route. Our route westward to Wiluna is via the left fork.

Continuing towards Wiluna, the road swings more in a southerly direction. At **Harry Johnson Water**, on the right 69km from Carnegie, is a camp site near the water, and a picnic table, shelter and barbecue.

The road continues to swing south, at one stage skirting the north-western extremity of the salt lake known as **Lake Carnegie**. The turn-off to Wongawol station homestead is on your left, 97km west of the Glen-Ayle turn-off. The station, which has no facilities for travellers, is also on your left.

Heading almost due south, the road passes the turn-off to Prenti Downs on the left, 20km south of Wongawol. The road

begins to swing more westerly, through mulga country with lots of kangaroos, and 164km from Wongawol the turn-off to Barwidgee station is on the left. Another 16km further on is a track off to the right which leads north to Glen-Ayle station.

The small community of **Wiluna** is entered another 43km west, 350km west of Carnegie station. For all intents and purposes this town is the end of the road. There is the choice of heading north up the Canning Stock Route; continuing westwards 181km to Meekatharra on the Great Northern Hwy; heading south to Leinster, Leonora and Kalgoorlie; or swinging south-west for

The Abandoned Gunbarrel

The section of the Gunbarrel from Warakurna west to Jackie Junction has been abandoned for many years, and the section west from Jackie Junction to Mt Samuel and the Heather Hwy is now experiencing the same fate. Interestingly, people who have travelled these sections say that they're actually in better condition than the 'used' section from Mt Samuel west to Carnegie station because they see far less traffic. However, whole stretches of the abandoned sections can get washed away in one downpour and you might find yourself facing tracks going off in all directions. It's easy to get lost, and chances of meeting other vehicles are slim. For this reason, the abandoned sections require a special permit that's hard to obtain, and they should only be attempted by two to five vehicles travelling in convoy with radio communication (one vehicle won't get a permit, and groups of more than five should be broken into two groups travelling a day apart).

The abandoned Gunbarrel Hwy begins 16km west of the Warakurna Roadhouse, where it veers off to the right from the Great Central Rd. It then swings along the southern ramparts of the Rawlinson Range and comes to a Len Beadell–marked tree, 66km from the Great Central Rd. Twenty kilometres further is another marked tree. Off to the north is Lake Christopher, which is the closest known point to the gold reef that Lasseter talked about.

Another 13km along this route sees you at another marked tree, and another one 16km after that. The road alternates from chopped-up to quite sandy. At 56km from the last marked tree, or 171km from the Great Central Rd, is a turn-off to the Patjarr Aboriginal community, 67km to the northwest. It has a craft centre and you're welcome to visit, but check with the Ngaanyatjarra Council (☎ 08-8950 1711) about permission to drive up there.

Turn left at this junction and follow the Gunbarrel as it swings further and further south. At Jackie Junction, 276km from the Warakurna Roadhouse, you need to turn right (west). Continuing south will take you to the Warburton Aboriginal community, 66km away.

Forty-six kilometres west of Jackie Junction is a turn-off to the left that also takes you to Warburton, although this particular road is in bad shape and you wouldn't want to take it anyway. Continue on the Gunbarrel and cross the Todd Range, passing just to the south of Mt Charles. Thirty-one kilometres past the turn-off you get to Mt Samuel to the left of the road, which has a lookout and a cairn on the top. Shortly after are some rockholes with crystal-clear water close to the road, but you have to explore on foot to discover them. Six kilometres after Mt Samuel and 83km from Jackie Junction you meet the Heather Hwy coming in from your left. This is the main used route that heads north from the Great Central Rd to join the 'real' Gunbarrel at this point.

455km through Sandstone to Paynes Find, itself 424km north of Perth on the Great Northern Hwy

Wiluna can supply fuel (but unreliably, so fill up at Carnegie), limited repairs and groceries. For more details on services in this community, see the Canning Stock Route section in the North-West chapter.

ALTERNATIVE ROUTE
Warburton to Laverton (558km)
Instead of taking the real Gunbarrel, you can continue to roar down the Great Central Rd, which is a far more direct route to Perth and Western Australia's south-west. From Warburton to Laverton it's 558km of very good dirt road in typical desert country. Allow six to seven hours if the grader has been through recently; add a couple more if there's been rain.

The Route From Warburton, head west on the Great Central Rd, but sail past the right-hand turn that leads to the Gunbarrel proper, congratulating yourself that you won't be enduring the pain of the Heather Hwy.

After 249km you reach *Tjukayirla Roadhouse (☎ 08-9037 1108, fax 9037 1110; open 7am-6pm Mon-Fri, 8am-5pm Sat & Sun)*. Owned by the people of the remote Papulankutja (Blackstone) Aboriginal community, almost 500km away to the north-east, Tjukayirla is a well-maintained and welcoming place that offers camp sites for $7 and beds in twin-share or four-bunk rooms for $28 per person. There are also limited supplies and regional art for sale.

As you approach a large salt lake called Lake Throssell on your right, the **Beegull Waterhole and caves** are on your left, 329km from Warburton. They're unspectacular, but a good place to stretch your legs.

The first turn-off to **Cosmo Newberry** is struck 138km further on, and a second road leads the same way a few kilometres later. This Aboriginal community is very serious about its dry status and has a *community store (☎ 08-9037 5969; open 10am-noon & 3pm-5pm Mon-Fri, 10am-noon Sat, closed Sun & public holidays)* that sells fuel and some supplies.

Some 85km later, you come to the bitumen. Turning left will take you to the mining community of Laverton, just 6km away (see the Anne Beadell Highway entry in the Bomb Roads section later for accommodation options); turning right will take you to Leonora, 119km to the south-west.

ORGANISED TOURS
Nobody really runs tours of the Gunbarrel as a stand-alone destination. *Swagman Tours (☎ 03-5222 2855, e info@swagmantours.com.au, W www.swagmantours.com.au)* includes the entire route as part of a longer safari that takes in the Canning Stock Route and Tanami Track. Otherwise, a couple of operators traverse the Great Central Rd section (but not the original Heather Hwy to Carnegie station stretch) as part of Perth to Alice Springs itineraries. These include *Travelabout Outback Tours (☎ 08-9244 1200, e travel@travelabout.au.com, W www.travel about.au.com)* and *Global Gypsies (☎ 08-9341 6727, e info@global gypsies.com.au, W www.globalgypsies.com.au)*. Swagman and Global Gypsies also allow you to tag along with your own vehicle. For the latest list of operators, contact the Perth Visitor Centre (☎ 1300 361 351, e travel@westernaustralia.net, W www.westernaustralia.net).

FACILITIES
It's sensible to take roadhouse opening hours into account when plotting your route – there's no 24-hour service out here. Fuel is generally available weekdays from around 9am to 5pm, with a break over lunch, but on weekends the pumps are likely to shut at 3pm. Some stations will open the pumps for you outside these hours for a fee of about $20. There's also a 90-minute time zone shift between Warakurna and Warburton, which is fine if you're going east-west but a real factor for refuelling if you're heading west-east. Diesel is the most readily available fuel, and supplies of leaded and unleaded are pretty reliable.

Outside of Yulara, accommodation is generally limited to unpowered and powered camp sites, plus prefab cabins.

Yulara

For information about the facilities this well-serviced township, see Facilities in the Uluru, Kata Tjuta & Kings Canyon section earlier in this chapter.

Docker River (Kaltukatjara)

The **Docker River Store** (☎ 08-8956 7373, fax 8956 7696; open 9.30am-noon & 2pm-4pm Mon-Fri, 9.30am-noon Sat, closed Sun & public holidays) has fuel plus a small selection of supplies and a hot food takeaway (open 11.30am to 1.30pm and 3.30pm to 5.30pm Wednesday to Sunday). Follow the signs from the main road. The community's spacious **Kaltukatjara camping ground** is the best on the entire Gunbarrel, with large, shady trees, plumbed toilets, a lookout and plenty of fresh water. It's just off the main road, a couple of kilometres past the turn-off, and operates on an honour system charging $5 per person per night.

Warakurna

Warakurna Roadhouse (☎ 08-8956 7344, fax 8956 2850, ⓔ warakurnaroad house@bigpond.com; open 8.30am-6pm Mon-Fri, 9am-3pm Sat & Sun) Unpowered/powered sites $8/12 per person, beds in 4-bed rooms $45, cabins from $115. A short distance from the Giles weather station, the roadhouse offers all fuels, a few supplies, takeaway food (including frozen meals that they'll heat up for you in the microwave), local artworks and has limited garage facilities. Note that Warakurna runs on Northern Territory time even though it's in Western Australia.

Warburton

Warburton Roadhouse (☎ 08-8956 7656, fax 8956 7645; open 8am-5pm Mon-Fri, 9am-3pm Sat & Sun, 9am-noon public holidays) Powered and unpowered sites $7 per person, single/double budget rooms $20/35, twins with shared facilities $70, doubles with private facilities $90. This large Aboriginal community's roadhouse sells all fuels, Avgas, spare parts and the best selection of fresh and packaged food between Yulara and Wiluna.

Carnegie Station

Carnegie station (☎ 08-9981 2991) Camp sites $10 per person, cabins $33. It's a good place to camp – green lawns fed by the near-unlimited water, with hot showers and cooking facilities. There's unleaded and diesel, the shop sells souvenirs (lots of Len Beadell memorabilia), basic food supplies and cool drinks, and there's a public telephone. Emergency repairs are also available. Only cash is accepted as payment.

Wiluna

This is the biggest and best-equipped supply centre you will see after leaving Yulara, though that's not saying much. It has most of the things you need to keep going, including food, fuel (though the supply occasionally runs out), general supplies, accommodation and camping, though opening hours can be a bit limited (eg, no fuel on weekends after 3pm).

For details on Wiluna, see the Canning Stock Route section in the North-West chapter.

ALTERNATIVE TRANSPORT

Regular bus and air services link Yulara with Alice Springs, which has connections to the rest of Australia. Once you leave Yulara, however, there are no regular transport services, aside from tour groups.

Bomb Roads

Highlights

- Rough camping under the vast night sky
- The austere beauty of the Rudall River National Park
- Red-sand deserts along the Anne Beadell Hwy
- The roller-coaster dunes of Googs Track

The Bomb Roads cover the desert country of western South Australia, inner Western Australia and the lower reaches of the Northern

Territory. Constructed by Len Beadell (mid-1950s to the early 1960s) to provide infrastructure for the Woomera rocket tests and Emu atomic tests, they encompass over 6000km of desert tracks. While the east-west Gunbarrel Hwy remains the most heavily trafficked route (and, as such, has its own separate section in this book), there's much more to explore within this vast grid of interconnecting tracks, showcasing some of Australia's most beautiful, remote and serene desert country. But be well prepared, some of these tracks are *very* remote.

Suggested Itineraries
The interconnected nature of the Bomb Roads allows you to construct some brilliant trips, taking in very varied terrain and a mix of rough camps and roadhouses. Here are a couple of long-distance options – with plenty of time allowed for camping, resting and exploring – but there are many more smaller loops you could explore.

Southern Australian Loop Alice Springs south-west to Yulara (Stuart & Lasseter Hwys), west to Warburton (Great Central Rd), south to Cocklebiddy (Connie Sue Hwy), east to Ceduna (Eyre Hwy), north to Malbooma (Googs Track), east to Glendambo (Trans Access Rd), north to Alice Springs (Stuart Hwy).

This terrific two- to three-week trip takes you first to the biggest attraction of them all – Uluru – before heading down the Great Central Rd to follow the remote Connie Sue Hwy through the spare beauty of the Great Victoria Desert. The caves and rugged coastline of the Bight follow, before a roller-coaster run up the Googs Track takes you back to the Stuart Hwy and Alice Springs, via the surreal town of Coober Pedy.

Central-West Figure Eight Alice Springs west to Kintore (Papunya Rd), south to Docker River (Sandy Blight Junction Rd), south-west to Leonora (Great Central Rd), north to Newman (Goldfields & Great Northern Hwys), east to Windy Corner (Talawana Track), south to Warburton (Gary, Gunbarrel & Heather Hwys), north-east to Uluru (Great

Central Rd), north to Kings Canyon, (Lasseter Hwy & Luritja Rd), east to Alice Springs (Mereenie Loop Rd & Larapinta Dr).

More remote and demanding, this three-to four-week route is an absolute cracker, taking in isolated communities, the magnificent desert oak country north along the Sandy Blight Junction Rd, the tranquillity and harsh beauty of the Talawana Track and Gary Hwy and then the holiday options of Kata Tjuta, Uluru and the Kings Canyon on the way back to Alice.

Information
Radio Frequencies You'd be mad not to carry an HF radio or emergency beacon on most of these roads, given their extreme isolation and infrequent traffic. If you're using an HF radio along the Gary Junction Rd or Sandy Blight Junction Rd, your best bet is the RFDS base at Alice Springs (call sign VJD; primary frequency 5410kHz and secondary frequency 6950kHz). For the Anne Beadell Hwy and Googs Track try Port Augusta (VNZ; 4010kHz, 6890kHz and 8165kHz) and for the Connie Sue Hwy contact Kalgoorlie (VJQ; 5360kHz and 6825kHz). Finally, along the Gary Hwy and Talawana Track contact the base at Meekatharra (VKJ; 4010kHz, 2280kHz and 6880kHz).

See also the Radio Frequencies entry in the earlier Gunbarrel Highway section.

Maps The majority of the Bomb Roads are covered by Hema's 1:1,250,000 *Great Desert Tracks* series ($15.40 each). Features of this four-map series include useful global positioning system (GPS) points, interesting historical snippets, and the facilities and services available in towns, communities and roadhouses. If, however, you require every single road and track marked on your map, then get hold of Landinfo's more detailed (if less user-friendly) 1:1,000,000 *World Aeronautical Chart* series ($8.35 each). A GPS unit is also very useful along these tracks.

ANNE BEADELL HIGHWAY (1340km)
This predominantly sandy road runs west from Coober Pedy to Laverton, through the

atomic bomb test site of Emu and the stark beauty of the Unnamed Conservation Park on the way to the Serpentine Lakes saltpans at the South Australian–Western Australia border. The thick sand gradually peters out as you reach the Neale Junction, where another Bomb Road – the Connie Sue Hwy – is crossed. The road improves markedly in the run home to the small mining community of Laverton, via the attractive Yeo Lake Nature Reserve and Yamarna station.

Built in several stages between 1953 and 1962, this is a long, remote and rugged track, where some severely corrugated sections and long periods of narrow, twisting track conspire to keep your speed down; a trailer or caravan is a significant liability on this road. It is possible to complete the 1340km run in five days, but you'll spend most of your time in the car and you'll be selling short the abundant natural beauty around you. Also ensure you're adequately stocked with fuel, water, food and spares as there are no facilities whatsoever.

While the Anne Beadell is increasing in popularity, it still carries comparatively little traffic and there's every chance you won't even see another vehicle while you're out there, which is just another reason to take your time and bask in the isolation and stillness of the Great Victoria Desert.

Permits & Maps

The Anne Beadell Hwy crosses land owned by the Maralinga-Tjarutja people, the South Australian Department for Environment and Heritage, and the Federal Department of Defence and you need permits from each. It's also polite to inform the owners of Mabel Creek station (☎/fax 08-8672 5204) that you're coming through, even though you no longer need written permission.

To enter Aboriginal land you need a permit from the Maralinga-Tjarutja Council (☎ 08-8625 2946, fax 8625 3076), PO Box 435, Ceduna, SA 5690. It's free, but allow four to six weeks for processing.

A permit to transit and explore the old atomic test sites around Emu is available free of charge from the Woomera Area Control Officer, Defence Support Centre

(☎ 08-8674 3370, fax 8674 3308), PO Box 157, Woomera, SA 5720.

The entry permit for the Unnamed Conservation Park is free, but a nightly camping fee of $6 per vehicle applies. Contact the Administrative Officer, Far West District, at the Department for Environment and Heritage (☎ 08-8625 3144, fax 8625 3123), PO Box 569, Ceduna, SA 5690.

The *South East* and *South West* sheets in Hema's *Great Desert Tracks* series cover this track very well. The Landinfo sheets are Nos 3354 (Tarcoola), 3353 (Nullarbor Plain) and 3352 (Kalgoorlie).

The Route

Coober Pedy to Emu (279km) From Coober Pedy, a very good dirt road takes you 46km west to **Mabel Creek** homestead in well under an hour. The road remains good through the station's lands, with a number of steeply humped fence crossings to be negotiated, before deteriorating somewhat on the run into Tallaringa Well. Occasional sandy ridges start to appear after you cross the vermin track 48km past Mabel Creek – a foretaste of the next four days' travel. **Tallaringa Well**, found opposite a Len Beadell marker, appears to be dry more often than not, but there's a pleasant camp spot beyond the marker. The remaining 125km to Emu isn't much fun, with long stretches of heavily corrugated track to test both your suspension and temperament. All up, the 279km from Coober Pedy will take five to six hours.

Around Emu there is little left from the atomic-test days apart from a couple of small **memorials** at the bombsites, known as Totem I and Totem II, plus some twisted remains of the metal towers that supported the bombs. There's also a good number of forbidding warning signs on the dangers of prolonged exposure to radiation. To get to the sites, turn right at an obvious crossroads 16km before the ruins of Emu township. Going left takes you to the official viewing area for the tests – a low rise 2km along a fair road.

There are a number of tracks in the area around the barely discernible ruins of Emu township; a GPS is useful here to confirm you're on the correct path. From the main road, you need to dogleg left (to the right is an airstrip) and then right to head north-west and into the desert proper.

Emu to Vokes Hill Corner (159km) The 159km from Emu to Vokes Hill Corner takes between four and six hours (depending on your approach to corrugations) on a pretty rough and winding track. The vegetation starts to thin out – with spinifex, acacia and occasional stands of mallee evident – while ridges of red sand appear more regularly. At Anne's Corner, 52km from Emu, there's a Len Beadell marker where the Mt Davies Rd heads north-west towards a cluster of Anangu Pitjantjatjara communities around the junction of the South Australia-Northern Territory-Western Australia borders. This is a permit-only road. Enter the **Unnamed Conservation Park** 127km from Emu and a further 32km takes you to a lush and shady camp site at Vokes Hill Corner that's suitable for large groups.

Vokes Hill Corner to Serpentine Lakes (171km) From Vokes Hill Corner it's 171km (five to six hours) to the Western Australia-South Australia border. The road south from Vokes Hill leads 250km through Maralinga-Tjarutja land to the small railway siding of **Cook** on the Trans Australian Railway. Heading west the track softens appreciably, making for much more comfortable driving, but the huge number of sidetracks that avoid wash-outs have turned this stretch into a slow, sinuous exercise in steering technique. Camels also infest this region and can slow your progress appreciably.

The Western Australian border is marked by the appearance of the salt-encrusted Serpentine Lakes, which twist south for almost 100km. Push on past the border (and the ubiquitous Len Beadell marker) for 10km to reach a left-hand turn that takes you to a truly delightful wooded *camp site* about 1500m in. Several hundred metres past the camp there's another spectacular salt lake that's well worth a wander.

Serpentine Lakes to Neale Junction (353km) West from the border, the track settles into a long, long series of flat, straight sections interrupted by corrugated, east-west sandy ridges. You can make good time, but there are a number of treacherous wash-outs and blind corners, so keep your wits about you. This is glorious red-sand desert country, with grass wrens, thornbills and honeyeaters plentiful in the hardy mallee and acacia vegetation, and raptors soaring overhead. If you're pushing on to Neale Junction, however, you'll be watching the road for most of the day, as the 353km will take you between eight and 10 hours.

At Neale Junction, where you cross the Connie Sue Hwy, there's a large if uninspiring camp site. The area from about 60km east to 30km west of the junction is proclaimed as the **Neale Junction Nature Reserve**.

Neale Junction to Laverton (378km) It's 235km (five to six hours) from Neale Junction to Yamarna station along a good sandy track with few surprises. Enter the **Yeo Lake Nature Reserve**, and pass through the attractive Pitcher Range and then the rugged mesa country of Morton Craig Range. The ruins of Yeo station are almost halfway through the reserve and have been transformed into an excellent *camping spot*, complete with two clean sleeping rooms, a stove, freshwater tanks, outdoor table and chairs, and a reliable well. It's a great place to break your journey.

The run into Laverton, via Yamarna station, is pretty anticlimactic as the road steadily improves and the numerous sidetracks make it clear you're nearing civilisation again. If you're planning to head up the Great Central Hwy (and don't need supplies at Laverton) the **Point Sunday Rd**, which leaves the Anne Beadell Hwy 25km from Yeo station, is a picturesque, soft and winding road that brings you out only 116km south-west of Tjukayirla Roadhouse.

The small goldmining town of **Laverton** offers fuel and a good range of supplies, as well as motel, pub and caravan park accommodation. *Laverton Chalet Accommodation* (☎ 08-9031 1130, 29 Augusta St) has clean and basic single/double/family rooms for $79/98/105. Across the road the pleasant *Laverton Caravan Park* (☎ 08-9031 1072, fax 9031 1673, e hamo3@tel stra.easymail.com.au, Weld Dr) charges $16/18/22 for unpowered/powered/en suite sites and has on-site vans from $60. The other option is the *Desert Inn Hotel* (☎ 08-9031 1188, fax 9031 1806, Laver Pl), which offers self-contained units for $93.50 or very basic singles for $40.

From Laverton it's an hour's drive southwest on a good dirt road to the larger and more attractive town of Leonora, from where you can head north to Wiluna (309km) or south to Kalgoorlie-Boulder (246km).

CONNIE SUE HIGHWAY (801km)

Built by Len Beadell's crew between August and October 1962, the Connie Sue is accessed from Cocklebiddy on the Eyre Hwy and begins in the small lime-mining town of Rawlinna on the Trans Australian Railway and heads north through Neale Junction (intersecting with the Anne Beadell Hwy) and up to the Great Central Rd a few kilometres west of Warburton. The road continues north for another 66km to meet the old Gunbarrel Hwy at Mt Charles, but the Ngaanyatjarra Council rarely issues permits for it, preferring to direct traffic up the nearby Heather Hwy. So the modern Connie Sue effectively starts from the only realistic access point – Cocklebiddy – and finishes at Warburton – and there are no facilities in between. It is achievable in two days, but more comfortable in three.

Permits & Maps

You need a permit from the Department of Indigenous Affairs in Perth (☎ 08-9235 8000, fax 9235 8088, w http://203.17.214.135/access.htm) for the section between Neale Junction and Warburton.

The *South East* and *South West* sheets in Hema's *Great Desert Tracks* series both cover the entire track. The corresponding Landinfo sheets are Nos 3352 (Kalgoorlie) and 3344 (Petermann Ranges).

The Route

Cocklebiddy to Neale Junction (490km)

The road to Rawlinna is directly across the road from the Wedgetail Inn roadhouse at Cocklebiddy on the Eyre Hwy. If you're coming from the west, you'll be tempted to take the Wool Rd 17km before Caiguna, but this is a privately maintained road that's not open to the public. The 146km to Rawlinna is hard, rough and rocky (perfect conditions for sluggish shingleback lizards) and can take up to three hours.

Rawlinna has no facilities, save for a fridge full of cold drinks in the main building, but they do ask you to drop in and let them know of your plans. Having crossed the railway line, the road heads north through chopped up and treeless cattle country past Seemore Downs station and the turn-off to the ruins of Premier Downs station, which is not a bad place to *camp*. The road then straightens through arid grasslands dotted with trees as you approach the fringes of the Great Victoria Desert. The track improves along with the countryside as you leave the farmland behind and eventually enter the Neale Junction Nature Reserve.

The 344km section from Rawlinna to Neale Junction is in pretty good nick, but allow about eight hours for the trip. A couple of major sandy roads join and leave the route, but these lead to mining camps or Aboriginal communities, so don't divert. At Neale Junction there's a large *camping area* about 100m to the west that's suitable for multiple vehicles. If you're not going to make it that far, you can camp anywhere north of Seemore Downs and south of the nature reserve (it's all unallocated Crown land), but try to select a site that's been used before.

Neale Junction to Warburton (311km)

North of the Neale Junction is authentic red-sand desert country with the track alternating rapidly between corrugated dunes and flat stretches of sparsely vegetated plain. The going is good until you enter the Baker Lake area where the sand dissipates and the track turns hard and rocky. The dark red surface makes it difficult to spot wash-outs, so slow down and keep your eyes peeled. The track skirts some rare high points, including Hanns Tabletop Hill, Skipper Knob and Point Brophy, before taking you up **Manton Knob** with fine views in all directions.

After another 40km or so, highlighted by majestic stands of desert oak, you arrive at a Y-junction where you veer right on a good track to continue to Warburton (see Facilities in the earlier Gunbarrel Hwy section for information on services and accommodation). The left-hand track, which is in very poor condition, hits the Great Central Rd only 8km west of the Heather Hwy turn-off, but it's probably quicker to go the long way around. From Warburton, you can head north-east towards Uluru, south-west to Laverton, or south-west to the junction of the Heather Hwy, which takes you north to link up with the Gunbarrel Hwy or Gary Hwy.

GARY HIGHWAY (368km)

The remote and beautiful Gary Hwy heads north from Everard Junction on the Gunbarrel Hwy past Windy Corner and Gary Junction to join up with the Canning Stock Route at Well 35. Built in April and May 1963, it hasn't been graded for decades and is dotted with severe wash-outs and occasionally crowded by unyielding foliage. However, the ever-changing desert terrain, sense of isolation and rich birdlife make for an outstanding experience. If you're on the Canning and seeking some solitude, a slow detour up the Gary via the Gunbarrel Hwy from Wiluna is well worth considering.

From the east, the Gary is accessed from Warburton, via the Heather Hwy and the Gunbarrel Hwy. Wiluna is the gateway from the west. The 368km from Everard Junction to Well 35 is a longish two-day drive, but chill out and do it in three if you have the time. You need good stocks of fuel and water for this route as it finishes a long way from anywhere.

Permits & Maps

No permits are required to use this road. The *North West* sheet in Hema's *Great Desert Tracks* series covers the entire track. The Landinfo sheets are Nos 3345 (Wiluna) and 3230 (Oakover River).

The Route

Everard Junction to Windy Corner (184km)

From the Len Beadell marker at Everard Junction, the narrow, single-track Gary Hwy initially meanders north through a sandy plain in a deceptively comfortable manner. The rough stuff starts soon enough though, with long sections of severe wash-outs from the 15km mark. Once you've cleared these, the convoluted nature of the track keeps your speed slow, until things start to even out after about 30km and you can start to drink in the desolate splendour of the **Gibson Desert Nature Reserve**.

The remaining 50km to Lake Cohen takes you through changeable terrain, with undulating spinifex plains dotted with small trees and termite mounds alternating with hard, rocky desert. It's pretty comfortable, although occasional rough patches ensure you don't let your guard down. Around 11km before the lake you pass a right-hand turn that heads 30km down a rugged track to **McPherson's Pillar**, where there are breathtaking 360-degree views. **Lake Cohen** itself is a large seasonal freshwater lake that's a great spot for a camp. When full, it attracts swarms of birds, including bustards, avocets, banded stilts, herons, native hens and coots.

The road junction of **Windy Corner** – where the Talawana Track heads west – is another 104km north through much the same terrain and there's a book (or glass jar stuffed with notes) for you to add to. All up the 184km from Everard Junction will take between six and seven hours.

Windy Corner to Well 35 (184km)

From Windy Corner, the Gary deteriorates a little, but you can still make good time as you cross lightly rolling plains for 56km, where a cleared line track to the north-east leads to **Veevers Crater**. This meteorite crater, 16km off the main track, is only 80m in diameter and 7m to 8m deep, but it's a near-perfect circle.

Soon afterwards, the track starts snaking through a series of dunes, but the open country and easier driving conditions soon return as you head towards the **Kidson Track** (also referred to as the Wapet Rd), which takes you to the Canning Stock Route 64km to the north-west. A further 31km to the north is **Gary Junction**, complete with Len Beadell marker, where the Gary Junction Rd heads due east for 874km to link up with the Tanami Track and eventually Alice Springs. To the west the Jenkins Track takes you to the Canning Stock Route, meeting the Kidson Track on the way. Continuing resolutely onwards, the Gary's last 41km stretch starts with some dunes and then gets pretty rough on its way into the junction with Canning near **Kidson's Bluff**. From here, Well 35 is a mere 4km away along the main Canning Stock Route. The 184km from Windy Corner can take up to seven hours.

TALAWANA TRACK (636km)

The last road built by Len and his crew between August and November 1963, the Talawana Track heads west from Windy Corner on the Gary Hwy into the Pilbara region, ending at the Marble Bar Rd, which you can follow south for about 50km to hit the Great Northern Hwy just south of the iron ore mining town, Newman. Overlapping briefly with the Canning Stock Route, it's a popular entry point for 4WDs taking on the Canning from Western Australia's central coast.

Strictly speaking, the Talawana ends after 428km, at the turn-off to the ruins of Talawana station, but it's a further 208km to Newman via the Marble Bar Rd, taking the total to 636km. This can be just managed in two days, but it's much better to allow yourself three or four days and spend some time exploring the spartan tracts of the Rudall River National Park. Again, you need to be fully prepared to tackle this track.

Permits & Maps

No permits are required to use this road. The *North West* sheet in Hema's *Great Desert Tracks* series covers the entire track, as does Landinfo sheet No 3230 (Oakover River).

The Route

Windy Corner to Georgia Bore (227km) Leaving the Gary Hwy, the track crosses hard gravelly country through the thick spinifex before entering a long, very

overgrown section about 10km in. Whether you tackle this at speed or slowly, you're going to scuff up your paintwork, so just grit your teeth and keep moving. Around the 40km mark, you skirt the **Connolly Basin**, an ancient, eroded meteorite crater some 9km in diameter, notable for its superb purple and yellow wildflowers if there's been any rain about.

The red, rocky terrain continues over a series of low hills for much of the next 40km, punctuated by some very nasty wash-outs and still more spinifex, before you start entering dune country. Around the 90km mark, a drum on the right marks the approximate position of the **Tropic of Capricorn**. Alternating sections of thick sand and washed-out gravel make for demanding driving all the way to the salt lakes of **Curara Soak**, about 10km short of the junction with the Canning. The short drive to the junction is both fun and picturesque, with sinuous sections of very deep, rich sand connecting flat stretches of blindingly white salt lake.

For the next 26km you travel on the popular Canning Stock Route – the heavy traffic it carries is evident in the deep track and severe corrugations. After 14km you reach **Well 23** where most Canning travellers pick up the vital stocks of fuel that have been delivered there for their use. After bumping along for another 22km, you kiss goodbye to the Canning and its corrugations at **Georgia Bore**, where there's an acceptable *camp site* and water source. All told, the 227km from Windy Corner will take between six and eight hours.

Georgia Bore to Newman (409km) At the Georgia Bore intersection, you head west towards Rudall River National Park on a hard, roughish track that soon emerges from the sand. The drive to the national park turn-off is dominated by the flat-topped mountains of the Harbutt Range that loom on your right, followed by the McKay Range on your left.

Ignoring the turn-off to the closed Parnngurr Aboriginal community at the 61km mark, continue 39km to meet the track that heads north into **Rudall River National Park**.

The park takes in a vast area of arid, unforgiving desert country that features the low-lying Fingoon and Broadhurst Ranges, and the salt lakes of **Lake Dora** and **Lake Blanche**, although these harsh elements are softened by the seasonal, gum-lined Rudall River. One of the most isolated national parks in Australia, Rudall River has an almost pitiless grandeur about it and is well worth exploring by foot or mountain bike – as long as you have plenty of water and sun protection. The best place to *camp* is under the trees by the hand pump at the southern fringe of the park; the camp sites further in are hard and uncomfortable.

Leaving the park behind, the Talawana flattens and widens gratifyingly on the run towards the **Talawana station ruins**. This 111km section should take less than two hours if the road is dry. Five kilometres later you take a left-hand turn and go south for 61km on a fairly rough road to Walgun station. If you're really short on fuel, turn left for Jiggalong 20km away. Otherwise, go right on to a better dirt track and follow it for 89km to the junction of the very good Marble Bar Rd, which you follow down to the sealed Great Northern Hwy. Less than 10km away are the bright lights and modern facilities of **Newman** where you can stock up on almost anything you need.

The day's driving is fairly humdrum, particularly once you pass the Talawana ruins, but you can make very good time, with the entire 409km stretch achievable in seven to eight hours.

GARY JUNCTION & PAPUNYA ROADS (894km)

Depending which map you look at, this road is known variously as the Gary Junction Rd, Papunya Rd or the Canning-Papunya Rd, which is curious because Len Beadell dubbed it the Gary Junction *Highway* on the completion of the Gary Junction–Sandy Blight Junction link in late 1960. We've split the difference, going for 'Papunya Rd' between Sandy Blight Junction and where Papunya Rd turns off the Tanami Track, and 'Gary Junction Rd' west from Sandy Blight Junction to Gary Junction itself.

No matter what you call it, it's a very long and remote section of track. Principally used by travellers from Alice Springs to access the Canning Stock Route, it heads pretty well due west for 894km from its origin at the Tanami Track, 136km north-west of Alice Springs. At the other end, Well 35 on the Canning is a further 45km past the Gary Junction along the Gary Hwy, taking the total distance from Alice to the Canning to 1030km.

Like most of Len's roads, it follows the easiest country possible, avoiding high dunes most of the time. However, the road is prone to severe flooding; in fact, heavy rains caused its closure west of Sandy Blight Junction for almost the whole of 2001 and forced a long-term evacuation of the isolated community of Kiwirrkurra. As always, check the conditions before you go, but this is a pretty comfortable three-day drive under normal conditions.

Permits & Maps

You require a permit from the Central Land Council (☎ 08-8951 6320, fax 8953 4345, e permits@clc.org.au, w www.clc.org.au, PO Box 3321, Alice Springs, NT 0871) to travel west of Papunya to the border. There's no charge, but allow three or four weeks for processing.

The *North East* and *North West* sheets in Hema's *Great Desert Tracks* series cover the entire route. The Landinfo sheets are Nos 3232 (Alice Springs), 3231 (Lake Mackay) and 3230 (Oakover River).

The Route

Papunya Rd Turn-Off to Sandy Blight Junction (365km) To get to the start of the Papunya Rd, head north from Alice Springs along the Stuart Hwy for 20km, then turn north-west along the Tanami Track to the Papunya turn-off, 136km from Alice. This is where the bitumen ends, but the next 110km to **Papunya** is good, graded dirt through low-lying scrub and takes about two hours. *Papunya Store (☎/fax 08-8956 8506; open 8.30am-noon & 1.30pm-4.30pm Mon-Fri, 9am-11.30am Sat)* has fuel and limited supplies.

Between Papunya and Kintore the road deteriorates somewhat, with harsher corrugations and occasional wash-outs, but you can still make good time. About 50km out of Papunya off to your left you will see **Mt Liebig**, the highest peak at the western end of the Amunurunga Range and soon afterwards you come to the turn-off to the community of the same name. Mt Liebig's **store** (☎ 08-8956 8591; open 10am-noon & 2pm-4pm Mon-Fri, 10am-noon Sat) offers fuel and some supplies. From here the road begins to follow Beadell's route west.

As you begin to approach the Ehrenberg Range, around the 100km mark, the first of the sand hills begin to appear. The road continues to be sandy and wash-outs become more common, but it's still generally in pretty good nick. **Sandy Blight Junction** is 250km west of Papunya, and nearby is the community of **Kintore (Walungurru)**. The main access to this dry community, where you can get fuel and limited supplies at the **Kintore Store** (☎ 08-8956 8575, fax 8956 8576; open 10am-noon & 2pm-4.30pm Mon-Fri, 10am-noon Sat & Sun), is 17km west of the junction. The drive from Papunya to Kintore takes between three and four hours.

Sandy Blight Junction to Gary Junction (484km) Beyond Kintore the road improves a little and is usually in fair condition. The Western Australia–Northern Territory border is crossed 40km further west, and 165km from Sandy Blight you see the remains of **Len's burnt-out ration truck** on the right side of the road. The story is told in Len's book *Beating About the Bush*.

Just 31km further on you come to the **Kiwirrkurra**, possibly the most remote community in all Australia. Fuel and limited supplies are available here, but only if you have had prior contact with the Kiwirrkurra community (☎ 08-8956 8305). The trip from Sandy Blight Junction to Kiwirrkurra will take between two and three hours.

To continue to the Canning Stock Route, head west out of town and past the airport. The road quickly becomes a sandy track, showing a definite lack of maintenance. In places it has been washed away and a new

track skirts the original. In other spots the sand along the road can be deep, forcing you to crawl along in second gear for kilometre after kilometre. This can really chew the fuel, so ensure you're carrying adequate supplies.

Jupiter Well is found in a magnificent stand of desert oak 327km west of Sandy Blight, about five hours' drive west of Kiwirrkurra, and it's a good place to *camp*. There's an Aboriginal community outstation beside the track just before you get there. No fuel or supplies are available, and don't rely on getting water here either.

You hit Gary Junction 161km (about five hours) further west, where you will find a Len Beadell marker. Continuing northwest, you reach Well 35 on the Canning Stock Route (see the earlier section on the Gary Highway for more details).

SANDY BLIGHT JUNCTION ROAD (297KM)

The Sandy Blight Junction Rd through central Australia strikes north from the Great Central Rd at a point 27km west of Docker River Aboriginal community, finishes at Sandy Blight Junction, 331km to the north, close to Kintore Aboriginal community and takes around eight hours on a dry track.

Built by Len Beadell between March and July 1960, and named after a particularly bad bout of this common desert eye disease he was enduring at the time, the Sandy Blight Rd is a relatively easy run north. For most of the way it crosses sandy country, and where it does traverse sand ridges they are generally small and present no problem. For much of the way the road passes through quite dense stands of magnificent desert oak.

Permits & Maps

You require a permit from the Central Land Council (☎ 08-8951 6320, fax 8953 4345, e permits@clc.org.au, w www.clc.org.au, PO Box 3321, Alice Springs, NT 0871) to travel this road. There's no charge, but allow three or four weeks for processing.

The *North East* sheet in Hema's *Great Desert Tracks* series covers the entire route, as do Landinfo sheets 3231 (Lake Mackay) and 3344 (Petermann Ranges).

The Route

The route begins 27km west of Docker River (Kaltukatjara) on the Great Central Rd. Docker River isn't a bad place to pick up last-minute supplies and fuel (see the earlier Gunbarrel Highway section for details) before you head out to the junction of the Sandy Blight Rd. Veering right off the highway, the road parallels Rebecca Creek and passes the western end of the **Scherwin Mural Crescent**, 13km north of the junction. Another 14km further on, with the Walter James Range off to the west, there is a track that leads to **Bungabiddy Rockhole**, deep within the range. It's a nice spot and popular with the locals.

The road continues north, and while it can be a little washed out, it is generally fairly easy, but slow, travelling. Past the junction to the closed community of Tjukurla, 66km north of the Great Central Rd, the track swings around the western end of the salty **Lake Hopkins**, and the first of the sand ridges are crossed 17km further on.

Around 150km from Docker River, keep your eyes out for a large desert oak bearing an original Len Beadell marker. From here the road crosses sand-ridge country and passes through the Sir Frederick Range on its way to the Northern Territory-Western Australia border, which features a log blazed by Len on the left.

From the border the road heads almost due east for 25km, before heading north again and crossing the Tropic of Capricorn – marked yet again by Len Beadell. Heading on, the horizon is dominated by the bulk of the **Kintore Range**; Mt Leisler (901m) is the highest point around for quite some way. At the far north of the range is Mt Strickland. It's a magnificent scene – one to which your eyes are drawn time and again.

Tietkins Tree, an old, dead tree emblazoned by the explorer William Tietkins in 1889, stands below the bluff of Mt Leisler. From here it's a pleasant 28km drive to Sandy Blight Junction and the Gary Junction and Papunya Rds, which lead you east to Alice Springs or west to the Canning Stock Route (see the earlier Gary Junction & Papunya Roads section for details).

GOOGS TRACK (188km)

Len and his crew had nothing to do with its construction, but Googs Track is a terrific linking road (and shortcut) from the Eyre Hwy to the Stuart Hwy, and provides access to the central Bomb Roads. Even better, its huge roller-coaster sand dunes are both technically challenging and enjoyable to drive, and the scenery in the Yellabinna Regional Reserve is magnificent.

Built between 1973 and 1976 by Goog Denton, Martin 'Dinger' Denton and Denis Beattie, of Lone Oak homestead, this 172km track is accessed via a 29km-long graded dirt road that leaves the Eyre Hwy about 5km north of Ceduna. It continues north to meet the Trans Access Rd (which shadows the Trans Australian Railway) at the Malbooma siding. Glendambo on the Stuart Hwy is a further 161km to the east, via the small town of Tarcoola. Rangers request that all vehicles traverse this route from south to north to minimise the chance of accidents while cresting the almost endless series of towering dunes. Assuming your vehicle is properly set up for sand driving, it's a comfortable two-day drive, unless you linger for a day around Goog's Lake.

Permits & Maps

There's no charge to enter the Yellabinna Regional Reserve, but you do require a permit to camp there and this costs $6 per person per night. Contact the Administrative Officer, Far West District, at the Department for Environment and Heritage (☎ 08-8625 3144, fax 8625 3123), PO Box 569, Ceduna, SA 5690.

The *South East* sheet in Hema's *Great Desert Tracks* series covers the entire route, as do Landinfo sheets 3354 (Tarcoola) and 3459 (Port Augusta).

The Route

Ceduna to Goog's Lake (82km) This is a very short day for a couple of reasons: First-time dune drivers will probably take things pretty slowly while they get a feel for the track; and the best *camping spot* along the route is at Goog's Lake, which is a great place to kick back for the afternoon.

The dirt access road 5km out of Ceduna is clearly marked so follow it through farmland for 29km to **Lone Oak** homestead, where the owners request that you check in. Enter **Yellabinna Regional Reserve** and the fun starts, with dune after dune climbing steeply in front of you and then dropping exhilaratingly away on the other side.

After 32km of dunes you reach the turnoff to Goog's Lake, marked by a poignant **memorial** to Goog and Dinger Denton. The large salt lake is 4km down a narrow track, which finishes at a large, well-wooded *camp site* suitable for large parties. The hills that fringe the lake feature some steep 4WD tracks to explore and there's good hiking to be had along the shores of the lake.

Goog's Lake to Glendambo (275km)

It's worth getting an early start, as the dunes continue for about 70km and you'll average 25km/hour. Still, the rolling track takes you through superb, lightly wooded desert country, thick with birdlife and native grasses.

Soon after the turn-off to Mt Finke, 105km from Lone Oak, the sand starts to dissipate and the track becomes harder and rockier. About 20km short of Malbooma, the track meets a fence, which it hugs all the way to the Trans Access Rd. This section of the track is narrow, very overgrown and painfully slow. It'll take between four and five hours, but the remaining 161km to Glendambo is straightforward on a broad, well-maintained dirt road that crisscrosses the Trans Australian Railway. It's usually takes a little less than two hours to get to Glendambo. At that point, turn south to get to major regional centre of Port Augusta or head north for the opal-mining town of Coober Pedy.

The South

From western New South Wales across South Australia to the eastern fringes of the south-west of Western Australia, 'the South' takes in a vast sweep of semi-arid saltbush and scrub plain that is, in the main, flat! Only through the heart of South Australia does a line of spectacular hill country, the Flinders Ranges, provide a different vista to the long, straight roads and distant, level horizons.

Much of the region is pastoral country, with the properties, mainly sheep stations, taking up huge areas. Often the only signs of human habitation are kilometres of straggly wire fences; slowly turning windmills bringing water to the surface; and the occasional silver, galvanised roof of a homestead glinting in the unrelenting sun. Towns (even small ones) are generally few and far between: the only one of any significant size in the area covered in this chapter is the mining centre of Broken Hill.

Distances between towns, although still measured in hundreds of kilometres, aren't as great as other areas of the outback. In the far west of South Australia and across into Western Australia the pastoral land gives way to the spinifex and sand ridges of the Great Victoria Desert. In this region the outback meets the sea, but the meeting is not a gentle one and beaches are few: the arc of the Great Australian Bight is mostly an unbroken line of cliffs where the Nullarbor Plain plunges into the wild Southern Ocean.

Eyre Highway

HIGHLIGHTS

- Driving or walking along the beaches of the Great Australian Bight near Eyre Bird Observatory
- Exploring the caves and the lonely expanses of the Nullarbor Plain
- Watching the whales and their calves at Twin Rocks

Ask Australians what they think the ultimate road trip is and most will answer 'crossing the Nullarbor'. The Eyre Hwy is the accepted way to do this, but this long and sometimes lonely road only briefly crosses the southern edge of the vast Nullarbor Plain – the vast majority of the route traverses coastal fringe country that receives regular rain and supports the trees that the Nullarbor lacks (*nullarbor* is dog Latin for 'no trees').

Unlike the wilder days of the '50s and '60s, when crossing the Nullarbor meant several days on a dirt road with few facilities and fewer vehicles, today the route forms part of the National Hwy around the continent; it's completely sealed, well serviced by roadhouses and carries a vast amount of tourist and commercial traffic.

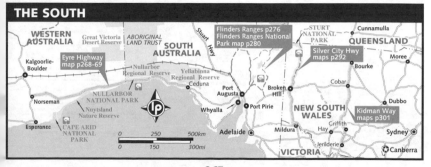

THE SOUTH

As such, the focus of this route has switched from an adventurous journey to an exploration of the attractions along the route between long, long stretches of tarmac road.

From the seaside town of Ceduna, the road stays inland, passing the resort town of Fowlers Bay and some good surf beaches. Entering Nullarbor National Park, the road runs parallel to the dramatic Bunda Cliffs of the Great Australian Bight and Yalata Aboriginal land, where there's superb whale-watching. The road swings back inland on the way into Norseman, passing the Nuytsland Nature Reserve, Newman Rock and a detour to the Eyre Bird Observatory.

The best time to do this journey is in winter or early spring, when the weather is cool and you spot hundreds of southern right whales and their calves cavorting in the Bight. All up it's 1219km from Ceduna to Norseman (which you can do in three days and still see some sights), but when you add the 761km from Adelaide to Ceduna and the 721km from Norseman to Perth, it's a mighty 2701km journey that will take you five days at least. It is, in the immortal words of a trans-Australian truck driver, 'a bloody long way'.

History

The highway across the Nullarbor takes its name from John Eyre, the explorer who, in 1841, made the first east-west crossing. In 1877, a telegraph line was laid across the Nullarbor, roughly delineating the route the first road would take.

Later in the century, miners en route to the goldfields followed the telegraph line across the Nullarbor. In 1896 the first bicycle crossing was made and in 1912 the first car was driven across, but over the next 12 years only three more cars managed to complete the route.

In 1941 the war inspired the building of a transcontinental highway, just as it had the Alice Springs–Darwin route. It was a rough-and-ready track when completed,

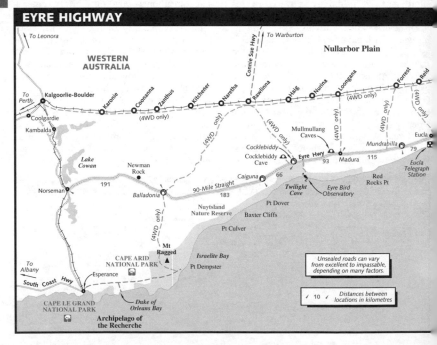

and in the 1950s only a few vehicles a day made the crossing. In the 1960s the traffic flow increased to more than 30 vehicles a day, and in 1969 the Western Australian government surfaced the road as far as the South Australian border. Finally, in 1976, the last stretch from the South Australian border was surfaced, making the Nullarbor crossing a much easier drive, although still a long one.

Information

Tourist Offices Ceduna has a friendly and well-stocked visitor information centre (☎ 1800 639 413, e travelce@tpg.com.au), at 58 Poynton St on the main drag, which also offers Internet access at very good rates. The Norseman Tourist Bureau (☎ 08-9039 1071, e nsmntour@wn.com.au), at 68 Roberts St, is the next official information centre, but all of the roadhouses en route have at least some information on the attractions in their area.

Books & Maps The tourist information centres in Ceduna and Norseman have all the information you're ever likely to need about the Eyre Hwy, its history and attractions; the free booklet *Ceduna: From Smoky Bay to the Nullarbor Whales* is particularly informative. The National Roads and Motorists Association's (NRMA) *Great Driving Adventures* and Ron & Viv Moon's *Discover Australia 4WD* detail some off-road options from the Eyre Hwy; the latter also has good national park information. If you follow the highway, no special maps are required.

Permits No permits are required to travel the Eyre Hwy, even though Yalata Aboriginal land is crossed at one stage. If you want to go off-road in Yalata land, you will need a permit from the Yalata Roadhouse (☎ 08-8625 6986). A permit is also required to bush camp in Nullarbor National Park or Nullarbor Regional Reserve. Contact the administrative officer, Far West District, at

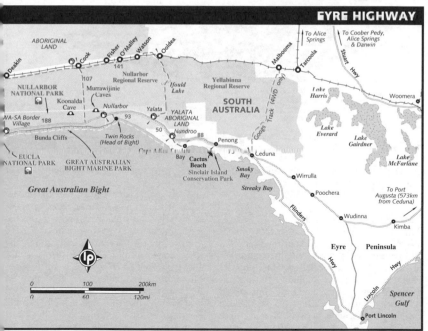

A Right Whale of a Time

Between 1790 and 1845 southern right whales were hunted to the brink of extinction in the waters of the Great Australian Bight. Considered by whalers as the 'right' whale to hunt, they could be found close to the coast, provided high oil yields and had the good grace to float after they'd been killed. From the 18 whaling stations along the South Australian coast during this period, thousands of southern rights were taken each year as they entered the Bight to mate, calve and nurse.

The remnant population has been slowly recovering and the world's southern right whales are now estimated to number 4000 (down from an estimated 100,000 in the 1790s). About 800 travel to the Bight every winter. Weighing up to 80 tonnes, the whales and their young spend several months in the sheltered waters of the Great Australian Bight Marine Park while the calves fatten up and learn the skills they'll need to traverse the great southern oceans.

While whales can be seen along much of the South Australian coast, Twin Rocks at Head of Bight (the Bight's northernmost point) is the prime viewing area. Between June and September it's common to see more than 100 animals breaching, rolling and blowing at the base of the cliffs that edge these waters. It's a captivating sight.

The turn-off to Twin Rocks is 79km west of Yalata Roadhouse; it's an easy 11km drive on a good dirt road to the coast. As the area is on Yalata land, you need a permit (adult/child $8/6.50) to enter. These are available at Yalata Roadhouse (see Ceduna to Eucla under Facilities, later in this section) and White Well Rangers Station (☎ 08-8625 6201), open 9am-5pm daily from May to October, just inside the turn-off.

KATE NOLAN

the Department for the Environment and Heritage (☎ 08-8625 3144, fax 8625 3123), PO Box 569, Ceduna, SA 5690.

Special Preparations

Although the Eyre is no longer an isolated torture trail of potholes and corrugations, it's still wise to take some simple precautions.

The longest distance between fuel stops is 188km, so you really shouldn't run out of petrol. More expensive and time-consuming is a mechanical breakdown, as there's currently no mechanic between Nundroo and Norseman, and a tow-truck may have to travel some hundreds of kilometres to get you. Make sure your vehicle is in good shape and that you've got plenty of fuel and decent tyres at the right pressure. Savvy motorcyclists fit a cheap rear tyre for the trip, as the centre of the tread will wear quite markedly.

Petrol prices vary alarmingly along the route, ranging from 15 to 30 cents a litre above city prices. When we went through, Mundrabilla and Yalata had the cheapest fuel, but jerry cans are still a good idea. Also bear in mind that this area lies close to the Roaring Forties, the strong winds that blow from west to east around the south of the globe, so travelling from east to west (the way we describe the trip) tends to cost more fuel than the other way round. Cyclists in particular should keep the wind in mind.

Carry plenty of drinking water (4L per person) in case you do have to sit it out by the roadside. Fresh water supplies are limited on the Western Australian side, so stock up where you can. All roadhouses have Eftpos facilities and accept major credit cards, but there are no banks between Norseman and Ceduna, so take some cash with you.

Finally, take it easy behind the wheel. The long, flat road makes it tempting to crank up the speed, but you're a long way from medical help and there are plenty of big 'roos waiting to mess up your car, particularly at night. The police also pull out their radar guns every now and then to collect revenue, especially near the Western Australian/South Australian border.

THE ROUTE
Ceduna
Ceduna (from an Aboriginal word meaning 'a place to sit down and rest') is a rather attractive little seaside town with six caravan parks, a backpackers, several hotels and a smattering of B&Bs, plus well-stocked supermarkets, banks, newsagents and all the other comforts you won't see until Norseman. It has several tour operators offering 4WD, fishing and whale-watching trips and the seafood here is superb, particularly the whiting and oysters. Drop into the information centre (☎ 1800 639 413, e travel ce@tpg.com.au) on Poynton St for more detailed information.

Ceduna to Nullarbor (304km)
Leaving Ceduna it's 73km to the small town of **Penong**, where you can detour south to Pink Lake, Sinclair Island Conservation Park and **Cactus Beach**, a famous surf beach with left and right breaks – a must for any serious surfer.

Another 35km brings you to a turn-off to **Fowlers Bay**, a small village that's managed to reinvent itself as a holiday destination, boasting large dunes, clean beaches, good fishing and some whale watching.

Back on the highway you pass Nundroo Roadhouse, where you enter the Nullarbor Plain for the first time and, shortly afterwards, Yalata Aboriginal land. This area of 6000 sq km takes in Twin Rocks (Head of Bight), where you'll find the best **whale-watching** along the coast (see the boxed text 'A Right Whale of a Time' for details). The community has its own roadhouse 93km before Nullarbor – see Ceduna to Eucla under Facilities, later in this section.

Nullarbor to Eucla (188km)
Nullarbor to the Western Australian-South Australian border is the journey's most picturesque stretch. You're in the Nullarbor National Park (5930 sq km) the entire way and the road soon hugs the coast, providing spectacular views of cliffs and ocean.

First, however, you can get a taste of the Nullarbor's famous caves, by taking a dirt road north for about 8km from the rear of the Nullarbor Roadhouse (ask for directions at the front counter). The three **Murrawijinie Caves** are clearly visible, as their roofs have collapsed, opening them up to the elements. You can scramble down and poke around, but be extremely careful and keep your eyes peeled for snakes.

The run to the border is highlighted by eight lookouts from the sheer **Bunda Cliffs** that tower up to 100m above the waters of the Bight – stop and check out at least a couple. Hand over your fruit and vegies to quarantine officials and turn back your watch 1½ hours (or 2½ hours during daylight savings) at the border; you enter Eucla 13km later.

The tiny town of Eucla grew up around an 1877 telegraph station whose ruins are gradually disappearing beneath the shifting sands 5km south of the modern town. Apart from a small but engaging **museum** at the motel, Eucla's attractions are natural, with the Delisser Sandhills and the high limestone Wilson Bluff the highlights of the 33.4 sq km **Eucla National Park**.

Eucla to Caiguna (353km)
After the excitement of cliffs, whales and caves, this stretch is comparatively dull. You pass Mundrabilla Roadhouse, with its strange

little menagerie, on the way to **Madura**, where horses were once bred for the Indian Army. On your way into Cocklebiddy you pass the turn-off to the Eyre Bird Observatory (see the following entry) in the Nuytsland Nature Reserve. Just 10km west of Cocklebiddy, an unmarked track leads you 10km to **Cocklebiddy Cave**, the largest of the Nullarbor caves. You can get about 300m inside before you hit the water – in 1983 a team of French explorers set a new record here for the deepest cave dive in the world. Take at least two light sources and wear good boots as it's pretty rough underfoot (also see Activities, later in this section).

Caiguna is a good place to stop for the day. Some 10km to the south is the memorial to John Baxter, Eyre's companion, who was killed on 29 April 1841 by Aborigines.

Eyre Bird Observatory The Eyre Bird Observatory *(☎ 08-9039 3450, fax 9039 3440; adult/child $5.50/2.20; open 8.30am-5.30pm daily)* is housed in the Eyre Telegraph Station in the **Nuytsland Nature Reserve**. Refurbished by Birds Australia in 1977, this 1897 stone building is in a peaceful setting surrounded by mallee scrub, and looks up to spectacular sand dunes. Regular activities and courses are held here, such as banding and census-taking of some of the 240 species of birds recorded, which include Major Mitchell cockatoos, mallee fowl, bronzewings, honeyeaters, waders and terns.

The *observatory* sleeps 16 people and charges adult/child $77/38.50 for the first night, with good discounts available for longer stays; bookings are essential. Meals can also be arranged with advance notice.

It's about 40km south-east of Cocklebiddy and you definitely need a 4WD to get here. The turn-off from the Eyre Hwy is 16km east of Cocklebiddy. Follow it south for about 20km to a microwave tower, then turn right and drive 5km to the lookout car park. Here you can see the huge migrating dunes that you're about to traverse. Reduce the pressure in your tyres and wind your way through soft sand for the last 11km. If you don't have a 4WD, you can arrange for return transport for $22 per person.

Caiguna to Norseman (374km)

From Caiguna you're on the famous 90-Mile Straight – one of the longest stretches of straight road in the world. After 146km the road finally turns (to the right) and soon passes the expensive Balladonia roadhouse. Good places to break for lunch are **Newman Rock**, 50km to the west, or **Ten Mile Rocks**, another 50km on. It's then an unremarkable drive into Norseman.

Norseman

Norseman is a pleasant enough little town with useful shops, a cinema and the **Historical & Geological Collection** *(Battery Rd; $2; open 10am-1pm Mon-Sat, but check first with tourist bureau)* of items from the gold-rush days. You can get excellent views of the town and the surrounding salt lakes from the **Beacon Hill Mararoa Lookout**, on the eastern edge of town, and **Mt Jimberlana**, about 5km east of town on the Eyre Hwy.

There are plenty of accommodation options, including a caravan park, backpackers hostel, two motels and two hotels. The hotels and motels also have restaurants; in addition, there's a cafe, deli, health food shop and pizza parlour in town. For details on the town's facilities, drop into the tourist bureau (☎ 08-9039 1071, **e** nsmntour@ wn.com.au) on Roberts St.

The Last Place on Earth

A latter-day visitor to the Eyre Bird Observatory was eccentric US millionaire Harold Anderson. Convinced that nuclear Armageddon was imminent, he decided to donate to the remote observatory all of the books he thought would form the perfect account of the earth and its history.

Anderson returned to the USA, collated the books and despatched them to Australia. Not long afterwards he was mugged and died, in his early 40s, never to see the books on the shelves at the observatory. They are still there, alongside all the written paraphernalia any avid bird-watcher could need.

DETOURS

Few roads head south off the Eyre, but a number lead north towards the *Indian-Pacific* railway line. Two detours from the normal route are described here. One leads south to the Great Australian Bight; the other takes you north to the railway, east along it and back south to the Eyre Hwy.

Two other routes that leave the Eyre are described in the Bomb Roads section of the Central Deserts chapter – Googs Track, which heads north from Ceduna, and the Connie Sue Hwy, which heads north from Cocklebiddy to meet Warburton on the Great Central Rd.

Into the Nullarbor

This detour, which gives you a taste of the true Nullarbor, takes you north through Yalata Aboriginal land to Ooldea, west along the Trans Access Rd to Cook and then south through the Nullarbor National Park and Nullarbor Regional Reserve back to the Eyre Hwy. It's a 384km route that's best done in a 4WD over two days, although you could do it in a single day in a pinch.

You'll need two permits: one to camp in the Nullarbor Regional Reserve and one to cross Yalata Aboriginal land (see Permits under Information, earlier in this section). There are no facilities along the route so ensure you have sufficient fuel, water and supplies.

From Yalata, you head roughly north on a passable road for 146km to Ooldea, a siding on the *Indian-Pacific* railway line, crossing the shimmering saltpan of **Ifould Lake** on the way. Turning west, you follow the generally good Trans Access Rd for 130km to Cook, passing Watson, O'Malley and Fisher stations. Finally, head south from Cook for 105km along a rougher road through the mallee, bluebush and saltbush scrub of the Nullarbor Plain to meet the Eyre 145km east of the Western Australian/South Australian border.

Balladonia to Norseman via Esperance

This is a substantial detour in which you head almost due south from Balladonia on a 4WD-only road into the superb beaches and rugged mountains of **Cape Arid National Park**, with its rare flora and fauna. You pass **Mt Ragged**, the highest point in the Russell Range, on the way; there's a tough 3km, three-hour walk to the peak if you're feeling fit. For more information on the park, contact the Esperance Office of the WA Department of Conservation and Land Management (CALM; ☎ 08-9071 3733). Ensure you're fully equipped with fuel, food, water and camping gear, as there are no facilities until Esperance.

Once you've taken in enough of the area's beauty, follow the road out of the park into the holiday town of Esperance. It's well set-up for visitors, with loads of accommodation and activities along a pristine section of coast. From Esperance it's an easy 202km run north into Norseman.

ACTIVITIES

Bird-Watching

The Eyre Bird Observatory is one of the best places in the country to bird-watch (see the entry under Eucla to Caiguna, in The Route section earlier). Otherwise, you'll see many birds of prey – including the majestic wedge-tailed eagle – dispensing with road kills along all sections of the highway.

Caving

The Nullarbor conceals one of the largest karst (limestone) cave systems in the world. Within South Australia, only Murrawijinie Caves, just north of Nullarbor Roadhouse, are accessible to the public (see the earlier route description). You can also visit Koonalda Cave, 20km north up a dirt track from a point halfway between Nullarbor Roadhouse and the border. You can't enter it, but you can peer down the 50m drop. You pass the heritage-listed ruins of Koonalda homestead on the way. Otherwise, only research and mapping parties are permitted to enter caves in South Australia. Contact the Department for the Environment and Heritage (☎ 08-8625 3144) in Ceduna for permit details.

On the Western Australian side of the border, Cocklebiddy Cave and Mullamullang Cave (on private land) are worth visiting, but check with CALM's Esperance Office (☎ 08-9071 3733) before you head in.

Cycling
Presumably it's the challenge of the sheer distance involved that attracts cyclists to the Eyre Hwy, because the scenery really isn't much chop. On the bright side, the many long flat sections will allow you to make pretty good time. If you're planning to tackle this road, it's sensible to go west-east to take advantage of the prevailing winds. You'll need excellent equipment, a lot of water, protection from the sun, and be sure to check the location of viable water tanks (and there are some) on the way.

Water Sports
Surfers and swimmers should think hard before succumbing to the siren song of the white-sand beaches and crashing waves along the Bight. There are *big* white pointer sharks out there.

FACILITIES
Ceduna and Norseman are well set up, but there's really only basic facilities on offer along the way. Most have a dusty caravan park, some hard tent sites, a number of tired but very clean motel rooms and a pub with a telly. With a couple of exceptions, the food is equally uninspired – if it's not meat, fish or a deep-fried vegetable, it's not on the menu. Truckies really have a lot to answer for.

Ceduna to Eucla
Nundroo Hotel Motel (☎ 08-8625 6120) Unpowered/powered camp sites for two $15/17.50, dorm beds $16.50, single/double/family rooms $71/82/119. This is a clean, simple place with good facilities, including a pool and the last mechanic until Norseman.

Yalata Roadhouse (☎ 08-8625 6986, fax 8625 6987) Unpowered/powered camp sites for two $5/10, double cabins $65. Owned by the nearby Yalata community, this roadhouse has a decent restaurant and good prices for its fuel, plus an interesting array of local art and craft.

Nullarbor Hotel Motel (☎ 08-8625 6271, fax 8625 6261) Unpowered/powered camp sites for two $10/16, budget singles/doubles $18/30, motel singles/doubles $76.50/92. A rocky, noisy camp site makes the refurbished motel rooms an attractive option. Scenic flights operate from here, too.

WA-SA Border Village (☎ 08-9039 3474, fax 9039 34733) Unpowered/powered camp sites for two $8/15, backpacker singles/doubles $23/41, motel singles/doubles $82/87. Acceptable rooms sit next to a brand-new service station, bar and restaurant rebuilt after a 1999 fire. Showers for campers cost $2 and fuel is available 24 hours.

Eucla Motor Hotel (☎ 08-9039 3468, fax 9039 3401) Unpowered/powered camp sites $2/11 per person, budget singles/doubles $22/38, motel singles/doubles $71/82. Spacious rooms, a wooded camp site, cottage garden and decent restaurant make this the best roadhouse on the route.

Eucla to Norseman
Mundrabilla Roadhouse (☎ 08-9039 3465, fax 9039 3200, e mundrabilla@bigpond .com.au) Unpowered/powered camp sites $10/15 for 2 people, motel singles/doubles/family rooms $55/65/90. This is a very friendly, if unprepossessing, place with clean rooms, a great range of home-cooked meals, an odd collection of animals and well-priced fuel.

Madura Pass Oasis Motel (☎ 08-9039 3464, fax 9039 3489) Unpowered/powered camp sites $12/16.50 for 2 people, budget - singles/doubles $60/69.50, motel singles/doubles $79/99.50. This is a well-maintained but expensive place with good pub meals, an overpriced restaurant and a shady camping ground. Go for the motel rooms over the worn budget accommodation.

Wedgetail Inn Cocklebiddy (☎ 08-9039 3462, fax 9039 3403) Unpowered/powered camp sites $8/16.50 for 2 people, budget singles/doubles $40/50, motel singles/doubles/family rooms $71/82.50/105. Wedgetail is an unexceptional place with the usual services, plus expensive fuel.

John Eyre Motel (Caiguna; ☎ 08-9039 3459) Unpowered/powered camp sites $7.70/16.50 for 2 people, motel singles/doubles/family rooms $65/88.50/115. This is a dusty but welcoming place with clean rooms, spacious bathrooms and a hard camping ground.

Balladonia Hotel Motel *(☎ 9039 3453, fax 9039 3405,* **W** *www.users.bigpond.com/ balladonia)* Unpowered/powered camp sites $12/18 for 2 people, beds in 4-bed dorms $16.50, motel singles/doubles/triples/family rooms $69/86/96/105. You'll see the signs well before you see it. Balladonia has a slick museum and pricey food.

ALTERNATIVE TRANSPORT

As the Eyre is the most important trans-continental route in Australia, there are daily scheduled bus services on the Adelaide-Perth route with McCafferty's (☎ 13 14 99, **W** www.mccaffertys.com.au). There is also a rail option, one of the great railway journeys of the world (see the *Indian-Pacific* section in the Getting Around chapter).

Flinders Ranges

For many seasoned travellers the Flinders Ranges in South Australia are the epitome of the outback. Certainly they are, for the vast majority of Australians, the easiest outback destination to get to. Another thing is certain: Of all the regions in Australia's outback, the Flinders have had more glossy coffee-table books produced about them than any other. That does say something about their grandeur and attraction.

While the Flinders officially begin near Crystal Brook, just 195km north of Adelaide, it is further north that they take on their distinguishing outback characteristics.

It's also further north that they reach their highest point and are at their grandest.

On these pages we describe the route from Hawker north via Wilpena Pound, Blinman and the Arkaroola Wilderness Sanctuary to Copley. While it could be done as a stand-alone trip, it is also an enjoyable route north to Lyndhurst or Marree and the start of the Strzelecki, Oodnadatta and Birdsville tracks.

Much of the route could be travelled in a normal car, as the conditions vary from good bitumen to slow but reasonable dirt. A notable exception is the 4WD alternative route from Arkaroola to the Copley-Balcanoona road near Mt Serle station. But in most cases it's in the far north, beyond Arkaroola, that the tracks become real 4WD.

All told, this trip covers around 450km of rugged outback range country. You could travel it in a longish day, but you wouldn't see much and you'd enjoy it even less. There are a number of places to stock up with supplies, and you could stay in a motel or hotel every evening you are away.

History

The Adnyamathanha (Hill People) have inhabited the Flinders Ranges for many thousands of years. The ranges and the people who lived there were an integral part of the long-distance trade routes that crossed the continent. Ochre and *pituri*, a mildly narcotic drug, were traded, as were stones for axes and tools, and shell for decoration.

Dotted among the hills and valleys are important archaeological sites including ochre quarries (the ochre being used as a paint decoration in ceremonies), rock quarries (sources of tools) and art sites. The Flinders are rich in rock engravings, or petroglyphs, a form of art that probably predates the painted art which, in the Flinders, lacks the richness and variety found at sites in northern Australia.

The last full-blooded Adnyamathanha died in 1973, but all the descendants of the tribal groups that inhabited the ranges and the surrounding country still have strong ties to the land. Most of them live in the towns of the region; Nepabunna, east of Copley, is a small Aboriginal community.

THE SOUTH

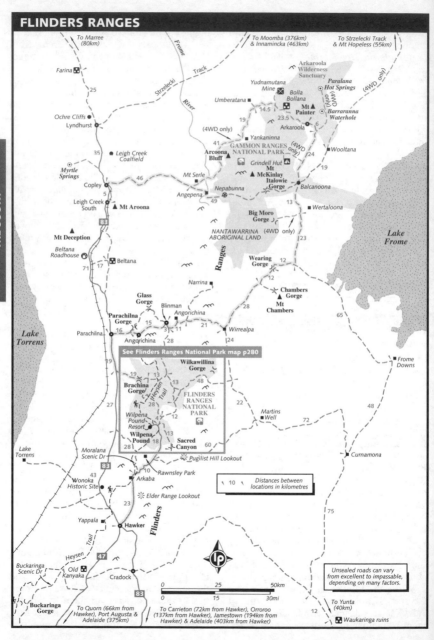

FLINDERS RANGES

THE SOUTH

To Marree
(80km)

To Moomba (376km)
& Innamincka (463km)

To Strzelecki Track
& Mt Hopeless (55km)

Farina

Frome

Track

Strzelecki

River

(4WD only)

Arkaroola
Wilderness
Sanctuary

Yudnamutana
Mine

Paralana
Hot Springs

Umberatana

14.5

Bolla
Bollana

Mt
Painter

Barraranna
Waterhole

25

(4WD only)

Ochre Cliffs
Lyndhurst

Leigh Creek
Coalfield

35

Myrtle
Springs

Copley

5

Leigh Creek
South

Mt Aroona

83

Mt Deception

Beltana
Roadhouse

71 17

Beltana

46

Mt Serle

Nepabunna

Angepena

49

19

Yankaninna

GAMMON RANGES
NATIONAL PARK

41

Arcoona
Bluff

Grindell Hut

Mt
McKinlay
Italowie
Gorge

23.5

Arkaroola

6

(4WD only)

24

19

Wooltana

Balcanoona

13

Wertaloona

Big Moro
Gorge

NANTAWARRINA
ABORIGINAL LAND

(4WD only)

23

Lake
Frome

Wearing
Gorge

12

Narrina

12

Chambers
Gorge

Mt
Chambers

Ranges

Glass
Gorge

Blinman

Angorichina

Parachilna
Gorge

15

3 11

21

28

Wirrealpa

28

65

Parachilna

16

Angorichina

24

Lake
Torrens

19

See Flinders Ranges National Park map p280

Wilkawillina
Gorge

19

13

13

48

Brachina
Gorge

Heysen Trail

13

FLINDERS
RANGES
NATIONAL
PARK

22

Martins
Well

48

27

28

Wilpena
Pound
Resort

12

72

Frome
Downs

Wilpena
Pound

28

18

13

Sacred
Canyon

60

Lake
Torrens

Moralana
Scenic Dr

83

10

Pugilist Hill Lookout

Curnamona

Wonoka
Historic Site

43

Arkaba

Rawnsley Park

10 Distances between
locations in kilometres

Elder Range Lookout

23

Yappala

Hawker

Flinders

75

Heysen Trail

47

Buckaringa
Scenic Dr

Old
Kanyaka

Cradock

83

Unsealed roads can vary
from excellent to impassable,
depending on many factors.

Buckaringa
Gorge

To Quorn (66km from
Hawker), Port Augusta &
Adelaide (375km from Hawker)

0   25   50km

0   15   30mi

To Carrieton (72km from Hawker),
Orroroo (137km from Hawker), Jamestown (194km from
Hawker) & Adelaide (403km from Hawker)

To Yunta
(40km)

12

Waukaringa ruins

The first white person to see these ranges was Matthew Flinders, from the deck of his ship *Investigator* in March 1802 as it sailed up Spencer Gulf. From his anchorage south of present-day Port Augusta he sent a group to climb a nearby peak, naming it Mt Brown after his intrepid botanist.

Edward John Eyre was next on the scene, in 1839. Over a two-year period, he explored along the western edge of the range, striking west and north, but ran into a series of salt lakes that he thought were one giant ring of salt blocking his way north. His last expedition saw him push east, from north of Mt Deception, past Mt Aroona and deep into the ranges near Mt Serle, before following the Frome River north out of the labyrinth of gorges and rugged ridges surrounding him. Following the edge of the range north-east, he climbed a low hill that he named, supposedly before he even climbed it, Mt Hopeless, and once again spied a barrier of salt.

Just four years later the pastoral expansion had reached the southern edge of the Flinders Ranges near Gladstone, and slowly but surely pushed north. William Chace was the first man to encounter Wilpena Pound, one of the natural wonders of the Flinders. He had been sent by the Browne brothers, two doctors who by 1851 had taken up the Wilpena, Aroona and Arkaba runs. The runs incorporated some of the best watered and most scenic country in the Flinders Ranges – today Wilpena and Aroona make up the picturesque Flinders Ranges National Park, while Arkaba is still privately owned but operated in part as a tourist lease.

Others followed, and by the early 1860s all of the range country was held under pastoral lease.

In 1846, copper had been found near Mt Remarkable and in 1859 it was also discovered at what became known as Blinman. Other discoveries followed, but while some were fantastically rich, most were small. Most ventures were plagued by isolation, little water and poor or non-existent roads, and never made a profit. Today the ruins of those mines are some of the best preserved and most poignant reminders of our recent past, scattered throughout the ranges in narrow, forgotten valleys.

From the 1870s the area south of Hawker was opened up to more intensive farming. This was in conflict with the view of the surveyor-general, GW Goyder, whose name is immortalised in Goyder's Line. That east-west line, Goyder said, indicated where the rainfall and the country changed from prospective farming land to pastoral country. A run of good seasons pushed the wheat farmers well north, towards and even into Wilpena Pound, but in the end, normal seasons returned and Goyder was proven right. The scattered stone ruins of old farm houses around Hawker, and the occasional abandoned old wheat harvester, are all that remains of their dreams and aspirations.

In the far north, among the convoluted ridges and gorges of the area we know as the Gammon Ranges, WB Greenwood found a wealth of different minerals, triggering a gem rush that had prospectors combing the hills for sapphires and rubies.

His discovery of the uranium-rich ore torbernite around Mt Painter in 1910 is what he is most remembered for, but it was many years before the new mineral could be identified. Working with Douglas Mawson, later of Antarctic fame, the two pegged many claims in the region. With the ore being used to produce radium, which in 1924 was worth, supposedly, the modern equivalent of $2 million an ounce, other prospectors rushed to secure leases in the rugged range country of the northern Flinders. Bigger, more easily worked discoveries of the ore overseas saw the Flinders mines wane, only to be revived again when the USA was developing the atomic bomb in the 1940s.

Information

Flinders Ranges & Outback South Australia Tourism (☎ 1800 633 060, 08-8463 4612, e wadlata@portaugusta.sa.gov.au, w www .flinders.outback.on.net) is at Level 10, 50 Grenfell St, Adelaide.

For national parks information for the Flinders Ranges northern region, contact National Parks and Wildlife SA – Hawker (☎ 08-8648 4244). For the southern region, contact Mt Remarkable National Park (☎ 08-8634 7068).

For information on desert conditions, contact the Department for Environment and Heritage – Outback Region (☎ 1800 816 078).

Radio Frequencies There is really no need for an HF radio in this region. If you have one fitted to your vehicle, the frequencies to have are the Royal Flying Doctor Service (RFDS) base at Port Augusta (call sign VNZ; primary frequency 4010kHz; secondary frequencies 6890kHz and 8165kHz) and the Telstra base in Sydney (call sign VIS).

Road Reports This trip is relatively easy. Distances between facilities are not great, the roads are generally pretty good by outback standards, and well used. Contact the Department of Road Transport's Road Conditions Report (☎ 1300 361 033) for current conditions. You can also get information from National Parks and Wildlife SA (☎ 08-8204 9000) and the Department for Environment and Heritage – Outback Region (☎ 1800 816 078).

Books & Maps *The Story of the Flinders Ranges*, by Hans Mincham, is the best book on the history of the area. Most of the towns, including Hawker, Quorn and Port Augusta, have local history books published about them. The murder at Grindell Hut in the Gammon Ranges is detailed in the book *Cloud over the Gammon Ranges* by Alan Bailey.

Flinders Ranges – An Australian Aura, by David Berndstoecker, and *The Flinders Ranges – A Portrait*, with photography by Eduard Domin, are just two of the coffee-table books on the region. The glossy books *Flinders Ranges, South Australia: The Art of the Photographer* and *An Australian Landscape – The Flinders Ranges*, by Stavros Pippos, are some of the best.

If you are into the natural delights of the area, *The Story of the Flinders Ranges Mammals*, by Dorothy Turnbridge, is worth reading. There are also *Fossils of the Flinders and Mt Lofty Ranges*, by Neville S

Pledge, and *Corridors Through Time – The Geology of the Flinders Ranges*.

The best guidebooks for those wanting to camp and 4WD is *The Flinders Ranges – An Adventurer's Guide*, by Ron & Viv Moon, and *Explore the Flinders Ranges*, by Sue Barker and others. Probably the best walking guide is *Grant's Guide to the Flinders Ranges*, by Grant Da Costa. *A Climber's Guide to Moonarie* is available from outdoor shops in Adelaide.

The *Flinders Ranges & Outback Visitor Guide* covers facilities, places to stay and commercial tours of the region. It has one big advantage: its free! It is available in many stores and visitors centres in region.

The Department of Recreation and Sport publishes maps that cover the length of the Heysen Walking Trail. The best maps of the area for general touring are *Flinders Ranges, South Australia*, produced by the Flinders Ranges & Outback South Australia Tourism Inc, and *The Flinders Ranges* by Hema. These maps are readily available locally or from map shops, Australia wide.

Permits Permits are required for visiting or camping in outback parks, and Flinders, Gammon and Mt Remarkable National Parks. Permits can be obtained at the rangers headquarters at Wilpena (☎ 08-8648 0048) or the district office in Hawker (☎ 08- 8648 6419). Day visitors with cars or motorcycles require a day pass ($6/$4). People walking or cycling don't need to pay.

Desert Parks Passes cost $50 for cars, $40 for motorbikes, and cover camping and entry fees. They are required for camping in the Witjira National Park, Elliot Price Conservation Park, Simpson Desert Conservation Park, Simpson Desert Regional Reserve, Innamincka Regional Reserve and Lake Eyre National park. Alternatively you can obtain an Annual Statewide Pass costing $140/70 for a car/motorcycle, with reduced costs for pensioners and renewal. For more information contact the Desert Parks Hotline (☎ 1800 816 078, ✉ desertparks@saugov.sa.gov.au).

Big Moro Gorge is now on Aboriginal land and a permit is required if you want to visit. For an update, go and see the rangers at Balcanoona (☎ 08-8648 4829), in the Gammon Ranges National Park.

Emergency Hawker has a police station (☎ 08-8648 4028) on Eighth St; the Great Northern War Memorial Hospital (☎ 08-8648 4007) is on Fifth St.

Quorn's police station (☎ 08-8648 6060) is on Railway Terrace. The town's hospital (☎ 08-8648 7888) is on Hospital Rd.

In Leigh Creek South, the police station (☎ 08-8675 2004) and hospital (☎ 08-8675 2100) are both on Black Oak Drive.

THE ROUTE

The route described is one of a number that traverse the ranges from south to north. It offers a good insight into the delights of the ranges, the variety of landforms and the mix of history that lies within these rocky ramparts.

Hawker

The adventure begins at the small township of Hawker, 375km north of Adelaide. You can reach it by travelling the blacktop via Port Augusta and Quorn or via Melrose, Wilmington and Quorn. Or you can travel via Jamestown and Orroroo, which is also now a sealed route. The routes via either Melrose or Orroroo are the most picturesque.

Established in 1880, Hawker originally serviced the many wheat farms that were established in the area and now caters for the sheep properties that took their place. Since 1970, when the railway ceased operating, tourism has become an important industry.

Hawker is a good place to use as your major resupply point. It has everything a traveller needs, including a choice of stores, fuel outlets, vehicle repair places and accommodation (but only one pub). From here north the price of accommodation sky-rockets, with the average price of caravan park cabins often doubling to around $60.

Hawker Motors (see Facilities later) in the centre of town is where most tourists go for fuel, minor repairs, souvenirs and information. The business was established by Fred Teague, who was something of a legend in the Flinders. His family, who still run the business, are a good source of information on the area. Inside the store is an informative little **museum** and a wide range of books for sale.

Many travellers use the town as a base to explore the area, but Quorn is better if you are travelling around the area south of Hawker. Wilpena is more central if you are exploring the north.

Hawker to Blinman (157km)

Heading north-east on the bitumen to Wilpena Pound, the road initially traverses gently undulating country, with the main range away to the left. Dominating the distant vista to the north are the bluffs of the southern wall of Wilpena Pound. As you progress, the Elder Range off to the west begins to draw the eyes more and more.

Arkaba Station The turn-off to Arkaba station (☎ 08-8648 4195) is 23km north of Hawker. This historic working woolshed is just a few hundred metres off the main road and caters to passing travellers with coffee, scones and cool drinks, as well as a good range of local art, craft and souvenirs. Arkaba runs 4WD self-drive and tag-along tours, with trips along the Elder Range and the southern ramparts of the Wilpena Range, which offer some of the best country in the Flinders (see Organised Tours later). Accommodation is also available.

Arkaba station one of the first properties taken up in the area, and with its good supply of spring-fed water it remains one of the best drought-protected properties in the Flinders. Surprisingly, much of the property was completely inaccessible to vehicles up until a few years ago. Then the new owners, members of the well-known Rasheed family, who own and manage Wilpena Pound, pushed a couple of tracks into the country bordering the Elder Range and began to control the rabbits and goats that had bred unchecked for generations. The results have been spectacular, and the family were recognised for their work by winning a major state conservation award in 1992. The tracks also make much of the range country accessible for keen 4WD travellers.

Arkaba Station to Wilpena Pound (33km) Less than 5km further along the bitumen, the **Moralana Scenic Drive** veers off to the left. This road is a private road that cuts across Arkaba station; public access is allowed, but straying from the road or camping is not! The 28km drive (one way) gives splendid views of both the Elder Range and the southern wall of Wilpena Pound.

Rawnsley Park station (☎ *08-8648 0030, Hawker-Wilpena Rd, Hawker*) a sheep property of just over 30 sq km, on the left of the main road 5km further north, offers a large caravan and camping ground, and self-con-

tained cabins and bunkhouse-style accommodation. It's popular during school holidays but quiet the rest of the time. Worthy of note is that pets are allowed, provided they are kept under control, and there is horse riding, bushwalking and more.

As you continue north along the bitumen, the southern rampart of the Wilpena Pound Range, Rawnsley Bluff, crowds in from the west. Seven kilometres from the turn-off to Rawnsley Park is a minor signposted track on the left to **Arkaroo Rock**, an Aboriginal art site within the national park. A short walk from the carpark brings you to this

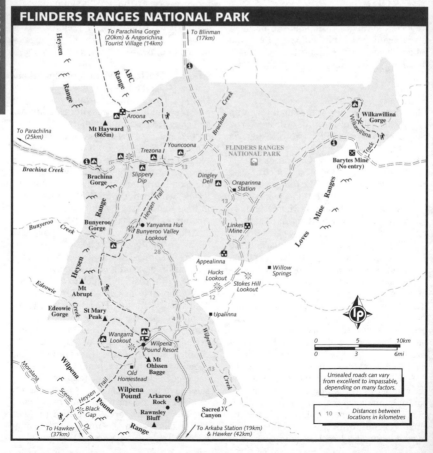

FLINDERS RANGES NATIONAL PARK

small but important site. It's an enjoyable walk through open forest alive with birds. Keen rock climbers can reach the 100m-high sandstone walls of Moonarie via a longer walk from the carpark; there are many routes up the cliffs to challenge even the most dedicated climber.

Back on the bitumen, you enter the **Flinders Ranges National Park** 3km further along the road, with the road now running parallel to the main range of the Pound. The drive is very enjoyable, with a red gum-lined rocky creek beside the road and a dense forest of smallish native pines crowding the road and the creek.

Wilpena Pound The turn-off to Wilpena Pound Resort, and the only entrance into Wilpena Pound, is 18km north of Rawnsley Park, or 52km north of Hawker. Turning left here will lead you 4km to the main parking area, the ranger's office and entrance to the resort and the camping ground. Fuel and supplies are available. If you can, stop here for at least two days. The walking is superb and there are a number of trails you can take, depending on your fitness and keenness; the Heysen Trail (see the boxed text later) passes through the national park.

Wilpena Pound is one of the most sensational visual features of the Flinders – a natural amphitheatre 11km long and 5km wide. Wilpena is an Aboriginal word that is taken to mean 'the place of the bent fingers' or 'a cupped hand', both of which are very appropriate.

The range that forms its perimeter slopes gently up from the inside to a line of bluffs and high peaks that drop steeply on the outside to the surrounding hills and plains. **St Mary Peak** (1190m), the highest peak in South Australia, is on the northern extremity of the Pound. The summit gives fine views of the encircling ranges, as well as occasionally attracting snow.

Only two creeks flow out of the Pound. One is **Wilpena Creek**; where it flows out of Wilpena Pound is where you will find the caravan park and all the facilities of the resort. The gums that line the creek are magnificent and it is no wonder that the area is popular with travellers. The second creek is Edeowie Creek, which leaves Wilpena Pound by a series of waterfalls and a tortuous course through **Edeowie Gorge**, in the far north-west of the Pound's surrounding ramparts.

The flat, well-watered floor of Wilpena Pound was used by the pioneers to graze sheep and cattle; for many years much of it was ploughed and wheat was grown, the tall peaks attracting more than their fair share of rainfall. In 1914 a flood down Wilpena Creek washed away the only track access into the Pound, and wheat growing was abandoned. In 1920, on the expiration of the lease, the area was declared a forest reserve.

In 1945 tourism had reached the stage where Wilpena Pound was proclaimed a National Pleasure Resort. A couple of years later a resort was built at the entrance to the Pound, and this was taken over in the 1950s by Kevin Rasheed, whose family still run this popular operation.

In 1970 the state government purchased Oraparinna station, proclaiming Oraparinna National Park. In 1972 Wilpena Pound was added to the national park to form the Flinders Ranges National Park.

Wilpena Pound to Blinman (106km)
Back on the main road north, the bitumen quickly ends. Just before you cross Wilpena Creek, 1km north of the turn-off to Wilpena Pound, a track heads off to the right to **Sacred Canyon**. This small gorge contains some of the best of the easily accessible Aboriginal rock engravings in the Flinders.

Nearly 5km north of the turn-off to Wilpena Pound, at a major road junction, take the road to the left. This is the start of one of the best drives in the Flinders; early morning, when the sun lights up the walls of the distant Heysen Range, is the time to go. The road is reasonably good dirt with the odd rough patch, so a normal car should have no problems.

For the first 12km to **Yanyanna Hut** the road traverses rolling hills cut by charming, tree-lined creeks. In the early morning, kangaroos and emus are commonly seen, as are flocks of raucous pink and grey galahs and snow-white corellas. Yanyanna Hut and

The Heysen Trail

The Heysen Trail is one of Australia's premier long-distance walking tracks. It starts far to the south at Cape Jervis, 110km south of Adelaide, and wanders through the Mt Lofty Ranges to Parachilna Gorge in the northern Flinders Ranges. The total walking distance is around 1500km and the trail is marked throughout.

In 1967, long before a recognised trail was established, CW Bonython became the first to walk the complete length of the range, a story told eloquently in his book *Walking the Flinders Ranges*.

The trail is named after one of Australia's greatest painters, the late Sir Hans Heysen, who painted extensively in the areas around Aroona and Arkaba near Wilpena Pound. He first visited the ranges in 1926, returning again and again to capture the mood of the ranges that he described later as 'the bones of nature laid bare'. Many artists have visited the Flinders, but it was Heysen more than any other who really opened people's eyes to the grandeur and the majestic beauty of the Flinders.

The trail takes you through some of the state's most scenic country, and you don't need to mount an expedition to enjoy it. Good vehicle access via dedicated tracks, or where the trail crosses a public road, means there are plenty of places you can go on a half-day or day walk.

A book and a series of 15 1:50,000 topographic strip maps ($6.50) produced by the South Australian Department of Recreation and Sport give you all the required information. The maps not only provide the normal geographical information, but also give good descriptions of the route, places to see, and some timely reminders about walking in this essentially arid country.

To walk the Heysen Trail you must be fit, have the right equipment, and know how to use it. A good knowledge of map-reading and route-finding is essential. It is surprising how many people get lost following the well-marked trail.

Remember that the trail traverses private land for much of the way. Treat the privilege of crossing it with consideration. Be extremely careful with fire, obey all the regulations, leave gates as you find them, don't disturb stock and don't camp right beside water so stock can't come and drink.

The Heysen Trail is closed to walkers from 1 November to 30 March, except for a couple of short walks within the Flinders Ranges National Park. Contact the Heysen Trail Management Unit, part of the Department for Environment and Heritage/National Parks and Wildlife, SA (☎ 08-8648 5300, [e] heysentrail@saugov.sa.gov.au, [w] www.environment.sa.gov.au/parks/heysen.html, GPO Box 1047, Adelaide, SA 5001). You can also contact the Friends of Heysen Trail Inc (☎ 08-8212 1930, [e] heysentrail@heysentrail.asn.au, [w] www.heysentrail.asn.au).

Information on the Heysen Trail is available from map shops throughout Australia and from a number of stores in the Flinders. For the latest information on the Heysen Trail, contact the main South Australian tourism and wildlife offices (see Information under the Flinders Ranges section).

its nearby yards testify to the days when this area was a working property.

From here the road swings in a big arc, the vegetation changes to native pine, and the scenery improves. The **Bunyeroo Valley Lookout**, 2km from the hut, is worth a stop to admire the view. The Heysen Range dominates the background to the west, while a lower range of more rounded peaks between the lookout and the main wall of rock is the ABC Range. To the south are the battlements of the eastern wall of Wilpena Pound, dominated by St Mary Peak.

For the next 2km the road traverses a ridge with spectacular views, before descending steeply to run beside **Bunyeroo Creek**. The next 2km is through a winding gorge with the road running, in typical Flinders fashion, along the creekbed. Normally the creek has water through it, and after heavy rain it is closed to normal traffic. Heed the 'Road Closed' signs if they have been erected. There are a couple of good camp sites along this section but none have any facilities.

Leaving the gorge, the road swings up out of the creek and heads north. A carpark on the left is a good spot to stop and take a walk down into Bunyeroo Gorge proper. For the next 10km the road heads north, with the rugged Heysen Range off to the left and the ABC Range directly off to the right.

Turn left at the T-junction 10km north of the carpark. (Turning right here will lead you east to a number of good camp sites in the Aroona Valley or along Brachina Creek and its tributaries; from there you can head either north to Blinman or south to Wilpena Pound.) Heading west, the road quickly becomes confined by the surrounding bluffs and cliffs of the Heysen Range into **Brachina Gorge**. The road seems to spend more time in the creekbed than out of it. After heavy rain this road is also closed to normal traffic, so take heed of the warning signs.

There is some excellent camping through here; although it is popular during school holidays, especially in spring, as it is one of the best places in the Flinders. The creek is fed by natural springs and it is rare for there to be no water in the gorge. From any of the camp sites, there are walks to be enjoyed down along the creek or up the steep hills for a great eagle's-eye view of the surrounds. Brachina Gorge is a good place to see the endangered yellow-footed rock-wallaby.

Seven kilometres west of the T-junction, the road crosses the creek for the last time and climbs a low rise and leaves the park. A lookout on the right gives an enjoyable view of the western battlements of the range, while to the west the flat plains of the desert country begin and sweep away to the shores of Lake Torrens and beyond.

The road improves as it leaves the range country and strikes west for another 12km before reaching the bitumen at a T-junction. Here you turn right (north) towards Parachilna. Hawker is 70km south along the bitumen. In the evening, as you head north, the ranges look superb, rearing up from the plain you are now travelling on.

The small railway siding of **Parachilna** is 19km north of where you joined the bitumen road; you need to turn off to the left to get to the Prairie Hotel or the public showers and toilets that are available. The historic pub

can supply accommodation, fuel and a top meal that would do a city restaurant proud.

About 100m past the turn-off to the hotel, take the road that strikes east towards the range and the township of Blinman. Nine kilometres later you enter **Parachilna Gorge**, and 2km further on a road junction is met. Keep right at the junction, although the left-hand route makes a pleasant scenic drive through Glass Gorge to Blinman. Good camp sites beside the creek become available just before the road junction off to the left and continue for the next few kilometres.

Parachilna Gorge is not within the national park: It's a recognised camping area maintained by the local shire. A camping permit is not required, and you can take the family pet. Because of that, the spectacular nature of the area, and the almost constant water supply in the spring-fed creek, the gorge is very popular. Even so, you could have a camp site to yourself. The experience of camping here among these red-raw ranges, with a trickle of water running past and a lazy wind sighing through the gum trees, is hard to beat.

Camping spots are numerous for the first few kilometres after they appear, but once you arrive at the **Angorichina Tourist Village**, 16km east of the bitumen, you are really out of the best of the camping areas. Angorichina caters for campers, caravanners and those wanting self-contained cabins, units, on-site vans and bunkhouse-style accommodation. The small general store has fuel, groceries, souvenirs and limited repair facilities.

There is some excellent walking around the gorge, with the **Heysen Trail** (see the boxed text) heading south from a picnic site close to the road, about 3km before Angorichina. This part of the long-distance walking trail leads along the Heysen Range all the way to Wilpena Pound and, while you don't need to go that far, you can enjoy a day walk. Another walk is along Oratunga Gorge (on the north side of the road, less than 1km before the picnic area), but the best one is along Parachilna and Blinman creeks up to the Blinman Pools and waterfalls. The small township of Blinman is 15km east of Angorichina.

Blinman

At the T-junction on the edge of Blinman, turn left for the hotel, general store, post office and the **old mine** about 1km north of town. In reality the main centre of the town is Blinman North. Blinman, a few kilometres south, is deserted and offers no facilities.

Copper was discovered here in 1859 by Robert 'Peg Leg' Blinman, and the original town of Blinman was surveyed in 1864. It was too far for the miners to walk from the mine, so in 1867 a new town was established a little closer, and Blinman North took over as the main centre of the community. In those years the population was around 1000 – about 985 more than at present. The mine closed in 1874 but was used spasmodically over the next 30 years. About the only person who ever really made any money out of it was Peg Leg, when he sold the mine to the Yudnamutana Copper Mining Company for £70,000 – a lot of money in 1862!

An excellent walking trail with information signs has been established around the site of the old mine and smelter, and it is worth more than just a passing glance.

Fuel (no LPG), meals and a choice of accommodation are available in Blinman and if it's a hot day you can enjoy a swim in the pub's swimming pool ($2). If you have taken the route described, you are 157km north of Hawker, but by the shortest route, directly north from Wilpena, the distance is only 113km.

Blinman to Copley (297km)

To continue on the loop, head south past the road junction you came in on to another road junction 3km further on. This is the original township of Blinman. Turn left here, and 6km further east, keep right at the junction. A few kilometres further on, the road begins to wind through a small gorge, and 14km from the Blinman Hotel, you pass the turn-off on your left to Narrina station.

The road passes through the Bunkers range before levelling out across lightly undulating country as Wirrealpa homestead is approached, 35km from Blinman. Just past the homestead, which is on your right, you meet with a major dirt road coming

from the south. This is another route, shorter but nowhere near as scenic, to Wilpena Pound and Hawker.

Turn north and follow the road as it traverses a relatively flat plain with the ranges off to the left. Numerous creek beds are crossed but these are nearly always dry, except after heavy local rain when they run for a few hours, or maybe a day, before being soaked up by the sands. The turn-off to Chambers Gorge is 28km north of Wirrealpa.

Chambers Gorge Chambers Gorge offers some enjoyable camping in an area vastly different to gorges further south. Here the country is harsher, the vegetation thinner, and the majestic red gums and native pines no longer dominate. The gorge itself starts about 9km from the turn-off; within 400m there is a prominent bluff on the left and a small, normally dry creek coming in from the same direction. Access past this point is 4WD. On the southern rim is the cube-capped dome of Mt Chambers, resplendent with scree slopes down its flanks.

While there's often water in the gorge, it should not be counted on, especially as a source of drinking water. Most of the camps are close to the creek, before the bluff, while the one at the bluff is the most popular and has the most spectacular setting.

Walking in the gorge is worthy of a few hours, especially in the cool of the morning. Within a few kilometres the gorge opens out and finally, at the edge of the expansive Frome Plains, ends at an impressive rock column known as **Windsor Pillar**.

Back near the first prominent bluff, a short walk up the creek will bring you to one of the best Aboriginal rock engraving sites you will find anywhere. It's worth spending an hour or so here, resting in the shade and pondering on what this country must have been like when these people chipped their designs thousands of years ago. Certainly it was more temperate and water was more abundant than it is now.

Chambers Gorge to the Arkaroola Wilderness Sanctuary (99km) On the main route north, 12km beyond the turn-off

to Chambers Gorge, the road begins to pass through **Wearing Gorge**. About 2km long, the gorge is a pleasant respite from the sun and heat of the flat plains. Once out of the gorge, the road runs east for 10km, meeting the main access road north from the small township of Yunta. This route south is the shortest to Adelaide from this point, as Yunta is on the main road between Broken Hill and Adelaide.

Turn left at the T-junction and head north with the immense salt expanse of Lake Frome occasionally visible off to the right. Wertaloona homestead, 23km north of the road junction, is off to the right, while almost directly opposite is the track to **Big Moro Gorge**. The track west to the gorge is 4WD and the 15km trip takes around 40 minutes. While the gorge isn't as spectacular as those further south, it's still worth exploring and enjoying – this area is now Aboriginal land, so check with the rangers at Balcanoona (☎ 08-8648 4829) as to permit requirements.

Heading ever northwards, there's a major T-junction, 13km north of the Big Moro Gorge turn-off. This is the main Copley-Balcanoona road. Turning left (west) at this junction will lead you on a good dirt road 95km back to the bitumen at Copley, 5km north of Leigh Creek South and 165km north of Hawker. Turning right will take you across a creek, and on your right is **Balcanoona**, now the main rangers station for the Gammon Ranges National Park.

The **Gammon Ranges National Park** covers an area of over 1280 sq km; it takes in a strip of land from the edge of Lake Frome and includes all the country from Arkaroola, Bolla Bollana and Umberatana in the north, to Arcoona Bluff, Mt McKinlay and Italowie Gorge in the south.

The park encompasses some of the most rugged country in the Flinders. John McKinlay explored much of the region on his travels looking for pastoral land in 1850, but so rugged and dry was the country that much of it wasn't taken up until later. In 1909 John Grindell secured most of the area in the east and south of what later became the national park. The Gammon Ranges themselves were not crossed until Warren Bonython and a friend walked across them in 1947. Today the ranges are a magnet for bushwalkers sufficiently experienced and well equipped to tackle the convoluted gorges and sheer ridges that make up the terrain.

There is some excellent camping within the park, and those with a 4WD can enjoy some good camping areas at places such as Grindell Hut, Lochness Well or Mainwater Well. Walkers have a much wider choice of camp sites. Water is often very scarce in the park, so travellers need to be self-sufficient.

Back at the creek crossing just before Balcanoona, a main dirt road heading off to the left, just north of the creek, is the main road to Arkaroola and the one to take.

Nine kilometres from the junction the main access road into the Gammon Ranges National Park heads off to the left. From this junction it is about 10km to **Grindell Hut**, about the only spot in the park a normal car has a chance of getting to.

Continuing north, the Arkaroola road skirts the main bulk of the range off to the west, running parallel to the national park boundary. Less than 9km further on, you enter the Arkaroola Wilderness Sanctuary, and 24km from the Balcanoona road junction you come to another road junction where you need to keep left. Heading right at this point takes you via a scenic drive to **Paralana Hot Springs**, 26km along the range.

Arkaroola Wilderness Sanctuary Less than 2km up the Arkaroola road from the junction, you pass the original Arkaroola station, and 6km from the junction, you come to a T-junction in the heart of Arkaroola village. You are about 300km north of Hawker by the way you have come, or 260km by the shortest route (via Wilpena Pound, past the barytes mine, and Wirrealpa to Balcanoona and Arkaroola).

Here you can camp, stay in the caravan park or choose from the wide range of other accommodation available. There is a store, service station, licensed restaurant and swimming pool. You could easily spend a couple of days here.

The **astronomical observatory** (☎ 08-8648 4848; admission $22; open nightly) shouldn't be missed. With the clear desert air and no artificial light to impinge on the scene, the views of our galaxy and beyond are unbelievable.

The Arkaroola Wilderness Sanctuary was established by Reg and Griselda Sprigg in 1968 when they took over the 610 sq km station lease. They immediately got rid of the sheep, and over the years that followed brought the rampant feral goat and rabbit populations under control. Now the Arkaroola Wilderness Sanctuary probably has a better example of the area's flora and fauna than the adjoining national park, all due to the eradication of the vermin on the place.

There are many geological features in this privately owned reserve, many of which, such as **Mt Painter** and the **Armchair**, are registered by the Geological Society as Rock Monuments, while a significant percentage of the area is listed on the Register of the National Estate.

There are many attractions worth visiting, and if you have a 4WD there are some enjoyable drives through the ranges to places of interest. These include Echo Camp Waterhole, Bolla Bollana mine and smelter ruins in the far north-west of the property, and the Yudnamutana Mine and smelter (a real highlight). The resort runs tours to these places for those without a 4WD.

One trip that you can only take in the resort's vehicles is the Ridgetop Tour. This tour is highly recommended and takes visitors through some of the most rugged country in the ranges to **Sillers Lookout**, where you can get fabulous views of the surrounding peaks and valleys, out across the plain to Lake Frome.

There are many good walks in the reserve. One of the most enjoyable is the 2.5km walk into **Barraranna Waterhole**, and many longer walks are available for those fit and well equipped.

Camping is only allowed in the camping area near the resort, and fires are only allowed in the fireplaces in the camping area.

Arkaroola to Copley (144km)

The route beyond Arkaroola, as it traces a path around the Gammon Ranges National Park, is definitely suitable only for 4WDs. It takes you through private property and no camping is allowed along the way. Normal cars will have to retrace their way to Balcanoona and head to Copley on the main road.

For those wanting to push on, turn left at the T-junction you met as you entered the village and head past the shops, down along Wywhyana Creek, keeping right at the next two track junctions that lead to the caravan and camping areas.

After the second junction, the road continues along Copper Creek and less than 7km from the resort a track heads off to the right to **Bolla Bollana Spring**. A short distance later the road crosses Bolla Bollana Creek and then, on the left, is the turn-off to the parking area for the short walk to the **Bolla Bollana mine and smelter ruins**.

Just a little over 9km from the resort, a turn-off to the right leads to **Nooldoonildoona Waterhole**. This is a pleasant spot, ideal for a lunch break and a bit of exploring.

The road divides 12.4km from the resort, both branches leading to the same place; the right-hand (northern) route is a little rougher, but it's more enjoyable than the left-hand (southern) route. The right-hand route passes along Wild Dog Creek to a track junction 23.5km from Arkaroola. From here, the right branch leads north 6km to the **Yudnamutana Mine** and smelter site. The left (south) branch is your route to Umberatana homestead.

Keep right at the next couple of track junctions, and 14.5km after you turned south, with **Umberatana** homestead on the right, pass through the gate and keep left. If you look up to the left along the ridgeline once you are past the windmill, you'll see the remains of a stone fence – imagine building it! The fence finishes a couple of kilometres later.

Nearly 19km south of Umberatana homestead you come to **Yankaninna** station. The track passes close to the homestead and outbuildings; keep the house on your left. Less than 1km past the homestead you will pass a track junction on your left, with a sign reading 'Yadnina'. This leads into the Gammon Ranges National Park and eventually back to Balcanoona.

Nine kilometres east of Yankaninna, with the track skirting the ramparts of the **Yankaninna Range**, cross Gammon Creek and then begin to swing more and more south as you pass **Arcoona Bluff**, which at 953m is one of the highest peaks in this part of the range. Just over 5km from the Gammon Creek crossing, a track heads off to the left, entering the national park and leading to a small camping area on Arcoona Creek.

Less than 500m south of this junction, the main track you are on crosses the same creek and 2km later passes through an outstation. The numerous small creeks that are crossed as you head south are all spawned in the rugged mountains to your left. Twenty kilometres from the outstation you pass **Mt Serle** station homestead on your right, and 4km later meet the main Copley-Balcanoona road, 46km east of the bitumen at Copley. The total distance from Arkaroola is 98km.

Turn right at this main dirt road and head west an easy 46km to Copley. At Copley you can head north 35km to Lyndhurst, or south 5km to Leigh Creek South, or 165km to Hawker. By the way you have come, the total distance is about 450km, but you have seen and experienced much more of these magnificent outback ranges than you would have if you had travelled up the bitumen.

Copley has a hotel, general store and a service station and can offer accommodation, fuel, repairs, food and meals. Leigh Creek South offers a more modern and extensive shopping facility, and the meals from the tavern restaurant are excellent.

ALTERNATIVE ROUTES

There are a number of alternative routes through the ranges, depending whether you want a quick trip or one that's a little different. Some of the shorter alternatives between such places as Wilpena Pound and Blinman, or Wilpena Pound and Balcanoona via the barytes mine road and Wirrealpa, have already been mentioned, but none are as scenic as the route described.

If you are in a hurry, the 165km run up the bitumen from Hawker to Copley is the way to go, but the Flinders Ranges will be just a line of blue mountains off to your right.

If you're coming from Adelaide and you want the shortest way to the northern Flinders, the quickest route is to head up the Barrier Hwy (the road to Broken Hill) from Adelaide 313km to Yunta. Here you turn north onto a good dirt road and, travelling via Frome Downs, reach Balcanoona in another 271km.

ACTIVITIES
Walks

Walking is the main activity in the Flinders. There is a host of day walks and marked walking trails, or you can wander the long distance Heysen Walking Trail (see the boxed text earlier) for a day or more.

Don't forget that this is an arid region and water can be scarce – be prepared!

Some of the walks that can be done in the gorges along the way have been mentioned already. At Arkaroola, in the far north, there are also many walks ranging from an hour to days. It's best to contact the visitors information centre at the Arkaroola Wilderness Sanctuary (☎ 08-8648 4848) for more details. In the nearby Gammon Ranges National Park there are no marked trails and much of the area is really only for experienced, well-equipped walkers. However, there are a couple of shorter walks, the most popular being a eight-hour 16km walk from Grindell Hut south through the park to the main Copley-Balcannoona road at Italowie Gorge. Another walk of about 5km heads from Grindell Hut east through Weetootla Gorge and Balcanoona Gorge to a carpark just west of Balcanoona. You should contact the ranger at Balcanoona (☎ 08-8648 4829) for more information; you should also let the ranger know details of your walk, route and expected time of return.

Wilpena Pound and the surrounding national park is the best set up area for walking, and there are a number of marked trails and short walks up to a day for those wanting to better experience the Flinders.

In Wilpena Pound itself, some of the walks include the old homestead and Wangarra Lookout, which take between one and two hours. The popular walk to St Mary Peak is a highlight, but it is a fairly strenuous one, taking eight to nine hours. The walk across Wilpena Pound to Edeowie Gorge takes about the same amount of time and leads north-west to Edeowie Creek and its waterfalls.

There are other walks in and around Wilpena Pound, while a little further afield, but still in the park, there are a couple of marked trails from the Aroona Ruins. From the ruins, you can follow the Heysen Trail north to Parachilna Gorge, a six-hour, one-way trip. In the east of the park there is Wilkawillana Gorge to enjoy for four to five hours.

At Yanyanna Hut, north of Wilpena and on the route described, there is an enjoyable six-to seven-hour walk across the undulating country to Elatina Hut. A bit further along the route is a two-hour walk, which includes a little rock-hopping into Bunyeroo Gorge.

ORGANISED TOURS

There is a huge choice of organised tours operating along this route. The most common tour options are 4WD tag-along tours (around $40 per day per vehicle) and 4WD self-drive tours (around $30 per day per vehicle). For those without 4WDs, most companies offer 4WD tours from around $70 per day per person.

Arkaba station (☎ 08-8648 4195, 23km north of Hawker), runs organised 4WD trips through the property (self-drive/tag-along $33/45 per vehicle). Trips are usually for one day, but you can camp in idyllic, secluded isolation on gum tree-lined flats beside the ranges. A few goats still exist in the rugged back country, but the native wildlife has flourished. Red kangaroos and the more stockily built hill wallaroo, or euro, are often seen at close quarters; the natural water points that dot the property are a magnet for animals, including a wide variety of birds.

Wilpena Pound Resort (☎ 08-8648 0004, 1800 805 802, e administration@wilpena pound.com.au, W www.wilpenapound.com .au) offers 4WD tours (adult/child $105/70 per day), and 20-minute scenic flights over Wilpena Pound (two people/three or more people $80/65). Longer flights can also be arranged.

For more information on the many other tour operators in the area, contact Flinders Ranges and Outback SA (☎ 1800 633 060, e wadlata@portaugusta.sa.gov.au, W www .flinders.outback.on.net).

FACILITIES

By outback touring standards, the Flinders Ranges has plenty of places where you can re-fuel, use Eftpos facilities and get basic supplies. Several of these outlets also offer mechanical repairs. Their bowsers are generally open from 7.30am to 5.30pm daily, although fuel outlets not attached to road-houses may well be closed Saturday after 12.30pm, and all day Sunday.

Throughout the Flinders there is a choice of bush camping – with or without facilities such as fire grates and toilet blocks – and camping in commercial camping grounds. The national parks offer a wide choice of camping spots. For details on permits, see that heading under the earlier Information section. During the school holidays, especially the spring and autumn holidays, and on long weekends, it pays to book in advance at the commercial camping areas.

If you don't fancy camping, there's a wide range of accommodation options – from dorm-style lodgings, simple cabins and cottages, to luxury hotel/motel rooms.

Angorichina

Angorichina Tourist Village (☎ 08-8648 4842, Parachilna Gorge Rd) Unpowered/ powered sites $6/15 for 2 people, dorm beds $16, single/double on-site vans $25/30, self-contained units & cottages $55-130 for 2 people. Pets are allowed at the manager's discretion. This is a well-equipped outpost within easy reach of spectacular scenery. The *store* here has a pay phone, sells groceries, souvenirs and all fuels (as well as camping gas), and can do minor vehicle repairs.

Arkaroola

Arkaroola Wilderness Sanctuary Resort (☎ 08-8648 4848, fax 8648 4846, e res@ arkaroola.on.net, W www.arkaroola.on.net) Unpowered/powered sites $11/16.50 for 2 people, dorm beds $10, singles/doubles

MITCH FEARDON

From New South Wales to Western Australia, the south is a vast sweep of salt-bush and scrub plain. Where the outback meets the sea, it's an almost unbroken line of cliffs, as the Nullarbor Plain plunges into the Southern Ocean.

The Barn Owl (Ninox connivens) – Mutawintji National Park, New South Wales (1). The mighty coastline of the Great Australian Bight – Western Australia (2). Early morning on the empty Nullarbor Plain – Eyre Peninsula, South Australia (3). Merino sheep at Fowlers Gap Station – Western New South Wales (4). Remains of the old telegraph repeater and weather station, opened in 1877, now almost engulfed by the desert – Eucla, Western Australia (5).

DIANA MAYFIELD

DENIS O'BYRNE

JOHN BANAGAN

MITCH REARLEON

Much of the south is pastoral country, with often the only sign of human habitation kilometres of straggly wire fences. Through the heart of South Australia, the spectacular hill country, the Flinders Ranges, breaks the distant horizons.

The Leaning Dunny of Silverton – New South Wales (1). Road sign to Camerons Corner where the borders of Queensland, New South Wales and South Australia meet (2). Wedge-tailed eagle (Aquila audax) on an outback road sign near Tibooburra – North-west New South Wales (3). The Flinders Ranges and surrounding countryside (4). 'Walls of China' dune, 30km long – Mungo National Park, New South Wales (5).

shared bathroom $35/43, with ensuite $48/59, air-con singles & doubles with en suite and fridge from $99. Rooms are basic but comfortable. The Arkaroola *service station* has a wide range of supplies, all fuels and limited spares and repairs.

Arkaba

Arkaba station (☎ 08-8648 4195, 23km north of Hawker) Bush camp sites $12 per vehicle. There is some excellent bush camping available here and you're guaranteed your own private spot – it's great! The station's lovely old two-bedroom stone cottage costs $140 per double. It's fully self-contained and sleeps up to six. There's a minimum stay of two nights. A camping area ($12 per vehicle) is also located on this renowned and strikingly spectacular property.

Beltana

Beltana Roadhouse (☎ 08-8675 2744) This roadhouse is just off the main highway, 35km north of Parachilna, and 17km west of the ghost town of Beltana proper. It offers fuel (no LPG), phone, ice and groceries along with food (eat-in and takeaway), and is licensed. Public toilets and showers are also available.

Blinman

Blinman Hotel (☎/fax 08-8648 4867) Unpowered sites $5 per person, singles/ doubles $75/85. At the Blinman Hotel campers and caravanners can pull up under the peppercorn trees, but space is limited. This historic pub has solid rooms and the added bonus of a heated indoor pool. Both the hotel and the *Blinman General Store (☎ 08-8648 4874)* on the main street sell fuel, but LPG is not available.

Copley

Copley Caravan Park (☎ 08-8675 2288, e copleycaravanpark@start.com.au) Unpowered/powered sites $16/19 for 2 people, single/double cabins $45/60. The friendly Copley Caravan Park, on the main street, has good facilities and dogs are allowed at the park. It also has a *store* offering supplies, all fuel, and repairs. From here it's just a

short walk to the brilliant *Bush Bakery & Quandong Cafe (☎ 08 8675 2683, open Easter to November, 8.30am-5pm daily)*.

Cooke's Outback Motors (☎/fax 08-8765 2618, e cookesobm@bigpond.com), on the main street, offers fuel, 24-hour towing, and top-notch mechanical repairs – this is your last chance to have any nagging problems fixed if you're heading into the remote north.

Packsaddle General Store (☎/fax 08-8675 2268) This store, on the main street, has a pay phone and three main types of fuel.

Farina

Farina (☎/fax 08-8675 7790) Unpowered sites $3.50 per person, dorm beds in shearers quarters $16.50. The ghost town of Farina, 2km from the main road, 60km north of Copley, offers some fine camping and opportunities to explore the ruins. The camping ground, a stone's throw from the once thriving town centre, has showers, firewood, flush toilets and an honesty-box payment set-up. You should ring in advance if you're planning to stay in the shearers quarters at the Farina homestead. Bookings are not required for camping.

Hawker

Hawker Hotel-Motel (☎ 08-8648 4102, e hawhotmot@internode.on.net, 80 Elder Tce) Singles/doubles with shared bathroom $44/50, en suite singles/doubles $71.50/ 77. This is a great old-style pub, with the cheaper rooms generally better value than the dearer motel rooms.

Hawker Caravan Park (☎ 08-8648 4006, e hawkcara@internode.on.net, w www .hawkersa.info/hcpark.htm, Cnr Wilpena Rd & Chace View Tce, Hawker) Unpowered/ powered sites $14.50/18.50 for 2 people, single & double self-contained cabins $66, single & double rooms with en suite $85. This place has a BBQ area and well-appointed cabins. No dogs are allowed here.

Flinders Ranges Caravan Park (☎ 08-8648 4266, e jsitters@flinderscpk.com.au, 1km north of Hawker, opposite the railway station) Unpowered/powered sites $14/18 for 2 people, double cabins with en suite $40-66. This is a large and friendly park, handy to the **Railway Station Restaurant**, and with a BBQ area. It's also pet friendly.

Hawker Motors (☎ 08-8648 4014, e john@hawkermotors.com.au, Cnr Wilpena & Cradock Rds) This is the service depot for automobile club members; it can supply all fuel types, parts and accessories, tyres, camping gas refills, souvenirs, books and maps, along with ice and cool drinks.

Range View Motors (☎ 08-8648 4049, Wilpena Rd) This shop has fuel (no LPG) and repair facilities; it is also the Toyota agent. It's open daily.

Leigh Creek South

Leigh Creek South Motors (☎ 08-8675 2016, Black Oak Dr) In Leigh Creek South, this establishment – on the main street into the town centre off the highway – is the only place to get all types of fuel. It can also supply tyres and repair facilities, along with food, cool drinks and the like.

Leigh Creek Tavern (☎ 08-8675 2025) Single/double self-contained air-con cabins $65/75, single/double motel rooms from $90/100. In the centre of town near the shopping centre and football oval, this large tavern includes a pool and a good **restaurant**. Bookings are essential for both accommodation and dining.

Parachilna

Prairie Hotel (☎ 08-8648 4844, e prairie _hotel@bigpond.com.au, Cnr High St & West Tce, Parachilna) Unpowered/powered sites $5.50/15 for 2 people, singles $70-165, doubles & twins $80-180. Caravanners can stay behind the hotel. The superbly well-run Prairie Hotel presents a good opportunity to sample some excellent 'feral' food, but it's very popular and the dining rooms can fill up fast. Breakfast and all meals are available. The rooms here range from tasteful to utterly luxurious. Fuel (no LPG) is sold. The publicans also operate the nearby **old Parachilna Schoolhouse**, which has basic doubles with shared bathroom for $20.

Rawnsley Park Station

Rawnsley Park station (☎ caravan park 08-8648 0008, holiday units ☎ 08-8648 0030, e info@rawnsleypark.com.au, W www .rawnsleypark.com.au, Wilpena Rd via Hawker) Unpowered/powered sites $15/21 per double, $7.50/10.50 per single, dorm beds $16, on-site vans $42 per single & double, self-contained cabins $55 per single & double, units $70-85 per single & double. This place has a large, pleasant camping ground with excellent facilities. Dogs are allowed, on leashes. The station's licensed shop has fuel (no LPG) and camping gas refills.

Wilpena Pound

Wilpena Pound Resort (☎ 1800 805 802, 08-8648 0004, e administration@wilpena pound.com.au, W www.wilpenapound.com .au) Single unpowered/powered sites $8/11, double unpowered/powered sites $16/22, doubles/triples/quads $105-165/127-187/ 149-209. This major tourist centre has a huge range of accommodation. There's also a large pool and BBQ area. Meals are available in the **restaurant**.

Wilpena Pound General Store & Coffee Shop (☎ 08-8648 0004) is part of the modern visitors information centre (open 8am to 6pm daily) and has all fuels and camping gas. Emergency repairs can be arranged. There also an ATM and an Internet booth ($7 per hour) in the visitors information centre.

Bush Camping

The stunning **Brachina Gorge** has several excellent designated camp sites with fireplaces and toilet blocks.

You can camp for free in **Parachilna Gorge**. There are no facilities and nobody to pick your rubbish up, so please look after this area – it is popular.

You can camp in the **Gammon Ranges National Park** if you have a permit issued by the ranger at Balcanoona (☎ 08-8648 4829). The same camping fees apply as for the Flinders Ranges National Park. The area around Grindell Hut is the most popular but there are others. Grindell Hut can also be rented – contact the ranger for details.

See the Farina entry earlier in this section for details of camping facilities available in **Farina**.

You need a 4WD to get to the ***Chambers Gorge*** camp site, but there are some good walks in the area. It's safest to bring your own water.

ALTERNATIVE TRANSPORT

If you don't have your own vehicle, there are a few ways of getting to and around the Flinders.

Car Rental

There are a couple of places where you can hire vehicles, but neither are very handy to the centre of the Flinders. The closest are Budget (☎ 08-8642 6040) and Thrifty Car Rental (☎ 08-8642 2445), both in Port Augusta.

Bus

Premier Stateliner (☎ 08-8642 5055, W www.premierstateliner.com.au) at 21 Mackay St, Port Augusta, makes regular trips between Port Augusta and Wilpena Pound.

For general information about South Australia's statewide and interstate public transport bus network, visit the Bus SA Web site (W www.bussa.com.au/index.shtml).

Train

From Port Augusta – if your timing is just right – you can hop aboard the *Afghan Express* or *Transcontinental* trains to make the trip to Quorn (via Stirling North). These old steam-driven beauties run semi-regularly between March and November on Saturday and Sunday. The one-way fare for children/concession/adults is $10/24/28

Several trains are also available for private functions. For more information on these, contact the Quorn-based Pichi Richi Railway Preservation Society (☎ 08-8395 2566, W www.prr.org.au).

Air

Kendell Airlines (☎ 02-6922 0100, W www.kendell.com.au) has scheduled flights between Port Augusta and Adelaide, with semi-regular flights between Port Augusta and Leigh Creek. Kendell is an Ansett Airlines subsidiary, but at the time of writing was likely to continue operations.

Silver City Highway

Highlights

- Discovering the rich heritage of the 'Silver City', Broken Hill
- Experiencing the wildlife of Sturt National Park
- Having a cold beer in a Tibooburra pub

For those travelling north from Melbourne, the Silver City Hwy is one of the best introductions to the vastness and uniqueness of the Australian outback. If you are journeying west from Sydney or east from Adelaide, the Silver City Hwy cuts across your course – you will probably meet it at the outback mining town of Broken Hill (Silver City), from which the highway gains its name. From here, travellers can head south to Wentworth and Mildura, both on the Murray River, or north through Tibooburra into south-eastern Queensland, and to Cooper Creek, Birdsville and places beyond.

Broken Hill, the largest town in western New South Wales, is a long way from anywhere: Sydney is nearly 1200km to the east, while Melbourne is 900km to the south. Adelaide, over 500km to the south-west, is the closest capital. It's the major source of supplies and the place where most Broken Hill residents go for holidays.

The Silver City Hwy starts on the New South Wales side of the Murray, opposite Wentworth. From here to 'the Hill' it's 266km, all of it good bitumen. North of the Silver City, the bitumen peters out after about 32km. It continues periodically, interspersed with sections of well-maintained dirt to Tibooburra, then as pure dirt to Warri Warri Gate on the New South Wales-Queensland border, 393km north of Broken Hill.

This is officially the end of the Silver City Hwy, and it shows. The road deteriorates as it heads north-west to Cooper Creek or north-east to Noccundra and Thargomindah, but in normal conditions it is still passable to ordinary vehicles. Although this

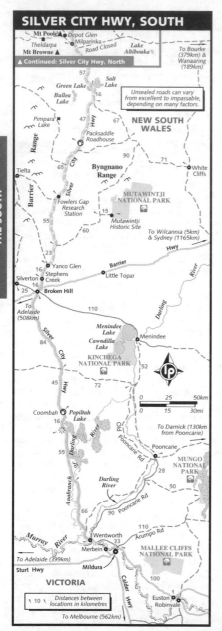

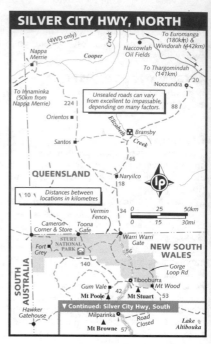

road is slowly being upgraded, it will be a long time before all of it is sealed.

History

The region west of the Darling River has been inhabited by Aboriginal people for millennia. While various groups were concentrated on the reliable water sources of the rivers, in the good seasons their wanderings took them across the rocky broken ground of the Barrier Range, where Broken Hill now stands, to the dunes of the sand-ridge country around Cameron Corner.

Charles Sturt was the first European to penetrate this country, in 1845. He named the Barrier Range but missed the wealth underneath, before pushing north to his Depot Glen near present-day Milparinka. Plagued by hot weather and a lack of water, he and his men continued northward to a point north of present-day Birdsville, but their effort was in vain. The inland sea that Sturt had set out to find had vanished a few thousand years before, and he and his men retreated the way they had come. It was one of the great survival feats of the European exploration of Australia, and a stark contrast to the next expedition that passed this way.

In 1860 Burke and Wills led their well-prepared expedition north from Menindee (on the Darling River) to a depot they established on Cooper Creek. At the depot, Burke, Wills and two others left the rest of the expedition and rushed to cross the continent. However, on their return, they discovered that the main party had left just hours before their arrival. The Burke and Wills team were left with just a few stores, and all but one (King) perished on the banks of the Cooper near present-day Innamincka. The search parties that went out looking for them found country that appeared to be ideal for grazing, and their reports soon had pioneer pastoralists moving into the region.

Wentworth, at the junction of the mighty Darling and Murray Rivers, 33km from Mildura, became a major port for the steamers plying these rivers from 1850 onwards, and Broken Hill came to prominence when Charles Rasp discovered the silver-lead-zinc deposit there in 1883. It is the richest deposit of its type ever discovered, and by the 1890s a town of 20,000 had been established. Since then, minerals worth over $2 billion have been extracted from the ground. The mine lead to the foundation of Broken Hill Proprietary (BHP), and the town of Port Pirie, on the coast of South Australia, where the ore is smelted. Broken Hill is now past its peak, the vast ore body stripped of its richest deposits. Within 10 or 20 years the ore will disappear, but the town will remain a tourist destination and an important service centre for this part of the country.

Both Tibooburra and Milparinka, a little further north, owe their existence to gold rushes that occurred during the 1870s and 1880s. However the gold was never in huge quantities, and the lack of water was always a problem.

Today Tibooburra is a charming little place offering basic facilities for the nearby stations and the ever-increasing numbers of tourists who come to experience the 'Corner Country'. But for the pub and a few hardy residents, Milparinka is a stunning, crumbling beauty of a ghost town.

Information

Tourist Offices Visitor centres in Wentworth and Broken Hill provide information on the Silver City Hwy and surrounds. The Wentworth Shire Visitor Information Centre (☎ 03-5027 3624, e tourism@wentworth.nsw.gov.au), at 66 Darling St, next to the post office, is open 9am to 4pm weekdays, and 10am to 3pm weekends. The Broken Hill Visitor Information Centre (☎ 08-8087 6077, e tourist@pcpro.net.au, w www.murrayoutback.org.au) is open from 8.30am to 5pm daily (except Christmas Day). It's on the corner of Blende and Bromide Sts. Also in Broken Hill, the district office of the National Parks and Wildlife Service (☎ 08-8088 5933) is on Argent St.

The Tibooburra district office of the National Parks and Wildlife Service (☎ 08-8091 3308), open 8.30am to 4.30pm weekdays, on Briscoe St, is an excellent place to find out a bit about the history and the fauna of that area.

For more information on Mutawintji and Sturt National Parks, contact the National Parks and Wildlife district offices in Broken Hill or Tibooburra; or the National Parks Centre (☎ within NSW 1300 361 967, other states ☎ 02-9253 4600, e info@npws.nsw .gov.au, w www.npws.nsw.gov.au), at 102 George St, the Rocks, Sydney. For details of Queensland Parks and Wildlife Service, visit its Web site (w www.env.qld.gov.au).

Books A wonderful recent publication takes you to into the heart of one of the Silver City Hwy's most magical towns – *Tibooburra: And the Legend of the Tree of Knowledge* by Julietta Jameson.

Emergency The Broken Hill Base Hospital (☎ 08-8088 0333) is on Thomas St, and the police station (☎ 08 8087 0299) is on Argent St.

The Wentworth police station (☎ 03-5027 3102) is on Darling St and the Wentworth

District Hospital (☎ 03-5027 2345) is on the Silver City Hwy.

The Tibooburra police station (☎ 08-8091 3303) and the Tibooburra District Hospital (☎ 08-8091 3302) are on Briscoe St, the town's main thoroughfare.

Road Reports Roads in these parts – particularly far north of Broken Hill – cop a beating whether it's wet or dry, and it's always worth checking conditions. An excellent source of info is Transport SA (☎ 1300 361 033, W www.transport.sa.gov .au/northern.htm).

The Royal Automobile Association of South Australia in Broken Hill (RASA; ☎ 08-8088 4999) handles emergency road services and recovery.

THE ROUTE

Officially the Silver City Hwy starts on the New South Wales side of the border, near Mildura, but it is at Wentworth, 30-odd kilometres further west, that it takes on its distinctive character and leaves behind the Murray River and its citrus groves.

From Mildura you can travel south of the river through Merbein, crossing the Murray 9km east of Wentworth. Alternatively, cross just north of the centre of Mildura, head a short distance north and turn left onto the Silver City Hwy at the small hamlet of Buronga. From here it is 24km to Wentworth.

Wentworth to Broken Hill (266km)

Regarded as the gateway to outback New South Wales, the township of Wentworth straddles the Darling River just upriver from its confluence with the Murray, but the main part of town is on the western bank of the Darling.

Just a few hundred metres past the Darling River bridge, turn right and follow the highway north. The manicured orchards and vineyards quickly give way to open grazing country, setting the scene for the drier, more expansive country further north.

The **Anabranch**, a major channel of the Darling River, is crossed 66km north of Wentworth. There is a spot to stop and enjoy

the slowly flowing waters close to the road bridge, and at a pinch you could stop here for the night.

Another 55km brings you to a high point overlooking the low-lake country to the east and **Popiltah Lake**, 121km north of Wentworth. It is a popular spot to stop and enjoy the view. It also makes a good overnight camping stop on the run north to Broken Hill. A bit further on is the Coombah Roadhouse (see the later Facilities section). From the roadhouse it is a steady run north, through country that gets progressively drier, to Broken Hill, 129km further on. The roadhouse is 16km north of Popiltah Lake.

Broken Hill

With a population of over 22,000, Broken Hill has much to offer the first-time visitor. Its rich mining heritage is well recorded in the **Railway, Mineral & Train Museum** *(☎ 08-8087 6077, Blende St; admission free; open 10am-3pm daily)*, and the mines that are open to the public. These include the **Daydream Mine** *(☎ 08-8088 5682, Silverton Rd; adult/child $11/5; open 10am-3.30pm daily)*, 28km north-west of the Hill just past Silverton, and **Delprats Mine** *(☎ 08-8088 1604, Access via Crystal & Iodide St intersection, Broken Hill town centre; adult/student $23/18; tours 10.30am Mon-Fri & 2pm Sat)*, the original BHP mine.

Broken Hill also offers travellers some fine **art collections**. For some years the town has been the centre for well-known Australian artists such as Pro Hart, Jack Absalom and Eric Minchin. Their galleries are well worth visiting, especially the **Pro Hart Gallery** *(☎ 08-8088 2992, 108 Wyman St; admission $2; open 9am-5pm Mon-Sat, 1.30pm-5pm Sun)*, which has one of the biggest private collections in Australia.

The **Heritage Trail**, which starts and ends at the tourist centre on the corner of Blende and Bromide Sts, can be completed in a couple of hours. This easy and enjoyable drive gives you a good idea of the history and development of the Hill, while the **Heritage Walk** covers about 2km and takes the visitor around many of the original buildings of the central commercial area.

The town is also a major centre for the Royal Flying Doctor Service (RFDS), and at their base at the airport they have an information shop and **museum** *(☎ 08-8088 1777, Broken Hill airport, Bonanza St; admission $3; open 9am-5pm Mon-Fri, 10am-4pm Sat & Sun)*.

South-east of the Hill are the **Menindee Lakes**, Broken Hill's watery playground, and the nearby **Kinchega National Park**. To the north-east of Broken Hill is **Mutawintji National Park**, with its rugged country and Aboriginal heritage, while a little further east is the opal town of **White Cliffs**.

Silverton One place not to miss is the nearby ghost town of Silverton, 25km north-west of the Hill. Once a rich mining centre, Silverton has been the location for a number of films, and the **Silverton Hotel** *(☎ 08-8088 5313)* and the **Gaol & Museum** *(☎ 08-8088 5317; admission $2; open 9 30am-4.30pm daily)* are beauties. **Penrose Park**, just a stone's throw from the Silverton Hotel, is a pleasant spot for a picnic, and its bush-like camping area is a quiet spot to put the tent up for a night or more (see Facilities later).

Broken Hill to Warri Warri Gate (393km)

Wind your way out of town, leaving the stark silhouettes of the mining headgear to the south. The Silver City Hwy twists and turns through the streets of the Hill before finally, about 2km from the centre of the city, heading towards Stephens Creek and places further north.

Stephens Creek, 16km out of the town, was once important to the townsfolk of Broken Hill as a pub and Sunday social centre, but is now just a name on the map, while **Yanco Glen**, another 16km up the road, is nothing more than a hotel. It offers a cool beer and that's about all.

A road junction 23km north (55km from Broken Hill) marks the turn-off for those heading east to the Mutawintji National Park, 75km away. This road also leads to the opal-mining community of White Cliffs, 221km from the junction. See Detours later for more about both destinations.

Mutawintji Turn-Off to Milparinka (240km) Continuing along the Silver City Hwy, the road heads almost due north, dipping through the occasional wide, low creekbed and skirting the infrequent rocky hill or low range. There's the occasional strip of dirt just to bring you back to reality and to give you an idea of what lies ahead.

Fowlers Gap, a research station, lies close to the creek of the same name, 55km north of the Mutawintji road junction, and here you'll find a pleasant wayside stop – if the weather isn't too hot.

Packsaddle Roadhouse (☎ 08-8091 2539), 65km further north (162km from Broken Hill) offers a cold beer, limited supplies and fuel. Basic double and twin rooms are $25. Note that Packsaddle is the only fuel outlet between Broken Hill and Tibooburra, and that it only has diesel and unleaded petrol – no LPG and no leaded petrol.

A reasonable dirt road joins with the Silver City Hwy 47km north of Packsaddle. This road, from the south-east, is the northern access to White Cliffs and Mutawintji National Park.

North of Packsaddle, the highway passes through a wide sweep of low sand-ridge and winds between a series of lakes (about 63km beyond Packsaddle). Off to the right is the normally dry **Salt Lake**, while to the left are the seasonal freshwater swamps of **Green Lake**. Neither of the lakes are signposted, but you can't miss them. There are basic *camp sites* without facilities at both lake areas, and several rough dirt roads connect them to the highway.

Milparinka Milparinka is 2km off the main road, 57km further on. While the main road continues north, you need to turn left at the signposted junction and follow the signs to the pub – the life centre of this virtually deserted town.

Milparinka was the centre of a brief, relatively rich gold rush that took miners into the surrounding hills searching for the elusive metal. During those heady days, the pub and the nearby courthouse and police station were built. While the pub survived intact, the other two fine buildings were destined to crumble, until recently when the locals got to work and saved these monuments. Plans were afoot at the time of writing to turn the beautifully restored courthouse into a museum.

About 15km from Milparinka is **Depot Glen**, where the explorer Charles Sturt and his party were trapped for months during their 1845 expedition to find the inland sea. So certain were they of finding a vast body of water that they had taken a boat with them – local legend has it that the boat was abandoned near here when the explorers retreated to the Darling River. A replica of the boat now stands in the main street of Tibooburra.

Depot Glen today is much the same as when Sturt and his men were there. Gums still line the creek, and corellas and galahs wheel in noisy profusion at the slightest disturbance. There's basic *camping* available here, but no facilities. Near the creek is a blazed tree and the grave of James Poole, Sturt's second in command, who died while the party were trapped here.

Eight kilometres north of the creek is **Mt Poole**. An impressive rocky monument known as **Sturt's Cairn** crowns this low but lofty prominence. There's a carpark at the foot of the hill, with a steep walking trail leading to the top, and magnificent views of the area. It's a 30-minute return hike. To keep his men occupied during their enforced stay, Sturt had them build a marker on top of this hill, stating in his journal:

I little thought when I engaged in that work, that I was erecting Mr Poole's monument, but so it was, that rude structure looks over his lonely grave and will stand for ages as a record of all we suffered in the dreary region to which we were so long confined.

These sites are well signposted and easy to find, but you should still drop by the pub for the latest local knowledge. Back on the main road heading north, it's an easy run to Tibooburra, 42km from Milparinka, unless, of course, you fancy the idea of a detour to Theldarpa Farmstay (see Milparinka in the Facilities section, later).

Tibooburra

For all intents and purposes, Tibooburra is a single street, which happens to be the main road north, with a few houses, offices and pubs along the way. Even so, it's the biggest town since Broken Hill and can supply all the general daily requirements for the traveller, such as food, fuel, basic repairs and a range of accommodation. The town's Web site (W www.tibooburra.com) is well worth a browse, as are the beautiful, rocky surrounds of the town, known to locals as 'the Common'.

Sturt National Park This park takes up 3440 sq km of the very north-western corner of New South Wales, having as its northern and western boundary the Queensland and South Australian borders, marked in this part of Australia by the famous **Dog Fence** (see Dingoes in the Fauna section in the Facts about the Outback chapter).

The protection the fence offers to sheep also benefits the kangaroos, which abound in the park. With their major predator kept under control and the water points put in for sheep and cattle, the roo numbers have increased since the coming of Europeans, and that makes the park and its inhabitants one of the major attractions of western New South Wales.

Here you will generally see the western grey kangaroo and the red kangaroo. The male of the latter species is easy to identify, but to the uninitiated, the female (or blue-flier) looks similar to the grey roo, a species where the male and female are less easy to tell apart. In the range country that cuts across parts of the park, the heavier-built hill wallaroo, or euro, may be seen.

Wedge-tailed eagles and emus are quite common in the park, as well as many other species of bird.

For most travellers who come this way, a visit to **Cameron Corner**, where the three states of New South Wales, South Australia and Queensland meet, is on the agenda. The Corner lies 140km north-west of Tibooburra and is reached by a good, well-signposted, dirt road (allow a good two hours). On the way, you will pass through Fort Grey, where

Sturt set up a base camp during his 1845 expedition. A camping area near the station of the same name is an ideal spot to enjoy this section of the park.

At Cameron Corner a gate through the Dog Fence leads to a small camping area in South Australia, while a drive of a few hundred metres will lead you past the Corner post to the *Cameron Corner Store* (☎ 08-8091 3872). Here you can get snacks, a cool drink and fuel (no LPG). From the Corner, you can head west to the Strzelecki Track and Cooper Creek, covered in the Central Deserts chapter.

Continuing north from Tibooburra, the road is good dirt all the way to the border at **Warri Warri Gate**, 56km from Tibooburra. Here you need to open the large gate through the Dog Fence; be sure to close it after you. You're now in Queensland and at the end of the Silver City Hwy, but as this is a hell of a place to stop, we'll push a little further north to take you to some form of habitation and a choice of places to go next.

North of Warri Warri Gate
Travelling through Queensland, the country remains much the same as before. A road junction 34km north of the border gives you your first choice of where to go. Turning left here will take you via Santos and Orientos stations north to Nappa Merrie on Cooper Creek, a total distance of 224km. Not so long ago, this was a sandy track, but recent years have seen it steadily upgraded north to Nappa Merrie, with a new bridge across Cooper Creek 5km east of Nappa Merrie.

Nappa Merrie is where the famous Burke and Wills 'Dig Tree' is located, about 50km east of Innamincka – see the Strzelecki Track section in the Central Deserts chapter. From Innamincka you can head north to Birdsville or Betoota, and from there to places further north.

Continuing along the main road north of Warri Warri Gate, **Naryilco** homestead is passed 18km further on, and another track to Santos comes in from the left just north of here. Yet another track to Santos meets the road 45km north from Naryilco. A few kilometres further on, just before the crossing of

the normally dry Elizabeth Creek, is the abandoned Bransby homestead, on the left.

Noccundra and its famous hotel (see the later Facilities section) are 88km north-east of the road junction, 185km north of the border, and 241km north of Tibooburra (at least a three-hour drive). From Noccundra you can head east on bitumen to Thargomindah, and from there to Cunnamulla and the Matilda Hwy (covered in The Tropics chapter). Alternatively, if you want to stay on dirt roads and tracks, you can continue north to Eromanga, Windorah and beyond.

DETOURS
Mungo National Park
This park makes for quite a detour at the start of the Silver City Hwy, but it's worth it. It covers 279 sq km and includes the superb 'Walls of China' eroded dunes, as well as a rich and ancient Aboriginal heritage. The visitors centre (☎ 03-5021 8900) is open daily and there are several excellent camping and picnic areas with facilities. From Wentworth, you head 90km north on the bitumen Pooncarie Rd, turning right at the unsealed, signposted road to the park, making it about 140km all up. If you're coming from Mildura, take the Arumpo Rd from Buronga (a hamlet just north of Mildura) and it's about 110km to the park.

Mutawintji National Park
Another worthwhile detour, approximately 130km north-east of Broken Hill, this park protects 689 sq km of the harsh sandstone country of the Byngnano Range, and the surrounding sand and gibber plains that are so characteristic of this part of New South Wales. Formerly Mootwingee National Park, the name change coincided with the handing back of the land to its traditional Aboriginal owners in 1998. The park is now jointly managed by Indigenous locals and the National Parks and Wildlife Service.

Near-permanent waters tucked into the narrow, rugged gorges that cut through the range made the area a welcome place to Aboriginal people in days gone by; the 1860 Burke and Wills expedition passed this way as well. There are many Aboriginal sites in the ranges, and the **Mutawintji Historic Site**, surrounded by the park and the most-visited area within it, gives a fine chance to discover this heritage. The Cultural Resource Centre, along with a network of trails and the guided walks led by Aboriginal rangers, helps people discover the art and imagine what life must once have been like in this region.

For more information, contact the National Parks and Wildlife Service district office in Broken Hill (☎ 08-8088 5933).

The area at Homestead Creek offers basic *camping* facilities, including showers. No bookings are required. Vehicle entry fee to the park is $6 per vehicle, camping fees are $10 for two people. No fuel or firewood are available.

White Cliffs

This small outback community north-east of Mutawintji is a little different from most: many of the inhabitants live underground. Their homes are extensive, multi-room affairs, some even sporting underground swimming pool areas and the like. Think about it – if you are an opal miner and your house becomes too small, what do you do? Well, you bring home the mining equipment you work with each day and add a room to your underground home – it's as easy as that.

A few houses and buildings aren't underground, and these include the hotel and the general store.

White Cliffs Hotel (☎ 08-8091 6606, e whihotel@ruralnet.net.au) Singles/doubles $25/35. This hotel can supply a cold beer or three.

PJ's Underground (☎ 08-8091 6626, e pjsunderground@bigpond.com, w http:// babs.com.au/nsw/pj.htm) Doubles & twins $99 (including breakfast), $24.50 for an extra person. This is a plush, cosy underground oasis with a popular restaurant.

White Cliffs General Store (☎/fax 08-8091 6611) This shop can supply fuel (no LPG) and a good range of foods; it is also the tourist information centre.

ORGANISED TOURS

Contact the various tourism bodies and regional tourist information centres (listed under Information earlier in this section) for details of local tour operators.

FACILITIES
Wentworth

Wentworth offers all facilities, including branches of most banks. There's plenty of accommodation – travellers can choose from a wide range of hotels, motels, holiday units and caravan parks. For a complete listing and prices, contact the tourist information centre (☎ 03-5027 3624, e tourism@ wentworth.nsw.gov.au) at 66 Darling St.

Willow Bend Caravan Park (☎ 03-5027 3213, southern end of Darling St) Unpowered/powered sites $10/12 for 2 people, cabins with shared bathroom/en suite $42/44. This park is in a very pretty riverside spot, and the cabins, by the river, are good value.

Two Rivers Motel (☎ 03-5027 3268, Silver City Hwy) Air-con singles/doubles with en suite $55/66-77. Rooms come with TV and fridge. This place has a pool and is well located near the river.

Coombah Roadhouse

Coombah Roadhouse (☎ 02-8091 1502, Silver City Hwy), roughly half way between Wentworth and Broken Hill, sells all fuels, plus takeaway foods and snacks.

Broken Hill

This major centre can supply all requirements. Bizbyte (☎ 08-8087 7352), 435 Argent St, has Internet access at $7 per hour. It's open 9am to 5.30pm weekdays.

There are over 20 hotels and nearly 20 motels, along with several caravan parks.

The Tourist Lodge (☎ 08-8088 2086, 100 Argent St) Dorm beds $16, singles/ doubles $18/30. This YHA-affiliated place is a well-run budget option in the town centre, with shared kitchen facilities and a small pool.

Broken Hill City Caravan Park (☎ 08-8087 3841, Adelaide Rd) Unpowered/ powered sites $14 for 2 people, on-site vans $29, double cabins without/with en suite $36/45. This park has plenty of shade and is about 3km from the town centre.

Lake View Caravan Park (☎ 08-8088 2250, 1 Mann St) Unpowered/powered sites $7/14 for 2 people, on-site vans $26, double cabins without/with en suite $34/40. This place has pleasant surrounds, and is close to the town centre, at the eastern end of Argent St. Dogs under control are allowed.

Mario's Palace Hotel (☎ 08-8088 1699, Argent St) Singles/doubles with shared bathroom $36/42, singles/doubles with en suite $45/55. This is a magnificent old pub with a huge balcony, impressive murals and excellent *meals* served daily. It also starred in the film *The Adventures of Priscilla, Queen of the Desert.*

Silverton

Penrose Park (☎ 08-8088 5307) Unpowered sites $3, dorm beds $16-20. Accommodation here is rustic, but includes coin-operated showers, BBQ and free hot water. There are three basic bunkhouse cabins. There's good food at the nearby *Silverton Hotel (08-8088 5313).*

Milparinka

Albert Hotel (☎ 08-8091 3863) Rooms $20 per person. This pub dates back to 1882 and is still a favourite watering hole. The solid-stone building offers a welcome respite from the heat, and the open courtyard with its water fountain is very pleasant. Rooms are basic but good, and there's free *camping* available nearby. The pub can also supply plenty of tourist info, *meals* and fuel (no LPG).

Theldarpa Farmstay (☎ 08-8091 3576) is 50km west of Milparinka, beyond Depot Glen on the road to Hawkers Gate. There's a wide range of accommodation on offer, including unpowered camp sites (with shower) from $5 per person, and bed & breakfast from $27 per person.

Tibooburra

The Tibooburra Telecenter, on Briscoe St next to the church, has free Internet access and is open 9am to 6pm weekdays.

Family Hotel (☎ 08-8091 3314, fax 8092 3430, Briscoe St) Rooms from $22. This popular place has good basic rooms with

ageing shared bathrooms. It also operates the *Family Lodge Motel* opposite, where very comfortable upmarket en suite cabins are $60.50 per double.

Granites Caravan Park (☎ 08-8091 3305) Unpowered/powered sites $14/18 for 2 people, en suite cabins $42 for 2 people, en suite motel doubles $60. This park is operated from the service station on Briscoe St. Dogs are allowed, under control. Motel accommodation allows use of a communal kitchen.

Just 1km north of town, at Dead Horse Gully, a small *camping area* ($6 for two people) is run by the National Parks and Wildlife Service.

The wonderful *Corner Country Store (☎ 08-8091 3333)* on Briscoe St, diagonally opposite the Family Hotel, has fuel (no LPG), souvenirs, groceries and some of the finest homemade food you're likely to find on your trip.

Noccundra

Noccundra Hotel (☎ 07 4655 4317) Here you can get a beer, meals and accommodation (basic singles/twins/doubles $15/25/35). Fuel (no LPG) and emergency repairs are also available, as well as up-to-date information on all the roads in the region.

ALTERNATIVE TRANSPORT
Car Rental

If you are hoping to hire a vehicle around Wentworth, you will need to check the hire-car companies based in Mildura. In Broken Hill, however, all major car-hire companies are represented: Avis (☎ 08-8087 7532), Budget (☎ 13 27 27), Hertz (☎ 08-8087 2719) and Thrifty (☎ 08-8088 1928).

Bus & Train

There are regular bus services, run by private companies as well as by public state transport authorities, from the eastern capital cities to Broken Hill and Mildura.

At the bus terminal in Broken Hill, 23–25 Bromide St, you'll find the booking office of McCafferty's/Greyhound (☎1800 801 294, 08-8087 2735). McCafferty's/Greyhound has a regular service from Adelaide to Brisbane, via Broken Hill and Dubbo. The Mildura-based bus company Junction Tours (☎ 03-8087 1400) also has a regular service between Mildura and Broken Hill.

Countrylink (☎ 13 22 32, e bookings @countrylink.nsw.gov.au, w www.country link.nsw.gov.au), run by State Rail in New South Wales, operates a rail/bus service to Broken Hill, with the XPT-Countrylink departing daily from Sydney, stopping in Dubbo, and connecting with an XPT bus to Broken Hill. The *Indian Pacific* runs from Sydney to Broken Hill every Monday and Thursday. Contact Countrylink ,Great Southern Railways (incorporating the *Indian Pacific*, the *Ghan*, and the *Overlander* train services; ☎ 13 21 47, 08-8213 4530), or the Broken Hill Railway Station (☎ 08-8087 1440), Crystal St, for current time-tables and costs of rail and coach transport. The station is open Monday to Friday, 8am to 5pm.

For details on bus services to Mildura (for connection to Wentworth), contact Country-link (☎ 13 22 32, e bookings@country link.nsw.gov.au, w www.countrylink.nsw .gov.au).

Air

Kendell Airlines (w www.kendell.com.au) has daily flights between Adelaide, Mildura and Broken Hill. There's also Hazelton Airlines (☎ 13 17 13, 02-6393 4222, e reser vations@hazelton.com.au, w www.hazelton .com.au), which connects Sydney to Dubbo and Griffith.

Both Kendell and Hazelton were subsidiaries of Ansett Airlines, at the time of writing, but were likely to contiue servicing regional centres. Southern Australia Airlines connects Broken Hill to Adelaide, Melbourne and Mildura. The airline is a subsidiary of Qantas, so bookings can be made via Qantas (☎ 13 13 13, w www.qantas .com.au).

There's also the Broken Hill-based Crittenden Air (☎/fax 08-8088 5702), which has single and twin-engine aircraft available for charter, as well as operating semi-regular flights to Tibooburra and several bush stations.

Kidman Way

Highlights

- Experiencing the outback that inspired some of Australia's earliest national literature
- Camping among the gum trees along the many rivers en route

Stretching for 800km through the heart of western New South Wales, the Kidman Way offers north-bound travellers the quickest route from Victoria. Many of Australia's best and most-loved poets, bush balladeers and writers drew their inspiration from this vast region; Henry Lawson, Will Ogilvie, 'Breaker' Morant and others all lived, worked and wrote about their experiences in this area of New South Wales.

The road is sealed most of the way and requires no specific travel preparation, but be aware that there's no fuel between Hillston and Cobar (257km).

History

This route crosses some of Australia's great rivers, and generations of Aborigines lived in this rich area before Europeans arrived in the early 1800s.

Across these vast plains and along the great rivers some of Australia's best-known early explorers sought to open the country up while vying for recognition and knighthood. Thomas Mitchell was one, and he was later knighted for his efforts, while Charles Sturt, the first European to discover the Darling River in 1829, never received the acclaim to which he was entitled.

Information

Tourist Offices Travellers will find tourist offices or information centres in most towns along the route.

The Griffith visitor information centre (☎ 02-6962 4145, e griffith@webfront.net .au) is on the corner of Banna and Jondaryan Aves. It's open 9am to 5pm weekdays, 9am

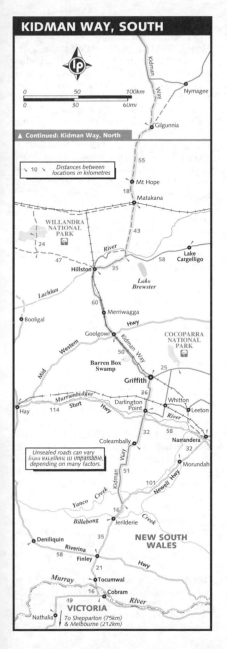

KIDMAN WAY, SOUTH

▲ Continued: Kidman Way, North

10 ↘ Distances between locations in kilometres

WILLANDRA NATIONAL PARK

Lake Cargelligo

Hillston

Lake Brewster

Lachlan

Booligal

Merriwagga

Goolgowi

Hwy

Western

Mid

Barren Box Swamp

COCOPARRA NATIONAL PARK

Kidman Way

Griffith

Murrumbidgee

Darlington Point

Sturt Hwy

Hay

Whitton

Leeton

River

Coleambally

Narrandera

Unsealed roads can vary from excellent to impassable, depending on many factors.

Morundah

Kidman Way

Newell Hwy

Yanco Creek

Billabong

Jerilderie

Creek

Deniliquin

Riverina

Finley

NEW SOUTH WALES

Murray

Tocumwal

Nathalia

Cobram

River

VICTORIA

To Shepparton (75km) & Melbourne (212km)

Kidman Way

Nymagee

Gilgunnia

Mt Hope

Matakana

River

KIDMAN WAY, NORTH

To Charleville (317km from Barringun)

Cunnamulla

Unsealed roads can vary from excellent to impassable, depending on many factors.

10 ↘ Distances Between Locations in Kilometres

QUEENSLAND

Mitchell Hwy

To Hungerford (82km from Yantabulla) & Currawinya National Park

Barringun

Yantabulla

Enngonia

To Collerina (74km from Bourke)

Fords Bridge

To Wanaaring (195km from Bourke) & Silver City Hwy

Bourke

To Brewarrina (95km from Bourke)

NEW SOUTH WALES

River

Darling

Louth

GUNDABOOKA NATIONAL PARK

Mt Gunderbooka

Oxley's Tableland

Mitchell Hwy

Byrock

To Nyngan (20km from Bourke)

Kidman Way

Mt Grenfell

Barrier

Cobar

Hwy

▼ Continued: Kidman Way, South

Nymagee

Gilgunnia

THE SOUTH

to 3pm Saturday, and 10am to 2pm Sunday. Contact the Goolgowi Council Chamber (☎ 02-6965 1306), on the corner of Cobram and Stipa Sts, for local tourist information. The Hillston visitor information centre (☎ 02-6967 2555, e touristofficer@ carrathool.nsw.gov.au) is on the corner of High and McGee Sts. It's open 9am to 5pm weekdays. The Bourke tourist information centre (☎ 02-6872 1222, e tourinfo@ lisp.com.au, w www.backobourke.com.au), in the Old Railway Building on Anson St, is open 9am to 5pm Monday to Saturday from November to Easter, and 9am to 5pm daily from Easter to October.

For excellent general information contact the Tourism New South Wales Sydney Visitor Centre (☎ 13 20 77, 02-9931 1111, w www.visitnsw.com.au; open 9am-6pm daily), at 106 George Street, the Rocks, and/or the Sydney National Parks Centre (☎ 1300 361 967 within NSW, 02-9253 4600, e info@npws.nsw.gov.au, w www.npws .nsw.gov.au), at 102 George St, the Rocks.

The Kidman Way Promotions Committee (w www.kidmanway.org.au) is a good source information on the route.

Books & Maps There are numerous books and maps that cover this region of Australia. See the nearest map shop or local automobile club, such as the NRMA in New South Wales, or the RACV in Victoria (see Useful Organisations in the Facts for the Visitor chapter for contact details).

THE ROUTE
Jerilderie
Jerilderie (population 1100) is on the Newell Hwy, 318km north of Melbourne on the main route to Brisbane. It is famous for wool, as well as wheat, rice and a host of other crops reaped from its verdant irrigation area. For travellers it supplies all one requires and has a good selection of accommodation.

The **Willows Historical Museum** (☎ 03-5886 1366; admission free; open 9.30am-3.30pm Wed, Fri-Sun), on Powell St near the lake, is well worth a look, and includes the tiny former post office that had its wires cut by the Kelly gang in 1879.

Jerilderie to Griffith (135km)
Head north out of town on the Newell Hwy for 16km and turn left for **Coleambally**. It's another 51km to this small township. Follow the main road past Coleambally (the huge dragline to your right is worth a quick look) and it's a straight run north, only interrupted by the major crossroad of the Sturt Hwy.

On the banks of the Murrumbidgee River, 3km north of the Sturt Hwy intersection and 32km from Coleambally, is **Darlington Point**. This small town was founded in the early 1860s and can supply a fair range of services. Follow the signposts out of town to Griffith, 36km north.

Griffith
Griffith (population 24,000) is by far the biggest town you will go through on this trip north and lies in the heart of the Murrumbidgee Irrigation Area, 680km west of Sydney. Proclaimed when the railway arrived in 1917, it was a flourishing town by 1922.

There's plenty to see and do in and around the city, with most of the nearby wineries putting on tours and wine tasting, while **Cocoparra National Park** (☎ 02-6966 8100, Myall Park Rd; admission free) 25km north-east of town, is worth a visit.

Griffith to Cobar (367km)
Once you've entered Griffith, keep a good lookout for road signs as the route through Griffith is a little convoluted. Basically, head north to the main street, Banna Ave, and turn left (west) looking out for signs. At the western end of town you need to get into Griffin Ave and onto Route 87 heading to Warburn, Goolgowi and Hillston.

Once on the right road out of Griffith it's a 50km run across flat land to the small town of **Goolgowi** on the Mid Western Hwy. From Goolgowi to Hillston it's another 60km, and you soon leave the irrigated country behind and enter wheat and grazing country.

Hillston On the banks of the **Lachlan River**, the town of Hillston (population 1100) is the original home of the Wiradjuri people. It offers a wealth of water sports as well as a good range of facilities and supplies. It's also the demographic centre of Australia. Yep, this is the point on the continent where there is an equal number of people in any direction you choose to face. This point shifts of course, and is currently travelling north-north-east at about 3m a day.

Willandra National Park (☎ 02-6967 8159, access via Hillston-Mossgiel Rd; admission free) is a pleasant day trip, 71km north-west of Hillston, where kangaroos and mobs of emus are very common. Check road conditions after rain – the access road can be impassable in wet conditions.

North of Hillston From Hillston, you need to turn right at the major intersection in the heart of town, and head for Lake Cargelligo and Mt Hope.

About 35km later you need to veer left, crossing the Lachlan River soon afterwards. You're now getting into more remote country and the road less travelled.

You can almost pass **Mt Hope**, 96km north of Hillston, without noticing. As the road climbs a small hill you pass the Mt Hope Royal Hotel and the general store – that's it!

Heading north, you enter Cobar from the south-east, meeting the main east-west Barrier Hwy just on the east side of town, where you veer left to the centre of town, past the majestic former office of the Great Cobar Copper Mine, which is now an excellent museum (see below).

Cobar

The 'Copper City' is on the Barrier Hwy, 705km west of Sydney, 161km north of Mt Hope and 502km north of Jerilderie. Centre of a large shire, the population of the town is around 4500, and while the town supports a rich grazing industry, mining is its lifeblood.

Don't miss the **Cobar Regional Museum & Visitor Information Centre** (☎ 02-8636 2448, ℮ cobarmus@cobar.net.au; adult/ concession/family $5.50/3.50/12; open 8.30am-5pm Mon-Fri, 9am-5pm Sat & Sun) on the Barrier Hwy, as you enter town from the south. Displays here include a simulated mineshaft, an ironstone xylophone and a lovingly restored Far West Children's Health Scheme train carriage.

Cobar to Bourke (160km)

Head north onto Bourke Rd and you are soon on your way. The road is sealed most of way between Gilgunnia and Bourke through scrub and grazing land. As you get closer to the Darling River town, signs of cotton growing begin to crowd the roadside.

You enter the outskirts of Bourke, cross over the railway line and meet with the main Mitchell Hwy. Following the main road north you come to the police station and the heart of town.

Bourke

On the banks of the mighty and muddy Darling River, Bourke (population 3400) is 780km north-west of Sydney, via the Mitchell Hwy, and 980km north of Melbourne, via the route just described. Brisbane is 950km to the east. This place features deep in the Australian psyche. Will Ogilvie and Henry Lawson both wrote about Bourke and its surrounds, giving it a larger-than-life character for many city people.

The Darling River is the lifeblood of the area and, at about 2800km long, is the longest river in Australia. In 1829 Charles Sturt was the first European to see the river, and graziers soon followed.

Bourke to Barringun (136km)

Follow the dog-legging Mitchell Hwy through town and you soon leave the built-up area behind and cross the Darling River to North Bourke, with its few houses and pub.

You are on bitumen as you head north along the Mitchell Hwy, and 99km from Bourke you come to the small hamlet of **Enngonia**, where the *Oasis Hotel/Motel* (☎ 02-6874 7577, Mitchell Hwy) has basic singles/doubles for $25/35.

Pushing ever north, it is just 37km to **Barringun** and the end of the Mitchell Hwy. Located 136km from Bourke, this small, sprawling village straddles the New South Wales-Queensland border, 1116km north of Melbourne and 798km north of Jerilderie. The pub, once a haunt of Henry Lawson, offers a traveller succour, while a road-house, just a short distance north, has fuel and food as well.

North across the border is Queensland and the all-bitumen Matilda Hwy (for details see The Tropics chapter).

ORGANISED TOURS

Contact the various tourism bodies and regional tourist information centres (listed under Information earlier) for details of local tour operators.

FACILITIES

Jerilderie

Jerilderie Motor Inn (☎ 02-5886 1235, fax 5886 1235, 4 Jerilderie St) Singles/doubles $55/65. This place has pretty swish rooms, and is nicely situated opposite the lake.

Jerilderie Caravan Lodge (☎ 02-5886 1366, 121 Newell Hwy at Jerilderie St) Powered sites $14 per double, cabins $38 for 2 people, motel units $44 for 2 people. This is a large park with good facilities, including a pool.

There's fine food to be had at the *Olive Tree Coffee Shop* (☎ 02-5886 1461, 6 Jerilderie St) in the old post office building, next door to the Jerilderie Motor Inn. It's open 5.30am to 'finish' (it closes at 8pm if no diners are in) daily. It's licensed, and hearty meals cost around $14.

Coleambally

Coleambally is a modern little town with a relatively large shopping strip. The *Coleamabally Caravan Park* (☎ 02-6954 4100), near the main road turn-off, has unpowered sites for $10 for two people, and caravans for $25 to $40 for two people. Pets are allowed, under control.

Darlington Point

The picturesque *Darlington Point Caravan Park* (☎ 02-6968 4237, e pcfrost@webfront .net.au, Kidman Way) has unpowered sites for $11 for two people, and en suite cabins for $38 to $50 for two people. This is a large, lush park on the banks of the Murrumbidgee.

Griffith

The Griffith City Library (☎ 02-6207 5723), Banna Ave, has free Internet access and is open 10am to 8pm weekdays.

It's worth noting that the town's budget accommodation attracts hordes of fruit-pickers from around November to April, so booking ahead is wise during these months.

Griffith Tourist Caravan Park (☎ 02-6964 2144, fax 6964 1126, 919 Wilandra Ave) Unpowered/powered sites $11/14.30, single/double on-site vans $22/27.50, dorm beds $35.20-38.50, single units/double units with en suite $44-49/55. This is a very efficiently run establishment. The units are attractive, set around a courtyard, and good value. There's also a swimming pool, barbecue area and public phone.

Acacia Motel (☎ 02-6962 4422, fax 6962 3284, 923 Jondaryan Ave) Singles/doubles $62/68. This is one of many modern motels close to shops and restaurants in the heart of Griffith.

Goolgowi

This small town can supply most requirements. The *Goolgowi Caravan Park* (☎ 02-6965 1266, 44 Napier St) has unpowered/powered sites for $12/14.

Hillston

There's free Internet access at the Public Library (☎ 02-6967 2503) on High St. It's open 10am to 6pm weekdays.

Hillston Caravan Park (☎ 02-6967 2575, Cnr Oxley Ave & Keats St) Unpowered/powered sites $9/12, cabins $55 for 2 people. This is a popular park with good facilities and pleasant surrounds.

Kidman Way Motor Inn (☎ 02-6967 2351, Cnr High & Keats Sts) Singles/doubles $60/70. This a spotless, modern place near the caravan park.

Hillston Motel (☎ 02-6967 2514, 25 McGee St) Singles/doubles $55/65. This homely establishment has tidy old-style rooms and a pool.

Cobar

Cobar Micro Bytes Internet Cafe (☎ 02-6836 1832), in the meticulously restored Cobar Railway Station (built in 1892), has Internet access at $6 per hour. It's on Railway Parade North, and is open Tuesday to Thursday, 10am to 4pm.

Copper City Motel *(☎ 02-6836 2404, 40 Lewis St)* Single/double units from $48 for 2 people. This is an unpretentious establishment with good, basic accommodation.

Cobar Caravan Park *(☎/fax 02-6836 2425, 101 Barrier Hwy)* Unpowered/powered sites $10.50/12 per double, en suite cabins $45 for 2 people. This large place has modern amenities, grassy tent sites, a shop and a public phone.

Bourke

The library (☎ 02-6872 2055), on Mitchell St, has free Internet access. It's open 9am to noon, and 1pm to 5pm weekdays.

Mitchell Caravan Park *(☎ 02-6872 2791, Brewarrina Rd)* Unpowered/powered sites $14/16 for 2 people, en suite cabins $52 for 2 people. This is a friendly, well-run park near the centre of town.

Kidmans Camp Caravan Park *(☎ 02-6872 1612, Kidman Way, North Bourke)* Unpowered/powered sites $12/14, single/double train carriage–style cabins with shared bathroom $36/42. This large, nicely laid-out park has excellent facilities, shared kitchen and attractive cabins. It's 7km north of Bourke proper.

Outback Motel *(☎ 02-6872 2288, Mertin St)* Singles/doubles $45/55. This is a no-nonsense motel with good basic rooms.

Bourke Riverside Motel *(☎ 02-6872 2311, fax 6872 2539, 3 Mitchell St)* Standard en suite singles/doubles $60/70, luxury suites from $82.50. This rambling historic place is set in beautiful riverside surrounds, with a pool. The rooms are large, if a little frayed at the edges for the price.

Jandra Chinese Restaurant *(☎ 02-6872 2190, Bourke Bowling Club, Mitchell St)* Main meals $12-14. This place is hidden away upstairs in the bowling club, but well

worth the search. It serves large, tasty meals in-house or takeaway. It's open noon to 2pm (except Monday) and 6pm to 9pm daily.

Morrall's Bakery *(☎ 02-6872 2086, 37 Mitchell St)* Light meals $6-8. Opposite the bowling club, Morrall's is open daily from 8am to 6pm and serves pastries and coffee. The same venue also offers good pizza (including vegetarian) thanks to ***Tiffanies Pizza*** *(☎ 02-6872 2086)* but it's only available 5.30pm to 9.30pm Friday and Saturday, and 6pm to 9pm Sunday.

ALTERNATIVE TRANSPORT
Car Rental

Representatives of major car-hire companies, such as Avis (☎ 1800 801 294), can be found in Cobar and Bourke, along with Thrifty Car Rental (☎ 02-6836 2607) in Cobar.

Bus & Train

There are no bus companies operating along the Kidman Way, although McCafferty's/Greyhound (☎ 1800 801 294) does have a service between Dubbo and Cobar.

To get to Jerilderie from Melbourne or Sydney, you can catch the XPT-Countrylink train to Wagga Wagga, and take the connecting bus to Jerilderie. For more information contact Countrylink (☎ 13 22 32, e bookings@countrylink.nsw.gov.au, w www.countrylink.nsw.gov.au).

Air

Dubbo-based Air Link (☎ 13 17 13) connects Sydney with Cobar and Bourke, as well serving Bourke, Dubbo, and Lightning Ridge. It is also available for charter.

Hazelton Airlines (☎ 13 17 13) also has regular scheduled flights to Charleville, Cobar and Bourke from Sydney, Brisbane and Dubbo.

The North-West

With its wide open spaces, stunning scenery and lure of adventure, Australia's north-west is a promised land for outback travellers. It includes the rugged Kimberley and Pilbara regions, spectacular coastlines of red cliffs and lonely beaches, and the vast, desolate expanses of the Great Sandy Desert. Towns are few and far between – a sprinkle of mining and pastoral centres in the Pilbara and Kimberley, and a few ports along the coast. Most famous of these is Broome, once the pearl capital of Australia and still with much of the atmosphere of its colourful past.

Unless you're mainly sticking to the few sealed roads, the north-west isn't really the place for inexperienced outback motorists. The region has numerous remote touring opportunities, including two of Australia's finest long-distance 4WD routes. The most challenging is the Canning Stock Route

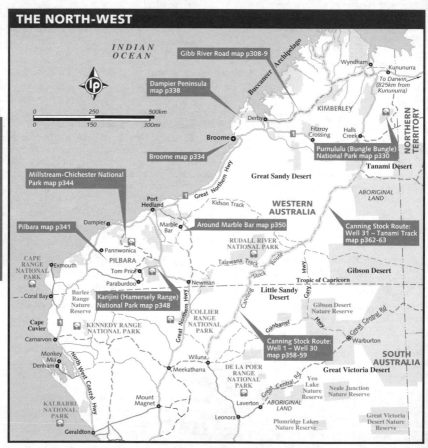

THE NORTH-WEST

THE NORTH-WEST

INDIAN OCEAN

Gibb River Road map p308-9

Buccaneer Archipelago

Wyndham

Kununurra

To Darwin
(825km from Kununurra)

Dampier Peninsula map p338

KIMBERLEY

Derby

Fitzroy Crossing

Halls Creek

NORTHERN TERRITORY

Broome

Broome map p334

Purnululu (Bungle Bungle) National Park map p330

Tanami Desert

Great Sandy Desert

Millstream-Chichester National Park map p344

Great Northern Hwy

Kidson Track

WESTERN AUSTRALIA

ABORIGINAL LAND

Port Hedland

Around Marble Bar map p350

Canning Stock Route: Well 31 – Tanami Track map p362-63

Pilbara map p341

Dampier

Marble Bar

RUDALL RIVER NATIONAL PARK

Pannawonica

PILBARA

Talawana Track

Gibson Desert

CAPE RANGE NATIONAL PARK

Exmouth

Tom Price

Paraburdoo

Newman

Tropic of Capricorn

Little Sandy Desert

Gibson Desert Nature Reserve

Coral Bay

Barlee Range Nature Reserve

Karijini (Hamersley Range) National Park map p348

COLLIER RANGE NATIONAL PARK

Gunbarrel Hwy

Great Central Rd

Cape Cuvier

KENNEDY RANGE NATIONAL PARK

Canning Stock Route: Well 1 – Well 30 map p358-59

Warburton

Carnarvon

North West Coastal Hwy

Wiluna

SOUTH AUSTRALIA

Monkey Mia

Denham

Meekatharra

DE LA POER RANGE NATIONAL PARK

Great Victoria Desert

Yeo Lake Nature Reserve

Neale Junction Nature Reserve

Great Central Rd

KALBARRI NATIONAL PARK

Mount Magnet

Laverton

ABORIGINAL LAND

Great Victoria Desert Nature Reserve

Geraldton

Leonora

Plumridge Lakes Nature Reserve

0   250   500km
0   150   300mi

(1700km), which cuts through the desert from Halls Creek in the Kimberley, to Wiluna in the south. There's also the Gibb River Rd (710km), running through the heart of the Kimberley between Derby and Kununurra.

If you're in a normal car, you can visit most of the national parks in the north-west, including Geikie Gorge and Tunnel Creek in the Kimberley, and Millstream-Chichester and Karijini in the Hamersley Ranges. The spectacular Bungles are, unfortunately, only accessible by 4WD – which is why most visitors confine themselves to a scenic flight. Although the north-west is extremely remote and sparsely populated, there's a good range of visitor facilities and organised tours. The latter include 4WD tag-alongs on the Gibb River Rd, fishing trips at various places, visits to a huge iron-ore mine at Tom Price, canoeing on the Ord River and boat cruises on the vast Lake Argyle.

Gibb River Road

Highlights

- Cooling off in the waterfalls of Bell Gorge
- Discovering the magnificent Aboriginal Wandjina art and the mysterious Bradshaw paintings
- Staying at Mornington Bush Camp and canoeing in Dimond Gorge
- Walking around Mitchell Falls and swimming in the pool at the top
- Observing freshwater crocs at Windjana Gorge

The Kimberley, that vast chunk of country that takes up the far north-west corner of Australia, is much bigger than the UK or Japan, nearly half the size of Texas and, for those who relate to Australia, bigger than Victoria and Tasmania combined.

It's closer to Asia than to most major cities of Australia: Indonesia is less than 500km away and Wyndham, northernmost port of Western Australia, is nearer to Jakarta than it is to Perth and closer to Singapore than to Melbourne. By road, it's 3400km from Melbourne to Halls Creek, while from Perth to Broome – on the other side of the Kimberley – it's a mere 2300km.

Less than 30,000 people live in the Kimberley, mainly in small towns such as Broome, Derby and Kununurra.

To the north and west, the area is bordered by a torn and twisted coastline and one of the most spectacular stretches of water in the world. Rugged sandstone ranges separate the Kimberley from the sandy desert that encroaches to the south.

The area represents one of the great outdoor travel destinations in Australia, rich in Aboriginal culture, European history and spectacular natural beauty.

Hwy 1 swings north-east from Broome to Derby and then east to Halls Creek, before heading north to Kununurra, but misses out on the 'real' Kimberley. To see that, you need to travel along the unsealed Gibb River Rd, which cuts through the very heart of the region. At 710km, it represents the shortest (but slowest) distance between Derby and Kununurra.

The road has been improved over the years, but one good wet season sees much of the past effort washed away. In 'good' years, after the graders have been out, the road is suitable for a normal car, if you don't mind it losing a few bits along the way. In 'bad' years, after heavy rain and no graders for months, the route is rough even for 4WDs that have been well prepared.

For the most part, the Gibb River Rd passes through pastoral country, with many beautiful gorges and some interesting national parks along the way.

History
The Kimberley was probably the first place on the Australian mainland where Aborigines landed when they arrived from Asia. A number of sites have been found that date back at least 18,000 years, but because the sea level has risen substantially in the past 50,000 years, many early occupation sites would now be under water.

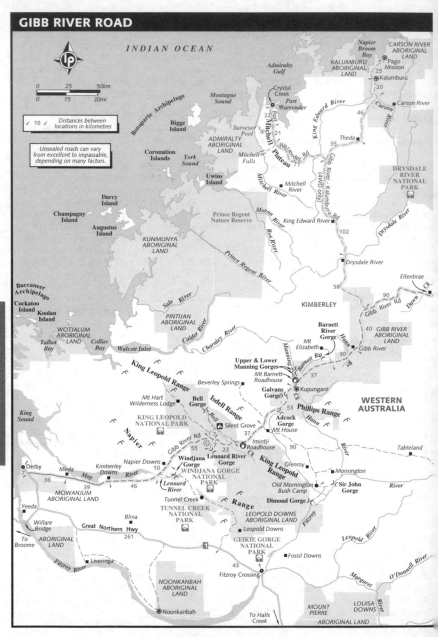

GIBB RIVER ROAD

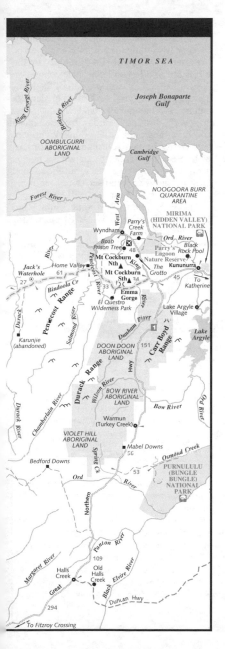

The richness of Aboriginal culture is vividly portrayed in the art that can still be found in the area – the Kimberley contains some of Australia's greatest collections of prehistoric art. If you are lucky enough to see a rock gallery of the distinctive, vividly painted Wandjina figures, then you, like many before you, will be impressed.

For hundreds of years, Macassan fishermen from islands far to the north had been sailing to the Kimberley coast to establish trepang (or sea cucumber) fishing camps there.

The first European known to have sailed along this coast was the Dutch navigator Abel Tasman in 1644. He went on to explore Australia's southern coast, where his name is immortalised in the island of Tasmania. The English buccaneer William Dampier was next on the scene, visiting in 1688 and 1699. His reports were less than favourable, curtailing English interest in the region until the early 1800s.

Nicolas Baudin's expedition in the ships *Le Geographe* and *Naturaliste* between 1800 and 1804 mapped much of the Australian coastline, resulting in the French names scattered along the Kimberley coast.

Matthew Flinders circumnavigated Australia at the same time without even seeing the Kimberley. Phillip Parker King led four coastal mapping expeditions to the area between 1818 and 1821, naming such places as Careening Bay (after the enforced landing of his ship) and the Buccaneer Archipelago (in memory of Dampier's voyage). He also travelled far up the Prince Regent River, sketching King's Cascade, still a favourite spot for remote boat travellers.

In 1837, Charles Darwin's famous ship, HMS *Beagle*, under the command of John Wickham and John Stokes, mapped much of the coast, including the area around Derby and Brecknock Harbour.

The first overland trip by Europeans in the Kimberley was attempted by George Grey. He landed late in 1837 at Hanover Bay, a spot that is just as remote today as it was then, and was the first European to see the Wandjina art that dots many of the caves and overhangs of the Kimberley. Although the expedition failed, Grey waxed so lyrical about the place that later a pastoral company was formed to establish a settlement near the Glenelg River. This venture failed too.

By the 1860s, pearlers were plying the coast from Broome and the first tentative steps towards a pastoral industry were being taken. In 1879 Alexander Forrest left Beagle Bay and followed the Fitzroy River upstream as far as Geikie Gorge, before heading towards the coast along the ramparts of the King Leopold Ranges. Failing to reach the coast, he returned eastward and discovered the Ord River. His reports of good grazing land along the Fitzroy and Ord Rivers sent settlers scrambling for a slice of the action. These included Nat Buchanan, the Durack family and the MacDonald family, who still own and operate the Fossil Downs station, just outside Fitzroy Crossing. The discovery of gold at Halls Creek in 1885 and 1886 resulted in a mini gold rush.

In the early 1930s, however, there were fewer than 10,000 people in the Kimberley and the cosmopolitan 'capital' of the area was Broome. Hundreds of boats worked out of Broome, searching for pearl shell and pearls. In the late 1930s a plan was developed for the formation of a Jewish home state centred on Argyle station in the eastern part of the Kimberley; it was not until the birth of modern Israel in 1948 that the idea died.

WWII brought raids by Japanese bombers, not only on Broome, Wyndham and Derby but on Aboriginal missions as well. Secret landfalls by Japanese troops occurred during these years, but the rugged terrain that had repulsed Grey and his followers served Australia well.

The population of Broome plummeted after the war as the new use of plastic for making buttons meant the demise of the pearling industry. In the 1950s, the main road north of Broome was improved from a horse track to a wide horse track. The road network was so poor that until the late 1950s, all police patrols were by horseback; Hwy 1 was finally sealed in 1987.

Pedalling through the Kimberley in the 1950s

Alex and Jacky Sklenica bicycled through the Kimberley back in 1954. Here's what they had to say about it many years later, after they had just completed a similar return trip in their trusty 4WD:

'Repacking our push bikes, we were considering possible routes from Wyndham to Derby. A shorter but very rough 700km on the Durack and Gibb River track, confusingly crossed by stock routes, petering out in the bush and no supply points along the way. Or the 1000km via Turkey Creek, Halls Creek, Fitzroy Crossing. This longer way, still rather a bush track than road in 1954, was used mainly by drovers and station vehicles. A decisive advantage was that food supplies would be available from shops at Halls Creek and Fitzroy Crossing.

The Wyndham Police and locals in the pub offered advice, wished us luck and one grinned: "You know what I am thinking".

We had to travel light and live mostly off the land. A limited amount of basic food supplies were bought in Wyndham. Water, still remaining after the previous *rainy*, and some edible plants would have to be found on the way. Not a beginner in the Australian bush, I carried also a few fishing hooks and a line, and a single-shot .22 rifle. We hoped to catch fish, but knew that our main food source would consist of pigeon, ibis, ducks, galahs and wallabies.

We were unable to ride our bikes over the frequently sandy or rock-strewn stretches, but had to walk, pushing the bikes or sometimes ride on firmer surfaces parallel to the road.

There were no camping grounds, national parks or tourists there. During four months, we met only one car with two Melbourne tourists and one Frenchman riding a motorcycle around Australia. When, on rare occasions, we met with station people, we stopped to boil a billy and to exchange news.

In 1963, the Ord Dam wall was completed and Lake Argyle, the largest lake in Australia, began to form. It took over two years to fill, even though the river in full wet-season flood would be capable of filling every dam that supplies Perth with water, from empty to full, in 20 minutes! The dam, and the irrigation area that was set up for it to serve, has only just recently reached its full potential.

The discoveries of oil at Blina, east of Derby, diamonds south of Lake Argyle in the late 1970s (now the largest diamond mine in the world), bauxite on the Mitchell Plateau around the same time, and oil and gas offshore really opened up the Kimberley. Much of the land is still for grazing, although cattle has waned in importance in recent years and many stations have either closed down, switched to tourism (with token herds of cattle to ensure tourist interest and to keep the authorities happy who might otherwise retract the lease) or reverted to Aboriginal control. Over 40% of the Kimberley is Aboriginal land of one form or

another, and this percentage is growing. More than 10% of the land is protected in national parks or conservation reserves, but much of this is inaccessible to travellers.

Information

Visitor Centres The Derby visitor centre (☎ 08-9191 1426, fax 9191 1609, PO Box 48, Derby, WA 6728) at 2 Clarendon St is a good source of information. The Kununurra visitor centre (☎ 08-9168 1177, fax 9168 2598) is found close to the heart of town at 75 Coolibah Dr. Wyndham's Information Centre (☎ 08-9161 1054, fax 9161 1341) is in the old port area at the Old Port Post Office, O'Donnell St.

The Western Australian Visitor Centre (☎ 08-9483 1111) at 469 Wellington St, Perth, can also provide information on the Kimberley.

The Department of Conservation and Land Management (CALM) has a regional headquarters at Kununurra (☎ 08-9168 4200), in the state government building on

---

Pedalling through the Kimberley in the 1950s

Once a passing stockman from Bohemia Downs stopped his truck near our little campfire for a bit of a talk, sharing with us a billy of tea. Looking over our scanty outfit, he said: "On bikes...but how...what do you eat?".

Pointing to our saddle bags I replied: "We have some flour, tea, sugar and such here, and there is plenty of game around waterholes".

When leaving our camp, he dropped an apparently empty plywood tea-chest: "Perhaps you can use this as a table".

Inside the tea-chest was his present: a loaf of bread and a pound of butter wrapped in sheets of newspaper. Fresh bread and real butter! Immediately, we boiled another billy, spread slices of buttered bread on the tea-chest and read every scrap of newspaper, including adverts. This was indeed a happy camp, still vivid in our memory.

There were no marked tracks through spear grass and spinifex leading to Geikie or Windjana Gorges. Near Tunnel Creek, overhanging rock shelters were still periodically inhabited by nomadic natives. We found and left undisturbed spears, stone knives and scrapers.

We met a mounted police patrol and sat till midnight smoking and talking, listening to natives singing around a campfire near the billabong.

A period in our life when we were not tied to conventions and restrictions of crowded civilisation. A time when we were free to walk over the horizon. A slice of damper and roasted wallaby washed down with Bushell's was a repast. A shady tree, the warmth of a small fire on cool nights, bright stars our roof. Unforgettable memories of an unfenced land, of outback people and times past'.

Alex Sklenica

Just such a short time ago, and much has changed. Yet so much remains the same.

Konkerberry Dr. You can contact them for any information on the national parks and conservation reserves in the Kimberley.

Radio Frequencies For those who have a High Frequency (HF) radio, the important frequencies to have are the Royal Flying Doctor Service (RFDS) bases at Derby, Port Hedland and Alice Springs.

For the RFDS base at Derby (call sign VJB), the primary frequency is 5300kHz with secondary frequencies of 6925kHz and 6945kHz. Port Hedland's call sign is VKL and its primary frequency is 4030kHz; secondary frequencies are 2280kHz and 6960kHz. Alice Springs (call sign VJD) is a good base to call from the eastern part of the Kimberley if you can't get through to Derby. Its primary frequency is 5410kHz and its secondary one, 6950kHz. However, communication is generally better through the RFDS base in Derby.

Books & Maps There are a number of good maps of this area. The Western Australian Department of Land Administration's Street Smart Touring Map entitled *The Kimberley*, Hema's *The Kimberley*, and Australian Geographic's *The Kimberley* are great for the general traveller.

The best guidebooks about the area are *The Kimberley – an Adventurer's Guide* by Ron & Viv Moon, *The Australian Geographic Book of the Kimberley* and Ben Knapinski's *Kimberley, Western Australia's Gibb River Road*. The latter is more a photo book but tells much of what you need to know and makes a fantastic souvenir. The surprisingly useful, 12-page *Gibb River and Kalumburu Roads Travellers Guide* is updated annually by the Derby visitor centre and is available from Kimberley visitor centres.

There are a host of other books that cover different aspects of the Kimberley, its people, history and natural wonders. Many of these are available in bookshops in towns of the region.

Permits There is no requirement for permits if you stick to the main road and the route described.

Emergency The following centres have basic services for assistance:
Derby The police station (☎ 08-9191 1444) is at the corner of Villiers and Loch Sts. The hospital (☎ 08-9193 3333) is farther west along Loch St. If you need towing, the Derby Royal Automobile Club of Western Australia (RAC of WA) agency is the BP Colac Service Station & Roadhouse (☎ 08-9191 1256) at 84 Loch St.

Wyndham The police station (☎ 08-9161 1055) is in the old port area. The hospital (☎ 08-9161 1104) is in the new part of town.

The RAC of WA agency in Wyndham, Branko BP Motors (☎ 08-9161 1305), on the Great Northern Hwy can arrange towing.

Kununurra The more modern town of Kununurra has its police station (☎ 08-9166 4530) just west of the main shopping centre, in Coolibah Dr.

The hospital (☎ 08-9168 1522) is in the same street, but a little farther west. Kununurra's RAC of WA agency, Elgee Toyota (☎ 08-9168 2236), at 231 Bloodwood Dr, can help with towing.

Special Preparations

Even in busy times, the road is remote and it's hard to expect any real help from the many passing tourists. Have a breakdown and you could be waiting for a while. Be prepared. The road can be very rough and tyre damage is common, so carry at least two spares. Most importantly though, *slow down.* Most problems occur because of excessive speed (some of those unexpected rocky outcrops can be very unforgiving).

That said, you're not in the middle of nowhere. Many of the cattle properties along the route (especially along the eastern half) are switching to tourism and offer camping or accommodation with dinner, bed and breakfast (DB&B) arrangements. Staff can fix tyres and help with minor emergency repairs. For anything major, your car will need to go to Derby or Kununurra on the back of a truck, which can easily cost $1000 or more.

To check on road conditions throughout the Kimberley, contact Main Roads WA

(☎ 1800 013 314, W www.mrwa.wa.gov
.au) or the department's offices at Kununurra
(☎ 08-9168 1755) and Derby (☎ 08-9191
1133). Alternatively, you could check with
the police stations at Derby, Kununurra or
Wyndham (see Emergency) or the visitor
centres (see Visitor Centres earlier).

The country dries out very quickly after
the wet-season rains and water can be scarce
along the way. Those contemplating walking or riding the route, please take note!

Fuel is available at Imintji (diesel), Mt
Barnett (diesel, unleaded and super) and El
Questro (diesel and unleaded), and along the
Kalumburu Road (see Detours later in this
section) at Drysdale (diesel, unleaded and
super) and Kalumburu (diesel, unleaded and
super). Motorcyclists in particular may need
to carry extra fuel if they don't want to
detour into El Questro. Note that the other
properties in the region, even if they cater for
tourists, are not allowed to sell fuel from
drums, though they may be able to help if it's
a real emergency and not just bad planning.

THE ROUTE

For the best views and lighting conditions
it's best to drive the Gibb River Rd from the
Kununurra end, and this is the way we've
described the trip.

Kununurra

The township of Kununurra is 45km from
the border of Western Australia and the
Northern Territory and owes its existence to
the construction of the Ord Dam in the 1950s
and 1960s. It is the Kimberley's most verdant
town, literally awash with green for most of
the year, courtesy of the nearby dams.

Today, Kununurra's population owes its
living not only to the irrigation area along
the river but also to the wealth of minerals
in the region (diamonds inland, oil and gas
offshore).

Via Hwy 1, Kununurra is 825km from
Darwin, 360km from Halls Creek and
1062km from Broome. It has good facilities
– everything the traveller needs, from camping and caravan parks to hotels and motels.

The town makes a good base for exploring the surrounding area, and you could join

in the fun at the many local festivals such as
the Ord River Festival or the Bushman's
Rodeo. Paddle a canoe on the Ord or go
fishing for the elusive barra, either on your
own or with the help of a guide. A couple of
national parks and nature reserves in the
area are also worth checking.

Mirima (Hidden Valley) National Park

On the edge of town, this small park
protects some Bungle Bungle–style rock
formations among a maze of cul-de-sacs,
amphitheatres and twisting, sheer-sided
valleys. There are examples of Aboriginal
art in some of the overhangs, but they're not
as spectacular as those found in other
galleries deeper in the Kimberley.

Animal life includes dingoes, agile wallabies, echidnas and a number of bats. Birds
are the most obvious and there are numerous
birds of prey, finches, pigeons and parrots.

The best way to see the park is on foot,
and a number of walks to good lookouts and
points of interest (up to 1km long) have
been established. An entry fee of $9 per ve-
hicle applies.

Ord River

There are two dams on the Ord
River. The first, just out of town where Hwy
1 crosses this mighty river, is the Diversion
Dam, holding back the waters of Lake
Kununurra. The main dam is 74km away,
via a good bitumen road, and its wall holds
back the waters of **Lake Argyle**. It makes an
enjoyable day trip, but if you have a boat or

KATE NOLAN

Echidna

a canoe or enjoy a spot of fishing, you can make something more of it (see Canoeing & Boating in the Activities section later).

Kununurra to Gibb River-Kalumburu Road (294km)

Heading west along the bitumen on Hwy 1 makes an easy start to this trip. A major road junction 45km west of Kununurra has you heading towards Wyndham and leaving Hwy 1 (the road to Halls Creek, Derby and Broome).

Seven kilometres north-west of this junction, a signposted dirt road turns off to the left (west). This is the start of the Gibb River Rd.

If, instead of turning left onto the Gibb River Rd, you continue straight ahead, you will reach **Wyndham**, 48km up the road. Despite Kununurra's size and importance, Wyndham is still the official centre for the huge Shire of East Kimberley. You may want to visit this historic port while you are in the area (see Detours later in this section).

Initially, the Gibb River Rd is well maintained and crosses the **King River** 17km from the highway. This river crossing is usually dry, except for during the wet season and two months into the Dry. The impressive ramparts of Mt Cockburn South can be seen to the north. In fact, for the next 50km, there are expansive views of the **Cockburn Range** and its towering cliffs of red, raw rock. In the evening light it is dramatically impressive.

The turn-off to **Emma Gorge** is another 7km along the road. This is part of El Questro Wilderness Park. At the Emma Gorge Resort you can pamper yourself, or you can just drive the 2km off the Gibb River Rd to the carpark, walk into the gorge and have a swim, but it will cost you $5.50 per adult. The resort is near the gorge, with a range of bush cabins, a bar and a shop.

The main access track into **El Questro Wilderness Park** is 10km further along the Gibb River Rd. This cattle station, 17km off the main road, takes in over 400,000 hectares of typically rough, broken Kimberley cattle country and has opened its doors to tourism in a big way. Camping is available along the Pentecost River or you

can stay in more luxurious accommodation – in fact, fancier accommodation in the Kimberley would be hard to find. Fishing, horse rides, boat trips and helicopter flights are all on the agenda. See Facilities later in this section for more information.

Until recently, El Questro Wilderness Park was known as El Questro station. It's still a working cattle station (with its distinctive 'ELQ' brand) but now caters for tourism in a major way with a staff of over 50 people. The over-the-top catering and general hype are not to everyone's liking, but there's no denying that the million-acre property has some stunning scenery and lovely walks, and provides a good summary of the beauty and joys of the Kimberley.

The **Pentecost River** is crossed 58km from the main highway. The causeway looks a bit daunting, especially early in the dry season when the water flows fast, but the foundation consists of firmly packed rocks and it's usually not a problem. There's good fishing downstream on the eastern bank of the river, but saltwater crocs inhabit the area so don't go swimming.

For the next kilometre or so, the road parallels the Pentecost River and on a sweeping corner just 9km from the crossing, a track leads off to the right to **Home Valley** homestead. Visitors are welcome and you can camp or be accommodated here (see Facilities).

Back on the road again, the route climbs the range. Near the top, 2km from the turn-off to Home Valley, a **lookout** gives an expansive view of the entire Cockburn Range. This is a top spot to sit on a cooling Kimberley evening, having a cold beer and enjoying the changing hues of the cliffs. From here you can also see, to the north, the twin Pentecost and Durack Rivers, as well as the West Arm of Cambridge Gulf.

Twelve kilometres further is a good *camping spot*. A track on the right leads down to a small camp beside a watercourse that generally has some water in it. There's only a little shade, but for an overnight camp it's fine.

Bindoola Creek is crossed for the first time just over 5km further and a second time 18km after. Both crossings are generally dry and present no problems.

After climbing Gregory's Jump-up at the 122km mark, it's just 3km to the turn-off for **Jack's Waterhole**. The waterhole (actually a billabong), once part of Durack River station, is less than 1km off the main road. Camping along the river is superb and you can fish, swim or canoe. Overnight accommodation and meals are also available, as are limited supplies (see Facilities).

Nearly 4km from the turn-off to Jack's Waterhole is the track to the abandoned **Karunjie** station. Durack River, Home Valley and Karunjie used to belong to the Sinnamon family but are now owned by the Indigenous Land Corporation.

From this junction, the road continues to be rough and stony – spare your tyres by taking it easy. For most of the time, the road winds across flat ground, occasionally climbing a jump-up or escarpment, where the going gets rockier and rougher. After a time on this plateau country, the road descends, via another jump up, to a flat or creek bed. This country is extremely harsh and unforgiving. Water is scarce between the rivers at any time, except during and straight after the Wet.

The **Durack River** is crossed 155km from the bitumen, just 27km past Jack's Waterhole turn-off. It's a wide crossing between quite high banks but is generally no problem. A number of tracks on both banks lead to camping spots up and downstream and there are some nice waterholes in both directions.

The main track to **Ellenbrae** homestead is passed just over 20km further on. Pleasant camping and accommodation are available here.

Dawn Creek is crossed 4km further and here you will find a reasonable camp site and permanent water down to the right. After another 24km of rock and dirt road, a track heads off to the right. Just 100m along this track is a good camp site on the Campbell River that comes with its own shade and water. Walkers and cyclists will appreciate both!

Just before the crossing of Russ Creek, 20km from the Campbell River camp, a track leads off to the right from the Gibb River Rd to a fair camp.

At the 242km mark from the highway (294km from Kununurra), 23km from the Russ Creek crossing, there's a major road junction. To continue on the Gibb River Rd, turn left. For a diversion to the Mitchell Plateau or the Aboriginal community at Kalumburu, turn right (see Detours later in this section). Both places are worthwhile, but if the Gibb River Rd is passable for a normal car during good times, the road to the Mitchell Plateau is definitely 4WD only and the road to Kalumburu is not much better.

Gibb River-Kalumburu Road to Derby (417km)

Veering left and continuing along the Gibb River Rd, you may notice an improvement in the road conditions if the grader has been out recently; if it's been a while, however, the road may be chopped up by the increased traffic that this section carries. By this time, if you have been crazy enough to tow a caravan along this road – and some people do – you'll be wishing you hadn't.

The track into Gibb River station is 40km from the Kalumburu junction and it's obvious from the sign on the front fence that they don't have fuel or supplies and want nothing to do with travellers.

Three kilometres further on is the Bryce Creek crossing and another 1.5km brings you to Mistake Creek. Generally both these waterways are as dry as a badger. Nine kilometres past the Mistake Creek crossing is the **Hann River** crossing. This is one of the major rivers in the central Kimberley and you are near its headwaters. The river often has water in it at the crossing. A couple of minor creek crossings follow.

Sixteen kilometres south of the Hann River you come to the turn-off to **Mt Elizabeth** station, run by the Lacy family. Their father pioneered this area in the 1920s and the family is keenly aware of the heritage, both Aboriginal and European, of this wild place.

The homestead is 30km from the main road, and accommodation and camping are available here. Booking is essential for accommodation and a phone call would be appreciated if you want to camp (see Facilities later in this section).

From the homestead, it's possible to travel to the remote western coast around the Walcott Inlet area, but you pay a fee to use the private road. This road is extremely rough and, unless you are experienced or travelling with others who are, it's not recommended. Bushtrack Safaris operate tag-along or fully organised tours out here – see Organised Tours later in this section. The Lacys offer plane trips to Walcott Inlet and also run 4WD day tours. They know the best art sites (some great Wandjina and Bradshaw figures) and the best fishing spots.

A little less than 10km down the main road from the turn-off to Mt Elizabeth is the track to **Barnett River Gorge**. This track heads west and winds around a little before getting to the river. The furthest point is about 4km from the main road but it's not the best camping spot, although the walking and river are excellent. A couple of earlier tracks that veer off this one give access to some exceptional camping. Across the river from the camping area, under an overhang, observant walkers will find some reasonable, but old and faint, Aboriginal art.

The Barnett River is crossed 27km further along the Gibb River Rd. It normally has water but is generally no problem for a 4WD.

On the right, 1km past the river crossing, is the turn-off to the **Mt Barnett Roadhouse** and camping area. The roadhouse dispenses fuel and all those things that hot, thirsty travellers love, such as ice creams. The camping down on the Manning River must be experienced to be fully appreciated – it's magic, though it can be crowded at times. Pay at the store to visit the gorge here ($5.50), even if you're not camping.

Spend some time lazing around the river – the sandy beaches, scattered rocks, cool water, sheer cliffs 100m upriver, shady trees and lily covered backwaters make this an idyllic spot. If you have a canoe, the waters of the river also make a pleasurable, gentle paddle. You can even snorkel in the **Lower Manning Gorge**.

There are some Aboriginal art sites around the area, which can be found on the opposite bank of the river at the end of the walking track.

A longer walk (about an hour each way) takes you to the **Upper Manning Gorge**. This track starts on the bank opposite the camping ground and cuts across country, following a marked trail of old drink cans hanging in trees, and the odd cairn.

The upper gorge has a small, sandy beach, but it's the waterfall and huge pool surrounded by cliffs that are the real attractions. Take lunch and spend the whole day up in the gorge – it's great.

Back on the Gibb River Rd and heading south, you pass, on your left, the Kupungarri Aboriginal community that owns Mt Barnett. The road improves from here; it's still stony dirt but the ridges of sharp rock jutting above the road surface that were so common north of Gibb River station have almost disappeared.

The turn-off to **Galvans Gorge** is 14km south of the roadhouse and the carpark is a few hundred metres in from there. A 10-minute walk takes you to the main pool and waterfall, a top swimming spot. A few harmless water goannas inhabit the pool. Beside the pool, in the shadiest part of the cliff-face, is a small sample of Aboriginal art, in this case a Wandjina head.

When the road passes the turn-off to Galvans Gorge, it begins to climb the Phillips Range. Over the next 10km there are good views of the surrounding country.

The Adcock River is crossed 13km from the Galvans Gorge track, and 5km further on, a track to the left leads off to **Adcock Gorge**. The 5km track into the gorge is pretty good, apart from the last few hundred metres. At the end is a small, idyllic camping area and the refreshing waters of the gorge. At the time of research, however, the camping area was closed because tourists had left too much mess. Whether it reopens remains to be seen.

Continuing along the main road, you cross a couple of minor creeks before coming to the turn-off to **Beverley Springs** station on your right, 49km south of the Mt Barnett Roadhouse. The homestead, 43km from the main road, offers accommodation, camping and tours in beautiful gorge country.

Just 4km past here and 160km from the Kalumburu junction, you will find the short access track to **Mt House** station on your left, a large, well-known Kimberley property that used to cater for tourists but now wants nothing to do with them. Travelling to the Old Mornington Bush Camp and the delightful Dimond and Sir John Gorges via Mt House is recommended (see Detours later in this section).

The first permanent water across the Gibb River Rd is to be found 25km south of the turn-off to Mt House. This is **Saddlers Spring**, and on the left, just 1km past the creek crossing, is the **Imintji Roadhouse** and Aboriginal community. Diesel and limited supplies are available here and camping is allowed at the creek. There's also a mobile mechanic (see the later Facilities section).

Some 8km west is the turn-off to **Bell Gorge**, probably the most scenic relatively accessible gorge in the heart of the Kimberley. The 30km run into the gorge is pretty reasonable and takes about an hour.

The access track parallels the northern face of the rugged **King Leopold Ranges**, coming to the camping ground at **Silent Grove**, 19km from the turn-off. The route swings north soon afterwards, before reaching and running beside Bell Creek. There are some excellent designated camping sights here. The shady trees and pandanus palms make a verdant scene, the canoeing and swimming are very enjoyable and you can wet a line for some sooty grunters or black bream, which make a great meal. Less than 4km on, the track ends beside a large boab tree with a bell carved into its trunk.

From this spot, a walking trail heads north a few hundred metres to the lip of one of the most spectacular waterfalls and gorges in the Kimberley, formed as the river slashes its way through the Isdell Range. Spend a bit of time enjoying the scenery, exploring the falls and the surrounding area.

This area was once a part of Mt Hart station and is now part of the King Leopold National Park, along with the station and the Lennard River Gorge.

About 4km from the Bell Gorge junction, the road turns to bitumen for a few kilometres and begins a long climb of the King Leopold Ranges. As the route winds its way up the battlements, it affords some good views of the surrounding area.

Over the next 10km, the road crosses a number of small creeks before coming to **Dog Chain Creek**, 21km south of the Bell Gorge turn-off. The road continues through range-country, and just over 2km from Dog Chain Creek, there's a major road junction with a good dirt road heading off to the left. This is the Millie Windie Rd. Two hundred metres along this road, a lesser track heads south into **Lennard River Gorge**.

It's about a 7km drive into the carpark that provides access to the gorge. The road is often very rough, passable only to 4WDs, but the drive and the walk down the hill to the gorge rim are worth it. A trail marked by some small cairns leads down to the water at one end of the gorge. Here, in the heat of the Dry, it is cool, and the deep, dark water always refreshing.

Seven kilometres south of the Lennard turn-off, a track heads off to the right to **Mt Hart Wilderness Lodge** (☎ *08-9191 4645*), formerly Mt Hart homestead, in the heart of the King Leopold National Park, some 50km from the Gibb River Rd. Upmarket accommodation is available (pre-booked only) but no camping.

A few hundred metres past this junction, the road crosses Apex Creek, which has a small camping area on its banks just after the crossing. Less than 1.5km later, pass through **Inglis Gap**; a small parking area on the left gives extensive views of the surrounding plains and ranges. From here, descend the final ramparts of the King Leopolds and head across rocky and undulating country towards the Napier Range, the final barrier before reaching the flat plains that border the great rivers of the western Kimberley.

The road gets better all the time. There are a few minor creek crossings in the next 40km but most of them are bridged. The turn-off to Napier Downs station is 278km from the Kalumburu junction and 53km south of Inglis Gap.

You begin to pass through Yammera Gap just 500m from the turn-off to Napier

Downs. This short pass leads through the **Napier Range**, a sheer-sided limestone range that was a coral reef millions of years ago. As you approach the gap, look out for Queen Victoria's Head on the right-hand side.

The Lennard River is crossed 9km south of the pass, and a track on the southern side of the river leads a few hundred metres west to a pleasant camp close to the stream.

Just 400m further is the **Windjana Gorge** turn-off, 21km from the Gibb River Rd, and **Tunnel Creek**, 35km further on from there. This road also leads another 68km east and joins the main highway, 43km west of Fitzroy Crossing.

Windjana Gorge is perhaps the best place in all of Australia to see freshwater crocodiles in their natural environment. Both Windjana Gorge and Tunnel Creek are national parks, but only the former allows camping ($9). Contact the ranger on arrival, or, if you're coming in a large group, CALM (☎ 08-9192 1036, fax 9193 5027) in Broome. Neither should be missed (see the Walking section under Activities later).

Once south of the Napier Range, the road passes through flat, lightly treed, pastoral country. The turn-off to Kimberley Downs station is 46km from the road junction to Windjana Gorge and the bitumen begins about 8km after the Kimberley Downs turn-off. You'll appreciate it!

The turn-off to Meda station and the **May River** is 39km further on. The access track to the homestead comes close to the May River after 6km. It's a popular spot with the locals and a good fishing area, but be careful where you swim: Big saltwater crocodiles have been seen there.

Back on the main road, a major T-junction is reached 36km beyond the May River turn-off; to the right is Derby and you'll hit the outskirts in less than 4km (it's about 7km to the centre of town). You're 416km from the Kalumburu junction and 710km from the green town of Kununurra.

Derby

Derby lies just above the high-tide mark on an ancient sandhill in King Sound, just north of the Fitzroy River mouth. Mud flats surround the town on three sides, subject to the highest tidal range in Australia (up to 11m). Derby may lack the all-season green of Kununurra and the razzmatazz of cosmopolitan Broome, but it's an honest and friendly place.

Derby was officially proclaimed in 1883, a couple of years after George Patterson founded Yeeda station on the banks of the Fitzroy River, 50km south. By 1890, the town boasted a jetty (used for the shipping of wool), a resident magistrate and a police force.

European settlement in the eastern Kimberley had been based on cattle brought overland from Queensland, but the western Kimberley was opened up by sheep graziers bringing their flocks from the south. By the mid-1890s, sheep swarmed over the flat plains, right up to the sheer rock walls of the Napier Range.

The local Aboriginal people resisted the white invasion and took to spearing European stock as a way of supplementing their food supply. During this time an Aborigine called Jandamarra, known to the whites as 'Pigeon', led a revolt that lasted for three years before he was killed near Tunnel Creek. The **Pigeon Heritage Trail** starts in Derby and takes in the cemetery where Pigeon's first victim is buried, plus the gaol and the **Prison Tree**. From there it leads out to Windjana Gorge and the ruins of Lillimilura (once a police post where Pigeon claimed his first victims), and on to Tunnel Creek where the final chapter was played out.

Apart from the heritage trail, there's also **Myall's Bore** next to the Prison Tree, said to be the longest cattle trough in the southern hemisphere (wow!), and **Wharfingers House**, which houses the local museum.

Derby is a good base for exploring the general area – it promotes itself as the 'Gateway to the Gorges and the Buccaneer Archipelago'. You can take a scenic flight over the coast and islands and the so-called **Horizontal Waterfall**, a 30m gorge at Talbot Bay where the tide squeezes through at a rate of 30 knots. Other tours include one around town, and day tours to Windjana

Fitzroy River Fishing

The Kimberley has the most spectacular and rugged coastline in Australia. The scenery is awe-inspiring and the fishing is fantastic, not only along the coast but also the inland rivers.

The Fitzroy River comes near the top of the list, helped by the very pleasant camping. There are several areas where you can indulge in both on the banks near Derby (ask at the visitor centre); elsewhere the river banks are off limits because most of the river downstream from Fitzroy Crossing is within the Noogoora burr quarantine area.

The most accessible area takes up the southern bank downstream from Willare Bridge, where Hwy 1 crosses the Fitzroy River, 58km south of Derby. The roadhouse (☎ 08-9191 4775) there offers accommodation and camping, and has a licensed restaurant. Fishing is popular among the trees within the first few hundred metres of the bridge, but there are spots all the way downstream to the old highway route at Langey Crossing – ask at the roadhouse.

For instance, cross Willare Bridge in the direction of Broome and turn right onto the dirt road at the first cattle grid. After a couple of kilometres, turn left at the Y-junction and keep going for a few kilometres: this takes you to a beach on the river with some superb camping and fishing, but beware of crocodiles. Don't leave rubbish, be careful with campfires, and seek permission from the owner of Yeeda station (☎ 08-9191 4766) for stays of more than one night.

If you're serious, other places to camp and fish are: downstream from Fitzroy Crossing to a point adjacent to Alligator Hill, about 10km south of the Fitzroy Bridge; east of Liveringa station, along the Camballin-Noonkanbah Rd; at Fitzroy Weir, 155km south-east of Derby; and at Myroodah Crossing just south of Liveringa, 120km from Derby.

Gorge and Tunnel Creek. Longer tours in 4WD vehicles are also available or you can hire vehicles from the local Avis and Budget dealers.

There is some excellent **fishing** from riverbank, jetty or boat. Boat-fishers will have more luck because they'll be able to access more places, including the offshore islands. Barra is prized, but many other species fight just as hard and are equally tasty. Threadfin salmon, sawfish, tarpon, catfish and sooty grunters are just some you can catch from the shore; boaties may get into queenfish or Spanish mackerel.

The jetty is a good spot to cast a line or net for mud crabs, but it also boasts the best fish and chips in Australia: a small restaurant beside the jetty caters for takeaways and sit-down meals.

Offshore are the 'Iron Islands' of Cockatoo and Koolan. **Cockatoo Island** has fishing and accommodation. The scenery is quite different from that inland but it's typical of the wild Kimberley coast.

Finally, Derby has some festivals that add so much to anyone's trip through the bush: the Boab Festival in July, with country music, a mardi gras, rodeo and more; the Derby Race horse race meeting in June; and, on 26 December, the annual Boxing Day Sports, just a little different to your normal sports day.

The town can provide all a traveller requires – see the later Facilities section. From Derby, it is just 222km to the bright lights, golden beaches and trendy boutiques of Broome. If you want to head further south, you are a mere 2520km from Perth!

DETOURS
Gibb River Road to Wyndham

It's worth making a short detour to visit the historic town of Wyndham, an easy run on bitumen from the turn-off where the Gibb River Rd starts. Fifteen kilometres north from this junction, or 22km from Hwy 1, you come to **The Grotto**. This secluded spot, a short drive left of the road, offers a chance for a swim. Early in the Dry the falls may still be running, adding more charm to this rocky defile, immersed in the green of trees, ferns and palms.

The **old road** to Wyndham veers off to the right just metres north of here and heads across the flood plains to Alligator Hole, Marlgu Billabong and Parry's Lagoon. **Alligator Hole** is a fine swimming spot, oddly enough, and the latter two areas are ideal for bird-watching (see the following section on Wyndham). This dirt road joins the bitumen again 12km north of The Grotto turn-off. Wyndham is 14km further north.

Wyndham Wyndham, on the shores of Cambridge Gulf, is the northernmost town and harbour in Western Australia. It was founded in 1886 to supply the cattle stations that were being established in the region and to allow easier access to the gold fields at Halls Creek.

In 1919, the meatworks opened and this enterprise kept the town going over the next 60 years. The factory closed down in the late 1980s and was gutted by fire soon afterwards.

Wyndham's proximity to South-East Asia meant that many great aviators, setting world air endurance records, passed through the town during the 1920s and '30s. The Ord River Dam revitalised the area in the 1960s, while in the late '70s, offshore gas, oil and mineral finds farther south maintained the impetus.

Much of the original character of the town has been retained, no doubt due to the fact that the old (port) area is 5km away from the newer hub of town, also known as Three Mile.

Wyndham has most of the facilities a traveller might need (see Facilities later in this section); there is also a hospital and police station.

In August, Wyndham stages its Top of the West festival, with 10 days of revelry, as well as a music festival, a gymkhana and the Wyndham Cup race meeting. If you can find accommodation then, it's a good time to be there.

Check the local **old port area**, which still reeks of the days when horses and carts rattled down the street and pioneers such as 'Patsy' Durack from Argyle station came into town. The three **old cemeteries** are also poignant reminders of days gone by, as is the

Boab Prison Tree found along the Karunjie Rd, just after it turns off the Moochalabra Dam Rd, 30km from Wyndham.

The **Moochalabra Dam** is Wyndham's main water supply and a pleasant picnic spot. There are also some Aboriginal rock paintings in the overhangs along the tall cliffs on your right, just before the picnic area.

One place not to miss is **Five Rivers Lookout**. From this spot above the old port area, you have a grand view of the old town, Cambridge Gulf and the rivers that feed it. The view is best in the morning. To the north is the mouth of the mighty Ord River, to the south are the King, Pentecost and Durack rivers, and to the west is the Forrest River.

The fishing is brilliant around Wyndham, and those with a boat will find it a mecca. Land-based fishers can try the wharf at the old port or any of the rivers in the area. The road out to the dam gives good access to the King River, which is a fine spot for barra. Otherwise, you can charter a boat for some fishing further afield.

If you enjoy bird-watching, the place to go is the **Parry's Lagoon Nature Reserve**. To get there, head south along the bitumen for 14km before turning left onto the unsealed Old Halls Creek Rd, which heads east across the flood plains of the Ord River. Parry's Lagoon, Marlgu Billabong and Police Hole hold water long after the dry season bleaches the rest of the plain a dusty gold. The birdlife is fantastic – right up there with Kakadu and far less crowded with tourists. Excellent camping and accommodation are available at Parry's Creek Farm (see Wyndham in the Facilities entry later in this section).

You can continue along this back road to Kununurra; it's a bit rough in places but usually OK for a 2WD driven with care. By all means visit **Black Rock Pool** (clearly signposted about 30km from Kununurra), one of the most impressive hidden waterholes in the Kimberley. A turn-off, shortly after, to the right takes you to the sealed Victoria Hwy and on to Kununurra. Straight ahead leads to **Ivanhoe Crossing** over the Ord River just north of Kununurra, which can be impassable well into the Dry, even to the most expert four-wheel-drivers.

The north-west is adventure country, with its lonely beaches, rugged Kimberley and Pilbara regions, vast and desolate Great Sandy Desert, and red-cliffed coastlines. Towns are few and far between. Most famous is Broome, with its colourful past as a pearl capital.

Looks different in an atlas: the North West 26th parallel – Western Australia (1). Frilled lizard (Chlamydosaurus kingii) – Kimberleys, Western Australia (2). The Purnululu (Bungle Bungle) National Park is an impressive rock formation 350 million years old – Western Australia (3). Pin cushion hakea grows wild in Western Australia (4). William Ramsay and his mates, from the Juwulinypany Aboriginal community, practise on a 44 – gallon drum for the forthcoming rodeo (5). Cockburn Range – Kimberley, Western Australia (6).

DIANA MAYFIELD

MARTIN COHEN

RICHARD I'ANSON

MITCH REARDON

RICHARD I'ANSON

JOHN HAY

The north-west roads are mostly for experienced outback motorists. It's a challenge to negotiate the Canning Stock Route or the Gibb River Road, which cut through the desert and the Kimberley. There are a few sealed roads and there's a range of scenic flights, 4WD tag-alongs and organised tours to the extraordinary sights in the region.

The heart of iron ore country – Karijini National Park, Western Australia (1). Major Mitchell Cockatoos – south-west Western Australia (2). Layers of ancient rocks: 120 million-year-old dinosaur tracks are visible at low tide – at Gantheaume Point, Broome (3). Large-blotched python (Stimsons, Pythonidae) – Kimberley, Western Australia (4). The Pinnacles in the early morning light – Nambung National Park, Western Australia (5). Four-wheel drive running a sand dune – Western Australia (6).

DIANA MAYFIELD

MARTIN COHEN

JOHN HAY

JASON EDWARDS

CHRIS MELLOR

COLIN K BARNES

Gibb River-Kalumburu Road

The road to the Mitchell Plateau and Kalumburu leaves Gibb River Rd 40km north of the turn-off into Gibb River station. There's an immediate decrease in the standard of the road and it certainly doesn't get any better – this is 4WD territory. The route north is nearly always closed for a few months of the wet season and even after the rains have stopped, no vehicles move across the black-soil plains for another month or so.

Drysdale River station (☎ 08-9161 4326), 58km north of the road junction, has fuel, limited supplies and accommodation. River-bank camping is also available close by.

Beyond here, the road continues to be rough and can be really chopped up at times. At the 102km mark north of Drysdale River is the turn-off to Mitchell Plateau, an interesting and enjoyable side trip.

Mitchell Plateau This plateau offers excellent scenery, good camping, a chance to get to the coast, and a good opportunity to see some fine Aboriginal art.

About 6.5km north-west from the junction is the **King Edward River**; across the river, there are some excellent camping spots close its banks. Swimming is very pleasant here and when walking walk upstream, the observant will find some exceptional art sites – some of the best in the Kimberley.

As the track continues it can become even rougher, depending on the previous wet season. About 15km from the river crossing, you climb up onto the plateau and begin to see the striking fan palms that are so distinctive in this area.

Nearly 71km from the turn-off from the Kalumburu road is the turn-off to **Mitchell Falls**. The Mitchell Falls track terminates 15km from the turn-off, at Mertens Creek. There is a small camping area with no facilities, although during the tourist season a helicopter operation is normally based there, offering scenic flights over the falls and the surrounding area (recommended, and surprisingly cheap if you can get a few people together).

From the camping ground, it's a half-hour walk to **Little Mertens Falls**. Ten minutes later is the spectacular **Big Mertens Falls**, and another 10 minutes will bring you to Mitchell Falls. You'll find some good Aboriginal art and spectacular scenery along the way and the water is delightful – take your bathers. Wear good, solid shoes, take a water bottle and be careful as the track isn't always easy to follow and the walk can be strenuous. Alternatively, take a $50 chopper ride, ask to be dropped off at the pool at the top of Mitchell Falls, and enjoy every leisurely minute of your visit.

Back on the main track heading north from the Mitchell Falls turn-off, it's 21km to the turn-off to **Surveyor's Pool**. The side track will take you nearly 7km west and then you need to walk another 4km to the pools. It's a top spot, but lacks the dramatic scenery of the Mitchell Falls walk.

Continuing farther north, the track leads to **Crystal Creek** and the nearby, mangrove-lined bay or into **Port Warrender**, a total of around 43km from Mitchell Falls junction. The tracks to either spot can be extremely bad – the track to Port Warrender can have 3m to 6m washaways in it, at which times it is, of course, impassable.

Drysdale River National Park Heading north to Kalumburu from the Mitchell Plateau turn-off, the road continues as before. **Theda** station (no tourist access) is passed 35km north (195km from the Gibb River Rd) and another 46km brings you to the **Carson River** crossing, which is another good spot to camp.

From here, a track leads to Carson River homestead (no facilities) and into Drysdale River National Park. This is one of the most remote parks in Australia and is only for experienced hikers – there are no roads, no marked trails, no facilities, no nothing. It includes rugged gorges, cliffs, waterfalls, pockets of rainforest and open woodland, and would be quite an experience if you could get in and see it. Unfortunately, at the time of research it was completely off limits as ownership and access issues were being sorted out. Contact the CALM office in Kununurra (☎ 08-9168 4200) for updates and information about access permits.

Kalumburu Twenty kilometres up the road from the Carson River crossing, enter the friendly Kalumburu Aboriginal community. You need a permit to enter – on arrival, visit the Kalumburu Community Council office (☎ 08-9161 4300, Mon-Fri 7am-noon) or the general store. Admission is $25 per vehicle, with an additional charge for a camping permit.

Visitors are welcome, but you are asked to respect the community's privacy and follow the rules and guidelines, the most important being no entry to the reserve without a permit and no alcohol brought in. You can purchase limited food supplies at the *general store (open Mon-Sat 8.30am-10.50am, and Wed, Thur & Fri 1.30pm-3.50pm Mon, closed Sunday)*. There's a little cafe and fuel (unleaded, super and diesel) is available from the *service station (open Mon-Sat 7am-11am, Mon-Fri 1.30pm-4pm, closed Sunday)*. Travellers should also note that repair facilities are very limited and virtually no spare parts are available. Cash only is accepted as payment.

Camping is possible at the reserve or along the coast at **McGowans Island Beach** and **Honeymoon Bay**. The latter two spots (with showers and toilets) offer excellent fishing but beware of crocodiles: there are some monsters in the area. If you don't have your own boat, it's possible to hire a fishing guide and equipment – ask at the store. Other attractions in Kalumburu include the **mission compound** itself, a surprisingly interesting **museum**, and the abandoned mission ruins, 25km out at **Pago**.

The Kalumburu Mission (☎ 08-9161 4333) has a licensed airstrip and there are no landing fees, though you're required to pay the normal visitor's fees to enter the community. Those wanting aviation fuel can arrange it through the mission – let them know in advance.

Gibb River Road to Old Mornington Bush Camp

This route leads east from the Gibb River Rd from the Mt House homestead turn-off, 53km south of the roadhouse at Mt Barnett, to the small camping resort at Old Mornington Bush Camp, 90km from the road junction.

Less than 10km from the Gibb River Rd you veer right to Old Mornington (left leads to the Mt House homestead, closed to visitors). About 53km from the main road another junction demands you veer right again and just over 10km later you pass the site of the old **Glenroy Meatworks**, a failed scheme that tried to fly processed meat out of the central Kimberley in the 1950s.

The ruins of the original **Glenroy** homestead are passed another 7km further south, and here the road deteriorates into a rough, single-lane track for the final 21km to the **Old Mornington Bush Camp** (☎ 08-9191 7046). You can camp here ($10 per person) or be accommodated in the permanent tents along the edge of a small, delightful creek with some interesting birdlife. There's a licensed *bar* (a big drawcard in these parts, especially its attempt at a wine collection!) and meals can be provided by arrangement.

Stockmen from nearby Mornington station used to camp here during cattle mustering. The station is now owned by the Australian Wildlife Conservancy, which is committed to preserving the area in its natural state (the remaining cattle will probably be moved out soon). At 3100 sq km, it's the largest non-government eco-sanctuary in the world. Mornington's former owner, Michael Curr, still runs the bush camp under contract. He's quite a character and a raconteur in the best outback tradition, who or will tell you all about life in the Kimberley past and present: 'I tell ya what, when I used to camp here during mustering with two white fellas and 10 Aborigines, I never once imagined I'd end up as a purveyor of fine wines to tourists!'

From here, travel 14km to **Sir John Gorge** on the Fitzroy River, or 24km to **Dimond Gorge** farther downstream. Both are magnificent places to visit. Access to the gorges is only possible by staying at the camp. There are a limited number of canoes for hire in Dimond Gorge ($40 for the day, booked at the camp) and you'll have the gorge pretty much to yourself – unforgettable.

ALTERNATIVE ROUTES

If you've been visiting Wyndham (see Detours earlier in this section, which includes information on the enjoyable back road between Wyndham and Kununurra), you can pick up the Gibb River Rd where it crosses the Pentecost River. Head back out of town the way you came for 6km to the airport and the signposted road to Moochalabra Dam. The road turns right, off the bitumen (when coming from town).

The turn-off to **Moochalabra Dam** is 19km further. Turning left here will take you to the dam and some Aboriginal art. Continuing straight ahead, there are some camp sites off to your right as you parallel the King River. Five kilometres past the dam turn-off, you will come to the **Boab Prison Tree**, once used by police patrols to hold their prisoners; it's a better example than the famed one at Derby.

Over the next few kilometres the road twists and turns through a few junctions, with few (if any) being signposted. Nine hundred metres from the Boab Prison Tree, turn right, then after 2.1km, turn left. Turn left again, 1.7km after this junction, and pass through a gate. You have covered just 35km from Wyndham.

You are now on the **Old Karunjie Track** and the route is now fairly plain to follow. Stick to the main track, which swings in a large arc around the great red massif of the Cockburn Range. Minor tracks spear off the main one, heading across the salt plains to the West Arm of Cambridge Gulf and some fishing spots. Be careful – get bogged out here and you are in the diabolicals!

You come close to the **Pentecost River** 39km after you pass through the gate. There are a number of camp sites on your right but they are for dedicated fishers. There are numerous tracks in this area, but just keep heading south and you'll end up in the right place. Less than 8km after first seeing the river, you pass through another gate. Another 2km will see you at the Gibb River Rd, just before the crossing of the Pentecost River.

The distance from Wyndham via this rough route is 83km and you are just 58km from the main highway via the Gibb River Rd. From here on, it is the Gibb River Rd all the way to Derby.

ACTIVITIES

Walking, canoeing (and boating), fishing and bird-watching would have to be at the top of the list of things you can do on your own. For good fishing and bird-watching spots, see the earlier route descriptions, the boxed text on 'Fitzroy River Fishing', and Canoeing & Boating information following.

Walking

There are some excellent walks beginning just outside of Kununurra. **Mirima National Park**, on the outskirts of town, has two short, marked trails, but you can spend hours wandering through here.

If you camp in **El Questro Wilderness Park**, there are ample walks into some of the magnificent gorges in the area. With a mud map from the store you can enjoy walks to El Questro Gorge, Moonshine Gorge or Zebidee Springs. The latter should not be missed – the springs run with hot water, and the small thermal pools and waterfalls they form as they run down the escarpment are divine. Shaded by lush tropical growth, there is no better place to spend a hot Kimberley day.

Hike around **Jack's Waterhole** and enjoy the birdlife.

At the **Barnett River Gorge**, take the walk up or downstream along the river. The shallow cascades, the deep pools lined with pandanus palms and the birdlife are most enjoyable.

If you stop at Mount Barnett Roadhouse and camp down on Manning River, the **Lower Manning Gorge**, just a stone's throw from the camping area, is worth exploring. There is some Aboriginal art on the north bank, below the gorge. A longer walk (about an hour each way) up to **Upper Manning Gorge** allows you to explore the falls and gorge. This walk is across rocky ground that blasts the heat back into your face at any time apart from early morning and evening. Spend the day at the top end of the gorge – you won't be disappointed.

In 1992, an expedition led by Peter Treseder and supported in part by Australian Geographic, walked from Mount Barnett down the Isdell River, through all its gorges to the sea at Walcott Inlet. They used rubber rafts (carried in their backpacks) to get over large sections of water, before heading back up the Charnley River to Mount Elizabeth station. From there, it was down the Barnett River to where they had started.

Galvans, **Adcock** and **Bell Gorges**, farther south along the Gibb River Rd, all warrant a little exploration.

At **Windjana Gorge**, take a walk up the gorge below its towering, shady cliffs. It offers a great opportunity to see freshwater crocs in their natural environment and you can also spot some reef fossils. A wander through the range at **Tunnel Creek** will probably mean getting wet and you may even have to swim. Carry a torch, preferably one that keeps working if it's wet. The 750m walk through the range can take as little as one hour (return) but is much more enjoyable if you take a bit longer. The far end is worth more than an hour on its own.

Canoeing & Boating

Taking a canoe or small boat to the Kimberley adds yet another dimension to the adventure.

Chamberlain Gorge in El Questro Wilderness Park is ideal for both a canoe and a small boat but no petrol motors are allowed, so it's a paddle or an electric-motor job only. Be warned that saltwater crocodiles have been known to reside in this stretch of water. The waters of the **Lower Manning** and **Windjana Gorges** are really only suitable for a canoe. On waters such as **Jack's Waterhole**, only non-motorised craft are allowed.

The best canoeing and boating, though, is around **Kununurra**. The waters of Diversion Dam, just outside town, can handle quite large craft, as the ski jumps testify, while Lake Argyle is so big that it is classed as an inland sea and can be dangerous to canoes.

The shallow waterways that adjoin the open waters of Diversion Dam are locally called **The Everglades** and the area is ideal for canoeing and bird-watching. There are a couple of places to launch a small boat or canoe adjacent to the highway or the caravan parks that abut the waterway. An evening paddle is great, but take notice of where you paddle: after a couple of hours,

paddling between reeds and trees, you might have trouble finding your launching spot.

One of the best trips is down the **Ord River**, from just below the wall at Lake Argyle to Kununurra, at Diversion Dam. The 55km trip can be done with a small outboard-powered boat. For much of the way, the river is lined with dense stands of paperbarks, coolabahs and pandanus palms. Carlton Gorge is about 15km downriver from the launching spot and there are a couple of reasonable camp sites in the gorge on the left. At the 23km mark, a creek joins the Ord where there's another good camp. For the next 10km, there are a couple of good sites to stop overnight, but then the river runs into the top end of Diversion Dam and access to the bank is limited. The water also slows, so it's a paddle without a current to help for the last 20km to the dam wall near the highway.

The Western Australian Department of Sport & Recreation's *Canoeing Guide (No 10)* to this stretch of water is sometimes available in Kununurra.

ORGANISED TOURS

Numerous tour operators around Australia go to the Kimberley. However, there are quite a few local tour operators based in Kununurra, Wyndham, Derby and Broome (see the Broome section later in this chapter) who offer more detailed and/or extensive trips by land, sea or air (or a combination of the three). Contact the relevant visitor centres for complete listings and further advice.

Kununurra

Alligator Airways (☎ *1800 632 533, fax 08-9168 2704,* e *fly@alligatorairways.com.au,* w *www.alligatorairways.com.au*) Runs daily flights over the Bungles from $185 ($430 full day, including ground tour). Also six-hour Kimberley flights over King George Falls, Mitchell Falls and a stopover at Kalumburu ($396). Also offers float-plane fishing safaris.

Belray Diamond Tours (☎ *1800 632 533, fax 08-9168 2704,* w *www.alligatorairways .com.au/belray, PO Box 10, Kununurra, WA*

6743) Tours of the Argyle Diamond Mine south of Lake Argyle (the largest in the world, famous for its pink diamonds) from $170 (by road) up to $325 (full-day tour including flight over the Bungle Bungle)

Desert Inn 4WD Adventure *(☎ 08-9169 1257, fax 9168 2271,* e *kimberleybookings@ wn.com.au,* w *www.kimberleyadventure.com, PO Box 819, Kununurra, WA 6743)* Darwin to Broome, and then back via the Gibb River Rd (11 days), $1560. Also two- and three-day tours to the Bungle Bungle from Kununurra, starting at $290. Under the name of Kimberley Canoeing, it also organises one/two/three-day canoe tours down the Ord River for $105/155/135 (three-day is cheaper because there's no boat pick-up and you paddle all the way).

East Kimberley Tours *(☎ 08-9168 2213, fax 9168 2544,* e *ektown.com.au* w *www .eastkimberleytours.com, PO Box 537, Kununurra, WA 6743)* A wide range of guided tours and fly-drive packages, from a one-day express tour to the Bungle Bungle for $160, to a nine-day, all-in package including the Gibb River Rd, Mitchell Plateau and Bungles for $2595.

Slingair Heliwork *(☎ 08-9169 1300, fax 9168 1129,* e *booking@slingair.com.au,* w *www.slingair.com.au, PO Box 612, Kununurra, WA 6743)* Offers plane flights (from Kununurra) and helicopter flights (Bellburn Airstrip) over the Bungles for $176. From Warmun (Turkey Creek) $165. Many other services, including fly-drive tours and plane/helicopter combos throughout the Kimberley.

Triple J Tours *(☎ 08-9168 2682, fax 9168 2562,* e *jjjtours@kimberley.net.au, PO Box 105, Kununurra, WA 6743)* Ord River and Lake Argyle tours from $80 to $135.

Wyndham

Kimberley Dreamtime *(☎ 08-9161 1288, 0429 922 01)* Bush tucker, bush medicine and Aboriginal culture tours in the Wyndham area for $70 (half day) or $135 (full day) in groups of 2-6 people. Overnight tours of El Questro and the Pentecost River region ($270 from Wyndham, $295 from Kununurra).

Look Sea Tours *(☎/fax 08-9161 1775,* e *lookseatours@bigpond.com, PO Box 187, Wyndham, WA 6740)* Many different charters and scenic tours along the river and out to the Cambridge Gulf, eg, one-day fishing tours $240 (minimum 2 people).

Derby

Golden Eagle Airlines *(☎ 1800 066 132, fax 08-9191 1201,* w *www.goldeneagleairlines .com, PO Box 61, Derby, WA 6728)* Flights over the Buccaneer Archipelago and Horizontal Waterfall (1¾ hours, $160), including a stopover and meal at Cape Leveque (4½ hours, $240).

Buccaneer Sea Safaris *(☎/ fax 08-9191 1991, PO Box 532, Derby, WA 6728)* Extensive boat tours of the Buccaneer Archipelago from Cockatoo Island (connecting flights from Derby or Broome), ranging from three to 12 days for $290/day.

Bushtruck Safaris *(☎/fax 08-9191 1547,* e *ricannbt@comswest.net.au,* w *www.com swest.net.au/~ricannbt, PO Box 7, Derby, WA 6728)* Luxury camping safaris of the Kimberley, including Mitchell Plateau and remote Walcott Inlet. Prices range from $1482 (six days) to $3458 (14 days). Also tag-along tours to Walcott Inlet ($50/day).

FACILITIES

Many homesteads along the Gibb River Rd offer accommodation on a dinner, bed and breakfast (DB&B) basis. Join family, staff and guests and eat whatever the cook rustles up. Prior notice is appreciated for obvious reasons, though if you arrive before late afternoon it's usually not too much of a problem to fit you in. Alternatively, you can camp and do your own thing, or join in the evening meal if the cook has a bit of notice.

Kununurra

Kununurra is a major regional centre. The town boasts a large supermarket complex, general stores, chemists, a laundry, a bakery, butchers, fishing-tackle shops, service stations and fuel supplies, as well as LPG and major repair facilities. The BP depot, about 3km east of town on the Victoria Hwy, usually sells the cheapest fuel in town.

Kimberley Exhaust & Spring Centre (☎ 08-9169 1463, Mango St) is the local agency for the RAC of WA and also does towing.

The Commonwealth and BankWest banks have ATM facilities and there's a National Australia Bank branch.

There's a wide choice of accommodation. The caravan parks are all quite pleasant:

Kona Lakeside Tourist Park (☎ 08-9168 1031, Lakeview Dr) Camp sites $8.50 per person, van sites $19.50, on-site vans $55 per double, cabins from $72 per double. In a picturesque, leafy spot on the edge of Lake Kununurra, about 2km out of town.

Town Caravan Park (☎ 08-9168 1763, Bloodwood Dr) Powered camp sites $9 per person, doubles $22, on-site vans $70, en suite villa units $105 double. A shady park, well situated in the centre of town but can get crowded.

Ivanhoe Tourist Village (☎ 08-9169 1995, Coolibah Dr) Unpowered/powered sites $20/22 double, cabins $65-95. A little out of town but very clean with pleasant views.

Hidden Valley Caravan Park (☎ 08-9168 1790, Weaber Plains Rd) Camp sites $9 per person, powered camp sites $20 per double. This park borders the national park.

Kimberleyland Holiday Park (☎ 08-9168 1280, Victoria Hwy) Camp sites $9 per person, powered doubles $20, cabins $80-95 double but can sleep up to 4 ($7 per extra person). Pleasant spot on the banks of Lilly Creek Lagoon about 1km out of town.

Hostels include:

Kununurra Backpackers (☎ 1800 641 998, 08-9169 1998, fax 9168 3998, e backpack@adventure.kimberley.net.au, 22 Nutwood Cres) Dorm beds $18, twins/triples $23/18 per person (YHA/VIP discounts available). Facilities include a swimming pool, spa, kitchens and a laundry. Bike hire is available as well as 4WD tours to the Bungles and canoe tours down the Ord River.

Desert Inn Backpackers (☎ 08-9168 2702, e adventur@comswest.net.au, Cnr Konkerberry Dr & Tristana St) Dorm beds/quads/doubles $18/19/46 (YHA/VIP discounts available). The Desert Inn has a pool and communal kitchen, organises tours of the Kimberley and canoeing trips along

the Ord River, and has a free pick-up service at the Greyhound bus stop.

Hotels and guesthouses include:

Country Club Hotel (☎ 08-9168 1024, e cchotel@bigpond.com, 47 Coolibah Dr) Units with en suite from $158.60 double. A pleasant, resort-style place, with swimming pool and two air-con restaurants.

Lakeside Resort (☎ 08-9169 1092, Casuarina Way) Doubles from $152, $17 extra person. A quiet place on Lake Kununurra, in a suburb a little way out of the town centre.

Hotel Kununurra (☎ 08-9168 1344, Messmate Way) Singles $35-90, doubles $66-125. The oldest hotel in town, right in the centre of the action (such as it is). In need of maintenance but friendly enough.

Lakeview Apartments (☎ 9168 0000, e lakeviewapartments@wm.com.au, 224 Victoria Hwy) Single/triple serviced apartments $154/$242. New and very comfortable, with views over the lake.

Duncan House (☎ 08-9168 2436, Coolibah Dr) B&B singles/doubles from $105/125. Arguably one of the most pleasant and relaxing places in town; pamper yourself after roughing it in the bush.

Wyndham

Wyndham lacks the variety and number of services available at Kununurra but has a wide range of facilities, including a supermarket, general stores, a hardware store, a bakery, service stations, a post office, fuel supplies, even a cute little Internet cafe. The RAC of WA agency is Branko Motors (☎ 08-9161 1305).

Accommodation is fairly limited:

Wyndham Community Club (☎ 08-9161 1130, along the hwy about 3km out of Three Mile) Single/double/triple units $55/66/77. Nothing fancy, but clean and good value.

Wyndham Town Hotel (☎ 08-9161 1202, O'Donnell St in the old port area) Fully self-contained singles/doubles $55/110. The social centre of town – it doesn't get any livelier than this.

Gulf Breeze Guest House (☎ 08-9161 1401, O'Donnell St, entry via Foreshore Rd) Singles/doubles $30/50. This is a ramshackle place, in the old postmaster's house.

Three Mile Caravan Park (☎ 08-9161 1064, Baker St) Camp sites $8 per person, $3 for power, single/double air-con cabins $25/35. Close to the shops in the new part of town. Has a huge, cordoned-off boab tree, said to be Australia's largest 'in captivity'. Pleasant and quiet, but the sandflies on the north-western edge of the camp near the billabong can be fierce.

Parry's Creek Farm Tourist Resort (☎ 08-9161 1139, at Parry's Lagoon via a dirt road 20km south of town) Camping $8 per person, power $2 extra, rooms and cabins also available (DB&B). Restaurant and bar. A beautiful little oasis in the Parry's Lagoon area (ask for the secluded bird-watcher's camping place). A top spot.

Gibb River Road

Emma Gorge Resort (☎ 08-9161 4388, fax 9161 4034) Double/quad tented cabins with fan $133/198. Only 2km off the Gibb River Rd and a short walk from the gorge, it's part of El Questro Wilderness Park and has an airstrip nearby. Facilities include a restaurant, bar, reasonably well-stocked shop, laundry and a large swimming pool.

Travellers who want to explore Emma Gorge but aren't staying overnight pay a fee of $5.50, plus $12.50 for a seven-day Wilderness Park Permit, also valid for El Questro, and available at either resort. This is waived if you stay at either place except camping at El Questro.

El Questro Wilderness Park (☎ 08-9161 4318, fax 9161 4355, for bookings ☎ 08-9169 1777, fax 9169 1383, e sales@elquestro .com.au, PO Box 909, Kununurra, WA 6743) Luxury homestead accommodation with everything included: twin share/singles per person $825/1025, non-luxury bungalows (up to four people) $170. Camp sites (close to the facilities or more secluded along the beautiful Pentecost River) $12.50 per person (children under 12 free).

Breakfast, lunch and dinner are available in the Steakhouse. Other facilities include a well-stocked store selling diesel and unleaded fuel, garage/workshop and private airstrip for those wishing to fly in. There's a wide range of guided and self-guided tours and activities.

Home Valley Homestead (☎ 08-9161 4322, fax 9161 4322) DB&B rooms $85 per person, camp sites $8 per person – check in advance, as the setup is likely to change. This station is surrounded by some spectacular scenery. The camping is pleasant – go fishing and bushwalking (fine views) or simply enjoy the pool.

Jack's Waterhole (☎ 08-9161 4324) DB&B rooms $85 per person, camp sites $8 per person. It's one of the best places to camp along the Gibb River Rd, with toilets and hot shower facilities, and many people who turn up for the night end up staying a few days to canoe, swim, fish or walk. A store provides limited supplies, and minor emergency repairs can be made to your vehicle. Rather surprisingly, camel rides are also available, including overnight trips to Oomaloo Falls. One of the managers used to run camel safaris in the Simpson Desert and claims that camels are well suited to the Kimberley. In the Wet most of the area around the waterhole is under water, except for the toilet/shower block at the camp site.

Ellenbrae Homestead (☎ 08-9161 4325, PO Box 132, Kununurra, WA 6743) DB&B bungalows $125 per person, camp sites $10-14 per person. The more expensive camping ground has a secluded, open-plan living room that you'll never want to leave. Ellenbrae is totally solar-powered and very much in tune with the surrounding flora and fauna. Future plans include natural-health programs.

Mount Elizabeth Station (☎ 08-9191 4644, PMB via Derby, WA 6728) DB&B rooms twin-share $130 per person, camp sites $11 per person. Enjoy the Lacy family's hospitality, although the main reason for travelling 30km in from the Gibb River Rd is to join a scenic flight or one of the 4WD day tours. On either, there's some of the wildest, most remote country in the Kimberley and fine examples of Aboriginal art (Wandjina and Bradshaw). It's also a working cattle station where you can view the action if you arrive at the right time.

Mount Barnett Roadhouse (☎ 08-9191 7007, fax 9191 4692, PMB via Derby, WA 6728) Open 7am-5pm. This roadhouse and the beautiful Manning Gorge are both on Mount Barnett station, which is owned by the Kupungarri Aboriginal community. The roadhouse has a good range of food supplies, snacks and cool drinks and all fuels, but no LPG. The workshop can carry out limited tyre and mechanical repairs. At the roadhouse, get your permit to visit the gorge ($5.50). The pleasant *camping area ($8 per person)* beside Lower Manning Gorge is a delightful swimming spot, and has toilets and fireplaces.

Imintji Store (☎ 08-9191 7471) This fairly well-stocked general store, part of the Imintji Aboriginal community, has Eftpos facilities and sells diesel fuel only. The Safari Camp at nearby Saddlers Creek charges $79 per person DB&B. There's also a garage/workshop for minor vehicle repairs, along with a mobile mechanic and vehicle retrieval service called Over the Range Tyre & Mechanical Repairs (☎ 08-9191 7887, 0407 991 094).

Derby

Derby is one of the original towns of the Kimberley region and can supply all a traveller's requirements. There are a couple of supermarkets that operate seven days a week charging Perth prices, along with a chemist, butcher, bakery, hardware and fishing stores.

Two service stations supply all fuels and LPG: the BP Colac Roadhouse & Service Station (☎ 08-9191 1256) is the RAC of WA agent; the Shell service station on Clarendon St, called Derby Tyre & Exhaust Centre (☎ 08-9191 1020), has a good reputation for its Toyota repairs. There are several other automotive repair facilities available.

The ANZ Bank has full banking facilities and the post office has both Passbook and Keycard facilities for the Commonwealth Bank. BankWest also has an agency here.

However, accommodation is rather limited for such a developed town:

Kimberley Entrance Caravan Park (☎ 08-9193 1055, Rowan St) Single/double sites with power $15/21, tent sites $9 per person. There are discounts for stays of more than three days. Leashed dogs are allowed. It's the only caravan park in town so there's no point being picky, but we've seen better.

King Sound Resort Hotel (☎ 08-9193 1044, Loch St) Single/double units $110/126. Could be better at that price, though the budget twins at $66 are OK.

West Kimberley Lodge (☎ 08-9191 1031, Sutherland St) Singles/doubles from $60, family rooms $120. Peaceful spot in tropical surroundings, shared kitchen; not a bad choice.

Spinifex Hotel (☎ 08-9191 1233, Clarendon St) Dorm beds $20, singles/doubles from $50/75. Rather basic and noisy but the central location helps, with lots of Aussie character.

Derby Boab Inn (☎ 08-9191 1044, Loch St) Budget singles/doubles $77/93.50, deluxe doubles $110. A bit less central than the Spinifex, but quieter and with slightly better rooms.

Airstrips

There are public aerodromes at Derby, Kununurra and Wyndham. The latter two are owned and maintained by the Wyndham-East Kimberley Shire (☎ 08-9161 1002). Aviation fuel is readily available.

Throughout the Kimberley are small, privately owned and maintained airstrips on station properties. Aviation fuel can often be purchased but you need to give prior notice of your requirements.

ALTERNATIVE TRANSPORT
Air

A wide choice of aircraft charters operate all over the Kimberley – see the earlier Organised Tours section or contact the Derby or Kununurra visitor centres.

Both major towns used to have regular Ansett Australia commercial flights to and from Perth, but at the time of research the situation was up in the air (so to speak) with that company's troubles.

In the case of Derby, Skipper's Aviation in Broome (☎ 08-9192 2887) has daily scheduled flights to and from Broome (except Sunday) for $170/340 one-way/return. Bookings are handled by Travelworld in Derby (☎ 08-9193 1488).

In the case of Kununurra, Air North in Darwin (☎ 08-8945 2866) has daily flights to and from Darwin for $295-360 return, and to and from Broome for $360-480 return. Local air charter services link Kununurra and Wyndham.

The Ibis Aerial Hwy, run by Northwest Airlines (☎ 08-9192 1369, fax 9192 2476, e nwregair@wn.com.au) at Broome airport, is a unique tourist setup for those who want to fly around the Kimberley and see all the best-known places. It operates services six days a week between Broome, Port Hedland, Karratha, Fitzroy Crossing, Halls Creek and (twice a week) Exmouth.

Bus

Kununurra and Derby are serviced regularly by McCafferty's/Greyhound (☎ 13 20 30), though its buses follow Hwy 1 around the south of the Kimberley. Bookings can be made at the Kununurra visitor centre (☎ 08-9168 1177) on Coolibah Dr, and at Broome Travel (☎ 08-9192 1561) on Hamersley St.

Car Rental

A number of companies in the Kimberley rent 4WDs to travellers. Drivers usually need to be over 25 years of age. Some companies also offer camping-equipment packages with the hire of the vehicle. Avis has offices in Derby (☎ 08-9191 1357) and Kununurra (☎ 08-9168 1258). Hertz also has offices in Derby (☎ 08-9191 1348) and in Kununurra (☎ 08-9169 1424). See also the Broome section later in this chapter.

Purnululu (Bungle Bungle) National Park

The beehive formations of the Bungle Bungle massif and its surrounding national park are one of the Kimberley's major tourist attractions. Rated by many as the top scenic wonder of Western Australia, the Bungles are more often than not viewed from the air, with visitors taking a scenic flight from Kununurra, Warmun (Turkey Creek) or Halls Creek. For the traveller with a 4WD, the diversion off the main highway around Australia is well worthwhile and allows you to get among the formations.

Secluded by distance and the surrounding ranges, the Bungles remained hidden from prying eyes until 1982. Previously known only to a few drovers, helicopter pilots and local Aboriginal people, the area became an instant hit when it was featured in a television documentary on the scenic wonders of Western Australia.

In March 1987, the Purnululu (Bungle Bungle) National Park was gazetted (the Kija word *purnululu* means sandstone). The 3200 sq km conservation reserve includes several ecologies but the Bungle Bungle massif is the only place that is readily accessible to the public. The surrounding country along the Ord River is prone to severe erosion – the reason this area and much of the country in the headwaters of the Ord River and surrounding Lake Argyle were proclaimed water catchment reserves as far back as 1967.

Since the park's formation, basic camping facilities have been established at a couple of places close to the range, and there's a ranger station.

The park is closed over the Wet, generally from 1 January to 31 March, but earlier or later rains can still make the access track impassable.

Information

Visitor Centres The Halls Creek visitor centre (☎ 08-9168 6262), on the Great Northern Hwy, is open from June to October. The Shire of Halls Creek (☎ 08-9168 6007) may also have useful information.

In Kununurra, the visitor centre (☎ 08-9168 1177, fax 9168 2598) is at 75 Coolibah Dr, while the regional headquarters of CALM (☎ 08-9168 4200) is on Konkerberry Dr.

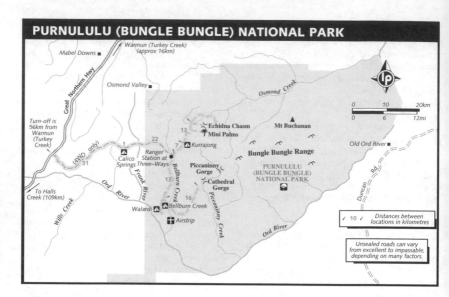

PURNULULU (BUNGLE BUNGLE) NATIONAL PARK

Another source of information is the Western Australian Tourist Centre (☎ 08-9483 1111) at 469 Wellington St, Perth.

Radio Frequencies It's not essential to have a HF radio for a trip into the Bungles. If you do have one, the frequencies required are the same as for the Gibb River Rd (see earlier).

Road Reports The track off the main highway into the national park has been realigned and upgraded in recent times but still remains a rough, dusty and rather tedious 4WD track, with a few potentially tricky creek crossings that can be fairly deep in water – motorcyclists may have to carry their gear across. Some 2WDs do make it in but they need good ground clearance and an experienced driver.

Books & Maps The best maps and books for the area are listed in the earlier Gibb River Rd section. Hema Maps also has a dedicated *Purnululu National Park* map.

Permits No permits are required to enter the park, other than an entrance and camping fee,

payable at the information bay adjacent to the ranger station near the 'beehives'. There are a couple of camping areas that have been set up with basic facilities. A day pass, payable for the first day, costs $8 per vehicle ($3 per motorcycle), with an additional camping fee of $9 per person per night.

Emergency There are hospitals at Halls Creek (☎ 08-9168 6002) and Kununurra (☎ 08-9168 1522). Police stations can also be found at Halls Creek (☎ 08-9168 6000) and Kununurra (☎ 08-9169 1122). There are also emergency services in Wyndham (see the earlier Gibb River Rd section).

THE ROUTE

From Kununurra, head west across the Ord River Diversion Dam wall to the intersection of Hwy 1 and the road to Wyndham, 45km from the town centre.

Turn left here and head down Hwy 1, admiring the great scenery of rolling hills and rugged mountain ranges. Initially, the Carr Boyd Range is off to the left (east), with the Durack Range far off to the west.

The **Durham River** crossing, about 35km south of the main road junction, offers a reasonable spot to camp, as does the Bow River rest area 95km further south.

Warmun (Turkey Creek) and its roadhouse are 151km south of the junction (196km from Kununurra).

Continuing south along the highway, the turn-off to Purnululu (Bungle Bungle) National Park is well signposted, 56km south of the roadhouse (or 108km north of Halls Creek). Turn left here onto a dirt road, which soon deteriorates into a dirt track. The information sign near the start is worth a read: it will let you know what the latest situation is with the track, camping in the park or whatever.

The first 40km of the east-bound track is across Mabel Downs station property and no diversions off it are allowed. Where there are private station tracks leading off from the main track, it is obvious (or marked) which track to stay on.

Calico Springs, 31km from the bitumen, is a popular camping and rest stop. Permission from the station owner is officially required to camp here but few people seem to bother. It's a top spot, with a couple of tall, rocky bluffs crowding in on a small area of flat land dotted with trees and palms. A small creek fed by the spring trickles through the gap in the range. With the shade and permanent cool water, it's a pleasant interlude from the dust and heat of the surrounding area.

The intersection known as **Three-Ways** is 53km from the bitumen and it is here that the ranger station (☎ 08-9168 7300) and the self-registration bay are located. The tedious drive in from the highway takes between 1½ and 3 hours. Fill in your visitor's form and from here you have a choice of places to go.

The *Kurrajong* camping area, 7km north, gives access to the western side of the Bungle Bungle range. This camping area has toilets, water and separate areas for campers with generators and those without.

This side of the range has a few gorges worth exploring, including Echidna Chasm, Frog Hole and Mini Palms. The walks are pleasant and less than 3km but do take water. Even if you are short of time, don't miss **Echidna Chasm**. As you progress up this gorge, it becomes narrower and narrower as the walls close in. Finally, it is just an arm-span wide and towers well over 100m upwards. It is a spectacular place.

The *Walardi* camping area is 13km south of the ranger station, and is just a little north of the *Bellburn Creek* camping area used by tour operators. Walardi is set up similarly to Kurrajong, with toilets and water as well as separate areas for groups and those with generators.

The Walardi and Bellburn camping areas give the easiest access to the southern section of the Bungle Bungle massif. From a track junction just north of the camp sites, it's a 16km drive to the end of the vehicle track. The last few hundred metres into the parking area can be tricky.

A 2km return walk to **Cathedral Gorge**, arguably one of Australia's most sensational and awe-inspiring natural wonders, takes you past spectacular domes and along an ever-narrowing ravine. Suddenly, around a corner, it opens up into a large amphitheatre. The walls encroach on all sides, a smallish patch of sky adding to the grandeur of this magical place. This sight makes the trek, and all the dust, worthwhile.

A much longer walk (30km return) leads to **Piccaninny Gorge**, farther north-east along the southern ramparts of the range.

About 5km from the Walardi camping area towards Cathedral Gorge is the airstrip and helipad. Scenic helicopter flights operate from here in the peak of the tourist season.

To return to the bitumen of the highway, retrace your steps.

ORGANISED TOURS

A number of tour operators around Australia and working out of Halls Creek and Kununurra, include the Bungles as a major destination in their trips around the Kimberley. For more information, see Organised Tours in the earlier Gibb River Rd section, contact the appropriate visitor centres or visit the Western Australian Tourist Centre.

Scenic Flights

Several scenic-flight operators are based in Halls Creek and Kununurra. See Organised Tours in the earlier Gibb River Rd section, or contact the Halls Creek or Kununurra visitor centres. Slingair Heliwork (see Organised Tours in the Gibb River Rd section) offers helicopter flights from Bellburn Airstrip in the park, or from Warmun (Turkey Creek).

FACILITIES

For full details on facilities at Halls Creek or Kununurra, see the earlier Gibb River Road section (for Kununurra) or the later Canning Stock Route section (for Halls Creek). Fuel and limited supplies are available at the *Warmun (Turkey Creek) roadhouse* (☎ 08-9168 7882), which has a camp site (dogs allowed) and accommodation.

Airstrips

Halls Creek and Warmun (Turkey Creek) have airstrips – contact the Halls Creek Shire Council (☎ 08-9168 6007) for details. Aviation fuel is readily available. Bellburn Airstrip in the park is normally not accessible to visitors, but ring CALM in Kununurra (☎ 08-9168 4200) to arrange advance permission and inquire about fuel.

Broome

Highlights

- Celebrating one of Broome's many annual festivals
- Discovering the town's colourful history
- Watching the stars under the stars at Sun Pictures outdoor cinema
- Enjoying beautiful Cable Beach after a long desert crossing

For many travellers, Broome is Australia's archetypal getaway: palm-fringed beaches, clear, blue waters and a relaxed atmosphere. But it is also noted for its very own Chinatown and the legacy of early Japanese pearlers. For outback travellers who have finished one of the long desert crossings, it is an absolute oasis.

History

The Roebuck Bay region was known to the local Aborigines of the Djuleun tribes as 'Nileribanjen'. The surrounding mud flats and shallows were rich in shellfish, fish and mud crabs and the Djuleun traded spears and pearl shell; the latter eventually contributed to the end of their traditional way of life.

In 1864, an syndicate of interested people was formed to investigate the story of a convict who claimed to have found gold at Camden Harbour, near Kuri Bay, in 1856. Many eager pastoralists backed this expedition and, when gold was not found, a number of them put together another expedition to introduce sheep to the region.

The Aboriginal inhabitants of Roebuck Bay resented the intrusion of the pastoralists, especially their fencing of traditional waterholes. In November 1864, three members of the pastoralists' expedition were murdered by Aborigines, which resulted in open conflict. The pastoralists withdrew in 1867 only to be replaced by pearlers, working their way north from Cossack in the 1870s.

Pearling in the sea off Broome started in earnest in the 1880s and peaked in the early 1900s when the town's 400 pearling luggers, worked by 3000 men, supplied 80% of the world's mother-of-pearl. Today only a handful of boats still operate.

When Japan entered WWII in 1941, the 500 Japanese in Broome were interned for the duration of the war. On 3 March 1942, following the bombing of Darwin in February, the Japanese bombed Broome. A number of flying boats were destroyed and about 70 Dutch refugees were killed.

Today, tourism and pearling are the major industries and Broome's attractions and festivals bring in hordes of visitors. The Aboriginal community is playing a major part in this renaissance.

Information

The busy Broome visitor centre (☎ 08-9192 2222, fax 9192 2063, e tourism@broome .wt.com.au, W ebroome.com/tourism) is on the corner of Great Northern Hwy and Bagot St, just across the sports field from Chinatown. It's open daily from 8am to

Broome's Special Events

Broome is something of a festival centre, offering visitors and residents many excuses to party.

Dragon-boat paddlers from all over Australia meet in Broome each April to take part in the Dragon Boat Classic carnival.

Accommodation is hard to find during Shinju Matsuri (Festival of the Pearl) in August. This excellent festival commemorates Broome's early pearling years and multicultural heritage, featuring many traditional Japanese ceremonies, including the Obon Festival at the start. When it's on, the town's population swells, so book ahead.

Also in August, world-class opera singers come to sing under the Kimberley's clear night skies during the appropriately named Opera under the Stars.

The sticky-sweet tropical fruit loved by many, but deplored by mothers with small children, is celebrated during the annual Mango Festival in November.

5pm April to November, and otherwise from 9am to 5pm Monday to Friday and 9am to 1pm on weekends. It publishes a useful monthly guide to what's happening in and around Broome, a *Broome Map & Information Guide* and a *Kimberley Holiday Planner* (all free).

THINGS TO SEE & DO

Some critics in the tourism industry say Broome has nothing to offer apart from a bit of history and a beach. But **Cable Beach,** about 4km west of the town centre, isn't any old beach: it's just about perfect and continues for 20km up the west coast. It was named for the telegraph cable that ran from here to what is now Indonesia. Many come here to watch the famous sunset.

The **cemetery** at the start of Cable Beach Rd testifies to the dangers that accompanied pearl diving when equipment was primitive and knowledge of diving techniques limited. In 1914, 33 divers died of the bends, while in 1908 a cyclone killed 150 sailors caught at sea. The Japanese section of the cemetery is one of the largest and most interesting.

The term **Chinatown** is used to refer to the old part of town, although there is really only one block or so that is multicultural and historic. Most of the distinctive, corrugated-iron buildings that line Carnarvon St are now restaurants, pearl galleries or tourist shops. The steel bars on the windows aren't there to deter outlaws but to minimise cyclone damage.

A must-see in Chinatown is **Sun Pictures**, the oldest outdoor cinema in Australia and possibly the world (it opened in 1916). Lie back in a deck chair under the stars and enjoy!

Another worthwhile sight, when conditions are be spot-on, is the **staircase to the moon**, an optical illusion caused by the full moon reflecting off the exposed mud flats of Roebuck Bay. It only occurs at extremely low tides between March and October – the visitor centre has a schedule.

Every Saturday, the **Courthouse Market** in the grounds of the Courthouse, on the corner of Frederick and Hamersley streets, brings together all the arty types and alternative lifestylers who are drawn to Broome.

ORGANISED TOURS

There are more organised tours in and around Broome than you can wave a $100 note at. Many businesses offer guided tours through the Kimberley (check with the visitor centre) but many more stay closer to home, including:

Spirit of Broome (☎ 08-9193 5025) This small hovercraft makes daily one-hour flights around Roebuck Bay, stopping at various points of interest including some dinosaur prints, for $66 per person. Breakfast and sunset flights are available too.

Broome Bushtucker Tours (☎ 08-9193 7778, e kimberleywild@mail.com) Explores the unique ecosystems of the area, from $29 for a two-hour mangrove walk to $78 for a full-day walk around the tip of the Broome peninsula.

Mamabulanjin Aboriginal Tours (☎ 08-9192 2660, e mabtours@wm.com.au) The six different Aboriginal groups of the

BROOME

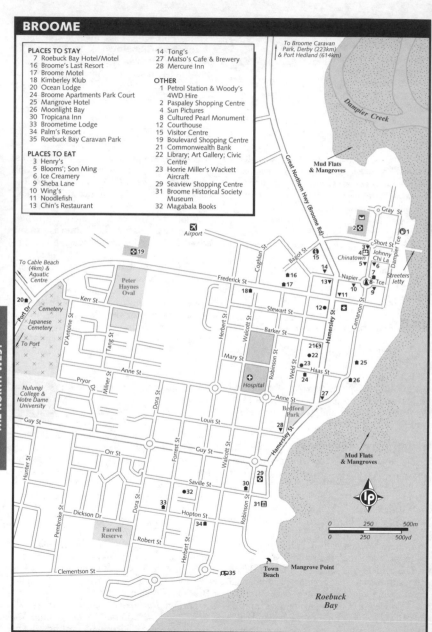

PLACES TO STAY
7 Roebuck Bay Hotel/Motel
16 Broome's Last Resort
17 Broome Motel
18 Kimberley Klub
20 Ocean Lodge
24 Broome Apartments Park Court
25 Mangrove Hotel
26 Moonlight Bay
30 Tropicana Inn
33 Broometime Lodge
34 Palm's Resort
35 Roebuck Bay Caravan Park

PLACES TO EAT
3 Henry's
5 Blooms'; Son Ming
6 Ice Creamery
9 Sheba Lane
10 Wing's
11 Noodlefish
13 Chin's Restaurant

14 Tong's
27 Matso's Cafe & Brewery
28 Mercure Inn

OTHER
1 Petrol Station & Woody's 4WD Hire
2 Paspaley Shopping Centre
4 Sun Pictures
8 Cultured Pearl Monument
12 Courthouse
15 Visitor Centre
19 Boulevard Shopping Centre
21 Commonwealth Bank
22 Library; Art Gallery; Civic Centre
23 Horrie Miller's Wackett Aircraft
29 Seaview Shopping Centre
31 Broome Historical Society Museum
32 Magabala Books

Broome area have all been influenced by the wide variety of foreigners who have settled here. For $88 you can spend a day learning about traditional lifestyles and how they have changed.

Willie Creek Pearl Farm *(☎ 08-9193 6000,* **w** *www.williecreekpearls.com.au)* Touted as Broome's most popular tour, this takes you to the pearl farm 40km north of Broome and includes a boat tour to see the suspended pearl panels. Cost is $55 per person, or $25 if you drive there yourself (4WD recommended). More interesting than it sounds.

Astro Tours *(☎ 0500 831 111,* **e** *mail@ astrotours.net)* Anyone who has camped in the outback has wondered about the southern hemisphere's rich sky. This recommended tour will answer many of your questions for $50 ($25 for children aged 6-16).

PLACES TO STAY

The Broome tourist season starts in April, peaks in July/August and slows down by October. Outside the season some good deals can be had but inside you'd be lucky to get a bed at all, let alone a cheap one. Book ahead.

Camping

Camping in Broome is not particularly good value, and in high season the 'no vacancy' signs go up by midday, especially if you're towing a van (tents can often be squeezed in). Most parks refuse reservations over the phone – your best bet is to turn up between 10am (check-out time) and midday.

Roebuck Bay Caravan Park *(☎ 08-9192 1366, Walcott St)* Camp sites without power from $10 per person, with power from $21 double, vans from $50. This is the most central place to camp (though still a fair walk into town), and you might get a spot overlooking Roebuck Bay if you're lucky (it gets very crowded in the high season).

Mango Camping Ground *(☎ 08-9192 1366, Walcott St)* Sites $8 per person, with camper's kitchen. Open April to September. In CALM's small mango plantation on Roebuck Bay, next to the Roebuck Bay park and run from the same office. Nice and shady, but sap from the trees will make your tent sticky.

Broome Vacation Village *(☎ 08-9192 1057, Port Dr)* Sites from $17 double. Some distance out of town, near the golf course and port.

Broome Caravan Park *(☎ 08-9192 1776, Wattle Dr)* Tent sites from $7 per person, on-site vans from $70 double. Off the Great Northern Hwy, 4km east of town.

Cable Beach Caravan Park *(☎ 08-9192 2066, Millington Rd)* Unpowered/powered sites $16/20 for 2 people, cottages from $110. A bargain, considering it's just behind the Cable Beach Intercontinental which starts at $350 a night! Gets crowded.

Hostels

Broome's Last Resort *(☎ 08-9193 5000, Bagot St)* Dorm beds/doubles from $16/50 (YHA discounts available). Close to the centre and just a short stagger from the airport. It's adequate but noisy, and has a pool, large kitchen and courtesy bus.

Broometime Lodge *(☎ 08-9193 5067, Forrest St)* Singles/twins with fan $55/75 (stay 7 nights and pay for 6). The rooms (shared facilities) are small but the friendly, knowledgeable owners and varied clientele make up for it. Pleasant pool.

Kimberley Klub *(☎ 08-9192 3233, Frederick St)* Dorms from $17, doubles $65. Close to the centre, this is one of the fanciest budget places you could ever hope to stay in. Great facilities.

Roebuck Bay Backpackers *(☎ 08-9192 1183, Napier Tce)* Dorms/doubles $14/55. Part of Broome's historic main pub, it's usually crowded with long-term residents.

B&Bs

McAlpine House *(☎ 08-9192 3886, 84 Herbert St)* Doubles with shared facilities/ private/executive from $200/300/340. Peaceful accommodation in the former home of Lord Alistair McAlpine, founder of the original Cable Beach Resort. Breakfast and airport transfers included.

Harmony Bed & Breakfast *(☎ 08-9193 7439, Great Northern Hwy)* Singles/doubles $55/88. About 5km out of town.

The Temple Tree B&B *(☎ 08-9193 5728, 54 Anne St)* Singles/doubles $80/95.

Hotels & Motels

The following is a selection – the visitor centre has a full listing.

Ocean Lodge (☎ 08-9193 7700, Cable Beach Rd) Doubles $104. Some distance from both the beach and the town centre, but it does have a peaceful central courtyard.

Broome Motel (☎ 08-9192 7775, Frederick St) Doubles from $115. Fairly central and comfortable.

Roebuck Bay Hotel-Motel (☎ 08-9192 1221, Carnarvon St) Doubles budget/ standard from $93.50/110. Legendary but noisy with lots of character – part of Broome's distinctive and historic main pub.

Palm's Resort (☎ 08-9192 1898, Hopton St) Motel rooms from $145. Unremarkable but OK.

Tropicana Inn (☎ 08-9192 1204, Cnr Saville & Robinson Sts) Doubles $132. OK rooms in a pleasant setting.

Broome Apartments Park Court (☎ 08-9193 5887, 2 Haas St) Self-contained, one-bedroom units $92. Small but OK for the price.

Mangrove Hotel (☎ 08-9192 1303, 120 Carnarvon St) Rooms from $165. Some rooms have great views across Roebuck Bay. Resort-style place.

Moonlight Bay (☎ 08-9193 7888, Carnarvon St) Rooms from $195. High quality with an enormous pool.

Habitat Beach Resort (☎ 08-9158 3520, Port Dr, beside the golf course) One-bedroom apartment $164. Other apartment options available. A pleasant place.

Cockatoo Island Resort (☎ 08-8946 4455) Doubles from $550, including all meals, but add $320 for return air transfer from Broome. In the middle of the Buccaneer Archipelago, it offers fishing, bushwalking, cruises and whale-watching during the season.

PLACES TO EAT

Finding a place to stay in Broome may be a hassle but eating out is no problem at all.

Bloom's Cafe (☎ 08-9193 6366, 2/31 Carnarvon St) Many people eat here after the movies at Sun Pictures. The evening meals are OK but the breakfasts are better and they serve a good cappuccino.

Henry's (☎ 08-9192 3222, Cnr Short & Carnarvon Sts) Another popular place to unwind after the movies, with good coffee and cakes.

Chin's Chinese Restaurant (☎ 08-9192 1466, 7 Hamersley St) A variety of dishes from all over Asia; has a popular takeaway section. Other Chinese specialists include: **Wing's** (☎ 08-9192 1072, Napier Tce); **Tong's** (☎ 08-9192 2080, 510 Napier Tce); and **Son Ming** (☎ 08-9192 2192, Carnarvon St).

Noodlefish (☎ 08-9192 5529, 2/6 Hamersley St) Casual, Asian-inspired meals. A favourite with the locals.

Sheba Lane (☎ 08-9193 6036, 6/12 Napier Tce) Upmarket, Asian-style restaurant in the building where the Japanese prostitutes used to live. Does great mud crab (order in advance).

Matso's Cafe & Brewery (☎ 08-9193 5811, 60 Hamersley St) Worthwhile international cuisine and some interesting brews in this old, restored shop dating from 1900.

Mercure Inn (☎ 08-9192 1002, Cnr Louis & Weld Sts) Modern hotel with bistro serving inventive, tasty dishes that don't cost a fortune. Popular with the locals.

Ice Creamery (☎ 08-9193 5400, 3/46 Carnarvon St) Lovely, home-made ice cream; also does luscious smoothies. There's another shop in the Paspaley shopping centre close by.

Coles supermarket (Paspaley shopping centre, Carnarvon St) Open 24 hours for self-catering.

The **kiosk** on the beach at Roebuck Bay Caravan Park is a pleasant place for breakfast in the cool of the morning.

GETTING THERE & AROUND

Qantas has regular flights to and from Perth and Darwin, and Air North in Darwin (☎ 08-8945 2866) links Broome to Kununurra and Darwin. For details on the unique Ibis Aerial Hwy, see Alternative Transport in the earlier Gibb River Rd section.

McCafferty's/Pioneer (☎ 13 20 30) has regular buses to and from Broome; its local bookings are handled by Broome Travel (☎ 08-9192 1561) in Hamersley St.

Car Rental

There are numerous car-rental options and it pays to ring around to find the deal that suits you best. Check the insurance cover and excess, and if you plan to drive to Cape Leveque (see the Dampier Peninsula section later in this chapter) or further afield to Windjana Gorge, Tunnel Creek or even the Gibb River Rd, make sure you have permission to take the car off the bitumen. Prices fluctuate 20% or more according to the season – prices quoted here are mid-year (high-season) prices:

Britz Campervan Rentals (☎ 08-9192 2647, Unit 1, 29 Clementson St) Toyota Hiace $206/day, unlimited km, sealed roads only. For unsealed roads, Toyota Prado $244/day or Land Cruiser campervan $281/day, both with unlimited km.

Broome Broome Car Rentals (☎ 08-9192 2210, Palm Ct) Toyota Echo $50/day or Toyota Seca $68/day, 50km free, sealed roads only. For unsealed roads, Toyota RAV4 $99/day, 50km free plus 33¢ per additional km.

Broome Discount Car Hire (☎ 08-9192 3100, Lot 103 McPherson St) Kia Mentor $55/day, 75km free plus 15¢ per additional km, sealed roads only (no 4WDs in stock).

Delta Europcar (☎ 08-9193 7788, Broome airport) Toyota Corolla $50/day, 100km free plus 22¢ per additional km, sealed roads only. Toyota RAV4 $80/day, 100km free plus 25¢ per additional km, sealed roads only. For unsealed roads, Toyota Land Cruiser $130/day, 100km free plus 28¢ per additional km.

Just Broome Car Hire (☎ 08-9192 6636, Hunter St) Second-hand Corollas, Lasers etc, for $32/day, 75km free plus 15¢ per additional km, sealed roads only. The cheapest place in town.

Topless Rentals (☎ 08-9193 5017, Hunter St) Second-hand Hyundais and Magnas $33.66/day, 50km free plus 22¢ per additional km, only around town. For farther out (but still only sealed roads), Ford Falcon $75/day, 50km free plus 22¢ per additional km. For unsealed roads, simple 4WDs (Daihatsu Terios, soon to be replaced with a different brand) $80-100/day.

Other companies around Broom include: Avis (☎ 08-9193 5980), on the corner of Frederick and Walcott Sts; Budget Rent A Car (☎ 08-9193 5355), on McPherson St at Broome airport; Hertz (☎ 08-9192 1428), at 69 Frederick St; and Maui (☎ 1800 998 029) at 1/29 Clementson St.

Motorcycle Rental

Road Runner Motor Cycle Hire (☎ 08-9192 1971) at 4 Farrell St, offers a choice of 50cc scooters ($40/day) or 250cc road bikes ($55/day) for running around the Broome area; 1000cc road bikes ($110/day) can be taken beyond Broome (say, to Derby), but none of the Road Runner bikes are allowed to be driven on dirt roads or beaches. For the road bikes, you will need a valid motorcycle licence that has been held for at least 12 months; for the scooters, a valid car licence held for at least 12 months will do. Road Runner also has free pick-up and delivery service.

Dampier Peninsula

Highlights

- Camping, walking and boating at Middle Lagoon
- Taking a boat tour from One Arm Point into the Buccaneer Archipelago
- Admiring the mother-of-pearl altar in the church at Beagle Bay

The Dampier Peninsula juts into the Indian Ocean north of Broome. It's a unique area in a transition zone between desert and tropics, with an interesting array of indigenous flora and fauna, striking red pindan cliffs along the western coast, and numerous white-sand beaches with azure-blue waters.

It's a very worthwhile two- or three-day excursion from Broome, but many people spend a week or more fishing, walking or simply enjoying the spectacular surroundings at the tip of the peninsula at Cape Leveque (pronounced a very un-French 'le-**veek**' by the locals), or at Middle Lagoon. You could also take a boat tour from One

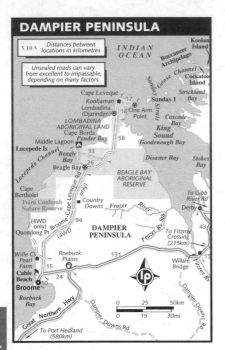

DAMPIER PENINSULA

Distances between locations in kilometres

Unsealed roads can vary from excellent to impassable, depending on many factors.

INDIAN OCEAN

Koolan Island
Buccaneer Archipelago
Sunday Goose Channel
Cockatoo Island
Strickland Bay
Cape Leveque 17
Kooljaman
Lombadina (Djarindjin) 18 One Arm Point
Sunday I
Cascade Bay
King Sound
LOMBADINA ABORIGINAL LAND
Cape Borda
Pender Bay 58
Goodenough Bay
Middle Lagoon
Lacepede Is
Beagle Bay 33
Beagle Bay 26
Disaster Bay
Stokes Bay
BEAGLE BAY ABORIGINAL RESERVE
Cape Bertholet
Point Coulomb Nature Reserve
Country Downs
Frazer River
To Gibb River Rd
Derby
(4WD only)
Quondong Pt
Broome (4WD) 94
DAMPIER PENINSULA
Fraser Sdtk
To Fitzroy Crossing (215km)
43
Wille Ck
Pearl Farm 15
Roebuck Plains
131
Willare Bridge
15
Cable Beach
Broome 10
24
Dampier Downs Rd
Roebuck Bay
Fitzroy Rv
Great Northern Hwy
Dampier Downs Rd
To Port Hedland (580km)

0   25   50km
0   15   30mi

Arm Point, a small Aboriginal community that offers the closest access to the hard-to-reach Buccaneer Archipelago; that group of islands is one of the most starkly beautiful areas in the world.

Originally the peninsula was inhabited by the Bardi people. During the early pearling days a number of Aborigines dived for pearl shell, and many of Broome's early pearling luggers were built from the local mangrove trees. The Aboriginal communities on the peninsula these days are highly religious, take pride in their relatively well-kept houses and lawns, and welcome visitors.

Information

Visitor Centres The peninsula is Broome's backyard, and the visitor centre in Broome provides information and also books tours and accommodation.

Books & Maps The StreetSmart and Hema maps mentioned in the earlier Gibb River Rd

section also include the Dampier Peninsula – StreetSmart's coverage is the most detailed. An excellent account of the plants and peoples of the peninsula is found in the CALM publication *Broome and Beyond* by K Kenneally, Daphne Choules Edinger & T Willing.

Radio Frequencies You don't really need a HF radio on the peninsula, but if you have one, the frequencies are the same as for the Gibb River Rd (see earlier).

Fuel The local communities shut down on Sunday and it's almost impossible to get fuel then, though the Kooljaman Resort (☎ 08-9192 4970) at Cape Leveque *sometimes* has fuel cards for 24-hour fuel at One Arm Point – ring ahead to confirm.

Road Reports The peninsula is a popular excursion from Broome, as evidenced by the many Toyota RAV4s and other (pseudo) 4WD vehicles with Broome car-rental stickers. Locals recommend a 4WD because the road is a bit sandy and corrugated and can be rough in places, though it can usually be negotiated by a 2WD driven with care. (Do check your rental agreement: Broome agencies don't allow their 2WDs here, nor some of their pseudo-4WDs.) Many people tow trailers and caravans all the way to Cape Leveque, so it's not too bad if you take it easy. In some weather the road and especially the sidetracks are definitely 4WD only. There are plans to upgrade the main road to good-quality gravel and to seal the final section at the cape, but locals say they'll believe it when they see it.

Permits Much of the peninsula is Aboriginal land, and though you don't need a permit to travel the road, you do if you want to visit the destinations described here. Camping in the bush is strictly prohibited and dogs and cats are not allowed.

THE ROUTE
The turn-off for the Broome–Cape Leveque Rd is 9km out of Broome, and from there it's about 210km to the Cape Leveque lighthouse at the tip of the peninsula.

About 12km after the turn-off the road turns to gravel, and 2.5km later a road to the left takes you to **Willie Creek Pearl Farm**. Tours of the farm must be pre-booked (see Organised Tours in the Broome section), though you can usually join here if you turn up at the right time, and you're welcome to browse around the shop. *Camping* (no charge) and fishing along the creek are good, but there are no facilities and a three-day limit applies – ask at the farm, and beware of crocodiles and the huge tidal differences.

North of here, on the western coast about a third of the way up the Dampier Peninsula, is the **Coulomb Point Nature Reserve**. This conservation area was set up to protect the unique pindan vegetation of the peninsula and may still harbour the endangered, rabbit-eared bandicoot (*Macrotus lagotis*) or bilby. Access is on foot (a five-day walk) or by 4WD depending on the tides – enquire at the Broome visitor centre.

From the Willie Creek turn-off to, it's 94km to the turn-off for the Aboriginal community, **Beagle Bay** (☎ 08 9192 4913), a welcome diversion. It has a beautiful church in the middle of a green, built by Pallotine monks and completed in 1918. Inside is an altar stunningly decorated with mother-of-pearl. The bell tower fell down recently and restorations may take a couple of years. A fee of $5 is charged to enter the community so contact the office on arrival. Petrol and diesel are available every day except Sunday, and there's no accommodation.

From the Beagle Bay turn-off, it's 26km to the turn-off to picturesque **Middle Lagoon**, 33km west on a manageable dirt road. The lagoon is a great place for snorkelling and swimming, boating and fishing – it's so attractive that many people who turn up for the night decide to spend a few days here. The half-moon bay with its impeccable sand-beach drains almost completely at low tide.

Just before Cape Leveque is the Aboriginal community, **Lombadina (Djarindjin)** (☎ 08-9192 4936), with its a lovely corrugated-iron church, lined with paper bark and supported by mangrove timber. Mass on Sunday at 5pm is quite an experience. There are a number of carved artefacts for sale in the shop nearby,

including trochus shell, ebony carvings and pearl-shell jewellery. A fee of $5 per vehicle applies, payable at the office.

Cape Leveque, about 220km from Broome, has a lighthouse and two wonderful beaches, but the many Aboriginal sacred sites in the area are off limits to visitors. The resort here, which goes by the name of Kooljaman, fills up quickly with guests. It tries to be upmarket but doesn't quite succeed, though it's pleasant enough and a good spot to unwind at what seems like the end of the world.

About 17km east of Cape Leveque is **One Arm Point** (☎ 08-9192 4930), another Aboriginal community where you can get petrol (leaded and unleaded) and diesel, as well as the trochus jewellery that's a speciality of the area, but no accommodation. An entry fee of $5 per vehicle is payable at the office. Drive through town, past the airstrip, to the beach with its shade structures for the boat tours (see the following section). A strong tidal current is often clearly visible just offshore.

ORGANISED TOURS

Ask at the Broome visitor centre (see the earlier Broome section) about tours, including the popular one to Willie Creek Pearl Farm.

One-day and overnight mud-crabbing and traditional fishing tours are conducted at Lombadina. Contact the community or the Broome visitor centre for details.

At One Arm Point, the McCarthy family runs boat tours to Sunday Island in the Buccaneer Archipelago for mud-crabbing, fishing or simply sightseeing, at $143 per person (minimum of four). These trips, which we highly recommend, can only be booked through the community (☎ 08-9192 4930) or through Kooljaman (☎ 08-9192 4970), not the visitor centre in Broome.

FACILITIES

The peninsula can get quite busy in the tourist season and it's best to book in advance, either direct or through the Broome visitor centre. If you go through the centre, they'll steer you towards Kooljaman unless you ask specifically about Middle

THE NORTH-WEST

Lagoon or Lombadina. No camping is allowed at Lombadina.

Middle Lagoon (☎ *08-9192 4002*) Unpowered sites $12, wonderful, double Robinson Crusoe-style beach shelters with pine floors $40 ($10 per extra person), cabins from $100. Limited supplies are available at the office/shop from 8am to 4pm daily, but no fuel. Strangley, this beautiful place was very quiet when we visited in the high season – everyone was crammed into Kooljaman when they could have had Middle Lagoon virtually to themselves. Still, it's wise to book ahead at the Broome visitor centre or direct with Middle Lagoon's friendly manager.

Kooljaman (☎ *08-9192 4970*) Camp sites $12 per person, self-contained units $88, bark cabins $110, safari tents $176. The restaurant, open for lunch and dinner from April to November (closed for dinner on Sundays), serves reasonable food considering the isolation. There's also a landing strip nearby ($20 landing fee).

Lombadina Djarindjin (☎ *08-9192 4936*) Backpacker units (4 people) $38.50 per person, self-contained cabins (4 people) $132. Book at the Broome visitor centre or direct with the community. Petrol (leaded and unleaded) and diesel, as well as supplies, are available weekdays from 8am to 11am and 1pm to 4pm.

The Pilbara

Highlights

- Witnessing the forces of nature at work in the wild Hamersley landscape
- The meeting of four gorges at Oxers Lookout – one of the outback's greatest sights
- Driving from Port Hedland to Karijini via Marble Bar

The Pilbara region encompasses some of the hottest country on earth. It also contains the iron ore that accounts for much of Western Australia's prosperity. Gigantic machines are used to tear apart the dusty red ranges of this isolated, harsh and fabulously wealthy area. The Pilbara towns are almost all company towns: either mining centres where the ore is wrenched from the earth or ports from which it's shipped abroad.

You get a good feel for the majesty and contrast of this ancient, raw frontier by driving through it. The major roads are sealed and there are no 'classic' routes that traverse it, but you can go deep into the arid areas and the fascinating Hamersley Range.

There's no doubt that the ancient Hamersley Range, with some of the oldest rock formations in the world dating back four billion years, contains some of Australia's most dramatic scenery. The landscape is dotted with spectacular red gorges, occasional waterfalls and palm-fringed waterholes. It's a land synonymous with the Dreamtime and abounds in Aboriginal sites. Eroded forms of prehistory are overlaid with the machinery of modern explorers in search of abundant raw materials and minerals.

South of Karratha and the Pilbara coastline are two magnificent interior national parks, one based on Millstream homestead and the Chichester Range, the other on the Hamersley Range. They contribute to part of an excellent loop journey from the coastal highway.

The description that follows assumes the loop starts in Karratha or Roebourne, passes through the Millstream-Chichester and Karijini National Parks, returning to Karratha via the western gorges, Tom Price and the Hamersley Iron (HI) privately owned Dampier-Tom Price railway road. The only backtracking is in and around the national parks. It is, however, a contrived route: there are many other possible points of entry and exit.

Information
Visitor Centres In Karratha, the Karratha & Districts visitor centre (☎ 08-9144 4600), on Karratha Rd just before you reach the T-junction of Dampier and Millstream Rds, has loads of information on what to see and

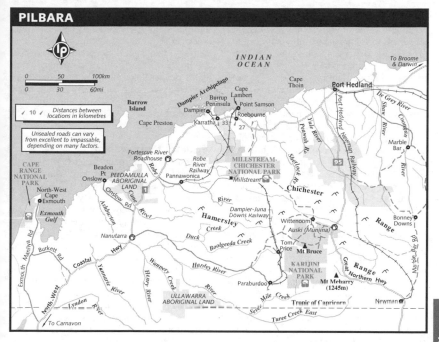

PILBARA

INDIAN OCEAN

To Broome & Darwin

do in the Pilbara. For information on the Pilbara's national parks, you could also contact CALM at its Karratha regional office (☎ 08-9143 1488), on Mardie Rd in the industrial estate. It's open Monday to Friday 8am to 5pm, but not really set up to handle general inquiries from the public.

In Roebourne, information is available at the visitor centre (☎ 08-9182 1060) in the Old Gaol complex, Queen St.

The Gem Shop (☎ 08-9189 7096) on Sixth Ave in Wittenoom acts as a tourist centre – probably until such time as the government succeeds in closing down the town completely and then bulldozing all evidence of it into the ground.

The Tom Price visitor centre (☎ 08-9188 1112) is on Central Rd. The Newman visitor centre (☎ 08-9175 2888) is at the corner of Fortescue Ave and Newman Dr. Port Hedland is also a popular starting point for a Pilbara tour; the visitor centre (☎ 08-9173 1711) is at 13 Wedge St, across from the post office.

The Millstream-Chichester visitor centre (☎ 08-9184 5144), at the old Millstream homestead (open daily 8am to 4pm), is usually unattended but has lots of good information. The new Karijini visitor centre (☎ 08-9189 8121, open daily 9am to 4pm), an award-winning steel structure near the junction of Dales Gorge Rd and the abandoned Yampire Gorge Rd, is run by descendants of the Panyjima, Innawonga and Kurruma people, the traditional occupants of Karijini.

Radio Frequencies If in trouble, it's unlikely that you'd have to wait long for another vehicle to pass by. For those with HF radios, the RFDS bases at Derby (call sign VJB, 5300kHz), Meekatharra (call sign VKJ, 4010kHz and 6880kHz) and Port Hedland (call sign VKL, 4030 and 6960kHz) monitor transmissions for emergencies 24 hours a day.

National Parks The Karijini and Millstream-Chichester and National Parks each charge an entry fee of $9 per vehicle ($3 per motorcycle), or you can buy a $17 annual local pass for both parks from visitor centres or CALM offices throughout the area. Camping in either park costs an additional $10 per night per site for one or two people ($5.50 per extra person, $2 per child).

The entry fee is payable at self-registration bays near entry points to the parks (honesty system, but rangers do check), and the camping charge is levied by so-called camping hosts at the camp sites (volunteers who spend a few weeks camping for free in wonderful surroundings) or else by the rangers who come by in the morning. The camp sites have drop toilets but no showers, and provide free cooking facilities on gas plates (open fires are strictly prohibited). Water is available at a few points but it's best to be self-sufficient.

Books & Maps A number of good publications cover this route. Useful publications by CALM include the pamphlets *Karijini National Park*, *Millstream-Chichester National Park* and *Pilbara National Park*, and the booklet *North-West Bound: From Shark Bay to Wyndham*. David Kirkland's *The Pocket Guide to the Pilbara* is available from visitor centres throughout the region, though you'd probably buy it more as a souvenir.

The Street Smart map of the Pilbara is indispensable for this trip and is favoured by the visitor centres for its wealth of useful detail. The Pilbara map published by Hema isn't bad either.

Permits A permit (no charge) is required to travel on private Hamersley Iron roads that run along the iron-ore railway lines. You will need one to travel on the Dampier–Tom Price Rd (used for the homeward part of the described loop). This is obtained easily from Hamersley Iron visitors centres in Tom Price and Parker Point (☎ 08-9143 3332, road report ☎ 9143 6464) in Tom Price, both open Monday to Friday 8am to 3.30pm; and you have to sit through an interesting, 10-minute safety video first.

Chances are that you may deviate onto Robe River Iron Associates' private road – it parallels Robe River's railway between

the shipping facility at Cape Lambert near Point Samson (☎ 08-9159 2150) and mining operations at Pannawonica.

If you can't get these permits because of the limited issuing points and opening hours, don't despair: you could simply backtrack the way you came, or return via the Great Northern Hwy and take the opportunity to visit Marble Bar (see Alternative Routes later in this section).

Special Preparations

Occasionally the roads are closed after rain – check road conditions with Main Roads Western Australia (☎ 1800 013 314). The roads are graded regularly in the tourist season and are generally pretty good, but the high iron content turns even innocuous-looking pebbles into tyre slicers. Carry two spares – the park rangers may be able to help in an emergency but don't count on any sympathy for bad planning. As always, the best advice is to slow down – travelling at more than 80km/h is asking for tyre trouble.

Always carry sufficient water and check that you have enough fuel to get to the next refuelling point. Fuel is available at a number of locations but is considerably more expensive than in the coastal towns – fill up those long-range tanks! The closest fuel to Millstream-Chichester National Park is in Karratha, Roebourne or at Auski Roadhouse (at the junction of the Great Northern Hwy and Munjina-Wittenoom Rd). Around Karijini, fuel is available at Tom Price, the Auski Roadhouse and a little farther away in Newman. There is no fuel at Wittenoom.

The parks lack resorts (a good thing, really) and the accommodation in the surrounding towns is a bit out of the way – come prepared to camp if you want to enjoy the parks to the full.

The only banking facilities in the area are at Tom Price, Newman, Karratha and Port Hedland, so bring plenty of cash. The Auski Roadhouse has Eftpos facilities.

THE ROUTE
Karratha

The town of Karratha ('good country'), the commercial centre for the area, owes its existence to the rapid expansion of the Hamersley Iron operations and the Woodside offshore natural gas project. The wealthy town is now the hub of coastal Pilbara. The area around Karratha is replete with evidence of Aboriginal occupation – carvings, grindstones, etchings and middens are all located on the **Jaburara Heritage Trail**, which starts near the visitor centre.

Just out of town on the **Burrup Peninsula** near Dampier is **Deep Gorge,** one of the most prolific Aboriginal rock-art sites in Australia, with ancient Jaburara etchings on many of the boulders. The tentative technique of crystal-erosion dating, which measures the erosion rate of exposed crystals in the rock, has dated these etchings back to the ice age, 27,000 ago.

The gorge is at the end of an unsignposted dirt track, 1.7km on the right along the road towards beautiful **Hearsons Cove**. The cove itself is one of the better places in Australia from which to view the 'staircase to the moon', an optical illusion caused by the full moon reflecting off the exposed mud flats at low tide – the Karratha visitor centre can tell you when conditions are right.

Also on the Burrup Peninsula, clearly signposted and only a couple of kilometres from the Hearsons Cove turn-off, is the **Northwest Shelf Gas Venture**. This huge resource development – the largest natural gas field in the world, in a cyclone-prone area out at sea – is transforming this part of Australia like a modern-day gold rush. The free **visitor centre** (☎ 08 9158 8292) is open daily 10am to 4pm April to October, 10am to 1pm November to March, and overlooks the onshore gas plant, shows how it all works and is well worth a visit.

Karratha to Millstream-Chichester

To get to **Roebourne**, head for the North-West Coastal Hwy from Karratha and turn left; Roebourne is 33km from this turn-off. It is the oldest existing town in the Pilbara. It has a history of grazing, gold and copper mining, and was once the capital of the north-west. There are still some fine old buildings to be seen, including an **old gaol**,

an 1894 **church** and the **Victoria Hotel**, the last of five original pubs in the area. Roebourne is close to the historic port of **Cossack** and the fishing village of **Point Samson**, both well worth a detour.

From Roebourne, follow the North-West Coastal Hwy for 27km to the turn-off for Millstream, then take the signposted gravel road. It passes through grazing land, with the occasional dry creek crossing. The most spectacular natural feature on this route is **The Pyramid**, a symmetrical pile of red rock and yellow spinifex dominating the landscape to your right.

Millstream-Chichester National Park

This 2200 sq km park is fed by a huge aquifer (natural underground reserve of water) contained in the porous dolomite rock. While Karijini, its sister park to the south-east, attracts hordes of tourists to its impressive gorges, Millstream-Chichester is more of an ecotourist destination with untouched wilderness. From the car it seems less impressive than Karijini but on foot you begin to realise how valuable it is. It's just as well that it attracts fewer visitors.

Thanks to the aquifer, the park features a number of freshwater pools – you don't have to climb down steep gorges for a swim like you do at Karijini. The turn-off to **Python Pool** is reached some 61km after you leave the North-West Coastal Hwy. This was once an oasis for Afghani camel drivers and still makes a good place to pause for a swim, though the water gets rather murky after the waterfall dries up in the dry season. The natural amphitheatre has good acoustics – a great spot to practise your operatic talents.

After Python Pool, the road becomes bitumen for 15km as it climbs **Mt Herbert**, from where there are great views of the Chichester Range and back towards the coast.

Once down the hill, the road reverts to gravel and you pass through undulating sandstone country. Ten kilometres from the end of the bitumen, the road crosses the Hamersley Iron railway line. At this crossroad go straight ahead and follow the road

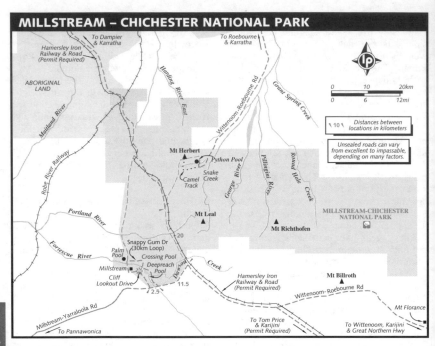

MILLSTREAM – CHICHESTER NATIONAL PARK

To Dampier & Karratha

To Roebourne & Karratha

Hamersley Iron Railway & Road (Permit Required)

ABORIGINAL LAND

Maitland River

Harding River East

Wittenoom-Roebourne Rd

Great Spring Creek

Robe River Railway

Mt Herbert

Python Pool

Snake Creek

Camel Track

George River

Pilingini River

Round Hole Creek

Portland River

Mt Leal

MILLSTREAM-CHICHESTER NATIONAL PARK

Mt Richthofen

Fortescue River

Snappy Gum Dr (30km Loop)

Palm Pool

Crossing Pool

Deepreach Pool

Millstream

Cliff Lookout Drive

2.5

20

11.5

Dampier Creek

Hamersley Iron Railway & Road (Permit Required)

Wittenoom-Roebourne Rd

Mt Billroth

Millstream-Yarraloola Rd

To Pannawonica

To Tom Price & Karijini (Permit Required)

To Wittenoom, Karijini & Great Northern Hwy

Mt Florance

0   10   20km
0   6   12mi

10   Distances between locations in kilometers

Unsealed roads can vary from excellent to impassable, depending on many factors.

for about 20km (a Hamersley Iron permit isn't needed if staying on the main road) until you reach the Millstream-Yarraloola Rd turn-off. Turn right (towards Pannawonica) and follow the road for 11.5km to the 30km loop road through the park, called **Snappy Gum Drive**.

This takes you to **Crossing Pool**, a pleasant camping spot. The lush environment is a haven for birds and other fauna such as flying foxes and kangaroos. Over 20 species of dragonfly and damselfly have been observed around the pool.

The road continues past some interesting lookout points to the visitor centre in the former **Millstream** homestead (see the earlier Information section). There's a lot of detail on Millstream ecosystems and the lifestyle of the Yinjibarndi people, the region's traditional inhabitants, here. It's usually unattended but you can still wander around. Note the kitchen building that was separated from the homestead for fire reasons.

The **Chinderwarriner Pool** next to the homestead is another pleasant oasis, with pools, palms (including the unique Millstream palm, *Livistonia alfredii*) and lilies. The owners of Millstream certainly knew how to make the area liveable, though the date palms they introduced threatened to edge out the original Millstream palms, which is why they are now being poisoned. A few date palms around the homestead are being kept for historical reasons but they'll probably be gone from the rest of the park by the time you visit.

Not far past the visitor centre at the old Millstead homestead is a 6km sub-loop called **Cliff Lookout Drive**, which has great views of Crossing Pool and the Fortescue River.

Near the end of Snappy Gum Drive, take a look at **Deepreach Pool**. You won't see it until you drive up to it, and then it will blow your mind. It's about 4km long, 120m wide and 19m deep (it's actually a flooded gorge that cuts right through the aquifer), and is lined with redgums. It's a great place to swim and camp – better than the other camping ground at Crossing Pool, though the latter has more shade and is probably better for a long-term stay.

The park has a number of walking trails, including the half-hour homestead walk, the 6km **Murlunmunyjurna Trail** (a great walk from the homestead to the Fortescue River and back, which traverses a wide range of ecosystems) and the 8km **Chichester Range Camel Track** (which follows in the footsteps of the old cameleers and offers great views). There are plans afoot (so to speak) for a number of serious bush trails through the less accessible regions of the park, as well as a number of walks in the delta wetlands. For the most up-to-date information, contact the CALM office in Karratha (☎ 08-9143 1488; see the earlier Information section).

Millstream-Chichester to Karijini

To get to the Auski Roadhouse (also known as Munjina after the nearby gorge) on the Great Northern Hwy, a possible base for exploring the Karijini (Hamersley Range) National Park, return the way you came to the Wittenoom-Roebourne Rd. Turn right here and after 28.5km you will cross the Hamersley Iron railway line. Keep a lookout for those 1km- to 2km-long iron-ore trains. In 2001, one of these trains set a world record with a length of 7.5km! A permit isn't requried to travel the main Wittenoom-Roebourne Rd.

The next 100km of driving takes you through relatively featureless country (with occasional patches of beautiful Sturt desert pea) occupied by stations such as Tambrey, Mt Florance and Mulga Downs (the former home of mining tycoon Lang Hancock). **Mt Florance** (☎ 08-9189 8151) offers camping for $5 per person and some beautiful, hidden waterholes. The spectacular Hamersley Range looms straight ahead on the other side of the Fortescue basin.

Wittenoom, once a main tourist centre, is at the northern end of the Karijini National Park. It used to be an asbestos mining town but mining stopped in 1966. A number of miners and baggers at the Wittenoom Gorge mine have subsequently 'died of the dust' and there are still many potential compensation cases outstanding. It is now virtually a ghost town, although a few inhabitants (30 at last count) cling tenaciously to almost beleaguered homes. Perth's bureaucrats are trying to close it down for good.

The now infamous but still very beautiful **Wittenoom Gorge** is immediately south of town. A sealed but somewhat dilapidated road runs the 13km through this gorge, passing the old asbestos mine (with everything still in place, as if they dropped their tools and simply walked out), smaller gorges and some very pretty pools, and ends at the so-called **Settlement**, the original Wittenoom township where a few inhabitants (mainly former miners) still reside.

If you're concerned about the asbestos risk, note the following warning and push on to the Auski (Munjina) Roadhouse on the Great Northern Hwy, 42km east of Wittenoom. After 24km, you pass the old northern access road into Karijini through **Yampire Gorge**, a site where asbestos was mined in the 1940s. This road has been washed away by floods and is no longer maintained (Perth bureaucrats wouldn't dare risk claims for asbestos-related diseases), so don't try to go through here into Karijini (Hamersley Range) National Park. Those who do (it's still marked on many maps) either turn back or get hopelessly stuck.

At both Wittenoom and Yampire gorges, blue veins of asbestos can be seen in the rock, and asbestos fibres are underfoot almost everywhere. It's a rather pretty mineral in its natural form, but in silicified form it's even prettier and known as tiger-eye.

Warning Even after 35 years, the government claims that there is still a health risk from airborne asbestos fibres around Wittenoom. The blue asbestos that used to be mined here is the most hazardous type of asbestos known and is a proven cancer-causing agent. Avoid disturbing asbestos tailings in the area and keep your car windows closed on windy days. If you're concerned, keep going and don't venture into Wittenoom or Yampire Gorges.

Asbestos – the Government vs Wittenoom

Asbestos in general and blue asbestos in particular (the variety found at Wittenoom) has a bad reputation these days and for good reason. It is well known that people who have worked with asbestos can later develop diseases. The most notorious of these is mesothelioma, a cancer of the outer lining of the lung that can emerge 40 years or more after exposure, though a third of known cases have no association with asbestos.

Asbestos is a general term given to a group of magnesium silicate minerals that occur in fibrous form. They are flexible, heat resistant, have high tensile strength with high binding properties, and are the only natural minerals that can be spun and woven. Among their many uses, they have been incorporated in brake and clutch linings, in the old-fashioned simmer plates for the stove that your mother used to love (and that worked so much better than modern versions), and in fire-retardant walls and ceilings in buildings, including many schools and hospitals built until the 1970s.

Blue asbestos, or crocidolite, which occurs in veins in ironstone and is found mainly in the Hamersley Range and in South Africa, has very thin fibres that can penetrate deep into the lung tissue and pass into the body more easily than other forms of asbestos. Research in Britain has indicated that the risk of contracting mesothelioma from blue asbestos is five times greater than it is from brown asbestos, while the risk from brown asbestos is 100 times greater than from white asbestos.

Nevertheless, the 30-or-so residents who remain at Wittenoom aren't crazy and claim with some justification that blue asbestos fibres in their natural form are unlikely to be a health risk. Even the WA government admits as much in its asbestos warning pamphlet. Asbestos dust, however, is far more dangerous. This occurs when car or truck mechanics clean out asbestos-lined brake drums (which are still favoured by some and aren't entirely a thing of the past), when demolition crews demolish old buildings that have asbestos panels – and when the miners at Wittenoom and Yampire Gorge used to mine asbestos, which involved crushing the ore and extracting the precious stuff with air, belching tonnes of dust into the atmosphere in the process.

Mining at Wittenoom ceased in 1966 (at Yampire Gorge it had already ceased in 1946) and the dust has since settled. The locals claim that the risk from airborne asbestos is now negligible – a claim

Karijini (Hamersley Range) National Park

Like the gorges in central Australia, those of Karijini are spectacular, both in their sheer rocky faces and varied colours. Unlike central Australia, however, the water in the gorges is icy cold in the winter months (April or May to October), which are also the main tourist season – forget about swimming unless you have a wetsuit. In early spring, the park is often carpeted with colourful wildflowers.

There's the sealed Karijini Dr from the Great Northern Hwy to the new Karijini visitor centre just west of the junction of Dales Gorge Rd and the abandoned track through Yampire Gorge. This access road starts about 35km south of the Auski Roadhouse and 160km north of Newman. After 30km, turn right (north) onto Banjima Dr

and follow the road to the visitor centre (see the earlier Information section). Pay the entry fee at the self-registration bay.

Dales Gorge is a good place to start your exploration of the many gorges. The 10km road into the gorge starts just east of the visitor centre; there's a freshwater tank close to the turn-off to replenish supplies.

At the end of this road, you can get to **Circular Pool** and a nearby lookout and, by a footpath, to the bottom of **Fortescue Falls**. The walk from Circular Pool along Dales Gorge to the falls is worthwhile, and you'll be surprised by how much water is permanently in the gorge.

Next, head west along Banjima Dr, past the visitor centre. After 19km, turn-off to the right leads to **Kalamina Gorge**, 6km from the main road. Another, after 10km leads to the **Knox Gorge** turn-off. Again the

Asbestos – the Government vs Wittenoom

backed by the last reliable measurements carried out in the region in 1995-6, which were supervised by Worksafe Australia. The locals also claim that there's more asbestos dust in the air in the Pilbara's iron-ore mines (where the mineral is often present) and in Perth (from asbestos-lined buildings, garden fences that often have asbestos reinforcements, and brake linings in vehicles), 'but no-one ever talks about that!'.

Since 1979 the Western Australian government, along with the agencies and departments under its control, have tried to eradicate all remaining evidence of Wittenoom, no doubt fearful of expensive legal claims arising from government activity that could be seen to promote the area in any way. Tourists are advised to keep going, and locals are told that their continued residence is entirely at their own risk.

Efforts to get residents to leave by cutting off their power, water and telephones were defeated by an injunction granted by the Western Australia high court, as cutting off paying customers would have been contrary to the constitutions of the utility companies. New residents, however, don't stand a chance of getting connected to power, which in effect rules out any newcomers. The government can't evict the remaining locals because they own their land under freehold title, but for them this is a catch-22: if they want to sell, the only buyer they're likely to find is the government, who will pay up to a maximum of $30,000 and then bulldoze everything into the ground.

What does this mean for a visitor to one of the most beautiful parts of the Pilbara? According to the locals there's no problem as long as you don't go out of your way to disturb the old mining tailings (waste) and sniff up the dust. The government would rather you didn't visit Wittenoom or Yampire Gorge at all, but realises that the no-go policy isn't entirely realistic. Its asbestos warning pamphlet states: 'Visits to contaminated areas should be avoided, but if undertaken should be of short duration, preferably for less than one day'. Either way, the choice is yours and you're on your own.

Some of the above was taken from the pamphlets Warning – *Blue Asbestos Present,* published by the Shire of Ashburton (for the prosecution), and *Wittenoom – Asbestos the Facts,* available at the Gem Shop in Wittenoom (for the defence).

gorge is 6km away from there. It's only 1km down this road to the often dry, but nonetheless spectacular **Joffre Falls**.

From the Knox Gorge turn-off, it's 3km west to a T-junction. Head north from this junction for another 14km to the remarkable **Oxers Lookout**, at the point where the Red, Weano, Joffre and Hancock Gorges meet. This is one of the outback's greatest sights, with a vertical drop of 80-100m from the two lookout platforms. If you want to go down into the gorge proper, take the steps down to Handrail Pool in Weano Gorge (turn to the right at the bottom, heading downstream). Use extreme caution – the rocks can be very slippery and accidents happen frequently.

Back at the T-junction, follow Banjima Dr south-west for 26km until it meets Karijini Dr and the Hamersley–Mt Bruce Rd. Turn right and head north-west along the Hamersley–Mt Bruce Rd until it meets the Nanutarra-Munjina Rd 30km later. Turn right (north) onto this road and after 22km you reach the turn-off to **Hamersley Gorge**, one of the most interesting gorges of the lot and only 4km from the main road. The evidence of the force of nature in the folded ribbons of rock adds to the awe-inspiring landscape. Intrepid adventurers should take the time to hike upstream above the waterfall for 1km or so (keep to the right-hand side for the best passage) to discover some hidden treasures – the Hidden Jungle, Spring Pool, Grotto and Moon World.

Just north of here, the Munjina-Wittenoom Rd leaves the Hamersley Range through the length of **Rio Tinto Gorge**, appearing like a dry gulch in those cowboy movies of old.

About 1km south of the Hamersley Gorge turn-off is a 29km short-cut to the

KARIJINI (HAMERSLEY RANGE) NATIONAL PARK

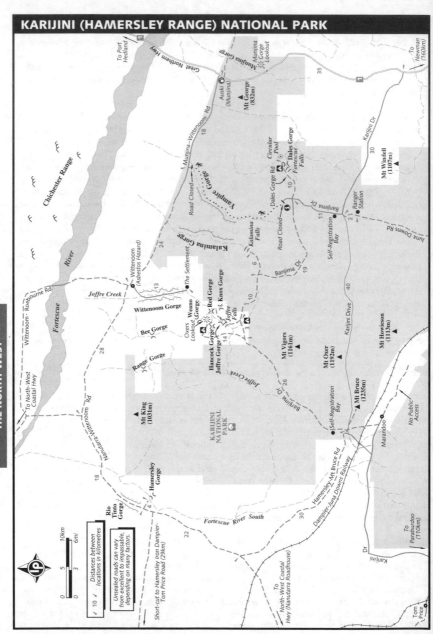

THE NORTH-WEST

Hamersley Iron Dampier–Tom Price Rd; it's quite clearly marked on the StreetSmart *Pilbara* map. From there it's plain sailing to Karratha. Alternatively, keep going north from the Hamersley Gorge turn-off, through Rio Tinto Gorge, and return to Karratha via the Wittenoom–Roebourne Rd along which you originally came via Mt Florance.

Tom Price

Tom Price is a pleasant town, scenically located among hills and mountains rich in iron ore. It's the site of the huge Hamersley Iron mine works that opened up this area. With an elevation of 750m it's also the highest town in Western Australia; temperatures can drop markedly at night.

Check with the Tom Price visitor centre about guided tours to the mine south-west of town – if nothing else, the scale will impress you. **Mt Nameless**, 4km west of Tom Price near the caravan park, is the highest mountain in Western Australia with vehicle access, and offers good views of the area, especially at sunset.

To get to Tom Price from the gorges, go to the intersection of Karijini Dr and the Hamersley–Mt Bruce Rd. Near here is **Mt Bruce** (1235m), the state's second-highest peak – incidentally, the it's highest mountain, **Mt Meharry** (1245m), is near the south-east border of Karijini National Park. From this intersection, follow Karijini Dr south-west for 40km until it meets the Paraburdoo–Tom Price Rd. Turn right and it's another 10km north-west to Tom Price.

When you've had your fill of a mining town, use your permit to travel the Hamersley Iron railway road back to the North-West Coastal Hwy and Karratha (use the map on the back of the permit). There are no real highlights on this 270km road, just the experience of using it. Slow right down on the exposed, rocky corrugations unless you enjoy changing tyres.

ALTERNATIVE ROUTES
Port Hedland to Karijini via Marble Bar

If you're coming from the north (or heading that way), your journey is likely to begin (or end) in Port Hedland, in which case you'd be doing yourself a favour by venturing off the Great Northern Hwy and including Marble Bar in your itinerary. Not only is the place itself worth visiting, but the route provides some of the prettiest outback scenery in Australia.

The route described here is generally OK in the dry season for a normal car driven with care, although there are a few rough sections south-west of Marble Bar. The manganese ore spilling from the huge trucks north-east of Marble Bar can play havoc with tyres so carry two spares. Bear in mind that the only fuel along this 450km route is at Marble Bar.

The Street Smart *Pilbara* map will do nicely for this trip.

Port Hedland to Marble Bar From Port Hedland, head east along the Great Northern Hwy for 50km (or 40km from the T-junction between Port Hedland and South Hedland) to the Marble Bar turn-off. Marble Bar Rd was sealed most of the way to Marble Bar when we travelled it, and will probably be sealed completely by the time you read this.

The scenery is fairly monotonous at first, but after about 90km it's more exciting as the road winds through the Gorge Range. At 108km is a turn-off to **Doolena Gorge** on your right, a delightful spot with permanent water a short drive off the road.

After the turn-off, the road crosses the Coongan River and at the 118km mark you come to a turn-off on your left heading towards **Coppin's Gap**. It's probably best to tackle this road only in a 4WD and the effort is worth it. The deep cutting is almost surreal, with impressive views and twisted bands of rock, and numerous pools fed by natural springs that are ideal for a swim. Nearby is **Kitty's Gap**, which is similar but strictly 4WD.

Back on Marble Bar Rd, another 35km takes you to Marble Bar itself.

Marble Bar The town takes its name from a bar of jasper (see the following section) across the Coongan River a few kilometres west of town. Reputed to be the hottest place in Australia, Marble Bar had a period in the 1920s when temperatures topped 37°C for 160 consecutive days. Once, in 1905, the temperature soared to 49.1°C. From October to March, day temperatures above 40°C are common – although it's dry heat and not too unbearable.

In spring, when the wildflowers bloom, Marble Bar is a pretty place and one of the most popular Pilbara towns to visit. Race Day on the first weekend in July is also a popular time but you'll need to book accommodation well in advance.

Tourist information is available from the service station (☎ 08-9176 1041) on Francis St opposite the Ironclad Hotel, or from the Ampol roadhouse (☎ 08-9176 1166) on Halse Rd, on your left as you enter town from Marble Bar Rd. The latter organises personalised tours of the area – ring details (ask for Bob or Jodi Howard).

In town, the 1895 **government buildings** on the corner of General and McLeod Sts, made of local stone, are still in use. The **Ironclad Hotel**, with its walls of corrugated iron, has remained unchanged since it was erected as the town's first hotel.

Unfortunately, accommodation and meal options are limited:

Marble Bar Caravan Park *(☎ 08-9176 1067, Contest St)* Camp/powered sites $7.70/9.90 per person. A pleasant little park situated in a hollow that gets cold at night.

Ironclad Hotel *(☎ 08-9176 1066, 15 Francis St)* Singles/doubles $77/88, single/double dongas $55/66. Distinctive and friendly but meals are available only to house guests.

Marble Bar Travellers Stop Motel *(☎ 08-9176 1166, at the Ampol roadhouse on Halse Rd)* Basic rooms with shared facilities $38, single/double motel rooms $77/96. Neat and tidy with a swimming pool. Dining room meals are available to non-guests.

Marble Bar to Woodstock Most people continue down the rough, unsealed Marble Bar Rd to Nullagine and Newman, but head south-west to Hillside homestead and Woodstock Aboriginal community to end up at the Great Northern Hwy 94km north of

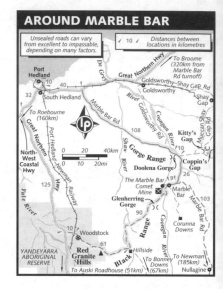

Auski Roadhouse. This would have to be one of the most scenic drives in the Pilbara.

But first we take a little detour 4km west of town to **Chinaman Pool**, a pretty swimming hole and picnic spot on the Coongan River (no camping allowed), where you'll probably see a few pelicans, egrets and cormorants, and hundreds of noisy corellas. One km further, at the end of the road, is the **Marble Bar** itself, a ridge of translucent, mainly red jasper across the Coongan River that the early settlers mistook for marble. Clamber over it and you'll see why.

Head back almost into town and out again on the road to Hillside homestead (during dry weather in winter, you can ignore the sign that instructs you to ring before proceeding). After 3km, a signposted turn-off on the left leads to a **Jasper deposit**, which is an extension of the Marble Bar ridge. Every now and then the authorities blow up a piece of the mountain so tourists can souvenir bits of jasper, which is strictly prohibited at the Marble Bar itself.

Ten kilometres out of town is the **Comet Gold Mine**, which operated off-and-on from 1936 to 1985. The mine itself is off limits but the museum (open 9am-4pm daily, admission $2) is well worth a visit. It also has beautiful mineral samples for sale. The mine's 75m smokestack, touted as the tallest in the southern hemisphere (another one of those southern-hemisphere records that Australians love to toss around), used to carry cyanide fumes away.

The road goes through some pretty countryside, and 21km past the Comet mine is a signposted turn-off on the left to **Glenherring Gorge**. This 4WD track winds along for 3.5km (bear right at the first Y-junction and left at the second one) and ends at a well-hidden little camping area next to a stream. It doesn't look like much, but walk downstream for about 1km into the gorge proper (stick to the left-hand side) and you'll see what it's all about. It's quite spectacular.

The main road continues for another 60km to Hillside homestead (no tourist facilities) as one scenic vista unfolds after another. As you get closer to Hillside, the stark **Black Range** with its distinctive black band of rock looms up on the left and keeps you company for some 30km.

At the Y-junction at Hillside, turn right towards Woodstock (left leads to Bonney Downs south of Nullagine). Shortly after, you cross the Shaw River – a big one during the Wet. There are no major sights along this 61km stretch to Woodstock, just more pretty scenery, including a couple of remarkably crumpled red granite hills on your left at the halfway mark.

Eventually you pass the Woodstock community on your left (no tourist facilities), and shortly after, cross the Port Hedland-Newman railway line. From here it's another 10km to the Great Northern Hwy. Turn left towards Auski (Munjina) Roadhouse (94km away) and Karijini.

ORGANISED TOURS

There are countless tour operators who cover the Pilbara from just about any town of any size in the region. The following selection just scrapes the surface – contact the visitor centres in the region for complete listings and further advice. For details on the unique Ibis Aerial Hwy, see Alternative Transport in the Gibb River Rd section earlier.

Design-a-Tour (☎ 08-9841 7778, fax 9842 2809, W www.dat.com.au, PO Box 627, Albany, WA 6331) Day tours of Karijini and the gorges for $99 (from Auski Roadhouse) or $120 (4WD from Tom Price); three-day backpacker camping tours $350 from Karratha or Exmouth; several other options.

Dingo's Tours (☎ 08-9173 1000, e dingos oasis@hotmail.com, 59 Kingsmill St, Port Hedland, WA 6721) Three-day, all-in Karijini camping tours from Port Hedland $380; one-day tours to Marble Bar and several other options; tagalong tours to Ruddall River National Park in planning. Several readers (young as well as middle-aged) have recommended Dingo's.

Red Rock Abseiling Adventures (☎/ fax 08-9189 2206, W www.redrockadventures .com.au, PO Box 559, Tom Price, WA 6751) Half-day walks through the gorges near Oxers Lookout (adventurous or sedate, depending on the group) and/or half-day abseiling trips in Hancock Gorge (no previous experience required), $104.50.

Snappy Gum Safaris (☎ 08-9185 3141, fax 9185 3141, PO Box 1545, Karratha, WA 6714) Two-day Karijini camping tour $275 all-inclusive; three-day Adventure camping tour (includes walks through the Karijini gorges) $375 all-inclusive; three-day North-West Explorer tour to Karijini (more comfort, with proper accommodation) $730 all-inclusive.

FACILITIES
Karratha

Karratha's resources boom means that accommodation is expensive and often full. Book ahead.

There are three caravan parks in town, none of them very central or scenic.

Balmoral Holiday Park (☎ 08-9185 3628, Balmoral Rd) Unpowered/powered sites $18/27 per double, vans from $39. On the western edge of town.

Pilbara Holiday Park (☎ 08-9185 3628, Rosemary Rd) Unpowered/powered sites $18/27 per double, cabins $85 per double. Also on the western edge of town.

Karratha Caravan Park (☎ 08-9185 1012, Mooligunn Rd) Double unpowered/powered sites $15.40/19.80, vans from $44. South of town in the industrial estate

Karratha Backpackers *(☎ 08-9144 4904, 110 Wellard Way)* Dorms $16.50 per person, singles $33, doubles/twins $44. A lively (and sometimes noisy) place near the centre of town.

At the other end of the scale (there's nothing in between) are:

Mercure Inn Karratha *(☎ 08-9185 1155, Searipple Rd)* Rooms from $142. Comfortable rooms set around landscaped tropical courtyards; free in-house movies and a licensed bar/restaurant.

Best Western *(☎ 08-9143 9888, Cnr Warambe & Searipple Rds)* Rooms from $168 ($110 on weekends) but mostly $200-plus. Formerly known as Karratha Central Apartments, this is a gleaming place near the centre of town.

Karratha International Hotel *(☎ 08-9185 3111, Cnr Hillview & Dampier Rds)* Rooms from $188 ($135 on weekends) but mostly $200-plus. A four-star hotel that prides itself on offering the best accommodation and dining in the Pilbara.

For snacks, try the cafes and takeaways in the Karratha shopping centre, including ***Boomerang***. The ***Tambrey Centre***, off Tambrey Dr a few kilometres west of the town centre, serves counter meals in its tavern and kids can play in the pool. The ***Mercure Inn*** has a sparkling bistro offering the usual meals.

Roebourne

Harding River Caravan Park *(☎ 08-9182 1063, 1km down a road on the north side of the bridge, just off the North-West Coastal Hwy)* Double camp sites $12, on-site vans $40. A bit dusty and windy but does the job.

Mt Welcome Motel Hotel This is the main place to stay in Roebourne. It was closed at the time of research but local advice suggested it would be reopening as the ***Victoria Hotel***. Contact the Roebourne visitor centre for current details.

Your only food option in Roebourne itself is takeaways at the ***BP service station***. However, most people continue 19km to ***Point Samson***, which has several places to stay and eat, while the historic town of ***Cossack*** (now virtually a ghost town) has backpacker accommodation in the old police barracks. The Roebourne visitor centre can provide details on all of this.

Millstream-Chichester & Karijini National Parks

In Millstream-Chichester, there are basic ***camping grounds*** at Snake Creek (near Python Pool), Crossing Pool and Deepreach. Snake Creek is really very basic and not as pleasant as the latter two places, which have drop toilets and gas barbecues. There are also several basic ***camping grounds*** within Karijini, including Fortescue (Dales Gorge), Weano Gorge and Banjima Dr at the Joffre turn-off. The Banjima camp site is probably not as pleasant as the other two.

See the National Parks earlier in this section for more information.

Wittenoom

The town's accommodation is very limited and under imminent threat of closure (the caravan park has already closed but you can camp for free in the gorge). The Gem Shop has basic supplies, and Elke's Coffee Shop has snacks and drinks.

Wittenoom Guest House *(☎ 08-9189 7060, Gregory St)* Camp sites/dorms $5/$10 per person, singles/twins with shared facilities $20/$35. In the old convent, with an oasis garden and very friendly owner – the sort of place it's hard to tear yourself away from.

Wittenoom Holiday Homes *(☎ 08-9189 7096, Fifth Ave)* Double cottages from $80. Run by the Gem Shop, worth considering for families and longer stays.

Auski (Munjina) Roadhouse

Auski Tourist Village *(☎ 08-9176 6988, open daily 6am-9pm)* Camp sites $12 per person, motel rooms singles/doubles $110/120. This roadhouse, at Munjina Gorge on the Great Northern Hwy, 42km east of Wittenoom, is so named because of its Aussie and Kiwi founders. It basks in a lack of competition and its services and products (including fuel) are overpriced.

A few kilometres south along the Great Northern Hwy is the Munjina Gorge lookout, down a track about 1km east of the road.

Tom Price

Tom Price Tourist Park (☎ 08-9189 1515, off Mine Rd, 4km west of town) Unpowered/powered camp sites $16.50/19.80, double chalets from $82.50. Under the shadow of Mt Nameless (walking trail from the caravan park, great views). The new owners are very keen to please.

Karijini Lodge Motel (☎ 08-9189 1110, Stadium Rd) Rooms from $120, budget twins $60.

Mercure Inn (☎ 08-9189 1101, Central Rd) Rooms from $115. Rather basic and showing its age.

The **Karijini Lodge** and **Mercure Inn** have restaurants. Other options include the **Red Emperor** (a reasonable steak and pasta house, BYO) and the **Karijini Cafe** (for light snacks), both in the shopping mall opposite the visitor centre on Central Rd.

Newman

Newman Caravan Park (☎ 08-9175 1428, Kalgan Dr) Double unpowered/powered camp sites $13.50/18. When we stayed here in the high season it was surprisingly quiet but the surroundings and facilities seemed fine.

Dearloves Caravan Park (☎ 08-9175 2802, Cowra Dr) Double unpowered/powered camp sites $15/19, motel room doubles $55, backpacker accommodation $27.50 per person ($22 if staying 2 nights or more). This camping ground was busier than the Newman, perhaps due to the tour buses parked out the front.

Mercure Inn Newman (☎ 08-9175 1101, Newman Dr) Doubles from $120. Slight discount with a pension card. In the centre of town.

All Seasons Newman Hotel (☎ 08-9177 8666, Newman Dr) Doubles from $140, budget singles/doubles $33/38. Good and clean. In the centre of town.

Capricorn Roadhouse (☎ 08-9175 153, fax 9175 2408, Great Northern Hwy 18km south of town, 7km past the Marble Bar turn-off) Double unpowered/powered sites $6.50/16, singles/doubles with shared facilities $22/33, single/double self-contained units $44/55, units (up to 5 people) $77. This place has a bar and restaurant, 24-hour fuel and meals. Fax the roadhouse (with six weeks notice) for fuel runs to Canning Stock Route ($350 per drum).

Restaurants are concentrated in three blocks of shops in the signposted 'Town Centre'. The **Chinese Kitchen** in the Boulevard Shopping Centre does tasty meals. Across the road from the Hilditch shopping mall is **TNT's Pizza**. Both the **All Seasons** and the **Mercure** have restaurants.

For tyres, batteries and breakdowns, you'll probably get good service from Newman Tyre & Battery Supplies (☎ 08-9175 2755), on Welsh Dr in the Light Industrial Area. Only 100m down the road, the **Outback Deli** does snacks and delicious home-made cakes.

Port Hedland

Accommodation at Port Hedland is directly affected by the boom and bust cycle of the iron-ore economy. In boom years, the newly employed hand out their hard-earned bucks for the most basic of dosshouses; in bust years (as at the time of research), you can get reasonable value. Most of the residents live 20km away in South Hedland, a modern suburb with shopping malls and tidy streets that holds little of interest for visitors.

Cooke Point Caravan & Camping Resort (☎ 08-9173 1271, Cnr Taylor & Athol Sts) Double powered camp sites $21, single/double backpacker accommodation $27/44, cabins from $62. This village-like park is adjacent to Pretty Pool. The sites are tidy and so are the cabins.

Dixon's Caravan Park (☎ 08-9172 2525, Lot 945 North West Coastal Hwy) Double powered sites $20, cabins from $50. A fair way out of town, but handy if you're in transit.

In South Hedland, there's **South Hedland Caravan Park** (☎ 08-9172 1197, Hamilton Rd) and **Blackrock Caravan Park** (☎ 08-9172 3444, North Circular Rd).

Port Hedland Backpackers (☎ 08-9173 3282, 20 Richardson St) Dorm beds $17, twins $38. Dusty but friendly, in the centre of town. Organises budget trips to Karijini.

Dingo's Oasis Backpackers (☎ *08-9173 1000, 59 Kingsmill St*) Dorm beds $17, doubles/twins $45. A 15-minute walk from town at a wonderful location looking out to sea (good sunsets). New, clean and tidy with very enthusiastic hosts. Runs trips to Karijini and Marble Bar (see Organised Tours).

Pier Hotel (☎ *08-9173 1488, The Esplanade*) Singles/doubles $65/80. Recently renovated. Busy, noisy pub with scantily clad barmaids.

Mercure Inn Port Hedland (☎ *08-9173 1511, Lukis St*) Rooms from $163. Enjoy the perfect sunsets and decent restaurant food.

South Hedland Motel (☎ *08-9172 2222, Court Pl*) Singles/doubles/family $80/90/100. Standard motel.

The Lodge Motel (☎ *08-9172 2188, Brand St, South Hedland*) Singles/doubles $129.50/151.50. Rates include all meals plus a packed lunch if you're travelling.

Thai restaurant ***Tip Pa Ros 3***, on Edgar St in the old Methodist Church, is a bit hit-and-miss, but on a good night the food is great. Good Thai food and fish and chips are available from the ***Yacht Club*** from Thursday to Sunday – enjoy the relaxed atmosphere as you watch the sunset. The ***Pier Hotel*** serves solid, cheap pub fare. The ***Mercure Inn*** has slightly better food, more upmarket surroundings and a brilliant view.

Canning Stock Route

Highlights

- The challenge of the world's longest, most remote stock route – the hardest 4WD trip in Australia

- Camping and exploring around the oasis of Durba Springs

- Walking through the Breaden Hills to Godfrey's Tank, with its reminders of the route's early explorers

The Canning Stock Route stretches over 1700km across the arid heart of Western Australia, between Wiluna in the south and Halls Creek in the north. It is the longest stock route in the world, most of it passing through uninhabited but vegetated desert country.

Just think: Here you can drive the same distance as the complete length of Great Britain and halfway back again; from Nagasaki in the south of Japan to the island of Hokkaido in the north; or from Los Angeles to Seattle – and hardly see a soul. It's a long haul in anybody's language.

It is the hardest and longest 4WD trip in Australia. The number of sand hills that need to be crossed varies, depending on who you believe and if they counted every hill or just the major sand-dune ridges. There are at least 800, but most people stop counting after day two or three.

The route crosses the Little Sandy Desert, the Gibson Desert, the Great Sandy Desert and, in its northern part, the western section of the Tanami Desert. Because of that, one may think the country or the scenery never changes. Nothing could be further from the truth. The variety of desert landforms and the subtle changes of vegetation weave their magic on all who travel this vast landscape.

Nobody travels the Canning in summer. It usually begins to see the first adventurers in late April or early May and by the middle of October, the season is coming to a close. June to August are probably the best months to travel. If you are the first of the season, you may be plagued by tall spinifex that can block your vehicle's radiator in less than 10 minutes. In places, you may find it difficult to see the track.

Needless to say, you need to be very well set up to travel the Canning. Most would consider the route to be out of the realm of small 4WDs. The ability to carry the huge amount of fuel, water and supplies for the minimum two-week trip means that anything smaller than a four-cylinder Jackaroo or Pajero is completely out of the question. While the four-cylinder utes, such as the Hilux and Rodeo, do well out here, the real kings of the Canning are the six-cylinder diesel Land Cruisers and Patrols.

Mind you, some people have walked the Canning. Alfred Canning, after whom the route is named, and his men did (when they weren't riding camels), but in more recent times, some adventurers looking for a challenge have walked or run the route. The handful who have, either pushed a specially designed cart to carry their supplies or had vehicle backup. Either way, it's a hard slog!

Cyclists and motorcycle riders are just as rare. The deep, soft sand and the distances between water tends to turn most off. Fuel is only available about halfway along the stock route, so carrying fuel and water is a problem requiring a backup vehicle.

Travelling the stock route in company is much safer than on your own. If you want to travel the Canning but don't know anyone who wants to go, 4WD clubs often have trips and there are a number of tour operators who take tag-alongs. Some of the latter even cook for you and they certainly supply the safety and companionship.

Wiluna and Halls Creek, at opposite ends of the stock route, are only small communities but service vast pastoral regions; you can find or get anything you want, as long as you have the time to wait. If you break down, parts may have to be flown in on the weekly mail plane. Forget the cost – you need the parts to keep rolling! The only other option is to sell your truck as it stands, hitch a lift to the more settled parts of the country and give up on exploring the real Australia.

History

One of the great attractions of travelling the stock route is the strong sense of history that pervades most of the 54 wells and water-holes dotting its course. It's impossible for the visitor not to be touched by this fairly recent saga in Australia's history.

Major Peter Warburton crossed from central Australia to the north-western coast in 1873, traversing the stock route's northern section on the way. In 1874, John Forrest and his party travelled from the coast of Western Australia to the Overland Telegraph Line, naming several points at the southern end.

On 2 June of that year, he found what he described as 'one of the best springs in the colony' and named it Weld Springs. When they were attacked by Aborigines here, Forrest and his men built a small stone fort to protect themselves. Rocks from the fort still remain at what became Canning's Well 9.

In 1876, Ernest Giles passed just to the north of Forrest's tracks on his return from the western coast. But it was to be another 20 years before other explorers travelled this region.

In 1896, two expeditions set out on south-to-north crossings. The Calvert Expedition was led by Lawrence Wells, but tragedy struck when two members, including his cousin, became lost and died of thirst. David Carnegie's party had better fortunes: All but one survived a double crossing of the desert (Charlie Stansmore died after a shooting accident). But they failed to find any gold or a stock route – the main reasons for the trip. Both expeditions advised the government that a cattle route was impossible and the search for one should be stopped. The stage was now set for Alfred Canning.

By the early 1900s, Kimberley cattlemen were clamouring for a stock route to be developed from the north-western station country to the southern gold fields. Earlier, in 1898, the movement of cattle from the East Kimberley to the coast around Derby had been banned to stop the spread of cattle tick. A desert route was seen as a natural barrier to the spread of the ticks.

In April 1906, Canning was already a surveyor with a good reputation and was chosen to lead a group of men to survey a route between Wiluna and Halls Creek.

In April of that year, the party of eight men, 23 camels and two ponies left Perth, heading via Day Dawn to Wiluna. Pushing north across the untracked wilderness, they arrived in Halls Creek at the end of October, spending Christmas there before heading south and back into the desert, at the end of February 1907.

Searching for water all the way, they used many rockholes that were sources of water for Aborigines. In April 1907, at a rockhole called Waddawalla (later to be known as

Canning's Well 40), party member Michael Tobin was speared to death.

In July, the group returned to Perth and Canning's report that a route could be made through the desert was met with a standing ovation in parliament. Canning was the obvious choice to lead a well-sinking party.

By the end of March 1908, the well-sinking party of 30-odd men congregated at Wiluna, ready to head into the harsh desert. When they reached Flora Valley station at the northern end of the stock route in July 1909, they had sunk, lined and set up 31 wells. They retraced their route a month later, reaching Wiluna in late April 1910, after establishing another 21 wells.

To line many of the wells, timber had to be cut and carted for long distances. The deepest well on the stock route is Well 5, dug to a depth of 32m, while the shallowest is Tank 42 at just 1.5m.

Canning, on his arrival at Wiluna, sent a three-word telegram back to Perth: 'Work completed – Canning.'

The first stock weren't far behind Canning and his men. In April 1911, two drovers, along with one of their three Aboriginal stockmen, were fatally speared near Well 37.

Over the next 30 years, the route was never used to anywhere near its full potential. Cattle were brought down it only occasionally, so in 1929, after much lobbying, the government sent out William Snell to refurbish the route. He only got as far north as Well 35. Canning was recommissioned at the age of 70 to finish the job!

From then until just after WWII, use of the stock route increased a little, with the last mob of cattle taken down in 1959.

The first vehicle to set wheels on the stock route was back in 1908, but the first to travel a section was Michael Terry's on a 1925 expedition. Other sections of the stock route succumbed to the motor vehicle, but it was not until 1968 that a group of surveyors drove the complete length. During the 1970s, a handful of travellers challenged the route and by the end of the 1980s, some 10 to 20 groups a year were travelling its length. Today, a few thousand adventurous souls travel the stock route each year.

Information

Track conditions can vary enormously from year to year. In 2001, for instance, the whole route north of Well 33 was impassable due to flooding. The route south of Well 5 is often closed due to flooding as well.

Visitor Centres The Wiluna Shire Council (☎ 08-9981 7010), on Scotia St, is a good place to seek information on the surrounding area and the stock route. The Visitor Centre in Halls Creek (☎ 08-9168 6262) is located in Hall St opposite the Shell Roadhouse. It's open Monday to Friday 8.30am to 4.30pm from June to October. This modern facility, with its statue of Russian Jack out the front, opened with much fanfare in 2001 as part of a new shire council complex. Staff are helpful and know the area well. In the wet season, when the office is closed, staff at the Halls Creek Community Resource Centre (☎ 08-9168 6007) around the back are also happy to provide information.

Radio Frequencies The RFDS bases at Meekatharra and Derby are the best radio bases to use. They are on call for medical and emergency calls 24 hours a day.

The primary frequency for the RFDS base at Meekatharra (call sign VKJ) is 4010kHz, while its secondary frequencies are 2280kHz and 6880kHz. Derby base (call sign VJB) has a primary frequency of 5300kHz and secondary frequencies of 6925kHz and 6945kHz.

The Australian National 4WD Radio Network (☎ 08-8287 1061) can be accessed through 3995kHz, 5455kHz, 8022kHz, 11612kHz and 14977 kHz. This voluntary network offers a service for travellers in remote areas, so contact it for further information and operational times.

Registration It is advisable to register with the police at your starting point (either Wiluna or Halls Creek) and complete a form called Notification of Travel in Remote Areas. Chances are they won't want to know about you but it pays to be safe. The Wiluna police station (☎ 08-9981 7024) is on Thompson St and the Halls Creek police station (☎ 08-9168 6000) is on the highway.

Books & Maps The best maps of the Canning are those published by Australian Geographic and Westprint Maps. A full range of 1:250,000 topographic maps is available, but these maps are unlikely to be required unless you are going off the beaten track.

Far and away the best books for travellers are *The Canning Stock Route – a Traveller's Guide* by Ronele & Eric Gard, and the *Australian Geographic's Canning Stock Route*. There is an interesting insight into Canning and his travels on the stock route in *The Beckoning West* by E Smith. It's hard to get but well worthwhile for history buffs. For further reading, *Blue Peaks & Red Ridges* by Peter Muir explores the delights on the lower Canning.

Permits No permits are required if you travel the stock route as detailed, though native title claims could change things in a few years time.

Both ends of the stock route cross private pastoral land, where the normal restrictions apply.

If you go via Glen-Ayle station (☎ 08-9981 2990), it costs $20 a vehicle to use the station tracks. It's best to make contact before you leave and visit as you pass through – the house is close to the track.

You need permission from Granite Peaks station (☎ 08-9981 2983) to use the track between the homestead and the stock route, and a fee of $20 per vehicle is payable. No payment is necessary to use the Cunyu station bypass track between Well 3A and Windich Springs.

Emergency Medical facilities are available at Wiluna Medical Centre (☎ 08-9981 7063) on Lennon St. It also has support from the RFDS in emergencies. In Halls Creek the hospital (☎ 08-9168 6003) is on Roberta Ave.

SPECIAL PREPARATIONS
Warning This is not an easy trip and you need to be thoroughly prepared and have your vehicle in first-class shape before you

start. People still die in this extremely remote region when their vehicles break down. In the last 10 years, the number has reached double figures. Others have survived because they either did everything right or luck was on their side. If your vehicle fails out here, you're in real trouble!

Food & Water Most people take about a fortnight to do the Canning, so you'll need plenty of food and water on board. For more on water, see Survival in the Facts for the Visitor chapter.

The countryside along the Canning is rapidly becoming stripped of firewood – many popular camping areas have no dead timber at all – so it's recommended that you take and use a gas stove for cooking.

Fuel To travel the route and see a few of the sites along the way (some are 50km or more off the main track), a six-cylinder diesel Land Cruiser will need to carry 280L to 300L of fuel, while a petrol Cruiser will need 350L to 370L. A big V8 Ford may need 500L or more, while a small four-cylinder diesel may get away with 200L to 220L. Basically, that is what you require to travel from Well 23 to Halls Creek or vice versa. From Wiluna to the resupply point at Well 23, a six-cylinder diesel will need about 160L to 180L.

That is a lot of fuel, but you'll only get away with that amount if you organise a fuel drop at Well 23. The Capricorn Roadhouse (☎ 08-9175 1535), just south of Newman, is the place to contact, but do it six weeks or so in advance. The fuel comes in 200L drums; work out your consumption before going, so that when you leave Well 23, you are fully fuelled for the run north. What doesn't fit in your tank, leave behind! Considering the remoteness of Well 23, $350 for a 200L drum is pretty good value.

Bulk fuel should also be available from the Kunawarritji Community (☎ 08-9176 9040) near Well 33, but ring ahead to check.

Tyres Carry at least two complete spares and a couple of extra tubes. A good tyre-repair kit and pump are essential. Tyre pressures will play a very important part in

THE NORTH-WEST

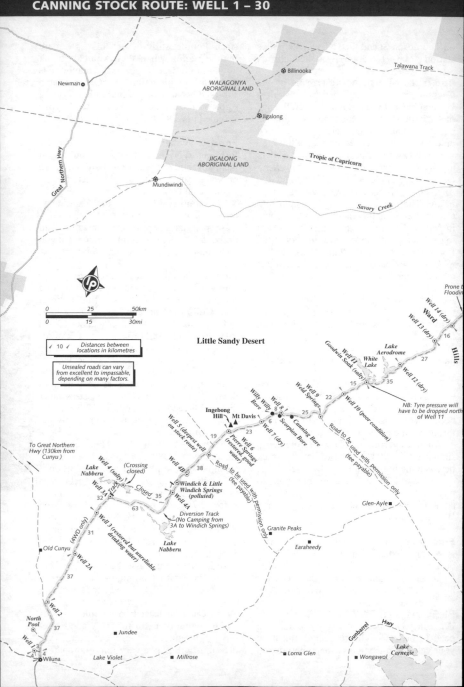

Rudall River

RUDALL RIVER
NATIONAL PARK

*Lake
Auld*

Well 30 (dry)   26

Well 29 (dry)   39

Parnngurr
(Cotton Creek)

Well 28 (dry)   32

Lake
George

Well 27 (fair)   16

Thring
Rock

Mujingerra
Cave
(extreme
caution
required)

Talawana Track

Well 26
(restored - good water)

15

Helen
Hill

31

35

Well 23 (not drinkable,
fuel dump)

Georgia Bore
(good water)

Well 25 (dry)

22

Separation Well
(Approximate
position)

McKay
Range

Savory Creek

Well 20 (dry)

44   19   22

14

23

Airstrip
(emergency)

Well 24 (dry)

Talawana   Track

Well 19-Kunawaggi
(dry)

10   8   40

Well 22 (dry)

To Windy
Corner

24   Well 21 (poor)

23

15
(Crossing can
be boggy)

'FX15'

Lake
Disappointment

Gibson Desert

Tropic of Capricorn

26

Water 17

Killagurra Springs

Onegunyah
Rockhole

33   5

Biella Spring (access
by walking trail)

Well 18 (restored - good water)

Durba Springs

Canning's
Cairn   24

Well 16 (polluted)

8   14   Sunday Well

Calvert
Range

38

Well 15 (restored - good water)

Continued on p374–375

DIANA MAYFIELD

*Lake
Brenner*

Lake Burnside

*Lake
Buchanan*

MUNGILLI
(ABORIGINAL LAND)

Gibson Desert
Nature Reserve

Gunbarrel Hwy

Carnegie

To Great
Central Rd

To Great Central Rd

Flora of the Canning

With luck, your trip up the Canning will coincide with rain somewhere along its course. The chances of that happening are, in fact, pretty good as the stock route traverses such a vast segment of land, from the more temperate south to the subtropical north. The occasional southern winter storm or tropical thunderstorm brings with it an unexpected bounty as the country bursts into new and colourful life. The hollows between dune ridges are often carpeted with flowers. For those who love wildflowers, the Canning can be a wondrous place.

Acacias, or wattles, are one of Australia's most common plants. On the Canning there are a number of species that colour the scenery. Prickly acacia, with its pale-yellow flower, is common along the complete length of the stock route, while gidgee is found along creeks in the southern section. Pindan wattle, found in the north, stands out with its yellow flowers. Another colourful wattle with bright-yellow flowers is locally called elephant-ear wattle; a good stand of these can be seen on the way to Rockhole 38.

Grevilleas are one of the most magnificent Australian flowers. There are about 200 species in Australia and you'll see a few different ones on the Canning. The holly grevillea, or Wickham's grevillea, has yellow flowers, while the similar prickly grevillea, found in the northern section of the stock route, has spectacular red-orange flowers. These plants can be found on rocky hills or sandy plains and dunes, but the desert grevillea and the honey grevillea are found only on dunes and sandy

successfully tackling the Canning. Too high and you won't get up the sand hills, too low and you will stake tyres. Because of the loads being carried, it's not necessary to drop pressure as low as you would for a day's run along the beach: 170kPa to 180kPa (25psi to 26psi) should do nicely.

In places, you will be travelling over very rocky and broken ground so extreme care is needed. Take it slowly and you should be OK. Travel too quickly, or with tyre pressures too low, and your tyres will start blowing.

Trailers The Canning is no place for a trailer. It is, of course, possible to take a well-constructed trailer but those who have done it once will never do it again.

THE ROUTE
Wiluna

Once considered the wildest town in Australia, Wiluna sits on the edge of desert country and was gazetted as a town in 1898. During its boom years in the 1930s, the population peaked at around 9000 and the town had four hotels. While its population waned after WWII, recent mining activities have seen the town gain a few more people.

Today the population is about 300. See the later Facilities section for more information.

Wiluna to Well 9 (295km)

This track lies across pastoral land and during times of heavy rain can be officially closed to all traffic. As with travelling across any pastoral land, leave gates as you find them and leave stock alone. Do not camp close to any stock-watering points. From Wiluna, a well-formed dirt road heads north with **Well 1** just 7km from town, while a little further on, 10km off the stock route, is **Water 1A**, called North Pool; it's on the Negrara Creek and is a popular swimming hole with locals.

Just before **Well 2**, you leave the main road and turn right onto a lesser station track reaching the well 2km later, 40km north of Wiluna. **Well 2A**, or the Granites, lies another 37km north and was blasted from rock. It was the last one built by Canning and his men.

Water from **Well 3**, 31km north of Tank 2A, is unpalatable, although the well was recently restored. Sections of the track between Well 3 and **Well 3A** can become boggy after even quite light falls of rain. The crossing of **Lake Nabberu**, which is really a

Flora of the Canning

plains. These two plants have bright yellow-orange flowers and are loaded with nectar. If there are not too many ants on them, the flowers are lovely to suck or to drop into a cup of water for a pleasant, refreshing drink.

Hakeas are closely related to the grevilleas and more than 90 of the 110 or so species found in Australia can be seen in Western Australia. The most common hakea on the Canning is the easily identifiable corkwood hakea, named for its distinctive bark. The flowers are a creamy yellow.

About 25 species of cassia can be found in the Australian inland, including several along the stock route. These shrubs are usually less than 2m high and all have yellow, buttercup-shaped flowers. The green cassia, desert cassia, blunt-leaf cassia and cockroach bush are just some you might see.

Found throughout the length of the Canning and elsewhere in inland Australia is the fluffy mulla mulla, sometimes called pussy tails. These low-growing plants have pink, purplish or white flowers that are commonly seen because they persist for a long time after rain.

Vivid displays of the delicate, star-shaped, pink flower of the desert-fringe myrtle can be seen on the dunes, and the yellow-green, bird-shaped flower of the parrot-pea bush is found north of Well 36.

Daisies of many sorts can also be seen, as well as bright-purple parakelia, and, if you are lucky, vivid displays of the magnificent Sturt's desert pea.

---

series of lakes, is now closed. Canning and his men built a corduroy log road across it. Access to **Well 4** is not permitted.

A bypass track to avoid this section through Cunyu station begins at Well 3A. It travels along the southern side of the Frere Range, climbs through Snell Pass to emerge at **Well 4A** and continues on to Windich Springs. No camping is permitted between Well 3A and Windich Springs.

Little Windich and Windich Springs were found and named by Forrest. These springs and waterholes are used today by numerous cattle but it's not the best place to camp as the water is polluted.

Well 5 is 214km north of Wiluna and 38km from Well 4A. It was the deepest well built by Canning and his men; more than a hundred tonnes of rock were blasted and removed by hand during its construction. Because of its depth, the water is hard to get. Here a track heads east to Granite Peaks homestead that can be used as a diversion around the lower Canning. A fee of $20 a vehicle, payable at the homestead situated by the track, is charged for using this route.

Well 6, or Pierre Springs as Forrest called it, is 19km further and was reconditioned by the Geraldton 4WD club in 1991. Its good,

reliable water and surrounds make it one of the best spots to camp on the Canning.

Ingebong Hill, 1km north of Well 6, is worth a climb. Once you have panted your way to the top, you'll have a great view of the surrounding country. Observant travellers may even find some Aboriginal art.

Set in a dense stand of mulga, 100m off the track and 23km from Well 6, **Well 7** is in a dilapidated state and has now collapsed. Willy Willy Bore, and **Well 8**, with its good water, are passed on the way to Well 9, a further 39km north.

Well 9 is Forrest's famous Weld Springs and is now contained in a historic reserve. Forrest and his men built a fort to protect themselves from attack by Aborigines – you can still see the remains. While the springs are now almost dry, the well, fitted with a windmill, still produces a good supply of water. The water looks crystal-clear as it overflows out of the tank, but you wouldn't want to drink it once you've looked inside. Pigeons and finches abound.

At this point, the track from **Carnegie** homestead via **Glen-Ayle** homestead joins the stock route; this track is often used by those coming from the east along the Gunbarrel Hwy. This diversion is also a wet-weather

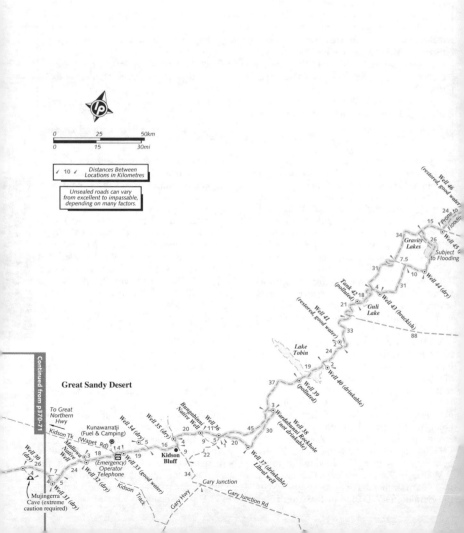

0 — 25 — 50km
0 — 15 — 30mi

✓ 10 ✓ Distances Between
Locations in Kilometres

Unsealed roads can vary
from excellent to impassable,
depending on many factors.

Great Sandy Desert

Continued from p370-71

*Well 46
(restored, good water)*

24
15 *Prone to
Floodir*

34 26 *Well 45 o*

*Gravity
Lakes*

7.5 *Subject
to Flooding*

31 10 *Well 44 (dry)*

Tank 42 18 4
(polluted) 31

21 *Well 43 (brackish)*

*Well 41
(restored, good water)* *Guli
Lake*

33 88

2

*Lake
Tobin* 24

19 2 *Well 40 (drinkable)*

37 *Well 39
(polluted)*

3

*Wardabunni Rockhole
(not drinkable)*

To Great
Northern
Hwy

Kidson Tk

Kunawarratji
(Fuel & Camping)
(Wapet Rd)

Well 34 (dry)
Well 35 (dry)
5

*Bungabinni
Native Well*

Well 36
20 11 16

45 30

Well 38

*Well 37 (drinkable)
Libral well*

*Mallowa
Native Well*
3 18
4
Well 31 (dry)
Well 32 (dry)
24
Well 33 (good water)
19
16

(Emergency)
Operator
Telephone

Kidson Track

4 1
16
**Kidson
Bluff**
9

4
9 5 20
22

*Well 30
(dry)* 26

4 5

*Mujingerra
Cave (extreme
caution required)*

34 *Gary Junction*

Gary Hwy *Gary Junction Rd*

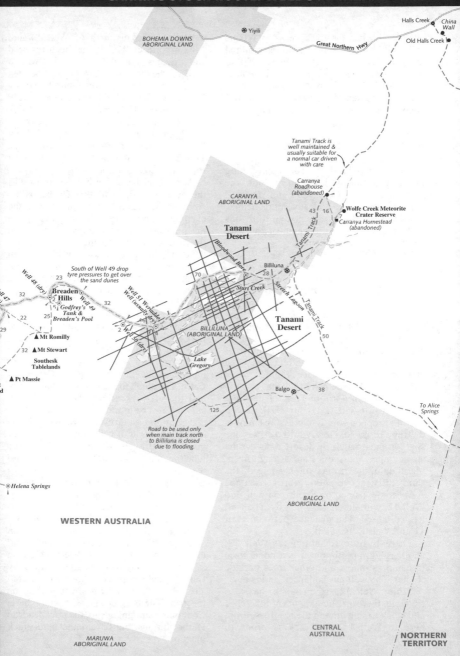

Halls Creek

China Wall

Old Halls Creek

Yiyili

BOHEMIA DOWNS
ABORIGINAL LAND

Great Northern Hwy

*Tanami Track is
well maintained &
usually suitable for
a normal car driven
with care*

Carranya
Roadhouse
(abandoned)

CARANYA
ABORIGINAL LAND

**Wolfe Creek Meteorite
Crater Reserve**
43   16
*Carranya Homestead
(abandoned)*

**Tanami
Desert**

Blauheard Bore

Billiluna

28

Sturt Creek

Stretch Lagoon

70

**Tanami
Desert**

Well 48 (dry)

*South of Well 49 drop
tyre pressures to get over
the sand dunes*   23

32   **Breaden
Hills**   32

*Godfrey's
Tank &
Breaden's Pool*

25

Well 51 Weriaddo
Well (usually dry)

2

50

22

29

▲ Mt Romilly

32   ▲ Mt Stewart

**Southesk
Tablelands**

▲ Pt Massie

BILLILUNA
(ABORIGINAL LAND)

*Lake
Gregory*

Balgo   38

To Alice
Springs

125

*Road to be used only
when main track north
to Billiluna is closed
due to flooding.*

Helena Springs

WESTERN AUSTRALIA

BALGO
ABORIGINAL LAND

CENTRAL
AUSTRALIA

**NORTHERN
TERRITORY**

MARUWA
ABORIGINAL LAND

alternative when the track between Wiluna and Well 9 is closed. Permission is required from Glen-Ayle station (☎ 08-9981 2990) to use this track; a fee of $20 per vehicle applies. It is about 200km from Carnegie station to Well 9 via Glen-Ayle. See the Gunbarrel Highway section earlier in this chapter for more information on Carnegie station.

Well 9 to Durba Springs (215km)

Once you leave Well 9 you are approaching the end of pastoral country. Soon the landscape changes and you enter sand-hill country, where the real adventure begins. The Durba Hills, at the very north of this section, are one of the gems of the trip: Allow time to enjoy them.

Well 10, 22km north of Well 9, was called the Lucky Well by the drovers of old, as they considered themselves lucky to have escaped the sand hill country and reached this far south. It is in poor condition now.

Heading for **Well 11**, you cross the first of the sand hills, but they really shouldn't be a problem. At this well on the edge of the salt expanse of **White Lake**, 15km north of Well 10, a sign for travellers has been erected by Australian Geographic. Water from this well is too salty to drink.

Nearly 21km north of Well 11, the first big sand hill will test your skill. If you haven't dropped your tyre pressures, now is the time to do so. Here you'll also see the southernmost patch of **desert oaks** on the stock route. These trees are a magnificent highlight of the trip. As you head north, the sand hills get bigger. North of Lake Aerodrome, named by Snell, you will find **Well 12**, with desert oaks nearby. The well has collapsed. The distance between Well 11 and Well 12 is 35km.

There is little remaining of **Well 13**, another 27km north, but it is a good place to camp as mulga and other trees provide shelter. The well has collapsed and is dry.

While **Well 14**, 16km north, has also caved in, there are the remains of the fence and stock trough among the tea trees. From here to Well 15, the track is prone to flooding.

Well 15, 25km north of Well 14 and 140km north of Well 9, has been restored and provides good water. About halfway to Well 16, the remains of a trolley can be seen beside the track. It was abandoned by Murray Rankin on his first attempt to walk the Canning in 1974. He succeeded in 1976.

A few hundred metres west off the track, and 38km north of the previous well, **Well 16** is set among picturesque white gums. This well normally has water but it's unfit for human consumption.

As the track heads north, it begins to skirt the western edge of the **Durba Hills**. Approaching the hills from the south in the evening is an unforgettable experience, as the rugged escarpment glows fiery red in the rays of the setting sun.

Sunday Well lies 14km north-east from the main track; the turn-off is nearly 9km north of Well 16. Now no more than a hole in the ground and surrounded by tea trees, it can be easily missed. This track also leads out to the **Calvert Range**, 45km east of Sunday Well, where there are Aboriginal rock engravings.

About 18km north of Well 16, a track leads north-east into the base of the escarpment, below the prominent **Canning's Cairn**. The climb to the top is relatively easy and the view excellent. Aboriginal rock carvings can be found on the southern wall.

The north-east turn-off to **Biella Spring** is about 7km north of Canning's Cairn. Once you have travelled the 2km from the junction, it is a pleasant half-hour walk into the gorge to the spring, where you will generally find water. There are a number of Aboriginal rock paintings here.

At the northernmost point of the range is a major track junction, 32km from Well 16. Turning north will keep you on the main stock route, while turning hard right will take you on a track into **Water 17**, also known as Killagurra Springs, named by Canning and a registered Aboriginal sacred site – the rock art is the best you will see on the trip. There is permanent water here. Continuing straight ahead, the track leads to Durba Springs, 5km from the main track junction.

Durba Springs is a place not to miss, and you should spend at least two nights here. The camping area boasts a solar-powered composting toilet courtesy of Track Care Western Australia. From the camping spot, you can explore the head of the gorge and the surrounding country. There are many Aboriginal art sites within the nearby hills and gorges and the area is a haven for birds. If nothing else, just relax and soak up the atmosphere of this tranquil place, though it does get busier than other spots along the Canning.

Durba Springs to Well 23 (205km)

North from the Durba Hills is some of the toughest country on the Canning, and further on, you skirt the western margin of the vast salt expanse of Lake Disappointment. North of Well 22, you meet the Talawana Track, a major escape route to the west, and just a little further on is Well 23 – site of the Capricorn Roadhouse fuel dump.

Well 18 lies only 33km north of the Durbas, but it will take you up to four hours to cover that distance. The well, about 1km east off the track, has been restored and yields good water.

Three kilometres further on a track heads east from the main track to the Terrace Hills and **Onegunyah Rockhole**, found at the base of a small, normally dry waterfall. A few kilometres south of **Well 19**, which is 26km north of Well 18, you will cross the **Tropic of Capricorn**, marked by a survey peg, FX15. Well 19 is on the edge of a claypan and is completely silted up.

Savory Creek, 23km north of Well 19, can be a major obstacle. While it often has water, it is very salty, as you can see from the creek banks. If the main crossing is too risky, there is another 6km west which should be drier and easier.

Once across, the track turns in towards **Lake Disappointment**, but swings north a short distance from the lake shore. A faint track continues to the lake and is worth a detour, but beware of boggy patches. This lake, a vast sea of salt, only has water in it after unseasonably heavy rains. The stock route travels along its western edge for over 70km, but this is about the only place you have a chance to see it at close quarters.

The turn-off to **Well 20** is 15km north of Savory Creek; the well is 10km west from the main track. All that remains is a hole in the ground.

You need to turn right at a track junction, 24km north of the turn-off to Well 20, which leads 8km to **Well 21** and its poor water. This route continues east and joins the other route just west of **Well 22,** in a picturesque white-gum flat between the dunes. The well, 40-odd kilometres north-east of Well 21 along this diversion, is dry.

The **Talawana Track**, graded by Len Beadell in 1963, meets the stock route some 9km north of Well 22. By heading west here, you reach the township of Newman within 460km. On the western side of the junction is Georgia Bore with its delightful water from a hand pump – a good spot to camp.

Well 23 – the **fuel dump** – is another 22km north. Most people stop here for fuel, but the well water is undrinkable.

For emergency evacuation there is an airstrip 2km beyond Well 23 on the way to Well 24, on the southern side of the track. A larger airstrip exists at the Harbutt Range, 36km north-west of Well 23, off the Talawana Track.

Well 23 to Well 33 (273km)

This section of the Canning brings variety and enjoyment as you revel in the waters of Well 26, the beautiful stands of bloodwood and desert oak and the secrets of its water-filled caverns.

Situated just off the track and 14km east of Well 23, **Well 24** is dry. Three kilometres further north, the **Windy Corner Track**, put in by Len Beadell, joins with the Canning. North of here a vast sea of waving spinifex leads to **Well 25** 20km away, once again dry with just a few surface timbers lying around. Just north of this well, a series of three big dunes will test your driving technique and tyre pressures. There will be plenty more like these between Wells 40 and 42. By the time you have covered the 59km to Well 26 from the refuelling point at Well 23, you'll be looking forward to stopping and enjoying this oasis. You are 760km from Wiluna, barring detours and side trips.

Well 26 was fully restored by a party led by David Hewitt in 1983 to commemorate the route's 75th anniversary. It provides good drinking water and a chance to freshen up. A visitor's book is also at the well and most travellers use it to record their thoughts and adventures.

A steady drive north for 31km leads to **Well 27**, which has fair water in an emergency. A further 15km brings you to a track which heads east for 35km to **Separation Well**. The drive to the well is a slow one and leads to a shallow depression where members of the 1896 Calvert Expedition split up to head for Warburton's Joanna Spring.

Warburton had plotted the position of Joanna Spring incorrectly and neither Calvert group found the spring. Charles Wells and his companion died, while Lawrence Wells, the leader of the expedition and in charge of the second group, made it to the Fitzroy River. Over the following few months, six search expeditions, all with Lawrence Wells as leader or member, pushed into the desert, finally finding both bodies at Discovery Well.

Little remains of **Well 28** and **Well 29**, which are both dry, but there is some good camping just before and just after Well 29, 153km north of Well 23.

What remains of **Well 30** lies 39km north of the previous well and among a glorious stand of bloodwood trees. It is an ideal camp site, although there is no water.

Just 4km east of Well 30 is **Mujingerra Cave**, a limestone cave with crystal-clear water. Reached through a narrow tunnel, it is not for the faint-hearted. Be careful when approaching the entrance and park your vehicle some distance away. Please do not pollute this fragile environment with soap.

Well 31 is 4km east off the main route and dominated by a good specimen of a cabbage-tree gum. The turn-off is 26km north of Well 30 and this route continues, joining up with the main track 5km later. The run 24km north from here to **Well 32** is easy and you may get a chance to hit top gear for a change. While Well 31 is dry, Well 32, alongside the main track on the eastern side has collapsed. About 3km west of Well 32, along a distinct track, is **Mallowa Native Well**, set among green acacias. Like many of these soaks, you will have to dig for water if there's none that is visible on the surface.

The Kidson Track (Wapet Rd) crosses the Canning 18km north of Well 32. Just 3km west along this relatively good road is the **Kunawarritji** Aboriginal community. Fuel and food are available from the community store (but see the earlier Fuel section) and you'll also find camping facilities with showers. Opening hours are on demand. If you keep heading west from Kunawarritji for another 575km you reach the Great Northern Hwy. East will lead to Gary Hwy, Windy Corner and Sandy Blight Junction, all just as remote as the junction you are at. There's a phone booth here that only takes operator-connected calls.

Well 33 is just 4km north of the Kidson-Canning junction on the eastern side of the stock route. It is a pleasant camp but the dingoes are friendly and will steal anything left lying around – smelly shoes seem to be a real favourite. The water from the well is generally drinkable.

Well 33 to Well 39 (161km)

Some of the most historic and poignant places lie along this section of the stock route. Take your time and make the effort to see it all.

Another good spot to camp is at **Well 34**, 5km west off the main track; the turn-off is 19km north of Well 33. Little remains at this spot and there is no water. The surrounding area gets very boggy after rain.

Once you pass **Kidson Bluff** to the east, there is a junction 16km north of the turn-off to Well 34. Here you can turn left and travel 4km to **Well 35**. This well was burnt out (like many on the Canning – a timely reminder to be careful with your own fire), but a bore casing does provide a limited supply of water. You're now just over 1000km north of Wiluna.

From Well 35, you can proceed north on an alternative route through a magnificent stand of desert oaks to **Bungabinni Native Well**, which has a plentiful supply of fresh water and a visitor's book. From there, you pass **Well 36**, with its fair water and nice camping spot among the desert oaks, before rejoining the main stock route just a few kilometres further on, 31km from Well 35.

At the junction before Well 35, you can also turn right, following the **Gary Hwy** for 9km before turning left (north) again back onto the stock route. About 27km north of this left turn, the alternative route described previously joins with the main stock route.

One kilometre past this junction a track veers off to the east, heading 20km to **Well 37**, or Libral Well. This well produces good water and the surrounding area makes for a pleasant camping spot; the history and the graves close by make for an interesting few hours of exploration.

Well 37 is often called the Haunted Well, because of its tragic history for the colonists. The first stockmen ever to take cattle down the Canning were attacked and killed by Aborigines at this point. The two drovers, along with their Aboriginal assistant, were buried about 50m to 60m almost due north of the well.

The grave of an oil prospector clubbed to death by Aborigines in 1922 can also be found here. He was killed some distance south of the well and was buried at the base of a desert oak about 250m north-east of the well. The tree is blazed but only the most observant will see the original blaze.

From Libral Well a diversion track leads for 30km to **Rockhole 38**, also known as Wardabunni Rockhole, which is normally dry, or green and stagnant. The walls of the rockhole reveal the initials of some of the early explorers.

Just 3km further on from Rockhole 38, you meet up with the old stock route track and swing north. Travelling another 37km north, you reach Well 39, which has reasonable water, in an emergency.

Well 39 to the Breaden Hills (300km)

From Well 39 to the Breaden Hills, history and a variety of desert landscapes vie with one another for attention and it's easy to spend days soaking up the atmosphere.

A few kilometres north of Well 39, a stand of desert oaks makes a good camp. The crossing of **Lake Tobin** is generally easy and speeding across the salt flat is something to enjoy! At the northern extremity of the lake, 19km north of Well 39, is the turn-off to **Well 40**. Two kilometres east from the main track, this well is the site where a member of Canning's 1907 survey party, was killed by an Aborigine. This is a good spot to camp and the well supplies reasonable water.

The turn-off to **Well 41** is 24km north of Well 40 and the well itself is another 2km west off the main stock route. Its tannin-stained water is quite good for drinking.

A bumpy scraped track, beginning 33km north of Well 41, leads to David Carnegie's **Helena Springs**. This track leads 88km east to the historic site and there is no water at the end. The track was put in by a group led by Peter Vernon, who has blazed a number of trails out here and, in July 1988, ran the length of the Canning from Wiluna to Halls Creek in 35 days.

On the south-western end of Guli Lake, **Tank 42** is 54km north of Well 41 and is the shallowest watering point constructed on the stock route. The trough timbers and the nearby bush have suffered from unthinking passing travellers looking for firewood, and the water is polluted.

Well 43 is 4km north-east off the main route. Just a few metres away from the original is a new well which can supply brackish water, drinkable in an emergency. The old well, which yielded thousands of litres per hour of good water, is now dry.

The distance between the turn-off to Well 43 and the turn-off to **Well 44** is 31km. Well 44 is some 17km east off the main route. It is nothing much more than a hole in the ground and is completely dry.

To continue to **Well 45** from Well 44, you can either backtrack to the main vehicle route or continue on a scraped track to join the stock route 26km north of Well 44, near the Gravity Lakes and about 15km south of Well 45. On the main route, the distance

THE NORTH-WEST

from the Well 44 turn-off to Well 45, located on the main stock route track, is 49km. Well 45 is caved in and generally dry.

From Well 45, you have the option of following the old vehicle route north-east, a distance of 90km, to a major track junction just south of Well 48. Here, you can turn off to the Breaden Hills. This route from Well 45 bypasses Wells 46 and 47 by up to 22km, but access tracks lead to each well.

A better choice is to head north along a scraped track that follows the original Canning Stock Route directly to **Well 46**, a distance of 24km, though this track should not be used following a heavy wet season. This well provides excellent water and is a great spot to camp.

You can head directly east from here, reaching the old vehicle route, 31km north of Well 45, after 15km. However, by heading north from Well 46 along another bumpy, scraped track for 29km, you will join up with the main access track to **Well 47**. Well 47 lies 4km further west and has collapsed.

From here, you can head back east, past the scraped track on which you came north, for 26km to join up with the old vehicle route, 63km north of Well 45 and 27km south of Well 48. This way, the total distance between Well 45 and Well 48 is 106km, compared to 88km via the main route, but you have seen all the wells along the way.

Alternatively, from Well 47 you can head 32km in a more northerly direction across faint, scraped tracks directly to Well 48, a total distance from Well 45 of about 90km. Whichever way you get to Well 48, it is worth visiting the nearby Breaden Hills.

From the track junction just south of Well 48, a track leads 5km north-east into the heart of the **Breaden Hills**. Breaden's Pool is a five-minute walk from the parking area, while the walk to **Godfrey's Tank** takes a little longer. Both are named after members of David Carnegie's 1896 expedition, and in the rock walls above Godfrey's Tank there are the initials of members of both the Carnegie and Canning parties. Aboriginal carvings can also be found.

Breaden Hills to Tanami Track (173km)

The end of the stock route looms and once north of the Breaden Hills, it's all pastoral country. Care needs to be taken here because of the large number of seismic survey lines that lead nowhere – several people have died in the past through taking the wrong track!

The turn-off to **Well 48** is just 2km north of the track junction that takes you into the Breaden Hills. The well lies a short distance to the west, just off the main route north. It once supplied small amounts of good water but is now dry.

The distance from the carpark at the Breaden Hills to **Well 49** is 30km, 23km east from the turn-off to Well 48. At the well, you'll find the grave of Jack Smith, a stockman, who died here after falling from a horse. This well also has some of the best water on the Canning, but to get a drink you'll need a long rope and plenty of energy.

As you head north, you pass the Australian Geographic's **notice to travellers** and then the last lot of desert oaks on the Canning. You are fast approaching civilisation; this spot is a good one for a last camp on the stock route proper. **Well 50** lies 2km south off the main track, 32km north of the previous well. It is caved in and dry.

The turn-off to **Balgo** Aboriginal community is 16km further and just 4km past here is **Well 51**, or Weriaddo, the last well on the stock route. The well has caved in and the bore next to it has water heavily laced with gypsum. You are now on Aboriginal-owned **Billiluna** station and there are many tracks and seismic lines throughout the area.

Stick to the main route north. About 70km north of Well 51, you will pass **Bloodwood Bore**. When you reach the first gate beyond the bore, make a right-hand turn, and travel 2km to an Aboriginal homestead. From here you will be directed to a delightful camping spot at Stretch Lagoon, where birds abound. Back on the main track and after a further 15km, you'll pass through the outskirts of the Billiluna Aboriginal community (no tourist facilities except in an emergency), just before the Canning Stock Route joins up with the Tanami Track.

While modern travellers head up or down the Tanami Track, the now-unused original stock route continues northwards along Sturt Creek with its occasional shady waterholes. North of present-day Sturt Creek station the original route leaves Sturt Creek following Cow Creek, crossing the Elvire River near the Old Flora Valley station before ending at Old Halls Creek, 16km east of present-day Halls Creek.

Turning west at the Tanami Track junction will lead you to **Halls Creek**, 175km away, but just 43km north along the Tanami Track is the turn-off to the **Wolfe Creek Meteorite Crater Reserve**, which is well worth a visit. See the Tanami Track section in the Central Deserts chapter for more about this unique crater.

At this stage, you'll feel elated that you have driven and experienced the Canning. If you are like most, you will be a little sad that this great adventure is over.

Take a well-deserved rest in Halls Creek, and while you do so, pay a visit to **Old Halls Creek**, a ghost town that presents a fascinating reminder of the Kimberley gold rush. About 6km east of the new town, along Duncan Rd on the way out to Old Halls Creek, you'll pass the turn-off to **China Wall**, a natural quartz wall that continues through the countryside for many kilometres.

All that is left of Old Halls Creek are the crumbling walls of the old post office, made from ant mounds and spinifex; the cemetery; and a new tourist venture – the modern building that sits forlornly at the top of the hill. The town is pleasantly located right on the banks of the creek of the same name. Nearby are the popular picnic and the swimming spots of Caroline Pool and Palm Springs.

ALTERNATIVE ROUTES

Some minor alternative routes between wells have been included. As well, there are a number of alternative ways to enter or leave the stock route.

The very southern section of the stock route is liable to be closed to traffic because of flooding around Lake Nabberu (Well 4). The alternative route for travellers during such times, or for travellers approaching from the east along the Gunbarrel Hwy via Carnegie station, is to travel to Well 9 via Glen-Ayle station. You will need permission from Glen-Ayle to travel these private roads and be required to pay $20 per vehicle.

Granite Peaks station, almost due west of Glen-Ayle, is reached via the Granite Peaks road from near Wiluna. This route will bring you out at Well 5; or from near Granite Peaks, you may head to Glen-Ayle and join up with the stock route further north. You need permission from Granite Peaks to use the track between the homestead and the stock route.

The Talawana Track joins the stock route 9km north of Well 22 and heads west 460km to the mining town of Newman. It's a relatively good dirt road, traversing remote desert country all the way to civilisation.

North of Well 24, the Windy Corner Track, graded by Len Beadell in 1963, joins the stock route. This track leads east 210km

Russian Jack

Australia's goldfields and gold rushes produced many heroes: successful speculators, the 'lucky' who found nuggets or struck it rich, Peter Lalor and the diggers of the Eureka Stockade, and the extremely odd and unusual. The latter category would have to include Russian Jack, the Kimberley's hero who is commemorated with a statue outside the modern Halls Creek Visitor Centre.

He was renowned for his feats of strength and endurance. He is believed to have carried a sick friend over 300km in his rough-and-ready wheelbarrow. He had originally pushed his barrow, with its 2m derbyshafts and extra-wide wheel for the sandy tracks, all the way from Derby loaded with food, tools, blankets and water.

His loyalty to his mates and the job became legendary. One day he fell about 23m to the bottom of an open pit at Mt Morgan in Western Australia. After lying there injured for three days, his only comment when they pulled him out was, 'I've missed a shift.'

THE NORTH-WEST

to the Gary Hwy. See the Bomb Roads section in the Central Deserts chapter for more details.

Just south of Well 33 is a crossroad. West is the Kidson Track (Wapet Rd) that runs over 900km to Broome or Port Hedland on the western coast. East takes you along the Kidson Track, 75km to the Gary Hwy.

At the T-junction before Well 35, you can turn west to the well or swing east, then north to Well 36. Where the Canning swings north, another track continues east 34km to Gary Junction at the northern end of the Gary Hwy. From this point you can either head south to the Gunbarrel Hwy (300km) or continue east to Alice Springs (900km). Both routes go through remote desert country but the going is easier than the Canning. The latter route passes through Aboriginal land and a permit is required. See the Bomb Roads section in the Central Deserts chapter for more details.

South of Well 51, the last section of the Canning heads north to Billiluna and the Tanami Track. This area can be flooded when Lake Gregory, to the east, overflows. A track heads south-east and then north-east 125km to the Balgo Aboriginal community, which is 38km south of the Tanami Track. Fuel, accommodation and limited supplies are available here in emergencies. Once again, you should have a permit but if the Canning is flooded, you should receive a sympathetic hearing. Travellers intending to visit the community should contact the Chairman, Balgo Hills Community Aboriginal Corporation, via Halls Creek, WA 6770.

ORGANISED TOURS

Portman's Australian Adventures (☎ 03-5786 1780, fax 5786 1818, e paa@hotkey .com.au) Operators, Geoff and Lisa Portman, have a trip along the Canning from Alice Springs most years. These are tag-alongs only and no passengers are carried.

Russell Guest's 4WD Safaris (☎ 03-9497 5877, W www.guest4wd.com.au) Russell Guest has been operating successful escorted convoys over outback Australia for quite a few years. You can join one of his trips to the Canning, either driving your own vehicle or travelling as a passenger in the escort vehicle.

Western Desert Guides (☎ 08-9341 2524, e wesdesgi@mail2me.com.au, W www .canningstockroute.info) This is run by Eric and Ronele Gard, who know the Canning better than most. They run tag-along trips and also carry passengers on their regular jaunts along the Canning.

FACILITIES

The Capricorn Roadhouse (☎ 08-9175 1535) and the Kunawarritji Community (☎ 08-9176 9040) can supply bulk fuel if given enough notice. See Fuel in the Special Preparations section at the start of this section.

Wiluna

Located 950km north-east of Perth, the town of Wiluna, you have to say, is remote. Nevertheless, most supplies are available and it is your last chance to stock up before tackling the Canning.

Wiluna General Store (☎ 08-9981 7034, Wotton St) Open Mon-Fri 9am-5pm, Sat & Sun 9am-3pm. This place has the only fuel in town, though it's not always available so ring ahead – you may have to continue to Carnegie station instead. At least you can get general supplies, hardware, clothing and ice here.

Canning Trading (☎ 08-9981 7020, Wotton St) This shop is open seven days a week. Along with food, it offers camping gas refills as well as mechanical and tyre repairs. It is also the local post office and the agency for the Commonwealth Bank. The store has Eftpos facilities.

Club Hotel Motel (☎ 08-9981 7012, Cnr Wotton & Wall Sts) Hotel rooms $45-55, motel rooms with air-con $100. This place offers cold beers and a range of *meals* for breakfast, lunch and dinner, while snacks are available throughout the day. On Sunday, weather permitting, there's a barbecue costing just $9 per head.

Wiluna Caravan Park (☎ 08-9981 7012, Lennon St) Unpowered sites $7.70 per person, powered sites $20.40 per double. Run by the Club Hotel Motel, it's dusty, small and barren, but after the Canning you'll appreciate the hot showers!

Halls Creek

Halls Creek is a major rural centre, catering reasonably well to the needs of the outback traveller. In the shire office around the back of the Visitor Centre (see the earlier Information section) you'll find the Halls Creek Community Resource Centre, including the public library and telecentre for Internet access. Halls Creek has a number of general stores including a bakery, butcher, liquor store and post office.

Kimberley Super Value Store (Great Northern Hwy) Open 8am-6pm Mon-Fri, 8am-noon Sat & public holidays, 9am-noon Sun. This shop has general food supplies, fruit, vegetables and hardware items.

Service stations and roadhouses have fuel supplies, and repairs can be carried out in one of the mechanical workshops in town. The service centre with the biggest range of spare parts (especially Toyota parts) is Baz Industries (☎ 08-9168 6150, 137 Duncan Rd). The Poinciana Roadhouse (Great Northern Hwy) can also be recommended for repairs.

Halls Creek Caravan Park (☎ 08-9168 6169, Roberta Ave) Camp sites $7.70 per person, powered sites $2.20 extra. Travellers not staying in the park can use the showers for $2.75. Dogs are allowed, on a leash ($25 good-behaviour bond). Facilities include washing machines, a reasonably stocked general *store* and a pleasant swimming pool.

It's a good place to check track conditions with other travellers who have just done the Tanami, Canning or Bungles.

Halls Creek Kimberley Hotel/Motel (☎ 08-9168 6101, Roberta Ave) Single & double budget rooms $86, single & double deluxe rooms $155, family rooms also available. Rooms are a bit pricey for what they offer, but there's a great pool and open bar to compensate, and a more than acceptable *restaurant* with fine seating.

Halls Creek Motel (☎ 08-9168 6001, 194 Great Northern Hwy) Singles/doubles from $70/88. More basic than the Kimberley and far less pretentious, it's a friendly place run by a young couple who've travelled all over the country and make you feel at home. There's a bar and licensed *restaurant*.

Halls Creek Backpackers (☎ 08-9168 6101) Dorm beds $18. This is part of the Kimberley Hotel/Motel, and is the place for budget-conscious travellers who don't have a tent. There is a dormitory with shower and toilet facilities, but no kitchen.

Airstrips Wiluna has a private airstrip – contact the Wiluna Shire (☎ 08-9981 7010) for details. Halls Creek also has an airstrip which is run by the Halls Creek Shire Council (☎ 08-9168 6007) and well used by charter and scenic flight operators. Avgas is available.

THE NORTH-WEST

The Tropics

The tropical north is a large slice of Australia that shows off some of the country's most spectacular scenery – bird-filled wetlands, ragged escarpment, deep rock pools, tall waterfalls, pristine coastline – and superb opportunities to experience Aboriginal art and culture. Darwin is the urban hub of the north and an ideal spot to kick back and restock before heading bush again. Cairns, on the far north Queensland coast, is another major centre and a stone's throw from reefs and rainforests.

While many of the region's sites can be accessed by conventional vehicle, it's behind the wheel of a well-prepared 4WD that you'll meet unforgettable adventures. Top of the list is perhaps the long trip to Cape York Peninsula, an isolated and rugged part of Australia and still one of the country's great 4WD expeditions. The Gulf

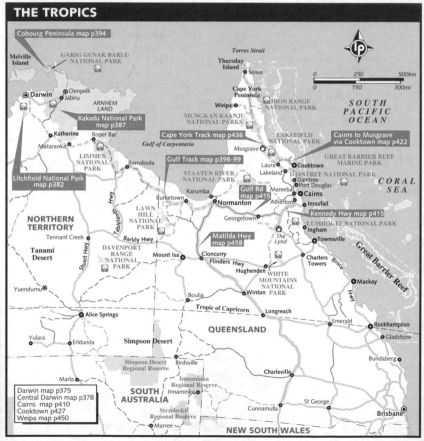

THE TROPICS

Track connects the Northern Territory with Queensland, and offers varied scenery, a bit of history and excellent fishing.

In the Northern Territory you can travel to one of the most remote corners of Arnhem Land and visit the Garig Gunak Barlu (Gurig) National Park on the Cobourg Peninsula – access is via Arnhem Land on a 4WD-only track. Kakadu National Park has superb wetlands, abundant birdlife and rock galleries of Aboriginal art, and 4WD tracks, billabongs and quiet spots to pitch a tent. Another great escape, and only around two hours south of Darwin, is Litchfield National Park, where you'll be impressed by waterfalls, swimming holes and places that can only be reached by 4WD vehicles.

Darwin

Highlights

- Watching a burnt-orange sun sink into the Arafura Sea
- Scoffing sizzling satays and tropical fruits at the Mindil Beach Sunset Market
- Hand-feeding huge, hungry milkfish at the popular Aquascene

Darwin is a city that, over the years, has taken a few batterings, including WWII bombings and the ferocious 1974 Cyclone Tracy; despite this it has emerged as a modern, optimistic city. This tropical northern capital, with a population of around 100,000, has a laid-back lifestyle, near-perfect climate and a vibrant, cosmopolitan flavour. Over 50 ethnic groups and nation-alities call Darwin home, and this is most evident at the city's restaurants and markets.

Adding to Darwin's appeal is its proximity to the Top End's natural attractions – and its remoteness from other big cities. For many people, Darwin is a great surprise and an 'oasis' after travelling many kilometres, and thousands choose to linger. When you're sitting by one of Darwin's beaches sipping a cool drink and watching one of its famous sunsets, you too may never want to leave.

Information

Tourism Top End (☎ 08-8981 4300, ⓔ info@ drta.com.au) is on the corner of Mitchell and Knuckey Sts. It's open from 8.30am to 6pm weekdays, 9am to 3pm Saturday and 10am to 2pm Sunday. It has an accommodation desk, free maps of the city and hundreds of brochures. This is a good place to ask about tours in, around and above Darwin and its harbour.

There are numerous banks and ATMs in the city, and the main post office is on the corner of Cavenagh and Edmunds Sts.

Parks Australia North (PAN; ☎ 08-8946 4300) is in the Commercial Union building on Smith St between Lindsay and White-field Sts; the Northern Land Council (NLC; ☎ 08-8920 5100) is at 9 Rowling St, Casuarina; and way out in Palmerston, 20km from the city centre, is the Parks and Wildlife Commission (☎ 08-8999 4814).

To obtain a fossicking permit, contact the Department of Business, Industry and Re-source Development (☎ 08-8999 5511), Centrepoint Building, Smith St Mall. For fishing information, call Fisheries (☎ 08-8999 2027) at Berrimah Farm.

Other useful organisations include:

Camping Supplies
The NT General Store (☎ 08-8981 8242) 42 Cavenagh St

Medical Services
Ambulance (☎ 08-8927 9000)
Royal Darwin Hospital (☎ 08-8922 8888) Rocklands Dr, Casuarina
Royal Flying Doctor Service Administration (☎ 08-8922 8110)
Royal Flying Doctor Service Emergency (☎ 08-8922 8888, ask for AMS doctor on call)

Other
Police (☎ 08-8927 8888) West Lane, off Mitchell St
Automobile Association of the Northern Territory (AANT; ☎ 08-8981 3837) 79–81 Smith St
Emergency Road Service (☎ 13 1111)
Wet-season road report for Top End (☎ 08-8922 3394)

Bookshops & Libraries Angus & Robertson (☎ 08-8941 3489), in the Smith St Mall's Galleria Shopping Centre, has a good selection of books. For maps, try the NT General Store (see earlier), or the Department of Lands, Planning and Environment's Maps NT (☎ 08-8999 7032) on the corner of Cavenagh and Bennett Sts. The library (☎ 08-8999 7177) at Parliament House has an extensive range of local and foreign newspapers, and Internet terminals.

Things to See & Do

Historic buildings in the city centre include the **Victoria Hotel** (1894) on Smith St Mall, the **old town hall**, **Brown's Mart** (1885), the 1884 **police station** and **old courthouse** on the corner of Smith St and the Esplanade, and **Government House**, built in stages from 1870.

At **Aquascene** (☎ 08-8981 7837, Doctor's Gully Rd, Larrakeyah; adult/child $5.50/3.30), near the corner of Daly St and the Esplanade, hundreds of fish head to shore for a bread-fest every day at high tide. It's quite an experience having a 1.5m, 18kg milkfish snatch soggy crusts from your fingers. As the feeding depends on the tides, call ahead for specific times.

The **Indo Pacific Marine** (☎ 08-8981 1294, Wharf Precinct, Darwin; adult/child $16/6; open 9am-6pm daily) is highly acclaimed for its fascinating displays of living coral ecosystems; admission includes a guided tour. Housed in the same building is the **Australian Pearling Exhibition** (☎ 08-8999 6573, Wharf Precinct, Darwin; adult/child $6.60/3.30; open 10am-5pm daily, last entry 4.30pm), which provides an insight into the local pearling industry.

The **Museum & Art Gallery of the Northern Territory** (☎ 08-8999 8201, Conacher St, Parap; admission free; open 9am-5pm Mon-Fri, 10am-5pm Sat & Sun) is by the beach in Fannie Bay, about 4km north of the city centre. It's modern, spacious and full of interesting displays, especially on maritime history, Cyclone Tracy and Aboriginal art. The cafe *Cornucopia*, with great snacks and an airy veranda, makes a great pit stop. **Fannie Bay Gaol Museum** (☎ 08-8999 8201,

WARNING

Deadly box jellyfish ('stingers') are prevalent in Darwin waters, so do not swim from October to May, and only swim between June to September at your own risk. There are crocodiles along the coast and rivers; any crocs found in the harbour are removed, and other beaches near the city are patrolled to minimise the risk.

Cnr East Point Rd & Ross Smith Ave, Fannie Bay; admission by donation; open 10am-4.30pm daily) is also worth a look-see; the self-guided tour is easy and informative. The gaol operated from 1883 to 1979.

East Point Reserve is perfect for in-line skating, jogging, cycling, walking and picnics; there's also the man-made saltwater Lake Alexander for year-round swimming. Just 2km north of the city centre are the beautiful **Darwin Botanic Gardens**, with thousands of tropical flora specimens and a self-guided Aboriginal plant-use trail.

Popular beaches include **Mindil** and **Vestey's** on Fannie Bay, both great spots to be wowed by the amazing orange-pink Darwin sunsets.

Places to Stay

Whether you're a prince or pauper, Darwin has no shortage of places to stay. For more assistance with accommodation hunting, contact Tourism Top End (☎ 08-8981 4300). All rates listed here are for the Dry; prices dip in the Wet season.

Camping There are some good caravan parks near Darwin, with shady sites, as well as dorm beds, cabins and motel rooms. All rates listed are per double.

Lee Point Village Resort (☎ 08-8945 0535, Lee Point Rd, Lee Point)* Unpowered/powered sites $22/24, cabins with shared bathroom $66. Located 15km north of the city and a short walk to the beach, the popular Lee Point is a spacious 'village' with excellent facilities.

Leprechaun Motel (☎ 08-8984 3400, 378 Stuart Hwy, Winnellie)* Unpowered/powered

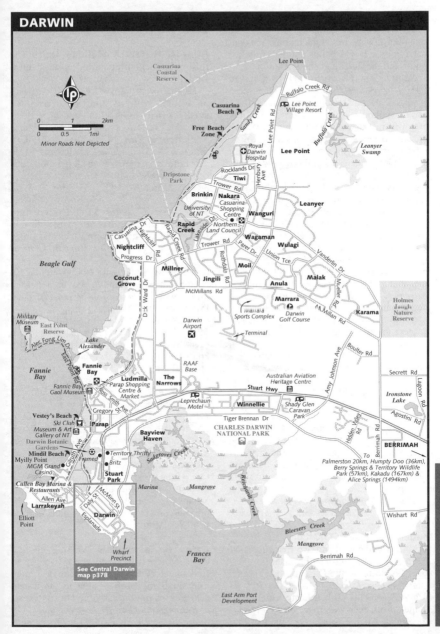

DARWIN

Casuarina
Coastal
Reserve

Lee Point

Buffalo Creek Rd

Casuarina
Beach

Lee Point
Village Resort

Free Beach
Zone

Sandy Creek

Lee Point Rd

Buffalo Creek

Lee Point

Leanyer
Swamp

0   1   2km
0   0.5   1mi
Minor Roads Not Depicted

Royal
Darwin
Hospital

Dripstone
Park

Rocklands Dr

Tiwi

Trower Rd

Brinkin

Nakara

Henbury Ave

Casuarina
Shopping
Centre

Wanguri

Leanyer

University
of NT

Lakeside Dr

Rapid
Creek

Northern
Land Council

Wagaman

Wulagi

Nightcliff

Casuarina Dr

Nightcliff Rd

Rapid Creek Rd

Progress Dr

Trower Rd

Parer Dr

Union Tce

Vanderlin Dr

Millner

Coconut
Grove

Dick Ward Dr

Jingili

Rothdale Rd

Moil

Anula

Malak

M. Millan Rd

Mueller Rd

Karama

McMillans Rd

Marrara

Holmes
Jungh
Nature
Reserve

Beagle Gulf

Darwin
Airport

Marrara
Sports Complex

Darwin
Golf Course

Terminal

Military
Museum

East Point
Reserve

Alec Fong Lim Dr

East Point Rd

Lake
Alexander

RAAF
Base

Australian Aviation
Heritage Centre

Amy Johnson Ave

Boulter Rd

Secrett Rd

Lagoon Rd

Ironstone
Lake

Agostini Rd

Fannie
Bay

Fannie
Bay

Ludmilla

The
Narrows

Stuart Hwy

Shady Glen
Caravan
Park

Hidden Valley Rd

Berrimah Rd

Fannie Bay
Gaol Museum

Ross Smith Ave

Parap Shopping
Centre &
Market

Leprechaun
Motel

Winnellie

Vestey's Beach

Ski Club

Museum & Art
Gallery of NT

Gregory St

Parap

Tiger Brennan Dr

Bayview
Haven

CHARLES DARWIN
NATIONAL PARK

BERRIMAH

Darwin Botanic
Gardens

Mindil Beach

Myilly Point

MGM Grand
Casino

Cullen Bay Marina &
Restaurants

Larrakeyah

Allen Ave

Smith Ave

Framed

Territory Thrifty

Britz

Stuart
Park

Saugroves Creek

Marina

Mangrove

Reichardt Creek

To
Palmerston 20km, Humpty Doo (36km),
Berry Springs & Territory Wildlife
Park (57km), Kakadu (167km) &
Alice Springs (1494km)

Wishart Rd

Elliott
Point

McMinn St

Daly St

Darwin

Esplanade

Wharf
Precinct

See Central Darwin
map p378

Frances
Bay

Bleesers Creek

Mangrove

Berrimah Rd

East Arm Port
Development

sites $15/22.50, rooms with en suite $65. This is the closest camping ground to the city (8km), with sites at the rear of the good-value motel. It gets bonus points for its two pools and the diner and shop next door.

Shady Glen Caravan Park *(☎ 08-8984 3330, Cnr Stuart Hwy & Farrell Crescent, Winnellie)* Unpowered/powered sites $20/22, cabins without/with en suite $69/89. Only 10km from Darwin's centre, this large park appears to get plenty of TLC from its owners. Clean, modern shower blocks and airy communal kitchens make this a good choice.

Hostels There's a swag of backpackers hostels in Darwin, most of them on or near action-packed Mitchell St and close to the transit centre. Standards vary so check rooms and showers before you part with your dollars. In the dry season, dorm beds typically cost between $16 and $23, while doubles and twins range from $48 to $58; in the Wet the rates decrease. Darwin gets *extremely* busy in June, July and August, so you should try to book at least a week ahead to avoid having to snooze on a park bench.

Here are four places to help your search:

Chilli's *(☎ 08-8941 9722, 69A Mitchell St)* Perched next to the transit centre, this popular hostel has clean rooms, two rooftop spas and an open-sided kitchen area over-looking Mitchell St. At the time of writing, the bathrooms had just been revamped and re-tiled.

Elke's Inner City Backpackers *(☎ 08-8981 8399, 112 Mitchell St)* Its six-bed rooms are a bit squeezy but the place is quiet, the facilities are good and there are pleasant places under mango trees to write your postcards.

Frogshollow Backpackers Resort *(☎ 08-8941 2600, 27 Lindsay St)* A short walk from the city centre, this spic-and-span hostel has plenty of OK rooms and breezy verandas, and a pool and two spas ringed by palm trees. The laid-back Frogshollow is a firm favourite on the Darwin hostel scene.

Wilderness Lodge *(☎ 08-8981 8363, 88 Mitchell St)* This 60-bed hostel offers ade-quate dorms, each with space for four budget travellers. All the rooms are smallish, but you can spend nonsleeping hours lounging around the large, cool swimming pool area.

Motels, Hotels & Holiday Units The following accommodation is in central Darwin unless otherwise stated:

Value Inn *(☎ 08-8981 4733, 50 Mitchell St)* Rooms with en suite $85. The Inn's small, no-frills rooms are good for a fleet-ing visit. Free street parking is available.

Poinciana Inn *(☎ 08-8981 8111, Cnr Mitchell & McLachlan Sts)* Rooms $119. The hotel's 51 rooms have all the mod-cons of most hotels, and it's centrally located.

Asti Motel *(☎ 1800 063 335, 08-8981 8200, Cnr Smith & Packard Sts)* Doubles $120, 4-person studios $143. Not far from the city centre, Asti has affordable, air-con rooms; studios have microwaves and sinks.

All Seasons Premier Darwin Central *(☎ 08-8944 9000, Cnr Smith & Knuckey Sts)* Rooms $227, with kitchenette $250. Neat rooms, an attractive pool area and the award-winning ***Waterhole restaurant*** make this a good bet for a plush stay.

Mediterranean All Suite Hotel *(☎ 08-8981 7771, 81 Cavenagh St)* 1-bedroom units $160, with spa $175. Built around a courtyard studded with a pool and foliage, the fully equipped units are bright and homey. It seems to get lots of return business.

Parap Village Apartments *(☎ 1800 620 913, 08-8943 0500, 39 Parap Rd, Fannie Bay)* 2-bed/3-bed units $171/220. If you'd prefer to be in the burbs, the 3½-star Parap offers comfortable self-contained units.

Places to Eat

One of the great things about Darwin is the diversity and quality of its food, whether it's Malay, Mexican or Mediterranean. Look for all-you-can-eat buffet deals, which seem to be a speciality.

Cafes & Takeaways Walking up and down Mitchell St, you won't struggle to find an eatery for breakfast, latte or dinner. The small *food centre* next to the transit centre turns out ordinary but cheap meals.

Rendezvous Cafe *(☎ 08-8981 9231, Off Smith St Mall)* Meals $6-12. Open 9am-

2.30pm Mon-Fri, 9am-2pm Sat, 5.30pm-9pm Thur-Sat. This hot spot for Malay/Thai dishes, tucked away off the Mall, serves laksa ($8.50) fondly referred to by locals as 'the best in Darwin'.

Salvatores (☎ 08-8941 9823, Cnr Smith & Knuckey Sts) Pizzas $6, pasta $7-11. Open 7am-midnight daily. The coffee here is so popular that the two machines often crank out 200 cups per hour; the meals and snacks are also delicious.

Roma Bar (☎ 08-8981 6729, 30 Cavenagh St) Meals about $10. Open 7am-5pm Mon-Fri, 8am-2pm Sat. Away from busy Mitchell St is this cosy cafe serving damn fine coffee and good breakfasts and snacks.

Gourmet Deli (☎ 08-8941 2744, 64 Smith St) Open 6.30am-6pm Mon-Fri, 8am-3pm Sat. This deli sells loads of sandwiches and focaccias bulging with any of 50 fresh ingredients – just look at that menu board.

Go Sushi (☎ 08-8941 1008, Shop 5, 28 Mitchell St) Sushi $3-5 per plate. Open 10am-9pm Mon-Sat, closed Sun. All aboard Darwin's only sushi train! The decor, Asahi beer and bona fide sushi chef make you feel like you're in Tokyo.

The *food centre* at the end of Stokes Hill Wharf (☎ 08-8981 4268) sells burgers, the ubiquitous barra and chips, espresso etc; it's all casual, alfresco eating at OK prices ($5 to $14).

North-west of the city centre is **Cullen Bay**, where a gaggle of pricey marina-side eateries trade mostly in the dry season.

Restaurants & Pubs These places are all in central Darwin.

Nirvana (☎ 08-8981 2025, 6 Dashwood Crescent, near Smith St) Mains $17-22. Good food, good live music, good atmosphere: Nirvana gets rave reviews one after the other and with reason.

Hanuman (☎ 08-8941 3500, 28 Mitchell St) Entrees $8-12, mains $17-23. Open 6.30pm-late daily, noon-2.30pm Mon-Fri. Head to this multi-award-winning Thai/Indian restaurant for a memorable wine and dine under dim lights.

Twilight on Lindsay (☎ 08-8981 8631, 2 Lindsay St) Entrees from $11, mains $18-29. Open 6.30pm-late daily. This restaurant, serving modern Australian cuisine, looks like it's leapt out of a glossy gourmet mag. It's good – just ask its loyal local following.

Hog's Breath Cafe (☎ 08-8941 3333, 85 Mitchell St) Burgers from $10, steaks from $21. Open from 11.30am till late daily. This eatery chain's speciality is its huge, juicy, slow-cooked prime rib steaks, but there's also vegie options. Roll up with a big appetite.

Rorke's Drift (☎ 08-8941 7171, 46 Mitchell St) Meals $7-22. Open 10am-2am daily. Being a 'British' bar, of course the menu lists bangers and mash, and a Sunday roast. Dine inside at booths or outside under the sprawling banyan tree.

Shenannigan's (☎ 08-8981 2100, 69 Mitchell St) Meals $7-22. Open 11am-2am daily. This pub is worth its weight in beer. The kitchen churns out big Aussie-Irish meals, including steaks and stews.

Self-Catering There are two Woolworths *supermarkets* in town – a bright, new one between Smith and Cavenagh Sts, near Peel St and an older, dingier one on the corner of Smith and Knuckey Sts. With all due respect to the latter, the former is much nicer to shop in (it also has a good bakery).

Markets Easily the best all-round eating experience in Darwin is the renowned **Mindil Beach Sunset Market** held on Thursday and Sunday night during the dry season. The throngs of locals and tourists begin arriving at 5pm to sample the incredibly delicious selection of food and then watch the sun set from the beach. Whether it's Japanese, Filipino, Indian, Brazilian, Thai or Greek, most food helpings will only cost you from $2 to $7. This bustling market also has art-and-craft stalls, pavement entertainment and New Age massage.

Similar food stalls can be found at the **Parap Market** on Saturday morning, the markets at **Rapid Creek** and **Nightcliff** on Sunday morning, the **Palmerston Market** on Friday evening (dry season only) and in the Smith St Mall in the evening (except Thursday), but the Mindil Beach one is the best for atmosphere and proximity to town.

CENTRAL DARWIN

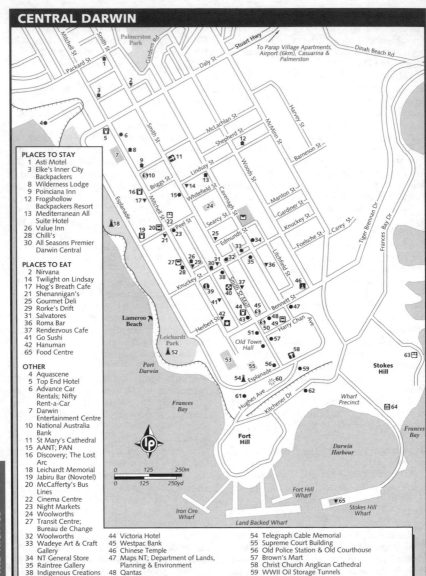

PLACES TO STAY
1 Asti Motel
3 Elke's Inner City Backpackers
8 Wilderness Lodge
9 Poinciana Inn
12 Frogshollow Backpackers Resort
13 Mediterranean All Suite Hotel
26 Value Inn
28 Chilli's
30 All Seasons Premier Darwin Central

PLACES TO EAT
2 Nirvana
14 Twilight on Lindsay
17 Hog's Breath Cafe
21 Shenannigan's
25 Gourmet Deli
29 Rorke's Drift
31 Salvatores
36 Roma Bar
37 Rendezvous Cafe
41 Go Sushi
42 Hanuman
65 Food Centre

OTHER
4 Aquascene
5 Top End Hotel
6 Advance Car Rentals; Nifty Rent-a-Car
7 Darwin Entertainment Centre
10 National Australia Bank
11 St Mary's Cathedral
15 AANT; PAN
16 Discovery; The Lost Arc
18 Leichardt Memorial
19 Jabiru Bar (Novotel)
20 McCafferty's Bus Lines
22 Cinema Centre
23 Night Markets
24 Woolworths
27 Transit Centre; Bureau de Change
32 Woolworths
33 Wadeye Art & Craft Gallery
34 NT General Store
35 Raintree Gallery
38 Indigenous Creations
39 Tourism Top End
40 Galleria Shopping Centre; Angus & Robertson
43 Ansett
44 Victoria Hotel
45 Westpac Bank
46 Chinese Temple
47 Maps NT; Department of Lands, Planning & Environment
48 Qantas
49 City Bus Depot
50 Commonwealth Bank
51 NT Government Publications Centre
52 ANZAC Memorial
53 Parliament House; Library
54 Telegraph Cable Memorial
55 Supreme Court Building
56 Old Police Station & Old Courthouse
57 Brown's Mart
58 Christ Church Anglican Cathedral
59 WWII Oil Storage Tunnels
60 Survivors Lookout
61 Government House
62 Helipad
63 Deckchair Cinema
64 Indo Pacific Marine; Australian Pearling Exhibition

THE TROPICS

Entertainment

Victoria Hotel ('the Vic'; ☎ *08-8981 4011, 27 Smith St Mall, Darwin)* Open 9pm-4am Wed-Sat. Live bands and lively young 20-somethings play upstairs and downstairs at this popular two-storey haunt off the Mall.

Top End Hotel (☎ *08-8981 6511, Cnr Mitchell & Daly Sts, Darwin)* The Top End comprises four venues open daily from 11am until late. *Lizards Bar & Grill* pulls in revellers of all ages, especially on Friday when the salsa show kicks off at 8pm. For a young clientele, *Hip.E Club* has techno and Top 40 thumping away until the wee hours. The other two rooms are *Sportsman's Bar*, and *Beachcombers Bandroom*, which has regular live bands.

Nirvana (☎ *08-8981 2025, 6 Dashwood Crescent, Near Smith St, Darwin)* Jazz & blues shows 8pm-2am nightly. This is one of Darwin's cosiest places to watch jazz and the occasional open-mike jam session.

Discovery (☎ *08-8942 3300, 89 Mitchell St, Darwin)* Open 9pm-late daily. A very popular venue where 18- to 23-year-olds 'git down' while DJs with interesting names spin discs. Part of the same complex is *The Lost Arc*, which has live music most nights. It caters for all ages, but there's a good sprinkling of late 20s and 30-somethings fond of 70s and 80s music.

Ski Club (☎ *08-8981 6630, Conacher St, Fannie Bay)* Open noon-late daily. This open-air bar on Vestey's Beach has jazz on Friday from 6pm and live music on Sunday from 4pm, and on any day it's a relaxed spot to raise a glass as the sun goes down.

Many a happy hour can be spent at *Rorke's Drift* and *Shenannigan's*, two of the better watering holes on Darwin's main drag (see Places to Eat, earlier). Karaoke, trivia nights, live music – there's always something abuzz here, mostly post-9pm until very late.

Most of the swish hotels lining the Esplanade have bars with low-key music tinkling in the background and comfy seats where you can spend a few civilised hours. One such place is *Jabiru Bar* at Novotel Atrium Hotel.

The *Darwin Entertainment Centre* (☎ *08-8980 3333, 93 Mitchell St, Darwin)* Box office open 10am-5pm Mon-Fri. You may be lucky and catch an opera, rock concert or play at this venue while you're in town; check papers or call to see what's on.

MGM Grand Casino (☎ *08-8943 8888, Gilruth Ave, Mindil Beach)* If you're feeling lucky, wander over to the casino with a fist full of dollars. If you lose it all, there's free jazz concerts on Sunday afternoon (dry season only).

For films, there's the six-screen *Cinema Centre (*☎ *08-8981 5999, 76 Mitchell St, Darwin)*. In the Dry, try the *Deckchair Cinema (*☎ *08-8981 0700)*, an open-air film venue near the Wharf Precinct.

Shopping

Raintree Gallery (☎ *08-8941 9933, 20 Knuckey St, Darwin)* Open 9am-5pm Mon-Fri, 9am-2pm Sat, 10am-3pm Sun (Dry only). Worth a browse is this shop selling fine artwork from Western Arnhem Land.

Wadeye Art & Craft Gallery (☎ *08-8981 9362, 31 Knuckey St, Darwin)* Open 9am-5pm Mon-Fri, 10am-2pm Sat & Sun. This is the only community-owned shop in Darwin and stocks a good collection of art, crafts and didgeridoos.

Indigenous Creations (☎ *08-8941 0424, 31 Smith St Mall, Darwin)* This is one of a chain of shops selling Aboriginal artefacts, specialising in musical-quality didgeridoos.

Framed (☎ *08-8981 2994, 55 Stuart Hwy, Stuart Park)* Open 8.30am-5.30pm Mon-Sat & 11am-5pm Sun. Welcome to one of Australia's largest commercial galleries, where T-shirts printed with Aboriginal designs go like hot cakes, and quality and prices vary.

Night Market (Cnr Mitchell & Peel Sts, Darwin) Open 5pm-11pm daily. A one-stop shop for all your tropical fashion needs, including sarongs, loud shirts and T-shirts, shark-tooth anklets and the like.

Getting Around

To/From the Airport Darwin's airport, about 6km from the centre of town, handles both international and domestic flights. Taxi fares into the city centre are around $16. Contact Darwin Radio Taxis (☎ 13 10 08).

There is an airport shuttle bus (☎ 1800 358 945) for $7.50/13 one way/return, which will pick up or drop off almost anywhere in the centre. When leaving Darwin, book a day before departure.

Car Rental All the major car rental companies are represented in Darwin, including Avis (☎ 08-8981 9922), Budget (☎ 08-89810148) and Hertz (☎ 08-8941 0944), all of which have offices at the airport. Most rental companies are open every day and have agents in the city centre to save you trekking out to the Stuart Hwy.

Nifty Rent-a-Car (☎ 08-8941 7090), 86 Mitchell St, offers deals as low as $34 a day for an early 1980s car, but you're restricted to within 70km of Darwin. The rate includes unlimited kilometres (well, up to a 2500km limit). Nifty also rents late 1990s vehicles with air-con from $59 a day, and offers one-day car hire to/from Litchfield for $89, free 400km included. 4WDs aren't in its fleet.

Advance Car Rentals (☎ 08-8981 2999), also at 86 Mitchell St, rents from $62 a day for its smallest cars, right up to $170 a day for a 4WD, with 100km per day plus around 30 cents per extra kilometre. To rent the same vehicles over seven days brings the costs down to $49 and $147 respectively. Advance also offers one-way rentals (unlimited kilometres) to Alice Springs.

Territory Thrifty (☎ 08-8924 2442), 64 Stuart Hwy, Parap, is probably the best value. Discount deals to look for include cheaper rates for four or more days' hire, weekend specials (three days for roughly the price of two) and one-way hires (to Jabiru, Katherine or Alice Springs).

Britz (☎ 08-8981 2081), 44-46 Stuart Hwy, Stuart Park, has great rates for long-term rentals on 4WDs and campervans, and you can do one-way rentals out of the Northern Territory. A two-person 2WD campervan for 21 days or more will cost around $160 per day, depending on the time of year.

Bicycle Darwin has a fairly extensive network of cycling tracks. It's a pleasant ride out from the city to the Botanic Gardens, Fannie Bay, East Point Reserve or, if you're feeling fit, all the way to Nightcliff and Casuarina. Many of the backpacker hostels hire out bikes for around $5/16 per hour/day.

AROUND DARWIN

Right on Darwin's doorstep are a number of attractions that can be visited as day trips or on the way to Litchfield or Kakadu. Ask at Tourism Top End (☎ 08-8981 4300) for tips and travel information. One of the must-sees near Darwin is the **Territory Wildlife Park** *(☎ 08-8988 7200, Cox Peninsula Rd; adult/child/family $18/9/40; open 8.30am-6pm daily, last entry 4pm)*, 57km south of Darwin, set in 4 sq km of bushland, this fantastic open-air zoo features a huge variety of Australian wildlife staring back at you from nocturnal houses, aviaries and the memorable aquarium. Not far away is the **Berry Springs Nature Park** *(open 8am-6.30pm daily)*, with waterfalls, hot springs and picnic spots.

If you're not in a hurry to get to Kakadu, there are plenty of worthwhile detours along the Arnhem Hwy. After passing the one-pub town of **Humpty Doo** and the **Fogg Dam Conservation Reserve** (where birds abound), you'll reach **Adelaide River Crossing**, known for its *river cruises (☎ 08-8988 8144; adult/child $33/18; trips 9am, 11am, 1pm & 3pm daily May-Aug, 9am, 11am & 2.30pm Sept-Apr)* and agile jumping crocs. Next along is Windows on the Wetlands (☎ 08-8988 8188; open 7.30am-7.30pm daily), a visitors centre full of information boards and interactive displays, and with mighty views across the floodplains. The proposed **Mary River National Park**, straddling the Arnhem Hwy, is a huge area brimming with lagoons, billabongs, monsoon forests and the highest concentration of salties (saltwater crocs) in the world. It's far less visited than nearby Kakadu, and campers, anglers, hikers, bird- and croc-watchers will all drive away satisfied. Part of the park is suitable for a 2WD but you'll see more in a 4WD; flooding may cause road closure in the Wet.

Litchfield National Park

The 650-sq-km Litchfield National Park, 140km south of Darwin, encloses much of the Tabletop Range, a rugged sandstone plateau with eroded cliffs dropping away to blacksoil plains. It is only a couple of hours' drive from Darwin and so is a very popular weekend getaway with the locals.

The main attraction of the park is its numerous superb waterfalls that tumble down from the plateau, creating plunge pools for swimming – but the beautiful country, excellent camping grounds, and the 4WD, bushwalking and photography opportunities are also major highlights. It's well worth a few days, although weekends can get crowded.

HISTORY

Aboriginal people have lived continuously in this area for around 50,000 years, and the many pools, waterfalls and other prominent geographical features had great spiritual and cultural significance.

In 1864 the Finniss Expedition explored the Northern Territory of South Australia, as it was then called. Frederick Litchfield was a member of the party, and some of the features in the park still bear the names he gave them.

In the late 1860s copper and tin were discovered, and this led to a flurry of activity with several mines operating in the area. The ruins of two of these are still visible today – at Bamboo Creek (which operated from 1906 to 1955) and Blyth homestead.

The area was then opened up as pastoral leases, and these were in existence right up to the proclamation of the park in 1986.

FLORA & FAUNA

The dominant trees of the open forest are the Darwin woollybutt and the stringybark, while below these grow sand palms, banksias, cycads, acacias and grevilleas. Around the waterfalls and permanent springs are pockets of surprisingly thick monsoon rainforest. The more open plains are covered with the high spear grass that is common throughout much of the Top End.

Birdlife is abundant. Two of the most commonly sighted birds are the distinctive red-tailed black cockatoo and the sulphur-crested cockatoo. Smaller parrots, such as the beautiful rainbow lorikeet, northern rosella and the red-winged parrot, are also common.

The jabiru, or black-necked stork, is found in the flooded areas of the park during the Wet, and predatory birds such as black kites, whistling kites and wedge-tailed eagles are often seen soaring in the thermals above the plateau.

The antilopine wallaroo is the largest mammal in the park, but dingoes are also sighted from time to time. Most of the smaller mammals are nocturnal, and so are not often seen – these include the rare northern quoll, the northern brown bandicoot and the northern brushtail possum.

An unusual feature of Litchfield is the so-called magnetic termite mounds that stud the blacksoil plains. The sight of thousands of these grey, tombstone-like structures is, at times, quite reminiscent of a large cemetery. Some mounds are up to 2m high and gain their name from the north-south orientation. It's believed they are aligned this way as a means of controlling temperature – during the hottest part of the day, only the narrow northern edge is exposed to the full sun.

Coastal banksia

INFORMATION

Permits are not required to enter the park, unless you plan to walk and camp in remote areas. There is a rangers station (☎ 08-8976 0282) at Batchelor, about 10km from the eastern edge of the park. Information about the park and its attractions is broadcast on FM radio 88MHz. Check road conditions by calling ☎ 1800 246 199.

The Parks and Wildlife Commission in Darwin publishes a very good map of the park. If you require more detailed maps, the topographic sheet maps that cover the park are the 1:100,000 *Reynolds River (5071)* and the 1:50,000 *Sheets No 5071 (I-IV)*. These are available from Maps NT (☎ 08-8999 7032) at the Department of Lands, Planning and Environment, corner of Cavenagh and Bennett Sts in Darwin.

Pets and firearms are prohibited. All dirt roads within the park are closed during the Wet, and usually re-open around the end of May.

Dangers & Annoyances

Scrub typhus, spread by tiny mites, has been reported in the area. Although the danger is small, wear insect repellent with

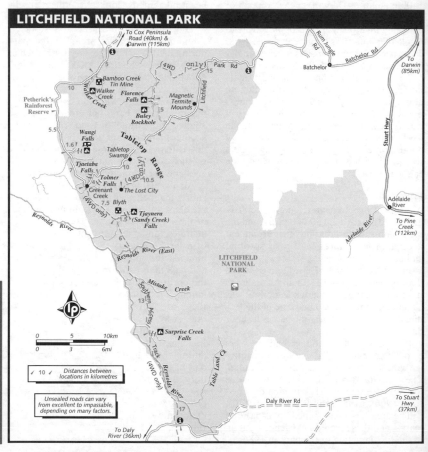

LITCHFIELD NATIONAL PARK

DEET and cover your feet and legs if you intend to walk in the area.

THE PARK

There are two routes to Litchfield National Park travelling south from Darwin, both about a two-hour drive. One, which enters the park from the north, involves turning south off the Cox Peninsula Rd onto the well-maintained Litchfield Park Rd, which is dirt but suitable for conventional vehicles during the dry season. A second approach, also called the Litchfield Park Rd, is along a bitumen road from Batchelor into the east of the park. The two access roads join up so it's possible to do a loop from the Stuart Hwy to the Cox Peninsula Rd. Another more exciting option in the dry season is along the southern access track (4WD), a detour west off the Stuart Hwy, just past Hayes Creek (see Stuart Hwy in the Central Deserts chapter).

If you choose to enter the park from Batchelor, it is about 15km to the first major batch of **magnetic termite mounds,** signposted just off to the right of the road.

Another 6km brings you to the **Florence Falls** turn-off on the eastern edge of the plateau. The double falls lie in a pocket of monsoon forest 5km off the Litchfield Park Rd along a sealed road. This is an excellent swimming hole in the dry season, as are the smaller cascades at the pretty **Buley Rockhole**, 2km before Florence; camping is an option at both. From Florence Falls, a 4WD track takes you north across the Florence Creek to a T-junction, from where you can turn right (east) and head back to the Litchfield Park Rd near the park's eastern boundary.

Back on the main road it's another 4km from the Florence Falls turn-off to the one for the **Lost City**, 10.5km south of the road along a rocky 4WD track (your vehicle will need ground clearance). Featured here are the large sandstone block and pillar formations that, if you suspend disbelief, resemble something akin to Inca ruins. You must return the way you came, as continuation of this track has been closed due to its badly pitted condition in all seasons.

Turn left as you hit the main road again and travel 4.5km to **Tabletop Swamp**, a peaceful place frequented by egrets, bee-eaters and lorikeets. It's a further 5.5km to the turn-off to **Tolmer Falls**, which are an easy 450m amble off the road. From the viewing platform you get superb views of the water tumbling over the ancient escarpment, but those seen while walking the 1.5km loop track are even better. As enticing as the plunge pools look, unfortunately they're off-limits to swimmers. Caves around the gorge here are home to the largest known breeding colonies of the rare orange horseshoe-bats.

It's another 4km along the main road to **Greenant Creek**, where there's a day-use area and a 2.7km (return) walking trail to **Tjaetaba Falls**, through pandanus and Carpentaria palms. As the falls are a registered Aboriginal site, you're not permitted to enter the water.

About 5.5km past Greenant Creek is the turn-off to the **Blyth homestead ruins**, which is about 1.5km along a very rough road (the Southern Access Track) with a few creek crossings. This corrugated-iron and cypress-pine homestead was built in 1929 by the Sargent family, and remained in use until the area was declared a national park in 1986 (a fact that beggars belief).

Just south of the homestead is where you turn off towards **Tjaynera Falls (Sandy Creek)**, which lie 1.5km off the Southern Access Track along a corrugated 4WD track. From the carpark and camp site it's a 1.7km walk to the falls along a track lined with lofty paperbark trees. The pool here is deep and cool, and is far less crowded than Wangi Falls (see later).

Before heading up to Wangi (or leaving Litchfield for Daly River Rd), you can head south on the 4WD track through the isolated southern reaches of the park. It's often a 20km/h crawl along this bumpy road and you'll have to ford **Reynolds River East** and **Mistake Creek**, but 19km later you'll be rewarded by the idyllic **Surprise Creek Falls**, where more often than not you'll be the only people. Don't be tempted to swim in the creek here as saltwater crocs may be lurking. The track crosses the Reynolds

River (East) and eventually links up with the Daly River Rd, 17km beyond Surprise Creek. From this intersection you can head east to the Stuart Hwy or south-west to Daly River. This track through the south of the park is impassable during the Wet.

Back on the track heading north, the road continues from the Tjaynera Falls (Sandy Creek) turn-off another 14.5km to the turn-off to the most popular attraction in the park, **Wangi Falls** (pronounced 'wong-gye'), 1.6km along a side road. The falls flow year-round and fill a beautiful, cool plunge pool, which is great for a dip during the Dry. It's not possible to swim here in the wet season, as the currents are dangerous. There's an emergency telephone at the carpark if someone gets into difficulty while swimming in the pool. For lovers of steep walks, there's a marked 3km, 1½-hour walking trail, which takes you up and over the top of the falls. There is also a large picnic and camping area, and a busy kiosk. The area can become tourist-infested on weekends, particularly in holiday periods.

From the Wangi Falls turn-off it's about 5.5km to **Petherick's Rainforest Reserve** *(admission $5)*, a small freehold forest reserve that actually lies outside Litchfield. There are waterfalls (including the Cascades), some thermal springs and monsoon rainforest, as well as the wreckage of a WWII Spitfire. The entry fee is waived if you camp here.

From here the road loops back into the park, and after about 10km there's a turn-off to **Walker Creek**, just 600m off the road, where there are more (less-visited) rock pools and a camping ground. At **Bamboo Creek**, reached along a short 4WD track just north of the Walker Creek side road, remnants of the tin mines can still be seen. A 750m signposted trail tells the story of the tin mines that operated here in the 1940s and 1950s. (For some reason, the flies here are vicious!)

It's only another 5km to the northern boundary of the park, and from there it's around 43km on an unsealed road to the Cox Peninsula Rd. Another 72km will get you to Darwin.

ACTIVITIES

Litchfield is dotted with idyllic waterholes and waterfalls, and saltwater crocodiles are absent from all but a few. Good, croc-free places for a dip are Buley Rockhole, Florence and Sandy Creek Falls and, although it can get crowded, Wangi Falls. *Do not swim* in the Finniss or Reynolds Rivers, which are inhabited by crocodiles.

During the dry season the rangers conduct a number of activities, such as slide shows, guided walks and talks, aimed at increasing your enjoyment and knowledge of the park. The schedule varies, but all details should be posted at the information bays on the way into the park.

Excellent *wetland cruises* on McKeddies Billabong, an extension of the Reynolds River, are available – book at the Wangi kiosk.

ORGANISED TOURS

Coo-ee Tours (☎ 1800 816 323, 08-8981 6116, Ⓦ coo-ee.downunder.net.au) 1-day tour $95, 2-day tour $220. The one-day tour includes visits to the four main falls, a 1½-hour billabong cruise and lunch; the two-day tour, of course, offers much more. Departures from 6.45am at Darwin accommodation.

Wild Thing (☎ 08-8931 3541) 1-day 'escape' $95, 2-day trek $199. Aimed at the young and/or energetic, these trips provide a 'bush' experience.

Travel North (☎ 1800 089 103, 08-8981 9910, Ⓔ info@travelnorth.com.au, Ⓦ www .travelnorth.com.au) 1-day tour adult/child $129/100. Departing Darwin at around 6.30am, this one-way tour takes you through Litchfield and on to Katherine; lunch is included.

FACILITIES
Camping

The Parks and Wildlife Commission (☎ 08-8976 0282 in Batchelor) maintains a number of *camping grounds* within the park. Those at *Wangi Falls*, *Florence Falls* (separate 2WD and 4WD areas), *Buley Rockhole* and *Sandy Creek* have facilities such as toilets, showers and fireplaces, and cost $6.60/3.30 per adult/child. The bush

Kakadu National Park is huge, stretching across Arnhem Land. It offers a great opportunity to delve into Aboriginal culture, with its significant rock-art sites and Kakadu is World Heritage listed for its cultural and ecological importance. The name Kakadu comes from the Gagadju people, one of the three major groups of traditional owners.

The South Alligator River winds its way straight through Kakadu in the Dry, while in the Wet it bursts its banks and floods the northern regions of the park (1). The art documents thousands of years of history, including the time of European contact (2). Kakadu's rock-art galleries, such as the one at Ubirr, are among the finest in Australia (3). Freshwater crocodiles share the park with their more lethal cousins, the saltwater crocs (4). Nourlangie and Anbangbang Billabong – Kakadu National Park, Northern Territory (5). Wetlands filled with water lillies (6).

Kakadu is famous for its diversity. It features six major ecosystems and passes through six seasons in the annual cycle, producing a wonderland of sights and experiences. There are both types of Australian crocodile here, along with a huge number of fish, frog, reptile, bird and insect species, some of them unique to the park.

Termites build their enormous mounds (1). Among the spear grass, which grows up to 2m during the Wet, the sulphur-crested cockatoo and the jabiru with its long red legs, are easy to spot (2, 3). The many waterholes in the park are a rich source of food and are excellent sites for birdwatching (4). The perfect mirror image of tranquil Jim Jim Falls – not to be missed (5). The fern-leaved grevillea, also known as the honeywattle, is a traditional Aboriginal delicacy (6).

MITCH REARDON

CHRIS MELLOR

RICHARD I'ANSON

MITCH READON

RICHARD I'ANSON

RICHARD I'ANSON

camp at **Surprise Creek** is very basic, but you'll only part with \$3.30/1.65 per adult/child. Note that only Wangi camping ground accepts caravans and you must book ahead for June, July and August.

It's also possible to camp at **Petherick's Rainforest Reserve** (*\$5 per person*), on the western edge of the park, but the facilities are very basic.

Motels

For an alternative to camping, you can stay in Batchelor, where there is a range of motels and powered caravan parks. One place to start with is **Jungle Drums Bungalows** (*☎ 08-8976 0555, 10 Meneling Rd*), which has dorm beds for \$22 and bungalows from \$66. The bungalows, each with air-con, en suite and veranda, are set in tropical gardens. When you share a dorm, you share a bathroom.

Fuel & Supplies

Fuel is available at Batchelor, where there's also a **supermarket**. The **Wangi kiosk**, not far from the waterfall, is open year-round (9am to 5pm daily) and serves snack meals, such as hamburgers and steak sandwiches.

Kakadu National Park

Highlights

- Seeing ancient Aboriginal paintings rock art galleries at Ubirr and Nourlangie
- Swimming through a cool gorge to reach the white beach of Twin Falls
- Cruising on the Yellow Water Wetlands, spotting birdlife, crocs and lily pads
- Soaring over the Arnhem Land escarpment in a wet-season scenic flight

Kakadu National Park is one of Australia's natural marvels, and in 1984 it gained a World Heritage Listing for both its natural and cultural heritage – one of the few areas in the world with such a listing. The longer you stay in the park, the more rewarding it is. It's a very popular destination, and there are some good 4WD opportunities, although these are gradually disappearing as tracks are upgraded.

Kakadu covers around 20,000 sq km and stretches more than 200km south from the coast and 130km from east to west, with the main entrance 166km by bitumen road east of Darwin. It encompasses a great variety of superb landscapes, swarms with wildlife and is home to some of Australia's best Aboriginal rock art.

The name Kakadu comes from the language of the local Gagadju people, and much of Kakadu is Aboriginal land, leased to the government for use as a national park. There are several Aboriginal settlements in the park, about one-third of the park rangers are Aborigines, and traditional elders advise on park management issues. Enclosed by the park, but not part of it, are a few tracts of land meant for other purposes – principally uranium mining leases in the east.

GEOGRAPHY

A straight line on the map separates Kakadu from the Arnhem Land Aboriginal land to its east, which you cannot enter without a permit. The Arnhem Land escarpment, a dramatic 100- to 200m-high sandstone cliffline, which provides the natural boundary of the rugged Arnhem Land plateau, winds circuitously some 500km through east and south Kakadu.

Creeks cut across the rocky plateau and plummet from the escarpment as thundering waterfalls in the wet season. They then flow across the lowlands to swamp the vast flood plains of Kakadu's four north-flowing rivers, turning the north of the park into a kind of huge vegetated lake. From west to east are the Wildman, West Alligator, South Alligator and East Alligator Rivers. Such is the difference between dry and wet seasons that areas on river flood plains that are perfectly dry underfoot in September will be under 3m of water a few months later. As the waters recede in the Dry, some loops of wet-season watercourses become cut off, but don't dry up. These billabongs are often carpeted with water lilies and are enticing for waterbirds.

CLIMATE

The great change between the Dry and the November-March Wet makes a big difference to Kakadu visitors. Not only is the landscape transformed as the wetlands and waterfalls grow, but also Kakadu's lesser roads become impassable in the Wet, cutting off some highlights such as Jim Jim Falls.

The local Aboriginal people recognise six seasons in the annual cycle. The build-up to the Wet, known as *Gunumeleng*, starts in mid-October. Humidity and the temperatures rise to 35°C or more and the number of mosquitoes, always high near water, reaches infestation point. By November the thunderstorms have started, billabongs are replenished and the waterbirds disperse.

The Wet proper, *Gudjuek*, continues through January, February and March, with violent thunderstorms and an abundance of plant and animal life thriving in the hot, moist conditions. Most of Kakadu's rain falls during this period.

April is *Banggereng*, the season when storms (known as 'knock 'em down' storms) flatten the spear grass, which during the course of the Wet has shot up to 2m or more in height.

Yekke, which lasts from May to mid-June, is the season of mists, when the air starts to dry out. It is quite a good time to visit: there aren't too many other visitors, the wetlands and waterfalls still have lots of water and most of the tracks are open.

The most comfortable time is the late Dry, July and August – *Wurrgeng* and *Gurrung*. This is when wildlife, especially birds, begins to gather in huge numbers around the shrinking billabongs and watercourses, but it's also when most tourists flock to the park.

FLORA & FAUNA

Kakadu's coastline has long stretches of mangrove swamp, which are important both for halting erosion and as a breeding ground for marine and bird species. The southern part of the park is drier, lowland hill country with open grassland and eucalypt woodland. Pockets of monsoon rainforest crop up here as well as in most of the park's other landscapes.

In all, Kakadu is home to over 900 plant species, and a number of them are still used by the local Aborigines for food, bush medicine and other practical purposes.

Kakadu also has about 25 species of frog, 60 species of mammal, 52 freshwater fish species, about 120 types of reptile, 280 bird species (one-third of all Australian bird species) and 10,000 different kinds of insect. There are frequent additions to the list as more species are identified, and a few of the rarer species are unique to the park. You'll only see a tiny fraction of these elusive creatures during a park visit since many of them are shy, nocturnal or few in number.

Kakadu's wetlands are on the United Nations List of Wetlands of International Importance, principally because of their crucial significance to so many types of waterbird. Take advantage of talks and walks led by park rangers – mainly in the Dry – to get to know and see more of the wildlife. You can obtain details from the Bowali Visitor Centre (see Information later). There are cruises on the East Alligator River and Yellow Water billabong that are an ideal way to see the water life.

Reptiles

Thousands of the world's largest reptiles – the estuarine (or saltwater) crocodile – call Kakadu home. There are also plenty of freshwater crocodiles, which are considered harmless but you wouldn't want to aggravate one. You'll most likely see a few of both varieties staring back at you during a South Alligator River or Yellow Water Wetlands cruise. *Exercise caution at all times* – dangerous salties stop for no man.

Kakadu's other reptiles include several types of lizard, such as the frill-necked lizard, and five freshwater turtle species of which the most common is the northern snake-necked turtle. There are numerous snakes, including three highly poisonous types but thankfully you are unlikely to

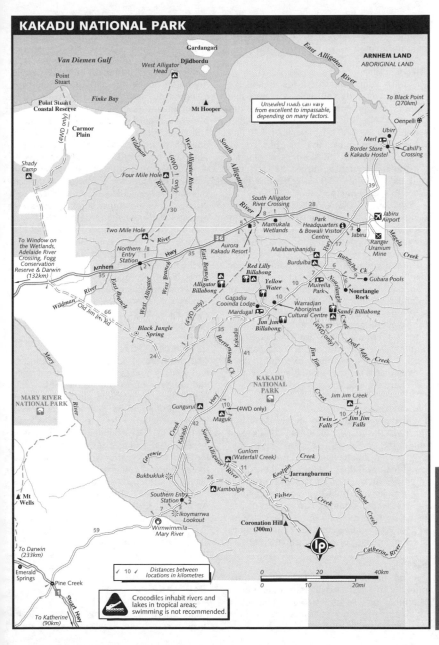

KAKADU NATIONAL PARK

Van Diemen Gulf

Gardangari
Djidbordu

West Alligator
Head

East Alligator River

ARNHEM LAND
ABORIGINAL LAND

Point Stuart

Finke Bay

Mt Hooper

To Black Point
(270km)

Point Stuart
Coastal Reserve

Carmor
Plain

(4WD only)

Shady
Camp

Wildman River

West Alligator River

(4WD only)

South Alligator River

Unsealed roads can vary
from excellent to impassable,
depending on many factors.

Oenpelli

Ubirr
Merl

Border Store
& Kakadu Hostel

Cahill's
Crossing

Four Mile Hole

30

South Alligator
River Crossing

28

39

To Window on
the Wetlands,
Adelaide River
Crossing, Fogg
Conservation
Reserve & Darwin
(132km)

Two Mile Hole

River

East Branch

8

Hwy

35

36

Mamukala
Wetlands

Aurora
Kakadu Resort

5 3

8

Park
Headquarters
& Bowali Visitor
Centre

Jabiru Airport

3

Jabiru

17

Ranger
Uranium
Mine

Magela Creek

Northern
Entry
Station

2

Arnhem

35

8

West Alligator

West Branch

Hwy

East Branch

Malabanbanjdju

Burdulba

Red Lilly
Billabong

Yellow
Water

Alligator
Billabong

Gagadju
Cooinda Lodge

Mardugal

10

Muirella
Park

Burdulba Ck

7

6

5

Gubara Pools

Nourlangie
Rock

Sandy Billabong

Old Jim Jim Rd

66

Wildman River

East Branch

(4WD only)

Black Jungle
Spring

35

Barramundi Ck

24

Kakadu

41

Warradjan
Aboriginal
Cultural Centre

Jim Jim
Billabong

10

57

(4WD only)

Nourlangie Creek

Deaf Adder Creek

Mary River

MARY RIVER
NATIONAL PARK

River

KAKADU
NATIONAL
PARK

Jim Jim Creek

Jim Jim Creek

Gungurul

Maguk

Hwy

10

(4WD only)

42

Kakadu

Gerowie Creek

South Alligator River

Twin
Falls

10

Jim Jim
Falls

11

Mt
Wells

Bukbukluk

26

Gunlom
(Waterfall Creek)

Kambolgie

11

Creek

Koolpin Creek

Jarrangbarnmi

Fisher Creek

Ginbai Creek

Southern Entry
Station

2

Ikoymarrwa
Lookout

Wirnwirnmila
Mary River

Coronation Hill
(300m)

Catherine River

To Darwin
(233km)

59

Emerald
Springs

Pine Creek

1

Stuart Hwy

To Katherine
(90km)

10 Distances between
locations in kilometres

0   20   40km
0   10   20mi

Crocodiles inhabit rivers and
lakes in tropical areas;
swimming is not recommended.

THE TROPICS

encounter any. Oenpelli pythons, probably unique to the Kakadu escarpment, were only discovered by white people in 1973.

Birds

Kakadu's abundant waterbirds inhabit the beautiful wetlands and make a memorable sight en masse, particularly late in the dry season. The park is one of Australia's chief refuges for several bird species, including the Burdekin duck and magpie goose. Kakadu supports 85% of the latter's Australian population during the Dry; Mamukala Wetlands (see later) are a good place to see a huge gaggle.

The jabiru, or black-necked stork, with its distinctive red legs and long straight beak, is another fine, commonly seen waterbird, as are the pelican, darter, heron, egret, ibis and cormorant.

In the open woodlands, you're quite likely to spot rainbow bee-eaters and kingfishers (of which there are six types in inland Kakadu). Majestic white-breasted sea eagles often soar near inland waterways too, and wedge-tailed eagles, whistling kites and black kites are also common sights. At night you might hear barking owls – they sound just like dogs. Also spectacular is the red-tailed black cockatoo, and there are also brolgas and bustards.

Mammals

Eight types of kangaroo and wallaby hop through the park, including black and antilopine wallaroos. At Ubirr, keep your eyes peeled at dawn and dusk for shy short-eared rock wallabies. In the woodlands, you might be lucky enough to see a nocturnal sugar glider or bushtail possum during daylight. Kakadu is home to 26 species of bat, including the fruit bat, and is a key sanctuary for four endangered varieties. Dingoes are sometimes spotted along roadsides.

Fish

Among the 52 species of fish are saratoga, rainbow fish and catfish. Barramundi are a common sight as they create a distinctive swirl near the water's surface; many grow well over a metre long.

ROCK ART

Kakadu has about 5000 Aboriginal rock-art sites dating from 20,000 or more years ago up to the mid-1980s. The art ranges from handprints to paintings of animals, people, mythological beings and European ships, constituting one of the world's most important and fascinating collections. They provide a record of changing environments and Aboriginal lifestyles over time. The dominant colours are yellow, red and white, obtained by grinding natural ochres to powder and mixing them with water.

In some places the paintings are concentrated in large galleries, with work from different eras sometimes superimposed over one another. Some sites are kept secret – not only to protect them from damage but also because they are private or sacred to the Aborigines; some sites are even believed to be the homes of dangerous spirits who must not be disturbed. Two of the finest sites, Ubirr and Nourlangie, are open to visitors, with access roads, walkways and explanatory signs. Park rangers conduct free art site tours once or twice a day from May to October.

INFORMATION

The entry fee of $16.25 (free for children under 16) is paid at the main park entrance, and entitles you to stay in the park for 14 days. There are random checks at various places throughout the park to check tickets.

The excellent Bowali Visitor Centre (☎ 08-8938 1121, Kakadu Hwy; open 8am-5pm daily) is a couple of kilometres south of the Arnhem Hwy. Here you'll find informative displays, a cafe and resource room, and details of guided art-site and wildlife walks.

At Cooinda, the circular **Warradjan Aboriginal Cultural Centre** (☎ 08-8975 0051; admission free; open 9am-5pm daily Sept-Jun, 7.30am-6pm daily Jul-Aug) gives a wonderful insight into the park's traditional owners with captivating displays, as well as a locally-made craft outlet.

THE PARK
Arnhem Highway

From where the Arnhem Hwy to Kakadu turns east off the Stuart Hwy, it's about

120km to the park entrance, and another 107km east across the park to Jabiru, sealed all the way. The Kakadu Hwy to Nourlangie, Cooinda and Pine Creek (also sealed) turns south off the Arnhem Hwy 2km before Jabiru.

A turn-off to the north, just past the park entrance on the Arnhem Hwy, leads to *camp sites* at **Two Mile Hole** (8km) and **Four Mile Hole** (38km) on the Wildman River, which is popular for fishing. The track is only suitable for conventional vehicles in the Dry, and then only as far as Two Mile Hole.

About 35km further east along the Arnhem Hwy, a turn-off to the south, again impassable to 2WD vehicles in the Wet, leads to *camp sites* at **Alligator** and **Red Lilly** billabongs, and on to the Kakadu Hwy.

The **South Alligator River Crossing** is on the Arnhem Hwy 64km into the park, about 3km past Aurora Kakadu Resort. There's a surfaced boat ramp here and it's a very popular fishing spot.

A short side road to the south leads to **Mamukala Wetlands**, 7km east of South Alligator River, with wide views over the South Alligator flood plain, an observation platform, a 3km walking trail and some bird-watching hides.

Ubirr

The spectacular Ubirr **rock-art site** *(open 8.30am-sunset daily 1 Apr-30 Nov, 2pm-sunset daily 1 Dec-31 Mar)* lies 39km north of the Arnhem Hwy. The road to Ubirr (pronounced 'oo-beer') is sealed all the way, although low-lying areas may be flooded during the wet season.

Shortly before Ubirr you pass the Border Store (Manbiyarra), the starting point for two walking trails close to the East Alligator River. Near the store are a riverside picnic spot, a *backpackers hostel* and a *camping ground*.

A 1.5km circular path from the Ubirr carpark takes you through to the main galleries and up to a lookout with stunning views over the Nardab floodplain. Stay for sunset if you can, when the views are particularly beautiful. There are paintings on numerous rocks along the path, but the

highlight is the main gallery with a large array of well-preserved X-ray-style native animals, plus a couple of *balanda* (white men). Also look for the Rainbow Serpent and Namarkan Sisters paintings.

The rock art at Ubirr, arguably the best in Kakadu, is in many different styles, and painted over a period ranging from 20,000 or more years ago up to the 20th century.

It's worth taking the ***Guluyambi Cruise*** *(☎ 1800 089 113; adult/child $30/15)* on the East Alligator River, near Ubirr. An Aboriginal guide accompanies the 1¾-hour trip and the focus is on Aboriginal culture. It runs daily at 9am, 11am, 1pm and 3pm, and bookings can be made at the Border Store, Jabiru airport and most travel agencies.

Jabiru

The township of Jabiru, built originally to accommodate the Ranger Uranium Mine workers but now a major service town, has a supermarket, Westpac bank, chemist, shops, petrol station and a public swimming pool. Eftpos facilities are available at the supermarket and petrol station.

Jabiru airport is 6km east, and nearby is the **Ranger Uranium Mine**. Minibus tours of the mine are run at 10.30am and 1.30pm daily by **Kakadu Tours** *(☎ 1800 089 113; adult/child $20/10)*.

Nourlangie

The sight of Nourlangie – the looming, mysterious, isolated outlier of the Arnhem Land escarpment – makes it easier to understand why it has been important to Aboriginal people for so long. Its long, red, sandstone bulk – striped in places with orange, white and black – slopes up from surrounding woodland to fall away finally at one end in sheer, stepped cliffs, at the foot of which is one of Kakadu's best known collections of rock art.

The name Nourlangie ('nor-**lan**-ji') is a corruption of *nawulandja*, an Aboriginal word that referred to an area bigger than the rock itself. The Aboriginal name of the upper part of the rock is Burrunggui (the lower section and surrounds are called Anbangbang). You reach the rock at the end of a 12km sealed road, which turns east off the Kakadu Hwy, 21km south of the Arnhem Hwy. The last few kilometres of the road are closed from around 5pm daily. Some worthwhile walks and lookouts in the Nourlangie area make it worth spending a whole day in this corner of Kakadu.

From the main carpark, a round-trip walk of 2.5km takes you first to the **Anbangbang Shelter**, which was used for 20,000 years as a refuge from heat, rain and the area's frequent wet-season thunderstorms. In the 1960s a respected Aboriginal artist repainted the art in this gallery. From there you can walk onto **Gunwarddehwardde Lookout**, where you can see the distant Arnhem Land escarpment. For a more thorough look at the area, there's a strenuous 12km marked walk all the way up, down and around the rock, for which Bowali has a leaflet.

Heading back towards the highway, you can take three turn-offs to further places of interest. The first, on the left about 1km from the main carpark, takes you to **Anbangbang Billabong**, with a dense carpet of lilies and a picnic site (check access in the Wet). The second, also on the left, leads to a 600m walk up to **Nawulandja Lookout**, with good views back over Nourlangie Rock.

The third turn-off, a dirt road on the right, takes you to another outstanding – but little visited – rock-art gallery, **Nangaluwurr**. A further 9km along this road brings you to **Gubara Pools**, an area of shaded pools set in monsoon forest, reached by a 6km return path.

Jim Jim & Twin Falls

Jim Jim Falls and Twin Falls are along a 4WD dry-season track that turns south-east off the Kakadu Hwy between the Nourlangie turn-off and Cooinda. The 57km track to Jim Jim Falls is lined by looming escarpment and the last 9km is slow going, taking about 35 minutes. You reach the falls and its icy pools by scrambling over 1km of rocks and tree trunks, so sturdy shoes are a must. The sheer 65m drop of Jim Jim is awesome during the Wet, but is reduced to a disappointing dribble in the Dry. More impressive for dry-season visitors are Twin

Falls, with water that gushes year-round. To reach the falls it's a 10km bumpy ride from Jim Jim, followed by a short walk and an 800m wade (or air-mattress ride) up a snaking, forested gorge. Twin Falls are memorable because of both their beauty and the unique way you reach them. Bush camping is available at Jim Jim Creek.

Yellow Water & Cooinda

The turn-off to the Cooinda accommodation complex and the superb Yellow Water Wetlands is around 47km down the Kakadu Hwy from its junction with the Arnhem Hwy. It's then 5km to Cooinda, and a couple more to the starting point for the **boat cruises** on the famous wetlands. A Yellow Water cruise is one of the highlights of most people's visit to Kakadu, thanks to the wetlands' beauty, the varied birdlife and regular sightings of a saltwater croc or four. Dawn is the best time to go, when the birds are most active, but other times of the day can be equally as good. It's usually advisable to book your cruise the day before – particularly for the early departures. The tours are operated by *Yellow Water Cruises* (☎ 08-8979 0145; adult/child $38/16.50; 2hrs) at Gagadju Cooinda Lodge. The number of tours and their duration vary according to the season, so it's worthwhile checking the details about all cruises.

Yellow Water is also an excellent place for watching sunsets, particularly in the dry season when the smoke haze from bushfires (common in the Dry) turns bright red in the setting sun. Bring plenty of insect repellent as the mosquitoes are voracious.

Cooinda Turn-Off to Pine Creek

Just south of the Yellow Water and Cooinda turn-off, the Kakadu Hwy heads south-west out of the park to Pine Creek on the Stuart Hwy, about 160km from Cooinda. On the way there is a turn-off to the very scenic falls and pools at **Maguk (Barramundi Creek)**, 10km along on a 4WD-only track; there's bush camping available here. Back on the Kakadu Hwy, it's 42km to the turn-off on the east towards **Gunlom (Waterfall Creek)**, but it does take you along an extra

37km of unsealed, dusty road to get there. Although a 4WD is preferable on this Dry-only track, a 2WD could make the distance.

ACTIVITIES
Walking

Kakadu is excellent, but often tough, bushwalking country. Many people will be satisfied with the marked trails, which range from 1km to 12km. For the more adventurous, there are infinite possibilities, especially in the drier south and east of the park, but take great care and prepare well; tell a ranger where you're going and don't go walking alone. You need a permit from the Bowali Visitor Centre to camp outside the established camping grounds. The Darwin Bushwalking Club (☎ 08-8942 2909) welcomes visitors and may help with information. It organises walks most weekends, often in Kakadu. Or you could join a Willis's Walkabouts guided bushwalk (see Organised Tours later).

Fishing

Fishing is permitted in most areas, but there are some restricted areas so check at Bowali Visitor Centre to be sure. Fishing with anything other than hand lines and rods with lures is not permitted, and the usual Northern Territory bag limits apply. Boating on the East Alligator River is permitted, but as the river forms the boundary between the park and Arnhem Land, landing on the Aboriginal land on the eastern bank is not permitted. There are boat ramps at Yellow Water, South Alligator River, Mardugal, Jim Jim Billabong and Border Store (Manbiyarra).

ORGANISED TOURS

There is an enormous number of tours to Kakadu from Darwin and a few that start inside the park. You can get around Kakadu in two days but an extra day is highly recommended. Three-day tours typically take in most of the main rocks, falls and cruises, and cost from $360 to $850, depending on group size, creature comforts etc. Travel agencies and hostels can advise with bookings. Following are some popular companies.

Gondwana Adventure Tours (☎ 1800 242 177, fax 8941 7163, e info@gondwana.cc, w www.gondwana.cc, Shop 6, 69 Mitchell St, Darwin) This company's emphasis is on small groups and getting away from the crowds, and it has a good reputation. Some tours combine Kakadu with Katherine Gorge and Mary River National Park. Book at its office direct.

Wilderness 4WD Adventures (☎ 1300 666 100, e info@wildernessadventures.com.au, w www.wildernessadventures.com.au) Tours from $405. They do 'safaris for fit, active people' so if that;s you, choose a three-, four- or five-day Kakadu treks.

Billy Can Tours (☎ 08-8981 9813, e res@billycan.com.au, w www.billycan.com.au) have 3-day tours from $320 to $1150, depending on the style of accommodation. This award-winning outfit offers numerous tours of between two and five days' duration.

Lord's Kakadu & Arnhemland Safaris (☎ 08-8979 2970, fax 8979 3367, e lords@topend.com.au) 1-day tour $125. This local company has over 10 years' experience taking tourists to the two falls, Jim Jim and Twin.

Willis's Walkabouts (☎ 08-8985 2134, e walkabout@ais.net.au) 2-week trip, including evening meals and return transport from Darwin $1800. Willis's has bushwalks guided by knowledgeable Top End walkers, following your own or preset routes of three days or more. Many of the walks are in Kakadu.

Tours into Arnhem Land

All 4WD tours are accompanied by an Aboriginal guide and depart from Jabiru.

Lord's Kakadu & Arnhemland Safaris (☎ 08-8979 2970, fax 8979 3367, e lords@topend.com.au) 1-day tour $160. Travel is in groups of a maximum of nine people, and includes stops in Mikinj Valley, Sandbar Billabong and Kunbarllanjnja (Oenpelli).

Magela Cultural & Heritage Tours (☎ 08-8979 2114) 1-day tour $165. This Aboriginal-owned company offers tours around Arnhem Land and parts of Kakadu, concentrating on the less-visited sites.

Scenic Flights

Kakadu Air (☎ 1800 089 113) 30-min flights $75, 1-hr flights $125, both per person. Kakadu Air does a number of flights over Kakadu, leaving from Jabiru airport. The bird's-eye views are spectacular.

FACILITIES

There are a number of fuel stations within the park, and there's a wide variety of accommodation. Note that accommodation prices in Kakadu can vary tremendously depending on the season – dry-season prices (given here) are often as much as 50% above wet-season prices.

Fuel & Repairs

Fuel (super, unleaded and diesel) is available at South Alligator River (Aurora Kakadu Resort), Jabiru, Cooinda and at the Wirnwirnmila Mary River Roadhouse (☎ 08-8975 4564), just outside the park's southern boundary on the Kakadu Hwy to Pine Creek. The Border Store at Manbiyarra (☎ 08-8979 2474; open 8am-5.30pm daily) sells diesel and unleaded fuel only (no super), but fuel may not be available from December to April.

Mechanical repairs can only be done at Jabiru, although emergency repairs and towing can also be arranged at Cooinda.

Camping

There are camping grounds run by the Parks and Wildlife Commission, and also some (with power) attached to the resorts. *Aurora Kakadu Lodge & Caravan Park (☎ 1800 811 154, 08-8979 2422, fax 8979 2254, Jabiru)* has double unpowered/powered sites for $16/22. The *Aurora Kakadu Resort (☎ 1800 818 845, 08-8979 0166, fax 8979 0147, South Alligator)* offers double unpowered & powered camp sites for $15. *Kakadu Hostel (☎ 08-8979 2232)* has double unpowered/powered sites for $16/22. *Gagadju Cooinda Lodge (☎ 08-8979 0145, Cooinda)* offers double unpowered/powered sites $22/28.

The three main national park camping grounds, with hot showers, flush toilets, drinking water and generator zones, are:

Merl, near the Border Store; *Muirella Park*, 6km off the Kakadu Hwy a few kilometres south of the Nourlangie turn-off; and *Mardugal*, just off the Kakadu Hwy, 2km south of the Cooinda turn-off. The fee of $5.40 per person (adults only) is collected at the site. Check access during the wet season.

The National Park also provides about 14 more basic *camping grounds* at which there's no fee (or drinking water). If you want to camp away from these, you'll need a permit from the Bowali Visitor Centre.

Hotels

South Alligator The *Aurora Kakadu Resort (☎ 1800 818 845)* has rooms for $185. Just a couple of kilometres southwest of the South Alligator River on the Arnhem Hwy is this hotel, which has a *restaurant* and swimming pool, and a basic shop (open 6.30am to 7pm daily).

Ubirr The *Kakadu Hostel (☎ 08-8979 2232)* offers dorm beds & twins & doubles for $22 per person. This hostel has a well-equipped kitchen, breezy lounge room and an above-ground swimming pool. The *Manbiyarra Border Store (☎ 08-8979 2474; open 8am-5.30pm daily)*, right next door, sells snack foods (eg, barra or buff burger $6.50) and all sorts of supplies and souvenirs.

Jabiru The *Aurora Kakadu Lodge (☎ 1800 811 154)* has rooms for $121 and self-contained cabins for $199. A no-frills interior greets you at the lodges; the cabins are a bit better. There's a communal kitchen and some barbecues.

Gagadju Crocodile Hotel (☎ 1800 808 123, ℮ executivesec@crocodile.sphc.com.au) Rooms $190-230. This hotel is shaped like a crocodile, although this is only apparent from the air. There's nothing very exotic about the hotel itself, but it's comfortable. Apart from the resort's restaurants, the *cafe* in the town shopping centre serves burgers and such. There's also a *bakery* nearby.

Cooinda This is by far the most popular place to stay, mainly because of the proximity to the Yellow Water Wetlands and the early morning boat cruises. It gets very crowded at times, mainly with camping tours.

Gagadju Cooinda Lodge (☎ 08-8979 0145, e cooinda1@bigpond.com) Budget rooms $30.50 per person, lodge rooms $198. The lodge has comfortable rooms for up to three people, and there are ultra-basic 'budget rooms', which are in transportable huts ('demountables' or 'dongas') – the rate charged per bed is pretty cheeky. There are communal showers, and the only cooking facilities are barbecues.

The *bistro* here serves barbecue-it-yourself meals that are overpriced at around $22, and the *bar* serves forgettable bain-marie cuisine for around $11, but the beers are cold and the sitting area is pleasant enough. There's also the more expensive *Mimi Restaurant* next door, but book in advance.

ALTERNATIVE TRANSPORT

Greyhound (☎ 13 20 30, W www.greyhound .com.au) runs daily buses from Darwin to Katherine via Cooinda and Jabiru (and vice versa), with connections from Jabiru to Ubirr.

Cobourg Peninsula

The far-flung wilderness of Cobourg Peninsula, 570km north-east of Darwin by road, includes the **Cobourg Marine Park** and the Aboriginal-owned **Garig Gunak Barlu National Park**, also referred to as Gurig National Park. This expanse of land and coastline is much more remote than Kakadu and you must be behind the wheel of a 4WD to access and enjoy it.

The Cobourg Peninsula is on the Ramsar List of Wetlands of International Importance as it is the habitat of a variety of waterfowl and other migratory birds, while the waters are home to dugongs and six species of turtles. You're likely to spot a few introduced animals such as Indonesian bantang cattle and Timor ponies, all of which were imported by the British when they attempted to settle the Top End in the 19th century. The coastline here is beautiful but unfortunately the water is unsuitable for swimming due to salties, sharks, stonefish and sea snakes.

One of the drawcards here is fishing off the coast in waters well known as some of the best in Australia. There are a few resorts (see later in this section) that provide fishing trips. It's not really possible to explore the inland parts of the area as there are virtually no tracks within the park apart from the main access track, but you can still wander along the white sandy beaches.

The park is jointly managed by the local Aboriginal inhabitants and the Parks and Wildlife Commission. Alcohol must not be consumed while travelling through Arnhem Land, but it's permitted beyond the Garig Gunak Barlu entrance.

History

Although European navigators had explored along this coastline, it was the British who tried to make a permanent settlement. After two unsuccessful attempts (at Melville Island and then Raffles Bay), a third attempt was made at Port Essington in 1838. The garrison town was named Victoria Settlement, and at its peak was home to over 300 people. The British intention was that it would become the base for major trade between Australia and Asia, but by 1849, after the settlement had survived a cyclone and malaria outbreaks, the decision was made to abandon it.

Information

Entry to Garig Gunak Barlu is by permit. You pass through part of Arnhem Land on the way, and the Aboriginal owners here severely restrict the number of vehicles going through. Only 20 are allowed in at any one time, so you're advised to apply up to a year ahead for the necessary permit, which must be obtained from the Parks and Wildlife Commission (☎ 08-8999 4814), PO Box 496, Palmerston, NT 0831. The camping permit fee is $220 plus $12.10 transit fee per vehicle (five people) for a stay of up to seven days.

At Black Point (Algarlarlgarl) there is a rangers station and visitors centre, which doubles as a very informative culture centre detailing the Aboriginal, European and Macassan people, and the history of Victoria Settlement. No caravans or trailers are allowed into the park.

The Park

The track to Cobourg starts at Oenpelli (Kunbarllanjnja) and is accessible by 4WD only – it's closed in the wet season (usually opening early May). The 270km drive to Black Point from the East Alligator River takes about four to six hours and the track is in reasonable condition – the roughest part being the first 15km or so. The trip must be completed in one day as it's not possible to stop overnight on Aboriginal land.

Victoria Settlement (Murrumurrdmulya) at Port Essington is well worth a visit, but is accessible by boat only. The ruins still visible include various chimneys and wells, the powder magazine and parts of the hospital. Book trips at the *Gurig store* (☎ *1800 000 871; open 4pm-6pm daily; ½-day tours $95/50 adult/child*) at Black Point, where you can also hire a dinghy ($120 per day plus fuel) for fishing trips.

Facilities

The *Gurig store* sells a good range of provisions including frozen meats, dairy products, ice, camping gas and outboard mix. You'll need to bring your own alcohol, and fresh fruit and vegies. Credit cards are accepted and basic mechanical repairs can generally be undertaken. Fuel (diesel and unleaded only) is available at the jetty at 6pm only, daily – ask at the store. There's an

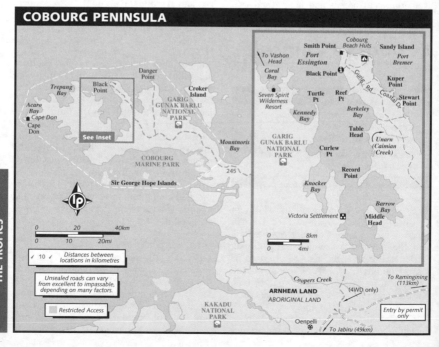

THE TROPICS

airstrip at Smith Point (Ngardimardi), which is serviced by charter flights from Darwin.

***Smith Point Camping Ground** (Smith Point)* Camping fees included in permit fee. About 100m from the shore and hidden among trees are 20 sites, with showers, toilets and barbecues. The grounds are split into No 1 and No 2; the latter allows generators. Call the Parks and Wildlife Commission (☎ 08-8999 4814) for more information.

***Cobourg Beach Huts** (☎ 1800 000 871,* ⓔ *cobourg@gurig.com.au,* ⓦ *www.cobourg .gurig.com.au, Smith Point)* Huts from $160. Fully equipped, six-bed huts with louvred window-walls, solar-powered showers and verandas overlooking Port Essington. The seclusion and views are fantastic.

***Cape Don** (☎ 1800 000 871,* ⓔ *capedon@ gurig.com.au,* ⓦ *www.capedon.gurig.com .au, Cape Don)* Doubles $550 per person. Packages also available. The rate includes comfortable accommodation, airfares to/from Darwin, all meals, and guided fishing and wildlife tours. Guests are limited to 10 at any one time.

***Seven Spirit Bay Wilderness Lodge** (☎ 08-8979 0277,* ⓔ *sales@sevenspiritbay.com,* ⓦ *www.sevenspiritbay.com, Vashon Head)* Singles/twins $490/390 per person. This award-winning resort is set in a secluded wilderness accessible only by air or boat. The price tag includes three meals daily, guided bushwalks and a sunset cruise. Accommodation is in open-sided 'habitats', each with semi-outdoor private bathroom. Return air transfer from Darwin costs $395 per person.

Gulf Track

Highlights

- Fishing and camping on the Gulf's many rivers
- Exploring the amazing 'lost city' sandstone escarpments
- Canoeing and hiking in Lawn Hill National Park
- Investigating the history of the 'wild north'

Steeped in history and lined by unmarked graves, the 1000km Gulf Track from Roper Bar in the Northern Territory's Top End to Normanton in north-western Queensland crosses some of tropical Australia's wildest and most remote country. Until recent times the track was little more than a set of wheel ruts winding through the endless bush. Those days are gone, but there is still a powerful sense of adventure, thanks to the Gulf's vast untouched forests, the lack of facilities and low population, and the crocodiles that lurk in its numerous rivers. Its attractions include some great fishing opportunities, detours to scenic coastline, abundant wildlife and bush camping beside flowing streams.

For the average traveller, complacency and excessive speed are the track's major motoring hazards. A 4WD may not be required during the dry season unless you plan to take the tracks that lead to the coast from the Hell's Gate and Wollogorang Roadhouses; however, conventional vehicles should have good ground clearance and solid suspension. The river crossings are usually no problem by June, when water levels will have dropped to no more than 600mm over the track.

Traffic varies from none in the Wet to an average of about 30 vehicles per day in July and August when days are warm and nights are cool. Travel is not recommended between December and April when it is extremely hot and humid, and heavy rain often closes the road for lengthy periods.

For almost its entire length, the Gulf Track passes through cattle stations, Aboriginal land and national parks, and the landowners will not be pleased to find you driving about on their land without permission. However access to bush camping at river crossings is generally unrestricted.

History
The Gulf Track more or less follows in the footsteps of the eccentric Prussian explorer Ludwig Leichhardt, who skirted the Gulf of Carpentaria on his trek from Brisbane to newly settled Port Essington (near Darwin). He left in October 1844 with 10 companions

including an Aborigine, a naturalist, two teenagers and a convict. He had 16 bullocks, 17 horses, six dogs and 1200lb of flour among his supplies, but his planned seven-month expedition took twice as long, so they had to live off the land. On the Gulf Track between Borroloola and Wollogorang Road-house is Seven Emu station which was named after the place where Leichhardt shot seven emus.

Leichhardt was attempting to find an overland trade route to India and many saw the new port becoming the Singapore of Australia – 'a safe harbour where the wealth of Asia could be exchanged for grain and horses'. However Port Essington was abandoned four years later, and the hardships of Leichhardt's route killed any hope that it could be used for trade.

After Leichhardt, the wilderness between Burketown (established in 1865) and the Roper River lay undisturbed until 1872, when D'Arcy Uhr took 400 head of cattle through to the Top End goldfields. But the first drover to follow Uhr starved to death near the Limmen Bight River after losing his entire mob to Aboriginal attacks, flooded rivers and stampedes.

In 1878 the legendary Nat 'Bluey' Buchanan drove 1200 cattle from Aramac in central Queensland to a station near Darwin. At the Limmen Bight River the drovers returned to camp to find their cook beheaded with his own axe. For hours afterwards the hills echoed with gunfire as the dead man's mates carried out a terrible vengeance.

Three years later Buchanan was back, this time in command of 70 men charged with taking 20,000 head of cattle from St George in south-eastern Queensland to the Daly River near Darwin. It was an epic in Australian droving history and established Leichhardt's hazardous track around the Gulf as the major stock route from Queensland to the Top End.

In 1886 the drovers were joined by a stream of desperadoes and penniless adventurers on their way to the Halls Creek gold rush in Western Australia's Kimberley area. The would-be diggers suffered unimaginable privations and many succumbed to

madness, starvation, thirst and Aboriginal spears.

Yet 10 years later, by which time the gold rush and the great cattle drives were over, traffic on the Gulf Track had dwindled to a trickle. In recent times, with the upgrading of the road, more travellers have been using this historical track. Even so, there are days even in the Dry when you can drive 200km and not see another vehicle.

Information

Tourist Offices The Gulf Local Authorities Development Association (GLADA; ☎ 07-4051 4658, fax 4031 3340, e info@gulf-savannah.com.au, w www.gulf-savannah.com.au), at 74 Abbott St, Cairns, has lots of information and publishes a useful free travel guide on the Gulf Track.

Tourism Tropical North Queensland (☎ 07-4051 3588, fax 4051 0127, e ttnq@tnq.org.au, w www.tnq.org.au), at 51 the Esplanade, Cairns, has information on the Queensland part of the track. Otherwise contact the roadhouses, council offices, camping grounds and hotels listed in the facilities section for local road conditions and other information.

Radio Frequencies For the track's western half contact St John Ambulance in Darwin (☎ 08-8922 6200). Their call sign is VJD and you can contact them on 2020kHz.

The eastern half of the track is serviced by the Mt Isa Royal Flying Doctor Service (RFDS) base (☎ 07-4743 2800). Their call sign is VJI, their primary frequency is 5110kHz and their secondary frequency is 6965kHz during the day and 2020kHz at night. The primary frequency is monitored between 9am and 9.15am Monday to Friday.

Before you set off, you should telephone the recommended organisations to check up-to-date frequencies and hours of operation. For emergencies press the emergency call button, which is monitored 24 hours a day.

Books & Maps Australian Geographic's *Gulf Country* by Sue Neales is good. *Eight Months with Dr Leichhardt* by JF Mann, published in 1888, is a very entertaining and interesting account of the Leichhardt expedition. *North Australian Fish Finder*, edited by Matt Flynn, has all you need to know about fishing up north.

Sunmap publishes a *Gulf Savannah* tourist map and Hema maps also cover the area.

Emergency There are medical clinics at Ngukurr, Borroloola, Doomadgee, Burketown and Normanton. Roper Bar Store and Wollogorang and Hell's Gate Roadhouses have RFDS medical kits and airstrips.

THE ROUTE
Roper Bar
The place where Leichhardt crossed the magnificent Roper River en route to Port Essington lies 174km east (by road) of Mataranka on the Stuart Hwy. Access from the Stuart Hwy (the turn-off is 6km south of Mataranka) presents no difficulty, as all but the last 40km is a one-lane bitumen strip. But remember: When you meet a road train or a large truck you must get right off the bitumen – they are the kings of the outback roads and it is up to you to get out of their way.

Named by Leichhardt after one of his expedition members, John Roper, the river is over 100m wide and lined by huge paperbark trees at the rock bar, which makes the river shallow. This popular fishing spot, renowned for barramundi and saratoga, lies at the river's tidal limit and has an airstrip, boat ramp, camping ground and general store that sells fuel. In the early days, steamships and large sailing vessels tied up at the bar to discharge cargo.

The road to **Ngukurr**, an Aboriginal community 30km east, crosses the river here, but to visit you need a permit from the Northern Land Council. For contact details see Travel Permits in the Getting Around chapter.

Roper Bar to Borroloola (373km)
The new **Limmen National Park** starts near Roper Bar and covers 10,000 sq km, almost all the way to Borroloola. Walking trails and camp sites are being developed. The red sandstone escarpments in the area have been eroded into all kinds of fantastic shapes, and

---

Absalom's Yabbies

My introduction to Roper Bar was memorable: Who should I meet there but the famous Australian bush artist and raconteur Jack Absalom? He and his wife, Mary, were on one of their regular pilgrimages to the Bar. Although it's a long way from their home in Broken Hill, most people who have camped by the Roper River will understand why they do it.

We were on the subject of fishing when Jack started waving his arms about to indicate the size of the local yabbies. I must have looked a bit sceptical because he went straight to his freezer and pulled out the biggest yabby I've ever seen – I didn't know they grew that big! He let me in on a little secret that he promised is much more effective than traps at catching yabbies: Simply toss a handful of chook pellets into the water near the bank to attract them, wait a minute, then snaffle them with a throw net.

Denis O'Byrne

---

one of these spectacular **'lost cities'** is only 6km from the main road. It is an amazing experience to wander among the remote sandstone columns that rear up into the sky all around you. Sculptured by the wind and rain, some of them look like ancient ruins, and they should be as well known as the Bungle Bungles in Western Australia. Contact the rangers at Nathan River Ranger Station (☎ 08-8975 9940, fax 8975 9761) for up-to-date maps and information.

This section of road is mainly good as it crosses undulating country carpeted with a mosaic of scrub, tall forest and open parkland. Along the way you pass lagoons and sandstone escarpments, wind through stony hills, ford several rivers and cross lots of creeks. Although the rivers are a feature of this region, their fording places can be disappointing: They are sited at constrictions in the main channels and so feel the full force of the wet-season flooding. However, the atmosphere and scenery a short distance away on either side are often superb. Downstream

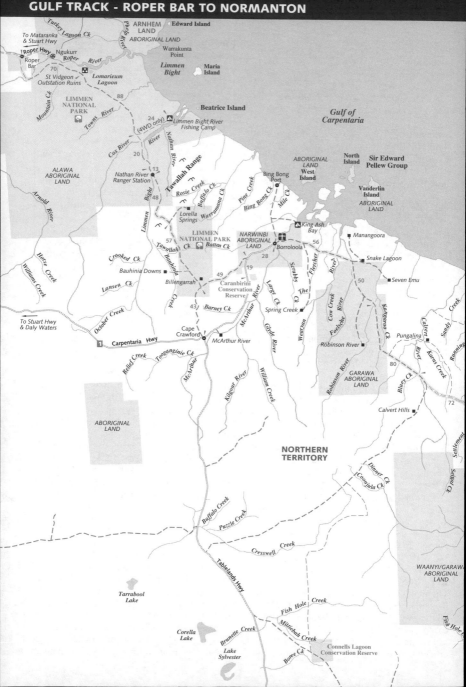

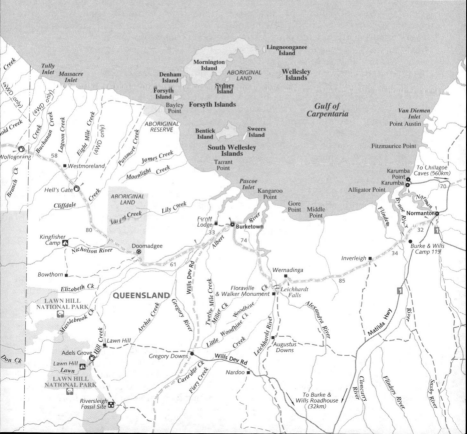

0   25   50km
0   15   30mi

✓ 10 ✓   Distances between locations in kilometres

Unsealed roads can vary from excellent to impassable, depending on many factors.

Lingnoonganee Island

Mornington Island

ABORIGINAL LAND

Wellesley Islands

Tully Inlet

Massacre Inlet

Denham Island

Forsyth Island

Sydney Island

Bayley Point

Forsyth Islands

Gulf of Carpentaria

ABORIGINAL RESERVE

Van Diemen Inlet

Point Austin

Fitzmaurice Point

Wollogorang

58

Westmoreland

Bentick Island

Sweers Island

South Wellesley Islands

Tarrant Point

Karumba Point

Karumba

To Chillagoe Caves (560km)

Hell's Gate

Pascoe Inlet

Kangaroo Point

Alligator Point

70

Cliffdale

ABORIGINAL LAND

Lily Creek

Gore Point

Middle Point

Normanton

80

Kingfisher Camp

Nicholson River

Doomadgee

Escott Lodge

33

Burketown

74

32

5

Burke & Wills Camp 119

Bowthorn

61

Inverleigh

34

Elizabeth Ck

Wernadinga

85

LAWN HILL NATIONAL PARK

QUEENSLAND

Floraville & Walker Monument

Leichhardt Falls

Adels Grove

Lawn Hill

Augustus Downs

Lawn Hill Lawn

Gregory Downs

Wills Dev Rd

Nardoo

LAWN HILL NATIONAL PARK

To Burke & Wills Roadhouse (32km)

Riversleigh Fossil Site

Matilda Hwy

from the crossings the rivers generally open out into broad stretches of water that go all the way to the Gulf.

Seventy kilometres from Roper Bar, a stretch in which there is little to delight the eye, you arrive at the old **St Vidgeon's Outstation** – a lonely ruin that conjures up stark images of pioneer battlers eking out a scant living from the hostile bush. Just behind the ruin is **Lomarieum Lagoon**, one of the park's gems. Fringed by paperbarks and covered by large water lilies, this oasis has many birds and a peaceful atmosphere – a great spot for a picnic.

After that the road mainly winds through scrub and forest, with occasional vibrant patches of flowering wattles and grevilleas early in the dry season. Large domed termite mounds and clumps of tall native pines are also of interest. Traffic is light and drivers usually wave to each other as they pass, so you have to adopt this outback custom and decide what kind of wave to do – a grand gesture or something casual.

From the lagoon it is 88km to a left turn that takes you 24km down a rough track, which is only suitable for 4WD vehicles, to **Limmen Bight Fishing Camp**. This is a good place to stay and has fuel and a small shop. You can catch mud crabs and fish, but the river is very wide here so crocodiles are often seen.

After this turn-off the track crosses the Cox and Limmen Bight Rivers, which have causeways, before reaching the Nathan River Ranger Station on the left. Drop in here for information on hiking and driving tracks in the national park.

The scenery improves soon after, but be careful crossing the unnamed deep creek 60km past the rangers station. If you get through this one, you should manage all the others! The next creek, **Tawallah**, has a delightful waterhole lined with pandanus palms and overhung with tall river gums and paperbarks. The pool looks ideal for a cooling dip, but up this way the sensible travellers do their swimming in a bucket because of the crocodiles.

About 105km from the rangers station is the **Cape Crawford** turn-off and its very own

Heartbreak Hotel, 43km south. Continuing on the main road, it is 49km to a junction with a bitumen road, Carpentaria Hwy. Turn left for Borroloola, 28km away, right for a short 19km drive along the bitumen to **Caranbirini Conservation Reserve**. It has no facilities and camping is not allowed, but there is a large waterhole that attracts a lot of birds and used to be a valuable food source for the local Gadanji people.

There is also a very pleasant one-hour, 1.5km walk around some **'lost city'** sandstone cliffs and towers. Squeezing through very narrow ravines with high cliffs on both sides of you is the highlight of this walk. The dramatic sandstone towers were originally sand that became rock and they are now becoming sand again. Sunset is a good time to visit because it brings out the beautiful rock colours. From the reserve it is 47km back to Borroloola.

Borroloola

Until 1885 there were no facilities between Burketown (then a busy little port) and the store at Roper Bar, except for a few widely scattered homesteads that were wooden forts armed against Aborigine attacks. Then 'Black Jack' Reid brought a boat loaded with alcohol and supplies up the McArthur River to the Burketown crossing, where he built a primitive store. So Borroloola was born.

A year later, the Kimberley gold rush greatly increased traffic on the Gulf Track and the new township soon had a population of 150 non-Aboriginal people – 'the scum of northern Australia', according to a government official. A decade later, the gold rush and great cattle drives were over and only six people remained. Borroloola survives as an administrative and supply centre for local cattle stations and nearby McArthur Mine, which produces zinc, silver and lead.

Sprawled along 2km of a wide main street, Borroloola was blown away by Cyclone Kathy in 1984 and most of the old buildings were destroyed. Its population swells to 1200 in the Wet, when Aboriginal cattle station workers stay in town.

Stories about Borroloola's colourful past of tough cowboys and pioneers are on show in the **museum** *(admission $2; open 10am-5pm daily)*, which is housed in the old, corrugated-iron police station. Built in 1886, it is packed with old photographs, newspaper articles and other displays, including a tree on which the famous explorer Leichhardt carved his initial. You can read about local characters such as the Freshwater Admiral, and the Hermit of Borroloola, who walked here in 1916 all the way from Cunnamulla, more than 2000km away, and lived in an old water tank.

Home-made booze with names like 'Square' and 'Come Hither' were once the cause of numerous incidents that kept the local police busy. The town is much quieter these days, although bloody re-enactments of what it was like a century ago occasionally take place when the booze is flowing freely.

Besides history, the other attraction is **fishing** – from the banks of the McArthur River in town, 40km downstream near King Ash Bay camping ground or by boat in the river, estuary or out in the Gulf around the Sir Edward Pellow group of islands.

Borroloola is connected to the outside world by bitumen roads leading to the Stuart and Barkly Hwys and by regular air services to Darwin and Katherine.

The **rodeo and show** is held every August, and the **Fishing Classic** at Easter draws a large number of enthusiasts. Barramundi is what they are usually trying to catch.

You can drive north to the sailing club at King Ash Bay and on to Port Bing Bong, which is used by the local mining company and is not a tourist attraction except for the Gulf views.

Borroloola to Wollogorang Roadhouse (258km)

This section of the Gulf Track is generally in good condition, with long, wide, straight and flat stretches that are like driving along an airstrip. It is easy to bowl along at 100km/h but it is best to tread lightly on the accelerator, as loose corners and occasional gutters cause numerous accidents and rollovers every year.

The creeks in this section are usually shallower than back towards Roper Bar, but the **Wearyan River**, 56km from Borroloola, has water and good bush camping just upstream from the crossing. Tall cycad palms grow here.

The Gulf rivers are notable for their wildlife, and the Wearyan River is no exception. If you decide to camp here you are likely to lie awake most of the night listening to mosquitoes whine, dingoes howl, curlews scream, fish splash, flying foxes screech and squabble, and heavy things go thump in the bush. This exercise in insomnia reaches its climax at dawn, when an army of kookaburras have a laughing competition in the trees above your head. The bird orchestra is louder than any alarm clock and starts early.

A lagoon on the right, 82km from Borroloola, is a good place for a picnic as is the **Robinson River**, 24km further on. Here mussel shells, yabby claws and fish scales on the sand give some idea of the river's bounty. Travellers with 4WD vehicles can reach some nice places to bush camp beside shallow flowing water, but the rubbish lying about shows that this is also a popular spot for drinking parties. The **Calvert River** crossing is 80km beyond the Robinson River and is another pleasant spot. The pink blooms of turkey bush – a nondescript species at other times – flower early in the wet season.

Turning right at the junction 23km from the Calvert River, the road heads south-west to the Tablelands Hwy. From the junction the Gulf Track heads east for another 17km through low but attractive open forest before entering an area of high, rocky hills. For 20km the road winds about, a pleasant change from the previous long straights, and crosses spring-fed creeks lined by lush tropical vegetation, and then you arrive on top of the range to be greeted by some dramatic scenery. From this lofty summit, a long descent takes you down into a narrow, rugged valley. Then the road straightens out again for the final 12km to Wollogorang Roadhouse, part of a cattle station that was first established back in 1881.

Covering 7000 sq km and supporting 40,000 cattle, this vast property has a licensed roadhouse, a camping ground and 80km of pristine sandy beaches on the Gulf of Carpentaria. The coast, which can only be reached by 4WD vehicle, is 90km away and takes three hours if you drive carefully. Most people camp by the beach under the shade of the she-oak trees and spend time fishing and crabbing. You can also visit **Massacre Inlet**, the scene of a slaughter of Aborigines by settlers in the early 1880s – the Aborigines had earlier attacked Westmoreland homestead killing all the Aboriginal and European women and children there except for one old Aboriginal woman. Contact Wollogorang Roadhouse to visit this interesting area, which is private property.

Wollogorang Roadhouse to Burketown (232km)

On this section of the Gulf track you can safely sit on 80km/h; unless, of course, a heavy Wet has destroyed the government's good work. The surrounding countryside has little going for it in the way of scenery, being mainly flat and covered with scrubby vegetation. In fact, apart from Hell's Gate and the Gregory River, there's little reason to linger on this section.

Just 6km from Wollogorang Roadhouse is the **Queensland border**, so put your watches forward half an hour. Another 52km brings you to **Hell's Gate Roadhouse** located among outcrops of grey conglomerate that rise like fat dumplings from the surrounding bush. In the old days the police escorted westbound travellers as far as these rocks, after which they were on their own until they reached Katherine. Afraid of the fierce Aboriginal people who lived in the area, they named the place Hell's Gate.

The roadhouse was established in 1986 by Bill and Lee Olive, and the friendly little oasis they have created in the middle of nowhere is a credit to these two battlers. Bill still runs 4WD tours of the area and is a very knowledgeable guide. The ladies toilet has an amusing notice: 'Lights attract insects. Insects attract frogs. Frogs attract snakes. SNAKES BITE. The Flying Doctors are two hours away. So please turn the lights out'.

Other than patches of open forest along occasional creek lines, there is little breaking up the mallee and paperbark scrub all the way from Hell's Gate to Doomadgee.

The turn-off to **Kingfisher Camp** is on the right, 51km from Hell's Gate. This road heads south to Kingfisher and some fine camping, and then on to **Bowthorn** station. From there continue south to Lawn Hill National Park or head east, joining up with the Gulf Track again east of Doomadgee. See Detours later in this section for more information on this area.

The Doomadgee turn-off is passed 30km further on. **Doomadgee** is an Aboriginal community of over a thousand residents; it has a well-stocked supermarket which also sells fuel.

Four kilometres past Doomadgee is the wide **Nicholson River** crossing which has a 600m causeway. In the Dry its bed of solid rock, scattered pools and shrubs presents a rather desolate picture. A swim would be nice but estuarine crocodiles may be waiting for the unwary.

Another 4km further on is a turn-off to the Lawn Hill National Park. Continuing on the track it's 53km to the **Gregory River** crossing with running water, lush vegetation and herons stalking their prey.

The **Tirranna Roadhouse**, 1km further on, has limited supplies, takeaways and snacks, and 8km later is a major junction. Turn right for Gregory Downs Hotel and the Lawn Hill National Park or turn left for Burketown, 24km away. Just 4km before Burketown is the turning for **Escott Lodge**, which offers camping, meals and accommodation.

Burketown

For many, Burketown is 'on the Gulf', but in reality it is over 30km from the coast. The little township shimmers on the biscuit-flat plains that border the waters of the Gulf. Just a stone's throw from the Albert River, it used to be a port with ships sailing upriver to service the town and its hinterland. While Burketown was named after the Burke and Wills expedition of 1860, Burke and his party were a long way east and nearer to Normanton.

Founded in 1865, Burketown almost came to a premature end a year later when a fever wiped out 30% of the residents. Then, in 1887, a cyclone and a tidal surge destroyed 98% of the town, including its three pubs. While nothing so dramatic has occurred since, the township is often cut off from the rest of Australia by flooded rivers.

Once said to be the wildest township in Australia, where everyone carried a pistol, Burketown today is much more peaceful and friendly. Not only is it the administrative centre for a vast region dotted with huge cattle properties, it is also a supply centre for travellers exploring the Gulf.

There are a few **historic sites** to see. In the salt pan area about 5km from town, a few rusty relics remain of a meat processing factory. Not far away is the tree blazed by Landsborough, the explorer sent to try and find out what had happened to the Burke and Wills expedition. Like many outback historic sites, this one is fast decaying under the onslaught of weather and white ants. The cemetery has some unusual gravestones including a fish-shaped one. The **Albert River** wharf is a popular place to fish – we only caught a catfish, but you might have more luck.

Burketown is also home to a phenomenon known as 'Morning Glory' – those unusual circular cloud formations that extend all along the horizon roll in from the Gulf in the early morning. The best time to see it is from September to November.

The Lawn Hill National Park and the Riversleigh (Myimba) Fossil Site should not be missed. See Detours later in this section.

Burketown to Normanton (233km)

From Burketown the track sweeps across the flat, grassy plains of the Gulf to Normanton, following the old coach route between Darwin and Port Douglas. Three kilometres out of town is the Albert River, first sighted in 1841 by Captain Stokes of HMS *Beagle*. He was enthusiastic about what he called the 'Plains of Promise', imagining that English villages and church towers would soon dot the landscape. But the plains were too dry in the Dry and too

wet in the Wet; the sheep died and only hardy cattle can be seen nowadays.

The bitumen ends at after 15km but the road continues to be reasonable, although corrugated patches, dips and cattle grids will keep your speed down. This end of the Gulf Track is drier, and most of the creek and river crossings have some kind of causeway. How bad the road is depends on when the graders have been out and how bad the preceding wet season was.

The grassland sometimes stretches as far as the eye can see, but it is bleached blonde by the sun. If the underground were was not so deep, irrigation could make this arid semi-desert bloom.

Turn right 73km from Burketown to visit **Frederick Walker's Monument**. He was the controversial founder of the Aborigine Trooper Police, who died here in 1866 of a fever while mapping a route for the Cardwell to Burketown telegraph line. Open the gate and drive towards **Floraville** station, then turn left at the sign, and you will soon see it. Please respect the privacy of the station people and stay away from the homestead.

Just 1km further along the main road, turn left to the carpark for **Leichhardt Falls**. There are sand dunes and pools of water, but often there's no water over the waterfall in the Dry. Explorers McKinlay and Landsborough camped here separately in 1861 as they searched for the missing Burke and Wills.

Only 2km from the Leichhardt River is a fork where you turn left for Normanton. The other road, Nardoo-Burketown Rd, heads south to the Burke & Wills Roadhouse, 146km away (see the Matilda Highway section later in this chapter). Just after the fork you cross the very rough bed of the Alexandra River.

Next, 113km later, you cross the Flinders, Bynoe and Little Bynoe Rivers. Turn right at the sign on the far bank of the Little Bynoe River and less than 2km away is Burke and Wills' **Camp 119**, their most northerly camp. Some of the 15 trees blazed by the expedition more than 150 years ago are still alive and are marked with metal discs.

Leaving their companions, Gray and King, to guard the camels and equipment,

Explorers' Bush Tucker

European explorers were often hungry and forced to live off the land.

Burke and Wills consumed a number of crows and hawks, but eating a snake made Burke ill. They also painstakingly collected seeds from the nardoo plant, crushed and baked them into a kind of bread, which they ate with 'weed and herb' soup.

Ludwig Leichhardt dined on stewed cocka-toos for Christmas dinner and at one stage his exploration party had to eat flying foxes for breakfast, lunch and dinner, eight a day each.

Edward Kennedy's expedition cooked up wallaby soup, horse blood pudding and even dog. The Jardine brothers ate iguana eggs, dried catfish and a cassowary bird, which they claimed was delicious.

Burke and Wills pushed north across the wet and flooded country to try and reach the waters of the Gulf. On 11 February 1861, they observed the water was salty and rose and fell with the tide, but the barrier of mangroves and mud kept them from seeing the actual Gulf.

Returning to their companions at Camp 119, they planned their return to the base camp on Cooper Creek in north-eastern South Australia. No longer an exploratory expedition with mapping and observing a prime consideration, it was now a desperate dash for survival. In the end, only King survived, kept alive by Aborigines.

Continuing on, you reach bitumen at the junction 32km beyond the Camp 119 turn-off. Turn left and 5km later you are in Normanton.

Normanton

On the banks of the Norman River, the town of Normanton is larger than Burketown with four pubs, a classic Victorian railway station, an ATM, shops, fuel outlets, a camping ground with artesian water, and a huge crocodile that is a life-sized replica of one of the largest ever caught. For more information see the Matilda Highway section later in this chapter.

From here you can drive south along the Burke Developmental Rd to Cloncurry, Mt Isa and beyond, or head east along the Gulf Developmental Rd to Croydon and Cairns – see the Kennedy Highway section later in this chapter.

Driving north will take you to **Karumba**, on the coast 70km away (see the later Matilda Highway section). On the way you can turn right onto the dirt road that goes to Dunbar station and then Chillagoe (famous for its limestone caves and rock art sites) and the coast. This rough, dusty road passes through remote country without any supply points.

DETOURS
Lawn Hill National Park & Riversleigh Loop (375km)

The wonderful gorge at Lawn Hill (Bood-jamulla) National Park is 220km from Burketown via the *Gregory Downs Hotel (☎ 07-4748 5566)* which offers accommodation, camping and fuel. The *general store (☎ 07-4748 5540)* is nearby and hires out canoes on the spring-fed Gregory River which flows all year. The famous Gregory Canoe Race is held every Labour Day weekend in May. The Wills Developmental Rd is gravel but straight and wide although with the usual cattle grids, dips and rough patches to slow you down.

Adels Grove (☎/fax 07-4748 5502, ⓔ *adelsgrove@bigpond.com)*, about 10km before the national park, has a small store that sells fuel and food. Camping costs $8 per person, on-site tents $22 per person. You can have some minor car repairs done and hire canoes. There are also tours of Riversleigh.

Lawn Hill's major creek has water all year and is fed by warm springs so it is great for swimming. Two-person canoes cost $8.80 an hour and you can paddle 1.5km between the high red sandstone walls of the middle gorge to a pretty waterfall. You may also be able to portage your canoe around the waterfall and canoe a further 1.5km along the upper gorge.

A delightful hike along the upper gorge among ghost gums, bush fig trees and pandanus palms ends at a spot where turtles and fish swim lazily by and fairy martins have plastered their nests to the vertical red cliff. Other hikes go up the Stack, with panoramic views from the top, and to an Aboriginal art site in a cave where the mounds of mussel shells point to a long period of occupation. In fact studies show that the local Waanyi people have lived in the area for more than 17,000 years. You can also visit the spooky lower gorge with its coral-like tufa rock, tangled tree roots and floodwater debris where freshwater crocodiles inhabit murky pools. Altogether there are seven different hikes to enjoy.

Back in 1889 there was a shoot-out at Lawn Hill and Senior Constable Alfred Wavell was killed by a notorious horse thief called Joe Flick. The wild north was Australia's version of America's wild west, but no one has written a song or made a film about it, so Joe Flick is not as famous as Jesse James.

Lawn Hill *camping ground* (☎ 07-4748 5572), has 60 sites but is very popular so book as far ahead as possible. Unpowered sites cost $3.85 per person.

Riversleigh (Myimba) Fossil Site

Riversleigh, 51km south-west of Lawn Hill camping ground, is a Unesco World Heritage site because of the huge range of prehistoric life, 20 million years old, preserved as fossils in the limestone outcrops. According to Sir David Attenborough, 'Only in one or two places in the course of the last 300 million years have conditions been just right to preserve anything like a representative sample of the species living at any one particular time. Those places are rare treasure houses of palaeontology and Riversleigh is one of them'.

Marsupial lions, a carnivorous kangaroo, a giant python, insects and creatures new to science have been found. But there is not much to see on the site except a hard-to-find fossil of a small turtle and a few fossilised bones of a 3m-tall bird. Some of the fossils that were found here are on display in the **Riversleigh Fossil Centre** at Marian St, Mt Isa (see Matilda Hwy later in this chapter). The boulder-strewn hillside has nice views and the walk around takes less than an hour.

George's Epic Hike

George Morrison was only twenty years old when he left Normanton on foot: alone, unarmed and with no compass or quinine. It was 19 December 1882 – the start of the wet season, just before Christmas and he was hoping to walk all the way across the hostile Australian outback to Melbourne, 3000km away.

Morrison waded through countless creeks and swam across rivers on his way to Cloncurry and Winton. He met a lot of different characters on the way including a kind, toothless African called John Smith. He visited Jundah, 'where every man in the township was more of less drunk'. He then walked past Cooper's Creek to Hungerford on the border of New South Wales and Queensland, then on to Wilcannia and Hay.

Living mainly on damper bread and billy tea, and sleeping in a swag or hammock, he suffered fever, sore feet and stomach cramp. He made it to Melbourne after four months of walking. Throughout the entire journey Morrison never saw a kangaroo.

Riversleigh has no camping or picnic facilities, but there is a toilet and some information boards. Carry on west from Riversleigh and 40km later you rejoin the main road, 70km north of Gregory Downs.

ORGANISED TOURS

Borroloola Fishing Estuary Tours (☎/fax 08-8975 8716, 8975 8980) offers half-day ($75) and full-day ($125) fishing tours.

Shawflight Aviation (☎ 08-8975 8688, fax 8975 8685) operates general charter and scenic flights from the bitumen Borroloola airstrip.

Bill Olive at *Hell's Gate Roadhouse* (☎ 07-4745 8258) runs half-day ($45) and full-day ($90) 4WD tours, which must be booked ahead.

Savannah Aviation (☎ 07-4745 5177, fax 4745 4211) organises fishing trips from Burketown ($110) and boat hire ($120 per day). It also flies to Mornington Island in the Gulf.

FACILITIES

Roper Bar

Roper Bar Store (☎ 08-8975 4636, fax 8975 4992) Open 9am-6pm Mon-Sat, 1pm-6pm Sun. Fuel, general supplies, takeaway food and clothing are available here. Unpowered sites cost $6 per person; there are hot showers and flush toilets.

Limmen Bight

Limmen Bight River Fishing Camp (☎ 08-8975 9844, 24km from Gulf Track) Unpowered/powered sites $10/20, air-con cabins $66, gazebos $25. There are hot showers, flush toilets, a small store, fuel, boat hire, a public phone and tyre repairs available here.

Cape Crawford

Heartbreak Hotel (☎ 08-8975 9928, fax 8975 9611, e lostcity@bigpond.com) Singles/doubles $55/66, unpowered/powered sites $12/15 per double. As well as accommodation, Heartbreak offers fuel, meals, a bar and helicopter flights over a nearby 'lost city' ($90 for 20minutes).

Borroloola

A post office, Commonwealth Bank, supermarkets, car repairers, fuel outlets, a clinic and a weekly dentist can be found in town. Activities include disco parties, country and western music, a rodeo in August and even a beauty contest and pet show.

McArthur River Caravan Park (☎ 08-8975 8734, fax 8975 8706) offers unpowered/powered sites $16/19.80 per double as well as budget/self-contained units for $49.50/77.

H & R Guesthouse (☎ 08-8975 5883) has rooms without/with en suite for $66/75 and cabins from $40 to $66.

Holiday Village (☎ 08-8975 8742, fax 8975 8741) provides bunkhouse/air-con units with en suite for $40/100 per double. There's also general store.

Borroloola Inn (☎ 08-8975 9670, fax 8975 8773) has single/double air-con rooms for $55/65. Camping may be possible at the back near the swimming pool and the dam area. There are also meals available, such as barramundi or steak with chips, for $15.

King Ash Bay Fishing Club (☎ 08-8975 9861, 40km north of Borroloola) has unpowered/powered sites for $50/85 per double per week. The club is licensed and serves meals.

Gulf Track

Wollogorang Roadhouse (☎ 08-8975 9944, fax 8975 9854) Unpowered sites $7.70 per person, power $5.50 extra, single/double air-con units $55/77, bush camping up on the coast $22 per vehicle per night. This is a licensed roadhouse serving good meals and snacks. Fuel is also available.

Hell's Gate Roadhouse (☎ 07-4745 8258, fax 4745 8225, e info@savannah guides.com.au, W www.savannahguides .com.au) Unpowered/powered sites $6/8 per person, cabin/safari tents $50/80 per double. Fuel and limited supplies are available. The licensed restaurant has a popular barbecue on Sunday nights.

Doomadgee

Turn right at the end of the access road to reach the well-stocked **supermarket** and **fuel outlet** which is open 8.30am to 4pm Monday to Friday and 8.30am to 12pm on Saturday. Vehicle repairs, a clinic and camping may also be available – check with the Community Council (☎ 07-4745 8188, fax 4745 8185) before you arrive.

Nicholson River

Kingfisher Camp (☎ 07-4745 8212, fax 4745 8202, 40km south of the Gulf Track) Unpowered sites $7 per person, budget units without/with air-con $20/25. Here you'll find fine camping, splendid gorge scenery, delightful birdlife, 4WD tracks, boating and fishing on the river.

Bowthorn Homestead (☎ 07-4745 8132, fax 4745 8202, e jbandidt@ozemail.com .au, W www.ozemail.com.au/~bowthorn, 33km south of Kingfisher Camp) Accommodation $75 per day including all meals. Bookings are essential. Get a taste of life on a working cattle station.

Burketown

The visitors centre (☎ 07-4745 5100, fax 4745 5181, e burkesc@bigpond.com,

W www.burkeshirecouncil.com), on Musgrave St, offers fast Internet service at $1.10 for 20 minutes, tourist information and even loans out sports equipment.

Burketown Caravan Park *(☎ 07-4745 5118, fax 4745 5126, Sloman St)* has camp sites (unpowered/powered $13.20/16.50 per double), air-con cabins (single/double $33/44) and self-contained units ($93.50).

Albert Hotel-Motel *(Burketown Pub; ☎ 07 -4745 5104, fax 4745 5146, Beames St)* has rooms with fan ($45) or air-con ($55).

Normanton & Karumba

These towns have a wide range of facilities. See the Matilda Highway section later in this chapter for details.

Cairns

Highlights

* Scuba diving over the Great Barrier Reef
* Enjoying all the adventure sports and activities
* Exploring the World Heritage–listed rainforest north of Cairns
* Partying the night away in the many pubs and clubs

The tourist capital of Far North Queensland, Cairns (population 114,000) has become one of Australia's top destinations for travellers. It is a base for every kind of adventure sport and for excursions to the tropical beauty of Cape Tribulation and the wilds of Cape York. It lacks a beach, but there are some good ones to the north, just a short bus ride away.

Cairns marks the end of the Bruce Hwy and the railway line from Brisbane. The town came into existence in 1876 as a beachhead in the mangroves, intended as a port for the Hodgkinson River goldfield, 100km inland. Initially, it struggled under rivalry from Smithfield and Port Douglas further north, but was saved by the Atherton Tableland 'tin

rush' from 1880 and became the starting point of the railway to the tableland.

Information

Tourist Offices There are dozens of privately run information centres, such as the Cairns Tourist Information Centre (☎ 07-4031 1751), at 6 Aplin St, which are basically booking offices for tours. Also good for information are the various backpackers hostels, and most have a separate tour-booking service. Each booking agent and hostel sells different tours, depending on the commission deal they have with the tour companies, so shop around.

Tourism Tropical North Queensland (☎ 07-4051 3588, fax 4051 0127, e infor mation@tnq.org.au, W www.tnq.org.au), at 51 The Esplanade, is open daily from 8.30am to 5.30pm, for reliable information.

Queensland Parks and Wildlife Service (QPWS; ☎ 07-4046 6600, fax 4046 6751, W env.qld.gov.au), at 10 McLeod St, is open from 8.30am to 4.30pm Monday to Friday. It issues camping permits and has information on Queensland's numerous national parks.

The Royal Automobile Club of Queensland (RACQ; ☎ 07-4033 6433, 1300 130 59, W www.racq.com.au), at 520 Mulgrave Rd, is out of the centre of town, so call or check the web site for information on road conditions.

The post office on the corner of Grafton and Hartley Sts has a poste restante service. For general business (such as postage stamps), there is also an Australia Post shop in the Orchid Plaza on Lake St.

For books, try the Pier and Cairns Central shopping complexes. For maps, go to Absell's in the Andrejic Arcade at 55 Lake St.

Things to See

A walk around the town centre turns up a few points of historical interest, although with much recent development the older buildings are now few and far between. The oldest part of town is the Trinity Wharf area, but this has been redeveloped with ugly modern structures. But there are still some imposing neo-classical buildings from the 1920s on Abbott St, and the frontages around the corner of Spence and Lake Sts date from 1909 to 1926.

An evening stroll along the **Esplanade**, with views of rainforest-covered mountains across the estuary, is enhanced by the birdlife on show, including pelicans.

The **Pier** is an impressive, upmarket shopping plaza with expensive boutiques and souvenir shops downstairs, and some interesting eating places upstairs. On Saturday and Sunday mornings there is a food, souvenir and craft market inside.

Cairns Museum (☎ *07-405 5582, Cnr Lake & Shields Sts; adult/child $4/2; open 10am-3pm Mon-Sat*) is housed in the 1907 School of Arts building, an excellent example of early Cairns architecture. It has Aboriginal artefacts, a display on the construction of the Cairns-Kuranda railway, the contents of a now-demolished Grafton St Chinese temple, exhibits on the old Palmer River and Hodgkinson goldfields, and material on the early timber industry.

Rusty's Bazaar, between Sheridan and Grafton Sts is a bustling market all day Friday and Saturday and Sunday morning with dozens of stalls selling vegetables, tropical fruit, handicrafts and clothes.

North-west of town, in Edge Hill, are the **Flecker Botanic Gardens** in Collins Ave, which is west of Sheridan St (the Captain Cook Hwy) 3km from the centre of Cairns. The botanic gardens are 700m from the turning, and just before them is an art centre and the entrance to the **Whitfield Range Environmental Park** with walking tracks that give good views over the city and coast. On the other side of the road, an excellent **boardwalk** leads through a patch of rainforest to Saltwater Creek and the two small **Centenary Lakes**.

Also in Edge Hill is the **Royal Flying Doctor Service** visitors centre (☎ *07-4053 5687, 1 Junction St; child/adult $2.75/5.50; open 8.30am-5pm Mon-Sat*). You can sit in a plane, watch a video and support this world-famous good cause.

Activities

Cairns has an amazing number of organised activities for the hordes of adventurous tourists. Most hostels have more than 200 brochures on display so there is a lot to read. Prices of activities are only a rough guide since there are usually lots of short-term special offers.

Diving Cairns is the scuba-diving capital of the Barrier Reef, which is closer to the coast here than it is further south. Budget four-day dive courses include four dives and two day-trips to the reef and cost around $270. The five-day courses cost $400 to $650 and include two nights on the reef with all meals and nine dives.

White-Water Rafting Three of the rivers flowing down from the Atherton Tableland make for some excellent white-water rafting. Most popular is a day in the rainforested gorges of the Tully River, 150km south of Cairns, which costs about $145. A day on the Russell River costs $124, while half-day trips on the Barron River are about $83. River kayaking is another option.

Other Activities You can **bungee jump** all day for $129, **rap jump** down a cliff for $65, fall further and faster on a tandem **skydive** for $248, or go gently up and down in a **hot-air balloon** for $130. Half a day on a **horse** costs $77; it's $110 for half a day on an **all-terrain vehicle**. A short ride on a **go-kart** costs $27. On the water, you can **parasail** for $50, tube for $25, **jet ski** for $50, **water-ski** for $99 (half-day) or **sea kayak** for $140 (two days).

Organised Tours

Most of the hundreds of tours available from Cairns are specially aimed at backpackers and are good value. Special deals are possible so shop around before handing over your hard-earned money to a smooth-talking salesperson.

Barrier Reef There are dozens of options available for day trips to the reef. It is always a good idea to ask a few questions before you book, such as how many passengers the boat takes, what is included in the price (usually at least snorkelling gear and lunch), how much the extras (such as wetsuit hire and introductory dives) cost, and exactly where the boat is going. Some companies have a dubious definition of outer reef; as a general rule, the further out you go, the better the diving.

Snorkelling trips to Green Island start at $60 but the area is crowded. Expect to pay $125 for a couple of dives on the outer reefs, but this could change.

Daintree, Cape Tribulation & Cooktown Venture into the tropical rainforest with a cruise along the crocodile-infested Daintree River, a hike around Mossman Gorge and stay in some interesting accommodation. *Queensland Adventure Safaris* (☎/fax 07-4041 2418) runs two- and four-day tours for $195 and $265, but there are hundreds of others.

Atherton Tableland Cool and scenic, this is another area not to be missed. There are many one-day tour options starting at around $50 and an award-winning bicycle tour by *Bandicoot* (☎ 07-4055 0155) at $98. The cable car and scenic train ride up to Kuranda Village costs $66.

Wildlife Spotting For a chance to see rainforest wildlife, such as tree kangaroos and the elusive platypus, with the aid of a spotlight, *Wait-a-While* (☎ 07-4033 1153) has 4WD tours that leave at 2pm and return around midnight for $132.

Cattle Station *Mt Mulligan cattle station* (☎ 07-4094 8360) provides transport, meals and activities for one night ($120) or two nights ($155).

Cape York There are a number of companies that operate treks and 4WD tours between Cairns and the top of Cape York. Most of them involve going overland to the top and then flying back, but you can travel overland both ways. You can also go by sea instead of air. These tours are popular because Cape York is a remote area with unsealed roads that requires a 4WD vehicle, which is expensive to hire or buy.

Wilderness Challenge (☎ 07-4055 6504, fax 4057 7226, e info@wilderness-challenge.com.au, w www.wilderness-challenge.com.au) does an eight-day camping tour of Cape York for $1915 and an accommodated seven-day tour for $2385. *The Adventure Company* (☎ 07-4051 4777) runs similar tours.

Oz Tours (☎ 07-4055 9535, fax 4055 9918, e info@oztours.com.au, w www.oztours.com.au) has a range of tours including a six-day Cape York fly/drive tour for $1595.

Exploring Oz (☎ 0500 502 688, w www.exploringoz.com.au) has many tours including a seven-day fly/drive Cape York tour for $1599 and a 12-day overland Cape York trip for $1699.

Heritage Tours (☎ 07-4038 2628, Smithfield) runs tours including a seven-day Cape York tour for $1630 (including flight cost).

Billy Tea Bush Safaris (☎/fax 07-4032 0077, fax 4032 0055, e info@billytea.com.au, w www.billytea.com.au) runs many tours including a 9-day fly/drive tour of Cape York for $2100. All camping gear, meals and flights are included.

4WD Tagalong (☎ 07-4091 1978, fax 4091 2545, e gta@cyberworks.com.au, w www.guidestoadventure.com.au) lets you travel in your own car behind the tour guide's vehicle and the tour guide on hand to help if necessary.

Cape York Motorbikes (☎ 07-4059 0220, fax 4059 0801. e renae@capeyorkmotorcycles.com.au, Clifton Beach) has eight-day Cape York tours for $3750 or 16-day tag-along tours for $3350.

Stay Upright Tours (☎ 07-4032 1022) has eight-day Cape York tours for $2950 or tag-along tours for $1600 (excluding flight cost). Tours are also available all the way to Darwin, Broome and Alice Springs.

Places to Stay

Cairns has hostels and cheap guesthouses galore, as well as plenty of reasonably priced motels and holiday flats. But in the high season it can be difficult to find a bed, so book ahead. Some places knock off a few dollars when business is quieter (November to March) or offer a lower weekly rate.

THE TROPICS

CAIRNS

PLACES TO STAY
1 Pacific Cay
2 Castaways
4 Bel-Air
5 Silver Palm Guesthouse
6 Caravella 149
7 Tracks
8 Inn the Tropics
10 Parkview Backpackers
12 Cairns Girls Hostel
18 YHA on the Esplanade
19 Hostel 89
20 Bellview
21 Jimmy's
22 Caravella 77
23 International Hostel

33 YHA McLeod Street
50 Gecko's
51 Dreamtime Travellers Rest
52 Gone Walkabout

PLACES TO EAT
3 Cock & Bull
13 Yanni's Greek Taverna
14 Galloping Gourmet
16 The Meeting Place
24 The Woolshed
29 Beethoven's
30 Swiss Cake
31 Red Ochre Grill
32 John & Di's Breakfast &
    Burger House

37 Mozart's Pastry
47 Dundees
48 Sports Bar
49 Tiny's Juice Bar

OTHER
9 Miner's Den
11 24-Hour Medical Centre
15 Johno's
17 Cairns Tourist Information Centre
25 Qantas
26 City Place Amphitheatre
27 Cairns Museum
28 Cinema 5
34 Queensland Parks and Wildlife
    Service

35 Rusty's Bazaar
36 Shenannigans
38 Tropos; Fox & Firkin Hotel
39 Absell's Map Centre
40 Lake St Transit Bus Stop
41 Woolworth's
42 Orchid Plaza; Post Office
43 Courthouse
44 Tourism Tropical North
    Queensland
45 Trinity Wharf & Transit
    Centre
46 Playpen Nightclub;
    Court Jester Bar
53 Pickers Geo Camping
    Store

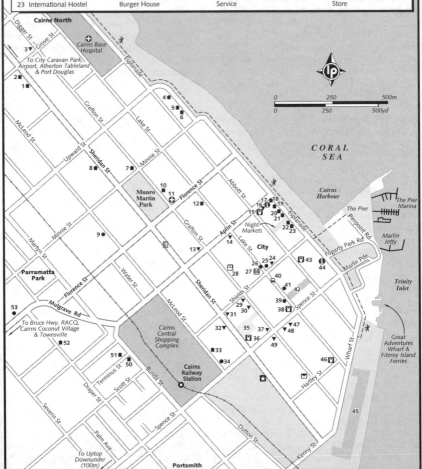

THE TROPICS

Camping Cairns has a couple of camping options.

City Caravan Park (☎/fax 07-4051 1467, Cnr Little & James Sts) Unpowered/powered sites $16/20 per double, on-site vans $35, cabin $45. This is the closest park to downtown.

Cairns Coconut Caravan Village (☎ 07-4054 6644, fax 4054 7591, Cnr Bruce Hwy & Anderson Rd) Unpowered/powered sites $24/28 per double, units $28-140. This place has lots of facilities.

Hostels The Cairns hostel scene is constantly changing as new places open up and old ones change hands; others rise and fall in quality and popularity. This type of accommodation is pretty standard: air-conditioned or fan-cooled dorms and double/twin rooms with shared hot shower and toilet facilities, a kitchen, TV lounge, laundry, small swimming pool and a tour desk. Some hostels also have metered air-conditioning ($1 for three hours).

As always, beware of theft – use lock-up rooms and safes if they are available. The hostel business is very competitive and many offer freebies such as meals, tours, Internet access, bicycle hire, tea and coffee. The Esplanade has the greatest concentration of hostels, and is a lively part of town. The hostels here tend to pack them in, and have very little space outside as they are usually have a swimming pool as well. The hostels away from the city centre offer much more breathing space and are generally quieter, and there are courtesy buses that make regular runs into town.

International Hostel (☎ 07-4031 1545, fax 4031 3804, e internationalhostel@internetnorth.com.au, 67 The Esplanade) Dorm beds/singles $21/27, doubles without/with air-con $44/48. Includes a free meal at the Rattle & Hum restaurant next door.

Caravella 77 (☎ 07-4051 2159, fax 4031 6329, e info@caravella.com.au, 77 The Esplanade) Dorm beds/singles/doubles $21/30/45. A wooden building, but nice with lots of air-con rooms.

Jimmy's (☎ 07-4031 4411, fax 4031 4924, e andrew@jimmyscairns.com.au, 83 The Esplanade) Dorm beds $18, budget/motel rooms doubles $42/55. A popular and friendly place and all rooms have air-con.

Bellview (☎ 07-4031 4377, fax 4031 2850, e bellviewcairns@bigpond.com, 85 The Esplanade) Dorm beds/singles/budget doubles $20/33/42, motel doubles $49-$65. The place is air-conditioned throughout and clean.

Hostel 89 (☎ 07-4031 7477, fax 4031 4924, e bluey@jimmys.com.au, 89 The Esplanade) Dorm beds/singles/doubles $18/38/48. It's all air-conditioned and there's free washing powder.

YHA on the Esplanade (☎ 07-4031 1919, fax 4031 4381, e cairnsesplanade@yhaqld.org, 93 The Esplanade) Dorm beds/doubles YHA members $20/46, non-members $22.50/51. Some rooms have air-con. Email costs $2 per hour and there's cable TV.

Caravella 149 (☎ 07-4051 2431, fax 4051 4097, e info@caravella.com.au, 149 The Esplanade) Dorm beds/singles/doubles are $17/32/40. Away from the crowds with motel-style rooms, Caravella 149 also has free evening meals.

Silver Palm Guesthouse (☎ 07-4031 6099, fax 4031 6094, 153 The Esplanade) Singles/doubles $35/40. Similar to a hostel, but without a tour desk, this small place offers clean and quiet accommodation.

Bel Air (☎ 07-4031 4790, fax 4052 1972, e belair@cairns.net.au, 155 The Esplanade) Dorm beds/doubles $17/40. This place has a spa and offers $1 meals.

Cairns Girls Hostel (☎/fax 07-4051 2016, 147 Lake St) Singles, twins & beds in 4-bed dorm per day/week $16/90 per person. Clean, friendly and a bargain, but only for women and girls.

Inn the Tropics (☎ 07-4031 1088, fax 4051 7110, e innthetropics@cairns.net.au, 141 Sheridan St) Dorm beds/singles $16.50/33, doubles without/with en suite $44/55. Clean with free tea and coffee and a TV in every room. The air-con is metered.

Castaways (☎ 07-4051 1238, fax 4052 1804, e castaways@castaway.com.au, 207 Sheridan St) Dorm beds/singles/doubles

$18/32/38. Castaways offers free wine and cheese twice a week, free bikes, free email (20 minutes) and a courtesy bus.

Tracks (☎ 07-4031 1474, fax 4031 8499, 149 Grafton St) Dorm beds/singles/doubles $18/31/38. Bike hire is only $8 a day here.

Parkview Backpackers (☎ 07-4051 3700, fax 4052 1133, 174 Grafton St) Dorm beds/singles/doubles $18/31/38. The hostel is housed in old wooden buildings.

YHA McLeod St (☎ 07-4051 0772, fax 4031 3158, e cairnscentral@yhaqld.org, 20 McLeod St) Dorm beds/doubles YHA members $20/46, nonmembers $22.50/51, family rooms $60. In a convenient location opposite Cairns Central shopping mall.

Uptop Downunder (☎ 07-4051 3636, fax 4052 1211, e uptop@castaway.com.au, 164 Spence St) Dorm beds/singles/doubles $18/32/38. A long way from the town centre, this hostel offers a courtesy bus, free email and free evening meals.

Behind Cairns Central are *Gecko's* (☎ 07-4031 1344, 187 Bunda St), *Dreamtime Travellers' Rest* (☎ 07-4031 6753, 4 Terminus Rd) and *Gone Walkabout* (☎ 07-4051 6160, 274 Draper St). All are fine if you want something basic and funky.

Motels & Holiday Flats Holiday flats are worth considering, especially for a group of three or four people who are staying a few days or more. Expect pools, air-con and laundry facilities in this category. Holiday flats generally supply all bedding, cooking utensils and so on. If you are staying for weeks or months, look at the notice boards for house-sharing deals which are much cheaper than hostels.

There is a string of motels and holiday units along Sheridan St. One of the cheaper ones is *Pacific Cay* (☎ 07-4051 0151, fax 4051 0077, e pacificcayhol@ozemail.com .au, 193 Sheridan St). One-bed/two-bed units are $70/90.

Places to Eat

For a town its size, Cairns has quite a variety of restaurants, some of which take advantage of the climate with open-air dining. There are Greek, Italian, Japanese,

Bush Tucker Fashion

More and more restaurants are offering exotic Aussie bush tucker. Dundees and the Red Ochre Grill in Cairns offer such delicacies as kangaroo-tail soup with wattle seed damper bread, possum cannelloni, emu sausages, camel meatballs, crocodile wonton and buffalo Kakadu. They also serve sauces made with quandong (a bright blue rainforest fruit), bush tomatoes (similar to raisins) and lemon myrtle leaves.

If this trend continues, maybe we'll soon be ordering Kentucky-fried crocodile and McBuffalo burgers.

African, Middle Eastern, Irish, Mexican, Thai, Chinese and Indian restaurants.

Cafes & Fast Food The Esplanade has a large collection of takeaway food joints and restaurants – the stretch between Shields and Aplin Sts is virtually wall-to-wall eateries, where you will find Italian and Chinese food, burgers, kebabs, pizzas, seafood and ice cream.

The Meeting Place (Aplin St near The Esplanade) Meals $8-15. This is a good food hall.

John & Di's Breakfast & Burger House (35 Sheridan St) Breakfast $7 or less. Open from 5am daily. John & Di's serves up every combination of cooked breakfast.

Galloping Gourmet (☎ 07-4051 6426, Cnr Aplin & Lake Sts) Full breakfast $6.50. Lunch specials go for only $4.50.

Beethoven's (☎ 07-4051 0292, Cnr Grafton & Shields Sts) competes with nearby *Swiss Cake* (☎ 07-4051 6393, 93A Grafton St) and *Mozart's Pastry* (☎ 07-4051 6085, Cnr Grafton & Spence Sts) for the cafe crowd. *Tiny's Juice Bar* (☎ 07-4031 4331, Cnr Grafton & Spence Sts) is a colourful place with juices and $5 snack meals.

Restaurants Cairns has a wide range of restaurants.

The Woolshed (☎ 07-4031 6304, 24 Shields St) Mains $9-14. At Cairns' most popular eatery, many of the customers are backpackers with free or cheap hostel meal vouchers. It really does look like a woolshed inside. At 10pm it turns into two discos.

Cock & Bull Pub *(☎ 07-4031 1160, Cnr Grove & Digger Sts)* Mains $12, dessert $6. It's outside the centre of town, but this pub has great atmosphere. It's a big place with big meals – one main course and desert is often enough to feed two.

Windows *(☎ 07-4031 2133, food court, Pier Complex)* Breakfast $11.90, lunch $8.90, seafood dinners $25.90. Windows offers good all-you-can-eat meals.

Sports Bar *(☎ 07-4041 2533, 33 Spence St)* Meals $10. The Sports Bar has good food and is also a busy nightspot.

Yanni's Greek Taverna *(☎ 07-4041 1500, Cnr Grafton & Aplin Sts)* Pasta and moussaka $18. Yanni's also does seafood meals for around $24.

Red Ochre Grill *(☎ 07-4051 0100, fax 4051 0025, e sales@redochregrill.com.au, w www.redochregrill.com.au, Cnr Sheridan & Shields Sts)* and **Dundees** *(☎ 07-4051 0399, 29 Spence St)* offer upmarket bush tucker, such as possum cannelloni, emu pate, kangaroo-tail soup and crocodile wonton. Lunches at Red Ochre Grill range from $6 to $22, dinner mains start at $25.

Entertainment

Many bars and clubs offer cheap drinks or free entry if you arrive before 9pm. In general drinks are reasonably priced, most places have pool tables, entry is $5 or free, and the action continues until late.

Johno's *(☎ 07-4051 8770, Cnr Abbott & Aplin Sts)* Johno's has live music every evening and no cover charge. The ageless, hard-working Johno and his band always put on a good show.

Tropo's *(☎ 07-4031 2530, Cnr Spence & Lake Sts)* Tropo's often has live bands and special events.

Sports Bar *(☎ 07-4041 2533, 33 Spence St)* This is another popular spot, especially when they offer five cheap drinks.

Playpen Nightclub *(☎ 07-4051 8211, Cnr Lake & Hartley Sts)* This is a nightclub disco, while the **Court Jester Bar** *(same address)* is more upmarket and quieter.

The **Fox & Firkin Hotel**, *(Spence & Lake Sts)*, the **Pier Tavern** *(Pier Complex)* and **Shenannigans** *(Cnr Spence & Sheridan Sts)* are both large pubs that serve cheap meals and often have live music and other kinds of entertainment.

For a touch of class try the bar in the old **Courthouse** *(☎ 07-4031 4166, 38 Abbott St)*. It often shows free outdoor movies.

City Place Amphitheatre *(Cnr Lake & Shields Sts)* hosts free lunch-time concerts from Monday to Friday.

Shopping

Many artists live in the Cairns region, so local handicrafts are available. Aboriginal art and didgeridoos are for sale all over town. The weekend markets at Rusty's Bazaar and the Pier Complex are worth a visit. The Night Market in Abbott St has enough souvenirs to satisfy anyone.

Getting Around

To/From the Airport The main domestic and international airlines use Cairns International Airport, which is 4km north of town up the Captain Cook Hwy, while small planes use the General Aviation Airport 2km further north. The Australia Coach Shuttle Bus *(☎ 07-4048 8355)* meets most flights, costs $7 and will drop you at your accommodation in Cairns. Since a taxi to downtown costs around $12, for two or more people it is cheaper by taxi.

Air Flights inland and up the Cape York Peninsula from Cairns are shared among a number of small feeder airlines. Companies, routes and prices are constantly changing. Macair *(☎ 13 13 13)* has frequent flights to Lizard Island (from $370 return), Yorke Island ($752 return) and Normanton/Burketown/Doomadgee for $695/908/959 return. Marine Air Seaplanes *(☎ 07-4069 5915)* does day trips to Lizard Island for $245 return. Skytrains/Air Swift *(☎ 07-4046 2462)* has daily flights to Cooktown (from $158 return) and Karumba on the Gulf ($341 one way). Qantaslink *(☎ 13 13 13)* flies to Horn Island (the airport for Thursday Island) every day for $361 return (including tax), but you must buy the ticket two weeks in advance or the cost goes up to $514 return. Aerotropics (☎ 07-4035 9138) flies to Bamaga ($325 one way) and all round the Torres Strait Islands.

For something completely different, Cape York Air (☎ 07-4035 9399, fax 4035 9108, ❸ enquiries@capeyorkair.com.au, ❿ www.capeyorkair.com.au), the local mail contractor, flies a different route every day with seven to seventeen stops at remote cattle stations. The cost varies from $240 to $670 depending on the distance travelled. You can also hop off (eg, at Normanton for $242) along the way. The same company also runs tours to Thursday and Horn Islands in the Torres Strait.

Car Rental Avis, Budget, Hertz and Thrifty have desks at the international airport terminal. In town, local firms have mushroomed, especially in Sheridan and Lake Sts. 'Cheap' deals are not always a bargain, so check out the details and shop around to find the deal that suits you. Generally, small cars start from $50, larger ones from $65 and 4WD vehicles with restricted destinations start at around $110. Rental companies prohibit you from taking conventional cars beyond Cape Tribulation, or to Cooktown or the Chillagoe Caves. However, Cooktown via the inland road will be no problem when it is bitumen all the way in 2005.

4WD Rental A few companies will hire 4WDs and allow you to take them to the tip of Cape York: Britz Rental (☎ 07-4032 2611, 411 Sheridan St), Cairns Leisure Wheels (☎ 07-4051 8988, 196A Sheridan St), Hertz Rentals (☎ 07-4053 1344, 436 Sheridan St) and Meteor (☎ 07-4051 6077, 137 Lake St). Expect to pay over $160 a day, a high insurance excess and to not be covered for single car accidents or water damage. You can also hire 4WD camper vans.

Motorcycle & Bicycle Rental Easy Rider (☎ 07-4052 1188, 144 Sheridan St) has every sort of motorcycle for rent, some of which you can ride up to Cape York. Bicycles are for hire all over town, usually at $15 a day.

Kennedy Highway

Highlights

- Exploring the unique Undara lava tubes
- Boating along magical Cobbold Gorge
- Finding topaz at O'Brien's Creek Gemfield
- Learning about gold-mining history in Croydon

This 720km route cuts across rainforested hills outside Cairns to the drier hills and plains that border the western side of the Great Dividing Range. Beyond Croydon, the vast, flat, billiard table–like plains of the Gulf begin and extend all the way to Normanton and the sea.

It is all bitumen, but be careful on the one-lane strips where road trains and other trucks stay on the bitumen and lesser vehicles have to get off it entirely.

History

Aborigines inhabited this part of the country for thousands of years before Ludwig Leichhardt and Edmund Kennedy passed through in the 1840s and James Mulligan discovered gold in the 1870s. Later, a series of mineral discoveries saw the founding of Chillagoe, Herberton, Mt Garnet, Forsayth, Georgetown and Croydon to service nearby mines.

Away from the timber mills, mines and mineral fields, sugar is the mainstay of the coastal farming land, while on the Atherton Tableland, dairy cattle, tobacco and a host of other crops are grown. Further west, cattle is the livelihood of the vast sprawling properties that sometimes cover of thousands of square kilometres.

Information

Tourist Offices Outback Tourism (☎ 07-3211 4877, fax 3211 4866, PO Box 13109, Brisbane, George St, Queensland 4003, ❸ oqta@a1.com.au, ❿ www.outbackholidays.tq.com.au) provides information on regional Queensland.

KENNEDY HIGHWAY & GULF ROAD

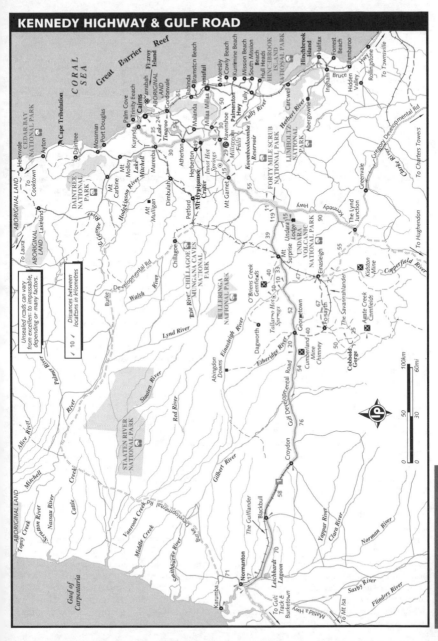

Unsealed roads can vary from excellent to impassable, depending on many factors.

Distances between locations in kilometres

CORAL SEA

Great Barrier Reef

Gulf of Carpentaria

THE TROPICS

Etheridge Shire Council Office (☎ 07-4062 1233, fax 4062 1285, ⓔ ethshire@ tpg.com.au), in St George St, Georgetown, has information on Georgetown, Forsayth, Mt Surprise and Einasleigh.

Croydon Visitors Information Centre (☎ 07 -4745 6125, fax 4745 6147, ⓔ croy don@bigpond.com.au) is open daily during the Dry and provides an excellent service.

Carpentaria Shire Council Office (☎ 07-4745 1268, fax 4745 1340) has information on the Normanton area.

The Miner's Den (☎ 07-4051 4413, ⓔ goldmine@ozemail.com.au, ⓦ www .nqminersden.com), at 55 Sheridan St, Cairns, can help with fossicking and permits (individual/family $5.10/7.20) that last for a month.

Hotels, caravan parks and stores usually also supply local information. See the Cairns section in this chapter for other tourist information services.

Books & Maps *The Reef to the Rock* published by the Queensland Tourism & Travel Corporation is good. Sunmap's *Gulf Savannah* map covers the area.

THE ROUTE
Cairns to Ravenshoe (145km)
The easiest route is to head north on the Bruce Hwy and, 13km from Cairns, turn left for Kuranda, onto the Kennedy Hwy.

Kuranda, 'the village in the rainforest', is 27km from Cairns and a popular place with day trippers. Another 35km takes you to **Mareeba** where you keep left and continue on the Kennedy Hwy.

Drive through **Atherton**, 30km south of Mareeba, and after 26km, turn right off the main road for a short rainforest walk to the spectacular **Mt Hypipamee Crater** and the **Dinner Falls** – called that because it has three courses. The crater is 130m deep with dark green water in it, and you might see the golden bowerbird around here. At the junction 23km beyond the crater turn-off, turn right onto the Palmerston Hwy and 4km later you will be in Ravenshoe.

For details on two other routes to Ravenshoe, see Alternative Routes, below.

Ravenshoe
Ravenshoe, an old logging town with a pioneer look, is the highest town (915m) in Queensland. It has an excellent tourist information centre and a wide range of shops and facilities. Just 4km south-west of the town are the **Millstream Falls**, the widest in Australia in the Wet, but still worth seeing in the Dry. Further south is the **Tully Gorge National Park** and the **Tully Falls**.

West to Georgetown (261km)
Twenty-nine kilometres from Ravenshoe are the **Innot Hot Springs**, where you can relax in hot mineral baths or dig your own hot pool in the river. You can also fossick for topaz at the Mt Gibson gemfield, 5km away. Camping here, you become aware of the variety of sounds made by Australian birds. The manic laughter of the kookaburras, the screech of the cockatoos, the croak of the crows, the racket of the galahs and other parrots, and the liquid melody of the butcher birds and curlews provide a musical accompaniment to camping in these parts.

A further 15km brings you to the small mining township of **Mt Garnet** and 55km further on is the **Forty Mile Scrub National Park**, an unusual dry rainforest. The short walk through it starts at the picnic area on the right-hand side of the road.

Just south of the park leave the Kennedy Hwy and turn right onto the Gulf Developmental Rd. Nineteen kilometres further on is the turn-off for the **Undara Volcanic National Park**.

You can only visit the lava tubes on an organised tour, but it should not be missed. The tour visits several sections of the huge, unique, 100km long lava tube or tunnel that was created by Undara Volcano. More than 160,000 years of erosion have caused most of the lava tube to collapse, but lots of sections have not fallen in and nine of them are open to visitors. Going inside is like entering a large, cool cave and you can only stand in awe at the power of the geological forces that play around with rock as if it were putty. The Undara lava flow was extremely hot for a volcano and continued for three months, creating the longest lava

From the tip of Cape York to the remote corners of Arnhem Land, the tropical north of Australia offers superb scenery, fabulous activities and a treasure trove of historical and cultural areas. Life is celebrated up here, with natural attractions springing from amongst the harsh realities.

A dirt road leading to the top of Australia – Cape York, Queensland (1). Graceful tree frog (Litoria gracilenta) – Jardine Creek, Cape York, Queensland (2). Stockmen at the New Dixie Station – Cape York, Queensland (3). Daintree River ringtail possum (Pseudocheirus cinereus) (4). Central Hotel, a traditional old building in Cairns – Queensland (5). Pajinka Beach – Cape York, Queensland (6).

OLIVER STREWE

ROHAN CLARKE

CHRIS MELLOR

MARTIN COHEN

RICHARD I'ANSON

MITCH REARDON

THE TROPICS

The tropics support a great variety of geological features, plants and wildlife, best seen in the many national parks. The people who live here are as different in race and culture as their surroundings. The cities are vibrant, exotic places while other communities range from resort to shanty towns.

Eliot Falls, on the tip of Cape York – Queensland (1). A green turtle (Chelonia mydas) laying its eggs on the Great Barrier Reef – Queensland (2). Children of the Injinoo perform a traditional dance (3). Bush tucker including Cedar Bay cherries found from the Daintree to Papua New Guinea (4). Mangroves on the beach – Daintree National Park, Queensland (5). Children celebrate multiculturalism at the Festival of Darwin, an outdoor arts and culture festival (6).

OLIVER STREWE

BOB CHARLTON

OLIVER STREWE

OLIVER STREWE

PETER PTSCHELINZEW

RICHARD I'ANSON

flow in the world at 160km. Camping, rooms and meals are available at the Undara Lava Lodge, 14km from the main road.

The road west continues through dry countryside and 56km from the Undara turn-off is **Mt Surprise**, which is full of surprises such as child tour guides. This lively little township of 70 people has stores, museum displays, restaurants, camp sites and tours and is on the route of the historic *Savannahlander* train to Forsayth. The weekly 5½-hour journey between Mt Surprise, Einasleigh and Forsayth is slower than driving but a lot smoother.

At Mt Surprise, turn right onto a track to find Oasis Camping, Digger's Rest and **O'Briens Creek Gemfield** which is 40km from the main road. It is one of the best topaz sites in the world and you can find some unusual colours as you sift through the gravel in the creek beds looking for glasslike topaz gemstones. The people at Digger's Rest hire out fossicking tools, give advice, sell maps and will identify and weigh your finds.

About 33km beyond Mt Surprise, turn left for a detour to Einasleigh Gorge, Forsayth and the delightful Cobbold Gorge. See Detours later in this section for more information.

Staying on the bitumen, 43km beyond Mt Surprise is the turn-off to **Tallaroo Hot Springs**, 10km down a gravel track. It has camping, a hot-spring bath and a small terrace of bubbling mineral pools that you can only visit with a guide. These ever-changing colourful pools have a wisp of steam and a whiff of sulphur.

Fifty-two kilometres along the Gulf Developmental Rd, from that turn-off is **Georgetown**, a service centre with the usual facilities for tourists, including a cafe with a museum. The golf course has black greens and there is a large, corrugated-iron Masonic hall which could hold the entire present-day population of 300.

Across the Gulf Plains to Normanton (302km)

About 20km beyond Georgetown is the site of **Cumberland Mine**, but all that remains is a tall chimney and a tailings dump. The nearby waterhole is shared by thirsty cattle and emus. The interesting township of **Croydon** is 150km from Georgetown. Established in 1885, Chinese and European gold miners rushed here so fast that the area had 8000 residents and 26 hotels by 1889. The gold mines had names like 'Golden Gate', 'Bobby Dazzler' and 'Homeward Bound'. Visit the site of Croydon's Chinatown, where there is not much to see but plenty to read about the people who used to live there. In 1890, Chinese residents operated 48 market gardens around Croydon; while others worked in the town as cooks, bakers, shopkeepers and doctors.

There are gold-mine relics, an interesting sculpture park and a number of renovated heritage buildings, including a corrugated-iron courthouse and police lock-up in Samwell St. You can read newspaper articles about life a century ago when blacksmiths did teeth extraction. Ouch! In 1902 this wry item appeared in the *Croydon Mining News*: 'Rose Morris. Drunk again; guilty; visited a lady friend and had 'one'; felt the need for another; then had several; finally got locked up; £1 or three days'.

The historic *Gulflander* train (☎ 07-4745 1391) runs between Croydon and Normanton once a week, leaving Croydon every Thursday at 8.30am and arriving in Normanton four hours later. It leaves Normanton for Croydon every Wednesday at 8.30am. A one-way ticket between the towns costs $40. The train also runs shorter excursions on Saturday for $25.

The Gulf Developmental Rd from Croydon follows the railway line to **Blackbull**, 58km away, where refreshments and a small museum with a thunderbox toilet can be enjoyed.

Seventy kilometres from Blackbull, turn left to visit the beautiful **Leichhardt Lagoon**, This is not only a camping ground but also a top spot for bird-watching. If you're lucky you can see 50 different bird species in one day. Just 17km from here is the town of Normanton. See the Matilda Highway section later in this chapter for more information on Normanton.

ALTERNATIVE ROUTES
Cairns to Ravenshoe via Palmerston Highway (165km)
Drive south out of Cairns, down the Bruce Hwy towards Innisfail. About 85km from Cairns, turn right onto the **Palmerston Hwy**. For the next 20km the road passes through sugar-cane fields and then begins to climb uphill, passing through the **Bartle Frere National Park**. Farmland dominates again as you enter **Millaa Millaa**, 50km from the Bruce Hwy junction. Another 30km across undulating, rich, green countryside brings you to Ravenshoe.

Cairns to Ravenshoe via Gillies Highway (135km)
Drive south from Cairns along the Bruce Hwy for 24km, then turn right onto the Gillies Hwy. Follow the Mulgrave River Valley up into the mountains, through Lake Barrine and Lake Eacham National Parks. Fifty-six kilometres from the Bruce Hwy junction, enter Atherton then turn left onto the Kennedy Hwy. See the earlier Cairns to Ravenshoe section for a description of the route from Atherton to Ravenshoe.

DETOUR
The Two Gorges Loop (244km)
Turn left down the dirt road 33km west of Mt Surprise, and 47km later you arrive in **Einasleigh**, an old copper-mining town with a population of 40. The road is corrugated and has some creek crossings but is not too bad. At Einasleigh, you can eat at ***Burger Man***; the ***Central Hotel*** *(☎ 07-4062 5222, fax 4062 5221)* has accommodation and fuel. **Einasleigh Gorge** is just past the hotel on the right. The gorge is grey lava rock but has sandy beaches and a waterfall.

The road and scenery improve driving across the Newcastle Range to **Forsayth**, population 90. Here the ***Goldfields Tavern*** *(☎ 07-4062 5374, fax 4062 5426)* offers accommodation ($62.50 for dinner, bed and breakfast), fuel and camping. There's an interesting display of agates in the bar and they also organise tours here.

Forsayth Homestay and Van Park *(☎ 07-4062 5386, fax 4062 5464, e forsaythhomestay@yahoo.com, Fourth St)* has bed and breakfast for $55, and camping is $11/13.75 a double for unpowered/powered sites.

A 50km drive south of Forsayth along a rough, winding road brings you to ***Cobbold Gorge Camping*** *(☎ 07-4062 5470, fax 4062 5453, e cobboldgorge@cyberwizards.com.au, w www.savannah-guides.com.au)* where unpowered sites are $5.50, and single/double units $35/70. Electric-boat tours that silently glide along the magical, narrow **Cobbold Gorge** cost $30.80 for 1½ hours and $66 for half a day. Azure kingfishers, agile wallabies and freshwater crocodiles may appear. You can only visit the gorge on a guided tour, but there are other nature walks you can do on your own.

Agate Creek is a further 20km if you want to do some fossicking. Otherwise drive back to Forsayth and it is another 40km from there to Georgetown and the bitumen.

ORGANISED TOURS
Contact tourist information centres for details of local tours in their area.

Coral Coaches *(☎ 07-4031 7577, fax 4031 7546)* runs coach tours of the whole savannah area. The four-day Gulflands Experience costs $560 while the five-day tour is $725 and includes Cobbold Gorge.

Undara Experience *(☎ 07-4097 1411)* runs one-day/two-day tours of the Undara lava tubes from Cairns for $92/271.

Down Under Tours *(☎ 07-4035 5566, fax 4035 5588, e res@downundertours.com, w www.downundertours.com)* runs three-day tours from Cairns to Alice Springs that pass through this area.

Gondwana Travel Co *(☎ 0500 555 354)*, based in Cairns, offers six- and an eight-day tours covering all the places mentioned in this route, and a 12-day tour that includes train journeys.

Oz Tours Safaris *(☎ 07-4055 9535, fax 4055 9918)*, in Cairns, has a seven-day Gulf Savannah tour for $1295.

Wilderness Challenge *(☎ 07-4055 6504, fax 4057 7226, e info@wilderness-challenge.com.au, w www.wilderness-challenge.com.au)* runs six-day tours for $1595, including accommodation.

Australian Pacific Tours (☎ 1800 675 222, fax 4052 1404) has one-day/three-day/nine-day tours operating out of Cairns for $92/595/1195.

FACILITIES
Atherton
Atherton has a long list of banks, stores, garages, camping and accommodation options. Try *Wrights Motor Inn (☎ 07-4095 4141, Simms Rd)*, *Woodlands Tourist Park (☎ 07-4091 1407, Herberton Rd)*, or *Atherton Backpackers (☎ 07-4091 3552, 37 Alice St)* and for vehicle repairs *All-Wheel Drive Centre (☎ 07-4091 1555)*.

Ravenshoe
Tall Timbers Caravan Park (☎ 07-4097 6325, Kennedy Hwy) has unpowered/powered sites ($9/13.50 per double), units ($40 to $50), a restaurant, a shop and fuel.

Club Hotel Motel (☎ 07-4097 6109) has double and single rooms at $28 to $55; *Tully Falls Hotel (☎ 07-4097 6163)* has doubles rooms for $29.50 and serves satisfying meals, *Kool Moon (☎ 07-4097 6407)* has double rooms for $52.80.

Bed & Breakfast places start at $65.

Innot Hot Springs
Innot Hot Springs Village (☎ 07-4097 0316) has unpowered/powered sites for $15.50/17.50 and units for $40/70 per double. Its seven hot pools are free to people who are staying there (otherwise entry costs $5.50). The hot springs in Nettle Creek are free for everyone. *Wayne Bowden (☎ 07-4097 0150)* does car repairs.

Mt Garnet
Norwestgate Motel & Van Park (☎ 07-4097 9249, fax 4097 9018) has unpowered/powered sites for $11/13 per double and units ranging from $40 to $50.

Undara Volcanic National Park
Undara Lava Lodge (☎ 07-4097 1411, fax 4097 1450, e info@undara.com.au, w www.undara.com.au) Budget accommodation/railway carriages $18/75 per person, unpowered sites $6 per person, power $6 extra per

site. Tours of the lava tubes are available (two-hour/half-day/full-day for $33/63/93). There's also a restaurant (popular with kookaburras) and a small food and souvenir shop. The guides give entertaining talks around the campfire in the evenings.

Mt Surprise
Mt Surprise Tourist Park (☎ 07-4062 3153, fax 4062 3162) Unpowered/powered sites $12/15.40 per double, motel rooms doubles $72. The park also has a book exchange; fuel; gemstone display; aviary; mini-horses; fossicking permits; good-value, tasty meals; and a pool. Some outback entrepreneurs cover a very wide range of services.

Bedrock Village Caravan Park (☎ 07-4062 3193, fax 4062 3166, e bedrockvillage@bigpond.com, Garnet St) Unpowered/powered sites $11/15.40 per double, units $38-50 per double. The park has a swimming pool, vehicle repair service and the enterprising owner organises lots of tours and activities.

Mt Surprise Hotel (☎/fax 07-4062 3118) has single/double rooms for $25/40. *Oasis Camping (☎ 07-4062 3001)*, near O'Briens Creek Gemfield, has camp sites for $10 per vehicle. *Digger's Rest (☎/fax 07-4062 5241, e diggersgems@bigpond.com)* is on the O'Briens Creek Gemfield.

Mt Surprise Motors (☎ 07-4062 3143) provides towing and car repair services.

Tallaroo
Tallaroo Hot Springs (☎/fax 07-4062 1221, e tallaroo@bigpond.com) Unpowered/powered sites $6 per person. Admission to the hot pools and tour costs $9.

Georgetown
Teresa's Museum and Coffee Shop (☎ 07-4062 1264) is worth a visit. *Butler's Auto (☎ 07-4062 1298)* provides towing and car repairs.

Latara Resort Motel (☎ 07-4062 1190, fax 4062 1262) Air-con budget/singles/doubles for $35/58/76. A pool and meals ($20 for barramundi or a steak) are available. It's modern and the best place to stay in the area.

Midway Caravan Park (☎ *07-4062 1219, fax 4062 1227, North St)* Unpowered/powered sites $11/14.30, cabins $44 per double. There's also a shop with takeaways and fuel.

Wenaru Hotel (☎ *07-4062 1208, fax 4062 1271)* Air-con singles/doubles with shared facilities $35/45. The hotel does meals from $14.

Goldfields Caravan Park (☎ *07-4062 1269)* has unpowered/powered sites for $10/13 per double.

Croydon

Croydon Caravan Park (☎/*fax 07-4745 6238, Sircom St)* has unpowered/powered sites for $12/15 per double and vans from $25 to $40. *Croydon Club Hotel* (☎ *07-4745 6184, fax 4745 6143),* on Brown and Sircom St, has double rooms for $45.

Leichhardt Lagoon

Leichhardt Lagoon Camping (☎/*fax 07-4745 1330)* has basic toilet and shower facilities, is a bird-watchers paradise and costs $5 per person.

ALTERNATIVE TRANSPORT
Air
Charter flights are the only way to get around this part of Queensland and there are a number available, mainly based in Cairns. Contact the companies listed under Getting Around in the Cairns section.

Bus
The service from Cairns to Karumba via Undara and Croydon with Coral Coaches (☎ 07-4031 7577, fax 4031 7546, Trinity Wharf Transit Centre, Cairns) costs $199 one way. The bus leaves Cairns at 6.45am, Monday, Wednesday and Thursday, arriving in Undara at 11.25am, Croydon at 3.15pm and Karumba at 6.15pm. The return journey, Tuesday, Thursday and Friday, leaves Karumba at 6.45am and arrives in Cairns at 6pm.

Car Rental
There are numerous car rental companies in Cairns to choose from. See the earlier Cairns section for details.

Cairns to Musgrave via Cooktown

Highlights

- Enjoying a Daintree River cruise through the rainforest
- Bird-watching in Lakefield National Park
- Strolling through historic Cooktown
- Relaxing on the beaches of Cape Tribulation

For those who do not have time to travel to the very top of Cape York, but still want to sample the delights of Far North Queensland away from the glitz and glamour of Cairns and Port Douglas, an interesting loop to do is from Cairns to Cooktown and on to Musgrave via Battle Camp and the Lakefield National Park, returning via Laura and the Peninsula Developmental Rd. For travellers who want to go to the top of Cape York, this route north is a much more enjoyable alternative to the more direct Peninsula Developmental Rd.

The route north from Cairns along the coast to Cape Tribulation and then through the ranges to Cooktown is one of the most scenic in Australia. The road north of Cape Tribulation was surrounded by controversy when it was built in the early 1980s because of concerns about the environmental effect it would have on the rainforest. Although the green movement was out in force, the road was pushed through anyway. Indeed some damage was caused, but for many travellers it offers a chance to see and appreciate this wild part of Australia. The locals in Cooktown also appreciate this shorter access road from Cairns, rather than having to take the inland route which is 70km longer.

Arguments still rage between environmentalists and landowners, some of whom want to develop their land for agriculture or tourism. The government has been buying up land, but another $50 million needs to be found to protect the existing environment.

North of Cooktown this route once again cuts across the Great Dividing Range before descending onto the vast flood plains that make up much of Lakefield National Park, famous for its birds, fishing and crocodiles. During the Wet the rivers often coalesce to make a shallow inland sea, which in turn is replaced during the dry season by a sea of waving grass, cut by lagoons and tree-lined billabongs.

At its northernmost point, the route described here passes very close to the shores of Princess Charlotte Bay, before swinging westwards to meet the Peninsula Developmental Rd at Musgrave Roadhouse. From here the route turns south to Cairns via the amazing Aboriginal rock art sites near Laura and the beautiful **Mareeba Wetlands**.

You could easily spend two weeks or more in this fascinating region of Far North Queensland.

History

Aborigines occupied much of this land long before the arrival of Europeans. They inhabited the flood plains and the escarpment country as well as the rainforested mountains along the coast. They travelled the rivers by canoe and at times made forays out to the close offshore islands.

Captain James Cook almost came to grief near Cooktown during his voyage to map the east coast of Australia. On the night of 11 June 1770 the *Endeavour* hit a reef and it was only after some heavy gear, including a few cannons, was dropped over the side that the ship was refloated. Eleven days later they pulled into the mouth of the Endeavour River and careened their ship for repairs. Cook stayed there until 6 August, his longest residence on the Australian mainland. In that time he managed to repair his ship while the botanist, Sir Joseph Banks, explored the river documenting flora and fauna (including the first kangaroo to be described by a European).

Cook decided to escape the intricate maze of the inner reef so he landed on and named Lizard Island. However he was later to return inside the reef, preferring to navigate the inner reef to the constant danger of being pushed onto the outer reef. With his departure the Aboriginal people were left in peace for a century.

In 1865 John Jardine, on his way back from Somerset on the tip of Cape York, sailed up the Endeavour River and later explored and named the Annan River, a little further south. For more information on the Jardine family, see the boxed story 'Frank Jardine & Somerset' in the Cape York section later in this chapter.

The area was changed for ever when James Mulligan discovered gold in 1873 on the Palmer River. By 1874 over 15,000 men were living and working on the Palmer River goldfield, most of them came via the newly founded port of Cooktown. The town quickly grew and by the end of that year there were 36 shanties where you could buy grog! There was a pub on every street corner.

The Aboriginal tribes of the area resisted the invasion of European and Chinese miners, and the first group of miners (which included a warden and police officers) to travel to the goldfield from Cooktown was attacked by a large group of Aborigines at a place later called Battle Camp. The Aborigines attacked in waves but were repulsed by heavy gunfire. After this defeat, the Aborigines resorted to hit-and-run tactics, which over the years left dozens of miners dead. How many Aborigines were killed it is impossible to say, but those who survived had to face the deadly threat of new diseases that the invaders had brought with them.

Information

The distances between fuel outlets along the route are not great, but there is no fuel available in the Lakefield National Park. Road conditions are generally fair, but with rough, corrugated and sandy sections. Traffic is light north of Cooktown and if you break down or get injured, you will probably be a long way from a vehicle repair centre or a hospital.

Entry permits are not required except for visiting Elim Beach past the Hope Vale Aboriginal Community. Camping in the Lakefield National Park requires a permit from one of the rangers stations.

THE TROPICS

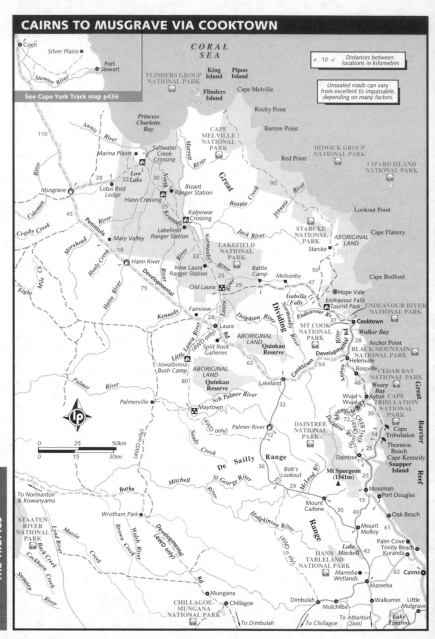

CAIRNS TO MUSGRAVE VIA COOKTOWN

CORAL SEA

Coen
Silver Plains
Port Stewart
Stewart River

FLINDERS GROUP NATIONAL PARK
King Island
Pipon Island
Cape Melville
Flinders Island

See Cape York Track map p436

Princess Charlotte Bay

Rocky Point
Barrow Point

Annie River

Marina Plains
Saltwater Creek Crossing
CAPE MELVILLE NATIONAL PARK

River

110

28
Low Lake
22
30
Bizant Ranger Station

Red Point
HOWICK GROUP NATIONAL PARK

LIZARD ISLAND NATIONAL PARK

Musgrave
Lotus Bird Lodge
Hann Crossing
Marrett River
North River
Great River
Kennedy

95

Kalpowar Crossing
Beattie Creek

Lookout Point

Coleman River

43
Peninsula River
Mary Valley
Lakefield Ranger Station

Jack River
STARCKE NATIONAL PARK
ABORIGINAL LAND
Cape Flattery

Crosby Creek
Morehead River
19
Hann River
33
New Laura Ranger Station

LAKEFIELD NATIONAL PARK
Normanby River
Battle Camp
Melsonby
Starcke

50
47

Cape Bedford

Healy Creek
Eight Mile Ck
Huan River
75
Developmental
Old Laura
29

Normanby River
Dividing
Isabella Falls
Endeavour Falls Tourist Park
Hope Vale
Endeavour Rv
ENDEAVOUR RIVER NATIONAL PARK

Kennedy
Fairview
28
Laura
Deighton River
Great Dividing
MT COOK NATIONAL PARK
37
Cooktown
Walker Bay

Split Rock Galleries
(4WD only)
Little Laura River
ABORIGINAL LAND
Quinkan Reserve
62
Developmental
54
28
Archer Point
BLACK MOUNTAIN NATIONAL PARK
Helenvale
Rossville
CEDAR BAY NATIONAL PARK

Jowalbinna Bush Camp
ABORIGINAL LAND
Quinkan Reserve
80
Lakeland
Cooktown
Annan River
46
Weary Bay
Wujal Wujal
Ayton
CAPE TRIBULATION NATIONAL PARK

Palmerville
Maytown
Nth Palmer River
32
Bloomfield
CREB Track (4WD only)
72
30
Cape Tribulation

(4WD only)
Palmer River
12
DAINTREE NATIONAL PARK
Daintree Rv
14
Thornton Beach
Cape Kennedy
Snapper Island

Palmer River
Sandy Creek
De Sailly Range
36
Bob's Lookout
29
Mt Spurgeon (1341m)
25
Daintree
11
25

Mitchell River
St George River
McLeod Rv
Mossman
Port Douglas

Butke
To Normanton & Kowanyama
Wrotham Park
Developmental (4WD only)
Mount Carbine
30
15
Oak Beach

STAATEN RIVER NATIONAL PARK
Lynd River
Massie Creek
Brown Creek
Walsh River
Hodgkinson River
HANN TABLELAND NATIONAL PARK
Mount Molloy
40
61
Palm Cove
Trinity Beach
Kuranda

Back Creek
Cockburn Creek
Strauben Creek
(4WD only)
Rd
Range
Lake Mitchell
42
Mareeba Wetlands
62
Cairns

Mungana
Chillagoe
CHILLAGOE-MUNGANA NATIONAL PARK
Dimbulah
Mutchilba
Mareeba
Walkamin
Little Mulgrave
Lake Tinaroo

To Dimbulah
To Chillagoe
To Atherton (2km)

Barrier Reef

10 Distances between locations in kilometres

Unsealed roads can vary from excellent to impassable, depending on many factors.

0   25   50km
0   15   30mi

THE TROPICS

Tourist Offices A variety of services are provided by Tourism Tropical North Queensland (☎ 07-4051 3588, fax 4051 0127, e information@tnq.org.au, w www .tnq.org.au) at 51 the Esplanade, Cairns.

Contact QPWS (☎ 07-4046 6600, fax 4046 6751, w www.env.qld.gov.au, 10 McLeod St, Cairns) for information about national park permits.

For information about tours, accommodation and free maps of the area contact the Cape Tribulation Tourist Information Centre (☎ 07-4098 0070) at Mason's Store in Cape Tribulation.

The Cook Shire Council Information Centre (☎ 07-4069 5446), in Charlotte St, Cooktown, has information on local parks and gardens as well as walking maps for the area.

Books & Maps Ron & Viv Moon's *Cape York – An Adventurer's Guide* is the most comprehensive guidebook for the do-it-yourself camper and 4WD enthusiast. Australian Geographic's *Cape York* also covers the area.

The best book on Cooktown is *Queen of the North* by Glenville Pike. *Daintree – Where the Rainforest Meets the Reef* (Australian Conservation Foundation and Kevin Weldon & Associates) is a beauty but may be hard to get.

The Hema maps on the Lakefield National Park and Cape York are both useful.

Emergency Head for Cooktown Hospital (☎ 07-4069 5433, Hope St), Mossman Hospital (☎ 07-4098 2444) or Laura Clinic (☎ 07-4060 3320), or contact the Flying Doctors.

The Cooktown Police Station (☎ 07-4069 5320) is on Charlotte St, and the Hope Vale Police Station (☎ 07-4060 9224) is at 4 Flierl St.

THE ROUTE
Cairns to Cooktown via the Coast (254km)
From Cairns, head north along the scenic coastal Captain Cook Hwy, past Cairns' northern beaches. If you haven't visited them already, drop in to a couple of these attractive, palm-fringed places.

At the turn-off to Port Douglas, 61km from Cairns, is the **Rainforest Habitat Wildlife Sanctuary** (☎ *07-4099 3235,* e *info@rainforesthabitat.com.au,* w *www .rainforesthabitat.com.au; adult/child $20/ 10; open 8.30am-5pm daily)* where there are 180 species in three habitats – wetland, grassland and rainforest. The species are mainly birds but there are also mammals, reptiles and fish. It is more of an 'eco-attraction' than a zoo, and you can see more wildlife close-up here than in the wild.

The town of **Mossman**, 20km further on, is in the middle of a sugar cane and tropical fruit area. Turn left into the town and drive 5km past the hospital to the famous and very popular **Mossman Gorge** (☎ *07-4098 2188)* within the Daintree National Park. This important park is part of the Unesco Wet Tropics World Heritage area. The 2.7km circular track passes under tall, shady, dripping rainforest trees and takes about an hour to walk. One unusual tree to look out for is the strangler fig, which starts life high on the branch of another tree and puts roots down to the ground. Gradually the roots join together around the trunk of the host tree, which is eventually strangled to death. Bird's nest ferns, orchids and brilliant blue Ulysses butterflies also features on the walk. Look closely for the tree-climbing kangaroo or a rare Boyd forest dragon clinging to a branch watching for insects to devour. Swim in pools in the river here, but take care as people have drowned.

Back on the main road, it is 25km to the turn-off to Cape Tribulation. But carry straight on for a scenic 10km trip to pretty **Daintree Village**, a mini-Kuranda, which has a timber museum, craft shops, restaurants, camping and accommodation. The CREB (short for Cairns Regional Electricity Board) Track starts from here and rejoins the main road up past the Bloomfield River. See Alternative Routes later in this section.

Turn right at the Daintree Village turn-off and 5km later you reach the **Daintree River Ferry** *($8 one way; operates 6am-6pm daily).* Very popular one-hour crocodile-spotting and bird-watching boat cruises leave from here and all along the river bank.

THE TROPICS

Cassowary

The Cape Tribulation Rd continues through dense rainforest where you might glimpse a cassowary bird, an endangered species found only in three small areas of rainforest in Queensland. They are large, flightless birds up to 2m tall with black plumage, a red and blue neck and a big bump on the top of their head. They are solitary birds and the male incubates the eggs and rears the chicks on his own. About 50 of them live in this area.

Stop at the **Alexandra Range Lookout** for superb views of the river mouth. At the **Rainforest Eco Centre** (☎ 07-4098 9171, $15), 10km from the ferry, climb a tower up to the rainforest canopy, go for walks and check out the environmental displays.

One kilometre further on is **Cow Bay** which has a hotel on the main road and a store that sells fuel on the road to the beach. You can also take a ride in a helicopter from the airstrip.

An ice cream factory is 4km further on. Try the ice cream made with sapote, a South American fruit known as the 'chocolate pudding fruit'. There are resorts scattered along both sides of the road as well as a tea plantation.

Seven kilometres past the ice cream factory, you reach Cooper Creek where you can take a one-hour day cruise or a 1½-hour night cruise with **Cooper Creek Cruises** (☎ 07-4098 9052).

Just past here is beautiful **Thornton Beach** which has a popular restaurant serving good coffee and interesting home-made food.

Marridja Boardwalk, 7km from Thornton Beach and 30km from the ferry, is an excellent 30-minute walk through rainforest and mangrove swamps. Put on insect repellent if you don't want to donate blood to various insects, some of which are microscopic but voracious. In many ways it's a more interesting hike than the much more popular one in Mossman Gorge.

A little further on is **Noah Beach** which has a small camping ground, but you must arrive early to get a site as bookings are not accepted.

Cape Tribulation, 8km further on, is also a place that has a lot to see and do. It was named Cape Tribulation by Captain Cook because this was where all his troubles began when his ship struck a reef. The area is famous for the lush rainforest that tumbles down the hills to the high-tide marks on the white sandy beaches, usually almost deserted. Just off the road on the left is Mason's Store, which is also a tourist information centre. The **Bat House** (☎ 07-4098 0063, **e** austrop@austrop.org.au, **w** www .austrop.org.au; admission $2 donation; open 10.30am-3.30pm Tues-Sun), staffed by volunteers, has various displays as well as a tame flying fox. At the nearby Cape Tribulation hostels, bed & breakfast places and upmarket resorts you can take part in activities such as night hikes, sea kayaking, horse riding, mountain biking, and diving and snorkelling trips to the Great Barrier Reef. Or else you can just laze around, enjoying the wonderful natural surroundings.

Here the Bloomfield Track (Cape Tribulation Rd) ends and the fun begins. The steep gradients can be a challenge after rain, even for a 4WD vehicle, so take care and use low gears. After a 43km roller coaster ride you cross the **Bloomfield River** which now has a concrete causeway and is not the obstacle it used to be. Once over, turn left for 1km to park and then walk to the **Bloomfield River Falls**.

The **Wujal Wujal** Aboriginal community is on the northern bank of the river, and 5km further on is the **Bloomfield Inn** which is not a pub despite its name and sells only food and fuel. The tiny village of **Ayton** (named after Captain Cook's home town), 5km further on, has a cafe and a good camping ground, from where you can walk down to the coast at Weary Bay, with its 9km of wilderness beach. Take a yacht or motorboat tour to the Great Barrier Reef from the Ayton wharf.

Beyond Ayton the road improves a bit and the creeks have wooden bridges over them. You soon reach the **Cedar National Park**, but at present it has no official tracks or facilities. **Rossville**, 25km beyond Ayton, has a store, takeaway (closed on Sunday) and budget camping and accommodation at the Home Rule resort. Another 9km brings you to the famous **Lion's Den Hotel**. Check out the corrugated iron and graffiti decor and have a beer or coffee under the century-old mango trees. Built in 1875, the pub was in the same family from 1875 to 1964 and since then all the licensees have been women. The place just oozes character: Such is the fame of this outback watering hole that Bert Cummings wrote *The Lion's Den – A Pub Yarn* about it. See Facilities for information about accommodation. The bitumen begins soon, so celebrate and get the dust out of your throat.

Carry on past the Lion's Den for 2km, then turn right onto the bitumen road and drive 3km to the **Black Mountain Viewpoint**. Have a close look at this strange mountain, which is a huge pile of black granite boulders: Is there anything like it anywhere else in the world? There's even species of frog, skink and gecko that only live on this mountain.

Cross over the wide Annan River on the smart, new bridge, and 2km later turn left and park beside the lily-covered bird zone called **Keating's Lagoon**. It's only a short walk to a hide where you can do some bird-watching and see cranes, ducks and the lily-pad walkers that some locals call 'Jesus

birds'. As usual, keep an eye out for any crocodiles that might have their eyes on you.

Back on the main road it's only 6km to Cooktown.

Cooktown

The 'Queen of the North', as it is often called, lies on the banks of the Endeavour River, close to where Captain Cook beached his ship for repairs in 1770. It is a well-established town with every facility, and an interesting place to spend a couple of days.

History Cooktown was founded with gold was discovered on the Palmer River in 1873. Within a year it had grown to a town of 15,000 people. There were 65 hotels, six butchers, five bakers, three watchmakers, seven blacksmiths, six barbers and three chemists. Other ports further south along the coast competed for the prize of being the port to feed and supply the Palmer River goldfield. But the demise of the goldfields due to the lack of rich reef gold heralded the slow decline of Cooktown.

There was still no road connection to Cooktown in 1930. The town relied on small coastal freighters for its supplies and mail. Cooktown and Laura were connected by a light rail from 1885, but the railway never reached the Palmer goldfield, despite that being its prime objective. Unfortunately, the railway has been closed and the track removed.

During WWII most of the town's population was evacuated and the surrounding area became a forward base for US and Australian servicemen fighting in New Guinea and the Coral Sea.

In 1949 Cooktown suffered a major setback when it was devastated by a cyclone. Much of it was completely flattened and those buildings that remained were badly damaged. However, Cooktown refused to die, and in the 1950s the tourists began to arrive. At first it was just a straggle of keen adventurers, but by the '70s it was a near flood, especially in the dry season.

Today the future of the town depends on tourism and the hinterland it has serviced for over 100 years. With the inland road to

Cairns being all bitumen by 2005, the future looks bright. The only danger is that too many tourists could spoil the somewhat seedy and laid-back charm of this frontier town.

Information The Westpac bank in Charlotte St has an ATM and a wonderful wooden interior.

Cape York Auto Centre (☎ 07-4069 5233, fax 4069 5274, e cytac@tpg.com.au), on the corner of Charlotte and Furneaux Sts, is the RACQ agent. FNQ Repairs (☎/fax 07-4069 6005), on the corner of Boundary and Adelaide Sts, is another option.

Things to See & Do The **waterfront**, which in the past saw so much action, is a pleasant place to wander, especially at sunset. Fish for barramundi off the wharf and wonder at the scene that hasn't changed since Captain Cook came ashore. Two-hour river cruises ($25) leave from here as do fishing expeditions and trips out to the Great Barrier Reef. You can also hire your own 'tinny' (a small fishing boat) for $88 a day.

A number of **monuments** line the river, including a statue of Captain Cook and an 1803 cannon sent to Cooktown along with some cannonballs and an army officer in 1889, when Russia was considered a threat.

The new **Milbi Wall** is a mixture of words and images on colourful tiles that tell the traditional stories and history of the local Gungarde Aborigines –from their own point of view. The missionaries arrived here in 1886 and Aboriginal children were taken away from their parents and put in school dormitories. The local cattle stations employed Aboriginal people as stockmen and maids, but the pay was low, conditions were poor and Aborigines didn't become Australian citizens until 1967. It's a complex and fascinating work of art that deserves more than a quick look.

Outside the post office in Charlotte St is what the locals call the **Tree of Knowledge** and they still pin notices to it.

The **James Cook Historical Museum** (☎ 07-4069 5386, Cnr Helen & Furneaux Sts; adult/child $5.50/1.65; open 9am-4pm daily Apr-Jan) is housed in a converted convent school, built in 1889 and staffed by Irish nuns. The displays cover Captain Cook's 48-day visit, the gold-rush days (knuckle dusters were common), pioneer household goods, Aboriginal artefacts and a few items left behind by the 20,000 Chinese who passed through or worked in Cooktown.

The **Cooktown Museum** (☎ 07-4069 5686, Cnr Walker & Helen Sts; adult/child $5/2; open 9am-5pm daily in the dry season) has a varied collection of pioneer examples of household goods and mining equipment.

Many of the town's **historic buildings** are over 100 years old, so just walking around is a worthwhile experience. Some of the old buildings have been put to new uses – for example the old hospital in May St has been recycled into a church hall. Only two pubs, the West Coast and Cooktown Hotels, have survived from the gold-rush days. The original Sovereign Hotel (built in 1874) was partially destroyed by the cyclone of 1949 and became known as 'The Half Sovereign'. Now it's been completely rebuilt and is Cooktown's only four-star hotel.

The **lighthouse**, built in 1885, is on Grassy Hill which was climbed and named by Captain Cook. It's no longer grassy (a better name would be Windy Hill), but still gives a great view of the surrounding area.

The **Botanic Garden** contains Vera's Cafe and **Nature's Powerhouse** (☎ 07-4069 6004, e keep@tpg.com.au, Walker St; admission $2; open 9am-5pm daily), which is small but excellent. Displays include information about the 185 creatures found only in Cape York and wonderful paintings of Queensland flora by local artist Vera Scarth-Johnson. From here it is just a short walk to the unspoilt **Finch Bay Beach**.

You can also hike through the **Mt Cook National Park** to the top of Mt Cook which takes about 90 minutes along a marked trail.

The **cemetery** has a unique Chinese shrine and some interesting gravestones, including that of Mrs Watson, the 'Heroine of Lizard Island'. Another intriguing epitaph simply states, 'Here lies the adventurer Modesto Spud Melino'. It would be interesting to learn more about that guy.

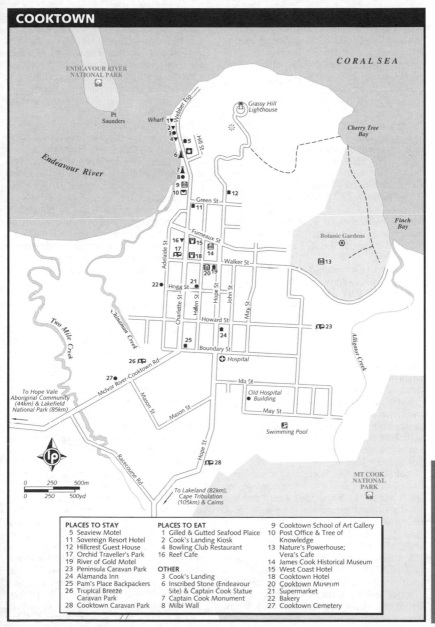

COOKTOWN

PLACES TO STAY
5 Seaview Motel
11 Sovereign Resort Hotel
12 Hillcrest Guest House
17 Orchid Traveller's Park
19 River of Gold Motel
23 Peninsula Caravan Park
24 Alamanda Inn
25 Pam's Place Backpackers
26 Tropical Breeze
Caravan Park
28 Cooktown Caravan Park

PLACES TO EAT
1 Gilled & Gutted Seafood Plaice
2 Cook's Landing Kiosk
4 Bowling Club Restaurant
16 Reef Cafe

OTHER
3 Cook's Landing
6 Inscribed Stone (Endeavour
Site) & Captain Cook Statue
7 Captain Cook Monument
8 Milbi Wall

9 Cooktown School of Art Gallery
10 Post Office & Tree of
Knowledge
13 Nature's Powerhouse;
Vera's Cafe
14 James Cook Historical Museum
15 West Coast Hotel
18 Cooktown Hotel
20 Cooktown Museum
21 Supermarket
22 Bakery
27 Cooktown Cemetery

In June the **Cooktown Endeavour Festival** is held over the Queen's Birthday weekend, and highlights of the three-day event include a re-enactment of Cook's landing in 1770, along with a colourful gala ball, sporting events, horse races and rides and a fishing competition. Contact the Cooktown Discovery Festival (☎ 07-4069 1566, PO Box 630, Cooktown, Qld 4871) for full details. There's also an **art show** in June.

In June and July there are popular **horse race meetings** run by the local Turf Club (☎ 07-4069 5309).

Cooktown to Musgrave Roadhouse (275km)

Drive out of Cooktown along McIvor River-Cooktown Rd past the cemetery, racecourse and airport. After 18km the bitumen ends but the dirt road should be reasonable.

In an idyllic setting near a waterfall, 37km from Cooktown, is the Endeavour Falls Tourist Park which sells fuel and has a well-stocked shop. Be careful at the junction 5km beyond the caravan park. Straight on there's a turn-off to the Aboriginal community of **Hope Vale** (☎ 07-4060 9185), which has shops and fuel, and a $10 permit allows you to visit the Elim coloured sand cliffs a further 20km away. A four-day carnival and rodeo is held here in August.

Turn left at the junction for Battle Camp and Lakefield National Park. The bush soon closes in, farmland is left behind and other vehicles become scarcer. If the road grader has not been around recently the corrugations can be bad.

Isabella Creek is 5km past the junction. Even late in the Dry it has water and on the left is a pretty little waterfall which makes a good spot for a picnic and even a swim. A few kilometres later is the Normanby River crossing. Expect some water but no problems. After that, drive along flat country and 20km from the river you reach the turn-off to Battle Camp station. The mountains to the south are the rugged Battle Camp Range.

After passing through cattle gates, you arrive at the **Lakefield National Park**, 91km from Cooktown. Attractive Emma Lake is

600m down a track on your right, while Horseshoe Lagoon, Leichhardt Waterhole and Welcome Waterhole are down the next turn-off on your right. The soft sandy tracks are a welcome relief after the hard corrugations on the main road. Bush camping is possible, but you must obtain a permit. For more information see the boxed section 'Lakefield National Park'.

It's 20km to Laura River which can be a little hairy early in the Dry, but should be no problem later. **Old Laura Homestead** is on the far bank. Two Irishmen bought a small amount of land here in 1879 for less than £9. Being on the track to the Palmer goldfields the station prospered and there were 9000 cattle here by 1894. But the homestead building, similar to many others built all over the Cape, is no cattle king mansion, just a two-storey structure made of corrugated iron and rough-hewn wood with an earth floor. The station owners believed they were on easy street, but now it seems like the hard life.

Just past the old homestead is a junction. Straight on takes you to Laura, 28km away. This is the nearest place for fuel and supplies if you need them. There is Old Laura, New Laura and Laura in this area. Try not to get all the different Lauras confused! To continue to Musgrave Roadhouse via the National Park, turn right.

The scenery is nothing special, but there are tracks to scenic waterholes that are patches of paradise in contrast to the dry grassland, scrub forest and termite towers that cover most of the park. From the junction it is 25km to the New Laura Ranger Station where you pay for camping permits.

After New Laura the corrugations may improve and you might see a couple of shy wallabies hop across the road, a mob of feral pigs digging up the ground, or a handful of stately Brolga cranes march by. The Lakefield Ranger Station is 34km away and you pay here for camping at the **Kalpowar Crossing**, 5km away on the banks of the Normanby River. This attractive camping ground has the best facilities in the park.

From Kalpowar you have a choice of routes to the Bizant Ranger Station, 32km

Lakefield National Park

Lakefield National Park is the second-largest national park in Queensland and covers over 5370 sq km. It encompasses a wide variety of country around the flood plains of the Normanby, North Kennedy, Morehead and Hann Rivers.

During the wet season these rivers flood the plains, at times forming a large inland sea. Access during this time is limited or nonexistent. As the dry season begins, the rivers gradually retreat to form a chain of deep waterholes and billabongs. Along these rivers, rainforest patches are in stark contrast to the surrounding grass plains and eucalypt woodland.

Flora & Fauna

To the north, around Princess Charlotte Bay, mud flats and mangroves line the coast and the estuaries of the rivers. It might be an area that is full of sandflies, mosquitoes and estuarine crocodiles, but this is the nursery for the marine life for which the area is so well known.

As the dry season progresses, the birdlife begins to congregate around the permanent waters, and at times thousands of ducks and geese create an unholy noise but a spectacular sight. Groups of brolgas dance on the open plain, and tall stately jabirus stalk their way through the grass. Birds of prey soar on the thermals looking for a meal, while in the deepest, darkest patches of the rainforest, pheasant coucals and Torres Strait pigeons can be found. In all, over 180 species of birds have been identified in the park. At times like these, a small pair of binoculars comes in handy.

Agile wallabies are probably the most commonly seen mammal in the park, but feral pigs are prevalent and a problem for the park staff. Flying foxes make up the largest group of mammals found here. They are an impressive sight as they burst from their roosting spots in their thousands on their evening search for nectar and fruit. You won't forget the sight, the smell, or the damage they can do to the trees in which they roost.

Camping

Camping is allowed in over 30 places in the park. There are camping facilities at only the Hann Crossing (pit toilets) and Kalpowar Crossing (flush toilets, tap water and cold showers).

Purchase a camping permit ($3.85 per person per night, maximum 21 nights) for the southern area of the park from the rangers at New Laura (☎ 07-4060 3260, PMB 79, Cairns Mail Centre, Qld 4871). Lakefield Ranger Station (☎ 07-4060 3271, PMB 29, Cairns Mail Centre, Qld 4871) issues permits for the centre of the park. Bizant Ranger Station (☎ 07-4060 3258, PMB 30, Cairns Mail Centre, Qld 4871) covers the northern section of the park. Bookings may be made six to twelve weeks in advance and it's a good idea to book as far ahead as possible. Say what you are interested in and the vehicle you have, and the ranger will let you know the best spots to camp. If you have the time, try a couple of different locations.

Boating

Many of the big waterholes make for excellent boating, and you can spend many enjoyable hours drifting along a quiet stretch of water, watching birds or animals as they come down to drink.

Crocodiles

Both freshwater and estuarine crocodiles are found in this park. Lakefield National Park is one of five areas in the state designated as important for the ongoing conservation of the estuarine crocodile in Queensland, and for many people it offers the best chance of seeing one of these animals in the wild.

Fishing

Lakefield National Park is one of the few parks in Queensland where fishing is allowed and barramundi is the prize catch. A closed season applies between 1 November and 31 January. At other times there's a bag limit of five fish per person. Only fish between 58cm and 120cm can be kept. Line fishing is the only method allowed to catch these magnificent fish.

Lizard Island

Lizard Island, north of Cooktown, is one of the better known islands of the Great Barrier Reef and is readily accessible by air or boat from Cairns.

Named by Captain James Cook in 1770 after the big goannas that still roam the island, this speck of rock in a turquoise sea is home to a marine research centre and an upmarket tourist lodge. Most of the island's 7 sq km area is national park and as such is open to anyone who takes the time and effort to travel there. The waters around it are part of the Great Barrier Reef Marine Park.

Most people heading out to Lizard Island are day-trippers on organised tours, or guests staying at the lodge. Don't expect any help from the lodge staff – campers do not rate too highly with them. They might be driving in a similar direction to you but you will be walking, while the lodge guests get the seats.

Things to See & Do
Don't go without taking some snorkelling gear. The waters off Mrs Watson's Beach are full of coral and fish, as are all the bays and headlands of this island. Spear fishing is not allowed, but the fish are friendly and the snorkelling is safe. Line fishing is allowed except for the area around the Blue Lagoon.

There are any number of walks to enjoy. Don't miss the walk up to Cook's Look, the highest point on the island. This is where James Cook looked out and planned his escape from the maze of reefs that surrounded the *Endeavour*.

The remains of Mrs Watson's cottage are at the opposite end of the beach to the camping ground. This remarkable woman lived here in 1881. While her husband was away fishing for beche-de-mer, she was attacked by Aborigines and her Chinese servant killed. Fearing more attacks, she collected some provisions and her diary, then, with her young child and a wounded servant, cast herself adrift in a large boiling-down tank. They drifted north-west at the whim of the currents, finally succumbing on one of the islands near Cape Melville. The last entry in her diary was dated 11 October 1881, a poignant '…nearly dead with thirst'. Her grave, and that of her child, is still well maintained in the Cooktown cemetery.

Places to Stay
If you have buckets of money, book and stay at Lizard Island Lodge (☎ 07-4060 3999). This luxury resort is one of the most exclusive and expensive on the reef. Dive trips, fishing, game fishing, sailing and boating are available.

Otherwise, camp on the island at the very pleasant designated camping ground just behind Mrs Watson's Beach. There are pit toilets, tables and water from a spring. Campers must be self-sufficient, and only charcoal fuel fires are permitted – fuel stoves are not allowed on flights to the island and all fallen timber, including driftwood, is protected.

A permit ($3.85 per person per night) is required from QPWS (☎ 07-4046 6600, fax 4046 6751, W www.env.qld.gov.au) to camp on the island (maximum stay 10 days). A permit is required to board the aircraft so plan ahead.

Getting There & Away
Flights from Cairns to the island with Macair (☎ 13 13 13) start at $370 return. Marine Air Seaplanes (☎ 07-4069 5915) does eco-friendly day trips ($245) from Cooktown. Day trips from Cairns are available with Aussie Airways (☎ 1800 620 022, 07-4055 9088, W www.amitytours.com.au).

away. At Red Lily Lagoon you might see flocks of magpie geese and galahs, perhaps a harmless water python curled up asleep, spoonbills busily feeding, or a pure-white egret standing as still as a statue waiting to strike. As with any safari what you see is a matter of luck and patience. But a great feature of the park is the excellent network of sandy tracks that provide access to out-of-the-way parts, so you can always find quiet places, however many visitors there are in the park.

The **Hann Crossing** of the North Kennedy River, 7km from Bizant, has pit toilets and camping but is not very attractive or shady. Be particularly careful of estuarine crocodiles here. One night in 2001 a crocodile grabbed a sleeping camper by the wrist and dragged him towards the river. Luckily he was rescued by his friend who then had to drive him hundreds of kilometres to the nearest hospital. Never camp within 50m of river banks. Crocodiles are not fussy eaters – they will eat humans, snakes, fish, frogs, crabs, dragonflies, and even other crocodiles. About the only thing they do not enjoy eating is a cane toad.

Just downstream from the crossing are a couple of waterfalls that drop into a large pool. If you want to see how many crocodiles are living there, take a spotlight down at night. Count the eyes and divide by two.

The road becomes sandy and single-tracked as you cross the Morehead River and the Nifold Plain, but 30km from the Hann Crossing, turn left for 3km to reach picturesque **Low Lake**. It is famous for its bird-watching and you might see a majestic eagle. You can drive part of the way round it, but walking is more rewarding.

Back on the main road, dips and deep sandy stretches slow you down but the road is being improved. A track on the right goes to the Saltwater Crossing and you can continue to the wetter areas near Princess Charlotte Bay.

From the Low Lake turn-off it is 25km to Lotus Bird Lodge, the perfect place for some relaxation and pampering as well as for spotting some more birds and crocodiles in the nearby lagoons. **Musgrave Roadhouse** is a further 28km and has fuel, beer, meals, camping and accommodation.

Musgrave Roadhouse Direct to Cairns (446km)

This route along the Peninsula Developmental Rd is detailed in the later Cape York section. While the road from Lakefield to

Flying Fox

Cairns is bitumen, before that there are rough, corrugated sections. Highlights along this route include Aboriginal rock paintings around Laura, the flying fox colony in Mary Valley and the Mareeba Wetlands.

ALTERNATIVE ROUTES
Cairns to Cooktown via the Inland Route (325km)

The bitumen road from Cairns to Lakeland is detailed in the later Cape York section. At Lakeland turn right for Cooktown, which is 82km away along a rather stony and corrugated road. However, the government has promised that the road will be bitumen all the way by 2005. You can camp near the **Annan River** and walk downstream to an impressive narrow gorge and a waterfall that really roars when it is in flood but is worth a look at any time. Soon after you can turn right to Helenvale for a short detour to the famous Lion's Den Hotel, and from here it is just 28km to Cooktown via the Black Mountain and Keating's Lagoon which are both worth a stop.

THE TROPICS

Cairns to Cooktown via the CREB Track (256km)

You must apply for a permit from QPWS (☎ 07-4091 8102, PO Box 975, Atherton, Qld 4883) before you attempt this challenging track, which can be impassable after rain and is closed in the wet season. It is easy to get lost and/or bogged. While it is the shortest route between Cairns and Cooktown, it is also the most difficult and the slowest.

It starts at **Daintree Village**, 112km north of Cairns, and follows the Upper Daintree Rd for 17km. Go through the gate on your right and cross the Daintree River.

For the next 55km the track passes through dense and varied rainforest, and crosses mountains and numerous picturesque creeks. The **Roaring Meg Falls** are a highlight and the track comes out on the road between Wujal Wujal and Ayton.

ACTIVITIES

Along the coast, **swimming** and **sunbathing** on the beaches are the way to go, but during the summer months, box jellyfish are a danger. Enclosures on some beaches provide some protection against these marine stingers, but always seek local advice before plunging in for a cooling dip. Vinegar should be poured on your skin if you are unlucky enough to be stung by one of them. **Snorkelling** is quite pleasant on the coast, but the water can be murky close to shore and boat trips to offshore reefs provide a much better experience. The resorts organise all kinds of activities, such as **sea kayaking**, **horse riding**, **mountain biking** and **guided rainforest walks**.

In Cooktown the **sport-fishing** clubs run tournaments between October and December each year. With barramundi and mangrove jack in the rivers and everything up to marlin in the offshore waters, the fishing and the catches can be spectacular.

While Lakefield National Park is one of the few that allow fishing, beware of crocodiles if you are on a river bank or in a small boat. The **bird-watching** is excellent so binoculars and a book about birds are useful items to take along.

ORGANISED TOURS

Numerous Cairns-based tour operators specialise in Daintree, Cape Tribulation and Cooktown – see the earlier Cairns section for details. The following are operators in Cooktown and Hope Vale.

Cooktown Cruises (☎ 07-4069 5712) has two-hour river tours that leave at 1pm every day (adult/child $25/12).

Reel River Fishing (☎ 07-4069 5346, e leonard@reelriverfishing.com, w www.reelriverfishing.com) offers fishing charter trips from Cooktown.

Endeavour Sportfishing Club (☎ 07-4069 5429) and **Cooktown Sportfishing Club** (☎ 07-4069 5775) are both based in Cooktown and welcome visitors.

Cooktown Bush Walkers (☎ 07-4069 5312) is a club that organises regular hikes and welcome visitors who want to join in.

Munbah Tours (☎ 07-4060 9173) runs cultural tours of the Hope Vale Aboriginal community. Ring for details.

Talk to the people at **Cook's Landing Kiosk** (☎ 07-4069 5101, Webber Esplanade) for details of local boat trips.

FACILITIES
North of the Daintree River Ferry

There is a string of accommodation and eating places along both sides of the road between the ferry and Cape Tribulation.

Cow Bay Hotel Motel (☎ 07-4098 9011, 10km north of the ferry) Single/double air-con units $55/66 includes bistro meals. Cow Bay Store on the road to the beach sells fuel and general store items.

Rainforest Retreat (☎ 07-4098 9101) Air-con, self-contained double/family units $66/95. In a rainforest setting, this place has a kitchen and pool.

Crocodylus Village (☎ 07-4098 9166, 2km from the main road) Dorm beds $20, en suite cabins $65. Located amid a rainforest, there's a pool, bar and restaurant that serves cheap meals. This place is popular with tour groups of young people.

Lync-Haven Rainforest Retreat (☎ 07-4098 9155, 16km from the ferry) Unpowered/powered sites $16/20 per double, new bungalows with shared facilities $95 per double, self-contained units $115 per double. Bungalows and units sleep up to six people. Meals are provided, there are hiking trails on 16 hectares of private rainforest and there's an animal sanctuary for injured or orphaned animals.

Rainforest Village (☎ *07-4098 9015*) Unpowered/powered sites $18/20 per double, and cabins are planned. Rainforest Village also sells fuel and food.

Thornton Beach Cafe & Bar (☎ *07-4098 9118, 20km from the ferry*) This place serves good coffee and delicious meals such as king salmon with chilli jam and home-baked coconut bread – a real treat.

Noah Beach Camping Ground (*29km from the ferry*) Single unpowered sites $3.85. You need to self-register (no bookings) at this national park camping ground.

Cape Tribulation

Coconut Beach Rainforest Resort (☎ *07-4098 0033, 4km north of Noah Beach*) $230/345 per double including breakfast. This place is almost five-star luxury. *Fern-tree Rainforest Resort* (☎ *07-4098 0000*), 2km further on, is similar.

PK's Jungle Village (☎ *07-4098 0040*) Double unpowered/powered sites $22/28, beds in 8-bed dorms $24, double cabins $65, double safari tents $70. Dorms, cabins and tents all have shared facilities and fans. PK's is near the beach and there's a kitchen, bar, restaurant, pool and 4WD hire.

Masons Store (☎ *07-4098 0070*) Set back from the road on the left, Masons sells food, general store items and alcohol, and provides information, a free map and a nearby swimming hole.

Bloomfield River to Helenvale

Once north of Cape Tribulation there is no accommodation until you reach Ayton, 10km beyond the Bloomfield River.

The Bloomfield Wilderness Lodge (☎ *07-4035 9166, Near Ayton*) $228 per person for 2 nights. This is a luxury resort.

Bloomfield Cabins & Camping (☎ *07-4060 8207, 20 Bloomfield Rd,* W *www.bloomfieldcabins.com, Ayton*) Single camp sites $9, cabins $49. Pizza is available but order in advance. Fishing and reef trips (☎ *07-4060 8234, 4060 8182*) are available and you can walk or drive to Weary Bay.

The Aboriginal community of Wujal Wujal has a *shop* and fuel for sale.

Home Rule Rainforest Lodge (☎ *07-4060 3925, Rossville*) Single camp sites $8, rooms $18. Turn right at the store in Rossville and it's 3km down a track. Meals can be provided and canoes hired ($5 per half day).

Lion's Den Hotel (☎ *07-4060 3911, fax 4060 3958,* e *lionsden10@bigpond.com .au, Helenvale*) Single camp sites $5, beds in shared safari tents $12, private 4-bed safari tent $60. Meals, snacks and souvenirs are for sale, and canoes can be hired.

Mungumby Lodge (☎ *07-4060 3158, fax 4060 3159,* e *mungumby@bigpond.com.au,* W *www.mungumby.com, Helenvale*) Double en suite wooden chalets $195 with breakfast. The lodge is 5km down a bumpy track, 1km past the Lion's Den Hotel. There are walks to old Chinese alluvial mining areas.

Cooktown

There are four caravan/camping parks.

Orchid Traveller's Park (☎ *07-4069 6400, fax 4069 6500, Cnr Charlotte & Walker Sts*) Single unpowered/powered sites $6/9. This is the nearest park to the town centre.

Peninsula Caravan Park (☎ *07-4069 5107, fax 4069 5255,* e *penpark@tpg .com.au, Howard St*) Unpowered/powered sites $15.40/18.70, vans $33, double self-contained cabins $60.50. Peninsula is in a bush setting and there's a walk through a paperbark forest to the beach.

Tropical Breeze Caravan Park (☎ *07-4069 5417, fax 4069 5740, Cnr Charlotte St & McIvor River-Cooktown Rd*) Unpowered/powered sites $14.50/17.50, self-contained units without/with air-con $65/76 a double, $55/60 a single. This place is quite spacious – it even has two swimming pools.

Cooktown Caravan Park (☎ *07-4069 5536, fax 4069 5592,* e *info@cooktown caravanpark.com,* W *www.cooktowncaravan park.com, 14-16 Hope St*) Unpowered/

powered sites $15.40/18.70. Cooktown Caravan Park is clean and new.

Apart from these, Cooktown also has a wide range of other accommodation.

Pam's Place Backpackers (☎ 07-4069 5199, fax 4069 5964, **e** *pamplace@ tpg.com.au, Cnr Charlotte & Boundary Sts)* Air-con dorm beds/singles/doubles $20/ 36/46. Rooms are small but with an interesting decor, gardens and lots of tame birds. Bike hire is $10 per day which is useful as Cooktown is very spread out.

Alamanda Inn (☎/fax 07-4069 5203, *Hope St)* Single/double self-contained units $55/75, single/double shared-toilet units $38/50, single/double shared-toilet & shower units $28/40. Alamanda is an excellent and fairly new place with a pool and meals available.

Seaview Motel (☎ 07-4069 5377, fax 4069 5607, Charlotte St)* Doubles $72, luxury units $155. Rooms have great sunset views over the Endeavour River.

River of Gold Motel (☎ 07-4069 5222, fax 4069 5615, **e** *river_of_gold@tpg .com.au, Cnr Hope & Walker Sts)* Stand-by doubles $71.50, double self-contained units $81.50. It has a pool and the restaurant serves good steaks and seafood.

Sovereign Resort Hotel (☎ 07-4069 5400, fax 4069 5582, **e** *gm@sovereign-resort .com.au,* **w** *www.sovereign-resort.com.au, Cnr Charlotte & Green Sts)* Double rooms/apartments $130/165. Cooktown's most upmarket hotel has a tropical lagoon pool and a balcony restaurant where you can enjoy steak and barramundi.

Hillcrest Guest House (☎ 07-4069 5305, fax 4069 5893, Hope St)* Single/double B&B rooms $40/60, double self-contained units $67-85. It also has a pool, a restaurant and a lovely garden.

Cooktown Hotel (☎ 07-4069 5308, Cnr Charlotte & Walker Sts)* Singles/doubles $30/50. Very basic accommodation at this place, known locally as the Top Hotel.

Most of the accommodation places in Cooktown offer meals. Otherwise here are a few other options.

The *bowling club* (☎ 07-4069 6173, Charlotte St; open 6pm-9pm daily)* offers dinners

that come highly recommended by the locals. *Gilled & Gutted Seafood Plaice* (☎ 07-4069 5863, On the wharf)* is a popular seafood and chips takeaway. *Reef Cafe* (☎ 07-4069 5361, Charlotte St)* does seafood meals, pizza, snacks, coffee and Devonshire teas.

For self-caterers the *supermarket* (☎ 07-4069 5633, fax 4069 5569)* is on the corner of Hope and Helen Sts.

Cooktown to Musgrave Roadhouse

Endeavour Falls Tourist Park (☎/fax 07-4069 5431, 33km north-west of Cooktown)* Double unpowered/powered sites $13/ 16.50, double self-contained units $55. It has a well-stocked shop, sells fuel and has a peaceful get-away-from-it-all atmosphere. The waterfall is pretty, too.

Lotus Bird Lodge (☎/fax 07-4059 0773, **e** *lotusbird@iig.com.au,* **w** *www.cairns.aust .com/lotusbird, 28km west of Musgrave Roadhouse; open mid-May to mid-Nov)* Stand-by wooden chalets $88. There's a pool, all meals are available ($11-27.50) as is free tea and coffee. Guided tours are available around nearby lagoons, and mountain bikes can be hired. It's a good place for bird-watchers and nature-lovers to unwind.

ALTERNATIVE TRANSPORT
Air
Most flights to Cooktown are from Cairns. See Getting Around in the Cairns section for full details. Cooktown Travel Centre (☎ 07-4069 5446, fax 4069 6023, **e** cook towntravel@bigpond.com) can help you with information on flights.

Bus
Coral Coaches (☎ 07-4031 7577, fax 4031 7546) runs a bus service from Cairns to Cooktown along both the coast and inland routes for $115 return each. The coast road route operates 1 May to 30 November on Tuesday, Thursday and Saturday. The bus leaves Cairns at 6am, reaches Cape Tribulation at 10am and Cooktown at 2pm. The return journey leaves Cooktown on Tuesday, Thursday and Saturday at 3pm and arrives back in Cairns at 9.30pm.

Cairns to Cooktown via the inland route operates all year on Wednesday, Friday and Sunday. The bus leaves Cairns at 7am and arrives in Cooktown at 12.30pm. The return journey on the same days leaves Cooktown at 2.30pm and arrives in Cairns at 7.45pm.

Another Coral Coach service runs twice a day between Cairns and Cape Tribulation. It leaves Cairns at 7am and 3.30pm and leaves Cape Tribulation at 7am and 1pm. Coral Coaches also runs from Cairns to Mossman and back 10 times a day.

Car Rental
Vehicles can be hired in Cooktown. Check out Endeavour Car Hire (☎ 07-4069 5860) or Cooktown Car Hire (☎ 07-4069 5694) at 1 Charlotte St, Cooktown.

Cape York

Highlights

- Standing on the northernmost tip of Australia
- Swimming and camping along the Telegraph Track
- Viewing the amazing Aboriginal rock art galleries around Laura
- Hiking and camping in the Iron Range National Park

Cape York Peninsula is one of the last great frontiers of Australia. It is a vast patchwork of tropical savannah cut by numerous rivers and streams, while along its eastern flank is the northern section of the Great Dividing Range. Among these ragged peaks and deep valleys are some of the best and most significant rainforests in Australia. Streams tumble down the rocky mountains to the sea, where just offshore the coral ramparts of the Great Barrier Reef stretch over thousands of square kilometres. The reef is protected in a marine park, and much of the land mass of the peninsula is protected in a number of spectacular but rarely visited national parks.

Giving access to this vast natural wonderland is the route to the cape. Initially the corrugated road you follow is known officially as the Peninsula Developmental Rd, but once that heads away to the mining town of Weipa you can follow the old and adventurous Overland Telegraph Line Track, with its numerous creek crossings. Avoid the creeks by taking the new but longer and very corrugated bypass roads.

From Cairns to the top of Cape York Peninsula is about 1000km via the shortest route, but a much more interesting route (described in the previous section) is to take the coast road to Cooktown via Daintree and Cape Tribulation and then drive through Lakefield National Park to Musgrave Roadhouse. Visiting the Iron Range National Park and Weipa also adds considerably to the total distance covered.

From the Archer River you can head north via Weipa and the Batavia Downs Road, or via the Telegraph Track. Further north again you have the choice of continuing on the Telegraph Track or taking the bypass roads, so called because they bypass nearly all of the river crossings – and thereby some of the best spots of the trip north.

Vast areas of Cape York Peninsula are designated Aboriginal land, while the rest is mainly taken up with large pastoral holdings and national parks.

Covering an area totalling around 207,000 sq km, about the same size as the state of Victoria, the peninsula has a population of only 15,000 people.

The largest towns in the region are Cooktown, on the south-eastern coast, and Weipa, a mining community on the central-western coast. A handful of small townships make up the remainder of the communities throughout the Cape.

History
Before the arrival of Europeans there were a large number of different Aboriginal tribal groups spread throughout the Cape, while a unique group of people inhabited the islands dotted across the reef-strewn Torres Strait. These Torres Strait Islanders came from Melanesia and Polynesia about 2000

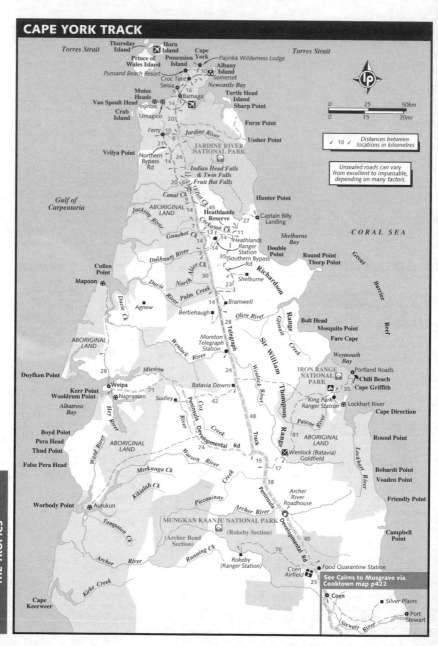

CAPE YORK TRACK

Torres Strait

Thursday Island
Horn Island
Prince of Wales Island
Possession Island
Cape York
Pajinka Wilderness Lodge
Albany Island
Punsand Beach Resort
Croc Tent
Seisia
Somerset
Newcastle Bay
Mutee Heads
Van Spoult Head
Injinoo
Turtle Head Island
Sharp Point
Crab Island
Umagico
Bamaga
Furze Point

Torres Strait

Ferry
Jardine River
Ussher Point
JARDINE RIVER NATIONAL PARK
Vrilya Point
Northern Bypass Rd
Indian Head Falls & Twin Falls
Fruit Bat Falls

Gulf of Carpentaria

ABORIGINAL LAND
Jackson River
Canal Ck
Elliot Ck
Hunter Point
Heathlands Reserve
Cockatoo Ck
Captain Billy Landing
Gunshot Ck
Heathlands Ranger Station
Shelburne Bay
Double Point
Round Point
Thorp Point

CORAL SEA

Dulhunty River
Nice Ck
North Ducie River
Southern Bypass Rd
Shelburne
Richardson
Great Barrier Reef

Cullen Point
Mapoon
Agnew
Palm Creek
Bramwell
Bertiehaugh
Olive River
Bolt Head
Mosquito Point
Fare Cape

Ducie Ck
Wenlock River
Moreton Telegraph Station
Telegraph
Sir William Range
Grenie Creek
Weymouth Bay

ABORIGINAL LAND
Duyfken Point
Mission
Batavia Downs
IRON RANGE NATIONAL PARK
Portland Roads
Chili Beach
Cape Griffith
Kerr Point
Wooldrum Point
Weipa
Napranum
Sudley
Cox
Peninsula River
Wenlock River
King Park Ranger Station
Lockhart River
Cape Direction
Albatross Bay

Boyd Point
Pera Head
Thud Point
False Pera Head
ABORIGINAL LAND
Hey River
Ward River
Creek
Developmental Rd
Watson River
Thompson Range
Pascoe River
ABORIGINAL LAND
Wenlock (Batavia) Goldfield
Round Point
Bobardt Point
Voaden Point

Worbody Point
Aurukun
Kikalah Ck
Merkunga Ck
Piccaninny
Archer River
Peninsula Developmental Rd
Archer River Roadhouse
Friendly Point

Tompaton Ck
MUNGKAN KAANJU NATIONAL PARK
(Rokeby Section)
(Archer Bend Section)
Running Ck
Rokeby (Ranger Station)
Campbell Point
Archer River
Kirke Creek
Coen Airfield
Food Quarantine Station

Cape Keerweer

See Cairns to Musgrave via Cooktown map p422
Coen
Silver Plains
Port Stewart
Stewart River

Distances between locations in kilometres

Unsealed roads can vary from excellent to impassable, depending on many factors.

0   25   50km
0   15   30mi

years ago and are culturally distinct from the Aborigines. While they had a close affinity with the people further north, they influenced Aboriginal tribal groups near the top of the peninsula and vice versa. The further south on the mainland, the less the influence from the north.

The rich Aboriginal and Torres Strait Islander heritage is alive today and travellers will see much of it on their way to the top. Of special importance is one of the world's most significant collections of prehistoric art in the escarpment country surrounding Laura. For further information, see the boxed text 'Quinkan Art' later in this section.

European history in Australia can trace its beginnings back to the early Dutch navigators who from 1606 explored much of the coastline. These included Janszoon and Tasman, reputedly the first Europeans to report seeing the great southern land. (It is unclear whether the Spanish navigator Torres, after whom the strait is named, actually sighted land.) Their exploits are remembered in the names of bluffs and bays dotted down the Gulf side of the peninsula.

James Cook mapped the eastern coast of Australia in 1770, and claimed the continent for England at Possession Island, just off the northerly tip that he named Cape York. Over the next 100 years other great English navigators, including Bligh, Flinders and King, mapped sections of the coast and bestowed their names upon it.

Ludwig Leichhardt was the first explorer to journey over a section of the peninsula during his 1845 expedition from Brisbane to Port Essington on the Cobourg Peninsula in the Northern Territory. South of the Mitchell River they were attacked and John Gilbert, the great collector of animals and birds for the naturalist John Gould, was killed by Aborigines.

Edmund Kennedy and his party had a horrific time in 1848 heading up the eastern coast along the Great Dividing Range. Continually splitting his party, Kennedy was fatally speared by Aborigines while among the swamps and waterways of the Escape River, south-east of the Tip. Only Jackey-Jackey, his Aboriginal guide,

reached their destination just a few kilometres north at Albany Passage.

Frank Jardine and his brother led a group taking cattle from Rockhampton to the new government outpost at Somerset in 1863. This was the start of the Jardine legend on Cape York Peninsula, with Frank Jardine dominating the top of the peninsula until his death in 1917.

Other explorers followed, opening up the region. The discovery of gold on the Palmer River in 1873 was the great catalyst for the development of Cooktown, Laura and, later, Cairns.

In 1887, the Overland Telegraph Line, from near Somerset to Palmerville and Cooktown, was finally completed, linking the northernmost outpost of the state with Brisbane. This is the route most travellers to Cape York follow today.

During WWII, Cape York was a major staging post for battles in New Guinea and the Coral Sea. Some 10,000 troops were stationed from Cooktown to Mutee Heads and Horn Island. Many relics of those days can still be seen, including wrecks of some of the 160 aircraft that were reported lost over the region.

During the 1950s bauxite was discovered along the coast near Weipa, and by the 1980s the world's biggest bauxite mine was located there.

In the late '80s there was much talk by the Queensland government about a space base being built on the Cape, but fortunately it did not come to fruition.

The Mer Islands in the Torres Strait were the subject of the Mabo claim, the first acknowledgement by the Australian legal system of native title as well as a rejection of the concept of *terra nullius*. Aboriginal people who had been living on land leased by pastoralists in the Weipa area, successfully claimed that native title could co-exist with pastoral leaseholds.

Information

The wet season greatly restricts vehicle movement on Cape York Peninsula. For that reason the best time to go is as early in the Dry as possible (June) when the countryside

The Legend of Frank Jardine

John Jardine was the government magistrate for the settlement of Somerset, established in 1863. Looking at the commercial aspects of the venture, he commissioned his sons Frank and Alick, both then aged in their early 20s, to overland a mob of cattle from Rockhampton to the new settlement.

That epic journey was the beginning of the Jardine legend on Cape York. It took them ten months to reach the Top, arriving at Somerset on 13 March 1865. Along the way they overcame lack of water, hostile Aborigines, flooded rivers when the Wet arrived, and the maze of swamps and waterways around the headwaters of the Escape and Jardine Rivers.

Frank Jardine was resisted all the way by local warriors and his party shot at least 30 Aborigines at the battle of Mitchell River, before making it to the Top. He gained a reputation as a ruthless murderer among local tribes. His legacy was mixed, however, because he also opened up the cattle industry on the cape in which many Aboriginal people were to find employment.

Jardine established outstations at Bertiehaugh, Galloway and Lockerbie and from his base at Somerset he ran a fleet of pearling luggers throughout the Torres Strait. Some say the family treasure came from a Spanish galleon he found wrecked on a remote reef south of New Guinea.

He married a Samoan princess called Sana, whom, the story goes, he kidnapped while she was being taken to New Guinea by missionaries.

Frank took over from his father as government magistrate. When he resigned, and the official government residence was moved to Thursday Island, he and Sana took over Somerset as their home. The grove of coconut palms they planted, some of which are still standing today, is the most visible reminder of their time at this outpost. The family lived relatively well in this wild place, entertaining ship's captains and any visiting dignitaries, and the Jardine hospitality was legendary.

In 1886, during the building of the Overland Telegraph Line, Jardine was in charge of transporting supplies to the workers building the northernmost section of the line. During that time he explored and named the Ducie River, establishing Bertiehaugh station on its banks some years later.

In 1890 the *Quetta* sank off the Cape, Queensland's worst shipping disaster. Jardine was responsible for saving many lives. From then on, ships passing through Albany Passage in front of Somerset would dip their flag in salute.

Frank died in 1919 and Sana in 1923. Both are buried on the foreshore at Somerset.

The Jardine story continued in this region until WWII when the family was evacuated from Somerset. Earlier, 'Chum' Jardine, the oldest son of Frank and Sana, had taken the family diaries to his new venture on the Aru Islands further west (now part of Indonesia). During the 1920s, the Australian Museum had offered the family over $10,000 for the diaries – an incredible sum for those days. In 1942 Chum was captured by the Japanese and beheaded for 'coast-watching'. The famous diaries and the family treasure, buried before the invasion, were lost.

Before they were lost, though, a number of books were written from those historic pages. The most famous writer to have access to them was Ion Idriess, who wrote *The Great Trek*, *Drums of Mer* and *Head-Hunters of the Coral Sea*.

What remained of the house at Somerset was burnt down in 1960, but there is still enough on the hill and down on the beach to remind people of this heritage. It is a great place to spend a few hours.

is greener, there is more water around, there are fewer travellers and the roads are generally better than later in the season. The peak period is between July and August, with the last vehicles leaving the cape by the end of October.

Tourist Offices There are no official tourist information centres but information is available from the hotels, roadhouses, camping grounds and rangers stations on the way. Collect as many leaflets as you can in Cairns before you go.

Road Reports If you plan to visit early or late in the season, it pays to check on the weather and road conditions with locals – contact the police in Coen, Weipa or Cooktown, or Archer River Roadhouse. Alternatively, you can contact the RACQ (☎ 1300 130 595, W www.racq.com.au).

Occasionally drivers get caught out by the early start of the Wet when they are at the very top of Cape York. Putting yourself and your car on the boat back to Cairns will cost around $1000.

You need to carry all the usual gear for travelling in a remote area so that you are as self-sufficient as possible, and you must carry water. Although you will cross a number of rivers, water can be scarce along this section, especially late in the Dry.

A well-constructed off-road trailer can be taken all the way to the top, but other trailers will fall apart along the way. Caravans can make it to Cooktown via the inland route, or even as far as Weipa if driven with care.

You are entering estuarine crocodile territory so always be careful when swimming, fishing or walking near water. Be aware that any dark, deep, long stretch of water can hide a big, hungry crocodile.

Excessive speed is the main cause of accidents on the gravel roads, particularly on the narrow, winding parts of the badly corrugated roads that bypass the Overland Telegraph Track creek crossings. Drive carefully and keep your wits about you.

Radio Frequencies Unless you are doing something way out of the ordinary, an HF radio, while nice to have, is not really necessary for the Cape.

The RFDS base in Cairns (☎ 07-4053 1952) uses VJN as a call sign and its primary channel is 5145kHz, with 7465kHz as the secondary one. The primary channel is monitored 9am to 9.15am Monday to Friday and the secondary channel between 9.15am and 9.30am Monday to Friday. For emergencies press the emergency call button, which is monitored 24 hours a day.

Road Reports Local police can be helpful with the most recent information on road conditions. Contact the following police stations: Coen (☎ 07-4060 1150); Weipa (☎ 07-4069 9119); Lockhart River Aboriginal community (☎ 07-4060 7120); and Bamaga (☎ 07-4069 3156).

Permits Permits are not required for travelling to Cape York via the main routes described. However, you need a permit to camp on Aboriginal land, which is nearly all the land north of the Dulhunty River. The Injinoo people are the traditional custodians of much of this land, along with other Aboriginal communities at Umagico and New Mapoon.

Please respect the signs and bylaws of the community councils. Contact the Injinoo Community Council (☎ 07-4069 3252, fax 4069 3253) for information about permits. At the top of the peninsula it's best to stay at the official camping grounds at Seisia, Punsand Bay, Loyalty Beach, Umagico and Pajinka.

In Weipa many roads and areas are off-limits to tourists because of mining operations. Permits are also required for camping along the beach south and north of the town. See Facilities later in this section for details.

Books & Maps See Books & Maps in the earlier Cairns to Musgrave via Cooktown section.

The Last Frontier: Cape York Wilderness, written and published by Glenville Pike, covers the history of the region well. The best book on the Palmer River goldfields is *River of Gold* by Hector Holthouse.

Percy Trezise has written three books on the Aboriginal rock art in the Laura area – *Quinkan Country*, *Last Day of a Wilderness* and *Rock Art of South-East Cape York* (published by the Australian Institute of Aboriginal & Torres Strait Islander Studies) which has excellent drawings of all the major paintings and is available in the reference section of the Cairns library.

A Wilderness in Bloom, written and published by B & B Hinton, is a good introduction to the flowers of the region. A book on Australian birds is a sensible idea as you will see and hear lots of them.

Emergencies There are hospitals in Cairns (☎ 07-4050 6333), Cooktown (☎ 07-4069 5433), Bamaga (☎ 07-4069 3166) and Thursday Island (☎ 07-4069 1109). Clinics exist in smaller centres and the Flying Doctor can get to the nearest airstrip.

If you need a tow, try Lakeland RACQ (☎ 07-4060 2133), Cape York Auto (☎ 07-4069 5233) in Cooktown, Weipa Towing (☎ 07-4069 7277) or Top End Motors (☎ 07-4069 3182) in Seisia. Expect to pay $66/hr or more. A good samaritan would be cheaper.

Special Preparations

Banking facilities are very limited on Cape York and ATMs are only available in Cooktown and Thursday Island. However, the good news is that major credit cards and Eftpos are widely accepted, even in the remotest places. One option is to have a passbook account with the Commonwealth Bank, which allows you to withdraw cash at any post office. Whatever you do, you still need to take plenty of cash.

Public telephones are available in the most surprising places, including Moreton Telegraph Station and Portland Roads.

Fuel Diesel, unleaded and super are generally readily available in the Cape, but it's 400km from the Archer River Roadhouse to Seisia via the bypass roads, without allowing for any detours or wrong turnings.

Weipa and Seisia have fuel and Bamaga should have it soon. The Jardine River Ferry usually has fuel but it isn't guaranteed. Lockhart River has fuel, but not always on Saturday and Sunday or in the afternoon Monday to Friday. Remote outlets charge a premium, which is fair enough as sales are low and transport costs high.

Fuel prices are highest in Seisia (37% above Cairns prices), followed by the Archer River, Hann River and Musgrave Roadhouses and Coen (22% above Cairns prices).

Camping Pickers Geo Camping & Canvas (☎ 07-4051 1944), at 108 Mulgrave Rd, Parramatta Park, has a range of camping equipment for hire. Adventure Equipment

Hire (☎ 07-4031 2669, fax 4031 1384, e service@adventurequip.com.au), at 133 Grafton St, Cairns, hires out all you need for hiking and camping, as well as kayaks and canoes.

THE ROUTE

NOTE: The map that covers the first part of this route is in the previous Cairns to Musgrave via Cooktown section.

Cairns to Lakeland (244km)

The journey is bitumen all the way. It heads out over the **Atherton Tableland**, west of Cairns, and most travel via Kuranda and Mareeba. This is a scenic drive up and over the Great Dividing Range, but be careful as impatient drivers and short overtaking lanes cause a number of accidents every year.

About 9km past Mareeba, in Biboohra, a left turn takes you to **Mareeba Wetlands**, which has a modern visitor centre (☎ 07-4093 2514), canoe and boat trips, and walks around lily-covered lagoons that attract thousands of birds. The staff are enthusiastic and volunteers are always welcome.

Back on the main road it's 33km to the small township of **Mt Molloy** which has cheap camping and real Mexican food. Another 30km brings you to **Mt Carbine**, which has cheap fuel. See the Facilities section for more details.

The road then climbs through the Desailly Range to **Bob's Lookout**, which offers good views and a photo opportunity. The vegetation is typical of what you will see for most of the trip. Forget deep, dark, impenetrable rainforest. Sure, you will see that at the Iron Range National Park, the Lockerbie Scrub and along the banks of major rivers. But for the most part, the open forests are dominated by stringy-barks, ironbarks, bloodwoods and other species of eucalypt.

From Bob's Lookout the road continues to wind through hilly country before the turn-off to the left, which goes to the **Palmer Goldfields Reserve** and Maytown.

For travellers with a little time, an excursion to **Maytown** is an interesting adjunct to a trip up the cape. Contact the ranger at Chillagoe (☎ 07-4094 7163, fax 4094 7213)

for a camping permit, information, maps and current track details. There are no tourist facilities or buildings to see there except a reconstructed miner's hut. The last family left in 1949; lone prospector Sam Elliot was the last person to live there.

The road is a challenge even in a 4WD, but there is a sense of history and the ghosts of the thousands of miners who came from all over the world to work in this remote district.

Back on the main road, the **Palmer River Roadhouse** is 12km further on from the Maytown turn-off and the artworks and small Palmer River goldfield museum (free admission) make it a worthwhile place to stop.

Another 32km brings you to **Lakeland**, a small rural hamlet with the usual facilities. The surrounding area produces crops such as papaya, watermelons, sorghum and peanuts.

Lakeland to Musgrave Roadhouse (202km)

A formed dirt road that is corrugated and stony in places takes you 50km north of Lakeland to the turn-off to the **Split Rock and Guguyaangi galleries**. See the boxed text 'Quinkan Art'.

Just 12km further on is **Laura** with a cafe and fuel on your right and the Quinkan Information Centre, which is often closed, on your left. Nearby is a camping ground and swimming pool. You must turn right beyond these for the Quinkan Hotel, which also has camping, and the general store and post office, which sells fuel.

The **Jowalbinna** and **Deighton River Bush Camps** offer camping and accommodation off the beaten track with guided tours of more rock art sites. The Brady Creek circuit is 3km long and encompasses 10 sites. Jowalbinna is a good place, with swimming in river pools and a walk up Frogs Hill past the bowerbird nests. See Facilities later in this section.

The Laura Dance & Cultural Festival is held 15km south of the township in June of odd-numbered years. It attracts thousands of visitors over three days, bringing together 25 communities of Aborigines and Torres Strait Islanders from Cape York Peninsula and the Gulf.

Locals from the surrounding cattle stations show off their skills and let down their hair at the rodeo and horse races, held the first weekend in July. People come from near and far to socialise and enjoy the entertainment.

Just past Laura, the Peninsula Developmental Rd to the right goes to Lakefield National Park and Cooktown, while the track on the left goes to the Jowalbinna Bush Camp. Carry straight on for Cape York: the road continues to be well-formed dirt but rough in places. Most creek crossings are dry by August, but a few – one just north of Laura, or the Little Laura or Kennedy Rivers – have water and make a good place to bush camp. The **Hann River Roadhouse**, 75km north of Laura, has food, fuel and camp sites.

From the roadhouse it is 19km to the turn-off to **Mary Valley** station, where camping and units are available down a 6km track. Nearby lagoons attract birds and freshwater crocodiles, and the station is also home to literally millions of little red flying foxes. During the day they roost together in the trees, but these noisy and restless creatures are always scratching and fanning themselves, squabbling with their neighbours, and are constantly on the move seeking the perfect twig to hang from. In the evening they all fly off in a big black cloud to search for food.

Back on the main road it is 43km to **Musgrave Roadhouse**, built on the site of one of the fortified telegraph stations. It provides fuel, meals, a bar, camp sites and accommodation. From here roads run east to the northern section of Lakefield National Park and west to Edward River and the Pormpuraaw Aboriginal community (camping permit required).

Musgrave Roadhouse to Moreton Telegraph Station (300km)

This section of road is usually maintained in a reasonable state, but there are always some corrugations, rough sections and dips,

Quinkan Art

Quinkan art is one of the great art styles of northern Australia. Vastly different to the x-ray art of Arnhem Land in the Northern Territory, or the Wandjina art of the Kimberley in Western Australia, Quinkan art gets its name from the human-shaped spirit figures with unusually shaped heads. The tall skinny ones are said to be 'good' spirits, while the squat ones with knobbly knees, arms and other parts are 'bad'.

Much study on the sites has been done since 1960 by Percy Trezise, and over 1200 rock art galleries have been discovered. All of these are around the settlement of Laura, in the escarpment country that surrounds the lowlands along the great rivers of Lakefield National Park.

This great body of art, some pre-historic, is testimony to the Aborigines who once lived in the region. When the Palmer River gold rush began in 1873, the Aborigines fought to defend their land against the well-armed invaders. Those who survived the bullets succumbed to disease, and the few remaining Aboriginal people became fringe dwellers on the outskirts of settlements, missions and cattle stations.

The rock art galleries contain many fine paintings of kangaroos, dingoes, wallabies, emus, brush turkeys, crocodiles, turtles, fish, snakes and flying foxes – in fact, all the wildlife and bush tucker that can still be seen along the rivers and plains today.

Spiritual figures, guardians and ancestral beings also point to a lifestyle that was rich in culture and religious beliefs. Numerous paintings of naked male and female human figures could be connected to fertility or love magic, while the upside down figures might be attempts at sorcery. Other figures seem to be dancing.

The Split Rock and Guguyaangi galleries are open to the public for a small donation. South of Laura and close to the main road, they are readily accessible with a walking track joining the two. It is a hot, steep, 20-minute climb up to the three Split Rock Galleries, so you might as well carry on and walk along the top of the escarpment and enjoy the panoramic views from the Turtle Rock lookout before looking round the Guguyaangi Galleries. The total loop takes two to three hours depending on how much time you spend looking at the rock paintings. Carry plenty of water and at least a snack.

---

so drive carefully. Some sandy stretches look like snow, but there is nothing much to see except the occasional wallaby or emu and a few hills.

About 80km north of Musgrave Roadhouse, a turn-off to the right crosses the Stewart River twice before reaching Coen. The first crossing makes a fine camp site with little traffic. The old road also leads to **Port Stewart**, on the eastern coast, which has good fishing (especially if you have a small boat).

Coen is the 'capital' of the Cape, with a shop, cafe, post office that also offers camping, pub with accommodation, guest house, two fuel outlets, clinic, ranger's office and car repair and towing service. Unless you take the turn-off to Weipa, it is the biggest town you will see north of Cooktown.

People have some funny times in this place, all of course in and around the pub, the social heart of any country town.

According to the locals the main road to Cairns has been improved so much in the past 15 years that the travel time has been halved. Think about that before complaining about the present-day road.

Just 2km north of Coen on the right is a pleasant camping and picnic spot near the Coen River where pit toilets are provided. This strip of bitumen continues for another 20km to the **Quarantine Station**. Since the authorities are worried about agricultural pests coming down the Cape rather than going up, travelling north is no problem.

Three kilometres from here is the turn-off on the left to **Mungkan Kaanju National Park** (☎ 07-4060 3256), which consists of

Quinkan Art

The first Split Rock gallery is an impressive array of art that is part Hieronymus Bosch and part Pablo Picasso. There is an evil frog-like spirit with knobbly knees, elbows and a large knobbly penis, an emu on its side, a turtle and other paintings in yellow, mauve, white and orange colours. The second gallery has lots of flying foxes, an important food. The third gallery is quite different and is viewed by some as a religious site. Tall Quinkans are painted on the rock, and look like elongated shadows.

There are a number of overhangs in the Split Rock group of galleries, and while Split Rock itself is the most visually stunning, within 100m there are smaller galleries containing flying foxes, tall Quinkans and hand stencils.

From this point the trail wanders through the open forest of the plateau for 1km to the Guguyaangi group of galleries. The views here are, once again, spectacular. If you are going to do this walk, save it for the late afternoon or early morning as it can get quite warm wandering across the plateau at midday. Take some water and food and enjoy the art and solitude of this place. The Guguyaangi group consists of over a dozen overhangs that are adorned with a vast array of figures, animals and implements, and are possibly the best of the lot.

The Giant Horse galleries, across the road from the Split Rock and Guguyaangi sites, are a little harder to see and consist of five shelters depicting many animals, including a number of horses. These galleries can only be visited with a guide from the local community, and pre-arrangement with a ranger is essential.

Percy Trezise and his sons, Steve and Matt, have established a wilderness reserve at Jowalbinna. The Jowalbinna Bush Camp and Deighton River Bush Camp are open to travellers and offer guided walking trips to the many marvellous galleries in the nearby area.

For more information on the Quinkan art around Laura, contact the Ang-Gnarra Aboriginal Corporation (☎ 07-4060 3214, fax 4060 3231). Self-guided tours of Split Rock are $5; $10 allows you access to the Guguyaangi gallery as well. Maps and brochures for self-guided walks around the art sites are obtainable from the information centre (if it is open) which is beside the caravan park in Laura.

two large separate areas that straddle much of the Archer River and its tributaries.

The Rokeby section has good bush camping on a number of lagoons and along the banks of the Archer River. Access to the more remote Archer Bend section of this park is only by rarely given permit. No facilities are provided and the ranger station is 70km away.

The **Archer River Roadhouse** is 65km north of Coen and provides food, drinks, fuel, accommodation and camping. The reward for crossing all those corrugations is an Archer burger, but you need crocodile jaws to eat it.

Just down the hill from the roadhouse is the **Archer River**. During the Dry it's a pleasant stream bordered by a wide, tree-lined, sandy bed and an ideal spot to camp.

As with many of the permanent streams on the Cape, the banks are lined with varieties of paperbarks, or melaleucas. Growing to more than 40m, they offer shade for passing travellers and, when in flower, food for hordes of birds and flying foxes that love the sweet-smelling nectar.

The Archer River crossing used to be a real terror, but now a bumpy causeway makes it easy to cross in the Dry. The road north of the Archer and all the way to Weipa is normally in reasonable condition.

Turn right 38km north of the Archer River to visit the **Iron Range National Park**, Chilli Beach, the Lockhart River Aboriginal Community and Portland Roads. See the Detours section later in this chapter.

Fifteen kilometres from this turn-off, the main road swings west to Weipa, so turn

THE TROPICS

right for the Overland Telegraph Line Track which heads north to Cape York.

Just before the **Batavia Downs** Station airstrip, a left turn marks the second turn-off to Weipa, 48km north of the first one. Two kilometres further on is the turn-off for Frenchmans Rd, which leads to Iron Range National Park. The Pascoe River crossing on this route is not safe until at least late August, so travelling this way is not recommended.

The final 22km to the **Wenlock River** is a reasonable stretch of road nowadays, and the new, $800,000 causeway has tamed the once fearsome river. **Moreton Telegraph Station** is on the far bank, but nothing remains of the original building except a concrete slab. It has very limited stores, a solar-powered public telephone and offers accommodation and camping. Hiking along a track and fishing in river pools are also possible here.

Moreton Telegraph Station to the Jardine River Ferry (180km)

This section is the best part of the trip, with some great creek crossings and excellent camp sites. Take your time and enjoy all the delights the Cape has to offer.

The challenge of following the rough track along the historic Overland Telegraph Line means that the trip will take at least a very long day, even if all goes well. There are many small diversions from the original route, especially where there is a creek or river to cross. Even in the Dry most major creek crossings have water in them; however, it's not the water that is the major problem but the steep banks on each side. Take care. Washaways demand you keep your speed down.

Among the scattered timber and blanket of grass you can see cycad palms, in places forming dense stands.

The turn-off to **Bramwell** station is 28km north of the Wenlock River. Camping and accommodation is available down a rough track, 10 km from the road.

The private road west (passing through Bertiehaugh station,) that goes to Weipa via Stones Crossing, is closed to the public these days.

The creeks or the corrugations – that is your choice 40km north of the Wenlock River. Crossing the creeks along the Overland Telegraph Line Track is shorter and more fun, but team up with someone with a winch just in case you get bogged. Also read the small print on your insurance policy, especially if you are driving a hired vehicle – you may not be covered on this track and are probably not insured for water damage.

Turn right if you want to follow the Southern Bypass Rd, which avoids the creek crossings. It starts off in reasonable condition but soon deteriorates into bad corrugations and deep sandy patches. Drivers go too fast, especially in the rainforest section where blind corners are a hazard.

A turn-off left, 58km from the start of the bypass, goes to the **Heathlands** ranger station (☎ 07-4060 3241, fax 4060 3314), which is 14km away. A turn-off to Captain Billy Landing on the coast is 11km beyond the turn-off for the ranger station. Another 45km from the Captain Billy Landing turn-off, you rejoin the track, 14km north of Cockatoo Creek. It's usually a relief to come to the end of this corrugated road.

For those who decide not to take the Southern Bypass Rd, Palm Creek is your first challenge, 40km north of the Wenlock. This is followed by Ducie, South Alice and North Alice Creeks, before you reach the **Dulhunty River**, 30km north of Palm Creek. The Dulhunty is a popular spot to camp and there are some lovely places to swim.

One more creek crossing and, 3km north of the Dulhunty River, a track on the right goes to the Heathlands ranger station. Use this road to bypass the notorious **Gunshot Creek**. This crossing, 15km north of the Dulhunty River, is the most daunting, although the banks are not quite as scary as they used to be thanks to some bulldozer work. There is a pleasant spot to camp on the far side of Gunshot.

Two kilometres north of the Gunshot crossing another track heads east to the Heathlands ranger station. The vegetation changes again: it is no longer dominated by straggly eucalypts such as ironbarks and bloodwoods, instead the country is covered

Walking to the Top

Many of the early explorers walked to the top of Cape York Peninsula, as did most of the pioneers who followed, searching for gold and rich grazing land. In more recent times, those who 'humped the bluey' are few and far between.

In August 1930, John Carlyon began his walk down the eastern seaboard, a couple of years after Hector Macquarie had made history by being the first to drive and push a car – a small Austin – to Cape York. It was not an easy trip – he had to raft the car over the Jardine River, and north of the Jardine he suffered 15 punctures in two days.

In the early 1950s Alex Sklenica and a couple of mates walked from Cairns to Cooktown and on to the Top where they joined the mail boat to travel around Torres Strait.

Sklenica was later to write about the trip:

'Cooktown, once a prosperous town with thousands of people and 60 pubs as we were told, was nearly a ghost town now.

A diesel, pulling two cars, maintained a once weekly rail service to Laura. Stockmen and prospectors using the train added to this romantic outback setting. Camping a few days on the Laura River, we shot a few wallabies to prepare jerky and pemmican for the long walk still ahead of us.

Further on the track we met Norman Fisher who offered to take us on his 4WD truck for $5 to Coen. We shared the top of the load with four prospectors who hoped to find a 'pocket' of gold nuggets in creeks around the Wenlock area.

Our travel was reduced sometimes to two miles per hour. We helped to fill holes, cut fallen trees and made a log causeway to enable the 4WD truck to cross the 70 yard wide sandy bed of the Stewart River…

…Supplies diminishing. Walking, we chewed tips of Yakka tree blades, and sticks of dried wallaby meat.

The track along the telegraph line path worsened, the uncut vegetation reaching nearly the wires. Our mainly meat diet lacked sustenance. We craved for carbohydrates, fruit and the kind of vegetables we were used to.

On 15 September, our remaining supplies consisted of half a pound of flour, three-quarters pound of tea, half a pound sugar, 1 spoon of cocoa and 4 spoons of salt.

Arriving at the Jardine River, we saw a small dinghy pulled up on the opposite shore. Nick, the best swimmer among us, brought the dinghy to our side while with Lad we stood guard with rifles. Gear loaded in the small dinghy, we swam across, holding onto the gunnels with one hand.

Later, Mr Cupitt from the Cape York telegraph station told us that he shot recently 14 crocodiles on the spot where we swam the river.'

In May 1987 Ian Brown and a couple of friends walked from Coen along much of the Great Dividing Range and the east coast to arrive at the Top 56 days later.

In September of that same year Barry Higgins and Steve Tremont began a trek in western Victoria that was to take them 15 months.

In June 1988 Peter Treseder walked and ran from the northernmost tip of Australia to Wilsons Promontory in Victoria. How long did this take him? He did it in an incredible 41 days – totally alone and unsupported. While those before him had taken to the coast and untracked wilderness of the range country, Peter had to average 134km a day, and to do that he stayed on the Overland Telegraph Track between Cape York and Musgrave. From there he went through Lakefield National Park to Cooktown and south through the Daintree and 50 other national parks, before finishing at mainland Australia's southernmost tip.

in heathland. Take a close look and you'll be surprised at the flowers you can find. The open plains are dominated by grevilleas, hibbertias and small melaleucas, to name just a few, while the creek banks and wetter areas are clothed in banksias and baeckeas.

One of the plants that observant nature lovers will spot is the pitcher plant. These are found along the banks of the narrow creeks, Gunshot Creek being a prime spot for them. These carnivorous plants trap insects in the liquid at the bottom of a 'pitcher', where their nutrients are absorbed. It is a unique adaptation to living in rocky areas that are poor in nutrients.

After the Gunshot Creek crossing the track is sandy until the **Cockatoo Creek** crossing, 89km north of the Wenlock River. Once again the actual river bed is no drama – although it is rocky and rough – it is the banks that are the problem. In this case it is the northern bank, which often has a long haul of soft sand.

For the next 23km the road improves slightly. A couple more creek crossings follow and, 14km past Cockatoo Creek, the Southern Bypass Rd rejoins the Overland Telegraph Line Track. Just 9km further on, the second major bypass, the Northern Bypass Rd, heads west away from the Telegraph Track to the ferry that crosses the Jardine River.

If you plan to take the Northern Bypass Rd, consider a quick detour to **Fruit Bat Falls**, just after the turn-off for the Northern Bypass Rd. The falls are only 2.6km away along a winding sandy track, to the right of the main track. It's a beautiful spot for a picnic or swim, and there are pitcher plants on your right as you step onto the boardwalk. Camping is not allowed but there is a pit toilet.

Drive back down along the Overland Telegraph Line Track and turn right at the Northern Bypass Rd, which heads west. For 55km shake, rattle and roll along another badly corrugated road through tropical savannah woodland to the Jardine River ferry. At least this bypass is shorter than the southern one. At the 18km and 30km marks, tracks join the bypass from the main track.

If you decide not to take the Northern Bypass Rd, the turn-off to **Indian Head Falls** and **Twin Falls** is 6.5km north of the turn-off to Fruit Bat Falls. Drive down the falls track for less than 2km to an excellent camping ground. On one side is Canal Creek and the delightful Twin Falls, while on the other is the wider Eliot Creek and Indian Head Falls, which drop into a small, sheer-sided ravine.

Pit toilets and showers are set up within the camping ground and the Heathlands ranger keeps the place in good condition – with your help. This is the most popular camping spot on the trip north, and although it can be crowded, it's still very enjoyable. A camping permit is required and a fee of $3.85 per person is charged. Contact Heathlands ranger station (☎ 07-4060 3241, fax 4060 3314) for a permit.

Spend some time here swimming and lazing in the creeks between lunch and dinner. If you have a mask and snorkel, the water is clear enough for a paddle and there are fish and turtles to see. Walk around and enjoy some bird-watching.

Back on the Overland Telegraph Line Track, the next 10km crosses the Canal, Sam, Mistake, Cannibal and Cypress Creeks. All offer their own sweet challenge. Just south of **Mistake Creek** a track heads west to join up with the Northern Bypass Rd, which leads to the ferry across the Jardine River. If you are having fun crossing the creeks, keep driving north at this point, but if you have had enough, it may pay to take the track out to the Northern Bypass Rd and the ferry.

From Cypress Creek it's nearly 8km to **Logan Creek**. From here the road is badly chopped up and often flooded in places. You are now passing through the heart of an area the early pioneers called the 'Wet Desert' because of the combination of an abundance of water but lack of stock feed.

Bridge Creek, or Nolan's Brook, 5.5km further on, once had a bridge, and when you get to it you will know why. It's a challenge to cross, and though short it does demand a lot of care. Less than 2km north of here the last track to the bypass heads west. Turn left unless you want to visit the southern side of the Jardine River first and then come back down here to get to the bypass road and the Jardine River ferry.

A deep creek has to be crossed before you reach the Jardine River, which has some magical camping spots along its southern bank, west of the vehicle ford. There are no facilities here, and because you are in a national park a camping permit is required from the ranger at Heathlands station.

The river is wide and sandy. If you want to swim, stick to the shallows where the sandbars are wide. Crocodiles do not like such open territory but may be lurking in the deep, dark, lily-covered holes that line sections of the river. Remember, the Jardine River is inhabited by estuarine crocodiles, and although you might not be able to see them they are definitely there. In December 1993 a man was killed by a crocodile while he was swimming to the ferry at the ferry crossing.

Fishing upstream is not allowed because you are in a national park. Downstream from this point there is no problem and at times the fishing can be good, although closer to the mouth it is better.

From here you have to take the road back down to the turn-off to the bypass road and the **Jardine River ferry**. The Far North welcomes you with tricky creek crossings, badly corrugated roads and a 'Land Access and Ferry Charge' of $88. This payment entitles you to a return ticket on the one-minute ferry crossing and a booklet. The chain ferry operates from 8am to 5pm every day from April to September. There is a fuel outlet on the southern bank with a camping ground behind it, but fuel is not always available.

North of the Jardine River Ferry

The roads to the Top are not very good but at least they are in better condition than the bypass roads, and by now you should at least be getting used to corrugations.

The road follows the Jardine River east to the old ford crossing, 10km from the ferry crossing. At the junction 22km north of the old ford, turn right. Left goes to the coast and the old wartime port of Mutee Heads.

Just 7km further on there is a small car park beside a fenced area that encloses an

plane wreck. Dating back to WWII, these are the remains of a DC-3, and while this is the easiest plane wreck to see in the area there are a few more scattered around the main airport, just a short distance away.

A couple of hundred metres past the car park there is a T-junction. Right leads to the main airport, while left leads to Bamaga.

Less than 5km from the T-junction, a signposted road heads off to the right leading to Cape York, Somerset and places close to the tip of the peninsula. This is the road you will require, but most travellers need fuel and other supplies, and so continue straight ahead to Bamaga and Seisia.

Bamaga is the largest community on the northern Cape and is a sprawling place with a resort, hospital, police station, supermarket and pub with a bottle shop that also serves chicken and chips. There is, however, no camping ground.

The Torres Strait Islander settlement of **Seisia**, 5km along a bitumen road north-west of Bamaga, is the perfect place for the weary traveller to relax after a long journey. There's an excellent camping ground with great sunset views on the beach front, among the coconut trees. It has useful kitchen huts, a restaurant, takeaway, shop and lots of information. Nearby is a good supermarket, fuel outlet, car mechanic and gas refill outlet.

The camping ground is also near the **wharf**, which is a top spot for fishing. In the evening watch the locals line fishing. The water is teeming with fish, and they have to be reeled in quickly before the sharks get to them. Catching dinner is almost guaranteed here – mackerel, jewfish, trevally, and barramundi abound. Notice the large black frigate birds bullying the smaller birds and stealing their food.

The wharf is also one of the places where you can board a ferry to Thursday Island – other ferries (same company, same price) leave from Pajinka Wilderness Lodge and Punsand Bay.

Seisia was established in 1949 by Mugai Elu (1910–90) and his family who came here from the Torres Strait Island of Saibai. Their home island was often short of fresh water. Mugai, the second son of a family of 13, was a trochus and pearl shell diver and lugger captain. Like many other island men he served in the armed forces in WWII. The name Seisia is made up of the initials of his father and brothers and there is a memorial to him outside the school. If you are in Seisia on a Sunday you can join the local church service.

A few kilometres north of Seisia is *Loyalty Beach Campground & Fishing Lodge*, located on land owned by **New Mapoon Village**. The lodge does fishing tours and the village has a fishing gear shop.

The village of **Umagico** was settled by Aboriginal people from the Lockhart River and is 4km west of Bamaga. It has accommodation and a camping ground on the beach and an unusual corrugated iron church that's unfortunately becoming derelict. There's a supermarket, fuel outlet and a pub, the Alau Hotel.

Injinoo, another 3km beyond Umagico, is where the traditional landowners of the whole peninsula area are based. Contact the Injinoo Community Council (☎ 07-4069 3252, fax 4069 3253) for bush camping permits.

To go to the tip of the cape, turn left 1km past Bamaga onto a well-formed but not well-maintained dirt road. After 16km you reach **Croc Tent** which sells souvenirs and refreshments. You should turn left here for the 11km drive to Punsand Bay.

Carry straight on at the Croc Tent and you soon enter the oddly-named **Lockerbie Scrub**, a small rainforest that is 25km long and from one to five kilometres wide. Be careful on the blind corners as the narrow road winds through the jungle.

Seven kilometres from the Croc Tent there is a fork. Turning right takes you down an 11km eroded track to the picturesque beach at **Somerset**, where the Jardines used to live (see the earlier boxed text 'The Legend of Frank Jardine'). Unfortunately, nothing much remains except a couple of graves and a monument. Fork left to continue to the Tip, and 3km further on is a small car park. Stop here and you can take a short **rainforest walk** (see the boxed text on the Lockerbie Scrub). From here it is another 7km to **Pajinka Wilderness Lodge**.

The Lockerbie Scrub

The Lockerbie Scrub is an important 100 sq km rainforest, despite being poorly named. It's regularly used as a stopover by migratory birds, and is home to some unique animals and insects. Surprisingly, it has been studied for some time, beginning with naturalists who visited the Jardine family at Somerset and their 'summer residence' at Lockerbie.

Vines and other climbing plants are common in this forest, while hickory ash, paperbark satin ash and cypress pines were the trees that first established a small logging industry. Probably the most spectacular tree is the fig tree, with its large, buttress-typeroots. Palms and ferns of all sorts can be commonly found right through the forest, including some huge bird's-nest ferns.

There's a short self-guided walk that starts opposite a small car park on the road to Pajinka Wilderness Lodge and the Tip, 3km north of the fork to Somerset and 7km before the lodge. Put on insect repellent before you start. Walking here is really enjoyable, and the thick canopy overhead keeps the area nice and cool. There is evidence that animals have been rooting around in the leaves and mulch that cover the forest floor. Sadly much of this is due to the feral pigs that infest the area, causing untold damage. The cane toad has also arrived, just to make matters worse.

Blue quandongs and blackfruit (which look like blueberries) are among the rainforest bush tucker along the path. There's a dome-shaped mound made by a male orange-footed scrub fowl. The male incubates the eggs in the mound, which is surprisingly large – at least 3m high. He regulates the temperature inside the mound by adding or taking away material and uses the same mound year after year.

Park by the camping ground and walk to the kiosk, but put on insect repellent before walking along the boardwalk through a patch of rainforest. Not far along is **Frangipani Beach**, a beautiful sandy bay that stretches away into the distance.

A scattering of mangroves line part of the beach, as they do most beaches on the cape, and sometimes it's almost imperceptible as to where the forest ends and the mangroves begin. Walk up the rocky cliffs and you can see the islands of the Torres Strait dotting the turquoise sea all the way to the island of New Guinea, just over the horizon.

Walking for 20 minutes brings you to the **tip of Australia**, a rocky headland with strong sea current. A much-photographed sign states that you have reached the northern-most point of Australia. Congratulations!

DETOURS
Iron Range National Park

Turn right off the Overland Telegraph Line Track, 38km north of the Archer River, for this interesting detour. Don't be fooled by the first few kilometres of road – which are excellent – it soon becomes narrow and rough with numerous creek crossings, all of which should be shallow or dry by June. At least the corrugations are not as bad as on the other roads. In fact, it's a slow but pleasant drive, with some of Cape York's best scenery towards the end.

The road crosses the Wenlock River 17km from the turn-off. Turn left at the top of the far bank and 2km later you reach the deserted **Wenlock (Batavia) Goldfield**. There's a rusting steam engine, a crushing mill and many old relics lying around the silent and deserted property.

Head back to the road and it's 70km to the start of the 346 sq km **Iron Range National Park**. This is a picturesque area with forested hills and a lookout across to Mt Tozer (543m). Beyond the lookout, the rainforest closes in with large trees festooned with creepers on both sides of the road. This is the reward for the hard travelling and it's well worth it.

This unusual rainforest has more in common with the island of New Guinea than Australia. Forget what you have heard about the Daintree, this place is better and wilder, with unique animals and plants: the rare and vivid eclectus parrot, the palm cockatoo and fawn-breasted bowerbird, the small red-bellied pitta and giant cassowary are just

some of the birds of the forest. Some 10% of Australia's butterflies also live in the park, including 25 species found no further south – the park being their stronghold.

Local mammals include the striped possum, the spotted and southern common cuscus (type of possum), and the spiny-haired bandicoot – all are confined to the rainforest habitats of Cape York and New Guinea. Another is the northern quoll, or native cat, which sometimes wanders into camps looking for food. If you are lucky enough to see one you will not forget the encounter – they are beautiful!

Eleven kilometres from the Mt Tozer lookout is a fork in the road. Turn right for the **ranger's station** (☎ 07-4060 7170), 3km away, where you pay for camping permits ($3.85 per person) and obtain information. Another 8km further along this road is the **Lockhart River** Aboriginal community, with its store, fuel and a health centre. Fork left back past the ranger station for the rainforest camping grounds, Chilli Beach and Portland Rds, which are close together but not much more than cleared areas. There aren't any facilities, though the Rainforest ground has a hiking trail. Expect to get your feet wet and look out for the very rare eclectus parrot, which often nests by the car park at the end of the track. The camping ground at Cook's Hut is next to an old miner's hut, and Gordon's Creek is near some old mine workings – where you can see an old stamper that's almost covered by vegetation. At one time, 45 miners worked there.

The famous **Chilli Beach** is another 35km on from here, but the road deteriorates, with lots of erosion channels and pot-holes making progress even slower. Facilities include two deluxe pit toilets and a well with an ancient hand pump that produces brownish water. It's generally either windy or very windy, but at least the mosquitoes get blown away. Coconut palms line the delightful sandy beach and it could be paradise – just turn a blind eye to all the plastic rubbish washed onto the beach from the sea.

Leaving Chilli Beach, turn right after 5km, and 6km later is the welcome sign to **Portland Rds**, a tiny community on a tiny

THE TROPICS

sandy cove surrounded by mangroves and fishing boats moored offshore. Accommodation is available but camping is not allowed. There are two public phones but no other facilities for travellers. Check out the notice board on the beach – someone might be selling fish or offering haircuts.

Weipa via the Peninsula Developmental Rd (145km)

Heading north along the Peninsula Developmental Rd, continue as it swings left, 53km north of the Archer River. The road is usually well maintained for the 145km to Weipa.

Around 3500 people live in this strange community with 'Keep Out' and 'Restricted Access' signs everywhere. Comalco's huge bauxite mine (bauxite is the raw material for aluminium) pays for everything: Comalco is both Big Brother and Sugar Daddy. There's a mine tour but it costs $19 and if there aren't enough people to make it profitable the company cancels.

The town has a hospital, a large supermarket, lots of takeaways and shops, and enough sports facilities to host the Olympic Games. Weipa has an obsession with lawn, so there are water sprinklers everywhere. There's a nature trail that no-one seems to use while the pub has 15 TV screens in the bar, which doubles as a gambling den. The town has an excellent library (with Internet service), a good camping ground by the sea, and two motels. There are three gun clubs and numerous cars with 'I have a gun and I vote' stickers on them.

Weipa via the Batavia Downs Road (113km)

This is a popular short cut to take if you are going to Weipa from the north. Twenty-four kilometres south of the Moreton Telegraph Station, turn right along the unsignposted road that runs beside the airstrip. Go past Batavia Downs homestead and through the barbed wire gate. The 42km track has some

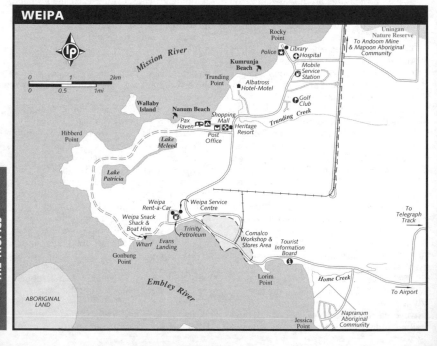

THE TROPICS

bad corrugations and a few creek crossings that can be difficult early in the Dry. Turn right on reaching the Peninsula Rd.

If you are coming from Weipa and heading north, turn left at the Batavia Downs sign, 71km from Weipa near Sudley station.

ORGANISED TOURS
Seisia
John Charlton (☎ *07-4069 3302*) runs one-day fishing or snorkelling tours for $99. *Ocean Gem* (☎ *07-4069 3900,* e *greg@ seafaris.com.au,* w *www.fishcapeyork.com)* and *Gary Wright's Sportfishing* (☎ *07-4069 3400, fax 4069 3155)* are other options.

Weipa
There's a 1½ hour tour of Comalco's Bauxite Mine for $19 but tours may not go every day. Book at the *Pax Haven Camping Ground* (☎ *07-4069 7871, fax 4069 8211)*. River, estuary and sea fishing trips can also be booked there. A full day of reef fishing costs $165 and a sunset buffet dinner cruise is $60.

Queensland Aviation Services (☎ *07-4069 9433)* do $250 scenic flights (25 minutes) for up to five people. Hiring your own boat is possible at *Evans Landing Wharf* (☎ *07-4069 7495)*.

Laura
Jowalbinna & Deighton River Bush Camps (☎ *07-4060 3236)* offer guided tours of Quinkan rock-art sites.

Contact the *Ang-Gnarra Aboriginal Corporation* (☎ *07-4090 3200)* for guided tours of Split Rock and other rock art sites.

FACILITIES
Mareeba
Mareeba Wetlands (☎ *07-4093 2514, 8km off the main road; adults $8; open 8.30am-4pm daily in the Dry but ring for opening times in the Wet)* At present camping is not allowed, but will be in the future. Twelve hectares of water spread over seven man-made lagoons that attract thousands of birds. Two-seater canoes can be hired for $11/hr and boat trips are $7 per person. It's run by a nonprofit organisation that always needs volunteers.

Mt Molloy
There is a pub, shops and a cafe that serves genuine Mexican food. One kilometre north of town is a *camping ground* which costs only $2 per vehicle. The amenities block is good but only has cold showers. *Mt Molloy Car Repair & Towing Service* (☎ *07-4094 1260)* is the RACQ agent.

Mt Carbine
Mt Carbine Village and Caravan Park (☎*/fax 07-4094 3160,* e *mtcarbinevill age@ledanet.com.au,* w *www.ledanet.com .au/~mtcarbine village/)*. Double unpowered/powered sites $13/15, double air-con units $45/50. Stay where the former mine workers lived. It's a ghost town that's been recycled into a place for tourists with its own tennis and basketball courts.

Mt Carbine Hotel-Motel (☎ *07-4094 3108, fax 4094 3180)* Single/double motel rooms $30/55. This is a typical outback pub that provides the usual fare.

Mt Carbine Roadhouse (☎ *07-4094 3043, fax 4094 3104)* Single/double budget air-con dongas $15/25. This roadhouse is open seven days a week and has meals, snacks, a small store and cheap fuel.

Palmer River
The *Palmer River Roadhouse* (☎ *07-4060 2152)* is an art gallery with a licensed restaurant and camping that costs $6.50 per person. With miners from the local area, it can be a colourful night's stay.

Lakeland
The small township of Lakeland caters for surrounding properties and travellers, and most facilities are available. The roadhouse is on the main road, but turn right towards Cooktown to find the other facilities.

Lakeland Roadhouse (☎ *07-4060 2188, fax 4060 2165, Peninsula Developmental Rd)* Open 7am-9pm every day. This roadhouse provides fuel, tyre repairs and wide range of tasty meals plus $10 specials.

Lakeland Hotel-Motel (☎ *07-4060 2142,* e *susankelly@bigpond.com)* Singles/doubles/backpacker rooms $45/65/20. This pub serves meals daily.

Lakeland Coffee House & Store (☎/fax *07-4060 2040, Sesame St)* Open every day, serving meals and selling fuel, and there's a general store that sells locally grown fruit and vegetable produce too.

Lakeland Caravan Park (☎ *07-4060 2040)* Unpowered/powered sites $6/14 per person. A small caravan park near the shop, it's a good place to store your van if you're heading north.

Laura

The cafe and camping ground are on the main road but you have to turn right for the Quinkan Hotel, the store and the town hall. *Laura Town Hall* has Internet service. *Laura Store* is also the post office and sells fuel. *Laura Cafe* is open 7am-10pm, provides the usual meals and also sells fuel and vehicle spare parts. The Quinkan Information Centre (☎ 07-4060 3124, fax 4060 3231) has useful information on Aboriginal rock art, but is often closed. The *camping ground* is $5 per person and has a swimming pool.

Quinkan Hotel (☎ *07-4060 3255)* Unpowered sites $5 per person, $3 extra for power, rooms/vans/dorms $28/15/13. Meals can be provided. There's a 30-minute nature trail loop that starts from the back gate.

Jowalbinna Bush Camp (☎ *07-4051 4777, 4060 3236, fax 4051 4888,* e *reser vations@adventures.com.au,* w *www. adventures.com.au, 37km from the main road)* Unpowered sites $8 per person, safari tents $60-80, dorms $15. The candlelit showers are romantic in this superb bush setting. Dingoes and bowerbirds are around, and yabbies live in nearby pools. The access road is sandy but no problem for a 4WD. Guided tours to the varied Quinkan rock art painting sites in the surrounding sandstone escarpments are available – $30 for two hours (10 sites on the Brady Creek circuit), or $75/100 for half-day/full-day tours. *Deighton River Bush Camp* (☎ *07-4060 3236)* is similar to Jowalbinna.

Hann River

Hann River Roadhouse (☎ *07-4060 3242)* Camp sites $6 per person, power $3 extra,

vans with/without bed linen $15/10 per person. The roadhouse also sells fuel, provides snacks and has a bar.

Mary Valley

Mary Valley station (☎ *07-4060 3254)* Camp sites with basic facilities $5 per person, 2 modern en suite units $25 for singles and $40 for doubles & triples. This is a good place for nature lovers, with birds, crocodiles and lots of flying foxes.

Musgrave

See Facilities in the previous Cairns to Musgrave via Cooktown section.

Coen

The facilities are close together and easy to find. The QPWS (☎ 07-4060 1137, fax 4060 1117) is on the left as you drive north out of town and can supply information on Cape York's national parks. Telephone first as the office may be unattended.

Clark's General Store, Car Repairs & Towing Service (☎ 07-4060 1120) is open every day but the workshop is usually closed on Sunday.

Post Office Store (☎ *07-4060 1134, fax 4060 1128)* Unpowered/powered sites $12/13 per double. Internet service should be available soon.

Wilderness Cafe (☎ *07-4060 1146)* Mains $10-20. Serves meals every day from 7.30am-8pm.

Exchange Hotel (☎ *07-4060 1133)* Singles/doubles $38.50/49.50, single/double motel rooms with en suite $55/77. Guests can order meals.

Homestead Guest House (☎ *07-4060 1157, fax 4060 1158)* Singles/doubles $38.50/55. Guests can cook their own food or order meals.

Archer River

Archer River Roadhouse (☎/fax *07-4060 3266)* Unpowered sites $6 per person, units with shared facilities $55 per double. Drinks and food, including a $7 Archer burger, are served here. Fuel is also available. Look for the epitaph to a local female truckie outside the roadhouse.

Wenlock River
Moreton Telegraph Station (☎ 07-4060 3360) Unpowered sites $6 per person, rooms $20. Although the facilities are run down, there are some pleasant camp sites under the mango trees.

Bramwell Station (☎ 07-4060 3237, 26km north of the Wenlock, 10km off the Overland Telegraph Line Track) Unpowered sites $8 per person, basic single/double units $35/55. Limited supplies and cooked meals are available.

Weipa
Weipa Service Centre (☎ 07-4069 7277, fax 4069 7156, Boundary Rd) is the RACQ agent and repairs all types of cars. It's open daily from 7am to 6pm. Weipa Mobile Repairs (☎ 07-4069 7708) is another option.

Pax Haven Camping Ground (☎ 07-4069 7871, fax 4069 8211, e ianandgail@bigpond.com.au, Nanum Beach) Unpowered sites $9 per person, power $2 extra, units $65-85 2-4 people. Set in a large shady area near the beach, there's lots of tourist information in the office.

Heritage Resort (☎ 07-4069 8000, next to the Shopping Mall) Singles/doubles with shared facilities $95/105. The resort is modern and smart with a restaurant and swimming pool.

Albatross Hotel-Motel (☎ 07-4069 7314, fax 4069 7130, Trunding Point) Singles/doubles $82.50/93.50. The Albatross has facilities similar to the Heritage Resort but isn't as smart.

Lockhart River Aboriginal Community
The *general store (☎ 07-4060 7192)* supplies most items as well as fuel. It's also a post office with a Commonwealth Bank agency. There's a health clinic, and a *guesthouse* may be available. Contact the Community Council (☎ 07-4060 7144, fax 4060 7139) for further information.

Portland Roads
Portland House (☎/fax 07-4060 7193) is a comfortable, almost luxurious house overlooking the sea that costs $50 per person.

It sleeps seven, but phone ahead to book accommodation and meals.

Jardine River Ferry
The *Jardine River Fuel Outlet (☎ 07-4069 1369, e injinoo@injinoo.com, W www.injinoo.com)* on the southern bank of the Jardine River has unpowered sites at $5 per person. Fuel should be available but do not rely on it.

Bamaga
Bamaga Resort (☎ 07-4069 3050, fax 4069 3653, e bamaga@resortbamaga.com.au, W www.resortbamaga.com.au, Lui St) Shared facility/self-contained units for two to six people $150/190. The resort has a swimming pool, a bar, serves meals and offers 4WD cars.

Bamaga Hotel is a pub and bottle shop that also does cheap chicken and chips. There is a post office and a bakery and a fuel outlet should open soon.

Seisia
Seisia Resort & Camping Ground (☎ 07-4069 3243, fax 4069 3307, e seisiaresort@bigpond.com) Unpowered & powered sites $8.80 per person, villas $185 per night, lodge doubles $105.60. A popular place with views over the Torres Strait.

Top End Motor Repairs & Towing (☎ 07-4069 3182) is on Tradesmans Way. Top Form Marine Engineering (☎ 07-4069 3230) will sort out boat and trailer problems.

New Mapoon
Loyalty Beach Camping Ground & Fishing Lodge (☎ 07 4069 3372, e fishcapeyork@bigpond.com, W www.loyaltybeach.com) Unpowered sites $8 per person, power $2 extra, lodge rooms with shared facilities $49.50 per person. Fishing trips and charter boats are also available.

Umagico
Umagico Camping & Wilderness Lodge (☎ 07-4069 3273, fax 4069 3108) has unpowered/powered sites at $7/9 per person and lodge rooms with shared facilities $45. Camp sites are located on the beach, and are

fairly quiet. *Alau Hotel* (☎ *07-4069 3228, fax 4069 3108)* is just a pub.

Punsand Bay

Punsand Bay Safari & Fishing Lodge (☎ *07-4069 1722, fax 4069 1403)* Unpowered/powered sites $9 per person, air-con cabins with shared facilities & meals $155 per person, safari tents with meals $115 per person. The lodge is surrounded by lush green grass and there's a swimming pool and a licensed restaurant with nightly specials; try the seafood extravaganza on Saturday nights. There's a regular ferry service, six days a week, from the resort to Thursday Island.

Pajinka Wilderness Lodge

The *Pajinka Wilderness Lodge & Camping Ground* (☎ *07-4069 2100, fax 4069 2110,* e *pajinka@bigpond.com,* w *www.pajinka .com)* is run by the Injinoo Aboriginal community and is only 400m from the northernmost tip of Australia. Unpowered sites cost $7 per person with the usual facilities and a kiosk. The upmarket lodge costs $275 per person but includes all meals.

ALTERNATIVE TRANSPORT
Air

A wide range of charter aircraft operate all over Cape York, with most based in Cairns. Contact Tourism Tropical North Queensland (☎ 07-4051 3588, e information@ tnq.org.au, w www.tnq.org.au) at 51 The Esplanade, Cairns, for up-to-date information on the fast changing airline situation.

Boat

A number of shipping companies service the coast of Cape York carrying a variety of cargo and stores. While many can transport vehicles, only a couple take passengers.

MV Gulf Cloud (☎ *1800 640 079)* $285 per person (including meals), vehicles around $450. This crew runs a weekly service between Weipa and Karumba on the Gulf.

Sea Swift (☎ *07-4035 1234,* e *bookings@ seaswift.com.au,* w *www.seaswift.com.au)* $325 per person including meals, vehicles $660. A weekly passenger and freight service

between Cairns and Thursday Island and Seisia that's very popular in the dry season – so book as far in advance as possible.

Kangaroo Cruises (☎ *1800 079 141,* e *enquiries@kangaroocruises.com.au,* w *www.kangaroocruises.com.au)* Offers regular cruises from Cairns to the top of Cape York and is an alternative to flying.

Based on Thursday Island, *Peddell's Ferry & Tourist Service* (☎ *07-4069 1551)* operates a regular one-hour ferry service between Seisia and Thursday Island using modern catamarans. During the peak tourist season, from June to October, the ferry runs from Monday to Saturday. The ferry leaves the jetty at Seisia at 8am and 4pm, and leaves Thursday Island at 6.30am and 2.30pm. A one-way ticket costs $40 ($75 for a day return). Children are half price. You can buy tickets at Seisia Camping Ground.

Peddell's also offer a package tour for $145.50, which includes a ferry to Thursday Island, tour around Thursday Island, ferry to Horn Island, Chinese buffet lunch, tour of WWII relics on Horn Island, and a ferry back to Thursday Island. As you can imagine it's hectic. The same company also runs a similar service from Punsand Bay and Pajinka Wilderness Lodge to Thursday Island.

4WD Rental

Hotels and resorts are best placed to provide the most up-to-date information on local car hire in the region. Otherwise, try Weipa Rent-a-Car (☎ 07-4069 7311) and Seisia Hire Cars (☎ 07-4069 3368).

Thursday Island & Torres Strait

Highlights

- Enjoying the South Sea atmosphere of tiny Thursday Island
- Discovering the history of the pearling industry
- Exploring WWII relics on Horn Island

No visit to the top of the Cape would be complete without a visit to Thursday Island, or 'TI' as it is more often called by locals and visitors alike.

There are a number of islands scattered across the reef-strewn waters of the Torres Strait, and they exhibit a surprising variety. There are three main types: the rocky, mountain-top extension of the Great Dividing Range makes up the western group that includes Thursday Island and Prince of Wales Island; the central group of islands that dot the waters east to the Great Barrier Reef are little more than coral cays; while the third type of islands is volcanic in origin and in the far east of the strait, at the very northern end of the Great Barrier Reef. These Murray Islands are some of the most spectacular and picturesque in the area.

While Thursday Island is the 'capital' of Torres Strait, there are 17 inhabited islands, the northernmost being Saibai and Boigu Islands, only a couple of kilometres from the Papua New Guinea coast.

HISTORY

There were often bloody tribal conflicts across the islands before the Europeans arrived, and inevitably the Islanders came off second-best against the weaponry of the whites.

When pearl shell was discovered in the shallow waters of the strait in 1865, it led to an invasion of boats and crews in search of this new wealth. It was a wild and savage industry back then, with 'blackbirding' – a form of kidnapping for sale into slavery – and murder quite common. Being on the very edge of the frontier, the strait and all those who worked in it and plundered its resources were out of reach of the law.

In 1871 the missionaries arrived and they were so successful that the people of Thursday Island are still one of the most church-going populations in Australia.

During the first half of this century the pearling industry was the lifeblood of the area. It was a dangerous job as there was little knowledge of the physiological aspects of deep diving, and death from 'the bends', or decompression sickness, was common.

Poor equipment and frequent cyclones were other perils that the divers and crews faced. In fact, it was a cyclone in March 1899 that caused the biggest loss of life and devastated the industry. That cyclone struck Bathurst Bay, where 45 boats from the Thursday Island pearling fleet were anchored, and in the following hours only one boat survived and over 300 men were killed.

While a number of nationalities made up the working population, the Japanese were considered by many to be the best divers. The price they paid for their expertise is evident in the Thursday Island cemetery, where 700 are buried.

During WWII, Torres Strait and the islands were part of the Allied front line in the battle against the Japanese. Horn Island, where the airport for Thursday Island is located, was bombed eight times. Thursday Island was never bombed. Some say that was due to the legend that a Japanese princess was buried on the island, but it was more than likely the fact that there was a large population of Japanese living there. Over 5000 Allied servicemen were stationed on Horn Island.

After the war, plastic buttons replaced pearl shell buttons and the industry collapsed, although cultured pearls are still grown on five sites on the island.

In 1975 Papua New Guinea became independent. Though there was some dispute over international boundaries, all the islands up to 2km off the Papua New Guinea coast remained part of Australia.

Today much of the wealth of the area still comes from the sea in the form of prawns from the Gulf, for which Thursday Island is a major port, and crayfish from the reefs of the strait. Tourism is also playing its part.

THURSDAY ISLAND

The island is little more than 3 sq km in area, with the town of Thursday Island on its southern shore. The population is around 2300. There are six churches, two posh hotels, three hostels, three pubs, four takeaways, a smart cafe, a supermarket, a bank, a hospital and two wind turbines that generate 30% of the island's electricity.

THE TROPICS

You can access the Internet at Jardine Motel and the library in Douglas St, but the best deal is at Torres Tech at 71 Douglas St. Unfortunately, there are no organised diving tours, which is a pity because there are lots of interesting diving sites in the reef-strewn tropical sea.

Things to See

Quetta Memorial Cathedral, the smallest cathedral in the world, was built in 1893 in memory of the *Quetta*, wrecked on an unchartered reef in 1890 with 133 lives lost. There is a visitors' book that dates back to 1945. The **cemetery** reflects the multicultural nature of the old pearl shell industry. Over 700 Japanese are buried there, far from their homeland. Other gravestones show that Chinese, Malays, Indonesians, Indians, Polynesians, Strait Islanders and Europeans also gave their lives. Walking around the cemetery it's hard not to wonder about all these people from different nations working together.

Green Hill Fort, on a hill on the western side of town, was built in the 1890s when the Russians were thought to be coming. Six other forts were built in other parts of Australia, and more were built in New Zealand. Three 19th-century, six-inch guns with a range of 8km guarded the only deep channel through the Torres Strait and are still in place. The fort was garrisoned by 40 soldiers from 1893 to 1926. An excellent new museum display has been set up in the underground chambers.

While there are places of interest around Thursday Island, it's the atmosphere of the island that sets it apart from the rest of Australia.

Special Events

The Torres Strait Cultural Festival (☎ 07-4069 1698 fax 4069 1658, PO Box 42, Thursday Island, Qld 4875), held every May, presents art exhibitions, traditional singing, ceremonial dancing and cooking, along with a colourful procession. Visitors can also wander through the stalls set up during the festival, many of which have local art and craft displayed.

Another major event, The Coming of the Light Festival, is held every July with the performance of traditional songs and choral hymns to celebrate the arrival of Christian missionaries in 1871.

Places to Stay

Grand Hotel (☎ *07-4069 1557, fax 4069 1327)* Singles/doubles from $110/150. All rooms have air-con, a fridge and TV. There's a spa and an upmarket restaurant overlooking the harbour.

Jardine Motel (☎ *07-4069 1555, fax 4069 1470, Cnr Normanby St & Victoria Pde)* Stand-by doubles including breakfast $150. The only place on the island with a swimming pool.

Federal Hotel (☎ *07-4069 1569, fax 4069 1407, Victoria Pde)* Doubles $134. Check out the 1960s mural in the bar.

Torres Hotel (☎ *07-4069 1141, Cnr Douglas & Normanby Sts)* Doubles with air-con, fridge and TV $50. It has a bottle shop and the meals are a good deal too with daily specials for $6.50.

Rainbow Motel (☎ *07-4069 2460, 57 Douglas St)* Doubles with air-con & shared facilities $99. It has a good-value takeaway restaurant.

Both *Jumula Dubbins* (☎ *07-4069 2212, Victoria Pde)* and *Cannon Boggin Pilot Hostels* *(Douglas St)* cater mainly for Aborigines and Torres Strait Islanders but sometimes take in other travellers.

Mura Mudh (House B'long Everybody) Hostel (☎ *07-4069 1708, fax 4069 2050, Douglas St)* Double with fan, fridge and TV $55. Guests are given a warm welcome and the lounge has an interesting collection of local craft.

Places to Eat

Try breakfast at *Jardine Motel*, coffee and cake at the *Gallery Cafe* (☎ *07-4069 2922)*, and lunch from *Rainbow Takeaway*. For dinner, how about a posh meal at the *Grand Hotel* or a $10 steak at the *Torres Hotel*.

Getting There & Away

See Facilities in the previous Cape York section for details of the ferry service.

Flights go to nearby Horn Island from Cairns. Contact Cape York Air (☎ 07-4035 9399) or Qantas (☎ 13 13 13) for details.

Getting Around

To see the island, grab one of the many local taxis (☎ 07-4069 1666) or join Peddell's tour, which meets the ferry from the mainland and costs $15.50 (children $7.50). Both the Grand Hotel and Jardine Motel have bicycles for their guests, although the island is small enough to walk around.

HORN ISLAND

Much bigger than Thursday Island but with a population of only 650, Horn Island is only 25 minutes away from Thursday Island by ferry. The main airport for the Torres Strait Islands is located here, and Cairns is less than two hours away by plane.

The airport was a key strategic base in WWII and you can join a tour of the bunkers, gun emplacements, slit trenches, crashed planes and empty beer bottles that they left behind. Every soldier was given two bottles of beer a week.

The *Gateway Torres Strait Resort (☎ 07-4069 1902, near the wharf)* has double rooms for $136, buffet meals and a fascinating museum about everyday life on the islands that costs $5.50 to browse. Car hire is also available.

Ferries run between Horn and Thursday Islands ($5 one-way) every hour.

OTHER ISLANDS

Other inhabited islands of Torres Strait are isolated communities wresting a living from the surrounding reef. These Islanders are proud of their heritage, with a separate identity to Australian Aboriginal people, who were based on Horn Island.

Outside of Thursday and Thorn Islands, the largest group of people are found on Boigu, close to the Papua New Guinea coast, where the population is less than 400. Most of the inhabited Torres Strait Islands have populations between 50 and 200. Most of them welcome visitors and have a guesthouse that generally costs around $50, but you need to contact them before you arrive.

There are regular flights to all the inhabited islands but they are expensive. Contact Torres Trait Travel (☎ 07-4069 1264, fax 4069 1691) for Qantaslink bookings to Thursday Island and Regional Pacific flights to the other Torres Strait Islands. You can visit a coral cay like Warraber Island for $290 return or Coconut Island for $350 return. Generally the nearer the island is, the cheaper it is. Yorke Island is around $420 return. Aerotropics (☎ 07-4035 9138, fax 4035 9985, ⓦ www.aero-tropics.com.au) have daily scheduled flights from Cairns to the Horn Island.

Torres Tours (☎ 07-4069 1586, fax 4069 1408, ⓦ www.torrestours.com.au) conduct package tours of Thursday Island. At present there is no passenger boat service for the outer islands. Giomi Ferries (☎ 07-4090 3611) is waiting on a government permit to establish one.

Matilda Highway

Highlights

- Discovering how the Outback was won at the Stockman's Hall of Fame in Longreach
- Experiencing railroad history on the tiny *Gulflander* train between Normanton and Croydon

Outback Queensland is a place where the dinosaur once roamed, the inspiration for Waltzing Matilda, the birthplace of Qantas and the home of the Stockman's Hall of Fame. It has many attractions for travellers with a sense of history and an appreciation of nature.

The all-bitumen, 1674km Matilda Hwy is the official nickname given to a route made up of sections of the Mitchell Hwy, the Landsborough Hwy and the Burke Developmental Rd. Beginning at Cunnamulla, it takes you north from the vast open plains of south western Queensland to Karumba, a prawn fishing centre on the Gulf of Carpentaria.

THE TROPICS

Mornington Island
Gulf of Carpentaria
Denham Island
Sydney Island
Forsyth Island
Bentinck Island
Sweers Island
To Borroloola (308km)
Hells Gate
Doomadgee
Burketown
Nicholson River
Lawn Hill
LAWN HILL NATIONAL PARK
Gregory
Riversleigh Fossil Fields
Gregory Downs
Camooweal
Wills Dev. Rd
117
217
230
Leichhardt River
Burke Developmental Rd
Smithburn
Staaten
Karumba
40
30
Normanton
Gulflander Railway Line
195
151
Croydon
Bang Bang Jump-up
Flinders River
Kajabbi
137
Quamby
Lake Julius
Mount Isa
Cloncurry
52
117
Mary Kathleen
104
Barkly
Camooweal
Leichhardt
Burke Developmental
Matilda Rd
Flinders
134
Julia Creek
144
Cloncurry River
Landsborough
Matilda
114
McKinlay
75
Kynuna
165
Combo Waterhole
Dagworth
164
Middleton
Carisbrooke
Developmental
Hamilton
Kennedy
Boulia
114
Diamantina River
Urandangi
Dajarra
Diamantina
Developmental Rd
Georgina River
Mulligan River
Tropic of Capricorn
SIMPSON DESERT NATIONAL PARK
Eyre Creek
Bedourie
Hamilton
Birdsville
Birdsville Developmental Rd
275
SOUTH AUSTRALIA
Innamincka
Noccundra
0 100 200km
0 60 120mi
10 Distances between locations in kilometres
Unsealed roads can vary from excellent to impassable, depending on many factors.

To Chillagoe (540km)
Staaten
STAATEN RIVER NATIONAL PARK
Mitchell River
Mossman
Walsh River
Chillagoe
Mareeba
Cairns
Gordonvale
Innisfail
BULLERINGA NATIONAL PARK
Einasleigh
Gilbert River
Walker Creek
Georgetown
Einasleigh
Mount Garnet
Ravenshoe
LUMHOLTZ NATIONAL PARK
UNDARA VOLCANIC NATIONAL PARK
The Lynd Junction
Ingham
Yappar River
Normanton River
Saxby River
BLACKBRAES NATIONAL PARK
GREAT BASALT WALL NATIONAL PARK
Homestead
Townsville
Great Dividing Range
WHITE MOUNTAINS NATIONAL PARK
Homestead
Charters Towers
Richmond
Flinders Hwy
112
Hughenden
Prairie
Torrens Creek
Pentland
Lake Dalrymple
Prairie Ck
Whitewood
Kennedy Developmental Rd
215
Muttaburrasaurus Byway
Winton
Lorraine
110
110
Morella
67
Muttaburra
Aramac
BLADENSBURG NATIONAL PARK
Lark Quarry Conservation Park
Diamantina River
Verbena Creek
Thomson River
QUEENSLAND
DIAMANTINA GATES NATIONAL PARK
Longreach
81
Barcaldine
Alp
Ilfracombe
Capricorn Hwy
To Emerald (166k) & Rockhampton (261km)
Outer Barcoo Byway
89
Alice Downs
103
Matilda
Landsborough
Dawson Developmental Rd (Wilderness Wa
Isisford
Blackall
101
Hwy
Barcoo River
Emmet
IDALIA NATIONAL PARK
Tambo
To Salvator Rosa (Carnarvon National Park 120km)
116
WELFORD NATIONAL PARK
Jundah
Windorah
HELL HOLE GORGE NATIONAL PARK
Adavale
MARIALA NATIONAL PARK
Augathella
Langlo Crossing
91
Cooper Creek
Thomson River
Diamantina
Bulloo River
Langlo River
Nive River
Quilpie
Cheepie
Developmental Rd
Eromanga
Toompine
Charleville
Warrego Hwy
209
Cooladdi
To Dalby (540km) & Roma (270k
Wyandra
197
Wilson River
Paroo River
Beechal Ck
Mitchell
Matilda
To St George (296km) & Dalby (598k
BINDEGOLLY NATIONAL PARK
Thargomindah
126
Adventure
Eulo
64
Way
Cunnamulla
To Barringun (119km) & Bourke (254km)
CURRAWINYA NATIONAL PARK
To Hungerford (52km)

History

Aborigines inhabited this country for thousands of years, and saw the comings and goings of animals that are now preserved in the stones of Riversleigh, a monumental deposit of fossils near Lawn Hill National Park, north-west of Mt Isa, and easily accessible from this route.

Dutch navigators were the first Europeans to sight this land, when Willem Janszoon sailed the Gulf coast in 1606. Others followed but found little to interest them, and it wasn't until the great British navigator Matthew Flinders sailed along the Gulf coast, careening his ship on Sweers Island in November 1802, that the British crown showed any interest in this region.

Ludwig Leichhardt crossed the Gulf plains on his way to Port Essington in the Northern Territory in 1844. Over the next 20 years, some of Australia's greatest explorers, including Thomas Mitchell, Burke and Wills, William Landsborough, Augustus Gregory and John McKinlay, crisscrossed the vast plains and the low rugged ranges of outback Queensland. In the process they opened up this land to the sheep and cattle graziers who quickly followed.

Information

Tourist Offices There are tourist information centres in most towns along the route.

For information on Cunnamulla, contact the Cunnamulla Visitor Centre (☎ 07-4655 2481, fax 4655 1120, ✉ pscinfo@grow zone.com.au) at Centenary Park.

Information is also available from Outback Queensland Tourism Authority (☎ 07-4743 7966, fax 4743 8746), at PO Box 356, Mt Isa, Qld 4825, and Gulf Savannah Tourism (☎ 07-4051 4658, W www.gulf-savannah.com.au) at 74 Abbott St, Cairns.

National Parks For information on any of the national parks, contact the Department of Environment and Heritage in Brisbane (☎ 07-3227 7111) or the regional headquarters in Townsville (☎ 07-4743 2055).

Books & Maps The Queensland state mapping authority's map *The Matilda*

Highway can be purchased from Sunmap centres or agencies and book/map shops.

THE ROUTE
Cunnamulla

The southernmost town in western Queensland, Cunnamulla (population 1600) is on the Warrego River 120km north of the Queensland/New South Wales border. It lies 805km west of Brisbane via St George and 1034km north-west of Sydney via Bourke (254km away).

The town was gazetted in 1868, and in 1879 Cobb & Co established a coaching station here. In the 1880s, an influx of farmers opened the country up to the two million sheep that graze the open plains today. The railway arrived in 1898, and since then Cunnamulla has been a major service centre for the district; in good years it is Queensland's biggest wool-loading rail yard.

The **Cunnamulla Bicentennial Museum** (☎ 07-4655 2481, John St; admission $1; open 9am-noon & 1pm-5pm Mon-Fri) tells the story of the pioneers of the district, and the **Robbers Tree** is a reminder of a bungled robbery in the 1880s.

In late August/early September, the town (along with neighbouring Eulo) celebrates the **Cunnamulla-Eulo World Lizard Racing Championships**, a week-long festival with arts & crafts, sports activities, a street party, and of course, lizard racing. Another major event is the annual show, held in late May.

Cunnamulla to Augathella (288km)

From Cunnamulla you can head east along the Balonne Hwy to Brisbane, or go west to Thargomindah and on past the Jackson Oil Fields to Innamincka, in north-eastern South Australia – see the Strzelecki Track section in the Central Deserts chapter.

Eulo, 64km west of Cunnamulla, is on the Paroo River close to the Yowah opal fields. In late August/early September it hosts the World Lizard Racing Championships (see the Cunnamulla entry). The **Destructo Cockroach Monument** was erected in memory of a racing cockroach who died when a punter stood on it; this granite plinth must be the only cockroach memorial in the world.

Our route from Cunnamulla lies north along the Mitchell Hwy, parallelling the Warrego River off to the west. The railway follows a similar route. A couple of railway sidings, the odd station homestead and tiny **Wyandra**, with the obligatory hotel and general store, make up the habitation profile of the 197km trip to Charleville. The mainly flat country is mostly clothed in mulga.

Charleville One of the largest towns in outback Queensland, Charleville (population 3330) is 760km west of Brisbane and situated on the Warrego River. Edmund Kennedy passed this way in 1847, and the town was gazetted in 1868, six years after the first settlers had arrived. By the turn of the century it was an important service centre for the outlying sheep stations.

From 1893 until 1920 Cobb & Co was building coaches in Charleville that were especially designed for Australian conditions. Aviation history was being made at the same time. In 1921 Qantas (Queensland & Northern Territory Aerial Services) was founded in Winton, and in November of the following year the carrier's first fare-paying passengers flew between Charleville and Cloncurry, to the north.

The excellent Charleville Visitor Information Centre (☎ 07-4654 3057) is in the large, tranquil Graham Andrews Parklands, on Sturt St (Matilda Hwy) south of the town centre. It's open 9am to 5pm daily April to October, and 9am to 5pm weekdays, November to March.

From a specially built observatory at the Charleville airport, **Skywatch** *(☎ 07-4654 3057, Off Sturt St near the information centre; adult/concession/family $8.80/6.60/22; open 7pm nightly)* offers visitors guided tours of the night skies through powerful telescopes.

Apart from its links with the stagecoach days and the birth of Qantas, Charleville offers history buffs the **Historic House Museum** *(☎ 07-4654 3349, Alfred St; adult/child $3/0.20; open 8am-4pm daily)*. This place is crammed with bygone-era curios. Some of the more interesting items include a working Edison cylinder phonograph and a 1920s rail ambulance car.

A worthy companion to the museum is the **historic tour** conducted through the beautifully preserved Corones Hotel (☎ 07-4564 1720), on Wills St. Tours leave daily at 2pm ($8) and include Devonshire tea. **Tarot card readings** ($30 per 30 minutes) are available at the Corones Hotel on Thursday, 10.30am to noon, and 2pm to 5pm.

North of Charleville From Charleville you can head east to Brisbane via Roma, or west to Quilpie, Windorah and Bedourie via the Diamantina Developmental Rd.

Our route, however, continues northwards along the Mitchell Hwy, paralleling the Warrego River. The river offers opportunities to dangle a line for Murray cod, yellowbelly, golden perch (one of the tastiest freshwater fish in Australia) or catfish.

Augathella

The quiet little town of Augathella is 91km north of Charleville. It lies at the junction of the Mitchell Hwy and the road southeast to Morven and the route to Brisbane. Travellers from south-east Queensland heading north to Mt Isa, the Gulf or the Northern Territory often join the Matilda Hwy at this junction. Surveyed in 1880, Augathella began as a bullock team camp beside the Warrego River.

Tourist information can be obtained from Russell's Roadhouse (☎ 07-4654 5255), on the Matilda Hwy. The roadhouse has all fuel types and is open 4.30am to 11pm daily. At the time of writing, the Augathella visitors centre was under construction on Main St.

Adjoining the site of the visitors centre is **Bodicea Arts & Crafts Shop** *(☎ 07-4564 5116)*, which is well worth a look.

Augathella to Barcaldine (320km)

From Augathella you continue north-west on the Landsborough Hwy (Matilda Hwy); 116km north of Augathella is the small township of **Tambo**, on the banks of the Barcoo River.

Tambo is surrounded by perhaps the best grazing land in western Queensland, and this small hamlet also has some of the earliest historic buildings in the region. In the main street are bottle trees and timber houses that date back to the 1860s, while the 'new' post office has been operating since 1904.

Tambo promotes itself as 'the friendly town of the west', and each year races are held at the local track, a tradition dating back to the formation of the Great Western Downs Jockey Club, in 1865. The information centre is on Arthur St (the main street), at the shire council chambers (☎ 07-4654 6133).

From Tambo you continue northwards, but if you're looking for a good excursion, there is access to the **Salvator Rosa** section of Carnarvon National Park (which also takes in Mt Moffatt National Park). The Salvator Rosa park is 120km east of Tambo via the Dawson Developmental Rd (also known as Wilderness Way) and the Cungelella station, generally a 4WD route. The turn-off to Salvator Rosa is 8km south of Tambo.

Discovered and named by the explorer Thomas Mitchell in 1846, the same year he discovered the downs on which Tambo is situated, Salvator Rosa's 26,000 hectares protect a maze of sandstone escarpments and gorges. It's a spectacularly rugged area with few facilities, and you need a permit from the national parks to camp. Try the park office (☎ 07-4684 4086) or the regional office in Longreach (☎ 07-4658 1761) for more information.

Continuing northwards along the Landsborough Hwy (Matilda Hwy), it's a pleasant run of 101km to the town of Blackall. The **Barcoo River** is crossed 59km north of Tambo; there's an excellent spot to camp off the eastern side of the road.

The Barcoo is one of the great rivers of western Queensland, and must be the only river in the world that in its lower reaches becomes a creek! The Barcoo initially flows north-west past Blackall, then swings southwest through Isisford and into the Channel Country of south-western Queensland, where it becomes Cooper Creek, probably the most famous of Australia's inland rivers.

While Mitchell had waxed lyrical about this river in 1846, thinking it was a route to the Gulf, it was left to his second-in-command Edmund Kennedy (later of Cape York fame) to discover the real course of the river and to call it the Barcoo in 1847.

Both Banjo Paterson and Henry Lawson mention the Barcoo in their writings. The name has also entered the Australian idiom, appearing in the *Macquarie Dictionary* in such terms as 'Barcoo rot' (basically scurvy), the 'Barcoo salute' (the waving about of hands to keep flies away from the face) and the 'Barcoo spews' (vomiting caused by extremes of heat).

Blackall Gazetted in 1868, Blackall is named after the second governor of Queensland, Samuel Blackall. The town is a pleasant spot to stop on trips north or south along the Matilda. The town prides itself on the fact that, in 1892 at nearby Alice Downs station, the legendary shearer Jack Howe set his world record of shearing 321 sheep in less than eight hours, with a set of hand shears! The record still stands today – even shearers using machine-powered shears didn't reach that number until 1950. Acclaimed as the greatest 'gun' (the best in the shed) shearer in the world, Jackie's name lives on in the working man's blue singlet which he made popular. After his shearing days were over, he ran one of the hotels in Blackall, and is buried here.

The Blackall Tourist Office (☎/fax 07-4657 4637) on the main street (Matilda Hwy), and is open 9am to 5pm weekdays.

North-east of Blackall is the **Blackall Woolscour** (☎/fax 07-4657 4637, **e** bhwa@ b190.aone.net.au, open 8am-4pm daily Apr-Nov), the only steam-driven scour (woolcleaner) left in Queensland. It stopped operating in 1978, but has since been painstakingly restored to working condition.

The **Blackall Aquatic Centre** (☎ 07-4657 4816, Salvia St; adult/child $1.50/0.80; open noon-6pm daily), one of the Matilda Hwy's greatest attractions for the dusty traveller, is a beautifully designed artesian pool and spa complex just off the highway. Cake and coffee are available poolside.

THE TROPICS

From Blackall you can travel into the Channel Country of southwest Queensland by heading out to Isisford or Windorah (respectively, 115km and 337km west of Blackall). Our route, though, lies north along the Landsborough Hwy.

North of Blackall Travelling these roads at night is not recommended. Kangaroos often reach plague proportions out in western Queensland, and the edge of the bitumen is a place where water gathers from any rain and where green feed is more readily available. At night in a 100km section of this road, you can see in excess of 1000 animals.

An hour's travelling on the bitumen across flat, lightly treed plains brings you to Barcaldine, 103km north of Blackall.

Barcaldine

Barcaldine (pronounced bark-**all**-den) lies at the junction of the Landsborough and Capricorn Hwys, 575km west of Rockhampton via Emerald, and is surrounded by sheep and cattle stations. It's known as the 'Garden City of the West', with a good supply of artesian water nourishing orchards of citrus fruits – Barcaldine was the first town in Australia to realise its underground bounty, in 1887.

The information centre (☎ 07-4651 1724) is on Oak St, and is open 8am to 5pm daily.

Established in 1886 when the railway arrived, Barcaldine gained its place in Australian history in 1891 when it became the headquarters of the historic shearers' strike, during which over 1000 men camped in and around the town. That confrontation saw troops called in, and the formation of the Australian Workers' Party, the forerunner of today's Australian Labor Party. The **Tree of Knowledge**, near the train station, was the meeting place of the organisers, and still stands as a monument to workers and their rights. The **Australian Workers Heritage Centre** (☎ 07-4651 2422, Ash St; adult/concession/student/family $9.90/7.70/5.50/27.50; open 9am-5pm Mon-Fri, 10am-5pm Sun) also commemorates the struggle – this unusual complex includes a number of exhibition halls.

Barcaldine's other attractions include the **Folk Museum** (☎ 07-4651 1724, Cnr Beech & Gidyea Sts; adult/child $3/free; open 7am-5pm daily), **Mad Mick's Funny Farm** (☎ 07-4651 1172, 84 Pine St; adult/child $7/4; open 9.30am-5pm daily Apr-Sept), and a number of National Trust buildings. The annual Show is held in May, while the town's Artesian Festival with its mardi gras, golf tournaments and more is usually held in June.

Barcaldine to Winton (285km)

From Barcaldine you can head east to Rockhampton and the coast, or you can head north through the small but interesting towns of Aramac and Muttaburra to Hughenden, 357km north of Barcaldine. The unsealed road from Muttaburra to Hughenden passes through flat country and can be a bit rough in places, but is usually quite manageable in a conventional vehicle with sufficient ground clearance. For more information contact the local shire office (☎ 07-4651 3311) in Hughenden.

From Hughenden, you can head east along the sealed Flinders Hwy to Charters Towers and Townsville, or continue up the Kennedy Developmental Rd to the bitumen at the Lynd Junction and on to Cairns – an interesting route that takes you past the stunning Porcupine Gorge. This road is rocky and rougher than the previous section, but is usually OK in a conventional vehicle driven with care.

Our route from Barcaldine, however, lies west along the Landsborough Hwy (Matilda Hwy), across the wide open plains towards Longreach.

Ilfracombe, a hamlet 81km from Barcaldine, contains several historic buildings and a good **Machinery & Heritage Museum** (☎ 07-4568 1639, Main Ave; admission free; open 8am-5pm daily during tourist season). Contact the shire council office (☎ 07-4658 2233) on Main Ave for tourist information.

Longreach Longreach, 27km further west, is on a 'long reach' of the Thomson River. It's western Queensland's largest town after Mt Isa, with a population of around 3500.

The surrounding region was explored by Augustus Gregory in 1858 and 1859, and though the area was settled in the 1870s, the town was not officially gazetted until 1887.

It was in 1870 that Harry Redford stole 1000 head of cattle from Mt Cornish, an outstation of Bowen Downs, north of Longreach, and drove them down the Thomson River and its continuation, Cooper Creek, to the present site of Innamincka. From there he followed the Strzelecki Creek south, finally selling his ill-gotten gains to a station owner north of Adelaide. His exploit opened up a new stock route south, and when he was finally brought to justice, in Roma in 1873, he was found not guilty by an admiring public!

The railway arrived in 1892, and during the early years of the 20th century the wool boom made Longreach into the town you see today. In February 1921 the first Qantas flight left here for Winton, and the following year Longreach became the operational base for the fledgling airline. The first seven aircraft built in Australia were constructed here, between 1922 and 1930.

The Longreach Shire Council Information Centre (☎ 07-4658 4111, e assist@long reach.qld.gov.au), on the corner of Swan and Eagle Sts, is open 8am to 5pm weekdays.

The **Stockman's Hall of Fame & Outback Heritage Centre** (☎ 07-4658 2166, e mus cum@outbackheritage.com.au, W www.out backheritage.com.au; Matilda Hwy; adult/ student/family $19.80/16/44; open 9am-5pm daily) is one of the finest museums in the country, honouring the explorers, stockmen, shearers and everyday folk who helped open up the Australian outback.

The **Qantas Founders' Outback Museum** (☎ 07-4658 2166, Matilda Hwy; adult/student/child $7.50/5.50/3.85; open 9am-5pm daily) is in the Qantas hangar at Longreach airport and houses, among other exhibits, a full-size replica of an Avro 504K, which was the first type of passenger aircraft used by Qantas.

The **Longreach Powerhouse Museum** (☎ 07-4658 3933, Swan St; adult/child $5/2; open 2pm 5pm daily Apr-Oct, 2pm-5pm Thurs, Sat & Sun Nov-Mar, 4.30pm-7.30pm Jan, closed Feb & Dec) is also worth a visit.

Longreach to Winton From Longreach you can head south along the Thomson Developmental Rd to Windorah and places further south along Cooper Creek. Northwards you can head to Muttaburra and Hughenden, 380km west of Townsville.

For those travelling the Matilda, head north-west out of Longreach along the Landsborough Hwy; just out of town you cross the Thomson River.

After passing the fabulously named Muttaburrasaurus Byway (an unsealed route to Muttaburra) at the tiny crossroad township of Morella, you reach Winton, 177km north of Longreach.

Winton

At the crossroads of the Landsborough Hwy and the east-west Kennedy Developmental Rd, Winton was settled in 1875. In 1895, Winton's original North Gregory Hotel was thought to be the venue for the first public performance of Banjo Paterson's *Waltzing Matilda*, which he had written after a visit to Combo Waterhole on Dagworth station (where a local shearer had committed suicide), 140km north-west of Winton. Or so the story goes – Kyuna begs to differ about where *Waltzing Matilda* originated.

An annual bush-verse competition, The Bronze Swagman Award, attracts interest from all over Australia, keeping alive the Banjo Paterson tradition. The Waltzing Matilda Festival held in April of each year features a race meeting, a rodeo and bush poetry.

The **Waltzing Matilda Centre** (☎ 07-4657 1466, e matilda@thehub.com.au, W www .matildacentre.com.au; Elderslie St; adult/ student $14/12; open 8.30am-5pm daily) is an Australiana extravaganza, with plenty of bells and whistles. It features many interactive displays, and should keep both adults and kiddies amused for hours. It doubles as the town's tourist information centre.

The **Royal Theatre** (☎ 07-4657 1289, Cobb Lane), off Elderslie St, is a unique and historic outdoor cinema in the heart of town. It hosts 'nostalgia nights' on Wednesday (and sometimes other nights as well during the tourist season), with old film clips.

THE TROPICS

The ticket box and theatre entrance is via the Stopover Cafe on Elderslie St. Nostalgia night sessions are $6/4 adult/concession, including tea and coffee after the show.

Southwest of the town is **Lark Quarry Conservation Park**, where fossilised footprints testify to a stampede of small dinosaurs 100 million years ago. It's a well-signposted trip of 115km each way on dirt roads to the site, which has no facilities other than a toilet and a rainwater tank.

Winton to Cloncurry (344km)

Heading north-west out of town on the Landsborough Hwy (Matilda Hwy), the country is rolling grassland dotted with the occasional mesa or patch of breakaway country. The wide thoroughfare is a recognised stock route, and it's not unusual to see cattle and drovers wandering the 'long paddock'. In those cases where there are sheep or cattle spread all over the road, you should slow down to a crawl, stopping if necessary, and let the people and dogs handling the stock work their way around you. Enjoy the passing parade – it is a way of life that brings back images of Australia's pioneering past.

The turn-off to Paterson's Combo Waterhole is signposted, 145km north of Winton. After another 20km you come to tiny **Kynuna**, where you can get fuel (no LPG) and limited supplies. This place claims to be the true birthplace of *Waltzing Matilda*, and as such, the biggest attraction here is the **Matilda Expo** (☎ 07-4746 8401), 'in the big red barn'. This unassuming, fascinating place tells the alternative tale of the Waltzing Matilda legend. Entry is by donation. Patrons can use the camping sites nearby which include showers.

McKinlay, 75km north of Kynuna, can also supply fuel and limited stores. Named after the explorer who passed through this region in the 1860s after searching for Burke and Wills, it's a little bigger than Kynuna, but that is not saying much! Once it would rarely attract many visitors, but ever since its **Walkabout Creek Hotel** starred in *Crocodile Dundee* trade has been brisk. It's an inviting place, dispensing cold beer, good meals and friendly banter. You can also stay here – see the Facilities section later.

The country begins to change north of McKinlay, the flat plain giving way first to low rolling hills and then to ever more rugged country. By the time the road crosses the Flinders Hwy just 14km east of Cloncurry, you are surrounded by low, craggy hills, scoured with veins of bare rock and cut by narrow, convoluted creeks that tear out the earth after any heavy rain.

The country remains the same for the run into Cloncurry, 335km north of Winton.

Cloncurry

Cloncurry (population 2000) traces its European heritage back to the days of the ill-fated Burke and Wills expedition, which passed this way in 1861 and named the Cloncurry River, on whose banks the town was built. There are a number of monuments to these explorers in and around the town.

As you come into town, it's hard to miss the **Tourist Information Centre & Museum** (☎ 07-4742 1361, McIlwraith St; open 8am-noon & 1pm-4.30pm Mon-Fri, 9am-3pm Sat & Sun). It's in the Mary Kathleen Memorial Park, and features relics of the uranium-mining town of Mary Kathleen, now just a spot on the map about 60km west towards Mt Isa. The park is a beauty, and the free museum has many reminders of the region's interesting history.

Cloncurry's major attraction is **John Flynn Place** (☎ 07-4742 1251, Daintree St; adult/child $6/3; open 7am-4pm Mon-Fri, 9am-3pm Sat & Sun). This ultra-modern museum tells the history of the RFDS, founded in this town by Reverend John Flynn, a minister with the Australian Inland Mission (which he also helped establish). In 1928, the first RFDS flight was from Cloncurry to Julia Creek, 134km to the east. Just a couple of years earlier, Alfred Traeger, an Adelaide radio engineer, had developed a 'pedal wireless' with Flynn's support, thus realising Flynn's dream for a 'mantle of safety' in the outback.

The **Afghan and Chinese cemeteries** here are a little different to the more commonly seen Christian ones, and are testimony to the area's rich cultural heritage. The town is also noteworthy for having recorded the highest shade temperature in Australia: 53.1°C (more than 130°F) in 1889.

Tours are available in the local area to as far afield as **Kajabbi** (100km north-west of Cloncurry) and **Lake Julius** (40km west of Kajabbi). For the do-it-yourselfers, there's river fishing and trips to the old mines dotted through the ranges. It's a good base from which to explore the surrounding area or even take a day trip to Mt Isa.

Cloncurry to Karumba (454km)

While the Matilda Hwy continues northwards, Cloncurry is a major stepping-off point for those heading west to Mt Isa and the Northern Territory. Eastwards, the Flinders Hwy stretches all the way to Townsville on the coast, 770km away.

Once across the Cloncurry River, the Matilda Hwy breaks away from the Flinders Hwy and takes to the narrower Burke Developmental Rd. It's not long before you leave the gentle pastoral country well and truly behind.

The stretch of highway between Cloncurry and Normanton is inferior to the road behind it. It's a mixture of good two-lane bitumen and narrow single-lane bitumen with soft, dusty edges. It's scenic, but tiring, driving. Beware the 50m road trains!

Quamby, just 8km north of the tiny hamlet of Urquhart, is 52km north of Cloncurry. Once a Cobb & Co coach stop and a centre for the gold mining that helped develop the region, Quamby now has nothing but the historic *Quamby Hotel (☎ 07-4742 5952)*. You can enjoy a beer here and fuel is also available. Rustic accommodation is available at $10 per person.

Continuing north across the rolling hills dotted with low, spindly gums, you reach the turn-off to **Kajabbi** 26km north of Quamby. Once the focus of the area, Kajabbi has been all but forgotten. The town was once the railhead for this part of the Gulf's cattle industry and the nearby copper mines, but all that has long since disappeared.

The *Kalkadoon Hotel (☎/fax 07-4742 5979)* is the focal point for locals and visitors alike. Time it right and you'll catch the Kajabbi Yabbie Races in April. From here there is much to explore, including the Mt Cuthbert Mine site, and the site of the last stand of the Kalkadoon people, who resisted the white invasion in bloody battles during the 1880s.

Just before the Burke & Wills Roadhouse along the Burke Developmental Rd, 180km north of Cloncurry, the Wills Developmental Rd from Julia Creek comes in from the right.

Nearly everyone stops at the **Burke & Wills Roadhouse**, where there's some welcome shade, ice creams to buy from the well-stocked store and, if you can afford it, fuel (including LPG).

From the roadhouse you can strike northwest along the Wills Developmental Rd to the fabulous Gregory River, where there is some excellent bush camping, and the famous *Gregory Downs Hotel (☎ 07-4748 5566; Wills Development Rd; singles/doubles $55/65)*. From there a reasonable dirt road leads north to friendly Burketown or westwards to the impressive **Lawn Hill National Park** – see the Gulf Track section earlier in this chapter.

For those travelling the Matilda, the route continues in a more northerly direction towards the Gulf. The country remains reasonably flat, but once you get to **Bang Bang Jump-Up** – a spectacular landscape of anthills – and descend about 40m to the Gulf plains proper, you really know what 'flat' means. This near sheer escarpment vividly marks where the high country ends, 80km north of the roadhouse.

From this point the road stretches across vast, billiard-table-flat plains covered in deep grass, which in the Dry is the colour of gold. Dotted here and there are clumps of trees, and wherever there is permanent water or shade there are cattle. In this country the cattle really stand out – during the day. At night, as everywhere in outback Queensland, they can make driving on the roads very hazardous.

On the Norman River, 384km from Cloncurry, Normanton marks the end of the 195km stage of the route from the Burke & Wills Roadhouse.

Normanton The most important town in the Gulf region, Normanton was established in 1868 and really boomed during the 1890s gold rush to the Croydon goldfields, 150km inland. So rich were these fields that the railway which was supposed to be built from Normanton south was eventually pushed through to Croydon. Today, the *Gulflander*, as it is called, is an isolated offshoot of the main Queensland railway network and caters more for tourists than for locals. Every Saturday it leaves Normanton railway station (☎ 07-4745 1391) at 10am for the two-hour trip to Croydon ($25 return). There's also often a 40-minute trip on the 1931 RM-60 train ($11 return).

As a base for fishing, Normanton is hard to beat, with the Norman River producing some magic-size barramundi. From here it's just a hop, step and jump across the plains to the Gulf port of Karumba. Travellers may also be interested in the **Normanton Rodeo & Gymkhana** held in June, the area's biggest social and sporting event of the year. In August the races and a ball take place.

There's plenty of tourist information at Gulfland Souvenirs (☎ 07-4745 1307), at Normanton railway station, Matilda St, open 8am to 5pm Monday to Friday, and 8am to 3pm Saturday.

Normanton to Karumba Heading out of town, the Burke Developmental Rd soon crosses the Norman River and, less than 29km up the road, a major tributary of the river, Walker Creek. At the 30km mark is a major intersection. Veer left here, sticking to the bitumen, and the road quickly swings almost due west.

Traversing these great plains, it is easy to see how, during the torrential rains of the wet season, this area becomes one huge lake. At times, with king tides backing up the waters of the rivers, the floods isolate towns like Normanton for weeks. But unlike the Cloncurry-Normanton leg, this stretch of highway is sublimely smooth in good weather. It's also the only sealed road to the coast in the Gulf Savannah region.

The bird life is rich and varied; this is the best region in Australia to see the stately brolga and the very similar sarus crane, a recent natural invader from South-East Asia. Another large bird that you'll see is the magpie-coloured jabiru, certainly one of the most majestic birds of the tropics.

Karumba

Karumba (population 600), 70km from Normanton, is right beside the Gulf of Carpentaria and the Norman River. Originally established as a telegraph station in the 1870s, it became a stopover for the flying boats of the Empire Mail Service in the 1930s. The discovery of prawns in the Gulf in the '60s brought Karumba alive, and today that industry keeps the town humming. It's hard to miss the boats as they sit beside the jetty, draped with nets, just a stone's throw from the pub and the centre of town.

Festivals held during the year include the Karumba Kapers in July, the Barra Ball in November, and the Fisherman's Ball in December.

The town lives and breathes fish and fishing, prawns and prawning. If you aren't interested in these things, you won't stay long. Sure, you can actually get to the sea at Karumba – one of the few places around the Gulf that you can – but once you've checked the town, been to the beach at Karumba Point and enjoyed a prawn or two at the pub, there is not much else to hold your attention. Of course, you could always fly to Mornington or Sweers Islands out in the Gulf, but once again, these are favoured fishing haunts and you need to love fishing to fully appreciate these wild, remote places.

Karumba marks the end of the Matilda, and if you have been travelling it from its humble origin in Cunnamulla, 1674km south, you have experienced one of the best bitumen trips in Australia. Like anything fine, it is to be savoured slowly – take your time and enjoy!

ORGANISED TOURS

Contact the various tourism bodies and regional tourist information centres for details of local tour operators.

If you don't have your own boat, hire one from Karumba Boat Hire (☎ 07-4745 9132) at Karumba Point. There are also a number of boating and fishing tours run from Karumba, and Air Karumba (☎ 07-4745 9354) has flights to Mornington and Sweers Islands, as well as further afield around the Gulf. Contact the Carpentaria Shire Council in Normanton (☎ 07-4745 1166) for full details.

FACILITIES
Cunnamulla
The Paroo Shire Library (☎ 07-4655 2052, John St; open Mon-Fri 9am-noon, 1pm-5pm) has free Internet facilities.

Corella Motor Inn (☎ 07-4655 1593, Cnr Emma & Wicks Sts) Air-con singles/doubles $55/65. This place is your standard, good-value motor inn.

Jack Tonkin Caravan Park (☎ 07-4655 1421, Watson St) Unpowered/powered sites $13/15, cabin doubles $35. Dogs are allowed here, if they are under control. This is a large park with a barbecue area and grassy camping area.

Charleville
Charleville Computers & Trophies (☎ 07-4564 1133), on Wills St in the Corones Hotel building, has Internet access at $6 per hour. It's open 8.30am to 5pm weekdays, and 9am to noon Saturday.

Bailey Bar Caravan Park (☎/fax 07-4654 1744, ☎ 1800 065 311, 196 King St) Unpowered/powered sites $14/16 for 2 people, double cabins $45. Bailey Bar is a friendly, popular park with shady grounds. Pets are allowed, under control.

Cobb & Co Caravan Park (☎ 07-4654 1053, Ridgeway St, off Alfred St) Unpowered/powered sites $14/16 for 2 people, single/double unit $40/48. This place is the closest park to the town centre, and has brand spanking new units. Pets are allowed, under control.

Corones Hotel (☎ 07-4654 1022, Wills St) Double & twin rooms $45-55. This grand old pub is an outback's gems, featuring historic displays and a huge balcony.

Waltzing Matilda Motor Inn (☎ 07-4654 1720, e waltzin@tpg.com, 125 Alfred St) Singles/doubles $44/52. This is a friendly

place with a pool and pleasant enough rooms, but beware of very thin walls.

Poppa's Coffee Shop (☎ 07-4654 1022, Wills St) Open 9am-late Mon-Fri, 9am-2pm Sat, 9am-1pm & 5pm-7pm Sun. Good breakfasts are served at this cafe in the former front bar of the Corones Hotel. Lunch and dinner are also available, including a $12 carvery from 6.30pm Monday to Saturday in the main hotel dining room.

Augathella
Augathella Motel/Caravan Park (☎ 07-4654 5177, Matilda Hwy near Russell's Roadhouse) Unpowered/powered sites $6.60/15.40 for 2 people, singles/doubles $55/66. This is a quiet place with tidy, motel-style rooms. Leashed dogs are OK.

Ellangowan Hotel (☎ 07-4564 5241, Main St) Singles/doubles $25/40. This is an attractive old pub with simple rooms and good meals available.

Tambo
Tambo Caravan Park (☎ 07-4654 6463, Arthur St) Unpowered/powered sites $11/13 for 2 people, single/double on-site van $22/30. This ramshackle place offers plenty of shade and a friendly canine welcoming committee.

Club Hotel/Motel (☎ 07-4654 6109, Arthur St) Dorm beds $12, singles/doubles $35/45. This pub has simple rooms and meals for around $8.

Royal Carrangarra Hotel (☎ 07 4654 6127, Arthur St) Singles/doubles with share bath $15/25. This is a friendly, rambling old place with very basic rooms and – it's said – a resident ghost. Meals are around $8.

Tambo Mill Motel (☎ 07-4654 6466, e tambomillmotel@bigpond.com, Arthur St) Singles/doubles $53/65. This is Tambo's upmarket option, featuring modern rooms and a pool.

Blackall
Coolibah Motel (☎ 07-4657 4380, Matilda Hwy) Singles/doubles $47/58. This is a friendly, well-run place, with a pool.

*Blackall Caravan Park (☎ 07-4657 4816, e ahcarr@ozemail.com.au, enter via

Hart Lane, off Matilda Hwy) Unpowered/ powered sites $12/15, double units $43, double cabins $49. This is a large and popular park, set back from the main road. Camp oven meals are served most nights ($10) during the tourist season. Pets are only allowed on application.

Barcaldine
There's a plethora of great old pubs in Barcaldine's main shopping strip of Oak St. The *Commercial Hotel* (☎ 07-4651 1242) and the *Globe Hotel* (☎ 07-4651 1141) offer basic rooms (singles/doubles $16/25) and cheap counter meals (around $10).

Homestead Caravan Park (☎ 07-4651 1308, Landsborough Hwy/Matilda Hwy) Unpowered/powered sites $12/15.40, single/double en suite units $30/45. This lively, good-value park has 24-hour fuel, and a barbecue every night (except Sunday) during the tourist season. Pets are allowed on application.

Ilfracombe
The Ilfracombe post office (☎ 07-4658 2197, Main Ave, open 9am-12.30pm & 1.30pm-5pm Mon-Fri) offers Internet access at $2 per hour.

The *Wellshot Hotel* (☎ 07-4658 2106, Main Ave) offers accommodation (singles/ doubles $30/40) and camping (powered sites $13 per double), while the *general store* provides fuel and takeaway food.

Longreach
Outback Queensland Internet (☎ 07-4658 3937) has Internet access available at $6 per hour. Open 10am to 6pm Monday to Friday, it's on Swan St, near the Eagle St intersection.

Accommodation-wise, there's a wide choice here, most of it centred around the main drag of Eagle St.

Gunnadoo Caravan Park (☎ 07-4658 1781, 12 Thrush Rd) Unpowered/powered sites $16.50/18.50, single/double huts $38.50/44, double cabins $60.50, double units $90. This is a large park with a swimming pool and a $10 smorgasbord is served every Wednesday evening.

Welcome Inn (☎ 07-4658 1361, Eagle St) Dorm beds $28, double units $57. The Inn is a classic big old pub with plenty of character.

Longreach Motel (☎ 07-4658 1996, 🄴 longreachmotel@tpg.com.au, 127 Eagle St) Singles/doubles $65/75. This is a modern motor-inn-style place with large, immaculate rooms.

Happy Valley Chinese Restaurant (☎ 07-4658 1311, 135 Eagle St) Mains $9.50-14. Open 11.30am-3pm and 5pm-midnight Fri & Sat, 11.30-3pm & 5pm-10pm Sun, Mon & Thur. This popular place near the Longreach Motel has a very good eat-in or takeaway menu.

Winton
The National Australia and Westpac banks have branches in Winton, but despite the town's size there is no ATM. The local RACQ depot is Winton Fuel & Tyre Service (☎ 07-4657 1305).

The North Gregory Hotel (☎ 1800 801 611, 07-4657 1375, 67 Elderslie St) has Internet access at $3 per 10 minutes, with access available from 8am till 'late'.

With many of Winton's places to stay connected to artesian bore water, showers can get a little sulphurous. Most travellers say this water stinks. Locals reckon it's just got a bit of 'body'.

North Gregory Hotel (☎ 07-4657 1375, 1800 801 611, 67 Elderslie St) Dorm beds $15, singles/doubles $33-55/44-55. Legend has it, this grand hotel is on the site of the first performance of *Waltzing Matilda*. Balcony rooms here are excellent, and all rates include a continental breakfast.

Tattersalls Hotel (☎ 07-4657 1309, Elderslie St) Singles/doubles with share bath $15/25. This is a wonderful old hotel, with friendly service and good food.

Matilda Country Tourist Park (☎ 07-4657 1607, 1800 001 383, 🄴 matpark@tpg .com.au, 43 Chirnside St) Unpowered/ powered sites $14/16 for 2 people, double cabins $60. This is a very popular Caravan and cabin park where you can enjoy campfire dinners and bush poetry most nights from April to September.

Kynuna

Blue Heeler Hotel (☎ 07-4646 8650, Kynuna, e stephen@blueheeler.com.au, W www.blueheeler.com.au) Unpowered/powered sites $3.30/13.30, double hotel rooms $33, double motel rooms $55. This 100-year-old establishment is decoratively graffitied and a top spot for a cool beer.

Never Never Caravan Park (☎ 07-4646 8683, Kynuna) Unpowered sites $5 per person. The park is conveniently located close to the Blue Heeler Hotel.

McKinlay

Walkabout Creek Hotel (☎ 07-4746 8424, Matilda Hwy) Unpowered sites $6, singles/doubles $42/52. Rooms here are basic but good. Pets are allowed.

Cloncurry

Curry Byte (☎ 07-4742 1630) on Ramsay St, the main drag, has Internet access at $6 per hour. It's open 9am to 6pm weekdays, and 9am to 3pm Saturday. The town has several hotel-motels and caravan parks, plenty of fuel outlets, and a supermarket.

Gilbert Park Tourist Village (☎ 07-4742 2300, e gilpark@topend.com.au, McIlwraith St) Unpowered/powered sites $14/18 for 2 people, single/double cabins with en suite $60.50/64.50. This is a busy, well-developed park with pricey but spacious balconied cabins. There's a pool and picturesque natural sunset viewing area.

Post Office Hotel Motel (☎ 07-4742 1411, Sheaffe St) Single/double hotel rooms $32/45, single/double motel rooms $60/70. This is a grand old place with basic hotel rooms.

Central Hotel (☎ 07-4742 1418, Scarr St) Singles/doubles $27.50/38.50 with share bath. Diagonally opposite the similar-vintage Post Office Hotel Motel, the Central has simple accommodation but is perfectly positioned to soak up glorious sunsets.

Wagon Wheel Motel (☎ 07-4742 1866, fax 4742 1819, 54 Ramsay St, next to the bowls club) Budget singles/doubles $54/60, deluxe singles/doubles $69/75. This is a friendly, well-run place with a **licensed restaurant** (☎ 07-4742 1480) serving,

among other things, eat-in or takeaway pizza. The budget rooms are a little on the cramped side.

Burke & Wills Roadhouse

The **Burke & Wills Roadhouse** (☎ 07-4472 5909; Matilda Hwy; open 7am-10pm Mon-Sat, 8am-10pm Sun) has unpowered/powered sites for $4.50/16.50, and pleasant, cabin-style singles/doubles for $38.50/49.50.

Normanton

Normanton has more than enough hotel/motels and caravan parks, as well as fuel (all types) and a supermarket.

Gulfland Motel & Caravan Park (☎ 07-4745 1290, fax 4745 1138, Landsborough St) Unpowered/powered sites $6.60/17.60, self-contained motel singles/doubles $77/88. This place actually lives up to its publicity blurb as 'a little oasis'.

Normanton Caravan Park (☎ 07-4745 1121, Brown St) Unpowered/powered sites $5.50/11-14.30. This park is run by the council and has all the facilities, including a heated pool. Pets on leashes are allowed.

Central Hotel (☎ 07-4745 1215, Landsborough St) Budget singles/doubles $25/40, motel single/doubles $55/60. This is a good-value option, next to the post office.

Purple Pub & Brolga Palms Motel (☎ 07-4745 1324, Cnr Landsborough & Brown Sts) Hotel singles/doubles $28/49, motel singles/doubles $63/85. This is a lively place with a good range of accommodation, and a pool.

Karumba

There's a large, modern pub here (the Sunset Tavern), several caravan parks, and plenty of cabins; the former can really be jumping when the boats come in for a short break or for resupply. There are heaps of holiday cabins for rent at Karumba and Karumba Point – contact the shire office in Normanton (☎ 07-4745 1166) for a full listing.

Gulf Country Caravan Park (☎ 07-4745 9148, Cnr Yappar St & Massey Dr) Unpowered/powered sites $15.80/17.95 for 2 people, double cabins $58. This is place has shady grounds and a pool.

Karumba Point Sunset Caravan Park (☎ *07-4745 9277, Karumba Point Rd*) Unpowered/powered sites $16/18 for 2 people, double cabins $65. This is a very popular place right next to the beach, with a pool.

Gee-Dee's (☎ *07-4745 9433, Karumba Point Rd*) Self-contained units $60. This place is good value, with spacious, new, family-size cabins with balconies; near the Sunset Tavern.

Sunset Tavern (☎ *07-4745 9183*) Main meals $12-14. This massive, open-air pub offers an equally massive menu and serves fantastic food (especially seafood). It's right on the beach and is open daily for lunch and dinner.

ALTERNATIVE TRANSPORT
Car Rental
Offices of Avis (☎ 13 63 33, 07-4743 3733) and Thrifty (☎ 1300 367 227) can be found in the larger towns, such as Charleville, Longreach and Mt Isa.

Bus
McCafferty's/Greyhound (☎ 1800 801 294, 07-4771 2134) services all towns between Townsville and Mt Isa on the Flinders and Barkly Hwys; and all towns on the Warrego, Landsborough and Capricorn Hwys between Brisbane and Mt Isa, as well as Rockhampton and Longreach.

Campbell's Coaches (☎ 07-4743 2006), based at Mt Isa, travel once a week from Mt Isa to Cloncurry, Quamby, Burke & Wills Roadhouse, Normanton and Karumba.

Cairns-based Coral Coaches (☎ 07-4031 7577) run several times a week between Cairns, Karumba and Mt Isa (with connections to Undara), as well as connecting to the Gulflander train in Normanton.

Train
QR Traveltrain operates rail services from Brisbane to Charleville on the *Westlander* (with bus connections to Cunnamulla and Quilpie), from Brisbane to Longreach on the *Spirit of the Outback* (with a bus connection to Winton), and from Townsville to Mt Isa on the *Inlander*. QR Traveltrain also operates regular 'scenic routes' from Normanton to Croydon on the *Gulflander*, and from Cairns to Forsayth on the *Savannahlander*.

The *Inlander* departs for Mt Isa from Townsville on Sunday, Monday, Wednesday and Thursday, stopping along the way in places such as Hughenden, Julia Creek and Cloncurry. From Mt Isa to Townsville, it goes Monday, Tuesday, Friday and Saturday.

The *Gulflander* departs Normanton on Wednesday at 8.30am, arriving in Croydon at 12.30pm the same day, then departing Croydon Thursday at 8.30am and arriving back in Normanton the same day at 12.30pm.

The *Savannahlander* departs Cairns Wednesday morning, and does a round trip via Almaden, Forsayth (with connections to Undara available) and Mt Surprise. It arrives back in Cairns on Saturday.

For bookings and information for any of these routes, contact QR Traveltrain (☎ 13 22 32, 07-3235 1122, e res.traveltrain@ qr.com.au). Bookings can also be made at the following train stations: Brisbane Central (☎ 07-3235 1323), Railcentre 1, 305 Edward St, Brisbane; Brisbane Transit Centre (☎ 07-3235 1331), Roma St, Brisbane; Robina railway station (☎ 07-5562 0539), Robina Town Centre Dr, Robina, Gold Coast; Cairns railway station (☎ 1800 620 324), McLeod St, Cairns; Rockhampton railway station (☎ 07-4932 0234), Murray St, Rockhampton; and Townsville railway station (☎ 07-4772 8546), Flinders St, Townsville. Bookings for the *Gulflander* can also be made at the Normanton railway station (☎ 07-4745 1391).

Air
Macair (☎ 07-4035 9722, fax 4035 9663, w www.macair.com.au) has a booking service hosted by Qantas (☎ 13 13 13, w www .qantas.com.au), and operates scheduled and charter services from its base in Cairns to destinations such as Cooktown, Normanton, Karumba, Burketown, Mt Isa and Cloncurry.

Virgin Blue (☎ 13 67 89, w www.virgin blue.com.au) operates daily flights from Brisbane to Cairns and Townsville.

Macair (☎ 13 15 28) operates general charter flights out of Thargomindah, with semi-regular flights to/from Brisbane, Cunnamulla and Toowoomba.

Savannah Aviation (☎ 1800 455 445, 07-4745 5177, e savair@ozemail.com, w www.savannah-aviation.com) has bases in Burketown, Karumba, Normanton and Mt Isa, and operates general charter services as well as day trips to Lawn Hill National Park.

The Karumba-based Heli-Man Aviation (☎ 07-4745 9588, 0408-088 872, fax 4745 9533) specialises in helicopter outback adventure tours, including heli-fishing, wildlife tours and general charter.

There's also a number of Cairns-based charter operators serving the Savannah region including: Air Swift Aviation (☎ 07-4035 9288, fax 4035 9245), specialising in charter flights throughout Cape York and the peninsula area; and Cape York Air Services (☎ 07-4035 9399, fax 4035 9108) which offers long-haul mail run flights to/from Cairns.

Boat

Gulf Freight Services (☎ 1800 640 079, 07-4051 3367, fax 4031 5847) operate a weekly freight service between Karumba and Weipa, with several cabins available to the public. Caravans and vehicles can also be carried. This is a popular tourist service and early bookings are essential. The boat departs Karumba Friday morning or Saturday evening, arriving in Weipa Sunday evening or Monday morning. It then departs Weipa Monday evening, arriving in Karumba (via Aurukun) Wednesday evening.

Checklists

Before You Go

- Pre-plan – where, time of year, time needed, distance, fuel range.
- Research – things to see and do, history, fuel availability, resupply, road conditions.
- Make an itinerary – and use it as a guide only. Keep it flexible to allow for breakdowns, advice or ideas you receive while underway and places you fall in love with.
- Apply for permits – to national parks and Aboriginal land. Some parks operate on a ballot system in the busy seasons so it's wise to enquire about bookings well in advance. Restrictions are also placed in parks such as Gurig in the Northern Territory, where bookings must be made at least 12 months in advance because only 15 vehicles are allowed in at any one time.
- Book accommodation – if you want to stay at a popular spot, for instance Monkey Mia in Western Australia over the school holidays, you may want to book. Remember that if you book too many places, your flexible itinerary will go out the window.
- Let someone know your itinerary – if you change it greatly, let them know so they don't hit the panic button. Keep in touch with someone at home at prearranged intervals.

Always Carry

- basic car recovery gear (see below)
- first aid kit plus manual (see the Health section in the Facts for the Visitor chapter)
- fire extinguisher
- HF radio, satellite phone or EPIRB if you're heading to remote country
- vehicle tools and spare parts (see below)
- plenty of water (at least 5L of drinking water per person per day)
- good maps
- matches
- compass
- torch (flashlight) and spare batteries
- knife
- space blanket

Camping & Personal Gear

- tent, swag and/or stretcher (camp bed)
- sleeping gear
- mosquito net (fine mesh)
- broad-brimmed hat (maybe with fly net)

- good-quality sunglasses
- wet-weather gear
- portable light (gas, spirit or electric – one that operates off the car battery)
- portable fridge or ice chest/Esky
- folding chairs
- folding table
- heavy-duty plastic rubbish bags
- toilet paper
- toiletries bag
- clothes (including sweater)
- camera, film and spare batteries
- sunscreen lotion (rated 30+)
- insect repellent
- paper and pencils
- string
- plastic sheet
- tarpaulin
- poles, ropes & pegs
- 10L bucket (square packs best)
- clothesline and pegs
- laundry detergent
- axe or bow saw (the latter is far safer)

Campfire Cooking Equipment (Essential)

- medium to large cast-iron camp oven – pack carefully so it doesn't bounce around and crack
- two or three steel saucepans or billies of varying size, with lids. Choose saucepans that will fit inside one another for better packing
- at least one large steel billy with lid
- large, steel frying pan
- steel barbecue plate with legs
- heat-resistant gloves with lower-arm protection (eg welding gloves)

Campfire Cooking Equipment (Optional)

- cake rack or similar to place in the bottom of your camp oven
- jaffle iron
- toasting forks
- metal fire grate with legs (preferably adjustable)
- long-handled barbecue utensils
- natural-fibre brush – to brush coals off camp oven lid
- fire starters

General Cooking Items
- gas stove
- eating utensils
- plates, bowls, cups (plastic is best)
- sharp knives
- mixing bowls, large mixing spoons
- flat plastic grater
- sieve
- chopping board
- can opener, bottle opener, corkscrew
- peeler
- small measuring cup
- small plastic funnel
- aluminium foil
- plastic food-wrap
- snap-lock plastic bags
- heavy-duty plastic rubbish bags
- tea towels
- dishwashing detergent (concentrated)
- pot scourer
- sponges (for dishwashing)
- square 10L bucket (for dishwashing)

Car Tools
- repair manual
- set of ring and open-end spanners (to suit your vehicle)
- adjustable spanner, plug spanner
- wheel brace, jack and jacking plate (30cm square x 2.5cm thick board)
- 1m length of steel pipe (to fit over handle of wheel brace for extra leverage when removing stubborn wheel nuts)
- screwdrivers (selection of standard and Phillips head)
- Allen keys (if applicable)
- hammer, chisel
- hacksaw and spare blades
- file, including a points file
- thread file
- pliers and wire cutters
- tie wire, nylon 'zip-ties'
- heavy-gauge low-tensile wire (handy for tying broken bits together)
- Araldite epoxy resin
- feeler gauges
- tyre levers
- bead breaker (if required)
- good-quality tyre pump and pressure gauge
- tube/tyre repair kit
- battery jumper leads
- WD40, or similar
- funnel and hose
- rags, octopus straps and spare rope

Car Spares
- radiator hoses
- heater hoses
- fan belts
- fuses
- globes
- electric wire
- electrical insulation tape
- thread sealing tape
- spark plugs (petrol engine)
- plug leads (petrol engine)
- points (petrol engine)
- coil (petrol engine)
- condenser (petrol engine)
- tyre tube, valves and caps
- bolts, nuts, self-tapping screws, washers
- grease
- gasket cement
- second spare wheel (for remote areas)

It's always wise to carry some extra fuel and engine oil. On longer trips, you could include a more comprehensive range of tools and spares, such as a socket set plus any of the commonly needed special tools for your vehicle, exhaust sealant, wheel bearings, air filters and gear oil. It's easy to carry too much, though, so be critical. If there are similar vehicles in your group, save weight by sharing. On remote trips or rough, rocky roads, an extra spare tyre should be high on your list of priorities.

Car Recovery Gear
- snatch strap
- two 'D' shackles
- long-handled shovel
- axe
- jack and jacking plate (to provide a stable base for jacking in mud or sand)

The above are the basics. Depending on the nature of the trip and the problems likely to be encountered, consider adding the following:

- Tirfor (or similar) hand winch, or power winch
- tree protector strap
- winch extension straps
- snatch-block
- extra 'D' shackles
- high-lift jack and base plate
- air-bag jack (particularly good in sandy areas)
- chainsaw (with fuel, spare chain, chain file etc)

Glossary

amber fluid – beer
ankle-biter – small child, *tacker*, *rug rat*
arvo – afternoon
avagoyermug – traditional rallying call, especially at cricket matches
award wage – minimum pay rate

back o' Bourke – back of beyond, middle of nowhere
backblocks – *bush* or other remote area far from the city
bail out – leave, depart
bail up – hold up, rob, *earbash*
Balmain bug – see *Moreton Bay bug*
banana bender – resident of Queensland
banker – a river almost overflowing its banks (as in 'the Cooper is running a banker')
barbie – barbecue, BBQ
barra – barramundi (a type of fish)
barrack – cheer on a team at sporting event; support, as in 'who do you barrack for?'
bastard – general term of address which can mean many things; mostly used as a good-natured form of greeting ('*G'day*, you old bastard!'); can also denote the highest level of praise or respect ('He's the bravest bastard I know!'), or it can be the most dire of insults ('You lousy, lying bastard!')
bathers – swimming costume (Victoria, Western Australia)
battler – hard trier, struggler (the outback is full of 'great Aussie battlers')
beaut, beauty, bewdie – great, fantastic, excellent
big bikkies – a lot of money, expensive
big mobs – a large amount, heaps
bikies – motorcyclists
billabong – waterhole in dried-up riverbed, more correctly an ox-bow bend cut off in the dry season by receding waters
billy – tin pot used to boil tea in the *bush*
bitumen – asphalt, surfaced road
black stump – where the *back o' Bourke* begins

blaze – (a blaze in a tree) a mark in a tree trunk made by cutting away bark, indicating a path or reference point; also 'to blaze'
bloke – man
blowies – blowflies, bluebottles
bludger – lazy person, one who won't work and lives off other people's money (originally, a prostitute's pimp)
blue, have a – to have an argument or fight with someone
bluey – *swag*; also nickname for a red-haired person
bonzer – great, *ripper*
boomer – very big; a particularly large male kangaroo
boomerang – a curved flat wooden instrument used by Aborigines for hunting
booze bus – police van used for random breath testing of drivers for alcohol levels
boozer – pub
bottle – 750mL bottle of beer
bottle shop – a retail outlet for alcohol
bottlo – see *bottle shop*
bowser – fuel pump at a service station (named after the US inventor SF Bowser)
Bradshaw paintings – in the Kimberley, mysterious and very ancient rock paintings of unknown origin
brumby – wild horse
bruss – brother, *mate* (used by central Australian Aborigines)
Buckley's chance – no chance at all ('Across the Tanami? They've got Buckley's in that *shitbox*'). The origin of this term is unclear. Maybe it derives from the Melbourne department store of Buckley's & Nunn; or from the escaped convict William Buckley, whose chances of survival were considered negligible but who ended up living with Aborigines for 20 years; or from the Sydney escapologist Buckley, who had himself chained-up in a coffin and thrown into Sydney Harbour, with dire results
bug – see *Moreton Bay bug*
Bulamakanka – beyond the *back o' Bourke*, way beyond the *black stump* (see *never-never*)

bull bar – outsize front bumper on car or truck used as the ultimate barrier against animals on the road

bulldust – fine, powdery and sometimes deep dust on outback roads, often hiding deep holes and ruts that you normally wouldn't drive into; also bullshit

bunfight – a quarrel over a frivolous issue or one that gets blown out of proportion

bungarra – any large (1.5m-plus) goanna, but specifically an Aboriginal name for Gould's goanna, prized as food

bunyip – mythical bush spirit said to inhabit Australia's swamps

burl – have a try (as in 'give it a burl')

bush – country, anywhere away from the city; *scrub*

bush, (ie, go bush) – leave civilisation

bushbash – to force your way through pathless bush

bushranger – Australia's equivalent of the outlaws of the American Wild West (some goodies, some baddies) – the helmeted Ned Kelly was the most famous

bush tucker – food available naturally

BYO – Bring Your Own (booze to a restaurant, meat to a barbecue etc)

caaarn! – come on, traditional rallying call, especially at football games (as in 'Caaarn the Crows!')

cackle-berries – eggs; also 'hen-fruit', 'chook-nuts' and 'bum-nuts'

camp draft – Australian rodeo, testing horse rider's skills in separating cattle or sheep from a herd or flock

camp oven – large, cast-iron pot with lid, used for cooking in an open fire

cask – cardboard box containing a plastic bladder filled with wine (a great Australian invention)

Chiko roll – deep-fried and battered cabbage roll

chocka – completely full (from 'chock-a-block')

chook – chicken

chuck a U-ey – do a U-turn

chunder – vomit, technicolour yawn, pavement pizza, curbside quiche, liquid laugh, drive the porcelain bus, call Bluey

clobber – clothes

cobber – *mate*

cocky – small-scale farmer; cockatoo

come good – turn out all right

compo – compensation, eg, money paid to a person injured at work

cooee – shouting distance, close (to be within cooee of…)

cop, copper – police officer (not uniquely *strine* but very common nevertheless); *walloper*

counter meal, countery – pub meal

cow cocky – small-scale cattle farmer

cozzie – swimming costume (New South Wales)

crook – ill, badly made, substandard, broken

crow eater – resident of South Australia

culvert – channel or pipe under road for rainwater drainage

cut lunch – sandwiches

cut snake – see *mad as a …*

dag, daggy – dirty lump of wool at back end of a sheep; also an affectionate or mildly abusive term for a socially inept person

daks – trousers

damper – bush bread made from flour and water and cooked in a *camp oven*

Darwin stubby – 2L bottle of beer sold to tourists in Darwin

dead horse – tomato sauce

deli – delicatessen; milk bar in South Australia and Western Australia

digger – Australian or New Zealand soldier or veteran (originally, a miner); also a generic form of address assuming respect, mainly used for soldiers/veterans but sometimes also between friends

didgeridoos – cylindrical wooden musical instrument played by Aboriginal men

dill – idiot

dingo – indigenous wild dog

dink – carry a second person on a bicycle or horse

dinkum, fair dinkum – honest, genuine ('fair dinkum? – really?')

dinky-di – the real thing

distillate – diesel fuel

divvy van – police divisional van

dob in – to tell on someone

Dog Fence – the world's longest fence,

erected to keep dingoes out of south-eastern Australia

donga – small transportable hut; also the *bush*, from the name for a shallow, eroded gully, found in areas where it doesn't rain often, so people don't go there

donk – car or boat engine

donkey – ingenious hot-water system for showers etc, consisting of a 44-gallon drum, piping and a wood fire

don't come the raw prawn – don't try and fool me

down south – the rest of Australia, viewed from the Northern Territory or anywhere north of Brisbane

drongo – foolish or worthless person

droving – moving livestock a considerable distance

Dry, the – the dry season in the north

duco – car paint

duffing – stealing cattle (literally: altering the brand on the 'duff', or rump)

dunny – outdoor lavatory

dunny budgies – *blowies*

earbash – talk non-stop

eastern states – the rest of Australia viewed from west of Queensland.

Eftpos – Electronic Funds Transfer at Point of Sale

Esky – trademark name for a portable ice box that keeps drinks and food cold

fair crack of the whip! – *fair go!*

fair go! – give us a break!

feeding the ants – being in a very deceased condition out in the *donga*

FJ – most revered classic Holden car

flagon – 2L bottle (of wine, port etc)

flake – shark meat, often used in fish and chips *down south*

floater – meat pie floating in gravy or thick pea soup

flog – steal; sell; whip

fluke – undeserved good luck ('they had three flat tyres, no spare, no puncture kit, no water, but they fluked a lift into town on the monthly mail truck. Otherwise they'd still be there *feeding the ants*')

fossick – hunt for gems or semi-precious stones

from arsehole to breakfast – all over the place

furphy – a misleading statement, rumour or fictitious story, named after Joseph Furphy, who wrote a famous Australian novel, *Such is Life*, then reviewed the book for a literary journal of the time and criticised it; the public bought it by the ton. Or maybe this is a furphy and the term instead derives from the water or sewerage carrier made by his brother's company in Shepparton, Victoria; in WWI these carriers were places where the troops met, swapped yarns and information and no doubt construed a few furphies

galah – noisy parrot, thus noisy idiot

game – brave (as in 'game as Ned Kelly')

gander – look (as in 'have a gander')

garbo – person who collects your garbage

gibber plain– stony desert; gibber is an Aboriginal word for stone or boulder

gidgee – a type of small acacia (shrub)

give it away – give up

g'day – good day, traditional Australian greeting

good on ya – well done

grade – (to grade a road) to level a road, usually by means of a bulldozer fitted with a 'blade' that scrapes off the top layer and pushes it to the side

grazier – large-scale sheep or cattle farmer

Green, the – term used in the Kimberley for the wet season

grog – general term for alcoholic drinks

grouse – very good, unreal

homestead – the residence of a *station* owner or manager

hoon – idiot, hooligan, *yahoo*; also 'to hoon' or 'hooning around', often in a vehicle; to show off in a noisy fashion with little regard for others

hotel – a place to stay, or a pub, or both

how are ya? – standard greeting (expected answer: 'Good, thanks. And you?')

how ya goin'? – *how are ya?*

HQ – second-most revered Holden car

Hughie – the god of rain and surf ('Send her down, Hughie!', 'Send 'em up, Hughie!'); also God when things go wrong ('It's up to Hughie now')

humpy – Aboriginal bark hut ('it was so cold, it would freeze the walls off a bark humpy')

icy-pole – frozen *lolly water* or ice cream on a stick

jackaroo – young male trainee on a *station*
jaffle – sealed toasted sandwich
jerky – dried meat
jillaroo – young female trainee on a *station*
jocks – men's underpants
joey – young kangaroo or wallaby
journo – journalist
jumped-up – arrogant, full of self-importance (a 'jumped-up petty Hitler')
jump-up – escarpment

kiwi – (also 'kay-one-double-you-one') a person from New Zealand
knackered – exhausted, very tired
knock – criticise, deride
knocker – one who *knocks*
Koori – Aboriginal person from Victoria or New South Wales

lair – layabout, ruffian
lairising – acting like a *lair*
lamington – square of sponge cake covered in chocolate icing and coconut
larrikin – a bit like a *lair*; rascal
lay-by – put a deposit on an article so the shop will hold it for you
lemonade – soft drink
lockup – *watch house*
lollies – sweets, candy
lolly water – soft drink made from syrup and water
lurk – profitable strategem, plan, dodge or scheme

mad as a cut snake – insane, crazy; also insane with anger
mallee – low, shrubby, multi-stemmed eucalypt *scrub*. Also 'the mallee' – the *bush*
manchester – household linen
March fly – horsefly, gadfly
mate – general term of familiarity, whether you know the person or not (but don't use it too often with total strangers)
Matilda – *swag*

middy – 285mL beer glass (New South Wales, Western Australia)
milk bar – general store
milko – milkman
mob – a herd of cattle or flock of sheep while *droving*; any bunch of people (group, club, company)
Moreton Bay bug – (also known as *bug* or *Balmain bug*) an estuarine horseshoe crab closely related to the shovel-nosed lobster (good *tucker* with an unfortunate name)
mozzies – mosquitoes
mud map – map drawn on the ground with a stick, thus any rough map drawn by hand
mulga – arid-zone acacia *scrub*; the *bush*, away from civilisation (as in 'he's gone up the mulga')
Murri – Aboriginal person whose ancestors are from Queensland or parts of New South Wales around Moree
muster – round up livestock
mystery-bags – sausages

never-never – a place even more remote than *back o' Bourke*
no-hoper – hopeless case
northern summer – summer in the northern hemisphere
north island – mainland Australia, viewed from Tasmania
no worries – *she'll be right*, that's OK
nulla-nulla – wooden club used by the Aborigines for hunting

ocker – an uncultivated, usually opinionated or boorish Australian
ocky strap – octopus strap: elastic strap with hooks for tying down gear and generally keeping things in place
offsider – assistant or partner
on the piss – drinking alcohol ('they're on the piss tonight'), an alcohol binge
o-s – overseas (as in 'he's gone o-s')
Oz – Australia

pad – animal track, as in 'cattle pad'
paddock – a fenced area of land, usually intended for livestock (paddocks can be huge in Australia)
pal – *mate*
pastoralist – large-scale *grazier*

pavlova – traditional Australian meringue and cream dessert, named after the Russian ballerina Anna Pavlova

perv – to gaze at a person with lust

pineapple, rough end of the – *stick, sharp end of the*

piss – beer

pissed – drunk

pissed off – annoyed

piss turn – boozy party

plonk – cheap wine

pocamelo – camel polo

pokies – poker machines

pom – English person

pommy's towel – a notoriously very dry object, 'the desert is as dry as a pommy's towel'

possie – position, pronounced 'pozzy', eg, to be 'in a good possie'

postie – postal worker

pot – 285mL glass of beer (Victoria, Queensland)

push – group or gang of people, such as shearers

quid – a British pound; also a common term in the *bush* for a non-specified amount of money, as in 'can you lend me a quid?' (enough money to last me until I'm no longer *skint*)

Quinkan – on Cape York, spirits depicted in two forms (the long and stick-like Timara and the crocodile-like Imjim) in rock paintings at Laura

rapt – delighted, enraptured

ratbag – friendly term of abuse (friendly trouble-maker)

rat's coffin – meat pie of dubious quality

ratshit (R-S) – lousy

razoo – a coin of very little value, a subdivision of a rupee ('he spent every last razoo'). Counterfeit razoos made of brass circulated in the goldfields during *two-up* sessions, hence 'it's not worth a brass razoo'

rego – registration, as in 'car rego'

ridgy-didge – original, genuine, *dinky-di*

ripper – good, great, also 'little ripper'

road train – *semi-trailer*-trailer-trailer

roo bar – *bull bar*

root – have sexual intercourse

ropable – very bad-tempered or angry

rubbish, to – to deride, tease, criticise

rug rat – small child, *ankle-biter, tacker*

saltbush – dry, shrubby plants of the Chenopodiaceae family named for their tolerance to saline conditions, widespread and sometimes dominant over vast areas

Salvo – member of the Salvation Army

sandgroper – a person who comes from Western Australia

sanger – sandwich

scallops – fried potato cakes (Queensland), the edible muscle of certain molluscs (north Queensland), shellfish (elsewhere)

schooner – a 425mL beer glass in New South Wales, or a 285mL glass in South Australia (where a 425mL glass is called a 'pint')

scrub – stunted trees and bushes in a dry area; a remote, uninhabited area

sealed road – bitumen road

sea wasp – box jellyfish

sedan – a closed car seating four to six people

see you in the soup – see you around

seismic line – *shotline*

semi-trailer – articulated truck

septic tanks – rhyming slang for Yanks, also 'septics'

session – lengthy period of heavy drinking

shanty – pub, usually unlicensed, common in gold-rush areas

sheila – woman, sometimes derogatory

shellacking – comprehensive defeat

she'll be right – *no worries*, it'll be OK

shitbox – a neglected, worn-out, useless vehicle

shonky – unreliable

shoot through – leave in a hurry

shotline – straight trail through the bush, often kilometres long and leading nowhere, built by a mining company for seismic research

shout – buy round of drinks (as in 'it's your shout')

sickie – day off work through illness or lack of motivation

singlet – sleeveless shirt

skint – the state of being *quidless,* to have no money

slab – four six-packs of cans (375mL) of beer, usually encased in plastic on a cardboard base; also called a 'carton' when packaged in a box (Victoria, Western Australia)
sleep-out – a covered verandah or shed, usually fairly open
sling off – criticise
smoko – tea break
snag – sausage
sooty grunter – black bream, a kind of fish
spinifex – dense, dome-shaped masses of long, needle-like grass on sandy soils and rocky areas, among the hardiest of desert plants
sport – *mate*
spunky – good looking, attractive, as in 'what a spunk'
squatter – pioneer grazier who occupied land as a tenant of the government
squattocracy – Australian 'old money' folk, who made it by being first on the scene and grabbing the land
squiz – inquisitive look or glance, as in 'take a squiz'
station – large sheep or cattle farm
stick, sharp end of the – the worst deal
stickybeak – nosy person
stinger – box jellyfish
stoush – physical or verbal fight or brawl
stretcher – camp bed
strides – *daks*
strine – Australian slang that comes from how an *ocker* would pronounce the word 'Australian'
stubbies – trademark name for rugged short shorts
stubby – 375mL bottle of beer
sunbake – sunbathe (well, the sun's hot in Australia)
super – superannuation, money paid by employer and/or employee to a retirement fund
surfaced road – tarred road
surfies – surfing fanatics
swag – canvas-covered bed roll used in the outback; also a large amount
swaggie, swagman – itinerant worker carrying his possessions in a *swag* (see *waltzing Matilda*)

ta – thanks
table drain – rainwater run-off area, often quite deep and wide, along the side of a dirt road
tacker – small child, *ankle-biter*, *rug rat*
takeaway – fast food, or a shop that sells it
tall poppies – achievers (*knockers* like to cut them down)
Taswegian – resident of Tasmania
tea – evening meal
terrorist – tourist
thingo – thing, whatchamacallit, hoozameebob, dooverlacky, thingamajig
thirst you could paint a picture of – the desire to drink a large quantity of foaming, ice-cold, nut-brown ale
thongs – flip-flops
tinny – 375mL can of beer; also a small aluminium fishing dinghy
Tip, the – the top of Cape York
togs – swimming costume (Queensland, Victoria)
too right! – absolutely!
Top End – northern part of the Northern Territory, sometimes also Cape York
Troopie – Toyota Land Cruiser Troopcarrier (seats up to 11 people)
trucky – truck driver
true blue – *dinkum*
tucker – food
turps – turpentine, alcoholic liquor, as in 'he's on the turps' (he's an alcoholic – a common condition in the outback)
two-pot screamer – person unable to hold their drink
two-up – traditional heads/tails gambling game

uni – university
ugg boots – sheepskin boots
up north – New South Wales and Queensland when viewed from Victoria
ute – utility, pickup truck

vegies – vegetables

waddy – wooden club used by Aborigines
wag, to – to play truant, eg 'to wag school'
wagon – station wagon, estate car
walkabout – a lengthy walk to get away from it all

wallaby track, on the – to wander from place to place seeking work

walloper – police officer (from 'wallop', to hit something with a stick)

waltzing Matilda – to wander with one's *swag* seeking work or a place to settle down; as used in Australia's unofficial national anthem *Waltzing Matilda*

Wandjina – in the Kimberley, a group of ancestral beings associated with fertility who came from the sky and sea, often depicted in rock images

washaway – washout, heavy erosion caused by running water across road or track

watch house – a prison cell at a police station for temporary detention

waterhole – permanent and usually small body of freshwater, either spring-fed or stream-fed (may be stagnant in the *Dry*)

weatherboard house – house clad with long, narrow planks of wood

Wet, the – the wet or rainy season in the north

wharfie – dock worker

whinge – complain, moan

whoa-boy – small, dirt ridge laid diagonally across a steep track for water run-off, often unexpected (hence the name)

willy-willy – whirlwind, dust storm

wobbly – disturbing, unpredictable behaviour as in 'throw a wobbly'

wobbly boot – (as in 'to put on the wobbly boot') to have consumed too much alcohol

woof wood – petrol used to start a fire (also 'bushman's lighter fluid')

woolly rocks – sheep

woomera – stick used by Aborigines to propel spears

wowser – spoilsport, puritan

yabby, yabbie – small freshwater crayfish

yabby, to – to catch yabbies, a relaxed activity often involving *mates* and a *slab* or two, 'they're going yabbying this *arvo*'

yahoo – noisy and unruly person, *hoon*

yakka – work (from an Aboriginal language)

yobbo – uncouth, aggressive person

yonks – ages, a long time

youse – plural of you, pronounced 'yooz'

yowie – Australia's yeti or bigfoot

LONELY PLANET

You already know that Lonely Planet produces more than this one guidebook, but you might not be aware of the other products we have on this region. Here is a selection of titles that you may want to check out as well:

Northern Territory
ISBN 0 86442 791 3
US$16.95 • UK£10.99

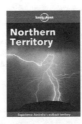

Western Australia
ISBN 0 86442 740 9
US$15.99 • UK£10.99

New South Wales
ISBN 0 86442 706 9
US$19.99 • UK£12.99

Sydney
ISBN 1 74059 062 7
US$16.99 • UK£10.99

Melbourne
ISBN 1 86450 124 3
US$14.99 • UK£8.99

Queensland
ISBN 0 86442 712 3
US$19.99 • UK£11.99

**Aboriginal Australia &
the Torres Strait Islands**
ISBN 1 86450 114 6
US$19.99 • UK£12.99

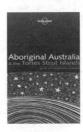

Sean & David's Long Drive
ISBN 0 86442 371 3
US$10.95 • UK£5.99

Watching Wildlife Australia
ISBN 1 86450 032 8
US$19.99 • UK£12.99

Sydney City Map
ISBN 1 86450 015 8
US$5.95 • UK£3.99

Australia Road Atlas
ISBN 1 86450 065 4
US$14.99 • UK£8.99

**Healthy Travel Australia,
NZ & the Pacific**
ISBN 1 86450 052 2
US$5.95 • UK£3.99

Available wherever books are sold

Lonely Planet Guides by Region

L onely Planet is known worldwide for publishing practical, reliable and no-nonsense travel information in our guides and on our Web site. The Lonely Planet list covers just about every accessible part of the world. Currently there are 16 series: Travel guides, Shoestring guides, Condensed guides, Phrasebooks, Read This First, Healthy Travel, Walking guides, Cycling guides, Watching Wildlife guides, Pisces Diving & Snorkeling guides, City Maps, Road Atlases, Out to Eat, World Food, Journeys travel literature and Pictorials.

AFRICA Africa on a shoestring • Botswana • Cairo • Cairo City Map • Cape Town • Cape Town City Map • East Africa • Egypt • Egyptian Arabic phrasebook • Ethiopia, Eritrea & Djibouti • Ethiopian Amharic phrasebook • The Gambia & Senegal • Healthy Travel Africa • Kenya • Malawi • Morocco • Moroccan Arabic phrasebook • Mozambique • Namibia • Read This First: Africa • South Africa, Lesotho & Swaziland • Southern Africa • Southern Africa Road Atlas • Swahili phrasebook • Tanzania, Zanzibar & Pemba • Trekking in East Africa • Tunisia • Watching Wildlife East Africa • Watching Wildlife Southern Africa • West Africa • World Food Morocco • Zambia • Zimbabwe, Botswana & Namibia
Travel Literature: Mali Blues: Traveling to an African Beat • The Rainbird: A Central African Journey • Songs to an African Sunset: A Zimbabwean Story

AUSTRALIA & THE PACIFIC Aboriginal Australia & the Torres Strait Islands •Auckland • Australia • Australian phrasebook • Australia Road Atlas • Cycling Australia • Cycling New Zealand • Fiji • Fijian phrasebook • Healthy Travel Australia, NZ & the Pacific • Islands of Australia's Great Barrier Reef • Melbourne • Melbourne City Map • Micronesia • New Caledonia • New South Wales • New Zealand • Northern Territory • Outback Australia • Out to Eat – Melbourne • Out to Eat – Sydney • Papua New Guinea • Pidgin phrasebook • Queensland • Rarotonga & the Cook Islands • Samoa • Solomon Islands • South Australia • South Pacific • South Pacific phrasebook • Sydney • Sydney City Map • Sydney Condensed • Tahiti & French Polynesia • Tasmania • Tonga • Tramping in New Zealand • Vanuatu • Victoria • Walking in Australia • Watching Wildlife Australia • Western Australia
Travel Literature: Islands in the Clouds: Travels in the Highlands of New Guinea • Kiwi Tracks: A New Zealand Journey • Sean & David's Long Drive

CENTRAL AMERICA & THE CARIBBEAN Bahamas, Turks & Caicos • Baja California • Belize, Guatemala & Yucatán • Bermuda • Central America on a shoestring • Costa Rica • Costa Rica Spanish phrasebook • Cuba • Cycling Cuba • Dominican Republic & Haiti • Eastern Caribbean • Guatemala • Havana • Healthy Travel Central & South America • Jamaica • Mexico • Mexico City • Panama • Puerto Rico • Read This First: Central & South America • Virgin Islands • World Food Caribbean • World Food Mexico • Yucatán
Travel Literature: Green Dreams: Travels in Central America

EUROPE Amsterdam • Amsterdam City Map • Amsterdam Condensed • Andalucía • Athens • Austria • Baltic States phrasebook • Barcelona • Barcelona City Map • Belgium & Luxembourg • Berlin • Berlin City Map • Britain • British phrasebook • Brussels, Bruges & Antwerp • Brussels City Map • Budapest • Budapest City Map • Canary Islands • Catalunya & the Costa Brava • Central Europe • Central Europe phrasebook • Copenhagen • Corfu & the Ionians • Corsica • Crete • Crete Condensed • Croatia • Cycling Britain • Cycling France • Cyprus • Czech & Slovak Republics • Czech phrasebook • Denmark • Dublin • Dublin City Map • Dublin Condensed • Eastern Europe • Eastern Europe phrasebook • Edinburgh • Edinburgh City Map • England • Estonia, Latvia & Lithuania • Europe on a shoestring • Europe phrasebook • Finland • Florence • Florence City Map • France • Frankfurt City Map • Frankfurt Condensed • French phrasebook • Georgia, Armenia & Azerbaijan • Germany • German phrasebook • Greece • Greek Islands • Greek phrasebook • Hungary • Iceland, Greenland & the Faroe Islands • Ireland • Italian phrasebook • Italy • Kraków • Lisbon • The Loire • London • London City Map • London Condensed • Madrid • Madrid City Map • Malta • Mediterranean Europe • Milan, Turin & Genoa • Moscow • Munich • Netherlands • Normandy • Norway • Out to Eat – London • Out to Eat – Paris • Paris • Paris City Map • Paris Condensed • Poland • Polish phrasebook • Portugal • Portuguese phrasebook • Prague • Prague City Map • Provence & the Côte d'Azur • Read This First: Europe • Rhodes & the Dodecanese • Romania & Moldova • Rome • Rome City Map • Rome Condensed • Russia, Ukraine & Belarus • Russian phrasebook • Scandinavian & Baltic Europe • Scandinavian phrasebook • Scotland • Sicily • Slovenia • South-West France • Spain • Spanish phrasebook • Stockholm • St Petersburg • St Petersburg City Map • Sweden • Switzerland • Tuscany • Ukrainian phrasebook • Venice • Vienna • Wales • Walking in Britain • Walking in France • Walking in Ireland • Walking in Italy • Walking in Scotland • Walking in Spain • Walking in Switzerland • Western Europe • World Food France • World Food Greece • World Food Ireland • World Food Italy • World Food Spain **Travel Literature:** After Yugoslavia • Love and War in the Apennines • The Olive Grove: Travels in Greece • On the Shores of the Mediterranean • Round Ireland in Low Gear • A Small Place in Italy

Lonely Planet Mail Order

onely Planet products are distributed worldwide. They are also available by mail order from Lonely Planet, so if you have difficulty finding a title please write to us. North and South American residents should write to 150 Linden St, Oakland, CA 94607, USA; European and African residents should write to 10a Spring Place, London NW5 3BH, UK; and residents of other countries to Locked Bag 1, Footscray, Victoria 3011, Australia.

INDIAN SUBCONTINENT & THE INDIAN OCEAN Bangladesh • Bengali phrasebook • Bhutan • Delhi • Goa • Healthy Travel Asia & India • Hindi & Urdu phrasebook • India • India & Bangladesh City Map • Indian Himalaya • Karakoram Highway • Kathmandu City Map • Kerala • Madagascar • Maldives • Mauritius, Réunion & Seychelles • Mumbai (Bombay) • Nepal • Nepali phrasebook • North India • Pakistan • Rajasthan • Read This First: Asia & India • South India • Sri Lanka • Sri Lanka phrasebook • Tibet • Tibetan phrasebook • Trekking in the Indian Himalaya • Trekking in the Karakoram & Hindukush • Trekking in the Nepal Himalaya • World Food India **Travel Literature:** The Age of Kali: Indian Travels and Encounters • Hello Goodnight: A Life of Goa • In Rajasthan • Maverick in Madagascar • A Season in Heaven: True Tales from the Road to Kathmandu • Shopping for Buddhas • A Short Walk in the Hindu Kush • Slowly Down the Ganges

MIDDLE EAST & CENTRAL ASIA Bahrain, Kuwait & Qatar • Central Asia • Central Asia phrasebook • Dubai • Farsi (Persian) phrasebook • Hebrew phrasebook • Iran • Israel & the Palestinian Territories • Istanbul • Istanbul City Map • Istanbul to Cairo • Istanbul to Kathmandu • Jerusalem • Jerusalem City Map • Jordan • Lebanon • Middle East • Oman & the United Arab Emirates • Syria • Turkey • Turkish phrasebook • World Food Turkey • Yemen **Travel Literature:** Black on Black: Iran Revisited • Breaking Ranks: Turbulent Travels in the Promised Land • The Gates of Damascus • Kingdom of the Film Stars: Journey into Jordan

NORTH AMERICA Alaska • Boston • Boston City Map • Boston Condensed • British Columbia • California & Nevada • California Condensed • Canada • Chicago • Chicago City Map • Chicago Condensed • Florida • Georgia & the Carolinas • Great Lakes • Hawaii • Hiking in Alaska • Hiking in the USA • Honolulu & Oahu City Map • Las Vegas • Los Angeles • Los Angeles City Map • Louisiana & the Deep South • Miami • Miami City Map • Montreal • New England • New Orleans • New Orleans City Map • New York City • New York City City Map • New York City Condensed • New York New Jersey & Pennsylvania • Oahu • Out to Eat – San Francisco • Pacific Northwest • Rocky Mountains • San Diego & Tijuana • San Francisco • San Francisco City Map • Seattle • Seattle City Map • Southwest • Texas • Toronto • USA • USA phrasebook • Vancouver • Vancouver City Map • Virginia & the Capital Region • Washington, DC • Washington, DC City Map • World Food New Orleans **Travel Literature:** Caught Inside: A Surfer's Year on the California Coast • Drive Thru America

NORTH-EAST ASIA Beijing • Beijing City Map • Cantonese phrasebook • China • Hiking in Japan • Hong Kong & Macau • Hong Kong City Map • Hong Kong Condensed • Japan • Japanese phrasebook • Korea • Korean phrasebook • Kyoto • Mandarin phrasebook • Mongolia • Mongolian phrasebook • Seoul • Shanghai • South-West China • Taiwan • Tokyo • Tokyo Condensed • World Food Hong Kong • World Food Japan **Travel Literature:** In Xanadu: A Quest • Lost Japan

SOUTH AMERICA Argentina, Uruguay & Paraguay • Bolivia • Brazil • Brazilian phrasebook • Buenos Aires • Buenos Aires City Map • Chile & Easter Island • Colombia • Ecuador & the Galapagos Islands • Healthy Travel Central & South America • Latin American Spanish phrasebook • Peru • Quechua phrasebook • Read This First: Central & South America • Rio de Janeiro • Rio de Janeiro City Map • Santiago de Chile • South America on a shoestring • Trekking in the Patagonian Andes • Venezuela **Travel Literature:** Full Circle: A South American Journey

SOUTH-EAST ASIA Bali & Lombok • Bangkok • Bangkok City Map • Burmese phrasebook • Cambodia • Cycling Vietnam, Laos & Cambodia • East Timor phrasebook • Hanoi • Healthy Travel Asia & India • Hill Tribes phrasebook • Ho Chi Minh City (Saigon) • Indonesia • Indonesian phrasebook • Indonesia's Eastern Islands • Java • Lao phrasebook • Laos • Malay phrasebook • Malaysia, Singapore & Brunei • Myanmar (Burma) • Philippines • Pilipino (Tagalog) phrasebook • Read This First: Asia & India • Singapore • Singapore City Map • South-East Asia on a shoestring • South-East Asia phrasebook • Thailand • Thailand's Islands & Beaches • Thailand, Vietnam, Laos & Cambodia Road Atlas • Thai phrasebook • Vietnam • Vietnamese phrasebook • World Food Indonesia • World Food Thailand • World Food Vietnam

ALSO AVAILABLE: Antarctica • The Arctic • The Blue Man: Tales of Travel, Love and Coffee • Brief Encounters: Stories of Love, Sex & Travel • Buddhist Stupas in Asia: The Shape of Perfection • Chasing Rickshaws • The Last Grain Race • Lonely Planet • Lonely Planet ... On the Edge: Adventurous Escapades from Around the World • Lonely Planet Unpacked • Lonely Planet Unpacked Again • Not the Only Planet: Science Fiction Travel Stories • Ports of Call: A Journey by Sea • Sacred India • Travel Photography: A Guide to Taking Better Pictures • Travel with Children • Tuvalu: Portrait of an Island Nation

Index

Text

Bold indicates maps.

Boxed Text

MAP LEGEND

BOUNDARIES

.... State
.... Disputed

.... International
.... Cliff

AREA FEATURES

.... Aboriginal Land
.... Beach
.... Building
.... Campus
.... Cemetery
.... Mall
Park, Gardens, Path
.... Urban Area

HYDROGRAPHY

.... Coastline
.... River, Creek
.... Dry River, Creek
.... Lake
.... Dry Lake; Salt Lake
.... Spring; Rapids
.... Waterfalls
.... Swamp

REGIONAL ROUTES

.... Primary Road
.... Secondary Road
.... Minor Road
.... 4WD only

CITY ROUTES

Fwy .... Freeway
Hwy .... Primary Road
Rd .... Secondary Road
St .... Street
La .... Lane
.... On/Off Ramp
.... Unsealed Road
.... One Way Street
.... Pedestrian Mall
.... Tunnel
.... Footbridge

TRANSPORT ROUTES & STATIONS

.... Train
.... Underground Train
.... Metro
.... Tramway
.... Described Route

.... Cable Car, Chairlift
.... Ferry
.... Walking Trail, Head
.... Walking Tour
.... Pier or Jetty

POPULATION SYMBOLS

Capital ...... National Capital
Capital .... State Capital
City .... City
Town .... Town/Village
.... Aboriginal Community

MAP SYMBOLS

.... Place to Stay
.... Place to Eat
.... Point of Interest

...... Airport, Airfield
...... Airplane Wreck
.... Bank/ATM
...... Bus Stop, Terminal
Bird Sanctuary/Park
.... Camping
.... Caravan
.... Cave
.... Church
.... Cinema
...... Disabled Access

...... Embassy/Consulate
.... Golf Course
.... Homestead
...... Hospital/Clinic
.... Internet Cafe
.... Lighthouse
.... Lookout
.... Monument
..... Mountain/Range
.... Museum/Gallery
.... National Park

.... Parking
.... Petrol/Roadhouse
.... Picnic Area
.... Police Station
.... Post Office
.... Pub or Bar
.... Ruins
.... Shipwreck
.... Shopping Centre
.... Snorkelling
.... Surfing

.... Stately Home
...... Swimming Pool
.... Taxi
.... Telephone
.... Theatre
................Transport
.... Toilets
...Tourist Information
.... Windsurfing
.... Winery
.... Zoo/Wildlife Park

Note: not all symbols displayed above appear in this book

LONELY PLANET OFFICES

Australia
Locked Bag 1, Footscray, Victoria 3011
☎ 03 8379 8000   fax 03 8379 8111
email: talk2us@lonelyplanet.com.au

USA
150 Linden St, Oakland, CA 94607
☎ 510 893 8555 TOLL FREE: 800 275 8555
fax 510 893 8572
email: info@lonelyplanet.com

UK
10a Spring Place, London NW5 3BH
☎ 020 7428 4800 fax 020 7428 4828
email: go@lonelyplanet.co.uk

France
1 rue du Dahomey, 75011 Paris
☎ 01 55 25 33 00 fax 01 55 25 33 01
email: bip@lonelyplanet.fr
www.lonelyplanet.fr

World Wide Web: www.lonelyplanet.com *or* AOL keyword: lp
Lonely Planet Images: lpi@lonelyplanet.com.au